HOUGHTON MIFFLIN COMPANY

Editorial Advisory Committee in Education

Remedial Teaching:

Research and Comment

EDITED BY

Wayne Otto
UNIVERSITY OF WISCONSIN

Karl Koenke
UNIVERSITY OF ILLINOIS

HOUGHTON MIFFLIN COMPANY · BOSTON

New York · Atlanta · Geneva, Illinois · Dallas · Palo Alto

To Elvira

Editor's Introduction

The literature on remedial teaching not only is vast but is spread among numerous books and journals. For the student, teacher, and scholar the task of retrieving this scattered literature is well nigh impossible without computer aids, condensed reviews, and/or books of readings such as this one. To bring to the attention of readers a generous sampling of the best articles in the area of remedial teaching—articles that are important and discrete, that point up the diversity and divergences in the field, that stimulate the reader to probe further in the literature on his own—an editor must assimilate much material and make his selections carefully.

The author-editors of *Remedial Teaching: Research and Comment* have done just this. From several thousand printed articles on remedial and corrective education they have selected a wide diversity of significant research reports as well as numerous treatises describing varied programs and procedures. Instead of evaluating each of the forty-nine selections herein, Otto and Koenke have provided in the Prologue a refreshing innovation; they have suggested a procedure for the reader to follow in analyzing and determining for himself the validity of the research reports and the worth of the descriptive articles. Certainly development of the critical faculty is particularly important for the reader in a field that boasts such a vast and varied literature, including textbooks with widely divergent viewpoints.

The book leads off with general articles on remedial teaching and then turns to the basic skills. There are selections not only on reading but on handwriting, spelling, arithmetic, and written expression as well. This is the only anthology I know of covering remedial teaching in the *several* basic skill areas. The volume is divided into eleven parts, each containing two to six articles. The part titles show the book's unusual breadth: Problems of Underachievement, Correlates of Learning Disability, The Diagnosis of Learning Problems, Approaches to Corrective and Remedial Teaching, The Case Report, Reading, Handwriting, Arithmetic, Spelling, and Written Expression. With a few exceptions the articles were published within the last five years.

Otto and Koenke have made a major contribution in *Remedial Teaching: Research and Comment,* which can serve as a companion book for the text *Corrective and Remedial Teaching* by Otto and McMenemy, published in 1966. This work should be of immeasurable assistance to students and teachers of remedial education, as well as to all classroom teachers.

Samuel A. Kirk

Preface

Three main concerns have shaped the contents of this volume. First, we have chosen the selections as a whole on the basis of their usefulness and appeal to both classroom and remedial teachers. Corrective and remedial teaching must necessarily be the concern of classroom teachers as well as remedial specialists. Special help outside the classroom is often unavailable; in many cases corrective and/or remedial help is most effectively given within the context of the regular classroom program; and in all cases in which a remedial specialist is involved, carefully planned coordination of the efforts of the specialist and of the classroom teacher is needed. Each selection is not likely to be equally germane to the immediate concerns of both classroom and remedial teachers, but all the articles taken together should help to develop the perspectives of both groups and strengthen the working relationships between them.

Second, we have sought to present two basic types of selections: those with general relevance to corrective and remedial teaching and those with specific relevance to the several basic skill areas—reading, handwriting, spelling, arithmetic, and written expression. Much of what has been published to date is limited to the skill area of reading. Although this trend is reflected to some extent in this volume, here an effort has been made to balance the coverage by including the other basic skill areas. To a certain extent the prevalent focus on reading may be justifiable because in many ways reading is the most basic of the basic skills. Failure in reading virtually precludes achievement in all other academic areas. Nevertheless, to limit remedial teaching to reading is unrealistic. Learning problems seldom are confined to a specific skill area; hence remedial help confined to a single area is not likely to have the desired total effect of enabling a student to function well in every phase of classroom work.

Third, we have endeavored to provide comments that will guide the reader in personally evaluating the selections in this volume, particularly the research reports. A general discussion of the contents of well written research reports and the nature of descriptive and discussion articles is given in the Prologue; comments on specific selections are given in the chapter introductions. While we cannot claim to have completely withheld personal judgments and biases, our main intent has been to suggest some criteria for evaluating articles and to direct attention to specific points in the articles contained herein.

The scope of *Remedial Teaching: Research and Comment* is broad. Our purpose has been to sample not deeply but widely in order to explore both relationships and divergences in the area of corrective and remedial teaching. Recency of publication was not a criterion in our selection of articles. Early reports and articles that we consider classics as well as recent reports showing new research results and current thinking are included.

The collection should be useful to teachers in the classroom, remedial specialists, administrators and curriculum specialists, and interested lay people. It should be particularly useful to teachers in training, both as an introduction to the literature of corrective and remedial teaching and as a guide in evaluating this literature for themselves.

We are grateful to the authors and publishers of the selections included for giving us their permission to reprint. A number of authors and editors made helpful comments and suggestions, for which we are particularly grateful.

Wayne Otto

Karl Koenke

Contents

Part Four

Approaches to the Diagnosis of Learning Problems   *93*

Part Five

Approaches to Corrective and Remedial Teaching   *123*

Part Six

The Case Report   *175*

Part Seven

Reading   *192*

Spelling   *313*

Written Expression   *353*

Remedial Teaching: Research and Comment

~~~~~~

Part One

Prologue

In *The True Believer* Eric Hoffer quoted Bagehot: "To illustrate a principle, you must exaggerate much and you must omit much." Hoffer was expecting his readers to quarrel with what he was about to say because it was indeed necessary to exaggerate and ignore in order to convey his essential thoughts. The context here is different, but the expectation is the same. We fully expect readers of this collection to disagree with our decision to include or exclude selections from the vast literature relevant to corrective and remedial teaching in basic school subjects. Yet we are optimistically hoping that the exaggeration, which is a natural result of inclusion, and the omission that is necessary in a book of readings will facilitate the illustration of at least some principles, for the illustration of principles is the primary function of such a book.

It has been said with justification that the subtitle of every book ought to be *How to Be More Like Me*. Books of readings are not exceptions. Although they comprise the works of many authors, each book of readings is an embodiment of the biases of its compilers. Therefore, it seems appropriate to examine some of the personal biases that provided the impetus for this book.

Rationale for the Collection

Teachers in training and teachers in the field benefit from exposure to a variety of professional journals, for journal reports tend to reflect front-line activities. Such activities may be disorganized; breakthroughs and setbacks may be occurring simultaneously; results may not always—or even often—be definitive; and models may be less than exemplary. But the fact is that questions are being raised, research is being conducted, stands are being taken, and action requires reaction. The ideas presented in the journals must be encountered before they can be adopted, adapted, or rejected.

One reason, then, for a book of readings on corrective and remedial teaching is that it makes readily available a collection of articles from many different journals. Students, teachers, and professors know the problems involved in getting and keeping a journal collection. Thus convenience is a consideration. Yet convenience alone is a flimsy defense for a book of readings. If what has been said about the value of exposure to journals is true, then the limitations inherent in a preselected volume are overwhelming. Therefore, the aim is not to provide a substitute for personal probing but to furnish an initial stimulus, to whet the appetite.

The articles and reports in this volume do not purport to cover the field or even to provide a balanced representation of the work in the field. Selections have been included for various reasons: because they are timely, because they represent a point of view, because they are classic, because they make a point or demonstrate a principle, because we feel they may whet the appetite. As we pointed out in the Preface, the publication date of articles was not a factor of prime importance in making selections. Some were still "in press" when they were chosen, and at least one was published more than three decades ago. However, the majority of the reports and articles included appeared within the past five years. We decided to live with the selections we have made and consequently have provided no supplementary reference lists either for individual chapters or for the entire book. Reference lists that are part of the original selections are, of course, included; if the selections succeed in whetting the appetite, these lists will be useful to the reader.

Another and closely related reason for a book of readings on remedial teaching is that it helps to place textbook coverage of the field in perspective. Textbooks tend to be organized around two opposite extremes: high-level generalizations on the one hand and specifics and pat answers on the other. This is as it should be, for an author's purpose in writing a text usually is to point a way by adopting and developing a point of view. Our purpose here—although we have admitted that biases cannot be repressed even in a book of readings—was to sample from a sufficiently wide array of sources, approaches, and viewpoints so that we could at least begin to demonstrate the diversity that exists. The general area of corrective and remedial teaching has tended to be dominated by a few authority figures, whose pronouncements are eagerly awaited and uncritically accepted by a bedazzled—or is it befuddled?—profession. We do not expect that our efforts will cause an appreciable decrease in pronouncements, but we are hoping for at least a modest decline in uncritical acceptances.

Finally, the individual selections in a book of readings can be the foci of specific discussions. A research report, for example, can be examined in terms of its purpose, methodology, results, and implications. A description of a specific approach can be discussed in terms of its apparent impact, the need for further development or adaptation in other situations, and the research required to validate it. Most of the articles in this collection are either research reports or descriptions of programs and/or procedures. The introduction to each section of this book provides a contextual framework for the articles that follow, but we have not attempted to offer specific critical reviews of individual articles. This can best be done by each reader in terms of the idiosyncratic background and requirements of the individual student or situation. Some general guidelines for such evaluation are given in the discussion that follows.

A Guide to Personal Evaluation

The following discussion is devoted to (1) characteristics of a typical research report and points to consider in making a personal evaluation of it, (2) points to consider in evaluating descriptive articles, and (3) implications for corrective and remedial teaching to be drawn from the literature. Readers who have had experience in conducting or analyzing research are advised to skip the entire section.

RESEARCH REPORTS

An adequately written research report includes five essential parts: statement of the problem, description of the method, summary of results, discussion of results, and a succinctly stated summary of the entire study. We shall consider the nature and function of each part. In an actual report, however, each part may not be explicitly labeled.

The Problem. A research activity proceeds from the identification and statement of a problem. Sophisticated methodology and esoteric statistical treatment can do little to salvage a study in which inadequate attention has been given to the identification and lucid explication of a problem. There is no pat procedure for finding and sufficiently defining a problem so that you are able to tackle it and come up with solutions, but it can be said that early in the sequence the emerging problem must be placed within the context of existing knowledge. That is, new hypotheses or questions should be generated in terms of what has already been learned through empirical study and/or in terms of what seems reasonable on the basis of logical analysis and experience. Thus an adequate introduction to a research report includes a brief review of the related literature and/or thinking. Such a review is important, for it serves not only to clarify the rationale for a study but also to preclude efforts that would be merely repetitive or tangential to a straightforward line of research.

Problems are best explicated and laid open to objective scrutiny through the statement of hypotheses. We have said that the identification and definition of a significant problem set the stage for research activity, and we now add that the statement of one or more hypotheses provides the stage directions that guide subsequent activity. Hypotheses are possible explanations of conditions or events. As such they are based upon and include facts, but they transcend known facts in that they are carefully considered guesses about as yet unknown conditions. A well stated hypothesis is plausible in terms of what is already known, and it is testable in terms of resources that can be brought to bear. Once stated, a hypothesis provides the researcher with a framework for designing a study and gathering the relevant information that will be the basis for the support or rejection of the hypothesis.

As a reader attempts to evaluate a research report, he may profitably keep in mind three key questions:

1. Is the general problem unambiguously stated, and is it defensible in view of related facts and explanations? Objectivity in answering the question may be clouded by personal feelings about the importance of the problem. Teachers may tend to reject problems that do not appear to have relevance to practice in the classroom; theoreticians, on the other hand, may reject action-oriented problems as premature, not adequately based on demonstrated facts. The communication gap between the two viewpoints is a frequently discussed matter that will not be resolved here. The point is simply that a problem should be evaluated on its merits.

2. Has there been an adequate review of the literature, and is the review coherently summarized? A thorough review of all the literature relevant to the variables being investigated should be given. Equally important, sound judgments regarding the technical adequacy and the justifiable conclusions of the studies reviewed should be set forth.

3. Is the specific hypothesis (or hypotheses) stated in terms that demonstrate its testability and make clear its adequacy as a solution to the problem? Here it should be made clear that although hypothesis testing is desirable, many studies which have no formal statement of hypotheses are published. Instead, statements of more informal questions to which answers are sought may be

given. If the latter is true, there is no reason to reject the study so long as the questions are relevant to the problem and answerable.

The Method.   The methodology section of a research report is a detailed description of the approach taken by the researcher in attacking the problem. Since each problem is unique, the method of attack must also be unique. To provide some degree of focus, the present discussion is limited to a consideration of experimental studies.

The basic requirement of an adequate description of method is that it be so clearly and thoroughly presented that another researcher would be able to replicate the procedures and, theoretically, obtain the same results. If this requirement is not met, the reader can only guess what actually was done, and any attempt at further critical analyses is reduced to whimsical speculation.

When the reader is given an accurate description of what actually went on, a number of considerations merit his attention:

1. Were the subjects selected in such a way as to avoid systematic bias? For example, if the intent is to compare the performance of good and poor readers on a particular task, some means to ensure that the two groups were comparable in intelligence is required. Without such a precaution the comparison may in fact be between intelligence levels rather than reading ability levels.

2. Were the variables not under consideration or control randomized? For example, in a study comparing the results of two distinct instructional treatments, the preferred procedure is to randomly assign pupils from a large pool of pupils to the two treatment groups. This is much sounder than to assign pupils from one school or classroom to one treatment and pupils from another school or classroom to the other treatment. Expediency often dictates that the latter be done, but in such instances a problem arises. Many factors that may have produced systematic biases in pupils' backgrounds remain intact to affect the results of the study in ways that cannot be determined.

3. Was the possibility of a confounding effect considered or at least recognized? Take, for example, a study in which the intent was to compare the reading achievement of pupils who scored high on a test of visual perception with pupils who scored low on the same test. Perhaps the two groups differed as much—or more—in intelligence, socio-economic indices, exposure to instruction, etc., as they did in visual perception. Of course, it is not always possible or even desirable to "randomize away" the related factors. The point here is that the possibility of confounding effects should be considered in the rationale for the study and at least acknowledged in the method section. Another example is a study comparing the effects of two methods of instruction. Unless extreme care is exercised, many factors other than method per se can influence the outcome of such a study. We shall specify a few: If two different teachers taught the two methods, any difference in results might be attributable to teacher rather than method. Uncontrolled factors might have raised the motivation level in one group but not in the other. The time of day at which instruction was given, the physical setup of the classroom, the format of the materials used, etc., might have been working more favorably for one group than the other.

4. Was sufficient care taken to standardize procedures and to control the subjects' experiences during their participation in the study? When two or more groups are involved, small variations in procedure can inadvertently provide subtle cues or additional information to the advantage of a single group. Subjects tested early in an experiment can pass on information to

subjects run later. In some studies, rest periods may become rehearsal time unless precautions are taken. Seemingly trivial variations and breaks in routine can scramble the results of an otherwise well executed study.

5. Were any directions to the subjects clear enough to be understood by each individual? A worthwhile approach is to pilot directions, particularly when working with children, to see that the directions do in fact evoke the desired behavior—or at least an attempt to behave in the desired manner. The directions given to the subjects should be stated verbatim in the method section of the report so the reader can react specifically.

6. Were any tests and measures used in the study clearly identified or described? Were they chosen from among the best available, and were they appropriate for all the subjects (e.g., was the range of behavior sampled sufficiently great)? If judgments were required, were the judges qualified, and were the intra- and inter-judge reliabilities reported?

7. Was the design of the study clearly described? Were the assumptions underlying the statistical techniques met? In many instances an adequate answer to the latter question would require a great deal of statistical sophistication, and even then two sophisticated statisticians might not agree. Our advice to the statistically unsophisticated reader is to accept the judgment of the editors of the journal in which the study is published. This may amount to whistling in the dark; but if it is dark and if whistling helps, then why not whistle? One should, of course, make some judgments about the editorial policies and competencies embodied in specific journals.

This list of general questions is not comprehensive. It should be clear, though, that logical analysis and common sense are, as always, useful in reacting to the method section of a research report.

Presentation and Discussion of Results.   A research report may include a section summarizing the results and another section discussing them, or it may have a single combined section. When separate sections are given, the former is devoted to a straightforward presentation of the results of the study—the data obtained and analyses of the data. The latter includes a consideration of the hypotheses in the light of the results obtained, a discussion of the problem in terms of the confirmation or rejection of the hypotheses, and a statement of the limitations and implications of the study. When the sections are combined, results are presented and discussed in a systematic way, commonly in the order in which the hypotheses were initially stated.

Following are some questions to keep in mind when evaluating a presentation of results:

1. Are the results presented in an orderly and logical sequence? Perhaps the order that is the most straightforward is dictated by the arrangement of hypotheses or questions in the introduction to the study. In some instances, however, the tests of more than one hypothesis will be inherent in a single analysis—say, in an analysis of variance with several pertinent main effects. In that case it is imperative that the relevant findings be sorted out and directed back to the appropriate hypotheses.

2. Are the data presented completely but at the same time concisely and in the most meaningful and palatable form? There is seldom a need to report raw data; measures of central tendency, standard deviations, ranges, etc., ordinarily suffice. The presentation should be sufficiently complete, however, to lay a solid groundwork for all conclusions reached on the basis of the data.

Graphs, charts, etc., should supplement the traditional tables when they can help clarify the presentation.

3. If the results of *post hoc* tests are reported, has the researcher made explicit mention of their use and the reason for their use? *Post hoc* tests are used in after-the-fact examinations of data. Sometimes their use is very straightforward, as when three or more means occurring within a significant main effect are compared. But in other instances both the tests and the explanations derived from the results are purely opportunistic. There is nothing wrong with *post hoc* reasoning so long as it is recognized and labeled as such.

The following are some guide questions to consider in evaluating a discussion of results:

1. Do the results discussed relate to the hypothesis posed in the study? The requirement here is that each hypothesis be accepted or rejected on the basis of results of the study. On occasion the results may only partially support a hypothesis; this should be noted explicitly.

2. Is a solution to the original problem suggested? Sometimes the data seem to point in a direction that is tangential to the original problem. In such cases no clear resolution of the problem is likely to emerge, but even then the discussion should focus on the originally stated problem before moving on to alternatives or redefinitions.

3. Are suggested conclusions limited to the results actually demonstrated in the study?

4. Are limitations noted?

5. Are implications for practice and/or further research noted?

Summary of Entire Study.   A well written summary of a research report is a succinctly stated review of salient points regarding purpose, method, and results. In recent years the practice of a number of journals has been to run a brief abstract at the beginning of the article. The abstract then serves the same function as the traditional summary and therefore supersedes it. Abstracts are commonly limited by editorial policy to a maximum of 120 to 150 words.

DESCRIPTIVE ARTICLES

Several types of articles are included under the above designation: descriptions of programs and practices, discussions of issues and procedures, reviews of research and/or theory. Reactions to such presentations are apt to be quite subjective because the format and the rules of the game are not so explicitly prescribed as they are for research reports. Nevertheless, we are offering some general criteria for evaluating descriptive articles with the caution that all of them will not be appropriate for every article of this type.

1. The article should make clear the purpose for which it was written. The reader should never have to second-guess what exactly the author had in mind. A review of existing research, for example, may be written either to extract immediate implications for practice or to seek implications for theory development and/or further research. Unless the purpose of the article is made clear early, the reader may easily get lost in the shuffle. Likewise, an author should make clear his purpose in writing a description of, say, an existing program of instruction. He may be suggesting that it serve as a model, that it be modified on the basis of his observations, or that it be replicated only under certain conditions. This point may be so basic that it seems trivial.

But for a reader to be left wondering why an article was written is disconcerting—and may indicate that the author never bothered to come to grips with that basic question himself.

2. Sufficient detail should be provided in the article to accomplish its stated purpose. This is, of course, closely related to the need for a stated purpose. A case in point is a description of an all-school reading program: If the purpose is to provide a model, then sufficient details must be given to permit replication. Too many writers dangle goodies in front of their readers' noses without bothering to make them attainable.

3. References should be cited when they are available and pertinent. Articles in this "descriptive" category often turn out to be distillations of many ideas from diverse sources, and as such they may become general discussions lacking in the specificity that comes with the citation of references. But general discussions do serve an integrative function; in fact, more efforts to pull together and interrelate research results and thinking in the many areas of remedial teaching are needed. Such efforts, however, are generally strengthened by the identification of at least the key sources.

4. Through his style of writing as well as his use of references and/or behavior descriptions, the writer should clearly indicate when he is dealing in facts and when he is in the area of conjecture. The article by English and Lillywhite in Part Six of this volume includes everything that needs to be said on this point.

5. A personal evaluation of a descriptive article is, of course, likely to be deeply colored by the relevance of its content to the concerns of the reader. A person interested in basic research is likely to find relevance and value in articles that practitioners view as too esoteric. Practitioners may find great relevance in articles that basic researchers would reject as irrelevant to the development of theory or a line of research. The point here is that while immediate relevance is likely to be a critical factor in a personal evaluation, it is not an absolute criterion for judging the competency of an article.

DRAWING IMPLICATIONS FROM THE LITERATURE

We wish to make just one point with regard to drawing implications from literature read: Be skeptical.

Too much is often done too soon simply because a tentative finding is aggressively pushed for profit or prestige. Certainly we should all be flexible and open-minded. But at a time when few people even bother to point out that an "innovation" is apt to be nothing more than a redundancy, there is a particular need to proceed with some caution. In our haste to adopt the "innovations" and thereby join the currently fashionable trend in education, we often forget that it would be innovative to refine and really try out some of the older ideas. They were not all bad.

The selections in this book move from general coverage of the problem and of approaches to consideration of specific basic skill areas.

Part Two

Problems of Underachievement

Heitzman's and Bloomer's statewide survey of the need for remedial teachers and Krippner's comparison of correlates of reading disability between the academically talented and slow to average learners point up two problems in underachievement. Certainly the difficulties in measuring achievement also constitute a very real and complex problem, but this technical problem will not be discussed here.[1]

The survey by Heitzman and Bloomer not only shows that the need for remedial teachers is great but also indicates the various content areas in both the elementary and the secondary school in which the need exists. While it is true that the findings of a survey apply only to a specific time and place, it is also true that in this case the increasing general concern for the material well-being of the culturally disadvantaged and the resulting federally funded projects tend generally to reinforce the Heitzman-Bloomer finding. Furthermore, those interested in estimating the need for certain types of remedial teachers in other fairly large areas of the country may find that the sampling technique used in the Heitzman-Bloomer survey has much to recommend it.

In his study of underachievement among the academically talented, Krippner compares the conditions that may have caused the learning problem of the academically talented child with the possible causes of the learning disability of average and slow children. The term "etiological factors" as used in this type of study actually denotes correlates, i.e., conditions that coexist with a learning problem; and one cannot always be certain that they caused the learning disability. However, common sense tells one that a knowledge of things that may hinder learning and/or circumscribe teaching is of value.

1 R. L. Thorndike, *The Concepts of Over- and Underachievement* (New York: Bureau of Publications, Teachers College, Columbia University, 1963).

1   The Need for Special Remedial Teachers

ANDREW J. HEITZMAN

RICHARD H. BLOOMER

The number of reading disabilities in the public schools today is estimated to range from 10 to 25 per cent, an alarmingly large number to popular magazines and newspapers. However, in the last 10 or 15 years the number of teachers providing specialized assistance for pupils disabled in some aspect of the curriculum, and particularly in reading, has grown markedly. The purpose of this survey was to determine the extent of need for specialized assistance and the kinds of preparation which school administrators believed would best equip teachers to handle specialized problems. These findings may be interesting to planners of teacher education and to prospective graduate students.

Procedure

A questionnaire was sent to a straight random sample of superintendents of schools in New York State. Of the sample of 100 superintendents, 69 replied. For the purpose of this present survey it was assumed that they were representative of the total group of superintendents in New York State, forming a basis for the projection of state-wide needs.

The questionnaire presented a list of courses considered essential parts of a curriculum to train remedial reading teachers or reading consultants. The superintendents were asked to give the number of special remedial reading teachers currently employed in the specific areas listed and to project the needs of their districts for the next five years in each category. Table I gives the projected number of special remedial teachers in the state. If the sample is representative, there should be 1785 elementary level remedial teachers, of whom 1467 work with reading problems. Of the elementary school consultants reported, all specialize in reading. This projection should not be construed to mean that there are not consultants in other areas, but only that the great proportion of the consultants have reading as their major responsibility.

TABLE I   *Estimated Number of Special Remedial Teachers—1960–1961*

Area	Elementary Remedial Teacher	Secondary Remedial Teacher	Elementary Consultant	Secondary Consultant
Reading	1467	1193	291	NR*
Arithmetic	137	9	NR	NR
Language Arts	26	NR	NR	NR
Social Studies	13	NR	NR	NR*
Science	142	NR	NR	NR
Total	1785	1202	291	

* None reported.

From *Journal of Reading*, Vol. 9 (October, 1965), pp. 30–33. Reprinted with permission of Andrew J. Heitzman and the International Reading Association.

TABLE II   *Projected Need for Special Remedial Teachers—1961–1966*

Area	Elementary Remedial Teacher	Secondary Remedial Teacher	Elementary Consultant	Secondary Consultant
Reading	583	4	4	NR*
Arithmetic	60	NR	NR	NR
Language Arts	86	NR	NR	NR
Social Studies	43	NR	NR	NR
Science	86	NR	NR	NR
Total	858	4	4	NR

* None reported.

Table II shows projections for the next five years. The greatest need appears in the elementary school area and is proportionally greater in the language arts, social studies, and science areas than the number of special remedial teachers currently employed in these areas. By far the greatest number of special teachers required in the foreseeable future will continue to be elementary remedial reading teachers. The number of additional secondary teachers and consultants projected is relatively small.

Desired Preparation of Teachers

Table III shows the courses listed by superintendents as essential for training remedial reading teachers and consultants. The superintendents believed that courses in elementary reading methods, diagnostic and remedial teaching, psychology of learning, practicum in remediation, and measurement and evaluation were essential for elementary remedial teachers. Considered to be of relatively little importance were the survey of exceptional children, secondary reading methods, and administration and supervision of remedial programs.

TABLE III   *Preparation Superintendents Considered Desirable for Special Remedial Teachers*

Type of Position	Degree Required	Elementary Reading Methods	Secondary Reading Methods	Diagnostic and Remedial Teaching	Practicum in Remediation	Measurement and Evaluation	Survey of Exceptional Children	Administration and Supervision of Remedial Programs	Psychology of Learning
Elementary Remedial Reading Teacher	B.S.	89.8*	17.4	84.0	76.7	76.7	55.0	20.3	81.1
Secondary Remedial Reading Teacher	B.S.	66.7	84.0	79.7	72.5	73.4	55.0	21.7	78.2
Remedial Reading Consultant, Supervisor, or Coordinator	M.Ed.	89.8	85.8	88.4	81.1	86.9	79.7	86.9	88.4

* Percentages of respondents.

At the secondary level the picture is somewhat different. Secondary reading methods, diagnostic and remedial teaching, and psychology of learning were again the most important courses; measurement and evaluation and a practicum in remediation were of considerable importance. Furthermore, many superintendents believed that elementary reading methods were important for secondary remedial teachers. This conclusion indicates the awareness that a good foundation in reading is vital to reading success. Again the superintendents stated that the survey of exceptional children and the administration and supervision of remedial programs were of little value in the education of a remedial teacher.

For the remedial reading consultant, the superintendents thought that all the listed courses were important.

In addition, a number of other course suggestions were made. Some of these are relatively common and are even required for certification of the regular classroom teacher. Others, while generally available, are not so commonly taken by college students. Among the common courses were those in the child psychology-human development area, in which several superintendents affirmed their confidence. A second group consisted of courses related to curriculum sequence and curriculum development. A third group stressed audio-visual methods.

Among the courses which are less likely to be found in prescribed programs of teacher education were surveys of children's literature or intensive investigation of children's literature with emphasis on readability. A course in research design was recommended by several superintendents. Educational research is a common graduate course but usually is not part of the elementary teacher's curriculum. The third group suggested by the superintendents, one not customarily found on the undergraduate level, was a set of intensive courses in reading, reading curricula, and the design of reading programs. Most of these would clearly be advantageous to the remedial reading teacher. This suggestion, furthermore, seems to imply that the bachelor's degree is not a terminal one in the training of remedial teachers and that the last-mentioned courses would be more meaningful to the practicing teacher and therefore should be taken as graduate work.

Summary

This study investigated the needs of New York State for special remedial teachers in the next five years. The greatest need appears on the elementary school level, with an estimated 858 additional teachers required, a large proportion of whom will be in reading. There will be increasing demands, however, for special teachers in arithmetic, language arts, social studies, and science. In teacher education, superintendents see a strong need for specific methods courses as well as for courses in psychology of learning, diagnostic and remedial teaching, measurement and evaluation, and practicum in remediation.

2   Etiological Factors in Reading Disability of the Academically Talented in Comparison to Pupils of Average and Slow-learning Ability

STANLEY KRIPPNER

Abstract.—*Etiological factors in reading disability for a high intelligence group were compared to those in average and low intelligence groups. All subjects were elementary and secondary pupils, ranging from 7–1 to 15–10 in age. The twenty-six high intelligence subjects ranged from 113 to 128 in WISC IQ. The 146 subjects of average intelligence ranged from 88 to 112 in IQ. The thirty-four low intelligence subjects ranged from 70 to 87 in IQ. The subjects were administered several diagnostic tests to determine the etiology of their reading disabilities. When the etiological factors were divided into organic and functional categories, it was noted that the high intelligence group's disabilities were significantly more often functional in origin than those of the other two groups.*

In the education of gifted and talented children, the mastery of basic reading skills is essential. Gowan and Scheibél (5), however, have estimated that most gifted children are hidden remedial reading candidates. Wheeler and Wheeler (19) have stated that "the most seriously retarded readers in our schools are the mentally superior students" while Strang (15) has noted that the gifted child who reads only at his grade level is actually a remedial reading case. Witty (20), Torrance (17), and Goodman (4) have expressed similar opinions concerning "creative" pupils.

The etiological factors associated with reading problems among the gifted are similar to those affecting average and slow-learning pupils. Disorders may be present in the peripheral nervous system (especially in seeing and hearing), in the central nervous system, or in the endocrine system (1, 9, 14, 18). These disorders are usually referred to as "organic" in nature. In addition, there may be "functional" disorders—those arising from social, emotional, educational, or cultural handicaps (13, 16).

The purpose of this study was to determine whether organic or functional etiology was more characteristic of highly intelligent disabled readers as compared to pupils representing other intelligence levels.

Procedure

For the purposes of this study, the concept of reading disability proposed by Bond and Tinker (1) was utilized. The Bond-Tinker formula computes a pupil's expected reading grade (ERG) by multiplying the number of years a child has been in school by his IQ (divided by 100) and adding 1.0 (because his grade placement was 1.0 when he entered school). Although the IQ is not an adequate criterion of giftedness, it was felt that the goals of the study would be best served by using it both for the Bond–Tinker formula and as a cut-off point in delimiting the three mental ability groups.

Each pupil's observed reading grade (ORG) was estimated by taking the mean of his grade equivalent on the six reading tests of the Durrell Analysis of

From *Journal of Educational Research*, Vol. 61, No. 6 (February, 1968), pp. 275–279. Reprinted with permission.

Reading Difficulty. These tests included oral reading rate, silent reading rate, word recognition, word analysis, visual memory, and phonics. The pupil's ERG was computed by using the Bond–Tinker formula, and the degree of reading disability was established by subtracting each pupil's ORG from his ERG. The only pupils used in this study were those with a reading disability of one year or more.

Each pupil's diagnostic test data were utilized to arrive at the major cause of his disability. Contributing etiological factors were determined by the same procedure, which included diagnostic testing and interviewing, clinical observation, the examination of medical reports, school records, parent conferences, developmental histories, and clinical observations. The final diagnostic statement was made by one of several graduate clinicians working at the Kent State University Child Study Center under the supervision of the author of this report. An attempt was made to lean heavily on objective test scores, so as to prevent subjective judgment from becoming a biasing factor.

During the 1961–1962, 1962–1963, and 1963–1964 academic years, a total of twenty-six disabled readers with WISC IQ's of 113 or above were seen at the Kent State University Child Study Center. During the same period of time, 146 disabled readers were seen with WISC IQ's between 88 and 112; thirty-four poor readers were seen with WISC IQ's of 87 and below. It was decided to refer to these youngsters as "academically talented," "average," and "slow-learning" and to make comparisons among the three groups as to the etiology of their reading problems.

Fifteen etiological categories were established as well as criteria for assigning pupils to those categories. The categorization of *impaired seeing acuity* was made on the basis of a report from an ophthalmologist or optometrist. If the impairment in visual acuity had not been corrected when reading instruction began, this element was cited as an etiological factor. In much the same way, the pupil was placed in the *impaired hearing acuity* category if this problem had not been identified by an audiologist before reading instruction was inaugurated. A pure-tone audiometric screening test and the Keystone Visual Survey were administered.

Visual skills were negatively affected in all cases where seeing acuity was impaired. Many pupils displayed *poor visual skills* who had no eye disease and who did not need corrective lenses. These children typically had problems with the visual discrimination of letters, visual memory, visual closure, and visual-motor coordination. Pupils were classified as having poor visual skills if they were one year or more disabled on the visual memory section of the Durrell Analysis or if their performance on the Perceptual Forms Test (11) was below 60. Additional visual problems were also noted on the WISC on such subtests as Coding Mazes, and Picture Completion and on the Frostig Developmental Test of Visual Perception. Because the latter test was not available when these pupils were diagnosed initially, the only ones who were administered the test were those coming to the Center for supplementary or follow-up testing in 1964.

Pupils were assigned to the category of *poor auditory* skills if they made an unsatisfactory score, for their age, on the Wepman Auditory Discrimination Test. Poor auditory skills were also identified by the Roswell–Chall Auditory Blending Test, the Illinois Test of Psycholinguistic Abilities, and the WISC Digit Span subtest. Pupils with defective auditory skills could not discriminate between two similar phonemes, could not blend individual phonemes together into a simple word, and could not recall material presented auditorially.

As the young child grows and develops, listening and speaking typically precede reading and writing. Reading instruction assumes a certain level of speaking ability, vocabulary development, and articulation preciseness. In some cases, therefore, poor articulation can be a causal factor in reading disability. At the Center, each pupil was administered the Montgomery Look-and-Say Articulation Test (10). If one or more major speech sounds were defective, and if those sounds were characteristically mastered by the majority of youngsters of that mental age, the pupil was considered to have a *speech defect.*

Brain injury was suspected among pupils whose scores on the Graham and Kendall Memory-for-Design Test (6) fell outside the normal limits. In many cases, this suspicion was confirmed by electroencephalographic examination. In others, neurological diagnosis was not possible because of financial factors. In the latter cases, a tentative diagnosis of brain injury was made on the birth history, developmental history, clinical observation, and additional data.

Rabinovitch (13) has described *disturbed neurological organization* in terms of a "developmental lag" between the maturation of verbal and non-verbal intellectual capacities, with verbal capacities displaying a slower development. As a result, these children display reading disabilities coupled with a difference of 15 or more IQ points between their WISC Verbal Scale scores and their WISC Performance Scale scores. Other symptoms described by Rabinovitch include disturbed body image, poor revisualization, poor reauditorization, difficulties in conceptual thinking, confusion in dealing with time, confusion in dealing with numbers, and confusion in dealing with directions. Those pupils placed in this category by Center clinicians had a WISC Performance IQ that was at least 15 points higher than their WISC Verbal IQ. In addition, their behavior indicated problems in at least five out of the seven characteristic areas described by Rabinovitch. Frank brain injury was not found to characterize these children, either by Rabinovitch or (with two exceptions) by Center clinicians. As a result, they are often referred to as suffering from "developmental dyslexia" as opposed to "post-traumatic dyslexia," in which damage to the central nervous system, rather than a developmental problem, exists.

Directionality confusion was diagnosed by the Harris Tests of Lateral Dominance. If a pupil had poor left-to-right progression in reading, if he often confused "d" and "b," and if his performance on the Harris Tests was also unsatisfactory, the pupil was placed in this category.

In the case of certain pupils, *endocrinal malfunctioning* was felt to be an etiological factor. In each case, there was a medical report that endocrinal malfunction existed (or did exist when reading instruction began).

Pupils were diagnosed as *socially immature* for their chronological age if they scored below 90 on the Vineland Social Maturity Scale.

All pupils were administered the Purcell Incomplete Sentences (12) and either the Mental Health Analysis or the California Test of Personality. On the basis of these measures, as well as clinical observation and outside reports, the Center clinicians made judgments as to whether emotional disturbance was an etiological factor. A breakdown into the categories of *neurotic, psychotic,* and *sociopathic* tendencies was made on the basis of projective test data. No pupil was ever placed in more than one of the above categories, even though it was sometimes felt that an interaction of two or three conditions existed. Almost all children with reading disabilities have some degree of emotional disturbance, generally as a result of their academic frustration. In making their judgments, therefore, the clinicians attempted to classify those pupils as disturbed only if the emotional disturbances were the *cause* of the reading disability rather than the *result* of it.

Unfavorable educational experiences were found to be an etiological factor among many pupils seen at the Center. The placement of a pupil in this category was dependent on such subjective data as parental interviews, school reports, and the types of errors made by the pupil on reading tests.

As a fee was required for an appointment at the Child Study Center, very few culturally disadvantaged pupils were seen during the course of this study. However, a pupil was categorized as *culturally deprived* if his fee had been paid by a social agency. The influence of his disadvantaged condition was subjectively estimated on the basis of reports and interviews.

Rarely is one etiological factor responsible for a reading problem. The clinicians, therefore, cited both the *major* etiological factor and the *contributing* factors in their reports. Isolating the major factor was extremely subjective in many instances, and the multifactor causation of reading disabilities became apparent to the clinicians involved in this study.

Results

The mean WISC IQ of the academically talented group was 117.2, with a range from 113 to 128. The average group's mean IQ was 100.5, with a range from 88 to 112. The slow-learning group had a mean IQ of 80.2, with a range from 70 to 87.

The mean reading disability of the academically talented pupils was 2.1 years. The mean reading disability of the average pupils was 2.0 years; the slow-learning pupils had a mean disability of 2.0 years.

The mean age of the academically talented was 11–8, with a range from 7–6 to 14.0. The average group's mean age was 10–8, with a range from 7–1 to 15–10. The mean age of the slow learners was 10–8, with a range from 7–5 to 15–0.

Of the academically talented group, 88.5 per cent were boys. Of the average group, 89.0 per cent were boys, and of the slow-learning group, 74.2 per cent were boys. Of the total group, 87.4 per cent were boys.

Chi-square analysis was done on the major etiological factors divided into organic and functional categories. The organic factors included impaired seeing and hearing acuity, poor visual and auditory skills, speech defects, brain injury, disturbed neurological organization, directional confusion, and endocrinal malfunctioning. The functional factors included social immaturity, unfavorable educational experiences, cultural deprivation, and neurotic, psychotic, and sociopathic tendencies. The division was somewhat arbitrary as etiological boundaries are not clear-cut and a great deal of overlap exists. The results of this classification are shown in Table I.

A non-significant Chi-square of 0.1 was obtained when the average and slow-learning groups were compared in reference to organic versus functional major etiology. A Chi-square of 4.3, significant at the .05 level, was obtained when the average and academically talented groups were compared. A similarly significant Chi-square of 5.2 was obtained when the slow-learning and academically talented groups were compared. In other words, the academically talented group demonstrated significantly *less* organic etiology as a major factor and significantly *more* functional etiology as a major factor than either the average or slow-learning group.

TABLE I *Major and Total Contributing Etiological Factors in the Reading Disabilities of Three Clinical Groups of Pupils Divided by WISC IQ's into Academically Talented (N = 26), Average (N = 146), and Slow-learning (N = 34)*

| | Major Etiological Factors | | | | | | Total Contributing Etiological Factors | | | | | |
| | Talented | | Average | | Slow-learning | | Talented | | Average | | Slow-learning | |
	f	%	f	%	f	%	f	%	f	%	f	%
Organic												
Impaired Seeing Acuity	0	0.0	14	9.6	2	5.9	5	19.2	41	28.1	18	52.9
Impaired Hearing Acuity	0	0.0	1	0.7	1	3.0	1	3.8	13	8.9	5	14.7
Poor Visual Skills	2	7.7	19	13.0	5	14.7	14	53.8	91	62.3	30	88.2
Poor Auditory Skills	0	0.0	1	0.7	1	3.0	2	7.7	52	35.6	24	70.6
Speech Defects	0	0.0	0	0.0	0	0.0	2	7.7	27	18.5	10	29.5
Brain Injury	3	11.5	25	17.1	13	38.2	4	15.4	30	20.5	14	41.2
Disturbed Neurological Organization	6	23.1	27	18.5	1	3.0	7	26.9	30	20.5	2	5.9
Directional Confusion	1	3.8	9	6.2	1	3.0	10	38.5	38	26.0	23	67.6
Endocrinal Malfunctioning	0	0.0	5	3.4	0	0.0	1	3.8	17	11.6	6	17.6
Functional												
Social Immaturity	0	0.0	3	2.1	1	3.0	7	26.9	25	17.1	14	41.2
Neurotic Tendencies	9	34.6	25	17.1	2	5.9	17	65.4	50	34.2	15	44.1
Psychotic Tendencies	1	3.8	2	1.4	2	5.9	1	3.8	3	2.1	3	8.8
Sociopathic Tendencies	2	7.7	6	4.1	1	3.0	3	11.5	8	5.5	1	3.0
Unfavorable Educational Experiences	2	7.7	8	5.5	3	8.8	15	57.7	83	56.8	14	41.2
Cultural Deprivation	0	0.0	1	0.7	1	3.0	0	0.0	9	6.2	5	14.7

Discussion

This study demonstrates the existence of neurological problems among some disabled readers of high intelligence. Often a program of perceptual training, dominance establishment, and/or motor coordination improvement is needed before remedial reading will be helpful. Many pupils seen at the Center had received two or three years of remedial tutoring without positive results. A deeper understanding of the disability was gained through diagnostic testing. Tutoring in reading is a process of sinking shafts into sand if the basic physiological foundations for learning do not exist. Satisfactory auditory discrimination must be present before a child can memorize whole words. A child must know the difference between his right and his left hand before he can master the difference between such words as "was" and "saw."

Once the bases of perception and symbol-making have been established, the academically talented child who is a poor reader shares many of the same remedial needs as other children with neurological inadequacies. He needs to improve his visual discrimination of letters and to improve his ability to blend phonemes into words. Rabinovitch (13) suggests training in directional orientation, phonics, and tactile-kinesthetic tracing. His learning needs constant reinforcement as this training is often slow and unsteady. There are many word recognition skills—sight cues, phonic cues, context, structural analysis—and those best suited for each remedial reader should be emphasized.

The customary skills in abstract thinking and conceptualization which most academically talented children possess cannot be relied on if emotional disturbance, brain injury, or disturbed neurological organization is present. These factors, alone or in combination, may hamper the process of abstraction; as a result, concrete experiences and tangible materials are often called for. Field trips may provide a meaningful basis for symbol-making. Tactile–kinesthetic approaches to words (involving tracing, touching, and framing) may be needed to supplement visual and auditory approaches. Comprehension skills must be built slowly; once again, a variety of reinforcement techniques may be needed.

The reading process is probably the most complex task the child is called upon to master. It should be no surprise that a variety of factors can interfere with the mastery of this process. Pupils falling into different categories of disability should receive different treatment (3). Furthermore, the remedial clinician should start with the child where he is and proceed up the educational hierarchy until the symbol-making process is mastered (7, 14). Furthermore, attention must be paid to the fact that children of different intelligence levels demonstrate different modes of problem-solving (2, 8). Therefore, three critical variables to be considered are level of intelligence, degree of disability, and etiology of disability.

Diagnosis has little value unless it is the first step in remediation. Reading disabilities of the academically talented demand as close attention to the individual aspects of the problem as do the disabilities of the average and the slow-learning. The fact that a pupil has relatively high general intelligence does not mean that he will overcome his reading problem automatically.

Remedial techniques for the academically talented demand an adaptation to their specific problem areas with an inclusion of intellectually stimulating content whenever possible. This is especially valuable when unfavorable educational experiences have been the major etiological factor in the reading disability. Counseling of parents and teachers is often called for as the bright disabled reader suffering from emotional disturbances, seeks to improve his reading skills while simultaneously working out new ways of relating to himself, to his peers, and to adult figures. His giftedness demands a stimulating, challenging educational environment while his emotional difficulty necessitates a structured, controlled pacing of new challenges. If the neurotic, psychotic, or sociopathic tendencies afflicting the disabled reader prove to be deep-seated, remedial reading must be preceded by family counseling and psychotherapy.

REFERENCES

1. Bond, G. L., and Tinker, M. *Reading Difficulties, Their Diagnosis and Correction* (New York: Appleton-Century-Crofts, 1957).

2. Borg, W. "Study Habits and Methods of Superior, Average, and Slow Pupils in Ability-Grouped and Random-Grouped Classrooms," paper read at the annual meeting of the American Psychological Association, 1964.

3. De Hirsch, K. "The Categories of Learning Difficulties in Adolescents," *American Journal of Orthopsychiatry*, XXXIII (1963), pp. 87–91.

4. Goodman, P. *Growing Up Absurd* (New York: Random House, 1960).

5. Gowan, J. C., and Scheibel, R. W. "The Improvement of Reading in Gifted Children," *Educational and Administrative Supervision*, XLVI (1960), pp. 35–40.

6. Graham, F.K., and Kendall, B.S. "Memory-for-Designs Test: Revised General Manual," *Perceptual and Motor Skills*, XI (1960), pp. 147–188.

7. Hewett, F. M. "A Hierarchy of Educational Tasks for Children with Learning Disorders," *Exceptional Children*, XXXI (1964), pp. 207–214.

8. Klausmeier, H. J., and Loughlin, L.J. "Behaviors During Problem Solving Among Children of Low, Average, and High Intelligence," *Journal of Educational Psychology*, LII (1961), pp. 148–152.

9. Mayne, D. "The Intelligent Retarded Reader," *Journal of Developmental Reading*, VII (1963), pp. 62–66.

10. Montgomery, J. *The Look-and-Say Articulation Test* (Chicago: King, 1961).

11. *Perceptual Forms and Incomplete Copy Forms, Teacher's Test Manual* (Winter Haven, Florida: Lions Publication Committee, 1963).

12. Purcell, J. W. *The Purcell Incomplete Sentences* (Kent, Ohio: Kent State University Child Study Center, 1961).

13. Rabinovitch, R. "Reading and Learning Disabilities," in S. Arieti (Ed.), *American Handbook of Psychiatry* New York: Basic Books, 1959), pp. 857–869.

14. Sonnenberg, C., and Glass, G. C. "Reading and Speech: An Incidence and Treatment Study," *Reading Teacher*, XIX (1965), pp. 197–201.

15. Strang, R. "Gifted Children Need Help in Reading," *Reading Teacher*, VI (1953), pp. 23–27.

16. Strang, R. "Mental Hygiene of Gifted Children," in P. Witty (Ed.), *The Gifted Child* (Boston: D. C. Heath and Co., 1951), pp. 131–162.

17. Torrance, E. P. *Guiding Creative Talent* (Englewood Cliffs, N. J.: Prentice-Hall, 1962).

18. Wepman, P. "Auditory Discrimination, Speech, and Reading," *Elementary School Journal*, XL (1960), pp. 325–333.

19. Wheeler, L. R., and Wheeler, V. D. "Relationship Between Reading Ability and Intelligence Among University Freshmen," *Journal of Educational Psychology*, L (1949), pp. 230–231.

~~~~~~

Part Three

Correlates of Learning Disability

Two important points should be kept clearly in mind in any consideration of possible causal factors in learning disability. First, seldom is it possible to identify a single cause in an individual case. Learning problems are more likely to stem from a combination of factors, any one of which by itself would not be debilitating. The identification of causal factors is further complicated by the fact that once a learning problem begins to develop, secondary factors may begin to contribute to the chronic deterioration of learning efficiency. Single-factor theories and methods are likely to be appealing in the area of learning disability because they tend to be straightforward; the problem is that they tend also to be oversimplified. Second, a cause-effect relationship cannot be inferred directly from a demonstrated relationship. Many studies ostensibly of causal factors are in fact studies of correlates without clarification of the cause-effect relationship. The latter can be immensely complicated, and we do not have an easy solution to the problem; but recognition of the problem may be the first step toward its solution.

Otto's study of the relationship between inhibitory potential and achievement in handwriting, arithmetic, and spelling is an example of a fairly clearly demonstrated relationship: underachievers in handwriting and spelling appear to accumulate reactive inhibition more rapidly than achievers in those skill areas. While the relationship is consistent with predictions from theory, the fact remains that a cause-effect relationship was not demonstrated. It is possible that a set of underlying causes is responsible for both the underachievement and the performance on the task used to quantify reactive inhibition.

The Belmont and Birch study of the intellectual profile of poor readers is interesting not only in terms of the method employed but also in terms of the authors' critiques of related studies. Several points merit special attention.

1. The dual aim of the study is sensible. The authors sought both a clearer understanding of the intellectual deficits that underlie reading difficulty and information regarding the effect of poor reading on intellectual development. Attempts to assess the impact of learning disability upon subsequent development are rare but needed to round out our understanding of the chronic nature of learning disability.

2. The epidemiological approach to the problem makes it possible to work with a sample of subjects whose behavior as a group is not distorted by their membership in a special clinical population. Clinic populations, as a rule, are not representative even of the specific problem groups from which they are drawn because in practice referrals to clinics are often made in response to

bizarre, or at least atypical, behaviors. As a result, much of what is known about disabled readers in particular and disabled learners in general is flavored by the fact that it is based upon studies of clinical groups, which predominate in such studies because such groups are captive and most easily accessible to researchers.

3. The critique of WISC subtest pattern analyses is comprehensive and objective.

4. The data analysis is not confined to tests of statistical significance. Some researchers, in their zeal to play the sophisticate, shy away from anything that cannot be examined through the application of statistical tests. This amounts in some cases to throwing the baby out with the bath water. The study is worthy of thoughtful perusal.

The second study by Belmont and Birch included in this section appears to be emerging as a classic study of the relationship of lateral dominance/awareness and reading disability. The subjects apparently were the same children who participated in the intellectual profile study, and again there is the advantage of working with a nonclinical group from a restricted intellectual and chronological age range. Many of the limiting factors present in related studies were eliminated, so the Belmont and Birch study may have brought some order into an area that has tended to be chaotic. Their point that middle-class children in clinics tend to be younger than lower-class children in clinics is interesting and if valid, seems to have both moral and scientific implications.

Correlations between measures of verbal intelligence and measures of achievement in basic school subjects such as arithmetic and reading tend to fall in the .5 to .6 area, depending on the measures employed. While such correlations are evidence of a substantial relationship, the fact remains that much of the variance in achievement test scores is not accounted for by intelligence alone.

The study by Crandall *et al.* adds another dimension to the study of nonintellectual correlates of academic achievement with its focus upon possible antecedents for achievement motivation. Although the above-average IQ's of most of the subjects place severe limitations upon any generalizations to be drawn from the study, the techniques for examining parental attitudes are worth particular attention. With regard to specific findings, the demonstration of a sex difference appears to be most salient: girls' achievement is more closely related to parental attitudes than boys' achievement.

In the Leton and Holz article on discriminant analysis, the interrelationship of achievement, social traits, and emotional traits is recognized. The authors' idea is to seek a means to avoid indiscriminate placement of children in social adjustment classes because ". . . groups . . . appear to have limits to their acceptance of differences." The message with regard to corrective and remedial teaching is clear.

Gallagher's excellent paper on specific language disability is rather arbitrarily placed in this chapter on correlates of learning disability, for it covers diagnosis and treatment as well as possible causes. The paper is an exceptionally clear and balanced overview of specific language disability.

Perhaps the most prominent omission from this part is a paper having to do with visual perception. A profusion of methods for assessing perceptual development/functioning and for training now exists. In view of the lack of definitive research, however, our decision was to add nothing to the present state of confusion.

3   Inhibitory Potential in Good and
Poor Achievers

WAYNE OTTO

The relationship of reactive inhibition to skill attainment in spelling, handwriting, and arithmetic and the effect of "motivating" instructions upon inhibitory potential were investigated in two related studies. An inverted digit-printing task was used to quantify reactive inhibition with 340 pupils in Grades 4–8. Predicted relationships were demonstrated for the skill areas of spelling and handwriting: Poor achievers dissipated more reactive inhibition than did good achievers. There was some support for the suggestion that the relationship did not hold for arithmetic because of the effect of intrinsic motivation.

This investigation consists of two related studies. In the first study the relationship of inhibitory potential to achievement in the skill areas of spelling, handwriting, and arithmetic was examined. The purpose of the second study was to facilitate interpretation of data from the first; the effect of high motivation upon the inhibitory potential of good and poor achievers was examined. In both studies the task and the experimental variables, with the exception of motivation level, were the same.

Studies (Lynn, 1960; Otto and Fredricks, 1963) have shown that poor readers dissipate more reactive inhibition than good readers during rest and that an inverted digit-printing task appears to be a satisfactory measure of reactive inhibition. Support for the notion that poor readers actually accumulate reactive inhibition more rapidly and further demonstration of the generality of earlier findings were provided by a later study (Otto, in press) with Negro subjects. Although the existence of a relationship does not demonstrate cause and effect, the findings have been consistent in lending support to speculation that a tendency to generate reactive inhibition quickly may be detrimental to the acquisition of skill in reading.

In a Hullian framework, a tendency to accumulate reactive inhibition rapidly would be detrimental to the building up of reaction potential. Thus, Lynn (1960) argued that if the theory that acquiring basic educational skills is a matter of conditioning (Peel, 1956) is correct, the pupils who learn these skills readily should generate reactive inhibition slowly. The existing data support the prediction for the specific skill of reading. The general purpose here was to test the prediction for the skill areas of spelling, handwriting, and arithmetic.

Study I

The approach in this study was to replicate the essentials of the Otto and Fredricks (1963) reading study with good and poor achievers in spelling, handwriting, and arithmetic. Each skill was considered separately rather than in an overall design because (*a*) the intent was to make an explicit check of the relationship between reactive inhibition and achievement in each skill area, and (*b*)

From *Journal of Educational Psychology,* Vol. 56, No. 4 (1965), pp. 200–207. Copyright 1965 by the American Psychological Association. Reprinted with permission.

The writer is grateful to Jim Carlson of the Parkrose, Oregon, Public Schools and John Hulsey of the Walton County, Georgia, Schools for their help in securing subjects, and to the Office of General Research, Graduate School, University of Georgia, for support of the project.

the appropriateness of the digit-printing task for quantifying reactive inhibition in the several skill areas was not known.

METHOD

Subjects and Design.   Subjects were good and poor achievers in the basic skill areas of handwriting, spelling (in Grades 4–6), and arithmetic (in Grades 4–8). All potential subjects were required to have IQ's in the average (90–115) range according to test scores corroborated by teacher judgment. Pupils with average IQ's who could not be clearly classified as good or poor achievers according to the following criteria were rejected as subjects. Good achievers in arithmetic and in spelling were those pupils who, according to test scores and teacher judgment, were clearly in the upper third of their class in achievement in the appropriate skill area; poor achievers were those who were clearly in the lower third. Good writers were pupils whose handwriting, according to teacher judgment, clearly ranked in the top third of their class; poor writers' handwriting was clearly in the bottom third. Judgments of handwriting quality were made on the basis of legibility ("readableness") rather than aesthetic appeal. In no case was a pupil classified as good or poor in more than one skill area.

Ten good achievers and 10 poor achievers at each grade level—4, 5, and 6 for handwriting and spelling, and 4, 5, 6, 7, and 8 for arithmetic—provided data for the study. Thus, there were 60 subjects—30 good achievers and 30 poor achievers—from handwriting and spelling and 100 subjects—50 good achievers and 50 poor achievers—from arithmetic. The subjects were from six elementary schools in a suburban (Parkrose, Oregon) school district. All subjects were white.

Task and Procedure.   The details of the inverted number-printing task as a measure of reactive inhibition are described elsewhere (Otto and Fredricks, 1963). Briefly, the experimenter put the inverted numbers from 1 to 10 on a chalkboard while the subjects attempted to make the inversions on their own. When the task was clearly understood, subjects were assured that they were not being tested in the usual sense, but they were told that what they did would be useful in "showing how children learn." The attempt was to secure motivation without anxiety. Subjects were then told to print inverted numbers in the ½-inch squares on their data sheets as quickly as possible and simply to write over any errors. They were given 12 massed 30-second trials, a 5-minute rest, and 4 more massed 30-second trials. The assumption is that reminiscence (the gain in post-rest over pre-rest performance) reflects the amount of reactive inhibition dissipated.

Subjects were run in groups of 7 to 16. Two experimenters were always present to insure accurate timing and to supervise the activity. To preclude pretest practice, each group was asked not to discuss the task until the experimenters left the school. All testing was completed in a 2-week period.

RESULTS AND DISCUSSION

Analyses revealed no significant differences in the numbers of digits produced by either good or poor achievers on consecutive trials (Trial 1 versus Trial 2, Trial 2 versus Trial 3, etc.), so selected trials only were considered in subsequent analyses. Table I presents mean inverted numbers printed on selected trials for each skill area and *F* values resulting from comparisons by simple analyses of variance of good and poor achievers' performances on respective trials. Repeated-measures analyses of variance (Edwards, 1950) of numbers printed on appropriate trials—by achievement level and grade level—were used to compare the performance of good and poor achievers in each skill.

Handwriting and Spelling. As can be seen in Table I, good and poor achievers both in spelling and in handwriting did not differ in performance on any of the selected trials. Analyses of variance of first and last pre-rest trials (acquisition) showed significant gains in digits produced by both spelling ($F = 10.08$, $df = 1/54$, $p < .005$) and handwriting ($F = 10.46$, $df = 1/54$, $p < .005$) subjects; but the only other significant F value was for Grade Level with spelling subjects ($F = 10.33$, $df = 2/54$, $p < .005$). Analyses of variance of last pre-rest and first post-rest trials (reminiscence) for spelling and for handwriting revealed significant F values for (*a*) Trial for each skill (spelling: $F = 63.92$, $df = 1/54$, $p < .005$; handwriting: $F = 171.69$, $df = 1/54$, $p. < .005$), indicating gains due to reminiscence for both skills; (*b*) the Trial × Achievement Level interaction for each skill (spelling: $F = 4.26$, $df = 1/54$, $p < .05$; handwriting: $F = 12.77$, $df = 1/54$, $p < .005$), indicating disproportionately larger gains by poor achievers; and (*c*) Grade Level for spelling subjects ($F = 6.69$, $df = 2/54$, $p < .01$) and the Trial × Grade Level interaction for handwriting subjects ($F = 4.82$, $df = 2/54$, $p < .05$), suggesting that performance is influenced by grade placement.

TABLE I   *Mean Numbers Printed and* F *Values for Selected Trials (by Skill)*

Skill and Level	Trial 1	Trial 5	Trial 8	Trial 12	Rest	Trial 13	Trial 16
Spelling							
Good	8.76	9.57	10.23	10.93	—	13.23	12.90
Poor	8.80	9.37	10.03	9.80	—	13.70	11.10
F	.00	.05	.04	1.48	—	.17	2.45
Writing							
Good	8.60	9.10	9.87	10.43	—	13.23	11.13
Poor	8.40	8.98	9.67	9.23	—	14.13	11.93
F	.12	.04	.07	2.64	—	1.06	.82
Arithmetic							
Good	11.98	13.10	14.24	14.58	—	19.82	16.66
Poor	9.56	9.84	10.18	10.32	—	14.86	12.32
F	11.41***	15.51***	25.75***	23.19***	—	17.60***	13.87***

*** $p < .005$.

That poor achievers' performances after rest increased disproportionately more than good achievers' implies that the poor achievers dissipated more reactive inhibition. Thus, the classic finding of the earlier reading studies is replicated for spelling and handwriting. Furthermore, Table I reveals that the pre-rest performance of good and poor achievers in both skills was predictable: Despite almost identical initial performance, poor achievers made lesser gains, ostensibly because they accumulated reactive inhibition more rapidly. Yet the analyses of variance across acquisition trials yielded no significant Trial × Achievement Level interactions and, therefore, no clear, statistically reliable support for the argument that the poor achievers actually accumulated reactive inhibition more rapidly than the good achievers. However, the intercorrelations reported in Table II provide a basis for, at least, further speculation.

TABLE II   *Intercorrelations Among Digits Printed on Trials 1, 12, and 13, Acquisition Gains and Reminiscence Gains by Good, Poor, and Combined Subjects: Spelling and Handwriting*

Score	Group	2	3	4	5
Trial 1	Goods	.4364**	.5580**	.4684**	.3396**
	Poors	.2106	.4224**	.4588**	.3064**
	All	.3228**	.4992**	.4494**	.3032**
Trial 12	Goods		.7058**	.5906**	.0299
	Poors		.7519**	.7720**	.3361**
	All		.6887**	.7004**	.2157*
Trial 13	Goods			.1926	.6870**
	Poors			.4088**	.3682**
	All			.2736*	.5594**
Trial 12-1	Goods				.3340**
(Acquisition gain)	Poors				.5047**
	All				.4323**
Trial 13-12	Goods				
(Reminiscence gain)	Poors				
	All				

* $p < .05$.
** $p < .01$.

In order to clarify internal relationships, the intercorrelations of total inverted numbers printed on Trials 1, 12, and 13, the acquisition gain (Trial 12 − Trial 1), and the reminiscence gain (Trial 13 − Trial 12) by good and poor achievers and by all subjects combined in both spelling and handwriting were determined. Data from both skill areas were combined because no important differences between skills were revealed either by the analyses summarized above or by an analysis of variance of the combined data. Most of the coefficients reach acceptable significance levels and, in general, appear to suggest that performance across trials is fairly stable (i.e., high digit producers remain high) and that although performance on Trial 1 is negatively related to acquisition gains (i.e., pupils who start low make greater gains), the correlation with reminiscence gains is positive. Most pertinent in the present context are the correlations between acquisition and reminiscence gains; that they are negative and substantial is consistent with the prediction in the present theoretical framework that small acquisition gains resulting from rapid accumulation of reactive inhibition will be accompanied by large reminiscence gains when the reactive inhibition is dissipated. This finding supports the basic assumption underlying the investigation.

The interpretation that follows is post hoc and, therefore, perilous; but the point is that the nonsignificant coefficients also appear to be consistent with present theory. Lack of a substantial relationship between the Trial 1 and Trial 12 performance of poor readers is expected due to the confounding effect of rapid accumulation of reactive inhibition. Poor achievers' poor performances on Trial 12, then, are accompanied by substantial reminiscence gains; but this is not so for good achievers, whose performances are not so markedly influenced by reactive inhibition. And, finally, poor achievers' large reminiscence gains are accompanied by good performance on Trial 13; whereas the relative absence of reactive inhibition would again account for the lack of a similar relationship among the good achievers. Granted the luxury of post hoc interpretation, the data suggest not only that poor achievers dissipate more reactive inhibition during rest but also that they accumulate it more rapidly.

Arithmetic. Table I shows that, contrary to the performance of spelling or handwriting subjects, the performance of good and poor achievers in arithmetic differed on each of the selected trials. Analysis of variance of first and last pre-rest trials yielded significant F values for Grade ($F = 15.43$, $df = 4/90$, $p < .005$), Achievement Level ($F = 34.28$, $df = 1/90$, $p < .005$), Trial ($F = 21.09$, $df = 1/90$, $p < .005$), and the Trial $\times$ Achievement Level interaction ($F = 6.33$, $df = 1/90$, $p < .05$). The significant interaction implies that the acquisition gains of good achievers were disproportionately greater than those of poor achievers. Analysis of variance of last pre-rest and first post-rest trials yielded F values significant at the .005 level for Grade ($F = 14.31$, $df = 4/90$), Achievement Level ($F = 34.06$, $df = 1/90$), Trial ($F = 209.39$, $df = 1/90$), and the Trial $\times$ Grade interaction ($F = 4.68$, $df = 4/90$). That the Trial $\times$ Achievement Level interaction did not approach significance ($F = 1.07$, $df = 1/90$, $p > .05$) implies no difference in the magnitude of good and poor achievers' reminiscence gains.

Thus, the arithmetic results did not replicate those for reading, spelling, and handwriting; but the failure appears to be due largely to the bizarre—compared to the other good achievers—performance of the good achievers in arithmetic. The poor achievers in arithmetic produced about as many numbers per trial as other poor achievers; thus, there is little support for argument that they responded in an excessively negative manner to the digit-printing task. The converse argument was appealing: That the good achievers produced many more digits may be due to their inherent motivation to do well with a success-associated task. The data offer limited support to the latter.

Wasserman (1951) argued that high motivation should raise the critical (tolerable) level of reactive inhibition necessary to produce the automatic-resting response: Thus high motivation should produce both increased performance and more reactive inhibition. His data confirmed the prediction. The present good achievers in arithmetic performed like highly motivated subjects: They produced more digits on each trial, and they improved rapidly; but contrary to good achievers in the other skill areas, they apparently accumulated as much reactive inhibition as poor achievers. An argument that good achievers in arithmetic are simply more adept at number printing would account for their superior performance but not for their greater accumulation of reactive inhibition.

Thus, there was tentative support for speculation that motivation level may affect the inhibitory potential of good achievers. Study II was an attempt to clarify that effect, if any.

Study II

If intrinsic motivation is in fact responsible, at least in part, for higher digit production and greater accumulation of reactive inhibition in good achievers in arithmetic, then high extrinsic motivation should produce similar results with good achievers in other skill areas. One purpose of the present study was to test the validity of the prediction. Another purpose was to examine the effect of high motivation upon poor achievers' inhibitory potentials. If, as hypothesized, their poor achievement is due, to any degree, to their already demonstrated tendency to accumulate reactive inhibition more rapidly than equally motivated good achievers, then increased motivation would only worsen an already undesirable tendency.

METHOD

Basically, the method was the same as in Study I except that instructions were varied.

Task and Procedure. The only change from Study I was that instructions were varied in an attempt to increase extrinsic motivation. In the earlier study the aim with all subjects was to secure reasonable motivation without anxiety. (These instructions will be referred to as the *original* instructions.) In the present study, subjects received either the original or *revised* instructions, depending on their group (see below). In the revised instructions considerable stress was placed upon the idea that speed was important because the number of digits produced would reflect general intelligence and learning ability; thus, it was implied that the task was a "test" on which it was important to do well for personal reasons.

Subjects and Design. Study II was carried out in two discrete phases rather than a single overall design, mainly for reasons of expediency in obtaining subjects. Good and poor achievers in Grades 4–6 were chosen according to criteria already described.

First, good and poor achievers—10 of each from each grade level—in spelling were tested. The purpose here was to examine the effect of high extrinsic motivation upon the performance of good achievers, so the poor spellers got original instructions and the good spellers got revised instructions. The subjects were from a single school in a suburban (Parkrose, Oregon) district. Second, good and poor readers—10 of each from each grade level—were tested. Here the poor readers got revised instructions, and good readers got original instructions. The subjects were from a single school in a semi-rural (Monroe, Georgia) district. Because the settings for the two phases of the study were markedly different, data obtained in each setting were examined separately.

RESULTS AND DISCUSSION

Table III presents means and *F* values for comparison purposes. Repeated-measures analyses of variance were used to make acquisitions and reminiscence comparisons.

TABLE III *Mean Numbers Printed and* F *Values for Selected Trials (by Motivation Level)*

Achievement and Motivation Levels	Trial 1	Trial 5	Trial 8	Trial 12	Rest	Trial 13	Trial 16
Good, High	12.23	12.80	13.73	13.50	—	18.90	16.27
Poor, Low	8.30	8.43	9.80	9.90	—	13.77	12.07
F	39.17***	25.67***	22.56***	25.27***	—	31.23***	18.41***
Good, Low	8.27	8.73	10.37	10.90	—	13.50	12.17
Poor, High	7.40	8.27	9.97	8.87	—	13.06	11.06
F	.86	.20	.16	7.59**	—	.29	1.77

** $p < .01$.
*** $p < .005$.

On each of the selected trials good spellers who got revised instructions produced more digits than poor spellers who got original instructions. This is in contrast to the performance of good and poor spellers in Study I. The suggestion is that the revised instructions did indeed produce high motivation. An analysis of variance of first and last pre-rest trials yielded significant F values for Achievement (Motivation) Level ($F = 59.43$, $df = 1/54$, $p < .005$) and for Trial ($F = 11.56$, $df = 1/54$, $p < .005$) only. An analysis of variance of reminiscence trials (last pre-rest and first post-rest) yielded significant F values for Achievement (Motivation) Levels ($F = 36.81$, $df = 1/54$, $p < .005$), for Trial ($F = 181.42$, $df = 1/54$, $p < .005$), and for the Trial $\times$ Achievement (Motivation) Level interaction ($F = 4.97$, $df = 1/54$, $p < .05$).

The significant interaction is most interesting, for the suggestion is that good achievers made disproportionately greater reminiscence gains than poor readers. This is in direct contrast to the previously demonstrated tendency for poor readers to make the greater gains. The implication appears to be that the highly motivated performance of the good achievers was accompanied by a greater accumulation of reactive inhibition. Thus, the data support the prediction that high motivation will yield both increased performance and more reactive inhibition; and, thereby, there is implied support for the notion that the performance of good achievers in arithmetic was influenced by their intrinsic motivation to do well with a number-printing task.

The data from the good readers with original instructions and poor readers with revised instructions are more difficult to interpret. The revised instructions did not produce the predicted higher performance in the poor readers, for the two groups differed in performance only on Trial 12. The implication is that the Trial 12 difference is due to poor readers' more rapid accumulations of reactive inhibition, but whether high motivation contributed to this expected tendency is not clear. An analysis of variance of first and last pre-rest trials yielded significant F values for Grade ($F = 4.32$, $df = 2/54$, $p < .05$), Achievement (Motivation) Level ($F = 4.88$, $df = 1/54$, $p < .05$), and Trial ($F = 20.8$, $df = 1/54$, $p < .05$). An analysis of variance of reminiscence trials yielded significant F values for Grade ($F = 4.67$, $df = 2/54$, $p < .05$), Achievement (Motivation) Level ($F = 4.03$, $df = 1/54$, $p < .05$), Trial ($F = 72.28$, $df = 1/54$, $p < .005$), and the Trial $\times$ Achievement Level interaction ($F = 4.33$, $df = 1/54$, $p < .05$). The between-achievement-levels differences appear to be largely attributable to the relatively large difference demonstrated on Trial 12. The interaction implies that the poor readers did, as expected, dissipate more reactive inhibition; but again, whether high motivation contributed to the expected tendency is not clear.

Subjectively, inspection of Tables I and III shows that the highly motivated poor readers produced fewer digits that other poor achievers. If the differences had reached acceptable significance levels—but analyses reveal they did not—it could have been argued with some conviction that the revised instructions may have had a generally debilitating effect upon the performance of the present poor readers. As it is, the revised instructions appear to have had no clear effect at all upon the poor readers' performances.

Conclusion

At this point some fairly definite and some strictly tentative conclusions can be stated.

The data reported here demonstrate a relationship between reactive inhibition and attainment in spelling and handwriting as well as in reading. Given a fairly low motivation level, good achievers in these skill areas dissipate less reactive inhibition during rest than do poor achievers. The implication is that poor achievers accumulate reactive inhibition more rapidly, but direct support of this latter notion is rather elusive.

To hypothesize a causal relationship between the tendency to accumulate much reactive inhibition and poor achievement, at least in certain skills, seems reasonable despite the fact that Hull's notion of conditioned inhibition seems to have fallen into disrepute. Inefficient learning precipitated by a strong negative drive (or resting response, which is caused by the presence of critical—intolerable—amounts of reactive inhibition) could account for lack of skill mastery and resultant chronic underachievement without dependence upon so elusive a construct as conditioned inhibition. In fact, a basic assumption in remedial education is that lack of skill mastery is not a permanent decrement but a disability that can be overcome. Studies that manipulate distribution of practice should help to clarify the role, if any, of reactive inhibition as a cause of learning problems.

There is some evidence that both the performance and the inhibitory potential of good achievers is increased when motivation (intrinsic or extrinsic) is increased. Yet no such relationship was demonstrated with poor achievers. The possibility that highly motivated poor achievers are simply unable to produce as many inverted numbers as highly motivated good achievers is not rejected by the present data. Another possibility is that instructions that produce motivation and improved performance in good achievers may provoke anxiety and poorer performance in poor achievers. A recent study by Van De Riet (1964) lends some support to the latter notion. Meanwhile, it seems clear that digit printing is an inappropriate task for quantifying reactive inhibition in good achievers in arithmetic; perhaps inverted alphabet printing would yield more predictable results.

REFERENCES

Edwards, A. L. *Experimental design in psychological research.* New York: Holt, Rinehart, & Winston, 1950.

Lynn, R. Individual differences in introversion-extraversion, reactive inhibition, and reading attainment. *Journal of Educational Psychology,* 1960, 51, 318–321.

Otto, W. Inhibitory potential related to school achievement of Negro children. *Psychology in the Schools* (in press).

Otto, W., and Fredricks, R. C. Relationship of reactive inhibition to reading skill attainment. *Journal of Educational Psychology,* 1963, 54, 227–230.

Peel, E. A. *The psychological basis of education.* Edinburgh: Oliver & Boyd, 1956.

Van De Riet, H. Effects of praise and reproof on paired-associate learning in educationally retarded children, *Journal of Educational Psychology,* 1964, 55, 139–143.

Wasserman, H. N. The effect of motivation and amount of pre-rest practice upon inhibitory potential in motor learning, *Journal of Experimental Psychology,* 1951, 42, 162–172.

4   The Intellectual Profile of Retarded Readers

LILLIAN BELMONT

HERBERT G. BIRCH

Summary.—*In the present comparative study, intellectual profile in normal and re-tarded readers was studied for samples homogeneous as to age (9- to 10-yr. olds) and sex (boys) selected from a total population of school children. Ss were 150 retarded and 50 normal readers matched for birth date and school class placement. Systematic equating for WISC IQ level was carried out. In general, weaknesses in intellectual functioning for the retarded readers were restricted to the Verbal Scale. The re-tarded readers, when matched with normal readers for Full Scale IQ, were character-ized by better functioning on the sub tests of the Performance Scale and poorer func-tioning on the Verbal Scale. The finding that inadequacy in language functioning rather than in perceptual or manipulative skills characterized the retarded readers was sustained by an intensive evaluation of use of language.*

The present study is an analysis of the patterning of intellectual functions in an age-homogeneous, representative sample of children who are significantly re-tarded in reading. Knowledge of such patterning can contribute to a better understanding of specific intellectual deficits, if any, which may underlie reading disability in this age range and in this way be of potential worth both for the early identification of children at risk of becoming reading problems and for the more effective management of those requiring remediation. In addition, a study of this kind may provide data which will be of use in subsequent analyses of the effects poor reading may have on the course of intellectual development.

In Table I we have summarized certain of the pertinent features of the in-vestigations which have sought to use the Wechsler Intelligence Scale for Chil-dren as a device for analyzing the profile of intellectual abilities to be found in reading retardation. Unfortunately, the results of these studies cannot readily be interpreted as being representative of intellectual patterning in children with reading disability because of the presence in each study of one or more funda-mental methodological weaknesses. These defects in method represent a major obstacle to an interpretation of intellectual patterning in children who are re-tarded in reading. They, therefore, require some detailed consideration.

The most ubiquitous defect in the design of the studies summarized in Table I lies in the samples used. One must question whether Ss who were selected for study were representative of any definable population of readers. Unless such representativeness can be determined, generalization of the findings is not

From *Perceptual and Motor Skills*, Vol. 22 (1966), pp. 787–816. Reprinted with permission of authors and publisher.

The research on which this report is based was conducted in cooperation with the Family Study Group of the Medical Council Obstetric Medicine Research Unit in Aberdeen, Scotland. It is sup-ported in part by the National Institutes of Health, National Institute of Child Health and Human Development (HD 00719-05); by the Association for the Aid of Crippled Children; and by the National Association for Retarded Children.

The authors take this opportunity to thank the members of the Obstetric Medicine Research Unit (MRC) and the Department of Education of the University of Aberdeen, Scotland, and the educa-tional authority of that city for indispensable help in making this study possible. The specific in-vestigation reported is one part of a broad cooperative program for the study of social and biologic factors in child development. The authors also wish to thank Mrs. Susan Lerman for all statistical computations.

TABLE I   *WISC Studies of Retarded Readers*

Study	Retarded Readers			
	No.	Age/Grade	Sex	Source
Graham (13)	31	?	?	Educational Clinic
Rabinovitch (22)	20 primary	10–3 to 16–3*	20 M	Clinic
	20 secondary	10–2 to 15–1	15 M	Clinic
			5 F	
Burks and Bruce (7)	31	Grades 3–8	26 M	?
			5 F	
Altus (1)	25	Grades 3–8	24 M	Guidance Dept.
			1 F	
Sheldon and Garton (26)	11	7–0 to 14–8	7 M	Summer Remedial
			4 F	Reading Program
Dockrell (9)	34	8–2 to 14–9	29 M	Educational Clinic
			5 F	
Hirst (15)	30	8–0 to 13–6	?	Summer Reading
				Clinic
Robeck (23)	36	6–11 to 13–9	32 M	Summer Reading
			4 F	Clinic
Kallos, *et al.* (18)	37	9–0 to 14–0	37 M	Reading Center
Neville (19)	35		35 M	Reading Clinic
Robeck (24)	80	6–10 to 13–9	68 M	Reading Clinic
			12 F	
Paterra (20)	33	6–5 to 14–6	?	Public Schools
Robeck (25)	20	6–11 to 12–1	19 M	Reading Clinic
			1 F	

* Adult Wechsler Scale used for four cases.

possible. A detailed analysis suggests that they were not representative of any definable population of readers but rather were agglomerations of retarded readers for whom intelligence test date were either available or readily obtainable. Weaknesses in sampling include small sample size, wide age ranges, joint consideration of children of both sexes, patients from reading clinics whose referral and selection biases are frequently unreported or unknown, and inappropriate comparison groups of normal readers against whom the retarded readers were viewed. Each of these weaknesses, either separately or in combination, has served to produce an unrepresentative and potentially distorted picture of intellectual organization in retarded readers.

As may be seen from an inspection of subject characteristics (Table I), the samples studied have almost all been small. The number of retarded readers studied has been as few as 11, and in only one instance were as many as 80 children considered. The median number of *S*s was 31 and the mean 35. These small sample sizes, in conjunction with the wide age ranges, make for difficulty in interpreting findings. Thus, with a sample of 35 *S*s and an age range covering as many as 8 yr., internal analysis would, if the ages are evenly represented in the sample, yield as few as 4 *S*s at a given age level. Since age distributions were not specified in any of the studies it was not possible to view the reports in this manner.

The majority of the studies reviewed used *S*s who were attending reading or education clinics. The orientation, selection policies, catchment areas, and referral bases of none of these services were specified. It is not clear whether, in addition to academic disabilities, *S*s of most of the studies had any associated dysfunction. Poor readers who attend reading clinics may be referred for a variety of social, neurologic, and behavioral reasons, and frequently tend to have concomitant personality disorders or to exhibit socially disturbing behavior in

TABLE I (cont.) *WISC Studies of Retarded Readers*

Normal Readers				WISC Findings for Retarded Readers		
No.	Age/Grade	Sex	Source	M_{IQ}	$IQ_{V vs P}$	Low Subtest Scores
	None			100.3	V < P	Arith., Coding, Vocab.
	None			91.8	V < P	Vocab.
				94.6	V < P	Vocab, Coding
11†	Grades 3–8	5 M 6 F	?	101	None given	Coding, Arith., Info.
	None			98.6±09.2	V < P	Coding, Arith., Info.
11†	7–0 to 14–8	7 M 4 F	?	100.3	V < P	Coding, Info., Arith., Vocab.
	None			104.5±11.1	V < P	Info., Arith., Coding, Vocab.
	None			109.3	V < P	DS, Arith., Coding, Vocab. (?)
	None			109.8	V < P	DS, Arith., Info., Coding
	None			99.2	V < P	Info., Coding, Arith.
35	?	35 M	Reading Clinic	100.3	V < P	Info., Arith., DS
	None			108.5	V < P	Info., Arith., DS, Coding
	None			107.6	V < P	Vocab., Arith.
	None			98 to 136	None given	Info., Arith., DS, Coding

† Control group not used to compare the performance of retarded readers.

the classroom. Consequently, unless there is specification to the contrary, Ss from reading clinics may be at high risk of having different types of concurrent pathology. When the sample studied is drawn from clinic populations, its character will not necessarily be determined by the degree to which the children are characteristic of retarded readers in a population of readers but will rather reflect the selection biases used for referral and the nature of services available in the clinic.

In all the studies, the age or grade range of Ss was wide, in general, spanning 6 to 7 yr. When the age range of children studied is so wide, sources for erroneous conclusions can derive both from heterogeneity in the nature of reading disability and from factorial changes in intellect which occur with age. The use of age-heterogeneous groups tends therefore to involve the unverified assumption that reading incompetence represents a unitary disorder, unrelated to age and to stage of development. An analysis of the reading task suggests that early reading is largely a matter of the development and mastery of perceptual skills in the various sense modalities whereas later reading relies more heavily on conceptual factors (e.g., comprehension, reasoning). Thus, young children who have not acquired primary reading skills and older deficient readers who have inadequate fluency or comprehension may be intermingled when a wide age-range of retarded readers is defined by a fixed number of years of reading retardation. This practice may either potentially obscure or exaggerate differences in intellectual pattern that exist between normal and retarded readers.

A similar type of difficulty attaches to the analysis of intellectual patterning over a wide age range. Since the composition of intellectual factors does in fact vary with age (8, 17), a wide age range can result in findings which reflect artifacts of age distributions rather than real differences in the patterning of intellectual capacities. If different intellective assets cluster at different ages during childhood, variation in organization may be obscured by age heterogeneity. The findings might therefore reflect artifacts of age distributions rather than real differences in the patterning of intellectual capacities. Such a consideration is especially important in evaluating populations of presumably atypically developing individuals and strongly suggests the need to use age-homogeneous groups or to make age-specific analyses.

Reading disability is pre-eminently a male disorder (5), and although some of the studies were restricted to males, others contained a variable proportion of girls as well. Uncontrolled sex ratios represent potential sources of difficulty for two reasons: first, because there may well be differences in patterns of reading disability in boys and girls; and second, because of noted (2, 29, 32) sex differences in intellectual organization at different ages. Consequently, it is unclear to what extent the presence of varying sex ratios in the groups studied has influenced findings.

The failure to use appropriately selected comparison groups or the tendency to use the standardization sample of the intelligence test (WISC) as a "normal" comparison group may result in both the artifactual obtaining and elimination of differences because of uncontrolled background factors. Only if one draws the comparison group from the same population as the retarded readers, can a definitive statement be made about differences between normal and retarded readers.

The present study was designed to obtain a representative picture of the intellectual patterning of retarded readers and of the aspects of their functioning which differentiate them from normal readers. This was accomplished by using a special opportunity to study a total population of school children in a medium-sized city having a population large enough to provide a group of retarded readers capable of being divided into subgroups for detailed analysis. The base population was also sufficiently large to permit analysis to be limited with respect to age and sex and to allow a comparison group equivalent for age, sex, school placement, and grade to be obtained. These procedures resulted in an age-homogeneous sample of boys retarded in reading whose intellectual profiles could be compared with those of normal readers who were both their age- and class-mates.

Method

The present intensive analysis of intellectual pattern in retarded readers is based upon an epidemiologic study of reading ability in all children born between the years 1951 and 1955 inclusive who were attending public, private, independent, and parochial schools in the city of Aberdeen, Scotland. Through the cooperation of the educational authorities and local school administrators one whole morning was set aside in December, 1962, for the simultaneous administration of reading tests to the whole population of school children in this city. Children who were absent were tested as soon after return to school as was feasible. This resulted in the standardized reading testing of 99.87% of all children in the 1951–1955 birth years who were attending any school in the city. For the purposes of the present study, the children in one birth year, 1953, were selected for intensive examination.

The tests used for assessing reading skills were a British sentence reading test, Test 1, published by the National Foundation for Educational Research in England and Wales, and three parts of the American Metropolitan Achievement

Test, Elementary Battery, Form B, Test 1, Word Knowledge, Test 2, Word Discrimination, and Test 3, Reading. All tests (except for absentees) were given in the classroom by the standard procedures.

The distributions of reading performances from which the children selected for intellectual assessment were drawn excluded all identified mentally subnormal children and were restricted only to children who had achieved an IQ of 80 or more on a group test of intelligence (Moray House Picture Intelligence Test 1) administered routinely by the schools to all 7-yr.-olds. Six months after reading evaluation, intelligence testing was carried out. At the time of intelligence testing the selected sample of children were between 9 yr. 4 mo. and 10 yr. 4 mo. of age. In order to avoid sex heterogenization in the analysis of findings, only boys were used for the purposes of our inquiry. Boys were selected because of the greater frequency of reading disability among them.

To study differences in the patterning of intellectual abilities, two groups, one of boys who were retarded readers and the other of boys who were reading at normal levels, were selected. The groups were defined as follows: (1) The retarded readers were 150 boys who were randomly selected from the 173 boys in the 1953 birth year whose raw scores on 3 or more of the 4 reading tests fell at or below the tenth percentile of the population tested. (2) The normal comparison group was made up of boys in the same birth year whose performance was not in accord with the above criteria for identifying retarded readers. One hundred and seventy-three children were matched with the poor readers on the basis of birth date, sex, and school class. From this sample, 50 *S*s were randomly chosen to serve as a normal comparison group.

TABLE II   *Age Distribution for Retarded* (N = 150) *and Normal Readers* (N = 50)

Age (Yr., Mo.)	Number of Readers	
	Retarded	**Normal**
10–4	3	0
10–3	11	1
10–2	13	2
10–1	13	8
10–0	15	4
9–11	18	4
9–10	11	7
9–9	11	4
9–8	5	3
9–7	9	3
9–6	13	4
9–5	19	5
9–4	9	5
M	9 yr. 10 mo.	9 yr. 9 mo.
SD	0 yr. 3.6 mo.	0 yr. 3.3 mo.

The age distributions of both groups are presented in Table II. The mean ages of the retarded and normal readers were 9 yr. 10 mo. (*SD* = 3.6 mo.) and 9 yr. 9 mo. (*SD* = 3.3 mo.), respectively. The difference in age between the two groups was not statistically significant.

An analysis was made of the raw scores of the two groups on the four reading tests. As may be seen from Table III, the mean differences between the two groups were all significant (*p.* < .001). The functional meaning of the

TABLE III   *Comparisons of Retarded* (N = 150) *and Normal* (N = 50) *Readers on Four Reading Tests*

Reading test		Readers		
		Retarded	Normal	
British Reading	M	12.8	24.5	
	SD	4.0	4.3	t = 17.7; p < .001
Word Knowledge	M	18.4	36.0	
	SD	7.9	6.1	t = 14.7; p < .001
Word Discrimination	M	13.9	28.1	
	SD	5.6	5.0	t = 16.1; p < .001
Reading	M	12.7	26.6	
	SD	4.8	7.5	t = 12.3;* p < .001

* Since there was a significant difference in the variances, the Cochran correction of the *t* test was applied.

obtained differences in reading scores of the children is better indicated if Metropolitan Achievement reading scores are converted into grade equivalent scores. Although the assimilation of British children to American norms is not entirely justifiable, a consideration of the differences between the two groups in terms of school achievement years is descriptively useful. The over-all mean difference between the two groups on the three tests was 1.7 school yr. (Word Knowledge 2.0; Word Discrimination 1.7; Reading 1.5). Fig. 1 contains the cumulative percentage frequency distribution of the amount of retardation (in school achievement years) by which the retarded readers differed from the mean over-all performance of the normal reading group. It can be seen from the ogive that fully one-third of the group lagged by more than 2 yr. behind the average performance of the normal comparison group and that almost all Ss (97.3%) were at least 1 yr. below the normal reading group in their over-all performance on the three reading tests.

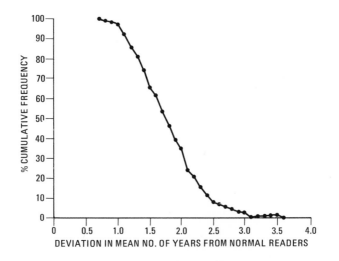

FIG. 1   *Cumulative frequency per cent distribution of the deviations in number of reading years of the retarded from the normal readers*

Such differences represent significant degrees of retardation especially when such retardation is related to the number of school years and the age of Ss. Two years retardation for older children with additional years of schooling would in fact not represent as severe a degree of retardation.

Ss of the present study were classified for social class based on the father's occupation at the time of the reading testing. The occupational categories are based on the British Registrar General's "Classification of Occupations, 1950." Social Class I represents individuals in administrative, managerial (industrial), professional occupations and officers. Social Class II contains professional and technical personnel (medical technologists, teachers, accountants) and farmers; Social Class IIIa contains non-manual white collar occupations and lesser civil service positions (e.g., post office, police). Social Class III contains skilled workers (engineering, metal, transportation, fishermen). Social Class IV contains semi-skilled workers. Social Class V contains unskilled workers. The unemployed were included with the lowest social class.

The distributions of social class in terms of number and per cent of Ss in both the reading retarded and comparison groups are presented in Table IV. As would be expected, since the children in the comparison group were drawn from the same school class as the retarded readers, the social class distributions of the two groups were basically similar. The retarded readers were somewhat underrepresented in Social Classes I and II, but the differences in the distributions by social class position were not statistically significant ($\chi^2 = 1.44$).

TABLE IV   *Social Class Distribution of 150 Retarded and 50 Normal Readers*

Social Class	Retarded Readers	Normal Readers
I and II*	9 (6.0%)	6 (12.0%)
IIIa*	14 (9.3%)	5 (10.0%)
III	73 (48.7%)	21 (42.0%)
IV	13 (8.7%)	5 (10.0%)
V and Unemployed	41 (21.3%)	13 (26.0%)
	$\chi^2 = 1.44; df = 3$	

* Frequencies for Social Class I and II were combined with those for IIIa since the theoretical frequencies did not otherwise meet the requirements for the use of the χ^2 test.

Intellectual assessment in both groups was carried out by means of the individual administration of the Wechsler Intelligence Scale for Children. To define most fully the patterning of intellectual performances, all 12 subtests of the WISC were administered to each child. Testing was carried out during school hours in the school attended by the child by one of 3 qualified examiners who had had previous experience in testing Scottish children. All testing was done "blind," in that the examiners had no knowledge of the reading group to which the child belonged, administrative personnel discussed no child with any examiner, and both retarded readers and comparison Ss were in the same school.

The WISC was administered using the test item alterations recommended for British children by the Committee of Professional Psychologists of the British Psychological Society. These changes represent the substitution of British money for American money in the Arithmetic subtest and specific substitutions on Information and other verbal items to take into account differences in national background.

All scoring of verbal items was checked by one additional examiner to ensure uniformity of scoring.

Results

In order to analyze the differences in intellectual patterning between normal and retarded readers in a comprehensive manner, a method of analysis was used which permitted the delineation of subgroups characterized by different levels both of intellectual functioning and of reading ability. The method used for the analysis of the patterning of intellectual performance was one in which successively greater delimitations were placed on the retarded readers identified in the population survey in terms of specifications of intellectual level and restrictions on level of reading ability. Such a method led to increasing clarity in the identification of differences in intellectual functioning between defined groups of retarded readers and their normal controls.

The results are presented in five sections. The first analysis is a delineation of the IQ and subtest profile characteristics of the entire group of 150 retarded readers and 50 normal controls. The second is one in which the retarded readers are divided according to level of intellectual functioning into a borderline IQ and a normal IQ group with separate analyses presented for these two groups and the normal comparison group. The third is a specification of the WISC subtest patternings of only those retarded and normal readers in the average range of intellectual functioning. The fourth is a comparison of the poorest readers within the normal intellectual range with normal readers individually matched to them for Full Scale IQ. Since the successive analyses of the subtest data increasingly focused attention on substantial differences in verbal performance between the two groups, a final intensive analysis of one aspect of language function is reported.

TOTAL GROUP FINDINGS

The mean IQ values for both the retarded readers and the normal comparison group are presented in Table V. Although the mean IQ's of both groups fall within the normal range, the retarded readers were significantly lower on all three IQ measures.

TABLE V   *Mean WISC IQ's for 150 Retarded and 50 Normal Readers*

WISC IQ	Retarded Readers	Normal Readers	t	p
Full Scale	92.1 ± 8.1	104.9 ± 10.1	8.26*	$<.001$
Verbal Scale	92.2 ± 8.5	106.6 ± 9.9	9.93	$<.001$
Performance Scale	93.5 ± 10.2	102.1 ± 11.8	4.30	$<.001$
$M_{\text{V-P Diff.}}$	-1.3	4.5		
t	1.42	2.86		
p	N.S.	$<.01$		

* Since there was a significant difference in the variances, the Cochran correction of the t test was applied.

A comparison of the mean Verbal and Performance IQ scores resulted in a small but significant difference favoring Verbal IQ in the normal comparison group and no significant difference between mean Verbal and Performance IQ's in the group of retarded readers. However, such mean comparisons perhaps obscure more than they reveal, and a more sensitive measure of differences in Verbal and Performance IQ patterning in the two groups may be obtained by determining the number of Ss in each group who had either higher Verbal or Performance IQ's. The results of this analysis indicate that there was a difference between the two groups in the numbers of individuals who had higher Verbal than Performance IQ's. Whereas 60% or 84 vs 58 of the retarded readers had higher Performance than Verbal IQ's, 60% (31 vs 17) of the normal comparison group had higher Verbal than Performance IQ's. This difference is significant ($\chi^2 = 7.19$, $df = 1$, $p < .01$).

Since there were significant differences between the two groups both in mean IQ levels and in verbal and performance patterning, it would be expected that the mean Scaled Scores and subtest profiles would reflect these trends. Table VI contains the mean subtest scores for the two groups. All but one (Coding) of the differences between mean subtest scores were significant. The greatest absolute differences in mean scores were significant. The greatest absolute differences in mean scores were found on the Arithmetic and Vocabulary subtests. Intratest scatter was small, with a mean range of 3.2 points for the normal readers and 2.2 points for the retarded readers between lowest and highest mean subtest scores.

TABLE VI   *Mean WISC Subtest Scores for 150 Retarded and 50 Normal Readers*

WISC Subtests	Retarded Readers	Normal Readers	t	p
Information	8.4 ± 1.9	10.5 ± 2.5	5.39*	<.001
Comprehension	7.7 ± 2.5	9.3 ± 2.5	3.90	<.001
Arithmetic	9.7 ± 2.3	12.5 ± 2.5	6.36	<.001
Similarities	9.1 ± 2.6	11.4 ± 2.8	5.23	<.001
Vocabulary	8.2 ± 2.3	10.9 ± 2.4	7.11	<.001
Digit Span	9.4 ± 2.3	11.5 ± 2.3	5.53	<.001
Picture Completion	9.9 ± 2.6	11.3 ± 3.0	3.18	<.01
Picture Arrangement	9.7 ± 2.5	11.0 ± 2.8	3.10	<.01
Block Design	8.7 ± 2.3	10.7 ± 2.9	4.88	<.001
Object Assembly	8.7 ± 2.9	9.8 ± 2.9	2.29	<.05
Coding	8.9 ± 2.2	9.5 ± 2.5	.16	N.S.
Mazes	8.5 ± 1.9	9.4 ± 1.9	2.90	<.01

* Since there was a significant difference in the variances, the Cochran correction of the *t* test was applied.

The relative similarity or dissimilarity in subtest profile between the two groups was explored in two ways. The first method employed was to determine the degree of relationship between the ranked mean subtest scores of the two groups. The rank-order correlation coefficient (*rho* = .70) indicated that the subtest profiles were similar in the normal and retarded reading groups.

The second method employed was graphic. A zero abscissa was established by using the deviations of each subtest score of the normal readers from the mean of their subtest scores as a base. Thus, if both the retarded readers and the controls had deviations of -1.0 from their own mean of subtest scores, the plotted difference would be zero and would fall on the abscissa. If, however, the control deviated by $+1.0$ from the mean of their subtest scores on a given subtest and the retarded readers by -1.0 on the same subtest, the retarded readers would be plotted as having a −2.0 deviation. This shifting zero permits a direct depiction of relative distance in subtest performance profile between the two groups. Thus, even when both the retarded readers and the normal readers have a subtest performance which deviates in the same direction from each group's own mean of subtest scores, greater positive deviation or a lesser negative deviation on the part of the retarded readers will both be reflected in positions above the abscissa. Conversely, greater negative deviations or lesser positive deviations in subtest score of the retarded readers will be reflected in positions below the abscissa.

This type of analysis of relative divergences from each group's mean of subtest scores (Fig. 2) indicates clearly a pattern of relatively greater negative deviation in Verbal subtests and relatively greater positive deviation in Performance subtests in the retarded readers. As may be seen from Fig. 2, five of six relative deviations on the Verbal Scale are in a downward direction and an equal proportion of the relative deviations on the subtests of the Performance Scale are in an upward direction for the retarded readers.

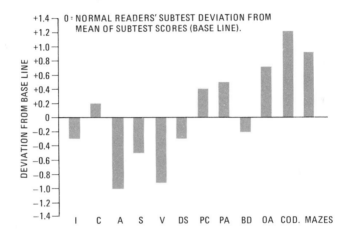

FIG. 2 *WISC subtest divergences of all retarded* $(N = 150)$ *from all normal readers* $(N = 50)$

Clearly, the graphic method provides a somewhat different picture from that provided by the correlational technique. The reason for this difference derives from the fact that each method asks a quite different question. The correlational method provides us with information on the degree to which the two groups tend to have similar subscore ranks. The graphic method determines differences in the relative magnitude of the individual subtest deviations. The findings suggest that, although the general direction of variation is similar for the two groups, the relative magnitudes by which they occur are different.

CONSIDERATION OF RETARDED READERS
WITH BORDERLINE AND WITH NORMAL IQ

When poor readers are identified solely on the basis of reading scores, individuals who are characterized by general slowness in mental development will necessarily be included in the sample. Such inclusion can potentially affect findings in two ways. One consequence can be the sufficient dilution of the retarded reading group by mentally backward individuals to provide pictures of intellectual functioning that are more characteristic of borderline normal mental ability than of reading disability. The second consequence of such dilution, even if it does not result in the first, is the inclusion of generally slow learners, whose reading level is not significantly more depressed than are other general aspects of functioning. Such heterogeneity makes it difficult, if not impossible, to explore characteristics of intellectual patterning which may be specific to reading disability *per se*. The design of the present study was intended to exclude all individuals whose IQ was below 80 on a group test of intelligence. Such a screen, however, was not entirely effective, and on individual testing it was found that 8 (5.3%) of the boys identified as poor readers had Full Scale IQ's below 80.

The distribution of WISC Full Scale IQ's for the two groups is presented in Table VII, from which it was clear that 60 of the retarded readers have IQ's below 90 and the remainder IQ's in the normal range. Thirty-four of the normal readers are in the normal range, and the remainder, with one exception, had

TABLE VII   *Distributions of WISC Full Scale IQ's for the Two Reading Groups*

IQ Range	Retarded Readers ($N = 150$)	Normal Readers ($N = 50$)
70–79	8	1
80–89	52	
90–109	88	34
110–119	2	10
120–129		4
130 and Above		1

scores falling at bright normal and superior levels. Since those poor readers with IQ's below 90 may not be specifically retarded in reading but generally slow in mental development, it is essential to separate them from those retarded readers without general slowness if one is to define intellectual patterns associated with poor reading as such.

An examination of the reading performances of the retarded readers with IQ's at or below the normal range is presented in Table VIII. As may be seen from this table, the degrees of reading retardation in the intellectually normal and below normal children are similar. In Table IX, reading level is related to

TABLE VIII   *Amount of Retardation (in School Years) from Normal Readers* ($N = 49^*$) *of Two Groups of Retarded Readers on Three Reading Tests*

IQ Group	N	Word Knowledge	Word Discrimination	Reading
IQ 89 or Less	60	2.4	1.8	1.7
IQ 90 and Above	90	2.0	1.8	1.5

* The one child with IQ below 90 in the normal reading group has been excluded from this and all subsequent analyses.

TABLE IX   *Reading Retardation Defined by Deviation in Reading Age from MA*

IQ Group	No. of Years Below MA of Reading Age in:		
	Word Knowledge	Word Discrimination	Reading
IQ 89 or Less	0.8	0.2	0.1
IQ 90 and Above	1.6	1.4	1.1

mental age. Those Ss in the borderline range appear to have no special reading handicap beyond that which would be expected by their general backwardness, except perhaps for Word Knowledge. In contrast, the retarded readers of normal IQ continue to exhibit more than 1 yr. of retardation in general reading, approximately 1½ yr. of retardation in Word Discrimination, and an even greater degree of retardation in Word Knowledge.

The intellectually defined subgroups of retarded readers were compared both with one another and with the normal comparison group. The groups differed from each other on all three IQ measures (Table X). There was a tendency for the group of retarded readers of normal IQ to have a slightly higher Performance than Verbal IQ ($t = 2.37$; $p < .20$). However, magnitude of difference was functionally insignificant.

TABLE X   *Mean WISC IQ's for Two Groups of Retarded Readers with Full Scale IQ of 89 or less and of 90 and Above and for Normal Readers with IQ of 90 and Above*

IQ Group	N	Mean WISC IQ's			$M_{\text{V-P Diff.}}$	t	p
		Full Scale	Verbal	Performance			
Retarded: IQ ≦ 89	60	84.4±4.2	86.1±6.7	85.5± 7.4	+0.6	.45	N.S.
Retarded: IQ ≧ 90	90	97.2±5.5	96.2±7.1	98.9± 7.9	−2.7	2.37	<.02
Normal: IQ ≧ 90	49	105.5±9.3	107.0±9.5	102.8±10.7	+4.2	2.66	<.02

This trend is more clearly seen in the analysis of Verbal and Performance IQ's in terms of numbers of Ss exhibiting a given Verbal-Performance difference. The retarded readers with IQ 89 and less had 27 Ss with relatively higher Verbal and 30 with relatively higher Performance IQ's. In contrast, the tendency to have higher Performance than Verbal IQ (54 and 31) was marked for the retarded readers of normal intelligence. The normal reading group contained significantly more Ss with higher Verbal than Performance IQ's (30 vs 17). The retarded readers of normal IQ, then, appear to have relatively greater difficulty with the demands of the Verbal, rather than of the Performance, portion of the intelligence test ($\chi^2 = 9.12$, $df = 2$, $p < .02$). The relationship applies even more strongly when one determines the numbers of individuals who had a difference of 10 or more points between Verbal and Performance IQ: at IQ 89 or less 14 retarded readers had higher verbal IQ's and 10 higher Performance IQ's; among retarded readers of IQ 90+ frequencies were 12 and 28; among normal readers of IQ 90+, frequencies were 15 and 4 ($\chi^2 = 13.40$, $df = 2$, $p < .005$).

The WISC subtest findings for the groups of retarded readers defined by intellectual level and for the normal readers are considered in Tables XI and XII and Fig. 3. As may be seen from Table XI, the absolute mean subtest score

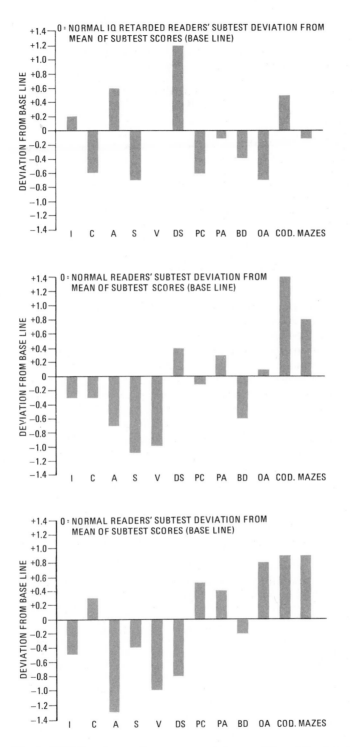

FIG. 3 (Top) *WISC subtest divergences of lower (N = 60) from higher (N = 90) IQ groups of retarded readers.* (Middle) *WISC subtest divergences of retarded readers of low IQ (N = 60) from normal readers (N = 49).* (Bottom) *WISC subtest divergences of retarded readers of normal IQ (N = 90) from normal readers (N = 49).*

TABLE XI   *Mean WISC Subtest Scores for Retarded Readers with Full Scale
IQ's of 89 or Less* (N = 60) *and of 90 and Above* (N = 90)

WISC Subtests	Retarded Readers		t	p
	IQ ≤ 89	IQ ≥ 90		
Information	7.5 ± 1.8	9.0 ± 1.7	5.36	<.001
Comprehension	6.3 ± 2.1	8.6 ± 2.3	6.22	<.001
Arithmetic	9.1 ± 2.4	10.2 ± 2.2	2.89	<.01
Similarities	7.6 ± 2.5	10.0 ± 2.3	6.00	<.001
Vocabulary	7.2 ± 2.0	8.9 ± 2.2	4.72	<.001
Digit Span	9.1 ± 2.5	9.6 ± 2.1	1.32	N.S.
Picture Completion	8.5 ± 2.2	10.8 ± 2.4	5.90	<.001
Picture Arrangement	8.6 ± 2.1	10.4 ± 2.4	4.62	<.001
Block Design	7.4 ± 2.1	9.5 ± 2.1	6.00	<.001
Object Assembly	7.2 ± 2.4	9.6 ± 2.8	5.33	<.001
Coding	8.2 ± 2.3	9.4 ± 2.0	3.33	<.001
Mazes	7.5 ± 1.4	9.3 ± 1.8	6.43	<.001

differences between the low IQ and average IQ groups for retarded readers were
fairly large; all differences were statistically significant, except for the mean
difference on the Digit Span subtest. The rank-order correlation between the
ranks of the mean subtest scores for the two groups (.72) suggests that the group
profiles were similar. As may be seen from Fig. 3, where the zero abscissa is
defined by the subtest performances of the retarded readers of normal intelligence, the low IQ group of retarded readers appeared to show relative weakness
on the Performance Scale, rather than on the Verbal Scale.

When the subtest performance of the low IQ group was compared to that of
normal readers, it was found that the two groups had essentially similar profiles
as reflected in a rank-order correlation coefficient of .71. However, when a profile was plotted, using normal readers' subtest performance as a zero abscissa,
marked relative weaknesses in Verbal Scale subtests were noted (Fig. 3, Middle).

In Table XII the mean subtest scores of the retarded readers of normal intelligence and of the normal readers are compared. As may be seen, the significant differences in mean subtest scores were restricted to Verbal Scale sub-

TABLE XII   *Mean WISC Subtest Scores for 90 Retarded and 49 Normal
Readers with Full Scale IQ's of 90 and Above*

WISC Subtests	Retarded Readers	Normal Readers	t	p
Information	9.0 ± 1.7	10.6 ± 2.5	4.00	<.001
Comprehension	8.6 ± 2.3	9.4 ± 2.5	2.00	<.05
Arithmetic	10.2 ± 2.2	12.6 ± 2.2	6.00	<.001
Similarities	10.0 ± 2.3	11.5 ± 2.6	3.75	<.001
Vocabulary	8.9 ± 2.2	11.0 ± 2.4	5.25	<.001
Digit Span	9.6 ± 2.1	11.5 ± 2.3	4.75	<.001
Picture Completion	10.8 ± 2.4	11.4 ± 2.8	1.50	N.S.
Picture Arrangement	10.4 ± 2.4	11.1 ± 2.6	1.75	N.S.
Block Design	9.5 ± 2.1	10.8 ± 2.8	2.83	<.01
Object Assembly	9.6 ± 2.8	9.9 ± 2.9	.60	N.S.
Coding	9.4 ± 2.0	9.6 ± 2.4	.50	N.S.
Mazes	9.3 ± 1.8	9.5 ± 1.9	.67	N.S.

tests, with the single exception of Block Design on the Performance Scale. All Verbal Scale subtest scores of the two groups differed significantly (*p*s of .05 to .001). Thus, the Full Scale IQ differences between the normal readers and the normally intelligent retarded readers reported in Table X appear, in the main, to reflect abilities tested by the Verbal Scale of the intelligence test.

The subtest profiles of the retarded readers of normal intelligence and the normal readers were in general similar (*rho* = .71). However, as may be seen from Fig. 3, Bottom, in which the subtest scores of the normal readers were used as the zero abscissa, relative weakness in Verbal subtest scores was present in the retarded readers of normal intellectual level.

COMPARISON OF RETARDED AND
NORMAL READERS OF AVERAGE IQ

Since the comparison of subtest patterns can be affected by differences in the intellectual levels of the groups compared, a further analysis was carried out in which IQ range was restricted to Full Scale IQ's between 90 and 109. This necessitated the elimination of 2 retarded readers from the group of *S*s with IQ's of 90 and over and 15 normal readers whose IQ's were above 109.

The reading levels of the two groups continued to be significantly different at the .001 level even though the magnitude of difference between the two groups was of course smaller than was the case when comparisons had been made without restriction of intellectual level. The over-all difference between the two groups of restricted IQ range was 1.4 school yr. Reading test differences were respectively 1.6 yr. (Word Knowledge), 1.5 yr. (Word Discrimination), and 1.1 yr. (Reading).

Even when IQ range was restricted, Full Scale IQ differences continued to favor the normal readers (Table XIII). This difference in IQ derives entirely from the normal reading group's superiority in Verbal Scale IQ. It is of further interest in this connection that whereas Verbal Scale IQ is significantly higher than Performance Scale IQ in normal readers, the reverse obtains for the retarded readers. In subtest scores (Table XIV), significant differences were all obtained on subtests of the Verbal Scale.

TABLE XIII   *Mean WISC IQ's for 88 Retarded and 34 Normal Readers with Full Scale IQ's in the Average Range (90 to 109)*

WISC IQ	Retarded Readers	Normal Readers	*t*	*p*
Full Scale	96.9 ± 5.2	100.6 ± 5.5	3.36	<.01
Verbal Scale	95.9 ± 6.8	102.8 ± 7.0	4.93	<.001
Performance Scale	98.6 ± 7.8	98.3 ± 6.7	.20	N.S.
$M_{\text{V–P Diff.}}$	−2.7	4.5		
t	2.33	2.88		
p	<.05	<.01		

The two groups had similar profiles as reflected in a rank-order correlation coefficient (*rho* = .66) between sets of subtests. In Fig. 4, with subtest levels of the normal readers in the 90- to 109-IQ range used as the zero abscissa, relative weaknesses in the subtests of the Verbal Scale were once again apparent for the retarded readers.

TABLE XIV   *Mean WISC Subtest Scores for 88 Retarded and 34 Normal Readers with Full Scale IQ's in the Average Range (90 to 109)*

WISC Subtests	Retarded Readers	Normal Readers	t	p
Information	8.9 ± 1.8	9.8 ± 1.9	2.50	<.02
Comprehension	8.5 ± 2.2	9.0 ± 2.2	1.14	N.S.
Arithmetic	10.2 ± 2.2	12.1 ± 1.9	4.52	<.001
Similarities	9.9 ± 2.3	10.5 ± 2.0	1.50	N.S.
Vocabulary	8.9 ± 2.2	10.1 ± 2.0	2.79	<.01
Digit Span	9.6 ± 2.1	11.0 ± 2.3	3.18	<.01
Picture Completion	10.7 ± 2.4	10.6 ± 2.2	.21	N.S.
Picture Arrangement	10.4 ± 2.5	10.8 ± 2.5	.80	N.S.
Block Design	9.5 ± 2.1	9.9 ± 2.2	.95	N.S.
Object Assembly	9.6 ± 2.9	9.0 ± 2.5	1.09	N.S.
Coding	9.4 ± 2.0	8.9 ± 1.9	1.25	N.S.
Mazes	9.2 ± 1.8	9.1 ± 1.7	.29	N.S.

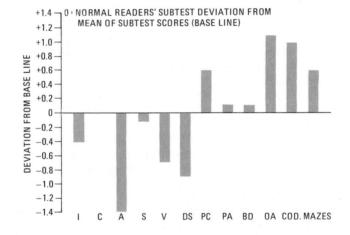

FIG. 4   *WISC divergences of retarded readers (N = 88) from normal readers (N = 34) both in the average IQ range*

COMPARISON OF THE MOST SEVERELY RETARDED READERS
WITH NORMAL READERS INDIVIDUALLY MATCHED FOR IQ

Clearly, factors of heterogeneity in intellectual level and in degree of reading retardation continue to influence comparisons even when IQ range is restricted. The restriction of IQ range only partially controls for differences in pattern which may derive from differences in IQ level. Stringent control for this factor can only be obtained when the individuals in the groups to be compared are matched for IQ.

An analysis of the reading scores indicated that retarded readers in the normal IQ range varied considerably in their degree of reading dysfunction. Such differences, too, could contribute to dilute the association between significant degrees of reading disability and intellectual patterning.

To control for both these factors a special subgroup of retarded readers of normal intelligence characterized by performance below the tenth percentile on all four reading tests was defined. This resulted in a group of 28 boys all with severe reading disability, 22 of whom could be matched for Full Scale IQ with normal readers (exactly in 15 cases, within 1 or 2 points in the remaining 7 cases). This definition of groups guaranteed that all retarded readers were in the normal IQ range, eliminated Full Scale IQ differences, and ensured that only significantly retarded readers were included in the reading retardation group. The over-all difference in reading between the matched groups of retarded and normal readers was 1.8 school yr. (Word Knowledge, 1.9 yr.; Word Discrimination, 2.0; Reading, 1.4).

TABLE XV   *Mean WISC IQ's for 22 Poorest Readers and 22 Normal Readers Matched for Full Scale IQ*

WISC IQ	Poorest Readers	Normal Readers	t	p
Full Scale	97.9 ± 4.8	98.0 ± 4.7	.71	N.S.
Verbal Scale	94.8 ± 7.4	100.5 ± 6.9	2.89	<.02
Performance Scale	102.0 ± 9.2	95.6 ± 6.2	2.67	<.02
$M_{V-P \text{ Diff.}}$	-7.2	4.9		
t	2.37	2.28		
p	<.05	<.05		

The WISC IQ data for the matched IQ groups presented in Table XV indicate that though equal in Full Scale IQ, the two groups differed significantly from one another in both Verbal and Performance IQ. The retarded readers achieved a significantly higher Performance IQ and a significantly lower Verbal IQ than did the normal readers. Within each group, the differences between Verbal and Performance IQ's were significantly different but opposite in direction. The Performance IQ was higher than the Verbal IQ in the retarded readers and the Verbal IQ greater than the Performance IQ in the normal readers.

The analysis of subtest scores (Table XVI) contributes further information on differences in the patterning of intellectual functioning for the two matched

TABLE XVI   *Mean WISC Subtest Scores for 22 Poorest Readers and 22 Normal Readers Matched for Full Scale IQ*

WISC Subtests	Poorest Readers	Normal Readers	t	p
Information	8.4 ± 1.7	9.5 ± 1.6	2.20	<.05
Comprehension	8.8 ± 1.7	8.6 ± 1.6	.40	N.S.
Arithmetic	10.3 ± 2.2	11.7 ± 1.9	2.33	<.05
Similarities	9.1 ± 2.8	10.0 ± 1.8	1.28*	N.S.
Vocabulary	8.2 ± 2.0	9.9 ± 2.0	2.83	<.01
Digit Span	10.1 ± 2.0	10.6 ± 2.3	.76	N.S.
Picture Completion	10.5 ± 2.7	10.1 ± 2.0	.57	N.S.
Picture Arrangement	10.8 ± 2.9	10.4 ± 2.7	.47	N.S.
Block Design	9.8 ± 2.4	9.3 ± 2.0	.76	N.S.
Object Assembly	11.0 ± 3.5	8.4 ± 2.6	2.77	<.01
Coding	9.9 ± 2.2	8.8 ± 1.8	1.83	<.10
Mazes	9.6 ± 2.2	9.2 ± 1.9	.67	N.S.

* Since there was a significant difference in the variances, the Cochran correction of the *t* test was applied.

IQ groups. The normal readers achieved a higher mean subtest score on all but one (Comprehension) of the Verbal Scale subtests. Conversely, the poorest readers achieved a higher mean subtest score on all of the subtests of the Performance Scale. This difference in pattern was significant ($p = .01$; Fisher's exact probability test).

When the various subtest differences were individually considered, the differences between the two matched IQ groups were statistically significant for the Vocabulary subtest ($p = .01$) and for the Arithmetic and Information subtests ($p = .05$). When individual subtests on the Performance Scale were considered, only one mean subtest score difference, that on Object Assembly, was statistically significant. Of particular interest, in light of frequent reports that Coding is especially poor in retarded readers (cf. Table I), was the finding that the retarded readers had a higher mean subtest score on the Coding subtest than did the normal readers.

When the mean subtest scores were ranked, the rank-order correlation coefficient between the relative position of subtests in the two groups was .20, a nonsignificant value, which indicates that there was no significant association between the patterning of subtest scores in the matched IQ groups of normal and retarded readers.

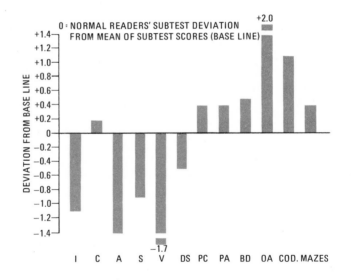

FIG. 5 *WISC subtest divergences of poorest readers* ($N = 22$) *from IQ-matched normal readers* ($N = 22$)

Fig. 5, in which normal reader's subtest scores were the zero abscissa, graphically illustrates relative and absolute strengths and weaknesses. These findings in the matched IQ group of poorest readers reaffirm and markedly strengthen the previously noted tendency for greatest weakness to exist on subtests of the Verbal Scale. Particularly noteworthy was the large divergence on the Vocabulary subtest, on which the retarded readers were very low and on the Object Assembly, and the Coding subtests on which the retarded readers presented exceptionally strong performances.

VOCABULARY SUBTEST ANALYSIS

In order better to understand the nature of the deficiency suggested by the generally poorer performance on the Verbal Scale by retarded readers, the Vocabulary subtest was more intensively analyzed. The analyses were related to two aspects of the vocabulary response. Did the differences in levels of ability found between the normal and retarded readers merely reflect the differences in the number of words the two groups of readers knew, or did the obtained differences in performance reflect differences in features of language style?

Failure on Simple Words. As a first step in the analysis, it was decided to determine whether there were differences between normal and retarded readers in the ability to define even the simplest words, i.e., the first five words on the WISC vocabulary list.[1] For the groups as a whole (Table XVII), a significantly greater proportion of Ss among the retarded readers than among the normal readers failed any of the first five words ($\chi^2 = 21.17$; $df = 2$; $p < .0005$). When a separate comparison was made between the normal readers and those retarded readers with IQ's of 90 and over, the relationship was sustained ($\chi^2 = 4.71$; $df = 1$; $p < .025$, one-tailed). When comparison is further restricted to those members of the normal and retarded groups who have IQ's in the 90 to 109 range, it may be seen that the relationship remains the same ($f = 17$ vs 71 retarded, 2 vs 32 normals). However, the smaller sample size resulted in χ^2 of 2.42 ($df = 1$, $10 > p > .05$).

TABLE XVII *Number of Ss Who Failed Any of the First 5 Words on the Vocabulary Subtest*

Group	Less Than 5 Correct	All 5 Correct
Retarded Readers: IQ $\leq$ 89	24	36
Retarded Readers: IQ $\geq$ 90	17	73
Normal Readers: IQ $\geq$ 90	2	47
	$x^2 = 21.17$, $df = 2$, $p < .005$ (one-tailed)	

Number of Words Known. An estimate of the number of words Ss knew could be obtained from the number of Vocabulary items passed. Passing could occur at two levels, which yield respective scores of "1" or "2." For purposes of assessing word-knowledge, either of these scores was considered to be equivalent as an indicator of acquaintance with the word. According to these criteria, retarded readers knew significantly fewer words than did the normal readers. A gradient of difference existed from the lowest to the highest IQ group. The group of retarded readers with IQ's below 90 knew fewer words than did the retarded readers of normal IQ [$Ms = 14.3$ (± 3.0) and 16.3 (± 2.9); $t = 4.00$; $p < .001$]. Moreover, the retarded readers of normal IQ knew fewer words than did the normal readers [$Ms = 16.3$ (± 2.9) and 18.4 (± 2.4); $t = 4.38$; $p < .001$].

When the analysis was carried out to control for IQ level by restricting both normal ($N = 34$) and retarded ($N = 88$) readers to the 90- to 109-IQ range, it

---

1 The findings of this analysis are based upon the standard administration for the WISC. In accordance with this procedure, Vocabulary testing for Ss 8 yr. and older begins at word 10. If full success (2-point definition) is achieved on all words 10 to 14, it is assumed that adequate knowledge of the earlier words in the list is present, and testing on these words is not carried out. If failure occurs on words 10 to 14, then testing of the earlier words is carried out until 5 consecutive full (2-point) successes are achieved (31, p. 68). It is of interest that a far greater number of retarded readers than of nonretarded readers had to be tested on the earliest words.

was found that even with these IQ restrictions the difference in number of words known [$Ms = 16.3$ (± 2.9) and 17.6 (± 2.1)] by the two groups was sustained ($t = 2.77$, $p < .01$, with t corrected by Cochran's procedure for significantly different variances). Furthermore, even when normal and retarded readers were matched for Full Scale IQ, number of words known [17.3 (± 2.1) and 15.4 (± 2.7)] was still significantly different ($t = 2.60$, $p < .02$). Retarded readers once again knew fewer words than did the normal readers. The findings indicate clearly that the readers even when of matched IQ were familiar with fewer words than were the normal readers.

Quality of Definition.   A further analysis of language function was made by comparing the quality of definition offered by normal and retarded readers.

Since the score of "2" for a given vocabulary item is presumed to represent a more abstract definition, a first analysis of the quality of language usage in the two groups of readers was made by determining the percentage of definitions which were scored as "2." The normal readers gave a higher proportion of "2" responses than did the retarded readers. However, when the comparison was restricted to the 90- to 109-IQ range, the difference was no longer statistically significant.

A careful perusal of Wechsler's criteria for a score of "2" indicated that such a score did not necessarily reflect a more abstract response. Therefore, an analysis of the quality of language usage was made on the basis of the scoring suggestions for the analysis of vocabulary responses first made by Feifel and Lorge (10) for the Binet and later developed for Wechsler Vocabulary items by Gerstein (11) and used by Stacey and Portnoy (28) with the WISC. In accordance with the latter methods, Ss' responses which had received any credit were scored on a three-point scale. Definitions were classified as (a) *descriptive* (bicycle—has wheels and handlebar), (b) *functional* (bicycle—you ride on it), or (c) *categorical* (bicycle—a vehicle). Only the responses made to nouns were scored, and Ss' definition was classified according to the highest level of response contained in the proffered definition. For example, a *functional* score was given to the definition of bicycle when the child defined the word by saying "it has wheels and a handlebar and you ride on it," because of the presence of the terminal phrase. If the child said "a bicycle is a vehicle that has wheels and a handlebar and you ride on it" a *categorical* score was given because of the initial phrase.

The analysis of the quality of definition was restricted to a comparison of the normal and retarded readers in the 90- to 109-IQ range. Each of the vocabulary responses of Ss was copied on a separate card and scored.[2] The percentage of Ss' responses in each of the three categories was then calculated. The data were treated in terms of these percentages.

It was found that normal and retarded readers of normal intelligence did not differ significantly in functional usage and that both groups gave a preponderance of functional definitions. These accounted for 55 to 60% of all definitions classified.

As may be seen from the mean percentage of descriptive and categorical definitions for the normal and retarded readers in the average IQ range, the two groups tended to show differences in the frequency of use of categorical and

2 Classification was done twice in order to establish reliability level. The cards were masked so that all identifying data were removed and after a lapse of 2 wk. were rescored. The degree of agreement between the first and second scoring was 93.4%.

descriptive definitions. The retarded readers defined words descriptively ($M = 25.4 \pm 15.0$) significantly more often than they defined words categorically ($M = 17.9 \pm 15.8$; $t = 2.87$, $p < .01$), whereas the normal readers had a higher percentage of categorical ($M = 23.2 \pm 15.0$) than descriptive ($M = 18.9 \pm 13.4$) definitions. This latter difference, however, was not statistically significant. The data further indicate that the retarded readers gave a significantly larger percentage of descriptive definitions (25.4 ± 15.0) than did the normal ($M = 18.9 \pm 13.4$) readers ($t = 2.24$, $p < 0.25$) and tended to give a lower percentage of categorical definitions ($M = 17.9 \pm 15.8$) than did the normal (23.2 ± 15.0) group ($t = 1.71$, $p < .05$, one-tailed).

Our analysis is necessarily incomplete because the WISC was administered in a standard way. The standard procedure, in which Ss over 8 yr. of age start with word 10, results in different ranges of verbatim responses from different Ss. This potentially results in a built-in advantage for the retarded readers since their language usage is being estimated for a sample of easier words than that upon which the estimation of usage in normal readers is based. Since previous analyses had indicated that the normal readers had a greater number of scorable responses, it was possible that any findings on quality of definition might have been a reflection of response number. Therefore, since the present analysis was restricted to nouns only, the numer of responses made to this word form was separately determined. When this was done, it was found that the mean number of responses for the two groups was not statistically significantly different for number of noun responses (12.7 for normal readers and 12.2 for retarded readers; $t = 0.69$). It was therefore decided to reduce the magnitude of possible influence of response frequency by comparing only those Ss who had been scored for quality of definition on no fewer than 10 nouns. This procedure necessitated the exclusion of 23 of the retarded readers and 8 of the normal readers from the analysis.

When low response frequency was controlled, all meaningful differences were magnified. The retarded readers gave a lower frequency of categorical as compared with descriptive definitions ($Ms = 13.7 \pm 10.6$ vs 25.1 ± 13.7; $t = 4.78$, $p < .001$). In addition, they gave a significantly higher percentage of descriptive definitions ($Ms = 25.1 \pm 13.7$ vs 19.0 ± 11.5; $t = 2.10$, $p < .025$) and a significantly lower percentage of categorical definitions ($Ms = 13.7 \pm 10.6$ vs 20.3 ± 11.7; $t = 2.75$, $p < .005$, one-tailed) than did the normal readers.

Discussion

The present study reports an attempt to define the patterning of intellectual functioning in a group of male retarded readers who were limited to a narrow age range and representative of retarded readers in a total population of school-children. The patterns of intellectual functioning in these 9- to 10-yr. old boys were compared with those found in a closely comparable group of boys from the same population who were not significantly retarded in reading. The characteristics of intellectual functioning on the WISC were considered by means of a series of successive comparisons, in the course of which increasing similarity in intellectual level between the two groups was achieved.

When the retarded reading group as a whole was compared with the normal readers, no sharp statistical differences were found in the patterning of Verbal and Performance subtest performances, and a significantly high correlation was obtained between subtest rank positions in the two groups. More refined graphic analysis, as well as the distributions of Ss with higher Verbal than Performance IQ's in the two groups, did, however, suggest relative weakness in Verbal Scale subtest performance in the retarded readers. However, no definite conclusions could be drawn from the first set of findings because of significant differences in intellectual level that obtained between the groups of retarded and normal readers.

An analysis of the distribution of IQ scores indicated that the group of retarded readers was made up of at least two subgroups. One of these contained Ss of borderline normal intellectual level whose poor reading performance was found to be one aspect of a generally low competence, whereas the other was composed of children at an over-all normal intellectual level whose reading competence was significantly discrepant from the level of their more general intellectual functioning. To homogenize the group for reading retardation *per se,* subsequent comparisons were restricted to children with normal Full Scale IQ's.

When comparisons were made between the retarded readers having IQ's of 90 and over and the normal readers, it was found that whereas the normal readers had significantly higher Verbal Scale than Performance Scale IQ's, the reverse relation obtained for the retarded readers. The differences in the patterning of Verbal and Performance IQ were also reflected in the fact that the proportion of Ss who had higher Verbal than Performance IQ's was significantly greater in the normal reading group. Profile similarities, as measured by a rank-order correlation among subtest positions, continued to be at a high level and suggested over-all similarity in subtest rank-position. However, graphic analysis indicated the presence of relative weakness in Verbal Scale subtests in the retarded readers.

However, restricting consideration to retarded readers in the normal IQ range does not fully eliminate IQ differences between retarded and normal readers. Therefore, as a third step in our analysis we equalized the IQ range (90 to 109) in the groups of normal and retarded readers who were compared. This analysis resulted in the strengthening of the previous findings, both as they reflected differences between Verbal and Performance IQ's and as they revealed relative weaknesses in the functioning of retarded readers on the Verbal Scale of the intelligence test.

The most stringent analysis of groups equal in Full Scale IQ was carried out by comparing intellectual organization in the most severely retarded of the poor readers and normal readers who were matched to them for Full Scale IQ. This procedure resulted in the magnification of all previously noted differences. Rank-order correlation of subtest positions between the two matched IQ groups resulted in a zero-order correlation, and the profile of subtest performance was markedly different. Graphic analysis indicated a marked depression of function on the Verbal Scale subtests for the retarded readers. This depression was most marked for the Vocabulary subtest and suggested the possible presence of significant difference in language style between the two groups.

This latter impression was substantiated by a detailed examination of definitions given on the Vocabulary subtest. The retarded readers of normal intelligence had greater difficulty with the simplest words on the scale and "knew" fewer words than did the normal readers. In an analysis of the quality of definition used by the two groups of readers, it was found that retarded readers of normal intelligence defined more words descriptively and fewer words categorically than did the normal readers.

The dual findings of difference in Verbal-Performance patterns and differences in language style between the two groups of retarded readers are highly compatible with previous reports (14, 16, 30) on the high correlation between verbal abilities and academic success. They suggest, too, that at the age-level studied, verbal abilities may have more relevance to academic competence, especially for reading, than do the performance skills measured on the WISC. It could be argued that the kind of "intelligence," e.g., verbal rather than performance, is of more relevance for children at this age level matched for Full Scale IQ than intellectual level, as such. The differences in language style may be seen as a reliance on more direct inputs on the part of the retarded readers than on a more indirect, symbolic use of language. Our findings do not answer the question of whether retarded readers have a verbal deficit because of their poor reading or because language is a primary deficit of etiologic significance for reading dysfunction.

Our negative findings are perhaps as important as the positive ones. Other workers, whose results are summarized in Table I, have repeatedly reported weakness in functioning in retarded readers on the Coding subtest. In none of our comparisons was this subtest performance found to be notably weak. Further, at all levels of analysis, in the age group of children studied, Performance Scale demands as a whole tended to be well responded to, and weaknesses were generally to the demands made by subtests of the Verbal Scale on the retarded readers. The difference in Coding score found in the studies of other workers may be a function of undetected sampling biases, inappropriate comparison groups, wide age ranges, or of the method of analysis of the data. The work of Neville (19), who used a valid comparison group and who found low Coding scores for *both* normal and retarded readers, suggests that the nature of the comparison groups used may be the reason for the finding.

Our findings of weaknesses on the Verbal Scale and strengths on the Performance Scale are not idiosyncratic. Rather, detailed analyses of the subtest patternings reported in other investigations are in accord with this general conclusion. However, little or no effort has been made in other studies to analyze this most general difference. It is probable that this failure derives in part from an excessive focus on perceptual and other performance factors rather than on language inadequacy in the intellectual organization of retarded readers. In general, the findings of the present study indicated that for 9- to 10-yr.-old retarded readers, intellectual weakness, when subnormal intellectual functioning is excluded, is sharply restricted to verbal demands. The intellectual problem appears to be one of language and its usage rather than of perceptual or manipulative skills as measured by the subtests of the WISC.

That these findings do not comprise the complete picture of cognitive lacks in retarded readers is clearly indicated by others of our studies of this group of children. In these studies we found evidence both of dysfunction in integrating auditory and visual information (6) and in lateral awareness (3). Further, whereas very young children with reading disability may well be ones in whom perceptual and performance skills are generally more markedly affected, in older groups of children retarded in reading one may find quite different patternings of defect (4). The findings, therefore, should be generalized only to children in the same age range.

One possible additional area of concern in the interpretation of our findings may derive from the manner in which the representative group of 9- to 10-yr.-old retarded readers was defined. These were not clinic cases but rather Ss drawn from the total body of male readers who were functioning at a level inferior to 90% of their age and classmates in a total normal school population. They therefore were selected epidemiologically for reading retardation, as such, and did not come to notice for a variety of other behavioral and conduct disorders that so frequently bring school children retarded in reading to clinical notice (12). They therefore were relatively free from the clinically associated neuro-behavioral concomitants that have been described in clinically obtained groups of retarded readers (21, 27). Our sample, then, is representative of the population of retarded readers in a community and not of any clinical group. In this sense our findings cannot be directly compared with those of other workers who have studied WISC intellectual patterning in retarded readers because of the undefined reference populations to which the earlier studies pertain.

A final difference stems from the fact that our retarded readers, as well as the normal comparison group, were Scottish children. It is possible that the noted differences in findings may derive from differences in educational practices and cultural milieu. Such a question, though fruitful for speculation, is presently not answerable. An answer must await the findings of a comparable epidemiologic survey currently being conducted in the United States (D. Bryant, personal communication).

RESUMÉ

The present study of intellectual profile of retarded readers differs from other studies in that it considers samples homogeneous as to age and sex selected from a total population of school children in a medium-sized city and compares their intellectual performance with that of a school class and age-matched group of normal readers. Intellectual profile of retarded readers was defined on the basis of their performance on the Wechsler Intelligence Scale for Children. Ss were 150 retarded readers and 50 normal readers matched for birth date and school class placement. Ss were all 9- to 10-yr.-old boys of a given birth year (1953) who were part of the total population of readers and were identified on the basis of an epidemiologic survey or reading competence in which 4 reading tests were used. From this available population of readers, the retarded readers were identified as those individuals whose scores on 3 of the 4 reading tests were at or below the tenth percentile. The WISC functioning of the retarded readers was compared with that of 50 normal readers.

The data were analyzed by a series of successive comparisons. (1) As a whole, the retarded readers were found to have significantly lower IQ's than the normal readers. (2) It was found that when borderline intellectual level was eliminated, the retarded readers were characterized in general by better functioning on task demands of the Performance Scale and relatively poorer functioning on the task demands of the Verbal Scale of the intelligence test. (3) With progressive delimitations of the groups studied, this finding was magnified. (4) When the subgroup of poorest readers in the average range of intellectual functioning was matched for Full Scale IQ with normal readers, it was found that the retarded readers were absolutely superior in Performance IQ and inferior in Verbal IQ to the normal readers. (5) These findings suggested that inadequacy in language functioning rather than that in perceptual or manipulative skills, as measured by the WISC, characterized this age group of retarded readers. (6) An intensive evaluation of Vocabulary subtest definitions in the retarded and normal readers in the average range of intellectual functioning indicated that retarded readers knew fewer words and defined significantly more words descriptively and fewer words categorically than did the normal readers.

The findings were contrasted with those obtained by other workers, and discrepancies were related to the nature of clinic samples as contrasted with samples of retarded readers representative of a population of school children.

REFERENCES

1. Altus, G. A WISC profile for retarded readers. *J. consult. Psychol.*, 1956, 20, 155–160.

2. Anastasi, A. *Differential psychology.* (3rd ed.) New York: Macmillan, 1958.

3. Belmont, L., and Birch, H. G. Lateral dominance, lateral awareness, and reading disability. *Child Developm.*, 1965, 36, 57–71.

4. Benton, A. L. Dyslexia in relation to form perception and directional sense. In J. Money (Ed.), *Reading disability; progress and research needs in dyslexia.* Baltimore: Johns Hopkins Press, 1962. Pp. 81–102.

5. Bentzen, F. Sex ratios in learning and behavior disorders. *Amer. J. Orthopsychiat.*, 1963, 33, 92–98.

6. Birch, H. G., and Belmont, L. Auditory-visual integration in normal and retarded readers. *Amer. J. Orthopsychiat.*, 1964, 34, 852–861.

7. Burks, H. F., and Bruce, P. The characteristics of poor and good readers as disclosed by the Wechsler Intelligence Scale for Children. *J. educ. Psychol.*, 1955, 46, 488–493.

8. Cohen, J. The factorial structure of the WISC at ages 7–6, 10–6, and 13–6. *J. consult. Psychol.*, 1959, 23, 23, 285–299.

9. Dockrell, W. B. The use of Wechsler Intelligence Scale for Children in the diagnosis of retarded readers. *Alberta J. educ. Res.*, 1960, 6, 86–91.

10. Feifel, H., and Lorge, I. Qualitative differences in the vocabularly responses of children. *J. educ. Psychol.*, 1950, 41, 1–18.

11. Gerstein, R. A. A suggested method for analyzing and extending the use of Bellevue-Wechsler Vocabulary responses. *J. consult. Psychol.*, 1949, 13, 366–370.

12. Gilbert, G. M. A survey of "referral problems" in metropolitan child guidance centers. *J. clin. Psychol.*, 1957, 13, 37–42.

13. Graham, E. E. Wechsler-Bellevue and WISC scattergrams of unsuccessful readers. *J. consult. Psychol.*, 1952, 16, 268–271.

14. Gunderson, R. O., and Feldt, L. S. The relationship of differences between verbal and nonverbal intelligence scores to achievement. *J. educ. Psychol.*, 1960, 51, 115–121.

15. Hirst, L. S. The usefulness of a two-way analysis of WISC sub-tests in the diagnosis of remedial reading problems. *J. exp. Educ.*, 1960, 29, 153–160.

16. Huge, D. S., and Stroud, J. B. Reading proficiency and intelligence scores, verbal and nonverbal. *J. educ. Res.*, 1959, 52, 258–262.

17. Jones, S. The Wechsler Intelligence Scale for Children applied to a sample of London primary school children. *Brit. J. educ. Psychol.*, 1962, 32, 119–132.

18. Kallos, G. L., Grabow, J. M. and Guarino, E. A. The WISC profile of disabled readers. *Pers. & Guid. J.*, 1961, 39, 476–478.

19. Neville, D. A comparison of the WISC patterns of male retarded and nonretarded readers. *J. educ., Res.*, 1961, 54, 195–197.

20. Paterra, M. E. A study of thirty-three WISC scattergrams of retarded readers. *Elem. Eng.*, 1963, 40, 394–405.

21. Rabinovitch, R. D. Dyslexia: psychiatric considerations. In J. Money (Ed.), *Reading disability; progress and research needs in dyslexia.* Baltimore: Johns Hopkins Press, 1962. Pp. 73–79.

22. Rabinovitch, R. D., Drew, A. L., De-Jong, R. N., Ingram, W., and Withey, L. A research approach to reading retardation. *Res. Publ. Assn. Nerv. Ment. Dis.*, 1954, 34, 363–387.

23. Robeck, M. C. Subtest patterning of problem readers on WISC. *Calif. J. educ. Res.*, 1960, 11, 110–115.

24. Robeck, M. C. Intellectual strengths and weakness shown by reading clinic subjects on the WISC. *J. developm. Reading*, 1962, 5, 120–129.

25. Robeck, M. C. Readers who lacked word analysis skills: a group diagnosis. *J. educ. Res.*, 1963, 56, 432–434.

26. Sheldon, M. S., and Garton, J. A note on "A WISC profile for retarded readers." *Alberta J. educ. Res.*, 1959, 5, 264–267.

27. Silver, A. A., and Hagin, R. A. Specific reading disability: follow-up studies. *Amer. J. Orthopsychiat.*, 1964, 34, 95–102.

28. Stacey, C. L., and Portnoy, B. A study of the differential responses on the vocabulary sub-test of the Wechsler Intelligence Scale for Children. *J. clin. Psychol.*, 1950, 6, 401–403.

29. Tyler, L. E. *Tests and measurements.* Englewood Cliffs, N. J.: Prentice-Hall, 1963.

30. Vernon, P. E. Ability factors and environment. *Amer. Psychologist*, 1965, 20, 723–733.

31. Wechsler, D. *Wechsler intelligence scale for children, manual.* New York: Psychological Corporation, 1949.

32. Wechsler, D. *The measurement and appraisal of adult intelligence.* Baltimore: Williams & Williams, 1958.

5   Lateral Dominance, Lateral Awareness, and Reading Disability

LILLIAN BELMONT

HERBERT G. BIRCH

Lateral preferences for hand and eye awareness of right-left relations were studied in an age-homogeneous sample of 200 boys selected from the total population of 9- and 10-year-old boys attending school in Aberdeen, Scotland. One hundred and fifty boys represented the poorest readers selected on the basis of four reading tests. The remaining 50 boys were controls matched for birth date and school placement and were drawn from the remaining readers. There were no differences in the lateralization of preferential hand and eye usage between the two groups. Significant differences were found in the level of right-left orientation. Confusion in right-left identification of own body parts in retarded readers was associated with the lowest scores on tests of sequential reading. Analysis of intellectual performance in the retarded readers indicated that disturbance in lateralization was more strongly associated with performance than with verbal IQ. The developmental course of the functions is considered, and the findings are compared with those found among samples in which selection biases may have occurred.

Two aspects of lateralization have frequently been examined in relation to reading retardation. Some investigators have sought to relate the emergence of lateral preferences in hand and eye usage to reading disorders. Children with reading disability have in some studies, but not in others, been found to have a higher incidence of inconsistent lateral preference or to be left-handed (Orton, 1937; Harris, 1957; Zangwill, 1962). Other workers have been concerned with spatial discrimination rather than lateral preference and have related failures in the ability to discriminate right and left to reading retardation. For example, Rabinovitch, Drew, DeJong, Ingram, and Withey (1954, p. 378) in their study of primary reading retardation reported that "directional (right-left) confusion was an extremely frequent finding."

The view that disturbances in right-left orientation underlie reading disability has recently been questioned by Benton and Kemble (1960). These workers have suggested that the reported differences in right-left orientation between normal readers and children with reading disability (Harris, 1957; Hermann and Norrie, 1958) are artifacts of IQ differences and that when IQ is controlled no significant differences in right-left orientation are to be found. However, the number of children with reading disability studied by Benton and Kemble was small; and the children studied were drawn from a remedial treatment center, the selection biases of which are unknown.

To a considerable degree the limitations enumerated for Benton and Kemble's study hold for almost all studies on the relation of right-left orientation and

From *Child Development*, Vol. 36 (March, 1965), pp. 57–71. Reprinted with permission of The Society for Research in Child Development, Inc. Copyright © 1965 by the Society for Research in Child Development, Inc.

The research on which this report is based was conducted in cooperation with the Family Study Group of the Medical Council Obstetric Medicine Research Unit in Aberdeen, Scotland, the same group as in previous report. See page 29.

lateral dominance to reading disability. The samples studied have frequently been drawn from clinic populations with unknown selection biases; IQ has either been unknown or unreported; and age and sex ratios have varied. Differences in findings, therefore, may derive equally as readily from differences in the samples studied as from correct or incorrect attributions of an association among the phenomena of lateral preference, lateral awareness, and reading disability.

The first step required to clarify the relationship between lateralization of function, lateral awareness, and reading disability is the analysis of these functions in poor readers and controls drawn from a total population of school children whose IQ's are known. The present paper reports the results of such a total population study.

Method

SUBJECTS

The subjects studied were drawn from the total population of school children of a single birth year (1953) in the city of Aberdeen, Scotland. At the time of the present study all the children were between 9 years 4 months and 10 years 4 months of age. Six months prior to this study, all children in the city's public, private, and parochial schools, representing 99.87 per cent of the total number of children in this birth year resident in the city, had received 3 hours of reading testing. The tests used for assessing reading skills were a British sentence-reading test, Form N.S. 6, published by the National Foundation for Educational Research in England and Wales, and three parts of the Metropolitan Achievement Test, Elementary Battery, Form B: Test 1, Word Knowledge; Test 2, Word Discrimination; and Test 3, Reading.

Reading disturbance has been shown to be significantly more frequent in boys than in girls (Bentzen, 1963). In order to eliminate sex differences and yet ensure an adequate number of retarded readers, only boys were selected for the present study. The distributions from which the subjects were drawn excluded children whose IQ's were below 80 on group tests administered by the school.

Two groups were compared: retarded readers and normal controls. The retarded-reader group consisted of those boys whose raw scores on at least three of the four reading tests were at or below the tenth percentile. This resulted in the indentification of a group of 173 seriously retarded readers, whose reading level was two or more years below age and grade expectation. From these, 150 children were chosen by random number for the present investigation. The normal comparison group was made up of 50 subjects not among the lowest 10 per cent of readers, chosen on a random basis from the 173 males who had been matched to the poor readers on the basis of birth date and school class placement.

As would be expected, the groups do not differ significantly in age. The mean age of the normal readers was 9 years 9 months (SD 3.3 mos.) and that of the retarded readers 9 years 10 months (SD 3.6 mos.).

At the time of the present study, intelligence-test data (WISC) were collected on all subjects. The mean WISC Full Scale IQ's of the normal and retarded readers were 104.9 (range 75 − 130; SD 10.1) and 92.1 (range 73 − 112; SD 8.1), respectively. The difference between mean IQ's is significant at better than the .01 level of confidence. The analysis of WISC findings forms the basis of a separate report (in progress), but certain features of the WISC data will be considered in connection with the analysis of the present results.

TABLE I   *Comparisons Between Retarded and Normal Readers on Four Reading Tests*

Reading Test	Group	
	Retarded Readers **(N = 150)**	**Normal Readers** **(N = 50)**
British reading:		
M	12.8	24.5
SD	4.0	4.3
	$t = 17.7; p < .001$	
Word knowledge:		
M	18.4	36.0
SD	7.9	6.1
	$t = 14.7; p < .001$	
Word discrimination:		
M	13.9	28.1
SD	5.6	5.0
	$t = 16.1; p < .001$	
Reading:		
M	12.7	26.6
SD	4.8	7.5
	$t^* = 12.3; p < .001$	

* Since there was a significant difference in the variances, the Cochran correction of the *t* test was applied.

The mean raw scores on all reading tests for both groups are given in Table I. It can be seen that differences in ability between the two groups on each of the four reading tests were significant at better than the .001 level of confidence.

PROCEDURE

The examinations for laterality and right-left awareness were carried out by three qualified psychologists. None of the three examiners was aware of the reading ability of any child tested. All children were tested individually, and all testing was conducted in a single session. Lateral preference was tested for hand and eye, followed by testing for right-left awareness.

Hand Preference.   The subjects were required to respond in pantomime to 10 hand preference items, drawn from the Harris scale (1947). The formats for presenting each item were almost identical. For example, in administering item 1, the experimenter says, "This is how I throw a ball" (demonstrate). "Now let me see you throw a ball." The items used were: (1) throw ball, (2) wind watch, (3) hammer nail, (4) brush teeth, (5) comb hair, (6) turn door knob, (7) hold eraser, (8) cut with scissors, (9) cut with knife, (10) write. The hand used by the subject for each activity was recorded.

Eye Preference.   The following items were used in determining eyedness:

1. Kaleidoscope. The child was handed the kaleidoscope and told, "Look through this."
2. Rifle-sighting. The experimenter handed the child a toy rifle and asked, "Do you know how to aim a rifle?" If the child said "Yes," he was asked to do so. If the child said "No," he was told to "close one eye, look through the sight, hold it on your shoulder, and make believe you are going to shoot."

3. Paper with hole. The experimenter handed the child a 6-inch square of paper with a ½-inch square hole in the center. The child was told, "Look at me through this hole."

4. Two pencils. The examiner handed the child two pencils and said, "Hold these two pencils in front of you and line them up with my nose."

5. Paper clip. The experimenter placed a paper clip on the table, handed the subject the paper with the hole in it, and said, "Look at this [clip] through the hole and tell me whether it looks larger or smaller than now."

The eye which was used for each task was recorded.

Rating Criteria for Lateral Dominance.   Handedness was scored as Total Right or Left if all 10 tasks were carried out with the same hand; Preponderantly Right or Left if on eight or nine tasks a given hand was used; Mixed if five, six, or seven tasks were performed with one hand and the remainder with the other hand.

Eyedness was scored as Total Right or Left if all five tasks were carried out with the same eye; Preponderantly Right or Left if on four tasks a given eye was used; Mixed if two or three of the tasks were performed with one eye and the remainder with the other eye.

Hand-Eye Dominance was rated as follows: If the subject had been rated Total Right or Total Left on both hand and eye preferences, his score was Total Right or Total Left. If the subject had been rated as Preponderantly Right or Left in eye and hand, his score was Preponderantly Right or Preponderantly Left. If the subject had been rated as Mixed on hand and/or eye or if he showed crossed preferences (e.g., right-handed and left-eyed), either with Total or Preponderant ratings, his score was Mixed for hand-eye dominance.

Awareness of Right-Left Relations.   In order to test the child's ability to make right-left discriminations on his own body parts, seven items were used. The first three questions were (1) "Raise your right hand"; (2) "Touch your left ear"; (3) "Point to your right eye." Four items form part of the Piaget schedule described below. These questions were: (1) "Show me your right hand"; (2) "Now show me your left hand"; (3) "Show me your right leg"; (4) "Now show me your left leg."

Each subject was also asked to respond to an additional series of questions derived from Piaget (1928) concerning awareness of right-left relations on other than his own body. The tasks included the identification of lateralization on the body of the examiner facing the child, as well as the degree to which awareness of right-left object relations exists. The conditions and questions involved in these tasks are indicated below. All responses were recorded, and any numbered group was scored as correct only when all of its component parts were answered appropriately.

The Piaget schedule of right-left awareness items follows:

1. Show me your right hand. _____ Now show me your left hand. _____ Show me your right leg. _____ Now show me your left leg. _____

2. (*E* sits opposite *S*) Show me my right hand. _____ Now my left. _____ Show me my right leg. _____ Now my left leg. _____

3. (Place coin on table left of a pencil in relation to *S*.) Is the pencil to the right or to the left? _____ And the penny, is it to the right or to the left? _____ (Have *S* go around to the opposite side of table and repeat questions.) Is the pencil to the right or to the left? _____ And the penny, is it to the right or to the left? _____

4. (*S* is opposite *E; E* has a coin in right hand and a bracelet [or watch] on left arm.) You see this penny. Have I got it in my right hand or in my left? _____ And the bracelet, is it on my right arm or my left? _____

5. (*S* is opposite three objects in a row: a pencil to the left, a key in the middle, and a coin to the right.) Is the pencil to the left or to the right of the key? _____ Is the pencil to the left or to the right of the penny? _____ Is the key to the left or to the right of the penny? _____ Is the key to the left or to the right of the pencil? _____ Is the penny to the left or to the right of the pencil? _____ Is the penny to the left or to the right of the key? _____

6. (*S* is opposite three objects in a row: a key to the left, a piece of paper in middle, and a pencil to the right. The following instructions are given to *S:* "Listen carefully, I am going to show you three things for a little while. You must look at them very carefully, and then afterwards tell me from memory how the things are arranged. Ready." The three objects are presented to *S* for 30 seconds and then covered, and he is then asked the following questions.) Is the key to the left or the right of the piece of paper? _____ Is the key to the left or the right of the pencil? _____ Is the paper to the left or the right of the key? _____ Is the paper to the left or the right of the pencil? _____ Is the pencil to the left or the right of the key? _____ Is the pencil to the left or the right of the paper? _____

Results

LATERAL DOMINANCE

The findings on lateral preferences for the two groups of readers are presented in Tables II, III, and IV. As may be seen from an examination of Table II, which contains the hand-dominance ratings of normal and retarded readers, in

TABLE II   *Hand Dominance of Normal and Retarded Readers*

	Normal Readers		**Retarded Readers**	
	N	**Per cent**	*N*	**Per cent**
Total Right	35	70	107	71
Preponderantly Right	6	12	26	17
Mixed	2	4	3	2
Preponderantly Left	4	8	7	5
Total Left	3	6	7	5
Total	50	100	150	100

both groups the majority of the subjects are clearly right-handed or show a strong tendency to right-handedness. When 100 per cent consistency for hand usage is taken as the criterion, the remaining subjects with mixed handedness, together with those who show some inconsistencies in handedness, account for less than one-fourth of either group. The differences in degree of hand usage between the two groups of readers are not statistically significant.

The findings on eye dominance presented in Table III indicate that a somewhat larger percentage of retarded readers had other than 100 per cent consistency in right or left eyedness. Whereas 86 per cent of the normal readers were consistently right- or left-eyed, 79 per cent of the retarded readers showed consistent eyedness. However, the differences in eye dominance do not reach a satisfactory level of statistical significance.

TABLE III   *Eye Dominance of Normal and Retarded Readers*

	Normal Readers		Retarded Readers	
	N	Per cent	N	Per cent
Total Right	33	66	85	57
Preponderantly Right	4	8	13	9
Mixed	2	4	10	7
Preponderantly Left	1	2	9	6
Total Left	10	20	33	22
Total	50	100	150	100

The data for the interrelation of eye and hand dominance in the retarded and normal readers are presented in Table IV. Approximately one-half of the subjects in each group achieved consistency in eye-hand dominance. Mixed eye-hand dominance was exhibited by 26 and 31 per cent of the normal and retarded readers, respectively. The over-all differences between retarded and normal readers in the consistency of eye-hand dominance are clearly not statistically significant.

TABLE IV   *Hand-Eye Co-dominance of Normal and Retarded Readers*

	Normal Readers		Retarded Readers	
	N	Per cent	N	Per cent
Total Right	25	50	69	46
Preponderantly Right	8	16	25	17
Mixed	13	26	47	31
Preponderantly Left	2	4	4	3
Total Left	2	4	5	3
Total	50	100	150	100

Because of the emphasis placed on mixed laterality in other studies of reading retardation (Orton, 1937; Zangwill, 1962), the reading scores obtained by the two groups were related to consistency in hand, eye, and hand-eye dominance. When the normal and retarded readers were divided into those who were consistently right or left dominant and those who showed any degree of inconsistency in lateral dominance, mean reading scores indicated small differences between the consistent and inconsistent groups. Among the retarded readers, those who were consistent in hand and eye dominance tended to have slightly higher mean reading scores. However, within the sample of normal readers, the inconsistent-dominance group tended to have somewhat higher mean reading scores than did those who were consistent in dominance. All of the differences were small, and none achieved an acceptable level of statistical significance.

In summary, the data on lateral preference presented in Tables II, III, and IV suggest strongly that the boys who were retarded in reading did not differ significantly in any type of mixed dominance from normal readers of the same age. Further, within each group no consistent relationship between lateral preferences and level of reading performance was found.

RIGHT-LEFT AWARENESS

Two sets of data on right-left awareness were available. One was concerned with the child's awareness of right and left on his own body; the other dealt with the subject's conceptions of right and left in relation to self, to others, and to the environment. As may be seen in Table V, the group of retarded readers included a greater number of children who were not able to identify right and left on own body parts with perfect accuracy. Whereas only one of the normal readers (who failed only one item) failed to achieve a perfect score, twenty-nine of the retarded readers misidentified left and right on their own bodies. This difference between groups is significant at the .01 level of confidence.

TABLE V   *Right-Left Awareness of Own Body Parts in Normal and Retarded Readers**

	All Items Correct	**One or More Items Incorrect**
Normal Readers	49	1
Retarded Readers	121	29

* $x^2 = 7.53$; $df = 1$; $p < .01$.

In Table VI the reading test scores of those retarded readers who passed all items concerned with right-left awareness of own body parts are compared with the reading performances of those in the same group who did not pass all own-body-part items. For all sections of the reading tests, and mean performances of those children who were consistently correct in the lateral location of parts of their own bodies were superior to those of the children who made any error in such lateral location. Two of these mean differences, both on tests which evaluated sequential reading, were statistically significant. On the remaining two tests, which were concerned with isolated word discrimination, the differences approached statistical significance.

TABLE VI   *Relation of Reading Score to Right-Left Awareness of Own Body Parts in Retarded Readers*

Reading Tests	Did Not Pass All Items (N = 29)		Passed All Items (N = 121)		t	p*
	Mean	Standard Deviation	Mean	Standard Deviation		
British Reading	11.7	4.5	13.1	3.8	1.71	<.05
Word Discrimination	12.7	6.6	14.2	5.4	1.30	<.10
Word Knowledge	16.9	7.6	18.7	7.9	1.12	<.15
Reading	10.7	4.7	13.1	4.8	2.47	<.01

* One-tailed test applied because of the directional nature of the hypothesis.

It is necessary to distinguish two groups among the 29 children who failed to perform perfectly in the lateral location of parts of their own bodies. One group was composed of nine children who consistently reversed right and left when dealing with parts of their own bodies. The remaining children exhibited no consistent reversal tendency. When the consistent reversers were compared for reading test performance with the children who passed all items concerned with the lateral location of body parts (Table VII), significant differences on all four tests of reading were obtained. For all measures the total reversal group was the poorer reading group.

TABLE VII   *Relation of Reading Score to Total Confusion in Lateralizing Own Body Parts in Retarded Readers*

Reading Tests	Failed All R–L Items (N = 9)		Passed All R–L Items (N = 121)		t	p*
	Mean	Standard Deviation	Mean	Standard Deviation		
British Reading	10.8	4.0	13.1	3.8	1.73	<.05
Word Knowledge	13.5	5.5	18.7	7.9	1.93	<.05
Word Discrimination	9.3	6.2	14.2	5.4	2.62	<.005
Reading	8.8	5.6	13.1	4.8	2.59	<.005

* One-tailed test applied because of the directional nature of the hypothesis.

The second body of data on right-left awareness is based upon Piaget's schedule of right-left conceptualization. Only the first item of this schedule is directly concerned with the child's own body parts. The remaining five items deal with the ability to make accurate right-left identifications on the body of the examiner and among environmental objects presented to the child. The age-specific norms available for the Piaget schedule, based upon Swiss (Piaget, 1928) and American (Belmont and Birch, 1963) samples, indicate that for the age group of children in the present study it would be expected that 75 per cent or more of the children would successfully pass items 1, 2, 3, and 4 of the schedule. Smaller percentages would be expected to respond appropriately to items 5 and 6.

The data presented in Table VIII indicate that the normal readers performed in accordance with age-specific expectation on items 1 through 4 of the schedule. In contrast, the retarded readers as a group performed at the 85 per cent level only for item 1 of the schedule, a level of performance which resembles that of the 6-year-olds in the standardization samples. The differences between the normal and retarded readers are sustained, too, for the more difficult items, 5 and 6.

TABLE VIII   *Subjects Who Passed Right-Left Conception Items on Piaget Schedule (Per Cent)*

Item	Normal Readers (N = 50)	Retarded Readers (N = 150)
1	98	85
2	76	63
3	90	73
4	82	69
5	46	25
6	36	21

In order to determine the general reliability of differences in right-left awareness between the groups of normal and retarded readers, the groups were compared with respect to the number of individuals who were differentially successful in dealing with the four tasks they would have been expected to pass at their age. As may be seen from Table IX, the greatest proportion (62 per cent) of the normal readers passed all four items. In contrast, only 37 per cent of the retarded readers did so. In addition, 37 per cent of the retarded readers passed two or less items, whereas only 16 per cent of normal readers passed as

TABLE IX *Performances of Normal and Retarded Readers on First Four Items of Piaget Schedule*

No. Items Passed	Normal Readers		Retarded Readers	
	N	Per cent	N	Per cent
4	31	62	56	37
3	11	22	38	25
2	8	16	44	29
1*	0		8	5
0*	0		4	3

* Steps combined in calculation of x^2. $x^2 = 11.96$; df = 3; $p < .01$.

few as two items. These differences between the normal and retarded readers are significant at better than the .01 level of confidence.

Because Benton and Kemble (1960) have suggested that the ability to locate right and left accurately may be a verbal function and that such ability is related to IQ differences, our data on lateralization were related to intelligence-test performance. Since there is a significant difference in the IQ's of the normal and retarded readers, no good purpose is served by inter-group comparison. We have therefore restricted our analysis to a consideration of the relationship between lateralization function and intellectual level to the reading retarded group. As may be seen from Table X, in which IQ is related to right-left aware-

TABLE X *Relation of IQ to Awareness of Right and Left on Parts of One's Own Body in Retarded Readers*

WISC	Failed R–L Items (N = 29)		Passed R–L Items (N = 121)		t	p*
	Mean	Standard Deviation	Mean	Standard Deviation		
Full-scale IQ	90.1	8.3	92.5	8.0	1.45	<.10
Verbal Scale IQ	90.4	7.5	92.6	8.6	1.28	<.10
Performance IQ	91.6	11.4	94.0	9.8	1.16	<.15

* One-tailed test applied because of the directional nature of the hypothesis.

ness of own body parts, none of the differences is statistically significant. When the intelligence-test performance of retarded readers is related to performance on the Piaget schedule (Table XI), only one of the differences, performance

TABLE XI *Relation of IQ to Performance on Piaget Schedule in Retarded Readers*

WISC	Two or Less Correct on Piaget Schedule (N = 56)		Three or More Correct on Piaget Schedule (N = 94)		t	p*
	Mean	Standard Deviation	Mean	Standard Deviation		
Full-scale IQ	90.8	7.8	92.8	8.2	1.52	<.10
Verbal IQ	91.6	8.2	92.4	8.5	0.56	<.30
Performance IQ	91.6	10.7	94.6	9.6	1.80	<.05

* One-tailed test applied because of the directional nature of the hypothesis.

IQ, is statistically significant. When the IQ's of the total reversal group of nine individuals are compared with the remainder of the retarded readers (Table XII), it is found that significant differences exist in full-scale and performance IQ but not in verbal IQ. The full-scale IQ difference is most probably a function of low performance IQ. The data in Tables X, XI, and XII, therefore, suggest strongly that differences in the ability to locate right and left in the group of retarded readers is not a function of verbal IQ.

TABLE XII   *WISC IQ's for Retarded Readers Failing and Passing All Items of Right-Left Awareness of Own Body Parts*

WISC	Failed All R–L Items (N = 9)		Passed All R–L Items (N = 121)		t	p^*
	Mean	Standard Deviation	Mean	Standard Deviation		
Full-scale IQ	87.5	5.7	92.5	8.1	1.84	<.05
Verbal IQ	89.9	9.1	92.6	8.6	0.91	<.20
Performance IQ	87.3	5.5	94.0	9.8	2.03	<.025

* One-tailed test applied because of the directional nature of the hypothesis.

Discussion

In the present study of the association of lateral preferences in hand-eye usage and awareness of right-left relations with reading retardation, no reliable difference in lateral dominance was found between a group of retarded readers and a group of normal controls. The amount of mixed laterality among the retarded readers was not distinguishable from the degree of mixed laterality found in normal readers. Further, types of lateral dominance (i.e., rightness or leftness), or degree of preference, did not serve to distinguish between better and poorer readers within each of the groups. However, the group of retarded readers was deficient in right-left awareness and contained a significantly greater proportion of individuals who were unable to identify right and left both with reference to parts of their own bodies and in the general environment.

Although differences in score on the Piaget schedule did differentiate the group of retarded readers from the controls, it did not serve to predict degree of reading retardation within the group of retarded readers. However, disturbance in the ability to identify right and left on one's own body was related to degree of reading retardation, and the retarded readers who had difficulty in identifying right and left on their own bodies had the lowest reading scores. These findings suggest that right-left awareness of parts of one's own body bears a more significant relation to reading performance that do later acquired (Belmont and Birch, 1963) and more complex features of right-left orientation.

These findings do not agree with those of Harris (1957), who found right-left confusion to be within the normal range in his 9-year-old group of children with reading disability. It should be noted, however, that Harris used a very brief three-item scale to test for directional confusion, whereas seven items were used in the present study. Benton and Kemble (1960) also report that children with specific reading disability tended to be somewhat poorer on all aspects of right-left orientation than were control subjects. However, in their study of a small sample these differences did not reach statistical significance.

It is of interest to relate the present findings to data dealing with the age-specific establishment of lateral dominance and right-left awareness. In an earlier study (1963) we found that in normal school children the awareness of the laterality of own body parts was fully stabilized by the age of 7, a point in development earlier than that at which fully stabilized lateral preferences for hand and eye were established. In normal school children, lateral hand preferences were fully stabilized at age 9, and eye and eye-hand preferences at age 10. At the age represented in the present sample, we would have expected both right-left awareness and lateral hand dominance to be fully stabilized. The present findings on lateral hand dominance for both the normal and retarded reading groups of children ages 9 and 10 agree fairly well with these expectations. Further, for the normal readers, the findings on lateral orientation are identical with the normative findings reported earlier. The retarded readers, however, perform significantly below normal levels of expectation on tasks of over-all right-left orientation, and the level of right-left awareness of own body parts is below that of the 7-year-old normal group. Whereas only 11 per cent of the normal children 7 years of age (Belmont and Birch, 1963) and only 2 per cent of the normal readers 9 and 10 years of age had difficulty with such right-left items, 19 per cent of the retarded readers had such difficulty.

It is apparent that our findings on lateralization differ from those of other investigators who have studied retarded readers selected from clinical settings (Orton, 1937; Zangwill, 1962) but are similar to those reported by investigators who have drawn the children studied from community samples (Gates and Bennett, 1933; Johnston, 1942). Generally, differences in lateral dominance relations between normal and retarded readers have been found when a clinic sample has been used and not when a school population or community has been examined. The present study sample is drawn from an unbiased, age-homogeneous total population, with the retarded readers representing the poorest readers in the total school population of children in a given birth year of a medium-sized city. The 200 subjects of the study were pupils at 30 different public and independent schools. Such a survey will, of course, include as a subgroup those children who may be receiving remedial treatment in clinics as well as other poor readers who have either not come to notice or been referred for diagnosis or treatment. It is different, however, from either a clinic population or a group of children selected for study merely because they are receiving remedial reading instruction. Children come to clinical notice or fail to do so for a variety of social, neurologic, and behavioral reasons and do not necessarily represent "pure" cases of reading retardation as such. In addition, such clinic samples represent extremely wide IQ ranges. Within remedial-reading centers there is a tendency for the younger poor reader to have associated behavioral difficulties and to be highly selected in terms of social class, with middle-class children more likely to be heavily represented at a young age than children from lower socioeconomic background. It is of particular relevance that in our representative sample lateral dominance bears no relation to reading dysfunction but that right-left awareness does.

Benton and Kemble (1960) have suggested that IQ differences among normal controls and retarded readers may serve to magnify or enhance differences in right-left orientation. In addition, they have indicated that confusion in right-left orientation may be a function of verbal facility. Our analysis of verbal and performance IQ's in the retarded readers suggests that such confusion is associated with differences in performance IQ rather than with differences in verbal IQ. This finding, when taken together with the fact that in the retarded-reading group as a whole the level of right-left awareness is more like that of normal younger children than of children of their own age, suggests the possibility of a defect in body schema and praxis rather than one of verbalization as such.

REFERENCES

Belmont, L., and Birch, H. G. Lateral dominance and right-left awareness in normal children. *Child Develpm.*, 1963, 34, 257–270.

Benton, A. L., and Kemble, J. D. Right-left orientation and reading disability. *Psychiat. Neurol.*, Basel, 1960, 139, 49–60.

Bentzen, F. Sex ratios in learning and behavior disorders. *Amer. J. Orthopsychiat.*, 1963, 33, 92–98.

Gates, A. I., and Bennett, C. C. *Reversal tendencies in reading: causes, diagnosis, prevention, and correction.* New York: Bureau of Publications, Teach. College, Columbia Univer., 1933.

Harris A. J. *Harris tests of lateral dominance.* Manual, 3d ed.) New York: Psychol. Corp., 1947.

Harris, A. J. Lateral dominance, directional confusion, and reading disability. *J. Psychol.*, 1957, 44, 283–294.

Hermann, K., and Norrie, E. Is congenital word-blindness a hereditary type of Gerstmann's syndrome? *Psychiat. Neurol.*, Basel, 1958, 136, 59–73.

Johnston, P. W. The relation of certain anomalies of vision and lateral dominance to reading disability. *Monogr. Soc. Res. Child Developm.*, 1942, 7, no. 2.

Orton, S. T. *Reading, writing and speech problems in children.* New York: Norton, 1937.

Piaget, J. *Judgment and reasoning in the child.* London: Kegan Paul, 1928.

Rabinovitch, R. D., Drew, A. L., DeJong, R. N., Ingram, W., and Withey, L. A research approach to reading retardation. *Res. Publ. Ass. Nerv. Ment. Dis.*, 1954, 34, 363–387.

Zangwill, O. L. Dyslexia in relation to cerebral dominance. In J. Money (Ed.), *Reading disability.* Baltimore: Johns Hopkins Press, 1962, 103–113.

6   Parents' Attitudes and Behaviors and Grade-School Children's Academic Achievements

VAUGHN CRANDALL

RACHEL DEWEY

WALTER KATKOVSKY

ANNE PRESTON

Problem

Since the time of Binet's pioneering attempts to predict children's academic achievements from their performances on intelligence tests, psychologists and educators have been concerned with factors producing individual differences in young children's scholastic attainments. Early research addressed to this question was primarily devoted to the role which general intellectual abilities played in academic performances. More recently, educational and child-development researchers have concerned themselves with factors other than ability which might also contribute to performance differences. Personality variables such as achievement motivation and anxiety have been brought into the picture. The achievement need has been the center of recent concerted research efforts by a number of investigators: e.g., McClelland and his colleagues (1, 6). So, too, has anxiety been used as a predictor variable for intellectual and academic performances: e.g., McCandless and Castaneda (5); Sarason, Davidson, Lighthall, Waite, and Ruebush (7).

Research on determinants of such achievement performances has indicated that both ability and motivational variables are useful and necessary predictors. Another broad, and basic, question still remains: What are the *antecedents* of differences in children's intellectual achievement motivations and performances? In other words, what environmental factors in children's everyday experiences facilitate or impede the development of intellectual and academic competence? Many persons and situations influence a child's personality development. Parents, teachers, siblings, and peers all interact with a child in the course of his daily experiences, and each of these individuals can be an important social reinforcer of the child's behaviors. This is true whether the area of personality under consideration is the development of aggressive, dependent, affiliative, or achievement behaviors.

Concerning the development of achievement motivations and behaviors, it is apparent to the careful observer that most children have developed by the time they enter grade school fairly consistent differences in the values they attach to intellectual and academic achievements, in their expectations of success in these activities, in the standards they use to judge their efforts, and in the methods and strategies they employ in their attempts to attain achievement goals. What factors produce these differences? This is the general question to which this research is directed. The present article describes one study of a larger research project concerned with parents as identification

From *The Journal of Genetic Psychology*, Vol. 104 (1964), pp. 53–66. Copyright © 1964 by The Journal Press. Reprinted with permission.

models and reinforcers of young children's achievement behaviors.[1] The investigation explored relationships between parents' attitudes and behaviors and their early-grade-school-age children's academic performances.

Methods

SAMPLE

The sample was comprised of 120 Ss: 40 early-grade-school-age children, and their fathers and mothers. The child sample contained 20 boys and 20 girls equally distributed in the second, third, and fourth grades at the time the children were administered academic-achievement tests. The socioeconomic status of the families was assessed by Hollingshead's Two Factor Index of Social Position (4). The proportions of families in Hollingshead's social classifications I through V were 10, 30, 29, 31, and zero respectively, indicating that all but the lowest social classification were reasonably represented. Slightly more than one-half of the fathers and one-fourth of the mothers were college graduates. Table I presents information regarding the intellectual levels and academic-achievement test performances of the children. The children's intellectual abilities were assessed with the Stanford-Binet Intelligence Test; their academic performances, with the California Achievement Test.[2] As indicated in Table I, the children of the study were intellectually superior to national norms; all but

TABLE I   *Intelligence and Academic-Achievement-Test Performances of the Children*

Number of Children	
Stanford-Binet IQ	
Below 100	2
100–114	9
115–129	13
130–144	14
145 and over	2
Reading Age vs. Chronological Age	
RA less than CA	2
RA 1–9 months beyond CA	7
RA 10–19 months beyond CA	19
RA 20–29 months beyond CA	5
RA 30–39 months beyond CA	4
RA 40–49 months beyond CA	2
Arithmetic Age vs. Chronological Age	
AA less than CA	5
AA 1–9 months beyond CA	12
AA 10–19 months beyond CA	13
AA 20–29 months beyond CA	7
AA 30–39 months beyond CA	3

1 This study was a part of the project "Parents as Identification Models and Reinforcers of Children's Achievement Development," partially supported by USPH Grant M-2238, awarded the first-listed author. The study was conducted under the auspices of The Fels Research Institute for the Study of Human Development in Yellow Springs, Ohio.
2 The second author of this report administered the academic-achievement tests. The authors wish to express appreciation to Dr. Virginia Nelson, who gave the Stanford-Binet Intelligence Tests to the children.

two had IQ's above 100, and approximately three-fourths of the children obtained scores more than one standard deviation above the national average. The mean IQ of the group was 124. Intellectual abilities within the sample, however, varied appreciably. The children's IQ's ranged from 79 to 164, with a *SD* of 16. As might be expected from their intelligence-test scores, the children's performances on the standard academic-achievements tests were generally above grade level. Only two of the children were reading below grade level, and only five were not performing at or above their grade level in arithmetic.

ASSESSMENT OF PARENT ATTITUDES AND BEHAVIORS

The parents were interviewed individually at the Fels Research Institute for the Study of Human Development, Yellow Springs, Ohio. To prevent communication between parents, each set of parents was interviewed concurrently but separately.[3] The interview sessions averaged from two and one-half to three hours and were electronically recorded for subsequent interview analyses. Two interviews were given each parent during the interview session. The first was concerned with the parent's attitudes and reported behaviors toward his child's everyday achievement efforts. This interview covered four achievement areas, only one of which—the intellectual achievement area—is relevant to the present study. The second interview covered several general (nonspecific to achievement) behaviors of the parents. These included parental affection, rejection, and nurturance.[4]

FIRST INTERVIEW

Interview I obtained information regarding the following parental attitudinal and behavioral variables:

The Parent's Attainment Value for His Child's Intellectual Performances. This referred to the degree of importance or value the parent attached to his child's intellectual achievements. This rating assessed the intensity of the parent's desire that his child show interest and participate in intellectual activities and assessed the value the parent placed on his child's effort, persistence, and competence in these situations.

The Parent's Evaluation of His Child's Intellectual Competence. This variable was concerned with the level of competence the parent felt his child characteristically demonstrated in intellectual activities.

The Parent's Satisfaction-Dissatisfaction with His Child's Intellectual-Achievement Performances. Ratings of this variable focused on the amount of satisfaction *vs.* dissatisfaction the parent expressed regarding his child's intellectual-achievement performances. This rating was exclusively concerned with relevant parental feelings as these were expressed to the interviewer; the parent's reported overt reactions (praise, criticism, etc.) to his child's efforts were *not* a part of the rating.

The Parent's Minimal Standards for His Child's Intellectual Achievement Performances. Here the "personal yardstick" the parent used to judge his child's intellectual performances was considered. The major judgment for this

3 The fathers were interviewed by the third-listed author; the mothers, by the fourth author.
4 A fourth general parental-behavior variable—dominance—was also assessed in Interview II for a study other than the present one and is not discussed in this report.

rating entailed the determination of the minimal level of intellectual competence below which the child's performance produced parental dissatisfaction and above which the parent felt more satisfied than dissatisfied with his child's efforts.

Parental Instigation of Intellectual Activities. This (like the remaining variables of Interview I) was concerned with reported parental behaviors rather than parental attitudes. Parental instigation referred to the frequency and intensity of the parent's attempts to increase his child's participation and competence in intellectual activities. The parent's reactions to his child's efforts *after* he had performed were not included here. To be a relevant behavioral referent for this variable, the parent's behavior must have preceded some activity on the part of his child. Examples of instigation included such events as the parent arranging for his child to receive special lessons or experiences in some intellectual pursuit, the parent making a special effort to convey to his child the importance of intellectual experiences, and the parent encouraging and/or demanding that his child participate in intellectual-achievement activities.

The Parent's Participation with His Child in Intellectual-Achievement Activities. This variable pertained to the extent that the parent actively engaged in intellectual-achievement pursuits with his child. Both the frequency of parental participation and the amount of personal involvement while so engaged constituted rating referents for this variable.

Positive Parental Reactions. Here the frequency and intensity of the parent's positive reactions to his child's intellectual-achievement behaviors were assessed. These included the degree to which the parent responded favorably to his child's interest and participation in intellectual-achievement activities, as well as the parent's positive reactions to the effort and the competence his child exhibited in these pursuits. Positive parental reactions might take the form of direct verbal approval or other less direct symbols of approbation, such as granting special privileges or giving rewards (e.g., money, gifts, etc.) for intellectual achievements.

Negative Parental Reactions. This variable was concerned with the frequency and intensity of disapproval and criticism which the parent expressed to his child for any lack of interest, participation, effort, and/or competence in intellectual-achievement activities.

SECOND INTERVIEW

Interview II sampled the parents' reported behaviors with their children which were nonspecific to the children's intellectual-achievement performances, but were aspects of parent-child interaction which might possibly influence (either directly or indirectly) children's intellectual-achievement efforts. The variables rated were:

Parental Affection. This variable pertained to the amount of overt affection and acceptance which the parent reported expressing toward his child.

Parental Rejection. Here the raters focused on the degree that the parent directly expressed dissatisfaction with, was critical of, or punitive about, his child's general personality attributes or characteristic behaviors.

Parental Nurturance. The behavioral referents for this rating were those relevant to the frequency and quality of emotional support and instrumental help given the child by the parent.

RATING PROCEDURES AND METHODS OF DATA ANALYSIS

The criterion rater for Parent Interview I rated all interviews of the 80 parents from typescripts of the interviews. Reliability raters rated 40 randomly picked father and mother interviews. All identifying information (e.g., parent, child, and sibling names, etc.) was removed before the interview protocols were rated. Interview II was rated after the rater listened to the interview recordings.[5] It was felt that, while the data in Interview I was concerned with specific parental attitudes and behaviors which could be assessed from typescripts, Interview II data included important parental feelings and expressions which were less likely to be represented accurately in typed protocols. For example, in Interview II two fathers (or mothers) might say that their children were "little hellions" in certain situations; yet one parent might mean (and convey) that he thoroughly disapproved of this behavior, while a second parent might make the same statement but indicate (through his intonation) that he actually approved of these behaviors on the part of his child.

The children's academic-achievement-test scores used in the study were achievement-ratio scores; the reading-achievement score for each child was his reading age divided by his chronological age, and his arithmetic score was obtained by dividing his arithmetic age by his chronological age.

Statistical analyses employed in the study were exclusively nonparametric tests. The rank-difference correlation was used for all measures of association, and Wilcoxon's Unpaired Replicates Test was employed for all assessments of differences (8).

Results and Discussion

INTERRATER RELIABILITIES

The interrater reliability coefficients for Parent Interview I are presented in Table II. The magnitude of rater concordance for these variables, with one

TABLE II *Interrater Reliabilities for Parent Interview I (Parent Attitudes and Reported Behaviors Toward the Children's Intellectual-Achievement Efforts)*

Parent Variable	Re Mothers	Re Fathers
Attainment Value	.50	.80
Evaluation of Competence	.78	.94
Satisfaction-Dissatisfaction	85	.96
Achievement Standards	.63	.57
Instigation	.63	.76
Participation	.70	.84
Positive Reactions	.86	.80
Negative Reactions	.22	.79

5 The criterion rater for Parent Interview I was the senior author. The reliability raters for this interview were the third author for the mother interviews and the fourth author for the father interviews. The criterion rater of Parent Interview II was Virginia Crandall. The reliability ratings (made from 40 randomly selected father and mother interviews) were done by the fourth author and the third author respectively.

noticeable exception (the mothers' reported negative reactions), ranged from moderately acceptable to highly acceptable agreement. Interrater reliabilities of the mother interviews of Parent Interview II were, for the variables of affection, rejection, and nurturance respectively, .87, .61, and .68. Correlations of interrater agreement for the same variables in the father interviews were .76, .85, and .78.

THE CHILD VARIABLES

Relations between the children's IQ's and their scholastic-achievement-test performances were assessed. Intelligence-test scores correlated .57 and .59 with reading and arithmetic-achievement-test scores respectively for the girls, and .66 and .50 for the boys. These correlations are similar in magnitude to associations found in previous studies of children's intelligence and their performances on standard academic-achievement tests. These data indicate, as have the results of previous investigations, that general intelligence is one major factor in children's academic achievements. However, the fact that less than one-third of the variance was held in common by these sets of variables (i.e., intelligence- and achievement-test performance) suggests that other factors may also be influential. Parents' attitudes and behaviors influencing children's intellectual-achievement motivations and behaviors may account for some of this variance.

RELATIONS BETWEEN GENERAL PARENTAL BEHAVIORS AND CHILDREN'S ACADEMIC-ACHIEVEMENT-TEST PERFORMANCES

Associations between general parental behaviors (i.e., affection, rejection, and nurturance) and the children's reading- and arithmetic-test performances were evaluated separately by sex of parent and sex of child. Of the 24 correlations run, only three were significant beyond the .05 level of confidence according to Old's Tables (8). This is only slightly better than might be anticipated by chance. That the significant correlations obtained were probably not chance occurrences, however, is suggested by the fact that all significant associations pertained *only* to the mothers and their daughters. Girls who were competent readers had both less affectionate and less nurturant mothers than did the girls who demonstrated less proficiency in that academic area; correlations between the girls' reading-achievement-test scores and their mothers' affection and nurturance were −.38 and −.43 respectively. In addition, girls who performed better on the arithmetic-achievement test had mothers who were also relatively low on nurturance; the Rho obtained was −.45.

Why should low maternal nurturance and affection seem to foster academic competence in the girls? Several possibilities are likely. First, the affectionate and nurturant mothers, by rewarding their daughters' affection-seeking and dependent behaviors, may have "taught" these girls to expect such overtures to be more effective means of attaining personal security than behaviors requiring independent initiative and achievement striving. In contrast, girls who did not receive as much maternal affection and support might have turned to other potential sources of satisfaction and security, such as achievement *per se*. Second, previous research has demonstrated the maternal nurturance fosters children's dependence and impedes the development of independence and achievement behaviors (3, 9). Restrictions of learning experiences in independence and achievement in the more highly nurtured girls of the present study may have produced (*a*) fewer possibilities for developing independent, problem-solving techniques to handle achievement situations and (*b*) less confidence (and more anxiety) regarding abilities to do so. One final explanation for the negative relations obtained between maternal nurturance and affection and the girls' academic achievements pertains to young girls' attempted identification with and emulation of their mothers. All parents act as learning models for, as well as direct reinforcers of, their children's behaviors. The mother who readily proffers love and help to her child may derive personal satisfaction from such maternal behaviors and may serve as a model to her daughter to this effect. On the other hand, the mother who withholds affection or rejects her child's help-seeking and emotional support-seeking may be less involved with the maternal role and be more achievement-oriented. Consequently, her daughter is—to the degree she uses her mother as an identification model—more likely to emulate her mother's achievement behaviors, values, and motivations and to attempt to become competent in academic achievement situations.

RELATIONS BETWEEN PARENTS' SPECIFIC ATTITUDES AND
BEHAVIORS TOWARD CHILDREN'S INTELLECTUAL ACHIEVEMENT EFFORTS
AND CHILDREN'S PERFORMANCES ON STANDARD ACHIEVEMENT TESTS

Data relevant to this portion of the study are summarized in Tables III and IV. The first four parent variables listed in these tables are attitudinal variables; the last four are behavioral variables. Each will be discussed in turn.

TABLE III   *Parents' Attitudes and Actions and Children's Reading Achievement**

Parent Variable	Mothers re		Fathers re	
	Girls	Boys	Girls	Boys
Attainment Value	−.14	.35	−.38	.03
Evaluations	.44	.48	.28	.21
Satisfaction-Dissatisfaction	.51	.48	.38	.23
Standards	.48	.18	.15	.26
Instigation	−.52	.18	−.43	−.07
Participation	−.10	.06	−.28	−.25
Positive Reactions	−.11	.09	.42	−.17
Negative Reactions	−.27	−.18	−.45	.06

* Italicized correlations are significant at or beyond the .05 level of confidence (one-tailed test).

TABLE IV   *Parents' Attitudes and Actions and Children's Arithmetic Achievement**

Parent Variable	Mothers re		Fathers re	
	Girls	Boys	Girls	Boys
Attainment Value	.17	.23	−.26	−.05
Evaluations	.23	.35	.20	.04
Satisfaction-Dissatisfaction	.76	.28	.19	.07
Standards	.50	.00	−.12	.34
Instigation	−.42	.05	−.38	−.31
Participation	.13	.05	−.09	−.55
Positive Reactions	.14	.01	.41	−.19
Negative Reactions	−.33	−.24	−.44	−.14

* Italicized correlations are significant at or beyond the .05 level of confidence (one-tailed test).

Attitudinal Variables. The *attainment values* the parents placed on their children's intellectual competence were essentially unrelated to their children's academic-achievement-test performances. In fact, the only significant correlation of the eight pertaining to this variable was an unanticipated negative one: fathers who expressed strong desires that their daughters be intellectually competent had daughters who performed less adequately on the reading-achievement test than did daughters of fathers who were less concerned with their daughters' intellectual activities and abilities.

The mothers' *evaluations* of their children's general intellectual competence were associated with their children's academic performances, but the evaluations of the fathers were not. Both the boys' and girls' reading-test performances were positively and significantly related to their mothers' assessments of their general intellectual competence. The children's arithmetic-test performances were positively correlated with the mothers' evaluations, though falling just short of statistical significance. In contrast, none of the fathers' evaluations of their children was related to these children's scholastic-achievement, test-taking behaviors. This finding—that the mothers' evaluation of their children's general intellectual performances were similar to their children's academic performances while the fathers' evaluations were not—may have been due to the fact that mothers are usually home to receive the after-school reports from their children regarding their academic successes and failures while most fathers are not. In addition, it is a common observation that mothers far outnumber fathers in school situations where concrete information is provided regarding their children's academic performances (e.g., PTA meetings and parent-teacher conferences). Finally, it may be that fathers more frequently based their judgments of their children's general intellectual competence on their intellectual performances observed in the home (e.g., efforts on puzzles, quiz games, etc.) than did the mothers.

Consistent with the findings on evaluations was the fact that the mothers' *satisfactions and dissatisfactions* with their children's general intellectual-achievement efforts were also more often positively associated with the children's achievement-test performances than were those of the fathers: three of the four significant correlations obtained pertained to the mothers' expressed satisfaction with the adequacy of their children's intellectual-achievement performances.

Parental *standards* for the children's general intellectual performances were unrelated to the children's demonstrated competence on the academic-achievement tests with two exceptions. Both of these pertained to the standards the mothers held for their daughters. Mothers who set high standards for their daughters' intellectual-achievement efforts, in contrast with mothers whose standards were less demanding, had daughters who were more proficient on both the reading- and arithmetic-achievement tests. These correlations, as well as a number of those found in the tables which follow, illustrate an inevitable problem inherent in most parent-child research. When significant correlations are obtained between parent and child behaviors, when might it be legitimate to assume the former caused the latter, and when might the opposite be true? The positive association of the mothers' achievement standards for their daughters and these girls' academic-test performances may have been a function of the following: (*a*) high maternal achievement standards induced the girls to strive for and become proficient in the academic areas under consideration, while low maternal standards produced the opposite effect; or (*b*) the mothers adjusted their intellectual-achievement standards for their daughters according to the girls' demonstrated academic proficiencies; or (*c*) the correlations obtained may be a function of both (*a*) and (*b*).

Behavioral Variables. The remaining correlations listed in Tables III and IV focus on reported parental behaviors rather than parental attitudes. The degree of the parents' *instigation* of their children toward intellectual-achievement pursuits was predictive of the children's achievement-test performances only for the girls. Girls who performed especially well on the tests had mothers and fathers who were *less* prone to encourage and push them toward intellectual activities than were parents of the less academically proficient girls.

Regarding the parents' *participation* with the children in intellectual activities, these parental behaviors bore little relation to the competence the children demonstrated on the academic-achievement tests. In only one instance—i.e., the fathers' participation and their sons' performances on the arithmetic-achievement test—was the correlation significant; fathers of boys who were especially competent in this area spent less time with their sons in intellectual activities than did the fathers of the less competent boys. There was, thus, no evidence in the present study that the amount of parental participation with children in intellectual activities *per se* had any positive impact on the children's academic achievements. The negative correlations obtained between parental instigation and participation and the children's achievement-test performances suggest, though cannot prove, that these parental behaviors might be reactions to the children's efforts rather than antecedent and causal factors in these performances. It is possible, for example, that many parents of grade-school-age children—when the child's academic efforts are competent ones—feel little need to encourage such endeavors or to spend additional time with the children in these pursuits. Conversely, parents of a child who performs relatively poorly in academic situations may become concerned with his ineptitude and increase their instigational efforts and participation with him in intellectual-achievement activities.

The two final antecedent variables of this study pertained to *parental reactions* to the children's intellectual-achievement behaviors as these predicted the children's academic-achievement-test performances. These variables, historically, have been the major focus of attention of researchers concerned with parent behaviors as determinants of children's personality development. In the current investigation an attempt was made to assess the reactions of the parents to their children's intellectual-achievement efforts and to relate these reactions to the levels of performance which the children evidenced on standard academic-achievement tests. The only finding indicating an influence of these parental behaviors on the children's performance—if a causal relationship is assumed—was a cross-sex one; both positive and negative reactions of the fathers to their daughters' intellectual efforts predicted their daughters' academic proficiency. The mothers' reactions, in contrast, were essentially unrelated to their daughters' performances, while neither the fathers' nor the mothers' reported praise or criticism was predictive of their sons' achievement-test scores. In short, the only evidence that the parents' direct rewards and punishments may have influenced their children's academic performances occurred exclusively between fathers and their daughters. Girls who performed especially well on the reading-achievement test had fathers who more often praised and rewarded and less often criticized and punished their general intellectual-achievement behaviors. A similar relation obtained for the girls' arithmetic performances.

Significant Findings

When the total pattern of significant correlations found in the current study is evaluated, the most striking finding is that the parents' attitudes and behaviors (both general and specific) were associated with their daughters' performances on the scholastic-achievement tests much more frequently than with those of their sons. Of the 18 significant correlations obtained between the Parent Interviews I and II data and the children's demonstrated academic competence, only three pertained to the boys. Why should these differences obtain? One possibility for this finding is that grade-school-age boys may differ from girls in their susceptibility to adult influence. Two unpublished sets of data by the authors of this report support this idea. First, ratings of free-play behavior of another sample of children in the same age range as the current child sample revealed that the amount of the children's achievement efforts and the amount of their approval-seeking from adults were positively and significantly related for the girls (Rho = .46) but unrelated (Rho = .03) for the boys. In other words, the girls' achievement strivings were directly related to their apparent desire for approval from adults, while the boys' achievement behaviors were more autonomously determined. It appeared that the boys had less need to use adults' reactions to define the competence of their efforts than did the girls, possibly because the boys may have developed more internalized achievement standards. Additional evidence suggesting that young boys' achievement performances may be less contingent on the reactions of others than are those of girls was obtained on the sample of Ss employed in the current study.

As a part of a different (as yet unpublished) investigation, the children were administered a specially constructed Children's Intellectual Achievement Responsibility Questionnaire. This questionnaire was designed to measure the extent a child attributes his intellectual-achievement successes and failures to his own instrumental behaviors rather than as a product of the behaviors and reactions of other persons. The boys' belief in self-responsibility correlated positively with their performances on the academic-achievement tests used in the current study, while these variables were not significantly related for the girls. The specific correlations between the boys' belief in self-responsibility and their reading- and arithmetic-achievement-test performances were .49 and .36 respectively. For the girls these correlations were −.16 and −.23.

In summary, to the degree that boys' achievement striving has been found to be unrelated to their approval-seeking from adults and to the degree that their academic proficiencies were associated with their belief in self-responsibility, their achievement behaviors appeared to be more independent and autonomous of adult reactions than those of the girls. Because of this, parental attitudes and behaviors may have less impact on and therefore be less predictive of the academic performances of boys of this age than of girls. The findings of the current study are congruent with this possibility. It should be strongly emphasized, however, that this reasoning rests on several assumptions, as well as limited research data, and must await more definitive tests in future investigations.

Summary

This study investigated relations between parents' attitudes and behaviors toward their children's general intellectual-achievement efforts and their children's performances on standard academic-achievement tests. The sample was comprised of 40 early-grade-school-age children and their fathers and mothers. The children were administered standard intelligence and scholastic-achievement tests. The parents were individually interviewed regarding their general parental behaviors (affection, rejection, nurturance), as well as their specific attitudes and reactions to their children's everyday intellectual-achievement efforts.

The following results were obtained:

1. Correlations between the children's IQ scores and their performances on the scholastic-achievement tests were of the same general magnitude found in most past research on children's intelligence and academic performances.
2. General parental behaviors which significantly predicted the children's academic-test performances pertained solely to mothers and their daughters; mothers of academically competent girls were less affectionate and less nurturant toward their daughters than were the mothers of the girls who were less proficient.
3. Certain specific attitudes and behaviors of the parents toward their children's intellectual-achievement behaviors were predictive of the children's academic-test performances; others were not. First, neither the mothers' nor fathers' expressed values for the children's intellectual experiences were positively associated with the children's observed performances. Second, both the mothers' evaluations of and satisfactions with their children's general intellectual competence were positively related to these children's actual academic performances, while those of the fathers were not. Third, parental instigation and participation, when correlations were significant, were negatively associated with the children's academic performances. Fourth, the positive and negative reactions of the parents to the children's intellectual-achievement efforts were predictive of the children's academic-achievement-test performances for father-daughter combinations only; the more proficient girls had fathers who more often praised and less often criticized their everyday intellectual-achievement attempts than did the less academically competent girls.
4. Many more significant relations obtained between the parents' attitudes and behaviors and their daughters' academic proficiency than occurred between these parental attitudes and behaviors and the boys' performances.

REFERENCES

1. Atkinson, J., Ed. Motives in Fantasy, Action and Society. New York: Van Nostrand, 1958.

2. Crandall, V., Katkovsky, W., and Preston, A. Motivational and ability determinants of children's intellectual achievement behaviors. *Child Devel.,* 1962, 33, 643–661.

3. Crandall, V., Preston, A., and Rabson, A. Maternal reactions and the development of independence and achievement behavior in young children. *Child Devel.,* 1960, 31, 243–251.

4. Hollingshead, A., and Redlick, F. Social stratification and psychiatric

disorders. *Amer. Soc. Rev.*, 1953, 18, 163–169.

5. McCandless, B., and Castaneda, A. Anxiety in children, school achievement and intelligence. *Child. Devel.*, 1956, 27, 379–382.

6. McClelland, D., Atkinson, J., Clark, R., and Lowell, E. The Achievement Motive. New York: Appleton-Century-Crofts, 1953.

7. Sarason, S., Davidson, K., Lighthall, F., Waite, R., and Ruebush, B. Anxiety in Elementary School Children. New York: Wiley, 1960.

8. Siegel, S. Nonparametric Statistics for the Behavioral Sciences. New York: McGraw-Hill, 1956.

9. Winterbottom, M. The relation of need for achievement in learning experiences in independence and mastery. In J. W. Atkinson (Ed.), *Motives in Fantasy, Action and Society*. New York: Van Nostrand, 1958. Pp. 453–478.

7   Discriminant Analysis of Achievement Profiles of Socially Maladjusted Pupils

DONALD A. LETON

MARGARET HOLZ

Criteria for grouping students in classes for socially maladjusted and emotionally disturbed are not clearly formulated nor experimentally validated at the present time. Various professional personnel, e.g., principals, teachers, social workers, counselors, and psychologists, are all instrumental in effecting the placement of such pupils. In referring pupils for social adjustment classes, teachers tend to consider classroom behavior and academic deficiencies as major factors in defining social maladjustment. Other specialists tend to consider such factors as relationship inadequacies, withdrawal and aggressive behavior, emotional immaturity, defective superegos, and sociopathic disturbances as criteria for such classification. This situation has led to inconsistent standards of eligibility and to heterogeneous groups of students in adjustment classes.

The socio-emotional criteria used by guidance specialists tend to be qualitative and subjective, whereas the classroom behavior and achievement criteria can be quantified. If the socio-emotional criteria were independent of achievement and classroom performance then two distinct bases of selection would exist. Since they are confounded in the child's personality, however, they cannot be considered separately. In a normal classroom situation the intra-group relationships are affected by the achievement skills of individual pupils. A number of pupils may show disdain, rejection, or perhaps sympathy toward other pupils for whom anxiety, immaturity, or social inadequacy impairs their achievement performance. In addition, they may also show an aloofness or social alienation from pupils who develop high academic achievement as a substitute for social participation. Groups as well as individuals appear to have limits to their acceptance of differences.

From *Psychology in the Schools*, Vol. 2 (1965), pp. 228–233. Reprinted with permission.

The authors are indebted to the Computing Center at the University of Hawaii for use of its computer facilities and programs.

Because of the interrelationships among achievement, social, and emotional traits there may be a communality of personality characteristics for socially maladjusted pupils. If a set of common characteristics do exist, the question arises as to whether this information may be of value for the identification and classification of such pupils. It is well recognized that indiscriminate placement may be harmful to an individual child. It may also disorganize the structure and functioning of an existing group.

Review of Literature

Quay (1963) concurs that the classification and placement of students in classes for emotionally disturbed are carried out on an impressionistic basis. He has concluded that there are two general classes of such students: the basic withdrawal and the conduct disorder types. The latter is also subdivided into the unsocialized aggressive, the neurotic delinquent, and the socially underprivileged-conning type. These conclusions are supported largely by the factor analyses of personality inventories administered to delinquent boys (Peterson, Quay, and Tiffany, 1961), and by analyses of delinquents' case histories (Quay, in press). The existence of these types among socially and emotionally disturbed students needs to be verified by factor scores on larger samples from the general student population.

Haring and Phillips (1962) discuss the problem of using achievement as a criterion of emotional disturbance. In agreement with most authors they report that emotionally disturbed pupils show achievement deficits. They conclude, however, that the magnitude of achievement loss without considerations of grade and intelligence levels would not be meaningful. Lambert (1963) obtained achievement data for pupils with varying levels of school adjustment. She pooled the reading and arithmetic scores from three different achievement batteries administered at different grade levels and then extrapolated to an expected achievement for the present placement in the second and fifth grades. She found that the reading and arithmetic grade scores for the preponderance of pupils from all levels of adjustment were within one-half year of their chronological age-grade placements. Because of the inconsistent categorizations for reading and arithmetic achievement and the gross classifications from three different achievement tests, these data have little value for defining the achievement characteristics of pupils with poor school adjustment.

Harris (1961) analyzed the socio-economic characteristics and family relationships of emotionally disturbed boys with or without learning problems. A higher proportion of disturbed boys with learning problems were from lower socio-economic classes. They also lived in family situations which were deterrent to school achievement. This illustrates the type of research needed for the educational classification of emotionally disturbed.

A number of authors recommend special classes and curricula for emotionally disturbed (Coleman and Hewett, 1962; Haring and Phillips, 1962; Topp, 1959; Berkowitz and Rothman, 1960). These are consistently oriented toward the emotional or social needs of the children rather than to their educational needs. The author recommends differential teaching to meet the developmental needs for various types of emotionally disturbed pupils (Leton, 1964); however, the specific educational needs are only hypothesized at the present time. In view of the fact that the teacher is the primary source of referrals for placements in adjustment classes, it is surprising to find that the achievement characteristics of these pupils are so vaguely defined.

Procedures

The purposes of this study were as follows: (a) to determine the achievement characteristics of pupils in Social Adjustment (SA) classes, and (b) to determine whether this information might hold value for classifying pupils of similar age, sex, grade, and intelligence levels into either SA or regular classes.

The experimental sample consisted of 89 students in intermediate SA classes who were administered the 1957 edition of the California Achievement Test Battery (CAT) in the 1962–63 school year.[1] The CAT yields subtest scores in Reading Vocabulary (RV), Reading Comprehension (RC), Arithmetic Reasoning (AR), Arithmetic Fundamentals (AF), Language (L), and Spelling (S). The control group was comprised of 89 pupils of the same sex, grade placement, age (± 3 months), and IQ (± 5 points). Matching for IQ scores was based on results of the California Tests of Mental Maturity. The mean age for the SA pupils was 10.81 and for the regular pupils was 10.78. There were 78 boys and 11 girls in each group. The frequency of boys and girls is consistent with that generally observed in such classes. The mean intelligence scores for the SA pupils was 84.5, and the matching procedure obtained a mean of 84.6 IQ for the regular pupils. The intelligence level of the SA pupils is below the school norm; and the age-grade distributions also indicated a slight educational retardation.

The means, standard deviations, and mean differences on the CAT subtests are shown in Table I.

The achievement levels of the social adjustment pupils show a retardation of approximately one grade in each subject area, whereas the regular pupils showed about .5 grade retardation. The configuration of the achievement profiles is similar for both groups. In view of the matching procedures a similar configuration could be anticipated. The decrement in the profiles of the SA pupils can be attributed to their social or emotional maladjustment.

TABLE I   *Summary of CAT Scores for Social Adjustment and Regular Class Groups*

Group	N	Reading Vocabulary		Reading Comprehension		Arithmetic Reasoning		Arithmetic Fundamental		Language		Spelling	
		Mean	SD	Mean	SD	Mean	SD	Mean	SD	Mean	SD	Mean	SD
SA	89	4.06	1.22	3.91	1.26	4.03	1.15	4.38	.83	4.06	.88	3.85	1.28
Reg.	89	4.56	1.40	4.49	1.32	4.65	1.28	4.89	.82	4.40	1.08	4.51	1.34
M. diff.		.50		.58		.62		.51		.34		.66	

Analysis

The distributions of achievement scores were analyzed for the discriminant classification of pupils' membership in SA or regular classes. Discriminant coefficients and distance functions (Mahalanobis, 1936) were obtained for the six subtests on the achievement profiles. The results of these analyses are presented in Table II.

1 The authors wish to express appreciation to Mr. Popenoe, Director of Research of the Los Angeles City Schools, for his permission to conduct this study and to the district superintendents, guidance supervisors, principals, and other staff who made the data available for this study.

TABLE II   *Discriminant Weights for CAT Subtests, D² Statistics and F Value*

CAT Subtests								
RV	**RC**	**AR**	**AF**	**L**	**S**	**D²**	**F value**	**df**
−.1036	+.0975	+.1097	+.3662	−.1987	+.1612	5.271	37.989*	6,171

* Significant at .001 level

For classifying pupils into the SA or regular groups the formula

$$Z_{ij} = X'S^{-1}d_{ij} - 1/2(X'_iS^{-1}X_i + X'_jS^{-1}X_j)$$

is applied in which Z_{ij} is the individual's discriminant score; X' is the one-by-six row vector of a given pupil's scores; d_{ij} is the six-by-one column vector of mean differences between the groups; S^{-1} is the inverse of the six-by-six dispersion matrix; X_i and X_j are the six-by-one column vectors of means for the $_i$ and $_j$ groups; and X_i and X_j are the respective transpose matrices.

This formula assumes equal groups and equal probability for membership in either group. To the extent that matching procedures were successful this assumption is met in this study. The obtained equation is:

−.1036 RV +.0975 RC +.1097 AR +.3662 AF −.1987 L +.1612 S −1.9738

The application of these discriminant coefficients to the combined samples led to correct classifications of 56 pupils and to misclassifications of 33 pupils from each group. Although 63% of each group was correctly classified, it is apparent that the group dispersions reflect a sizable overlap between groups. The use of this equation is illustrated in the following example. A vacancy occurs in the SA class, for which the counselor or administrator wishes to consider one of two eligible pupils from the waiting list, who have the following achievement scores:

	RV	RC	AR	AF	L	S
Pupil A	4.0	4.1	3.5	5.4	4.1	3.5
Pupil B	5.0	4.0	3.7	4.0	4.0	3.9

Each pupil shows one subtest score near his present grade level, and the remaining scores are approximately one year below grade level. If the subtest scores were to receive equal weighting, the composite achievement would be at the 4.1 grade level for both students. This composite is also comparable to the level of achievement observed in the SA classes. The counselor computes $Z_{ij} = $ .1225 for pupil A and $Z_{ij} = -.3972$ for pupil B. Since the discriminant score for the first pupil is positive, he concludes that this pupil should be classified with the regular class group. The negative discriminant score for pupil B indicates achievement characteristics similar to the SA pupils.

Discussion

This illustration of the use of discriminant analysis for the classification of socially maladjusted pupils requires further discussion. The assumption that the original selection procedures were suitable, i.e., the criteria employed for the existing group, is inherent in this application. The use of the procedure described here would insure that later placements would bring a similar pattern of achievement skills. To the extent that such direction is desirable for determining teaching objectives and curriculum planning for these classes, it would seem to be of value. It should not be construed that this procedure would refine the previous criteria or alter the composition of the group in terms of its social and emotional characteristics.

If profiles of personal and social characteristics were available, further progress on the classification problem would be possible. Opinions about the existence of syndromes and subdimensions among the emotionally disturbed (e.g. Quay, 1963) could be empirically tested. The intelligence and achievement characteristics which are associated with particular types of maladjustment could subsequently be analyzed for purposes of differential teaching. Finally, the criteria for the selection of homogeneous groups, as well as for the refinement of existing groups, could be established.

The discriminant model employed in this study assumes equal probability of assignment to either group. The application of the equation obtained in this study to a population of regular pupils would not be appropriate because the a priori probabilities for membership in the socially maladjusted or regular class groups are unequal. Probability coefficients which consider the sizes of the groups and the differences in group dispersions would need to be computed for membership in each of the possible socially maladjusted or regular groups.

There has been an abundance of academic prediction studies in educational research, and these have had an important impact on the field of guidance. Actuarial tables for success in specified college curricula are now generally available for educational guidance. Problems of classification and placement, however, are persistently handled by subjective opinions and clinical impressions. Studies of academic prediction will probably continue to show the usual attrition and failure rates until better criteria of educational classifications are developed.

REFERENCES

Berkowitz, P. H., and Rothman, E. P. *The disturbed child, recognition and psychoeducational therapy in the classroom.* New York: New York Univer. Press, 1960.

Coleman, J. C., and Hewett, F. M. Opendoor therapy: a new approach to the treatment of underachieving adolescent boys who resist needed psychotherapy. *Journal of Clinical Psychology,* 1962, 18, 28–33.

Haring, N. G., and Phillips, E. L. *Educating emotionally disturbed children.* New York: McGraw-Hill, 1962.

Harris, I. D. *Emotional blocks to learning.* New York: Free Press of Glencoe, 1961.

Lambert, N. M. *The development and validation of a process for screening emotionally handicapped children in school.* Sacramento, California: State Department of Education, mimeographed report, 1963.

Leton, D. A. Differential teaching techniques for emotionally disturbed children. *Mental Hygiene,* 1964, 48, 209–216.

Mahalanobis, P. C. On the generalized distance in statistics. *Proceedings of the National Institute of Science,* India, XII, 1936, 49–55.

Peterson, D. R., Quay, H. C., and Tiffany, T. L. Personality factors related to juvenile delinquency. *Child Development,* 1961, 32, 335–372.

Quay, H. C. Dimensions of personality in delinquent boys as inferred from the factor analysis of case history data. *Child Development,* in press.

Quay, H. C. Some basic considerations in the education of emotionally disturbed children. *Exceptional Children,* 1963, 30, 27–32.

Topp, R. F. Psychotherapy in the classroom. *Child Education,* 1959, 35, 406–408.

8   Specific Language Disability
(Dyslexia)

J. ROSWELL GALLAGHER

May I first thank those of you who invited me to give this fifth Joseph Wall Memorial Lecture. It is a real privilege to be with you at this time and to help you again to honor your beloved former chief of staff.

Today I would like to talk to you about a condition which not infrequently affects children. It is often the reason for their failure in school, and when this occurs both they and their parents become upset. I refer to specific language disability.

Specific language disability has also been termed specific reading disability, congenital dyslexia, congenital word blindness, etc., and is one of the many causes of scholastic failure (1–3). When present it is a handicap to a pupil, even though failure may not result. Its basic cause, though still unknown, would seem to be a disturbance in neurological function; but it should be distinguished from neurological disorders which are less amenable to treatment such as those following anoxia at birth or following encephalitis and those resulting from intellectual and sensory deficits and from learning problems primarily due to emotional disturbances.

A language skill as used here includes either talking, spelling, reading, penmanship, or expressing oneself in writing or in speech. The term "specific language disability" seems preferable to others because it implies that there is something wrong with one or more of these language skills and not only with reading or with visual or auditory perception; it furthermore implies that the learning problem is specifically in the language area and not also in other fields such as science and mathematics. It is a condition characterized by the inability of an individual readily to acquire, and subsequently to use, one or more language skills with a facility commensurate with his intelligence or with his facility in learning science and mathematics, and in addition not commensurate with the opportunities which have previously been offered him to learn; it is also characterized by that individual's tendency to reproduce language (in one or more of its forms) in an *unusual* fashion. Usually the term "specific language disability" is applied to those young people who have found it very difficult to learn to read and spell but who are otherwise intelligent and usually learn arithmetic more readily. It is to be remembered, however, that young children who have a language disability often confuse numbers (*6* for *9*, *15* for *51*, etc.) and that older children, because of their slow and inaccurate reading, may also experience trouble in arithmetic when they attempt "word problems."

This condition, which so clearly will handicap school performance, should be recognized before a boy or girl enters school and begins to try to learn to read or spell. Early unsuccessful efforts will in all probability produce little except frustration and discouragement and may adversely affect attitudes toward school and learning. Not infrequently, however, this condition will go unrecognized through oversight or because it is mild and compensated for by the individual's very

The Joseph Wall Memorial Lecture, presented as part of the Children's Hospital of D. C. Alumni Day, May 23, 1959. Reprinted (with permission) from *Clinical Proceedings of the Children's Hospital,* Vol. 16 (January, 1960), pp. 3–15. Studies upon which some of this material is based were supported by The Grant Foundation, Inc.

good intelligence. In any event it is likely that any boy or girl who has this handicap and who previously has been given neither special teaching nor even an understanding of why reading and spelling are so difficult to learn will find the demands of high school (with its longer reading and writing assignments and its foreign languages) more than can possibly be managed. If the difficulty of these young people is not then recognized and remedied, not only will there be failure in school but also excessive anxiety, loss of confidence, and family discord, following which any one of a number of psychosomatic symptoms may develop.

This disability may vary from the very mild to the extremely severe, a fact which at times makes for difficulty in clear-cut diagnosis and which is, no doubt, a reason for some of the disagreement and difference of opinion which exist in regard to its causes and management. One or many of the language skills may be inferior to the individual's intelligence or his ability to learn in other fields (such as arithmetic or science or handicraft or business). But for practical purposes, particularly when it is an adolescent who presents the problem, in deciding whether specific language disability is the *major* cause of failure for which the pupil should receive a specific type of remedial instruction, *the spelling should be peculiar.* This is not to say that specific language disability cannot be present if the spelling errors are not both frequent and odd. It is to say, however, that when this complicated language skill of spelling does not seem to be disturbed, other causes than those believed to be associated with a specific language disability should be sought as the explanation of the failure in school, the poor reading, poor writing, or the speech impairment. Spelling errors in specific language disability are not just numerous—they are often bizarre.

Most of these young people will also be poor readers; but by virtue of good intelligence or good cultural background, many will perform in a much better fashion when this skill is tested than one would expect from their spelling. Some will be hesitant talkers, awkward or slow in penmanship, poor in expressing themselves orally or on paper, have poor left-right orientation, or be noted for their inability to remember names of acquaintances or of places or people of whom they have read or heard. But to consider that all these young people have a specific language disability, providing their spelling and reading skill is at or near a level commensurate with their intelligence, is to court error.

Other considerations help to round out this clinical picture. The intelligence may be at any level; it is often high. The spelling is not only poor when compared with the intelligence but is also well below grade level. Often there is a reversing of letters (such as *flim* for *film*), a confusion of sounds (such as *graditude* for *gratitude*), and the omission of syllables in long words (such as *exceply* for *exceptionally*). The oral reading is hesitant: words are mispronounced, short words are omitted, and some words which are not present will be inserted. Silent reading is slow (again in comparison to the intelligence and in relationship to the previous schooling) and may also be inaccurate. The vocabulary, particularly the written one, is relatively meager. The handwriting may be slow, cramped and uneven, and may vary considerably in slant, pencil pressure, and in spacing between the letters—an uneven performance which suggests, as does the spelling and oral reading, that cerebral images for individual letters cannot readily, smoothly, and accurately be recalled and reproduced.

On questioning it is often learned that other members of the family—parents, siblings, aunts, uncles, grandparents—have had some manner of language difficulty. There is a considerable body of evidence which suggests that this condition is hereditary. These young people will also frequently be reported as having been late to learn to talk and to walk: their development often has the characteristics of maturation lag. Their coordination in the early years tends to be below the average, and they later choose, because they can be more successful in them, those large muscle sports such as football, swimming, and riding, which do not demand a high degree of fine coordination. It is usual to be told that such an adolescent had trouble learning to read and to spell from the very first, but that he had always done better in arithmetic; that he now avoids reading, has great difficulty learning a foreign language, is poor at writing themes and uses an immature vocabulary in them, excels in science and mathematics, and is "good with his hands." Some of these people have a poor sense of direction and rhythm and are unsure of which is right or left, are clumsy, and have trouble remembering names, in reading music, and in learning the Morse code.

These young people may be said to be indifferent to, and may want to leave, school; they may refuse to study and seem nervous, irritable, and disrespectful. Much of this is what one would expect to develop in an intelligent adolescent frustrated by his or her inability to learn as readily as his no more intelligent or industrious companions. He has become resentful, anxious, and discouraged by years of failure.

Specific language disability is nothing new. Nowadays much of the poor reading skill in the United States is blamed on teaching methods which avoid drill in phonics and emphasize developing interest, the ability to read rapidly, and the understanding of ideas rather than a focus on details. But the fact that many people taught in these ways read exceedingly well makes this conclusion suspect. It is certainly true that those who have even a mild language disability find it difficult if not impossible to learn when the whole word approach is used; remedial teachers know only too well that such people experience trouble in grasping and retaining even as much as a whole letter. But specific language disability exists in people of other countries where other methods of teaching than those now so prevalent in the United States are used; furthermore, descriptions of this sort of learning problem antedate the "whole word" method, which has been so widely blamed. Kussmaul (4) coined the term "word blindness" in 1878, and in 1897 an English school physician, Kerr (5), mentioned that reading disabilities occur in children of normal intelligence. In 1896 Morgan (6) suggested that a child who was incapable of learning to read in spite of normal sight and otherwise normal status suffered from congenital word blindness. He could find no evidence of an *acquired* brain injury in his patient, so he concluded that this 14-year-old boy who had good intelligence and yet very low reading ability had a condition "evidently congenital and due most probably to defective development of that region of the brain, disease of which in adults produces practically the same symptoms—that is, the left angular gyrus."

Over the years a considerable number of similar reports have appeared; a variety of clinical descriptions and neurological explanations and many names for this condition have been offered. In keeping with advances in our knowledge, there is less tendency now to think of this condition as being strictly limited to one area of the brain or as being confined to a single "pure" neurological defect. Orton (7), who, beginning in the 1920's, devoted years of his life to a careful, thoughtful study of this field, considered the term "word blindness" misleading and introduced the term "strephosymbolia" (twisted symbols). He developed the hypothesis that "reversals" and the omission and introduction of letters resulted from a defect in cerebral dominance. Skydsgaard (8), writing in 1942, preferred the term "constitutional dyslexia," a condition which he defined as covering "in analogy to acquired alexia, both the most serious defects (which might well be termed congenital alexia) and those of a milder character, which extend right up to the physiological variants."

More recently there has been considerable interest in comparing these young people with those who are thought to suffer from Gerstmann's syndrome (9) and/or some disturbance of Gestalt function. Drew (10) has described three cases of familial dyslexia which exhibit findings comparable to those abnormalities present in *acquired* word blindness due to involvement of the parietal lobes. He suggests that their difficulties were due to a disturbance in Gestalt function. Such a disturbance, he believes, is inherited as a dominant trait, and he feels that a delayed development of the parietal lobes is the anatomical substrate which underlies this condition. Hermann and Norrie (11) in Denmark have discussed the points of resemblance between dyslexia and Gerstmann's syndrome (which some believe to be an expression of difficulty in Gestalt formation and which is characterized by finger agnosia, right-left disorientation, acalculia, and agraphia). They emphasize the findings of right-left confusion (as do Zazzo and his associates (12) in France) and poor finger discrimination in dyslexia patients, and believe that these patients' difficulties and those of patients who suffer from Gerstmann's syndrome both derive from a disturbance of directional function. De Hirsch (13) and Bender (14) are among those in this country who regard congenital dyslexia to be a result of a fundamental disturbance in Gestalt function—a defect in the visual-motor field. It is of interest that Orton, some 25 years earlier, discussed three levels of cortical integration of vision and emphasized the relevance of visual association to dyslexia; those who nowadays refer to Gestalt function speak of its three states: Gestalt seeing, Gestalt recognition, and object comprehension or visual association.

From the time of the very earliest case reports it has been suspected that there has been a genetic factor in at least some forms of dyslexia. Many subsequent reports, personal experiences of clinicians, and such genealogical tables as those published by Skydsgaard (15) paved the way for acceptance of Hallgren's (16) recent statistical study from Sweden and his conclusion that "specific dyslexia with a high degree of probability follows a monohybrid autosomal dominant mode of inheritance"—that is, a single gene is involved in a dominant, non-sex, linked form of inheritance. His work has been subjected to some criticism, and furthermore he himself clearly qualified his conclusion. When one remembers the disagreements over the definition of this condition and the difficulties of accurate differential diagnosis, the problems and the criticism which such an investigator faces are obvious.

Studies of twins who have dyslexia are more convincing. In Hallgren's three pairs of monozygotic twins, there was concordance in all; in his three pairs of dizygotic twins there was concordance in but two pairs. Similarly, in Hermann and Norrie's (17) series of 39 Danish twins, the nine monozygotic twins all showed concordance; this occurred in only 10 of the dizygotic pairs. The other 20 dizygotic pairs were discordant.

These preceding comments from the medical literature are intended to indicate both the past and present trends in physicians' thinking on this subject, its universality, our lack of positive knowledge of its cause and therefore of its prevention and treatment, and the need for further research. Furthermore, they may serve to emphasize the fact that although the medical approach does not deny that emotional and environmental factors play a role, the physician's main concern over the years has been to discover what *basic* modification of brain functioning it is which accounts for this apparently hereditary rather than acquired disturbance.

Many psychologists, on the other hand, have taken the position that many factors result in poor reading and have concentrated on studying the reading process itself and on developing tests of reading skills rather than concerning themselves with the other interrelated language skills. Javal (18), as early as 1878, published observations on eye movements during reading. These were followed by studies by Dearborn (19), Buswell (20), and Taylor (21), who constructed a binocular camera—the ophthalmograph—which photographed eye movements. Concurrently, psychologists made studies of the perception of the printed word and developed tests designed to evaluate reading skill, and after 1910 also began to suggest ways in which their findings could improve the teaching of reading. In recent years there has been a trend for psychologists to leave the laboratory and go into the field to deal with this problem in the classroom. Gray (22), Gates (23), and Robinson (24) have been outstanding among the many very competent leaders in this area.

Many educational psychologists reject the belief that there are hereditary and cerebral causes of dyslexia and object to the use of the word "congenital," perhaps considering it to imply that the condition is unlikely to improve. This would seem to indicate a misunderstanding on their part regarding the susceptibility of hereditary traits to change. Finally, although many seem to emphasize one or another special factor, most tend to believe dyslexia the result of such causes as inadequate readiness for initial reading, intellectual backwardness, physical handicaps, social and cultural poverty, speech retardation, personality, emotional and adjustment difficulty, irregular school attendance, and defective teaching.

There are few who would question the importance of any of the foregoing and would not wish to give them consideration when dealing with any individual patient. But at the present time it is difficult to believe that any one of these, or any combination of them, can constitute the basic cause of difficulty in a high percentage of those young people who exhibit the characteristics of a specific language disability. The frequency with which any one of those factors seems to be the *primary* cause of trouble and the frequency with which *no* difficulty in learning to read or spell occurs in their presence need further to be investigated.

Most studies of this problem will, I believe, be best carried out as cross-sectional community ones rather than pursued in special schools, hospital clinics, or guidance centers; in these institutions selective factors inevitably operate. Malmquist's (25) recent study of school children in Sweden almost satisfies this condition even though it embraced only urban children. However, although Malmquist investigated numerous significant variables, he omitted such matters as auditory perception and auditory memory, and could not include those contributions which the collaboration of representatives of medicine, neurology, sociology, and education might have made. Malmquist made clear that the relationship which he found to exist between certain factors (intelligence, ability to concentrate, persistence, self-confidence, emotional stability, spelling ability, social and educational status of the parents, and the teachers' teaching experience) and reading disabilities should not be interpreted as evidence of their being *causes* of them. He further suggested that future studies should investigate the roles of heredity and of emotional patterns.

The primary difference in point of view between many educational psychologists and physicians has been that many of the former do not recognize the existence of such an entity as specific language disability and prefer to think of those persons who have experienced difficulty in learning to read and spell as representing no more than the sort of variation from the average (perhaps increased temporarily because of one or more environmental or emotional factors) which one would expect in any normal, unselected population. They do not regard these people as having any structural or functional disorder which sets them apart from others and modifies their ability to acquire language skills, and they point out that characteristics said to be indicative of a specific language disability (such as the reversal of letters, sound confusions, delayed speech, better skill in arithmetic, left-right confusion, et cetera) are also present in many other normal children. This certainly is true and is in fact one of the chief reasons that the early selection (at 6 years of age, for example) of those thought to have specific language disability is subject to considerable error. Many physicians, however, who regard specific language disability as a specific dysfunction point out that these children's difficulties persist to a significant degree in spite of time and schooling, that the kind of spelling errors they make and the other difficulties they have in acquiring and using language skills, though not pathognomonic, are more frequent and more persistent than is true of members of the general population, and finally that the genetic evidence for constitutional factors in them is strong.

In recent years some psychiatrists have suggested that emotional factors are basic in the causation of dyslexia, but not all psychiatrists fully agree. Pearson (26) although deeply concerned with the emotional factors in learning, has cautioned that "it is necessary to re-emphasize . . . [the organic] because at the present time when there is so much emphasis on the importance of intrapsychic processes in all phases of medicine and education, psychiatrists tend to become overenthusiastic about dynamic intrapsychic processes to the complete neglect of physiological and organic processes. . . ." Rabinovitch and his colleagues (27) recognize as one of three groups of children those who "present a basic defect in capacity to integrate written material and to associate concepts with symbols" (the others are those who have frank brain damage and those in whom personality or educational neglect factors are at fault). They consider their findings to suggest that in these patients they are dealing "with a developmental rather than an acquired brain injury" and that the specific areas of difficulty "are those commonly associated with parietal and parietal-occipital dysfunction."

There is no doubt that many very intelligent children are unable to learn because of their faulty emotional adjustment, and it is possible that because of some emotional disorder a few are unable to learn to read and spell but at the same time learn arithmetic. However, it would seem likely that those who believe emotional difficulties are the basic cause of all dyslexia, as we have defined it here, may hold this opinion because they have had the opportunity to study few children except those who are emotionally upset.

Few children and adolescents who suffer the frustration and defeat which follow excessive difficulty in learning to read and spell can hope to escape some degree of emotional, personality, and behavioral disturbance. However, many physicians feel that these disturbances are secondary and that when reading and spelling are later taught in a way which enables these people to learn, their emotional problems may begin to dissipate. Some young people will doubtless have become so upset by continued failure that a period of psychotherapy may have to precede or be concurrent with any effort at remedial instruction. Conversely, it will be necessary if a true language disability is present also to give subsequent remedial instruction to the boy or girl who has had a long period of psycho-therapy; the resistance to learning may have been removed, but the ability to learn to read and spell when taught in a conventional fashion will not have been affected.

The examination of young people suspected of having a specific language disability begins with an interview with the parents. This includes questions about their own scholastic history and interests, including the extent of their schooling, type of job, level of performance, relative ability in speech, reading, spelling, and mathematics; their ability to express themselves orally or to remember names; their handedness, tendency to confuse right and left; and their sense of direction. Similar questions should be asked about their own parents, their siblings, and their other children.

Information should then be obtained about the patient's birth, early health and development (speech and walking), as well as a history of convulsions, head injury or illness accompanied by high fever, early coordination and later athletic skill, sense of direction, tendency to confuse left and right, frequency and ex-tent of school absences, handedness, and adjustment at home and school with those older and younger than themselves. Such factors as slow neurological de-velopment, head injuries, encephalitis, speech disorders, cerebral dominance, and emotional maladjustment should be kept in mind and an effort made to deter-mine whether there is a time relationship between any relevant information dis-closed and the onset of the learning problem. Finally, a careful history of the patient's schooling is taken: when he entered school, his initial reaction to it, his teachers' early comments, his feelings about his teachers and theirs toward him, the relative ease with which he learned various subjects and what special help was given as well as how much, what kind, by whom, and how it was accepted by the patient.

Later, similar questions are asked the patient, and his attitudes, stability, his interest in his studies and in his own predicament are assessed. During the physical examination more attention is given to tests of central nervous system function (finger agnosia, hand grip, hand-to-face test, balance, gait, etc.) than is usual; and though positive unequivocal findings are not common, it is obvious that the more frequently one employs such tests, the more they are apt to yield. Vision (including tests of eye muscle balance, binocular vision, and amplitude of fusion) and speech and hearing should be carefully evaluated; the relative ability to read from left to right and from right to left and to write with each hand may be revealing. Handedness, eyedness, and footedness are also evaluated.

Next, standardized arithmetic, reading, spelling, and penmanship tests are given. The achievement tests are followed by an individual intelligence test (Weschler-Bellevue WISC or WAIS) since group tests are heavily influenced by reading skill and may therefore reflect this rather than intelligence; and by such evaluations of visual, auditory, and motor skills and of emotional stability as seem appropriate.

Finally, a combined evaluation of the person, his history, the physical find-ings, and the test results must be made. Given a boy (specific language disability seems to be about four times more common in males), a history of difficulty in reading and in using language in other members of the family, freedom from evidence or history of birth injury or of a subsequent illness which might have damaged the central nervous system, a history of being late to learn to talk, of having relatively poor coordination in early life, some ambidexterity rather than a strong single hand preference, some right-left confusion, early success at arithmetic and concurrent difficulty in learning to read and spell, a subsequent dislike of school and reading, little benefit from sporadic tutoring in reading, and persisting poor reading and bizarre spelling in spite of excellent intelligence —certainly the diagnosis of specific language disability is a reasonable one to entertain. When the intelligence is borderline or the defeatist or defensive attitudes strong, it will be more difficult to be sure. However, if the spelling has the characteristics of specific language disability, it is usually proper to consider a trial of remedial instruction, at least as a therapeutic test. If after a thorough trial, properly selected and properly administered remedial methods do not succeed, the evidence should be re-evaluated and another tentative diagnosis and treatment plan made.

It is assumed that these young people *can* learn to read, spell, and write with reasonable facility and that they can improve these skills at least to a point where they will no longer be seriously handicapped. But this assumption is made on the premise that those selected really have a specific disability and that the proper sort of remedial help can be provided. These young people have amply demonstrated their inability to learn when taught in the manner previously used. One method, no matter how effective for many, is not necessarily the best method for all. However, if we postulate that these highly intelligent young people have not learned to read and spell because their brains are such that they find it difficult to form clear, strong images of the look and sound and feel of letters, and are therefore subsequently unable quickly and accurately to recall them when they wish to employ them in reading or writing or spelling or saying a word, we should expect that some other method designed to produce sharper images and to reduce left-right confusion would be successful. This apparently is the case. Methods devised and practiced by such people as Gillingham (28) in this country, Borel-Maisonny (12) in France, and Norrie (29) in Denmark have basic similarities and have proven successful. These young people must have drill, they must have the advantages which accrue when the sound, the look, the feel of a letter are experienced simultaneously, they must develop and use most that sensory area—visual, auditory or kinesthetic—which yields them the best results and the least frustration. When the proper kind of remedial help is given them, these young people not only can learn to read and spell in an adequate fashion, but as they find themselves improving after years of failure, they may also be expected to gain in confidence, to regard school without dread, and to lose their symptoms of anxiety.

It furthermore seems true that when the child first learning to read is taught by an alphabetic-phonetic method which combines visual, auditory, and kinesthetic approaches to the learning of letters and which furnishes information which will enable to him to attack new and strange words in other than a random fashion, he will subsequently experience less difficulty and anxiety in acquiring that degree of language skill which one would expect on the basis of his intelligence and background. When a child has a considerable degree of language disability, it would seem likely that additional individual help would be necessary. But at the present time such group preventive methods as have been employed at the first grade level by Gillingham (30) at the Francis Parker School and elsewhere, by Spalding (31) in Honolulu's parochial schools, and by Filbin (32) (with Eustis' assistance) first in Peterborough and now in Lincoln seem successful in enhancing the ability to acquire adequate language skills in all but those whose language disabilities are very severe. Children so taught do not appear, because of the method's repetitious drill and emphasis on *first* learning single letters, subsequently to be slower or less understanding readers, nor do they seem to have become inhibited or resentful because of the method's insistence on careful observation and its flavor of regimentation. Instead, perhaps because they have acquired a thorough acquaintance with each component part of a word and have some knowledge of how each part affects the others, they seem to approach words with less anxiety, a feeling of being able to conquer, and with pleasure.

In concluding, I would like to urge the pediatrician and the family physician, who know both the child and his parents and who have a large share of the responsibility for children's proper all-round development, to keep this condition in mind; they particularly should do so when the family history or a child's early development or difficulty in acquiring language skills suggests that such a condition as specific language disability may be present (33). When this is done, early steps then can be taken which may prevent handicapping and upsetting personality and school problems.

REFERENCES

1. Cole, E. M.: Disabilities in speaking and reading, M. Clin. N. America 22: 607, 1938.

2. Eustis, R. S.: Specific reading disability; familial syndrome associated with ambidexterity and speech defects and frequent cause of problem behavior, New England J. Med. 237: 243, 1947.

3. Gallagher, J. R.: Specific language disability: cause of scholastic failure, New England J. Med. 242: 436, 1950.

4. Kussmaul, A.: Disturbance of Speech, Ziemssen's Cyclopaedia of the Practice of Medicine 14: 770, 1878. London, Sampson Low.

5. Kerr, J.: School hygiene in its mental, moral and physical aspects, J. Statistic Soc. 60: 613, 1897.

6. Morgan, W. P.: A case of congenital word blindness, Brit. M. J. 2: 1378, 1896.

7. Orton, S. T.: Reading, Writing and Speech Problems in Children, New York, W. W. Norton and Company, Inc., 1937.

8. Skydsgaard, H. B.: Den Konstitutionelle Dyslexi "Ordblindhed," Copenhagen, Busch, 1942.

9. Gerstmann, J.: Syndrome of finger agnosia, disorientation for right and left, agraphia and acalculia; local diagnostic value, A. M. A. Arch. Neurol. & Psychiat. 44: 398, 1940.

10. Drew, A. L.: Neurological appraisal of familial congenital word-blindness, Brain 79: 440, 1956.

11. Hermann, K. and Norrie, E.: Is congenital word-blindness a hereditary type of Gerstmann's syndrome, Psychiatria, Basel 136: 59, 1958.

12. Zazzo, R., Ajuriaguerra, J., Borel-Maisonny, S., Galifret-Granjon, N., Stambak, M., Simon, J., et Chassagny, D.: L'Apprentissage de la Lecture et Ses Troubles—Les Dyslexies D'Evolution, Paris, Presses Universitaires, 1952.

13. De Hirsch, K.: Specific dyslexia or strephosymbolia, Folia Phoniat. 4: 231, 1952.

14. Bender, L.: Problems in conceptualization and communication in children with developmental alexia. Chapter 11 in Psychopathology of Communication, Hoch, P. H. and Zubin, J., editors, New York, Grune and Stratton, 1958.

15. Skydsgaard, H.: Medfødt Ordblindhed, Om Ordblindesagen i Danmark 1: 8, 1944.

16. Hallgren, B.: Specific dyslexia ("congenital word-blindness"); clinical and genetic study, Acta psychiat. et neurol. (supp. 65) 1, 1950.

17. Hermann, K.: Om Medfødt Ord-blindhed, Copenhagen, Munksgaard, 1955. Revision and English translation by P. G. Aungle under title, Reading Disability: a neurological study of reading disability and of related language disorders. Published simultaneously by Manksgaard, Copenhagen; Charles C Thomas, Springfield, Illinois, and by the Ryerson Press, Toronto, Canada, 1959.

18. Javal, E.: Essai sur la Physiologie de la Lecture, Annales d'Oculistique 79: 97, 1878.

19. Dearborn, W. F.: Ocular and manual dominance in dyslexia, Psychol. Bull. 28: 704, 1931.

20. Buswell, G. T.: Fundamental reading habits: a study of their development, Suppl. Educ. Monograph 21, Chicago, University of Chicago Press, 1922.

21. Taylor, E.: Controlled Reading, Chicago, University of Chicago Press, 1937.

22. Gray, W.: The teaching of reading and writing. Monograph Fund, Educ. 286, New York, UNESCO. 1956.

23. Gates, A. I.: The Improvement of Reading: A Program of Diagnostic and Remedial Methods, ed. 3, New York, The MacMillan Company, 1947.

24. Robinson, H. M.: Why Pupils Fail in Reading: a Study of Causes and Remedial Treatment, Chicago, University of Chicago Press, 1946.

25. Malmquist, E.: Factors Related to Reading Disabilities in the First Grade of the Elementary School, Stockholm, Almquist and Wiksell, 1958.

26. Pearson, G. H. J.: Survey of learning difficulties in children, Psychoanalytic study of the child 7: 322, 1952.

27. Rabinovitch, R. D. et al.: A research approach to reading retardation, Neurol. and Psychiatry in Childhood XXXIV. Proceedings of the Association for Research in Nervous and Mental Disease 363, Baltimore, The Williams and Wilkins Company, 1956.

28. Gillingham, A., and Stillman, B. W.: Remedial Training for Children with Specific Disability in Reading, Spelling and Penmanship, ed. 5, Bronxville, New York. Privately Printed, 1956, (Distributed by Anna Gillingham).

29. Norrie, E.: Behandlingen paa Ord-blindein-instituttet, Landsforenigen for Ordblindesagen i Danmark 1: 27, 1943. (A revision and translation being prepared for publication in The Independent School Bulletin).

30. Report—The First Seven Years of the Gillingham Reading Program at Francis W. Parker School, Chicago, Francis W. Parker School, 1957.

31. Spalding, R. B., with Spalding, W. T.: The Writing Road to Reading, New York, Whiteside, Inc. and Wm. Morrow & Co., 1957.

32. Filbin, R. L.: A classroom experiment in remedial reading, New Hampshire Educator, November 1956.

33. De Hirsch, K.: Tests designed to discover potential reading difficulties at six-year-old level. Am. J. Orthopsychiat. 27: 566, 1957.

~~~~~~

Part Four

Approaches to the Diagnosis of Learning Problems

The literature concerning the diagnosis of learning disabilities may be thought of as comprising two categories. One is theoretical or position papers that present views concerning diagnosis and remedial treatment. Capobianco's discussion of diagnostic methods, of the classroom teacher's role in diagnosis, and of the usefulness of the classification "brain damaged" is an example.

The second category is studies estimating the reliability and validity of various tests used in diagnosis. The studies selected for inclusion here that belong to this category also present conclusions about psychological factors that may affect a test score and about the psychometric prediction of academic failure.

The first study within this grouping is by Chansky, who along with Finley investigated reading achievement tests. Chansky sought to determine what factors other than reading skill affect a standardized reading test score. Common sense tells one that conditions other than skill or knowledge influence a test score, and Chansky's study is an attempt to point out some of these influencing variables. On the other hand, Finley's conclusions about the relative difficulty of the arithmetic, language, and reading subtests of three widely used achievement tests have implications supporting the argument for the establishment of a district or school achievement testing program to identify underachievers who are to be included in a remedial program.

The Otto-McMenemy and Ivanoff-Tempero studies present data concerning the reliability and validity of two intelligence tests used in screening poor readers. Since, as Otto and McMenemy have noted, group IQ tests tend to penalize the poor reader, some other method of assessing potential seems necessary. Unhappily, the best measures—the WISC and the Stanford-Binet—are not usually available immediately. Therefore, it seems essential to present information about two IQ tests that can be quickly administered by remedial teachers with a minimum background in educational measurement. For comprehensive bibliographies and a review of all tests the reader can consult O. K. Buros' *Sixth Mental Measurement Yearbook*.

Keogh's brief report on a four-year longitudinal study of the Bender Gestalt's validity in predicting reading achievement should help to make the remedial teacher aware of some of the limitations of a popular diagnostic instrument. Note should be taken of the various Bender scoring systems used and the relationship of good and poor Bender scores to general academic achievement.

9   Diagnostic Methods Used with
         Learning Disability Cases

R. J. CAPOBIANCO

Abstract.—*The extreme variability of behavior characterizing the neurologically impaired, or more recently "children with learning disabilities," demands the educator's attention to symptomatology rather than etiology. Diagnosticians must strengthen their attempts to recommend corrective-remedial education for these children rather than serve as mere "classifiers" or intermediate "stop-gaps" between teachers and neurologists. Clinical educational techniques of proven value should be geared to the nature of the learning disability rather than to causative factors.*

Perhaps the one irrefutable characteristic attributed to children with learning disabilities is their wide variability of behavior. Considerable time, effort, and money have been expended in attempts to describe, measure, diagnose, and remedy the learning problems which are commonly regarded as the aftereffects of brain injury. Efforts to group these children into categories variously termed neurologically impaired, exogenous, cerebrally dysfunctioned, and the like have complicated the interpretation of research findings rather than provided a basis for operational definitions. With the intensity of effort to "pigeonhole" or classify these youngsters as one clinical entity, the behavioral descriptions which resulted have grown far out of proportion to functional diagnosis. Indeed, if the exhaustive list of behaviors attributed to neurologically impaired children were accepted at face value, then it would be difficult, if not impossible, to imagine a child who could not be labeled brain injured on the basis of one set of behaviors or another.

Modern educators and psychologists have attempted to skirt the problem of diagnostic difficulty by coining a new phrase for the old list of names—children with learning disorders (or disabilities). This new phrase provides for the inclusion of all youngsters with a syndrome of behaviors which interfere with the learning process and yet eliminates the inherent difficulty in establishing the existence of a brain injury. Hence, the modern special class for children with learning disabilities may be composed of youngsters who are brain injured, emotionally disturbed, visually impaired, auditorially handicapped, intellectually subnormal, or suffering from some motor imbalance—perhaps any one individual may be hampered by a combination of these handicaps.

The apparent heterogeneity of these children according to the multiplicity of labels is deceiving. They are no less homogeneous than groups of students collected together merely because they have been categorized as brain injured. Nevertheless, it is suspected that for some time to come, classes for children with learning disabilities will still be composed predominantly of youngsters who meet the psychoeducational criteria established for the brain injured—the only difference being that they will not be labeled brain injured.

Candidates for these special classes are selected primarily on the basis of the overt display of certain characteristics such as underachievement, hyperactivity, distractibility, poor motor coordination, impulsivity, and short attention span and secondarily on their performance on selected psychological tests of perceptual processes. There is no intent here to argue for or against this approach;

From *Exceptional Children*, Vol. 31 (1964), pp. 187–193. Reprinted with permission.

indeed, this author has suggested years ago that teachers should deal with symptomatology rather than etiology. Similar notes of caution have been voiced by Barnett, Ellis, and Pryer (1960), Gallagher (1957), Kirk and McCarthy (1961), and Newland (1963) among others. In the final analysis, the worth of the program will rest upon the adequacy with which specific methods tend to alleviate identifiable learning impairments without respect to causation.

Clinical-educational techniques have been devised which purport to lessen the difficulties in learning characteristic of brain-injured, or "Strauss syndrome," children. Varying degrees of success have been reported by psychologists and educators employing these methods. But who is to say that all children with learning disabilities need to be exposed to this intensive program of special education to insure learning? Certainly there would be less expenditure of time and effort and fewer demands for extensive professional training on the part of teachers if some of these children could learn without recourse to rigorous programs of education suggested by some professional educators. Hence, the importance of an exhaustive psycho-educational diagnosis to determine the need for specific clinical-educational techniques and devices which would eliminate or remedy certain behaviors detrimental to learning. Kirk and McCarthy (1961) have already differentiated between classification and diagnosis, as has Newland (1963) between testing and assessment. Mere classification and/or testing does not necessarily prescribe treatment; complete diagnosis or assessment implies a course of remediation with prognosis.

The diagnosis of brain injury is difficult to formulate. Even with identification, the problem is not so readily resolved; for the neurologically impaired do not follow any typical, preconceived set of behaviors. In fact, the behaviors exhibited vary so greatly that the differences observed are as variable intragroup as between brain-injured and normal populations. To complicate the situation further, many of the neurologically impaired children do not present any specific learning problem in the classroom, whereas non-brain-injured children with supposedly organic behaviors do have difficulty.

One attempt to isolate and refine some sub-populations of brain-injured mental retardates according to behavior was described by Capobianco and Funk (1958). The Rorschach test was administered to exogenous and endogenous subjects representing both sexes. A pathology gradient was established, based upon electroencephalographic tracings, which isolated four groups: endogenous-normal, endogenous-convulsive, exogenous-convulsive, and exogenous-focal. Omitting the first group, the remaining three may be considered brain injured. Although there may seem to be an apparent contradiction within the category endogenous-convulsive, let it be known that the original endogenous-exogenous dichotomy was based upon the Riggs and Rain (1952) classification system before administration of the electroencephalogram (EEG). Thus, convulsive tracings were found in records of children who had originally been diagnosed as familial retardates (endogenous) without evidence of brain damage. Although the EEG is admittedly not a foolproof test, the proportion of abnormal tracings (58%) found within the familial population far exceeded the expected error.

The emerging patterns on the selected Rorschach variables, followed closely the hypothesized gradient, reversals occurring occasionally between the endogenous-normal and endogenous-convulsive categories. Results were interpreted by the authors as follows: "If this function of pathology and etiology is 'real,' the exogenous-focal end of the distribution reflects more conceptualizing; more outward-directed affect; more interest in people; less immature, stereotyped thinking; more feelings of negative self-appraisal; less negativism; and more perceptual difficulty . . ." (Capobianco and Funk, 1958, p. 68). The authors caution that this pathology gradient is based upon the results of a very small sample of familial and brain-injured retardates but that it should promise to be a fertile area for research in the future.

Similar attempts to refine sub-populations of children according to specific kinds of brain damage and EEG tracings have been reported by Burns (1960) and Sievers and Rosenberg (1960).

Diagnostic Procedures

The asserted preponderance of learning difficulties exhibited by organically impaired children has been the mainstay of the argument presented by those professionals who view the education of these children as a distinct and separate process. The fact that some of the neurologically impaired children do not experience difficulties in the learning process and that some nonimpaired children do is not sufficient justification to eliminate special teaching methodology. Insofar as the teacher is concerned, the disturbing behaviors demonstrated by these children, brain injured or not, must be eliminated or modified. The teacher will find no difficulty in recognizing that all is not well with a child who:

Follows no logical pattern in his behavior.

Never sticks with anything over a long period of time.

Wanders aimlessly about the room, apparently concerned with everyone else's business.

Never sits still for a minute; always runs, never walks.

Acts before thinking, seldom considering the consequences of his behavior.

Repeats, excessively, a task or movement.

May be able to read but does not comprehend the significance of what has been read.

Experiences difficulties in arithmetic, performing at a level far below expectancy.

Demonstrates visuomotor difficulties.

Seems at times to be out of contact—does not hear you.

Rapidly changes his mood or temperament.

Performs inconsistently and with marked variability in the various school subjects.

These behaviors do not comprise a total list of indicators of potential organicity; however, they serve as specific examples of the many factors comprising the learning difficulty syndrome. It is not within the province of the schoolteacher's responsibility to make the diagnosis, but rather it is his duty to utilize techniques and methodologies which prove to alleviate the condition responsible for the inadequacy of the child's functioning. When the techniques at the teacher's disposal do not improve the situation, then it is time to request a diagnostic workup by the school psychologist.

It is a rare school system indeed which has available to its students the services of a neurologist. Hence, the problem of identification of the brain injury usually falls into the hands of the school psychologist. Working in collaboration with the classroom teacher and the school physician or nurse, a screening process is effected. If the evidence obtained is sufficient to warrant a referral to a neurological specialist, it is based upon the collective information gleaned from behavioral descriptions, medical evidence, and psychological assessment. Strauss and Lehtinen have established four criteria for a complete diagnosis of minor brain damage: (a) a history of trauma before, during, or after birth, (b) neurological (or "soft") signs are present, (c) evidence that the child comes from normal familial stock, and (d) indicative evidence gleaned from psychological tests (1947). In recent years the trend in diagnosis of brain injury has been to rely more and more upon the results and interpretation of psychological tests. Complete neurological examinations, including the administration of the electroencephalographic test, often fail to discover positive evidence of injury and perhaps equally often may discern an injury which is nonexistent. Positive identification through the utilization of multitudinous tests of perceptual and conceptual disturbances are equally questionable—but considerably less expensive and time consuming. Oftentimes, the behavior described by the classroom teacher may overtly appear to be an indicator of brain damage but may actually be the result of some emotional upheaval recently affecting the child. Other characteristic behaviors may be "read in" by the referring teacher, often in good faith but without basis in fact. The failure of his particular teaching methods with the child in question may lead to a request for diagnostic information out of sheer desperation in not knowing what next to do. Whatever the reason for the request for further information on the child, the psychologist must serve as the first recourse for the teacher in the total assessment process.

The diagnostician is often forced to make a decision regarding the role he must play—to serve as an ancillary aide to the neurologist or to provide some practical suggestions for the teacher. Usually, the suspected degree of impairment serves to decide the course of action. Mild cases are groomed for the educator; more severe suspects are assessed for future referral to the neurologist. For education purposes, the pychologist is better equipped than the neurologist to offer recommendations regarding remedial techniques. Only for cases requiring medical treatment, such as post-encephalitis or tumors, would the referral to the neurologist be of subsequent help to the educator.

Armed with an array of information on the child, which includes his cumulative record and the behavioral description prepared by the teacher, the psychologist then selects the particular instrument or battery of tests to administer in his search for diagnostic evidence. A multitude of tests are already available which purport to be of unique value toward the diagnostic evaluation of brain-injured behaviors. Many clinicians prefer to utilize various subtests from standardized instruments seeking to arrive at qualitative evidence in addition to quantitative scores. This type of assessment, a "cafeteria" approach, has been described by Newland (1963) as an effective approach in the absence of individual devices suitable for use. This method of diagnosis is only as proficient as the clinician who employs it. In the hands of an inexperienced clinician or untrained personnel, the method would be relatively useless and perhaps dangerous.

Scatter patterns on some tests of intelligence have been investigated to determine characteristic performance of brain-damaged patients. Unfortunately, the results of research efforts in this area of diagnosis are often misleading and confusing—indeed, the results of one investigator may be directly contradictory to the conclusions formulated by another. Reitan (1955), in his very comprehensive work on Wechsler-Bellevue patterning, found that brain-damaged subjects generally exhibited characteristic patterns based upon the extent and localization of the brain insult. Verified left-hemisphere damage usually resulted in lower Verbal than Performance IQ's, while the reverse was true of right-hemisphere lesions. Subjects with diffuse damage performed approximately equally well on both scales. Morrow and Mark (1955) reported characteristically low performance by brain-injured subjects on Digit-Symbol, Digit-Span, and Arithmetic in support of Reitan (1955) and Wechsler (1944). On the other hand, Beck and Lam (1955) found no characteristic subtest patterns for their brain-damaged subjects, and Taterka and Katz (1955) reported that Coding, as a subtest, was affected adversely by brain damage. In an extensive comparative study of exogenous and endogenous subjects, Capobianco and Funk (1958) found similar patterns on the Wechsler Intelligence Scale for Children for both groups and both sexes. The differences between groups was in the predicted direction on the Arithmetic, Block Design, and Coding subtests; however, these differences were not statistically significant.

Many workers in the field have reported varying degrees of success in diagnosis of brain injury using perceptual organization tests such as the Rorschach, Bender-Gestalt, Graham-Kendall, Ellis Visual Design, and a variety of cube, stick, marble, and mosaic tests. The results are inconclusive. Even though many of the studies demonstrated differences in performance between brain-damaged and nondamaged subjects, individual children who scored poorly on one of these tests did not necessarily score correspondingly on another. Many known cases of brain injury are not isolated by these instruments, and the number of over referrals is overwhelming.

Even if the reader were willing to accept the diagnostic patterning of test scores and/or inferior performance on perceptual tests as truly characteristic of brain-injured functioning, he would still be at a loss to explain why these deficiencies apparently do not hamper educational progress. Research reports by Bensberg (1958), Capobianco (1956), Capobianco and Miller (1958), Capobianco and Funk (1958), and Gallagher (1957) among others have failed to discern any significant differences in performance between brain-damaged and nondamaged subjects on a number of educational and psychological variables. In an exhaustive investigation of psychological and psychophysical abilities displayed by organic and familial retardates, Clausen found that of 51 variables measured, only one (critical flicker frequency) obtained significance at the .05 level (Personal communication, 1964). Although other investigators have reported poorer performance by brain-injured subjects on this test (but not consistently), this one significant difference out of 51 comparisons could easily have occurred on a chance basis. Barnett, Ellis, and Pryer (1960) suggest that the term "brain injury" be dropped since it has been demonstrated that all Ss so labeled do not exhibit distinct behaviors nor do they necessarily demand special modes of instruction.

The one significant finding pervading this research is the characteristic variability of performance by brain-damaged subjects, far in excess of the performance exhibited by the control subjects; mean performances, however, remained relatively consistent. Attempts to subgroup populations of brain-injured subjects along an ordered continuum (pathology gradient proposed by Capobianco and Funk [1958]) and new methods of differential diagnosis (Illinois Test of Psycholinguistic Abilities) recently developed by Kirk and McCarthy (1961) appear to offer keys to future success in the bothersome area of brain-injured functioning.

Classroom Behavior

One cannot expect the teacher to be proficient in the administration and interpretation of projective techniques, intelligence tests, and tests of perceptual organization. The responsibility of the teacher in the total assessment process is far removed from the one to one clinical setting. First and foremost, the teacher is expected to keep complete records, including achievement tests, samples of school work, anecdotal reports, and rating scales. One incidence of unpredictable behavior in the classroom is not sufficient reason to trot the child to the nearest psychologist. But periodic outbreaks of unexplainable behavior, short attention span, and hyperactivity, coupled with poor scholastic performance, would warrant genuine concern on the part of the teacher. Unlike the consistently poor achievement characteristic of the mentally retarded child, the brain-injured child displays an irregular pattern of performance. He may be very proficient in reading and far below capacity in arithmetic. He may excel in verbal facility but experience considerable difficulty in reasoning. He may display superficial charm in initiating social acquaintances, yet "wear off" with the passage of time. He may learn quickly some skills which emphasize rote, but fail miserably in tasks which require independent thinking. These inconsistencies should be noted in the teacher's anecdotal records.

The periodic use of sociograms within the classroom often gives significant information to the teacher. The hyperactive, disinhibited youngster is seldom accepted by his classmates. The individual's own choices of peers on the sociogram give some clue as to the personality he himself may desire to be. Gross distortions in the child's artwork serve to implement further the informal diagnosis within the classroom. The child at play exhibits behaviors which oftentimes yield more information regarding his problem than actual classroom performances. All too often the teacher does not take note of this particular fertile area for study. Obviously, the teacher cannot keep a complete, up-to-date, ongoing record on every child in his room, but behaviors of note should be included in the anecdotal record. Trusting to memory, the teacher often fails to record significant behaviors which occur during the school day. The practice of attempting to record all pertinent information at the end of the school day should be abandoned in favor of immediate recording—not total descriptions of the incident but a word or two to identify the behavior, who was involved, and the time it occurred. Later, the more complete description may be recorded. With information as complete as described, the teacher not only systemizes his own interpretation of the youngster's behavior but also preserves diagnostic information which would be an invaluable asset to the psychologist who may ultimately be responsible for the complete assessment of the child.

Rating scales, such as described by Gallagher (1957), force an orderly account of the children's behavior. These instruments provide insurance against the tendency on the part of many observers to record only the negative aspects of behavior.

Summary

The term "brain injury" has failed to serve any practical function. It is an etiological concept which offers little to the educator, psychologist, or other specialist who is interested in the behavioral symptomatology of the child with learning disabilities. The generic term adds more confusion to a field in which specialists are constantly seeking to differentiate sub-populations through newly formulated diagnostic systems. The term itself offers no help to the specialists engaged in the development of sound educational and therapeutic programs to ameliorate the problems demonstrated by children with special learning disabilities. Some investigators have proposed new titles for the general area of brain damage without essentially dismissing the criticisms leveled above. One of the effects of the newer terminology was to instill in the minds of the regular classroom teacher a greater fear of those youngsters labeled cerebral dysfunction, neurophrenia, or organically impaired. In the eyes of the teacher these newer diagnoses quickly joined those originally labeled brain-injured as youngsters "who cannot learn." Some attempts to isolate specific subgroups of brain-injured youngsters in accordance with differential characteristics are more rewarding. Differential diagnosis within this field, however, is still at the infancy stage of development.

Recently, parents of these children have established organizations which seek to collect and distribute information in an attempt to educate the layman regarding the disabilities of brain-injured children. This movement has been directly or indirectly responsible for the establishment of many public school special classes for these children. Psychologists and educators have collaborated with neurologists and pediatricians in helping the parent groups to present professional programs to their membership. Research and demonstration projects are currently on the upswing in this field. Specialists representing the allied areas of emotional disturbance, mental retardation, orthopedic handicaps, and remedial instruction have sought a reciprocal interrelationship with authorities in the field of neurological impairment to consolidate their respective gains made to date. State departments of education have included special classes for the brain-injured within their structure of reimbursement, special aids, and transportation allowances. The growth within the field is constantly supplemented by new discoveries in the areas of neurology and psychology. Clinical educational techniques which have proven value in the training of brain-injured youngsters are periodically described in the literature. Hence, in spite of the large gaps which exist in our knowledge of this area, the infant field of brain injury is starting to grow up.

Diagnostic procedures, at this writing, are still somewhat spotty. It is difficult, at best, to expect the classroom teacher to succeed in the technical aspects of diagnosis when the instruments of the neurologists and psychologists are still subject to gross errors. Whereas one particular clinician may experience a high degree of success with one battery of tests, a similarly trained specialist may question its validity. The research literature compounds the confusion by presenting conflicting results often within the same issue of a specific journal.

The burden of action, nevertheless, remains with the teacher. Keeping complete records on learning disability cases is one of his major responsibilities. Armed with an organized series of reports, including tests results, rating scales, sociograms, anecdotal records, and personal impressions, the teacher is in an excellent position to discuss the particular problem with the school psychologist. Prescriptions for teacher reaction to the child's behavior are supplied by the psychologist. He may recommend firm control for the hyperactive, disinhibited child and more permissiveness for the withdrawn, apathetic youngster. Gallagher (1960) describes a system of tutoring which was successful with brain-injured, mentally retarded children. Perhaps the new movement to establish special classes for children with similar learning disabilities may reduce some of the frustrations suffered by the diagnostician who no longer will find it necessary to "prove" that a brain injury exists.

REFERENCES

Barnett, C. D., Ellis, N. R., and Pryer, M. W. Learning in familial and brain-injured defectives. *American Journal of Mental Deficiency,* 1960, 64, 894–901.

Beck, H. S., and Lam, R. L. Use of the WISC in predicting organicity. *Journal of Clinical Psychology,* 1955, 11, 154–158.

Bensberg, G. J., Jr. The relation of academic achievement of mental defectives to mental age, sex, institutionalization and etiology. *American Journal of Mental Deficiency,* 1953, 58, 327–330.

Burns, R. C. Behavioral differences between brain-injured and brain-deficit children grouped according to neuropathological types. *American Journal of Mental Deficiency,* 1960. 65, 326–334.

Capobianco, R. J. Quantitative and qualitative analyses of endogenous and exogenous boys on arithmetic achievement. *Monograph of Society for Research in Child Development,* 1956, 19, 101–141.

Capobianco, R. J., and Funk, Ruth A. *A comparative study of intellectual, neurological, and perceptual processes as related to reading achievement of exogenous and endogenous retarded children.* New York: Syracuse University Research Institute, 1958.

Capobianco, R. J., and Miller, D. Y. *Quantitative and qualitative analyses of exogenous and endogenous children in some reading processes.* New York: Syracuse University Research Institute, 1958.

Gallagher, J. J. A comparison of brain-injured and non-brain-injured mentally retarded children on several psychological variables. *Monograph of Society for Research in Child Development,* 1957, 22, (2).

Gallagher, J. J. *The tutoring of brain-injured mentally retarded children.* Springfield, Illinois: Charles C Thomas, 1960.

Kirk, S. A., and McCarthy, J. J. The Illinois test of psycholinguistic abilities—an approach to differential diagnosis. *American Journal of Mental Deficiency,* 1961, 66, 399–412.

Morrow, R. S., and Mark, J. C. The correlation of intelligence and neurological findings on 22 patients autopsied for brain damage. *Journal of Consulting Psychology,* 1955, 19, 283–289.

Newland, T. E. Psychological assessment of exceptional children. In Cruickshank, W. (Editor), *Psychology of exceptional children and youth* (Second Edition). Englewood Cliffs, New Jersey: Prentice-Hall, Inc., 1963.

Reitan, R. M. Certain differential effects of left and right cerebral lesions in human adults. *Journal of Comparative and Physiological Psychology,* 1955, 48, 474–477.

Riggs, Margaret M., and Rain, Margaret E. A classification system for the mentally retarded. *Training School Bulletin,* 1952, 49, 151–168.

Sievers, Dorothy L., and Rosenberg, C. M. The differential language facility test and electroencephalograms of brain-injured mentally retarded children. *American Journal of Mental Deficiency,* 1960, 65, 46–50.

Strauss, A. A., and Lehtinen, Laura E. *Psychopathology and education of the brain-injured child.* New York: Grune and Stratton, Inc., 1947.

Taterka, J. H., and Katz, J. Study of correlations between electroencephalographic and psychological patterns in emotionally disturbed children. *Psychosomatic Medicine,* 1955, 22, 62–72.

Wechsler, D. *The measurement of adult intelligence.* (Third Edition) Baltimore: Williams and Wilkins, Inc., 1944.

10   A Note on the Validity of
Reading Test Scores

NORMAN M. CHANSKY

It is not unusual to find a competent reader whose scores on a standardized reading test would warrant a diagnosis of reading retardation. This disconcerting datum suggests that factors affecting a reading test score require investigation.

An incidental finding of a study by Voas (2) was that there were relatively high correlations between reading speed and two test validity checks, F and K Scores of the Minnesota Multiphasic Personality Inventory. The subjects in the Voas study were servicemen. The author undertook the present study to determine to what extent the relationships between F and K with reading scores existed in a college freshman population.

Procedure

Fifty-six college freshmen enrolled in a required Introductory Psychology course were the subjects. The validity checks were the F and K Scores of the Minnesota Multiphasic Personality Inventory (MMPI). The MMPI had been administered to the students early in the semester. The measure of reading, the Cooperative English Test, C2 (Coop), had been administered as part of the college entrance test battery.

It was decided that only the Total scale score of the Coop would be used in computing the correlations between the validity checks and reading because subtests correlate quite highly with it. In the present sample, Total Reading correlated with Vocabulary + .82, with Speed + .91, and with Comprehension + .93.

Results and Discussion

Table I reveals a substantial correlation between MMPI validity scores and reading. The F Score is a measure of testee carelessness or inability to comprehend the items in the test (1). The correlation between F and the Coop may mean that carelessness or inability to comprehend lessened the validity of the obtained measurements. The K Score, on the other hand, is a correction factor which serves as a suppressor variable and appears to measure "test-taking attitude." Response bias may be influencing reading scores. These findings compare favorably to those of Voas.

TABLE I   *Correlations Between Reading and Validity Checks of the MMPI*

	MMPI	Validity Checks
Reading	F	K
Coop Total Scaled	+.58	+.68
F		+.33

From *The Journal of Educational Research*, Vol. 58, No. 2 (October, 1964), p. 90. Reprinted with permission.

Furthermore, a substantial coefficient of multiple correlation was obtained between F and K and the Total scaled score of the Cooperative English Test, C2, specifically, R(F.K.) Coop $= + .79$; the regression equation is Total scaled score (Coop) $= + 0.3448F + 0.4397K$. This urges upon the writer the interpretation that the reading test scores contain the psychometric elements of carelessness, lack of understanding of the items, and response bias. This being the case, it would appear that diagnoses of reading behavior based on standardized reading tests may be in error unless carelessness and test-taking attitudes are controlled.

Summary

The combined effect of F and K, two validity scores of the MMPI, correlated quite highly with reading. At least part of the statistical relationship may be attributed to a test-taking variable.

REFERENCES

1. Hathaway, S. R., and McKinley, J. C., *Minnesota Multiphasic Personality Inventory Manual* (N.Y.: The Psychological Corporation, 1951).

2. Voas, R. B., "Personality Correlates of Reading Speed and the Time Reading to Complete Questionnaires," *Psychological Reports,* III (1957), pp. 177–82.

---

11   A Comparison of the California Achievement Test,

Metropolitan Achievement Test,

and Iowa Test of Basic Skills

CARMEN J. FINLEY

Much activity has been generated in California by the recent enactment of legislation making testing programs mandatory. In the area of achievement testing at the elementary level, six tests have been approved as acceptable in meeting the state requirement (1). One of the questions administrators and pupil personnel workers are asking is whether the results of these six tests are comparable. If the tests differ significantly from each other, this has implications not only for evaluating a pupil's status but also for evaluation of curriculum in a school district.

The purpose of this study was to compare the instrument currently in use in a county-wide testing program (California Achievement Test) with other achievement tests from the approved list. Although it would have been desirable to include *all* the approved instruments, limitations of time and personnel made it necessary to confine the investigation to two additional tests. A secondary

Paper presented at the California Educational Research Association conference in Los Angeles March 9, 1963. Reprinted (with permission) from *California Journal of Educational Research,* Vol. 14, No. 2 (March, 1963), pp. 79–88. Copyrighted by California Teachers Association, 1963.

The author wishes to express appreciation to Dr. DeForest Hamilton, Sonoma County Superintendent of Schools, and to teachers participating in this study.

purpose of the study was to evaluate teacher reaction to the administration and general appropriateness of the tests.

Other Studies

All of the achievement batteries considered here have had either major revision of content or been re-normed within the last five or six years. Hence it was not expected that there would be many pertinent studies in the literature.

However, Stake (3) did make a comparative study of the California Achievement Test with the Iowa Test of Basic Skills, Metropolitan Achievement Test, Science Research Associates Achievement Test, and Stanford Achievement Test. He collected achievement test data on 570 third-grade children who had been administered Stanford-Binet Tests for early entrance to kindergarten. For this superior group he concluded that the California Achievement Test overestimated the achievement of the pupils by more than one-half year. Differences among the other four tests were non-significant.

More recently Taylor and Crandall (4) compared the California Achievement Test, Iowa Test of Basic Skills, Metropolitan Achievement Test, Stanford Achievement Test, and the Science Research Associates Achievement Test using matched groups of fifth- and eighth-grade students. They found that children who took the California Achievement Test consistently received higher scores and that children taking the Metropolitan and the Stanford Achievement Tests fairly consistently received lower scores.

Procedure

Selection of instruments for comparison was made by a group of curriculum and guidance consultants in the Office of the Sonoma County Superintendent of Schools. On the basis of face validity the Metropolitan Achievement Test and Iowa Test of Basic Skills were selected to compare with the California Achievement Test.

Three subtest areas were chosen for consideration: (a) reading comprehension, (b) arithmetic reasoning, and (c) language skills. These were selected because they were the most comparable sections of the respective batteries. Thirty-six classes were selected to participate in the study—six classes for each subtest area at grade levels three and five. Each class was then administered a single subtest area, taking the respective parts of the three different batteries. Order of administration was rotated. All tests were administered in the spring between February and May. Following administration of the last test the teacher rated each of the three tests on thirteen criteria relating to ease of administration and interpretation.

Differences among mean achievement scores were tested by analysis of variance, and significant differences were further investigated using the q test as described by Dixon and Massey (2). Intercorrelations among the tests were also determined. Teacher ratings were summarized by obtaining the mean rankings assigned to each test on each of the thirteen criteria questions.

Results

Nine hundred twenty-five children and thirty-six teachers completed the study. IQ scores from the California Short Form Test of Mental Maturity were available on 771 of the children. Mean IQ's for the three third-grade groups were 102, 104, and 108, while mean IQ's for the fifth-grade groups were 99, 105, and 108. As may be seen from Table I there was a consistent tendency for children to obtain higher average scores on the California Achievement Test than on either of the other two tests. Analysis of variance indicated that all of the differences were significant at the 1 per cent level of confidence. Further comparison of the tests two by two using the q test is summarized in Table II.

TABLE I *Means and Standard Deviations on the Three Tests*

	Grade 3				Grade 5			
	Norm for Grade	Mean*	SD	N	Norm for Grade	Mean*	SD	N
Reading Comprehension								
California		4.24	1.10	159		6.01	1.67	159
Metropolitan	3.5	3.49	1.03		5.6	5.02	1.78	
ITBS		3.74	1.15			5.26	1.51	
Arithmetic Reasoning								
California		4.08	1.03	151		6.39	1.18	173
Metropolitan	3.7	3.41	.72		5.6	5.46	.92	
ITBS		3.50	.99			5.61	.99	
Language								
California		4.43	1.11	123		6.29	1.35	160
Metropolitan	3.8	3.85	1.43		5.8	5.15	1.33	
ITBS		3.88	1.08			5.87	1.57	

* Grade equivalent scores.

TABLE II *Contrasts Among All Possible Differences Among Means*

	Confidence Limits $H_1: \mu_1 - \mu_2 = 0$	Significance Level
Grade 3		
Reading Comprehension		
California vs. Metropolitan	.75 ± .356	.01
California vs. ITBS	.50 ± .356	.01
Metropolitan vs. ITBS	−.25 ± .286	—
Arithmetic Reasoning		
California vs. Metropolitan	.67 ± .311	.01
California vs. ITBS	.58 ± .311	.01
Metropolitan vs. ITBS	−.09 ± .250	—
Language		
California vs. Metropolitan	.58 ± .452	.01
California vs. ITBS	.55 ± .452	.01
Metropolitan vs. ITBS	−.03 ± .363	—
Grade 5		
Reading Comprehension		
California vs. Metropolitan	.99 ± .542	.01
California vs. ITBS	.75 ± .542	.01
Metropolitan vs. ITBS	−.24 ± .435	—
Arithmetic Reasoning		
California vs. Metropolitan	.93 ± .325	.01
California vs. ITBS	.78 ± .325	.01
Metropolitan vs. ITBS	−.15 ± .262	—
Language		
California vs. Metropolitan	1.14 ± .462	.01
California vs. ITBS	.42 ± .372	.05
Metropolitan vs. ITBS	−.72 ± .462	.01

It may be readily seen that in all cases, the California scores were significantly higher than either of the other two. In all cases but one (fifth-grade language) this difference was significant at the 1 per cent level of confidence. It should also be noted that there was only one significant difference between the Metropolitan and ITBS (fifth-grade language).

Intercorrelations among the three tests are given in Table III. A fairly high degree of relationship exists among the three tests in the reading comprehension and language areas. A marked but somewhat less degree of relationship exists in the area of arithmetic reasoning. So that while there are differences in the absolute scores obtained, the relative position of the child within the group tends to be the same regardless of which test is used.

A summary of the mean rankings obtained on the teacher evaluation questionnaire is presented in Table IV.

TABLE III   *Intercorrelations Among the Three Tests*

Grade	Subtest	N	Calif. & Metro.	Calif. & ITBS	Metro. & ITBS
3	Reading Comprehension	159	.79	.73	.79
3	Arithmetic Reasoning	151	.77	.71	.74
3	Language	123	.80	.78	.80
5	Reading Comprehension	159	.78	.87	.81
5	Arithmetic Reasoning	173	.74	.65	.70
5	Language	160	.79	.80	.76

TABLE IV   *Mean Rank Assigned to Each of the Three Tests on 13 Variables*

Which Test:	Mean Rank*		
	California	Metropolitan	ITBS
1. Provides instruction most easily understood by pupils?	1.5	1.9	2.6
2. Provides better practice exercises?	1.4	2.0	2.0
3. Appears to be better liked by the students?	1.9	2.3	1.7
4. Appears to have content more nearly in line with what you have been teaching?	1.9	2.1	1.9
5. Has the most pleasing format and general appearance?	2.3	1.8	1.8
6. Takes less time for you in preparing for administration?	2.0	1.5	2.4
7. Gives fewer problems in scheduling for time for administration?	2.2	1.4	2.3
8. Appears to give more value received for time spent?	2.1	2.0	1.9
9. Provides for easier handling of materials (both booklets and answer sheets)?	1.8	1.7	2.3
10. Appears to give you a better estimate of your class as a group?	2.0	2.1	1.9
11. Appears to give you a better estimate of individual children in your class?	1.9	2.2	1.8
12. Is easier to interpret to children and parents?	2.1	1.9	2.1
13. Would you rather use?	2.1	1.8	2.0

* On a 3-point scale with 1 = test most liked and 3 = test least liked.

Teachers tended to feel that the California Test provided instructions most easily understood and provided better practice exercises. On the other hand, they tended to feel that the Metropolitan took less time in preparation for administration and gave fewer problems in scheduling. Both the Metropolitan and the ITBS were preferred to the California for having the more pleasing format and general appearance. The ITBS was rated least liked on the matter of ease of handling of materials and at the same time was rated higher than the other two in its general appeal to students.

Question 13 asked the teacher to select which test he would rather use. The detailed choices appear in Table V.

TABLE V   *Ranking on Response to Question: "Which Would You Rather Use?"*

Test	1st	2nd	3rd	Mean Rank
California	9	8	12	2.1
Metropolitan	9	15	4	1.8
ITBS	12	4	12	2.0

TABLE VI   *Summary of Teacher Comments on Preference for One of Three Tests*

Test Preferred	Grade and Subtest Area	Reason
ITBS	Reading Comprehension Grade 3	Seems to give the children a much wider scope in this particular area. From looking at the test, it would seem to do the same in other areas. The group tested was average and above. Slow groups might have a little trouble with the answer sheets at third-grade level.
ITBS	Reading Comprehension Grade 5	This test seems so much more comprehensive. Poems included. Comprehension tested by various ways instead of by just one method.
ITBS	Reading Comprehension Grade 5	This section can be given in one block of time; the booklets are easier to manage; questions and answers demand comprehension and thought, not just choice of an item or number.
ITBS	Reading Comprehension Grade 5	More realistic test of the basic building skills that are needed for development. Material interesting.
ITBS	Arithmetic Reasoning Grade 3	Took longer for children to understand, but problems were more of a challenge, more children completed test, and more children had a feeling of accomplishment. They told me they enjoyed doing ITBS while others frustrated them.
ITBS	Arithmetic Reasoning Grade 5	Material and format best, harder material. Used as workbook with excellent results.

TABLE VI   (cont.) *Summary of Teacher Comments on Preference for One of Three Tests*

Test Preferred	Grade and Subtest Area	Reason
ITBS	Arithmetic Reasoning Grade 5	Strongly prefer ITBS and so does the class. It is based more on reasoning than on factual knowledge. The problems are the clearest of all. There is a wide range of difficulty. Interesting format. Work skills section especially valuable.
ITBS	Arithmetic Reasoning Grade 5	More comprehensive. This test taxes the children's thought processes more than does the CTA.
ITBS	Arithmetic Reasoning Grade 5	Because of its better content in relation to class material, its format, and decreased time in preparation and administering.
ITBS	Language Skills Grade 3	I feel this gives a clearer picture where the child stands.
ITBS	Language Skills Grade 5	Children like it. Easy to understand. Directions and thought contents matched learning experiences.
ITBS	Language Skills Grade 5	Seemed to have a more comprehensive coverage of content. Children enjoyed this test most.
Metropolitan	Reading Comprehension Grade 3	The format is clearer and is easier to administer.
Metropolitan	Reading Comprehension Grade 3	Easier to administer and children seemed less frustrated.
Metropolitan	Reading Comprehension Grade 3	Easier to prepare, easier to explain, less questions asked by children, and less cumbersome to handle.
Metropolitan	Arithmetic Reasoning Grade 3	With this slower group. With a faster group it would be ITBS.
Metropolitan	Arithmetic Reasoning Grade 3	Easy to administer. Children understand instructions easily.
Metropolitan	Arithmetic Reasoning Grade 3	No comment.
Metropolitan	Arithmetic Reasoning Grade 3	No comment.
Metropolitan	Arithmetic Reasoning Grade 5	Appearance, easy directions, wording on problems, easier administration. Only dislike—test a little too long.

TABLE VI   (cont.) *Summary of Teacher Comments on Preference for One of Three Tests*

Test Preferred	Grade and Subtest Area	Reason
Metropolitan	Language Skills Grade 5	Easily read, valuable for content covered, easily given and understood.
California	Reading Comprehension Grade 3	Because I am familiar with it and acquainted with its values.
California	Reading Comprehension Grade 5	Seems to take less of a time block and can be fitted into a schedule easier. Students are less tired with shorter time test.
California	Reading Comprehension Grade 5	No comment.
California	Language Skills Grade 3	Less difficulty in understanding directions.
California	Language Skills Grade 3	Covers material required of third-graders in a more complete fashion. Is simple to explain and conduct.
California	Language Skills Grade 3	Easier to administer. The machine-scored sheet was very confusing to many of my children.
California	Language Skills Grade 3	For my class at present I prefer the California test since I feel it gives a more accurate view of my slow learners also. The ITBS is quite complicated for them (vocabulary, the way it's set up, etc.), while the California has a more simple vocabulary and they actually tried to read where they just guessed on the ITBS. I also like the way the California test breaks down the mechanics on the Diagnostic profile page so weaknesses can more easily be seen at a glance.
California	Language Skills Grade 3	The California is the only one where the children put their marks directly on the word or sentence in question. Many third-graders have trouble transferring what they know to a different line or page. The instructions in California are shorter and simpler. The tests are shorter and less tiring. On the other hand, the children and I are more familiar with the California, and that may be why it seemed easier for them to take and for me to administer.
California	Language Skills Grade 5	Appears to have content more nearly in line with what has been taught.

While there is little difference in the mean rankings of these tests, it may be noted that a substantial number of teachers—12—ranked the California and ITBS in third place. At the other end of the scale ITBS was selected as most liked by 12 teachers!

Table VI gives the detailed comments of teachers as to the basis of their preference of one test over the others. The ITBS was more preferred by fifth-grade teachers than by third-grade teachers and was chosen by some teachers in each of the subtest areas. Reasons for their choice focused on the content of the test. A number of teachers indicated that this test demanded more thought, reasoning, and comprehension than did the other test instruments. It should also be noted that this is the only test of the three which requires third-graders to use IBM answer sheets. While there was some objection to this, many third-graders were able to handle IBM answer sheets successfully at this level.

Of the nine who chose the Metropolitan, seven were third-grade teachers. Reading comprehension and arithmetic reasoning were preferred more than the language section. Reasons for their choice centered on format and ease of administration.

Of the nine who chose the California test, six were third-grade teachers, and six were in the language subtest area. There were no first choices in arithmetic. Most comments indicated this test was preferred because of ease of administration, although there was also some comment favoring the content of the test.

Discussion

As may be seen from the results of this study, there is a definite tendency for the California tests to yield higher scores than either the Metropolitan or the ITBS. In relation to the norm for the groups tested, the California yielded scores from 4 to 8 months above the norm, while the Metropolitan varied from 1 month above to 6 months below, and the ITBS varied from 2 months above to 3 months below.

It might be argued that since the ability level of the groups is somewhat above average, achievement *should be* above the norm. However, the reader should be cautioned that the IQ test used was part of the dual standardization procedure used by the test publisher and hence any bias introduced into one could be expected to be present in the other!

Unfortunately, it is not possible from these data to conclude which test yields more "accurate" scores—whether the one is "overestimating" or the others are "underestimating," although the present findings are generally in agreement with those of Stake (3) and Taylor and Crandall (4). In addition, the most appropriate test for one district may not be the same as for another, depending upon their respective curricula and goals. Only an analysis of the test content as compared with the course of study can answer this question. However, it may safely be stated that significantly different scores *are* obtained depending upon the test used and that the standardization samples used by the various publishers do not come from a common population. The implications for this in a state testing program are obvious. Any comparisons made would have to be confined to districts using a common test.

In interpreting the results of the teacher questionnaire, it should be borne in mind that the California test had been a part of the regular county testing program for 10 years. This is a test with which all teachers had had previous experience, while the Metropolitan and ITBS were new to the teachers and students. Yet, the Metropolitan was rated quite highly on ease of administration. It is important, too, that although the ITBS was felt to be more demanding in this area, it was selected as the preferred test by the greatest number of teachers, and selection was based on superior content. However, there is some indication of serious limitations in the use of answer sheets by third-grade pupils.

Summary

Nine hundred twenty-five children and 36 teachers at grades three and five participated in this study investigating the subtest areas of reading comprehension, arithmetic reasoning, and language skills on the California Achievement Test, the Metropolitan Achievement Test, and the Iowa Test of Basic Skills. In all cases the children obtained higher average scores on the California Test. Average scores on the other two tests were quite similar.

There was little difference among the three tests when teachers evaluated them on thirteen criteria. Differences which did occur tended to favor the California and Metropolitan on items regarding ease of administration. However, when asked to choose which test they preferred to use, the Iowa Test of Basic Skills was more frequently chosen. Reasons for this choice were generally related to superior content of the tests. Teachers who chose the Metropolitan and California Tests did so mainly on the basis of ease of administration. Some objection was raised to the use of IBM sheets on the Iowa with third-grade children.

REFERENCES

1. Calif. State Dept. of Education. *Manual for Reporting Test Information.* Sacramento, California: Author, 1962.

2. Dixon, W. J. and Massey, F. J. *Introduction to Statistical Analysis* (2nd ed). New York: McGraw-Hill, 1957.

3. Stake, R. E. "Overestimation" of Achievement with the California Achievement Test. *Educational Psychology Measurement*, 21, 59–62, 1961.

4. Taylor, E. A. and Crandall, J. H. "A Study of the Norm Equivalence of Certain Tests Approved for the California State Testing Program." *California Journal of Educational Research*, 1962, 13, 186–192.

12 An Appraisal of the Ammons Quick Test in a Remedial Reading Program

WAYNE OTTO

RICHARD A. MCMENEMY

Poor readers are apt to perform poorly on the typical group intelligence test because they cannot respond successfully to items they cannot read. Yet remedial reading teachers outside of clinical settings seldom have ready access to the better individual tests such as the Stanford Binet or the Wechsler Intelligence Scale for Children (WISC). Often they are not qualified to give the tests personally; time is almost always at a premium; and referral possibilities usually are limited. Thus, there is a need for an intelligence test that permits quick, straightforward administration and interpretation by remedial teachers and yields reasonably valid scores with poor readers. The Ammons Quick Test (QT) clearly meets the first criterion; the purpose of this study was to determine if it meets the second.

The QT is a very brief intelligence test that is closely related to the earlier and more extensively researched Full-Range Picture Vocabulary Test (FRPV). A complete description of the test construction and details of administration and interpretation are given by Ammons and Ammons (1962). Briefly, each of its three forms, which can be administered in about two minutes, consists of a single plate comprising four line drawings. The examinee is asked to point to the picture that best illustrates the meaning of a work spoken (accompanied by the printed word at seventh grade level and up) by the examiner. Scoring is uncomplicated: the examinee is given credit for each correct answer regardless of the reason for his choice. Norms are provided—age two through adult—for each of the three forms and for each of the four possible combinations.

Researchers have reported that the antecedent FRPV appears to be a worthwhile screening test of intelligence both in general clinical use (Grossberg, 1964; Schramm, 1953) and for pupils with reading difficulties (Smith and Fillmore, 1954). Similar studies have not yet been reported for the QT; but validity studies have shown FRPV and QT results to be closely related (Ammons and Ammons, 1962). The purpose here was to make an appraisal of the validity of the QT as a screening test of intelligence for use by remedial teachers with poor readers in a naturalistic setting. Therefore, many of the careful considerations of the typical validity study were foregone in an effort to approximate the conditions under which the test might actually be used.

Method

SUBJECTS

The QT was given to a total of 110 pupils in grades 4–9 of a large metropolitan school district. All subjects met two criteria. First, they were certified participants in the remedial reading program. To be certified a child must have

From *Journal of Educational Measurement*, Vol. 2 (December, 1965), pp. 193–198. Reprinted with permission.

The authors are grateful to the Counseling Center for Adults, Portland, Oregon, Continuation Center, and to the Office of General Research, Graduate School, University of Georgia, for support of this project.

average or better intelligence and reading achievement at least 1 year below grade level in Grade 4 and 2 or more years below in Grade 5 and up. Second, they were pupils who had WISC scores (obtained by qualified psychometrists) not more than two years old. There were 22 subjects—18 boys and 4 girls—from Grade 4; 42 subjects—33 boys and 9 girls—from Grade 5; and 46 subjects—36 boys and 10 girls—from Grades 6–9 combined.

PROCEDURE

QT's were administered by regular remedial reading teachers during the 1964 spring semester. Forms were given—not more than one on a single day—in a 1, 2, 3 sequence.

Fifteen remedial teachers (about a third of the remedial reading staff) each administered two or more QT's. Specific training in giving the QT was minimal. Salient points regarding use of the QT were discussed with the teachers, and each was given the necessary testing materials and written instructions for administration and scoring.

Raw scores on each of the three QT forms (QT_1, QT_2, QT_3) and on combinations of forms 1 and 2 ($QT_{1,2}$) and of all three forms ($QT_{1,2,3}$) were converted to MA's according to the norms provided, and quotient IQ's were computed by dividing MA by CA. Validity checks were made by comparing the resultant QT IQ's with previous WISC IQ's from the Verbal Scale (WISC-V), the Performance Scale (WISC-P), and the Full Scale (WISC-FS).

Results and Discussion

TABLE I   *Group Means and Standard Deviations for Age, QT Scores, and WISC Scores*

	Grade 4 N = 22		Grade 5 N = 42		Grade 6–9 N = 46		Boys N = 87		All Ss N = 110	
	M	**SD**	**M**	**SD**	**M**	**SD**	**M**	**SD**	**M**	**SD**
Age	10.14	.49	11.03	.42	13.20	1.04	11.82	1.50	11.76	1.48
QT_1	108.73	14.73	103.81	15.67	100.46	15.01	104.47	15.24	103.39	15.38
QT_2	104.41	16.93	100.79	19.41	98.02	16.17	102.13	17.74	100.35	17.62
QT_3	107.55	15.83	106.52	18.60	101.48	13.62	105.60	16.25	104.62	16.19
$QT_{1,2}$	106.64	15.73	102.43	16.40	99.54	14.70	103.49	15.61	102.06	15.65
$QT_{1,2,3}$	107.46	14.51	103.43	16.03	100.09	13.92	103.91	14.95	102.84	14.99
WISC-V	92.00	8.08	94.38	8.21	92.59	6.92	93.35	7.88	93.15	7.66
WISC-P	102.00	9.50	100.95	7.87	99.46	9.11	100.79	8.63	100.54	8.72
WISC-FS	96.32	8.07	97.29	7.28	95.57	6.87	96.63	7.47	96.37	7.25
Range:										
$QT_{1,2,3}$	128–75		144–80		147–81		147–75		147–75	
WISC-FS	118–85		114–85		109–84		118–84		118–84	

Table I summarizes group means and standard deviations for age, QT IQ scores, and WISC IQ scores and gives the range of scores on total tests for each group. The mean QT scores are consistently higher than the mean WISC IQ's. This finding is similar to that previously reported for comparisons of FRPV and WISC scores (Grossberg, 1964; Smith and Fillmore, 1954; Schramm, 1953). There is a consistent tendency, too, toward decreasing QT scores with increasing grade level; and boys' QT means tend to be slightly higher than QT means for all subjects. There is greater variability in QT scores than in WISC scores.

TABLE II   *Intercorrelations Among QT Scores, WISC Scores, Chronological Ages, and Discrepancy Scores* $(N = 110)$ *

	2	3	4	5	6	7	8	9	10	11	12
1. QT_1	.77	.72	.93	.91	.40	.23	.39	−.18	.76	.75	.77
2. QT_2		.77	.95	.92	.34	.19	.34	−.10	.80	.78	.82
3. QT_3			.79	.90	.35	.25	.38	−.18	.77	.72	.77
4. $QT_{1,2}$				.97	.39	.21	.38	−.14	.83	.82	.85
5. $QT_{1,2,3}$					.39	.22	.39	−.18	.86	.84	.88
6. WISC-V						.32	.81	−.12	−.13	.20	−.01
7. WISC-P							.81	−.09	.07	−.35	−.18
8. WISC-FS								−.13	−.03	−.08	−.11
9. Chronological Age									−.12	−.12	−.13
10. $QT_{1,2,3}$-WISC-V										.79	.94
11. $QT_{1,2,3}$-WISC-P											.95
12. $QT_{1,2,2}$-WISC-FS											

* Coefficients of .19 and .24 required for significance at the .05 and .01 levels.

Table II gives intercorrelations among the several QT and WISC IQ's, chronological ages, and discrepancy scores for all subjects combined. Intercorrelations were also run for grades 4, 5, and 6–9 for boys only; but because the coefficients obtained were very similar in magnitude to those for all subjects, they are not reported here. Discrepancy scores are the differences between $QT_{1,2,3}$ IQ's and WISC Verbal, Performance, and Full Scale IQ's. Much caution must be exercised in interpreting the correlations between QT and WISC scores because of the special conditions under which the study was conducted and the restricted variability of WISC scores as compared to QT scores.

The substantial correlations between the various forms of the QT demonstrate reasonably high reliability and suggest that erratic performance on the QT was not a major problem despite minimal training of testers. This is important in view of the possibility that successful control of guessing could be a major problem with the QT. Part scores (Verbal and Performance) are, of course, highly related to Full Scale scores on the WISC; and it is interesting to note the significant but fairly low correlation between Performance and Verbal Scale scores. The latter value of .32 with the present poor readers is somewhat lower than the values of .68 and .58 reported with children unselected as to reading ability (Wechsler, 1949). There are consistently negative correlations between chronological age and IQ scores, but none of the values are statistically significant.

There are significant correlations between all QT and WISC IQ scores. The values are lower for WISC–P scores, which is logical in view of the verbal stress of the WISC–V and the QT. Yet, Table I shows that mean WISC–P scores tend to be closer to mean QT scores than do WISC–V scores. Thus, mean WISC–P and QT scores were more similar, but overall relationships were lower. All QT scores are substantially related to discrepancy scores. On the other hand, there appears to be no such relationship between WISC scores and discrepancy scores. These latter observations were corroborated by analyses of discrepancy scores at various IQ levels.

Table III examines discrepancies between QT scores and WISC scores. Discrepancies clearly favor the QT compared to the WISC–V and the WISC–FS; total discrepancies are about evenly divided on the WISC–P comparison, but the larger discrepancies result from higher QT scores. Most interesting is the fact

TABLE III *Number and Percentage of Children Showing Given IQ Differences Between QT and WISC Verbal, Performance, and Full Scale Scores*

IQ Difference	WISC-V		WISC-P		WISC-FS	
	N	%	N	%	N	%
Higher on QT[1,2,3]						
1–10	38	34.6	28	25.5	34	30.9
11–20	16	14.6	13	11.8	21	19.1
21 or more	27	24.6	15	13.6	17	15.5
Totals	81	73.8	56	50.9	72	65.5
Higher on WISC						
1–10	21	19.1	34	30.9	26	23.6
11–20	4	3.6	13	11.8	8	7.3
21 or more	1	0.9	7	6.4	2	1.8
Totals	26	23.6	54	49.1	36	32.7
No Difference	3	2.7	0	0	2	1.8

that the difference between WISC and QT scores was 10 points or less in more than half of the cases. This is not markedly different from the finding when WISC and Stanford-Binet scores of children unselected as to reading ability were compared (Krugman, Justman, Wrightstone, and Krugman, 1951): two-thirds of those subjects obtained Stanford-Binet scores within 10 points of WISC–V and WISC–FS scores and half were within 10 points on the WISC–P. On the other hand, discrepancies of 20 points or more were more frequent in the present study; about one-fifth were 20 points or more, most resulting from higher estimates on the QT.

Conclusions

While the validity coefficients obtained were statistically significant, the question of practical significance remains. Correlations between WISC and QT scores were low; but minimal values could be anticipated considering the conditions surrounding the study. Furthermore, the discrepancy comparisons showed that more often than not the difference between WISC and QT scores was less than 10 IQ points. Thus, while the QT is not a substitute for the WISC—the authors of the QT do not suggest that it is or should be—we feel that it has value in the present application. It appears to be a worthwhile device for use by remedial reading teachers—even with minimal training—in obtaining quick estimates of poor readers' IQ's. The test has the obvious advantages of quick administration and straightforward scoring, and it makes no reading demands of poor readers. In situations where group test scores are questionable (as with poor readers), testing time is at a premium, and outside psychometric services are limited, the QT can provide some additional objectivity where objectivity might otherwise be lacking.

With the present subjects, QT IQ's tended generally to be higher than WISC IQ's. This tendency should be kept in mind when QT scores are used for screening or general diagnostic purposes with poor readers. There is evidence, too, that a few extreme (over 20 points) IQ overestimates by the QT tended disproportionate to decrease validity estimates. In practice, such extremely deviant scores should not present any great problems to perceptive teachers: IQ tests are but one source of information regarding pupils' capacity. Whether guessing was responsible for the extreme overestimates is not clear from the present data; but high reliability coefficients suggest that wild guessing was not a major problem. Perhaps with more experience in giving the QT, testers would have obtained fewer extreme deviant scores.

Aside from its potential value in making quick IQ estimates, the QT can serve other functions for the remedial teacher. Children perceive the QT more as a game than a test; it is a good rapport builder. If a teacher wishes, he can preview a pupil's verbal fluency or general experiential background by encouraging discussion of answers. With some pupils, there may be evidence of habitual guessing or, conversely, of too much concern about making errors. The subjective judgment of the teachers who gave the QT in the present study was that it yielded information well worth the small amount of time involved.

REFERENCES

Ammons, R. B., and Ammons, C. H. The Quick Test (QT): provisional manual. *Psychological Reports,* Monograph Supplement 1–VII, 1962, 11, 111–161.

Grossberg, J. M. A comparison of the Full-Range Picture Vocabulary Test and the WISC in clinical use. *Journal of Consulting Psychology,* 1964, 28, 188.

Krugman, J. I., Justman, J., Wrightstone, J. W., and Krugman, M. Pupil functioning on the Stanford-Binet and the WISC. *Journal of Consulting Psychology,* 1951, 15, 475–483.

Schramm, C. An evaluation of the WISC and the Full-Range Picture Vocabulary Test in clinical use. Paper read at Kentucky Psychological Association, Lexington, 1953.

Smith, L., and Fillmore, A. The Ammons FRPV Test and the WISC for remedial reading cases. *Journal of Consulting Psychology,* 1954, 18, 332–335.

Wechsler, D. *Manual: Wechsler intelligence scale for children.* New York: Psychological Corporation, 1949.

---

13   Effectiveness of the Peabody Picture Vocabulary Test with Seventh-Grade Pupils

JOHN M. IVANOFF

HOWARD E. TEMPERO

Statistical data regarding the effectiveness of new measuring devices are typically limited and preliminary until evidence is accumulated through studies in the field. Such an instrument is the Peabody Picture Vocabulary Test (PPVT), an intelligence test constructed by Lloyd M. Dunn in 1959 (1). The test serves as a quick screening instrument and has been designed to require minimal verbal and/or motor responses. Such characteristics contribute to the instrument's suitability for use with subjects have serious verbal and motor impairments without affecting its utility for use with others.

Available evidence on the PPVT is primarily limited to the work of Dunn and his associates. Preliminary data in the manual suggest that the PPVT is a reason-

---

From *The Journal of Educational Research,* Vol. 58, No. 9 (May–June, 1965), pp. 412–415. Reprinted with permission.

ably stable and valid screening instrument for not only the "normal," but also handicapped individuals. Using 20 cerebral palsied children, Dunn and Harley (2) found the PPVT to be adequately stable and to correlate highly with arithmetic and reading achievement. Norris, Hottel, and Brooks (4), using 60 upper elementary school children of normal intelligence, reported that obtained scores were not a function of the test form nor of individual or group administration, and practice effects were found to be negligible. The present study was designed to supplement the available data on the PPVT.

Purposes

The purposes of the study were to obtain additional information concerning validity as well as the effects of practice and order on the administration of the PPVT. Scores obtained from 150 seventh-grade pupils were examined for evidence related to the effectiveness of the PPVT with regard to:

1. Equivalence of Forms A and B.
2. Practice effect as shown by a comparison of scores on the first and second administrations to the same sample.
3. Comparison of the order of administration of the two forms, i.e., BA or AB.
4. Validity as based upon correlations with scores on the Henmon–Nelson Tests of Mental Ability and on the California Test of Mental Maturity.
5. Validity as based upon correlation with the scores on the California Achievement Test Battery.
6. Reliability expressed as a coefficient of correlation calculated from the scores of 150 pupils who took both Forms A and B.

Instruments

The pupils' scores obtained on the PPVT, Forms A and B; the Henmon–Nelson Tests of Mental Ability, revised edition, Form A, level 6 through 9 (HNTMA); the California Test of Mental Maturity, Form 1957, elementary level (CTMM); the California Achievement Test Battery, 1957 edition, Form X, junior high-school level (CAT) were used in this study. All tests except the PPVT were administered as a part of the regular testing program.

The PPVT consists of 150 plates, each of which contains four pictures representing objects, concepts, or activities. The four pictures on each plate are numbered by position. In administering the test the examiner provides a stimulus word orally as, "Show me the butterfly." The subject then points to, or in some other way indicates, the picture on the plate which best illustrates the meaning of the stimulus word.

The plates are arranged by the author in ascending order as based upon difficulty level, which determined empirically. The mental age range is from 1–9 to 18–0. The same set of plates serves both forms of the test although for each form one and only one stimulus word is given per plate. The S must establish a basal of eight consecutive correct responses, and his score then includes the basal plus the correct responses through his ceiling, which is determined by six incorrect responses out of eight. Age, standard score equivalent (IQ), and percentile norms are provided in the manual as based upon a population of 4012 subjects ranging in chronological age from 2–6 through 18–0.

Subjects

The subjects were students in six sections from the seventh grade in a representative junior high school of the Lincoln (Nebraska) public schools.[1] Assignment of the students to sections had been on a random basis at the beginning of the year. Complete information was obtained for 150 students of whom 74 were male and 76 were female. These were students in regular classrooms of appropriate ages for their grade placement (C.A. 11–10 to 13–5 years).

Procedure

Although the test was originally designed as an individual test of intelligence, Dunn (1) in his manual, nevertheless, used group administration procedures in the test standardization on the upper elementary and high school levels. He adopted this method on the basis of the results reported by Norris, Hottel, and Brooks (4), who found no appreciable difference between scores obtained by individual and group administrations. The present authors, likewise, adapted similar group administration procedures for this study.

Three of the class sections were randomly selected, and Form A was administered during their first testing period. Two days later Form B was then administered to these Ss. In this group there was a total of 75 Ss of whom 39 were male and 36, female. For the 75 Ss (35 males and 40 females) in the remaining three sections Form B was administered first and two days later, Form A. The tests were administered to all sections by one of the school counselors.

Design

The experimental design used to test the first three purposes is essentially an analysis of variance based on the design for repeated measurements. Each subject received both Form A and Form B and both a first and a second administration. The procedure requires two separate error terms for the tests of significance: one for the possible correlated data obtained from the same Ss and one for the data obtained from the independent group of Ss.

Analysis and Discussion

Means and SD's for all 150 Ss on each form and for each order of administration are presented in Table I.

TABLE I   *PPVT Performance of 150 Seventh-Grade Students Under Experimental Conditions*

	Form		Administrations	
	A	**B**	**First**	**Second**
Mean	107.61	106.71	106.29	108.04
SD	13.67	14.85	14.61	13.89

[1] The authors wish to express appreciation to Dr. Steven N. Watkins, Superintendent of Schools; Julius A. Humann, Director of Guidance; Principal Emory G. Priefert; and Counselor Lucile L. Tempero for their cooperation in this study.

Either testing order (AB—BA) appears equally as effective since the differences between their means can be accounted for in terms of random sampling from a common population. With one degree of freedom an F value of .36 was obtained. Likewise, the obtained F value of 1.30 with one degree of freedom for Form A, Form B comparison is so small as to leave little question as to the equivalence of the two forms for this population. The obtained F value between the first and second administrations was significant at the .05 level, and the obtained difference of 1.753 standard scores equivalents appeared in the direction of practice effect. Consequently, whatever practice effect exists amounted to only about two I.Q. points. The coefficient of correlation computed between the two forms was found to be .75. This reliability coefficient is comparable to those reported in the manual for this age group.

These results are comparable to the present initial accumulation of data regarding the equivalence of the forms and of the order of administration of the PPVT. However, the present study finds a greater degree of practice effect than that reported previously by Norris, Hottel, and Brooks.

Means and SD's for the 75 students who were administered Form A during their first period as well as those for the 75 students who were first administered Form B are presented in Tables II and III along with the respective means and SD's of the other test scores for the entire group of 150. Validity coefficients are presented in Table IV.

TABLE II   *Means and Standard Deviations of Intelligence Test Scores*

	PPVT		HNTA	California Test of M. M.		
	Form A N = 75*	Form B N = 75*	N = 150	Language N = 150	Non- Language N = 150	Total N = 150
Mean	107.33	105.17	109.89	111.62	110.84	106.05
SD	12.36	16.42	16.06	19.47	15.89	13.71

* First administration scores of Forms A and B only were used; therefore N = 75.

TABLE III   *Means and Standard Deviations of California Achievement Test Battery*

	Reading		Arithmetic		Language	
	Vocab- ulary	Compre- hension	Reason- ing	Funda- mental	Mechan- ics	Spell- ing
Mean	7.44	8.64	8.03	7.76	7.75	7.23
SD	1.55	1.99	1.12	1.52	1.93	1.58

Inspection of Table IV reveals that the congruent validity coefficients for the PPVT against the criteria of the HNTMA and the CTMM are similar to those usually found for coefficients of this type. As might be expected, the relationship of the PPVT to the language factors of the CTMM is significantly higher than the relationship to the non-language factor.

The intercorrelations shown in Table IV consistently reflect higher correlations between the HNTMA and the other tests with the exception of correlations between PPVT (B) and CTMM (L), and CTMM (L) and CTMM (T). In

TABLE IV   *Correlations for PPVT and Three Selected Criteria*

| | PPVT | | HNTMA | CTMM | |
| | Form A | Form B | | L | NL |
	N = 75*	N = 75*	N = 150	N = 150	N = 150
I HNTMA	.64	.61			
II CTMM					
Lang.	.62	.65	.82		
Non-Lang.	.40	.34	.59	.58	
Total	.57	.58	.80	.85	.61
III CAT					
Reading					
Vocab.	.56	.58	.80	.73	.44
Comp.	.60	.63	.87	.69	.56
Arithmetic					
Reason	.50	.57	.75	.73	.59
Fund	.40	.49	.76	.57	.60
Language					
Mech.	.44	.45	.75	.66	.52
Spell.	.41	.45	.65	.51	.35

* First administration scores of Forms A and B only were used; therefore N = 75.

three other cases the difference was small, i.e., PPVT (A) and CTMM (L), CTMM (L) and CTMM (NL), and CTMM (L) and CAT (Arithmetic Reasoning).

Criterion measures of achievement against PPVT indicate significantly higher relationships in the reading area than in the arithmetic and language areas. All of the correlations, however, were statistically highly significant.

In general the correlations for the PPVT were consistently lower than those for the HNTMA or the CTMM (L). The comparison of the PPVT and CAT correlations with those of the CTMM (NL) and CAT show the PPVT with higher correlations in both reading subtests and in the spelling subtest under language for CAT. It will be recalled that the PPVT correlations are based on 75 subjects and the other correlations on the entire group of 150.

This study gives additional evidence that the PPVT test results may be relied upon with confidence whenever a quick screening device for intelligence is desired. Although this study used a representative public school population, this fact does not detract from the potential of the PPVT for use with children having speech and motor disabilities. Additional research in the applicability of this instrument with such handicapped children is desirable for clinicians, teachers, and other special education workers. Certainly the PPVT can be used successfully within the typical school situation.

Summary

This investigation was undertaken to provide additional data regarding the effectiveness of the PPVT. Analyses of the scores obtained from group administration of both forms of the PPVT to 150 seventh-grade Ss demonstrated that their scores were not a function of the order of administration nor of the form used, but influence of practice effect was indicated. Further evidence of the adequacy of the PPVT was found in the size of the validity coefficients between the test and two commonly used intelligence tests as well as with one popular test of achievement.

REFERENCES

1. Dunn, L. M. *Manual: Peabody Picture Vocabulary Test* (Nashville: American Guidance Service, 1959).

2. Dunn, L. M., and Harley, R. K. "Comparability of Peabody, Ammons, Van Alstyne and Columbia Test Scores with Cerebral Palsied Children," *Exceptional Children*, XXVI (1959), pp. 70–74.

3. Lamke, T. A., and Nelson, M. J. *Manual: Henmon–Nelson Test of Mental Ability*, Revised Edition (Boston: Houghton–Mifflin, 1957).

4. Norris, R. C., Hottel, J. V., and Brooks, Sadys. "Comparability of Peabody Picture Vocabulary Test Scores Under Group and Individual Administration," *Journal of Educational Psychology*, LI (1960), pp. 87–91.

5. Sullivan, Elizabeth T., Clark, W. W., and Tiegs, E. W. *Manual: California Test of Mental Maturity* (Los Angeles: California Test Bureau, 1957).

6. Tiegs, E. W., and Clark, W. W. *Manual: California Achievement Tests* (Los Angeles: California Test Bureau, 1957).

---

14   The Bender Gestalt as a Predictive and Diagnostic Test of Reading Performance

BARBARA K. KEOGH

This study evaluated the Bender Gestalt at kindergarten as a predictive measure of third-grade reading achievement and the Bender at third grade as a diagnostic test of reading performance, by utilizing measures on the same children at both grade levels. Complete data were available for 127 of an original sample of 221 public school children. The group Bender Gestalt was administered at kindergarten (Keogh and Smith, 1961). Third-grade data were the group Bender, California Test of Mental Maturity, three subtests of the California Reading Test, teacher ratings of reading ability (1–7), and teacher interviews. Bender protocols were scored with the Koppitz System (Koppitz, 1962), Keogh-Smith Rating Scale (Keogh and Smith, 1961), and a clinical check list of eight Bender performance characteristics: perseveration, truncation, rotation, verticalization, primitization, integration, erasure, and workover.

Results showed clear and significant improvement in Bender performance, reflected on all of the individual designs and for total score by both scoring systems; improvement was related to age or grade, rather than sex difference. Correlations between Bender total scores and major reading criteria were statistically significant and tended to be of similar magnitude regardless of specific scoring system or reading measure; the range of Pearson r was .23–.37 for these relationships ($p = .01$). The majority of correlations became nonsignificant when effect of intelligence was held constant.

Comparison of characteristics of extreme subgroups suggested a generalized pattern of school results associated with Bender performance. Only good performance on the Bender was predictive of reading performance. Cutoff scores

From *Journal of Consulting Psychology*, Vol. 29 (February, 1965), pp, 83, 84. Copyright 1965 by the American Psychological Association. Reprinted with permission.

defining good Bender performance at kindergarten or third grade clearly identified successful readers; poor Bender performance at either grade was nondefinitive for individual prediction.

Several points seem pertinent to the use of the Bender in educational diagnosis. Although correlations between the Bender and reading criteria were of statistical significance, magnitudes were too small to allow confident individual prediction of reading from the Bender. Individual design interpretation and use of the clinical check list items for differential diagnosis were not supported; the best prediction of reading was from total Bender score. The Bender reflected a general pattern of school performance, with greatest predictive accuracy based on good Bender performance. Poor Bender scores were not predictive, but attainment of certain levels on the Bender was associated with maturity in areas of development pertinent to reading; thus children who achieved well on the Bender were apt to achieve well in other aspects of the school program. Results suggest that the group Bender is of limited validity for prediction and diagnosis of individual cases of reading disability at primary grades, but that it warrants consideration as a possible screening technique for early identification of children likely to be successful in the school program.

REFERENCES

Keogh, B., and Smith, C. E. Group techniques and proposed scoring system for the Bender-Gestalt Test with children. *Journal of Clinical Psychology,* 1961, 17, 172–175.

Koppitz, Elizabeth M. *The Bender Gestalt Test with the Human Figure Drawing Test for young children.* Ohio: Ohio Department of Education, 1962.

Part Five

Approaches to Corrective
and Remedial Teaching

The only safe generalization regarding approaches to corrective and remedial teaching seems to be that there are few safe generalizations. The appeal, the use, and the ultimate success of an approach is likely to be determined as much by the point of view of the remedial teacher as by the specifics of the approach. The appropriateness of a principle may be dependent upon the interaction of disabled learner, teacher, and approach. The first article in this chapter has to do with general principles, while the focus of the remaining four articles is upon specific approaches. Each is an invitation, if not to outright disagreement, at least to reaction and comment.

While the results of the first article, Van De Riet's study, are by no means definitive, the possibility that good and poor achievers may react differently to praise and reproof has interesting implications for both research and application. The author has done an exceptionally thorough job of pointing out limitations and possible alternative explanations of the results reported; the discussion section of the paper deserves careful attention. The methodology section of the paper may also be of special interest to readers who are not familiar with laboratory studies of human learning. The task and procedures used by Van De Riet are typical for studies done with a paired-associate learning paradigm.

Children who have learning problems are likely to have social-emotional problems as well. We feel that in most cases it is less important to decide which came first than to accept the fact that if the problems exist concurrently, they must be attacked concurrently. Remedial teachers probably could not entirely avoid the role of counselor if they tried, but it seems clear that in some cases individual psychotherapy is needed. Bills' study of the use of play therapy with retarded (disabled) readers is an attempt to determine whether that particular approach would be useful in conjunction with remedial teaching. Since the publication of the results of the study in 1950, the paper has been cited frequently not only for the specific findings, but also because the "control period" idea lends itself to other hard-to-control situations.

Bills' finding that the provision of play therapy enhanced the reading performance of his subjects has implications for remedial teaching, but he recognizes the fact that the design of the study did not permit a direct answer to the question of whether the improved reading was due to improved personality adjustment. Subsequently he did another study[1] to seek an answer. The design was similar to that of the first study, but the subjects were chosen because they were

1 Reported in the *Journal of Consulting Psychology*, Vol. 14 (1950), pp. 246–249.

well adjusted according to projective and objective personality tests. Reading gains were not significantly greater during the therapy period. Thus it appears that play therapy may help to improve reading ability but only when emotional maladjustment exists with the reading problem. Therapy is not a panacea for reading disability.

The Staats and Butterfield article represents a quite different approach to remedial teaching. The authors have spelled out both their theoretical position and the specifics of their approach in sufficient detail to make further comment unnecessary here. The final point made in the report bears underscoring: The approach described demonstrates the possibility of testing learning principles and of working out applications within the same context. The study also demonstrates the potential usefulness of doing an exhaustive analysis of a single subject's behavior in an experimental setting.

Still another approach to the treatment[2] of learning problems has been offered by Doman and Delacato. They have suggested a sequence of exercises and procedures that they claim will enhance neurological organization and thereby lead to improved functioning of the student in basic school subjects like reading, handwriting, and spelling. The Doman-Delacato approach has received much acclaim in the popular press; but in the absence of objective data to support the often extravagant claims, most professionals in the related fields of medicine, psychology, and education have remained skeptical. The paper by Robbins represents an attempt by a disinterested outsider to test the Doman-Delacato rationale. The examination of a placebo group as well as a traditional control group in the study merits special attention.

In the final paper in Part Five, Hewett suggests a hierarchy of educational tasks for children with learning disabilities. Although he has limited his description of applications mainly to severely emotionally handicapped children, the concept of a task hierarchy should be useful to remedial teachers who work with children in traditional school settings. Although the idea of "behavior shaping" through the reinforcement of desired behaviors may be offensive to some workers, the establishment of a hierarchy of tasks is basic to any remedial teaching sequence. The parallels between Hewett's suggestions and the approach described by Staats and Butterfield should be noted.

---

2 While we would normally not use the term "treatment" in a discussion of approaches to learning problems, it is used advisedly in the present context.

15 Effects of Praise and Reproof on Paired-Associate Learning in Educationally Retarded Children

HANI VAN DE RIET

It is suggested that success constitutes a threat to underachievers because these Ss have a "need to fail." The present study sought to determine whether praise of underachievers would result in a decrement in subsequent learning performance. 45 underachieving boys in Grades 4, 5, and 6 were matched to 45 nonunderachieving boys with respect to ability. 2 equated lists of paired associates were learned by Ss. Between lists ⅓ of the Ss were praised, ⅓ were reproved, and ⅓ were told nothing. Results indicated that praise results in slower learning among underachievers while it results in faster learning among nonunderachievers.

An enigmatic phenomenon with which all teachers and many perplexed parents are familiar is the child who manifests an inability to learn in school in spite of test indications of normal or superior ability. One view of learning disabilities, and the one with which this study is concerned, is that the disability is a neurotic learning inhibition in which the learning problem is the major symptom. As Pearson (1952) points out, the learning process itself becomes involved in conflict.

Underlying many of the contributing factors involved in the neurotic condition appears to be the existence of a "need to fail" (Kunst, 1959) for any of a number of reasons. Among these reasons are the confusion between aggression and achievement (Klein, 1931; Liss, 1940), negative reinforcement in early mental exploratory experience (Oberndorf, 1939), and disturbance in experiences of receiving from the environment (Fenichel, 1937; Strachey, 1930).

If a need to fail is present in children with learning disabilities, then it would be expected that praise of their performance would be experienced as threatening and would act as a detriment to further learning. Indeed, the factor of level of achievement may be one of the uncontrolled variables which contributes to the contradictory results of prior research on the effects of praise and reproof on learning.

This study tested the following experimental hypotheses concerning the variables of praise and reproof in learning by these children:

1. Educationally retarded children require more trials to reach criterion of learning than do children who are not educationally retarded on initial paired-associate learning.

2. For educationally retarded children, praise results in a significantly larger number of trials to reach criterion on the second task than does reproof because success constitutes a threat.

3. For normal children, praise results in a significantly smaller number of trials to reach criterion than does reproof.

This article is based on a Ph.D. dissertation submitted to the graduate school of Florida State University. Reprinted (with permission) from *Journal of Educational Psychology*, Vol. 55, No. 3 (1964), pp. 139–143. Copyright 1964 by the American Psychological Association.

The author wishes to thank W. A. Kennedy for his assistance.

Method

The subjects for this research were boys drawn from the fourth, fifth, and sixth grades of schools in Gainesville, Florida. Only boys were used since most observers (Blanchard, 1936; Klausmeier, 1958) agree that boys constitute the vast majority of children with learning disabilities.

Boys considered to have learning disabilities were those who met the following criteria:

1. Subjects had at least average intelligence (an IQ equal to or above 90) as measured by an individually administered Binet, Form LM, abbreviated version. Prior to this subjects were screened for individual testing primarily by means of the Kuhlmann-Finch Group Tests.
2. A distribution of group intelligence test scores and a distribution of group achievement test scores for all boys in these grades were prepared and compared to each other. All boys who scored four or more deciles lower in the achievement distribution than they did in the intelligence distribution were selected as subjects. In addition, all boys having achievement scores at least 1 year below grade level while being of average intelligence were regarded as underachievers. Achievement scores used were total grade equivalent scores on the Stanford or California Achievement Tests.
3. Subjects were not in treatment for or recommended for therapeutic treatment for any major reason other than learning retardation prior to the onset of this study.

These children were assigned randomly to one of three groups: praise, reproof, and control. Fifteen boys were placed in each group. These underachieving boys constituted about 5% of the school population from which they were drawn.

For every boy placed in a learning disability group, another boy of similar grade level, school, and IQ who did not have a four-decile discrepancy in either direction between his achievement and intelligence test scores was placed in the corresponding condition (praise, reproof, or nothing) of control subjects. Thus there was a total of six groups: Experimental Praise, Experimental Reproof, Experimental Nothing, Control Praise, Control Reproof, and Control Nothing.

The means and standard deviations of the intelligence test scores and of the deviations from achievement test battery norms for underachievers and nonunderachievers in Grades 4, 5, and 6 are shown in Table I. It should be noted

TABLE I *Binet IQ Scores and Achievement Deviation*

Subject	Binet IQ		Achievement Deviation (in Years)	
	M	SD	M	SD
Underachievers				
Grade 4	108.2	11.10	−1.29	.67
Grade 5	106.6	7.71	−1.35	.74
Grade 6	106.8	10.23	−1.51	.82
Normal achievers				
Grade 4	109.9	11.09	+.69	.56
Grade 5	108.7	10.19	+.87	.53
Grade 6	107.8	10.58	+1.01	.89

that educational retardation increases with grade level among the underachievers while the nonunderachievers show accelerated progress.

TASK

Two lists of seven consonant-vowel-consonant (CVC) trigrams, each paired with colors, were used. These trigrams were drawn from the list of all possible three letter CVC combinations prepared and standardized by Archer (1960). Only those trigrams having an association value of 30% or less were used. Trigrams in each list were matched for percentile of association value. All five vowels were used and as many different consonants as were available meeting the above criteria. The two lists of trigrams and association levels are shown in Table II.

Each trigram was paired with 1 of 14 easily distinguishable colors which children of this age were able to identify in a pilot study. Trigrams were paired with colors rather than with other trigrams or forms because learning problem children are likely to be confused by the latter. Color-trigram pairs were placed in the center of 4 × 6 inch cards. Five different random orders of each list were prepared to reduce position learning.

TABLE II   *Trigram Lists and Percentile of Association Value*

List 1	Association Value	List 2	
FOV	27	ZOL	
YAD	25	DAX	
MIV	17	KIF	
TUZ	29	VUT	
JEG	29	GEF	
PUV	22	WOY	
BOJ	WUC	16	

PROCEDURE

All subjects were shown a card displaying the 14 colors and were asked to designate the appropriate color when requested by the experimenter. All subjects familiar with these colors were then given List 1 of the paired associates, followed by the administration of praise, reproof, or nothing. Following this all subjects learned List 2.

At the beginning each trigram-color pair was presented once for 4 seconds with 4 seconds between pairs, and the following instructions were given:

> Remember how you knew the name of every color I showed you? Well, I have new names for some of the colors that I showed you. The new name of each color is printed beside it on each of these cards. I'll say the new name first, then you say it to learn how to pronounce it.

After the series was completed in the above fashion, the trigram-color combinations were then presented for learning by the anticipation method in a procedure similar to that used by Otto (1961). The color alone was presented for 4 seconds, during which the subject was to guess CVC name. The color-trigram combination was then presented for 4 seconds, during which the trigram was pronounced by the subject. A 10-second inter-trial rest was given. The pairs were presented in the five orders until the criterion of one correct anticipation of each pair consecutively for the entire list was reached. Total score was the number of trials required to reach criterion level. The following instructions were used:

Now I want you to learn the new names for these colors. This is how we'll do it.
I will show you a color alone for a few seconds, during which you are to try to
guess its new name. Then I will show you the color and its new name together
so you can see if your guess was right. When you do see its new name, say it
out loud. We will go through all the colors and new names this way. Do you
understand?

After criterion level was reached on the first task the two groups receiving
praise were told:

Boy! You really did well. You know, you learned them faster than nearly any
of the other kids that took this test. I'll bet you are one of the best students in
your class. Now just to be sure, let's try another list like this first one to see if
you can do as well on it. Here are the new names for these colors.

After criterion level was reached on Task 1 the two groups receiving reproof
were told:

Well, that's it. You know, you took a lot longer to learn those names than I
expected, and I'm kind of disappointed. Do you think . . . maybe if we try
another list you could do better on it? I tell you what, we'll forget these scores
and try a new list.

The two control groups were asked some autobiographical questions to equate
time intervals with the praise and reproof groups and then were told:

I have another list of colors with new names which I want you to learn just like
the first list. Ready?

At the end of the second list, each student receiving reproof was reassured
about the adequacy of his performance.

Results

The means and standard deviations of all six groups before and after administration of the experimental condition are presented in Table III.

TABLE III   *Means and Standard Deviations of Number of Trials
for Tasks 1 and 2*

Condition	Experimental Subjects (Underachievers)		Control Subjects (Normal Achievers)	
	Task 1	Task 2	Task 1	Task 2
Praise				
M	63.07	81.73	40.33	29.53
SD	17.52	22.33	9.03	12.14
Reproof				
M	58.67	35.73	38.73	47.13
SD	17.16	17.90	9.58	13.01
Nothing				
M	63.07	65.73	32.80	34.67
SD	24.70	21.03	8.68	10.87

The first simple analysis of variance which was done compared the mean
scores on Task 1 for all three learning disability groups after Hartley's test for
homogeneity of variance resulted in a nonsignificant F. This analysis resulted in

an *F* value equal to .24, which is not significant. This finding is consistent with the assumption that all three samples were drawn from the same population prior to treatment.

The mean scores for all three normal groups prior to treatment were also compared by means of a simple analysis of variance after the presence of homogeneity of variance was established. The means of these groups also did not differ prior to treatment and thus may be assumed to have been drawn from the same population.

Hypothesis 1, that all normal subjects combined were superior to all learning disability subjects combined prior to treatment, could not be tested by the usual matched *t* test because the variability within the learning disability groups was greater than within normal groups. Instead, the *t* test for samples with unequal variances was used (Walker and Lev, 1913, p. 157). This *t* ratio was equal to 7.46, which is significant at the .001 level. Thus Hypothesis 1 was supported.

Following the administration of praise, reproof, or nothing, the three learning disability groups differed at the .001 level of significance ($F = 17.48$). At *t* ratio equal to 2.02 ($p < .05$) showed that praise results in more trials required to reach criterion than saying nothing to the learning disability subjects. A *t* ratio equal to 4.23 ($p < .001$) showed that reproof resulted in significantly less trials required to reach criterion than did saying nothing. Thus Hypothesis 2, that for educationally retarded boys, praise results in a larger number of trials to reach criterion on the second task than does reproof, was supported.

Following the administration of praise, reproof, or nothing, the three normal groups differed at the .01 level of significance ($F = 8.47$). The *t* ratio for difference between the means for the praise and no-treatment groups was equal to -1.22, which was not significant. The *t* ratio for the difference between the reproof and the no-treatment groups was equal to -2.79 ($p < .005$). Thus it can be seen that reproof resulted in slower learning than did saying nothing or praising the subjects.

Matched *t* tests showed that neither of the nontreatment groups changed in the number of trials required to reach criterion between the first and second tasks.

Discussion

The issue of whether praise or reproof is more effective in classroom teaching has received a great deal of attention. The weight of speculative opinion has been on the side of using praise. The results of prior research, however, have not been unequivocal in their support of praise as an incentive. It may seem reasonable to interpret the present results to mean that these educationally retarded boys should be criticized for their inadequate performance in order to obtain faster learning. It should be noted, however, that additional research is necessary before such a conclusion is justified. Other variables which may be related to the effect of praise and reproof include the type of task employed and the duration and type of praise or reproof given. It must be noted that praise and reproof are not absolutes, and no effort was made to control the amount or intensity of these effects. It is quite possible that the praise condition for the underachievers was unrealistic and so interpreted by them, whereas the reproof condition was realistic and invited them to do better. The praise condition was perhaps interpreted realistically by the normal achievers. In this study praise or reproof was given for only a brief period of time between two verbal tasks. It may well be that praise given continuously over a longer duration may affect performance in a different manner. In addition, it is not known whether the long-range consequences of praise or reproof would be similar to those of this experimental situation.

It should also be remembered that these boys were relatively severe underachievers and that the conclusions from this study may not be applicable to students with less severe educational retardation who may have different dynamics responsible for their underachievement.

REFERENCES

Archer, E. J. Re-evaluation of the meaningfulness of all possible CVC trigrams. *Psychol. Monogr.,* 1960, 74 (10, Whole No. 497).

Blanchard, Phylliss. Reading disabilities in relation to difficulties of personality and emotional development. *Ment. Hyg.,* 1936, 20, 384–413.

Fenichel, O. The scopophilic instinct and identification. *Int. J. Psycho-Anal.,* 1937, 18, 6–34.

Klausmeier, H. J. Physical, behavioral, and other characteristics of high- and lower-achieving children in favored environments. *J. educ. Res.,* 1958, 51, 573–581.

Klein, Melanie. A contribution to the theory of intellectual inhibition. *Int. J. Psycho-Anal.,* 1931, 12, 206–218.

Kunst, Mary S. Learning disabilities: Their dynamics and treatment. *Soc. Wk.,* 1959, 4, 95–101.

Liss, E. Learning: Its sadistic and masochistic manifestations. *Amer. J. Orthopsychiat.,* 1940, 10, 123–128.

Oberndorf, C. P. The feeling of stupidity. *Int. J. Psycho-Anal.,* 1939, 20, 443–451.

Otto, W. The acquisition and retention of paired associates by good, average, and poor readers. *J. educ. Psychol.,* 1961, 52, 241–248.

Pearson, G. H. J. A survey of learning difficulties in children. *Psychoanal. Stud. Child.,* 1952, 7, 322–386.

Strachey, J. Some unconscious factors in reading. *Int. J. Psycho-Anal.,* 1930, 11, 322–331.

Walker, Helen M., and Lev, J. *Statistical inference.* New York: Holt, 1953.

---

16   Nondirective Play Therapy
with Retarded Readers

ROBERT E. BILLS

The problem of the retarded reader has caused educators much concern and has stimulated much research. Retardation in reading is now thought to be the result of poor teaching or of the inability of a child to learn by customary instructional procedures; consequently the retarded reader is usually given enriched

A condensation of portions of a doctoral project submitted to the Advanced School of Education, Teachers College, Columbia University, in 1948. Reprinted (with permission) from *Journal of Consulting Psychology,* Vol. 14 (1950), pp. 140–149. Copyright 1950 by the American Psychological Association.

The author is deeply grateful to Professors Nicholas Hobbs, Ruth Strang, and Helen Walker for their encouragement and constructive criticism.

reading instruction of an individual and remedial nature which is designed to teach him what he has failed to learn in the usual way.

Often remedial reading instruction proves to be valuable, and the child does learn to read with skill commensurate with his ability. There are probably many causes of the gains in ability resulting from such individual instruction. Many retarded readers, however, fail to improve in spite of such instruction. Clinical experience has shown that some members of this group may learn to read when the remedial practice is preceded or accompanied by individual psychotherapy.

Lecky (6) and Axline (2) have postulated that poor reading may result from inconsistencies in the attitudinal system of a child or from difficulty in resolving a conflict between a concept of self as a poor reader and a concept of self as a good reader.

If the difficulty which some retarded readers show is due mainly to inconsistencies within their value systems, and if nondirective play therapy can aid the individual in changing his attitude toward self or in re-evaluating his concept, then corresponding changes should occur in subject matter ability after nondirective play therapy. The following experiment was designed to test the hypothesis that significant improvements occur in the reading ability of a retarded reader when he has been given a nondirective play therapy experience.

Design of the Investigation

SELECTION OF THE CLASS

Through the cooperation of the Bureau of Reference, Research, and Statistics of the New York City Board of Education and a principal of an elementary school in New York City, permission was obtained to work with a class of third-graders who had been previously classified as slow learners. It must be emphasized that the children included in this study were in this third-grade class because of an inability to learn at a normal rate and not because of intellectual or emotional factors. Intellectual or emotional factors may have caused these children to learn slowly, but they were not the criteria for placement in this class.

It is to be expected, because of their presence in this class, that the children in the study would be low in achievement and would exhibit some retardation in school, but it does not necessarily follow that these children would exhibit difficulty in emotional adjustment to a greater degree than a group of children not classified as slow learners.

At the beginning of the study twenty-two children were in the class. Of these, two were of foreign birth and had English language handicaps of such severity as to render their scores on standardized tests meaningless, and two others left the school district before the study was completed. Final test data are included for the remaining eighteen children.

THREE PERIODS OF THE STUDY

The plan of the investigation included three periods of thirty school days each. The first of these periods was the control period, the second the therapy period, and the third was considered as a period for noting lasting or cumulative effects of the therapy. It was thought that the most adequate comparison which could be obtained would be made between the gain of each child during the therapy and third periods and his gain in the control period. Each of the therapy children could have been matched with other children on the basis of certain objective factors such as sex, age, grade, and intelligence, but it is far from certain that these are the important factors in the problem.

Employing the children as their own control could possibly introduce certain invalidating features such as the instruction given in the different periods, the health of the child, home circumstances, the child's motivation, and school attendance. It is reasonable to expect that the influences operating on the therapy group during the control and therapy periods would be as constant as the influences operating on the therapy group and a selected control group during any one period. It was assumed, therefore, that the children could be matched with themselves during two periods of the experiment with a greater degree of control of important personality variables than if they were matched with another group of children on the basis of objective criteria.

TESTS EMPLOYED

Three types of test were used in the selection of the therapy group and in measuring the gains of this group and the rest of the class during the three periods of the study. They were: the Gates tests of paragraph meaning, the Gray Oral Reading Paragraphs, and the Revised Stanford-Binet, Form L.

On the first day of the control period all of the children were tested with the oral and silent reading tests. During the next two weeks they were tested with the intelligence test. At the end of the control period all of the children were retested with the oral and silent reading tests, and these tests were given again at the end of the therapy and third periods.

SELECTION OF THE THERAPY GROUP

The Gates Primary Reading Tests of paragraph meaning at the beginning of the control period gave a reading grade score and a reading age equivalent for each child, and the intelligence test gave a mental age. Any discrepancy between mental age and reading age was taken as a measure of reading retardation. The four children who showed the greatest discrepancy were chosen as part of the therapy group. Since these children had very high intelligence quotients the other four children were selected from the group with discrepancies and approximately average intelligence quotients in order to determine not only the effect of the experience on very intelligent children but also the effect on four children of average intelligence. These eight children made up the therapy group. The remaining children in the class may be thought of as a comparison group, but the inadequacies of this group for comparison purposes must be kept in mind.

TREATMENT OF THE THERAPY GROUP

After the testing with the Revised Stanford Binet nothing was done with any of the children during the control period. As has already been stated, all of the children were retested with the reading tests at the end of this period.

During the second or therapy period, the eight children of the therapy group were given a play experience of a nondirective, therapeutic nature following the principles established by Rogers (8), Axline (2), and others. For the first three weeks of this period the children met in individual sessions with the experimenter, and during the last three weeks each child attended an individual session and one group meeting each week. In all there were six individual sessions and three group meetings in a period of six weeks for five of the children, two of the children had six individual meetings, and two group contacts, and the remaining child had four individual meetings and one group contact.

Each session lasted forty-five minutes. All of the children in the class were re-tested at the end of this period with the oral and silent reading tests.

Nothing was done with the children during the third period. At the end of this time all of the children were tested for the fourth time with the oral and silent reading tests.

COLLECTION OF DATA

The collected data were of six types including: (a) the results of the standard-ized tests, (b) the recordings of the play sessions, (c) the school records, (d) the ratings of the judges, (e) the observations of the Binet examiner, and (f) observations of the reading instruction. The first of these has already been dis-cussed.

Each of the play sessions was recorded by means of a wire recorder and notes made by the worker, and these were used to supplement each other in the for-mulation of a verbatim transcription of what occurred during the individual play sessions. It was from these recordings that the judges made their ratings.

The school records supplied background information on the children, atten-dance records, and records of previous tests.

The three judges employed here were well qualified.[1] They had satisfactorily completed supervised counseling experience and were graduate students in the final stages of completion of their doctoral work. In addition each judge had several years of experience in dealing with psychological problems both in and out of clinical situations. Each judge adhered to a different therapeutic school, including eclectic, psychodynamic, and nondirective views.

The observations of the Binet examiner consisted of the subjective impres-sions which each child gave during the testing situation. This description in-cluded mainly those points which aided in understanding the performance of the child. The Binet examiner was well qualified and had considerable experience in testing children of the age range included in this class. The experimenter conducted no tests because of the possibility of biasing the data.

It was believed that any gains which the children made during the different periods might possibly be accounted for by differences in the methods of the teacher, a change in emphasis given to individual children, a remedial approach by the teacher, or other factors. To determine if such factors might be at work, the experimenter made several observations during each period to determine the constancy of the instruction and the emphasis given each child. In the third period of the investigation the writer and two well qualified teachers made three independent observations of the reading class. The three observers had con-siderable experience in teaching, amounting in two cases to seven years and in the third to four years, and two of the observers had experience in administra-tion and supervision. These observers concluded that the instruction was equal for all members of the class, that it was not remedial in nature, and that it was constant for each period of the experiment.

Group Data

The data of this study were obtained in two ways: by an intensive study of eight individual children and by the study of the children as a group. Because of limitations of space the results of the study of the eight children as individuals

1 The author is indebted to Miss Ruth Witty and Messrs. Leon Gorlow and Ija Korner for their services as judges.

are not presented in this paper but are set forth in detail by R. E. Bills(3). The group data are presented below.

COMPARISON GROUP

Since the intelligence and reading tests were given to the entire class, test data are available for ten children who were not included in the play therapy experience and who make up the comparison, or nontherapy, group. It must be emphasized that the therapy and nontherapy groups were not matched and that statistical comparison of the two groups is impossible.

The two most obvious differences between the therapy and nontherapy groups were the factors of intelligence and reading retardation. The average intelligence quotient of the therapy group was 130 and of the nontherapy group was 95. All of the children in the therapy group showed a negative discrepancy between mental age and reading age, but only three of the children in the nontherapy group showed this discrepancy.

The data for the nontherapy group are useful in showing the gains of this group during the three periods of the study and the relative equivalence of the tests employed. They have little value as a means of comparison with the gains of the therapy group.

TEST RESULTS

The chronological age, mental age, and intelligence quotient of each child in the class are given in Table I. The range of chronological ages for the entire class was from 7–4 years to 9–6 years, the range of mental ages was from 6–8 years to 14–9 years, and the intelligence quotients ranged from 70 to 159.

TABLE I   *Chronological Age, Mental Age, and Intelligence Quotient for Each Child**

Name	Chronological Age*	Mental Age	IQ
Therapy Group			
1. Nancy	8–1	8–0	99
2. Jean	8–0	8–2	102
3. Bernice	7–11	9–9	123
4. George	8–7	9–6	111
5. David	8–7	12–8	148
6. Janice	7–4	10–10	148
7. Mary	7–11	11–8	147
8. Jack	9–3	14–9	159
Nontherapy Group			
9. Dorris	8–11	7–4	82
10. Harry	9–6	6–8	70
11. Emily	8–3	8–0	97
12. Lester	8–4	7–8	92
13. Bob	7–10	9–9	124
14. Grace	9–1	7–10	86
15. Sibil	8–7	7–4	85
16. Roberta	8–0	8–11	111
17. Christine	7–10	9–11	127
18. Wally	8–8	10–8	123

* The chronological age is the age as of the date of testing with the Revised Stanford Binet, Form L. Ages are given in years and months.

The mental age and reading age for each child, and the results of subtracting the reading age from the mental age are given in Table II. Using the assumed criterion of reading retardation, eleven of the eighteen children in the class were classified as retarded readers, one child showed a reading age equivalent to his mental age, and the remaining six children had reading ages greater than their mental ages.

TABLE II *Discrepancy Between Reading Age and Mental Age for each Child**

Name	Reading Age	Mental Age	Discrepancy†
Therapy Group			
1. Nancy	7–3	8–0	− 0–9
2. Jean	7–7	8–2	− 0–7
3. Bernice	7–5	9–9	− 2–4
4. George	8–2.5	9–6	− 1–3.5
5. David	9–0.5	12–8	− 3–7.5
6. Janice	8–7	10–10	− 2–3
7. Mary	8–7	11–8	− 3–1
8. Jack	8–9.5	14–9	− 5–11.5
Nontherapy Group			
9. Dorris	7–4	7–4	0–0
10. Harry	7–3	6–8	+ 0–7
11. Emily	8–5	8–0	+ 0–5
12. Lester	8–8.2	7–8	+ 1–0.2
13. Bob	9–0.5	9–9	− 0–8.5
14. Grace	8–7	7–10	+ 0–9
15. Sibil	8–9.5	7–4	+ 1–5.5
16. Roberta	9–3.5‡	8–11	+ 0–4.5
17. Christine	9–0.5	9–11	− 0–10.5
18. Wally	8–7	10–8	− 2–1

* Reading age was determined from the first test of paragraph meaning of the Gates Primary Reading Tests.
† This discrepancy is obtained by subtracting mental age from reading age. The figure is given in years and months or fractions of a month.
‡ This is the highest score obtainable on this form of the test.

The grade scores of each child on the four tests of silent reading and the change in score for each child in the three periods of the study are given in Table III. The four tests included in this table showed that during the control period five of the eight children in the therapy group showed an increase in grade score, while only one of the ten children in the nontherapy group showed an increase. In the therapy period, all eight of the children in the therapy group and nine of the ten children in the nontherapy group showed increases in grade score. In the third period of the study six of the children in the therapy group and five of the children in the nontherapy group showed increases in grade score.

The average gain of the therapy group may be given a statistical treatment. The hypothesis to be tested is that the mean of the gains of the therapy group in the second period of the study was not significantly different from the mean of the gains of the same group in the first period of the study. The results of the statistical computations are given in Table IV. These results show that the gains

TABLE III   *Grade Score on the Gates Primary and Advanced Primary Reading Tests for Each Child**

Name	$T_1{}^a$	$T_2{}^b$	T_2—$T_1{}^c$	$T_3{}^d$	T_3—T_2	$T_4{}^e$	T_4—T_3	T_4—T_2
Therapy Group								
1. Nancy	1.95	1.95	.00	2.75	+ .80	2.80	+ .05	+ .85
2. Jean	2.30	2.40	+.10	3.75	+1.35	4.00	+ .25	+1.60
3. Bernice	2.10	2.20	+.10	3.10	+ .90	3.50	+ .40	+1.30
4. George	2.75	2.30	−.45	2.75	+ .45	2.60	− .15	+ .30
5. David	3.55	3.35	−.20	4.00	+ .65	6.00	+2.00	+2.65
6. Janice	3.10	3.35	+.25	5.40	+2.05	5.40	.00	+2.05
7. Mary	3.10	3.35	+.25	4.80	+1.45	5.40	+ .60	+2.05
8. Jack	3.35	3.55	+.20	4.00	+ .45	5.40	+1.40	+1.85
Nontherapy Group								
9. Dorris	2.00	2.00	.00	2.20	+ .20	2.80	+ .60	+ .80
10. Harry	1.95	1.65	−.30	1.60	− .05	1.70	+ .10	+ .05
11. Emily	2.90	2.90	.00	3.35	+ .45	3.20	− .15	+ .30
12. Lester	3.22	3.55	+.33	3.70	+ .15	3.30	− .40	− .25
13. Bob	3.55	3.22	−.33	3.50	+ .28	3.80	+ .30	+ .58
14. Grace	3.10	3.10	.00	3.30	+ .20	3.50	+ .20	+ .40
15. Sibil	3.35	2.75	−.60	3.20	+ .45	3.30	+ .10	+ .55
16. Roberta	3.75	3.35	−.45	3.50	+ .15	3.50	.00	+ .15
17. Christine	3.55	3.35	−.20	3.50	+ .15	3.50	− .20	+ .05
18. Wally	3.10	2.75	−.35	3.00	+ .25	2.90	− .10	+ .15

a Grade score on the first test of paragraph meaning. Form 1, Type III of the Gates Primary Reading Tests was used to obtain this score.
b Grade score on the second test of paragraph meaning, Form 2, Type III of the Gates Primary Reading Tests was used to obtain this score.
c This is the discrepancy between the first and second tests. This is given in terms of school grades and fractions of school grades.
d Grade score on the third test of paragraph meaning. Form 1, Type II of the Gates Advanced Primary Reading Tests was used to obtain this score.
e Grade score on the fourth test of paragraph meaning. Form 2, Type II of the Gates Advanced Primary Reading Tests was used to obtain this score.

TABLE IV   *Comparison of the Difference of the Means of the Gains of the Therapy Group in Silent Reading in the First and Second Periods of the Study*

Name	$T_3{}^a$	$T_2{}^b$	T_3—T_2	$T_1{}^c$	T_2—T_1	d^d	d^2
Nancy	2.75	1.95	.80	1.95	.00	.80	.6400
Jean	3.75	2.40	1.35	2.30	.10	1.25	1.5625
Bernice	3.10	2.20	.90	2.10	.10	.80	.6400
George	2.75	2.30	.45	2.75	−.45	.90	.8100
David	4.00	3.35	.65	3.55	−.20	.85	.7255
Janice	5.40	3.35	2.05	3.10	.25	1.80	3.2400
Mary	4.80	3.35	1.45	3.10	.25	1.20	1.4400
Jack	4.00	3.55	.45	3.35	.20	.25	.0625
			M_1=1.01		M_2=.03	Σd=7.85	Σd^2=9.1175

$$t = 6.125 \text{ Degrees of freedom} = 7$$
$$t > t_{.001}$$
$$P < .001$$

a T_3 is the grade score on the third test of paragraph meaning of the Gates Reading Tests.
b T_2 is the grade score on the second test of paragraph meaning of the Gates Reading Tests.
c T_1 is the grade score on the first test of paragraph meaning of the Gates Reading Tests.
d d is a difference and is obtained by applying the formula: $(T_3$—$T_2) - (T_2$—$T_1)$.

of the therapy group in the first and second periods of the study were significantly different and that the therapy group made a significantly greater gain in the therapy period than it did in the control period. (These results are significant at the .001 level of probability.)

The hypothesis may also be tested that there was no significant difference between the mean of the gains of the therapy group in the control period and the mean of the gains for this same group, measured by the difference in grade score of the second and fourth tests. The results of the statistical computations are presented in Table V. The statistical treatment shows that there is no evidence to assume that this hypothesis is correct. It is apparent that the gains of the therapy group during the second and third periods of the study were significantly greater than the gains during the first period of the study. (These results are significant at the .01 level of probability.)

TABLE V   *Comparison of the Difference of the Means of the Gains in Silent Reading of the Therapy Group in the Six Weeks of the Control Period and the Twelve Weeks of the Second and Third Periods*

Name	$T_4{}^a$	$T_2{}^b$	T_4-T_2	$T_1{}^c$	T_2-T_1	$2(T_2-T_1)^d$	d^e	d^2
Nancy	2.80	1.95	.85	1.95	.00	.00	.85	.7225
Jean	4.00	2.40	1.60	2.30	.10	.20	1.40	1.9600
Bernice	3.50	2.20	1.30	2.10	.10	.20	1.10	1.2100
George	2.60	2.30	.30	2.75	−.45	−.90	1.20	1.4400
David	6.00	3.35	2.65	3.55	−.20	−.40	3.05	9.3025
Janice	5.40	3.35	2.05	3.10	.25	.50	2.55	6.5025
Mary	5.40	3.35	2.05	3.10	.25	.50	2.55	6.5025
Jack	5.40	3.55	1.85	3.35	.20	.40	2.25	5.0625
			$M_1=1.58$			$M_2=.06$	$\Sigma d=14.95$	$\Sigma d^2=32.7025$

$$t = 5.241 \quad \text{Degrees of freedom} = 7$$
$$t_{.01} = 3.499$$
$$t_{.001} = 5.405$$
$$.01 > P > .001$$

a T_4 is the grade score on the fourth test of silent reading.
b T_2 is the grade score on the second test of silent reading.
c T_1 is the grade score on the first test of silent reading.
d The quantity (T_2-T_1) is multiplied by 2 to make the six week gain of T_2-T_1 comparable to the twelve week gain of T_4-T_2.
e "d" is obtained by applying the formula $(T_4-T_2) - 2(T_2-T_1)$.

It has already been stated that the children were tested with the Gray Oral Reading Paragraphs at the beginning of each period of the study and after the third period. The scores for each child in the class and the changes in score for each period of the study are given in Tables VI and VII. It was noted that these gains agreed, in general, with the gains measured by the tests of silent reading. During the control period, six of the eight children in the therapy group and eight of the ten children in the nontherapy group improved in oral reading ability. In the therapy period five of the children in the therapy group and two of the children in the nontherapy group showed gains in oral reading ability. During the third period, all eight of the children in the therapy group and four of the children in the nontherapy group gained in oral reading ability.

TABLE VI   *Time and Error Score of Each Child on the First and Second Tests with the Gray Oral Reading Paragraphs*

Name	First Test		Second Test		$T_2—T_1$[b]
	Set I[a]	Set II	Set I	Set II	
Therapy Group					
Nancy	60–12[c]		50–1		+
Jean	35–2		20–1		+
Bernice	50–5		45–5		+
George	50–5		35–1		+
David		65–0		70–1	−
Janice		70–2		55–0	+
Mary		75–4		75–2	+
Jack		70–2		80–2	−
Nontherapy Group					
Dorris	40–5		25–2	65–10	+
Harry	d		d		0
Emily	45–4		35–0	55–1	+
Lester		80–7		75–4	+
Bob		75–2		70–1	+
Grace		110–9		115–7	+
Sibil		95–11		85–8	+
Roberta		90–0		75–5	−[e]
Christine		65–3		60–0	+
Wally		75–3		70–1	+

a The Gray Oral Reading Paragraphs are in four sets of increasing difficulty. Each set has five equivalent forms. The sets which are reported under each test period are those which suited the ability level of the child.

b The gain during the period between test 1 and test 2.

c The first number is the time in seconds required to read the selection, and the second number is the number of errors made.

d Child could not read selection.

e The increase in errors is here considered to overbalance the decrease in time.

RATINGS OF THE JUDGES

To insure uniformity, the ratings of the judges were obtained by means of questionnaires. Jean, Bernice, David, and Janice were rated by all three judges as exhibiting significant emotional maladjustment. Nancy and Jack were rated by two of the judges as showing significant emotional maladjustment, while one judge felt that they were adequately adjusted. Mary was voted well adjusted by two judges and by the third judge as exhibiting significant social maladjustment. George was rated by all three judges as being well adjusted. The judges were agreed that Nancy, Jean, Bernice, David, and Jack had gained in emotional adjustment as a result of the play therapy experience. Two of the judges were agreed that George and Mary had not gained in emotional adjustment, and two were agreed that Janice did gain.

Conclusions and Implications

The data of this study indicate that some factor or factors were operative during the second and third periods of the study which caused the reading gains of the children during these periods to be greater than the gains which they showed in the control period. On the basis of the experimental design, the study of the individual child, the observations of the reading instruction, the study of the

TABLE VII *Time and Error Score of Each Child on the Third and Fourth Tests with the Gray Oral Reading Paragraphs*

Name	Third Test			T_3—T_2 [a]	Fourth Test			T_4—T_3 [b]
	Set I	Set II	Set III		Set I	Set II	Set III	
Therapy Group								
Nancy	59–3[c]			—	42–3			+
Jean	21–0	98–3		+		100–2		+
Bernice	46–3			+	35–2			+
George	32–2			0[d]	25–1			+
David		61–0	74–1	+			61–1	+
Janice		59–1	74–4	—			71–2	+
Mary		68–0	88–4	+			75–1	+
Jack		62–0	66–1	+			56–1	+
Nontherapy Group								
Dorris	35–3	e		—	27–2			+
Harry	e			0	e			0
Emily	33–2	e		—	29–1			+
Lester		80–1		+		77–4		—
Bob		56–2	74–9	0[d]			72–7	+
Grace		136–12		—		130–8		+
Sibil		82–8		0		91–9		—
Roberta		67–3		+		77–4		—
Christine		57–2		—		56–5		—
Wally		63–5		—		66–6		—

a The gain in the therapy period or between test 2 and test 3.
b The gain in the third period of the study between test 3 and test 4.
c The first number is the time in seconds required to read the selection, and the second number is the number of errors made.
d The increase in errors and the decrease in time are considered to counterbalance.
e Child could not read selection.

interview transcriptions, and all other available information, it appears that the play therapy experience which the children received could account for their changed reading skill. It may be concluded that when the eight retarded readers of this study received a nondirective play therapy experience, they showed significant gains in their reading ability.

The design of this study does not permit a conclusion on the effect of maladjustment on the reading ability of a child, but the results do suggest directions for future research. Future investigation might well take the form of an inquiry into the effects of play therapy on the reading level of children who show adequate emotional adjustment. If it can be shown that children who are making adequate emotional adjustment do not gain significantly in reading ability as the result of such play experience, then it can be assumed that the reading gains noted in the present study were possibly the result of treatment of the maladjustment which the child evidenced. If, though, well-adjusted children did gain in reading skill as the result of the play therapy experience, maladjustment should be regarded as irrelevant to the changes recorded in the present study.

The source of the reading gains which the children made in this study is in need of further investigation. It is possible that one of two things occurred: (a) these children were able to learn at a more rapid rate when they had received the play therapy experience, or (b) the gains which the children showed in reading skill resulted from information which the child already possessed but was unable to utilize with maximum effectiveness. Both of these alternatives are possibly true, but the size of the gains recorded in this study and the length of the study lend weight to the second interpretation. In a longer study the first possibility might assume more significance.

The data also indicate that the gains in reading ability which the retarded readers of this study made appeared immediately after therapy for some of the children and after a short period following therapy for the others who exhibited a gain. Further investigation is needed to determine if there is a relationship between the rapidity of appearance and the size of the reading gain following nondirective play therapy and the extent of the emotional disturbance which some retarded readers show.

This study was concerned with the gain in reading ability which a child shows following a nondirective play therapy experience. It is possible that such an experience may cause changes in abilities other than reading ability. There is a need for an investigation of the effects of a nondirective play therapy experience on the abilities of children who are classified as retarded in other subjects included in the school curriculum.

The conclusion that personal change follows nondirective play therapy is certainly not unique to this study. Many other studies have shown that this is the result to be expected. This study adds to the body of information on the length of therapeutic treatment necessary to produce personality changes. It has been shown that, as a result of six individual and three group play therapy sessions, personality changes may occur.

It appears that although seven of the eight retarded readers in this study did show emotional disturbances, and although there were common personality characteristics in these children, there were enough differences among them to preclude any broad classification of types of maladjustment. This finding tends to support the conclusion of other studies that there is no single type of personality maladjustment in the retarded reader. It likewise lends weight to the hypothesis that inability to read may be connected with the attitudinal system or the self-concept of the individual.

The causes of the changes in reading abilities recorded in this study are in need of further investigation. It has been suggested that the change which occurs in the child as a result of a nondirective, play therapy experience is a change in self-concept. More adequate measures of self-concept must be devised in order to test the hypothesis that the change in reading ability of some retarded readers following a nondirective play therapy experience is related to the change in the child's self-concept. Experimentation is also needed to determine how the therapy experience enables the child to change and what techniques are most valuable in facilitating this change.

This study shows that the change in reading ability which followed the nondirective play therapy experience was present six weeks after the therapy had ended. There is a definite need to determine if this changed ability is permanent or if it disappears after a time.

It cannot be concluded from this study that the child who is having difficulty with his reading is also having difficulty with his adjustment problems. Before this conclusion could be approached there would have to be a more thorough demonstration that the emotional maladjustment which the children in this study evidenced was not an accidental characteristic of the sample which was chosen for the study. Even though it might be found that emotional maladjustment does not exist in retarded readers to the extent found in the sample which was investigated in this study, the subject may not be dismissed lightly.

Schools have attempted to prevent emotional maladjustment from developing and have worked toward eliminating maladjustment that does occur. This is probably as it should be, and what is needed is not a greater desire on the part of the school but better tools with which to work in preventing and correcting emotional maladjustment.

This study and many other studies concerned with nondirective therapy have shown that personal changes do result from a nondirective, play therapy experience. Axline (1) has shown that the procedures of nondirective therapy can be used in the classroom. If personal changes do result from nondirective therapy and if these techniques are adaptable to the classroom, then an approach to teaching is indicated which would include a corrective mental hygiene aspect.

Summary

This study was an investigation of the effects of individual and group play therapy on the reading level of retarded readers. Eight retarded readers were selected for the play therapy experience. The criterion of reading retardation was a negative discrepancy between mental age and reading age. The study was designed to include three periods of thirty school days each. The first period was a control period, which was intended to measure the gains of the children during a period in which no play experience was given. During the second period, the therapy period, the children were given a play therapy experience of a nondirective nature. The third period was included to measure the gains which followed immediately after therapy. A measure of intelligence was obtained during the control period, and measures of silent and oral reading abilities were made before each of the three periods and following the third period.

As a result of the play therapy experience it was concluded: (a) significant changes in reading ability occurred as a result of the play therapy experience, (b) personal changes may occur in nondirective play therapy in as little as six individual and three group play therapy sessions, and (c) there appears to be no common personality maladjustment present in this group of retarded readers.

REFERENCES

1. Axline, Virginia M. Nondirective therapy for poor readers. *J. consult. Psychol.* 1947, 11, 61–69.

2. Axline, Virginia M. *Play therapy.* Boston: Houghton Mifflin, 1947.

3. Bills, R. E. An investigation of the effects of individual and group play therapy on the reading level of retarded readers. Unpublished Doctor's project, Teachers College, Columbia University, 1948.

4. Combs, A. W. Some dynamic aspects of nondirective therapy. In Roy W. Miner (Ed.), Current trends in clinical psychology, *Ann. N.Y. Acad. Sc.* 1948, 49, 878–888.

5. Hobbs, N. My understanding of nondirective psychotherapy. Unpublished paper, Teachers College, Columbia University, 1947.

6. Lecky, P. *Self-consistency: a theory of personality.* New York: Island Press, 1945.

7. Raimy, V. C. The self-concept as a factor in counseling and personality organization. Unpublished Doctor's dissertation, Ohio State University, 1943.

8. Rogers, C. R. A comprehensive theory of personality and behavior (tentative draft). Unpublished paper, University of Chicago, 1948.

9. Sheerer, Elizabeth T. An analysis of the relationship between acceptance of and respect for self and acceptance of and respect for others in ten counseling cases. *J. consult. Psychol.*, 1949, 13, 169–175.

10. Snygg, D. The need for a phenomenological system of psychology. *Psychol. Rev.* 1941, 48, 404–424.

17   Treatment of Nonreading in a Culturally Deprived Juvenile Delinquent: An Application of Reinforcement Principles

ARTHUR W. STAATS

WILLIAM H. BUTTERFIELD

A 14-year-old, Mexican-American delinquent boy who had a long history of school failure and misbehavior and second-grade reading achievement was given 40 hours of reading training which extended over a 4½-month period. Science Research Associates reading materials were adapted for use in conjunction with a token system of reinforcement. During the training, S's attention and participation were maintained in good strength by the reinforcers, he made many reading responses and learned and retained 430 new words, his reading achievement increased to the 4.3-grade level, he passed all his courses for the first time, and his misbehaviors in school decreased to zero.

Staats (1964c; Staats and Staats, 1963) has previously discussed behavior problems and their treatment in terms of learning principles. In doing so it was indicated that problem behaviors can arise in part (1) because behavior that is necessary for adjustment in our society is absent from the individual's repertoire, (2) because behaviors considered undesirable by the society are present in the individual's repertoire, or (3) because the individual's motivational (reinforcement) system was inappropriate in some respect.

Although a complete account is not relevant here, several points pertinent to the above conceptions will be made in introducing the present study. The notion that many behavior problems consist of deficits in behavior is important in the study of child development. Behaviorally speaking, a child is considered to be a problem when he does not acquire behaviors as other children do. It is conceivable that a deficit in behavior could arise because the child simply cannot

From *Child Development*, Vol. 36 (December, 1965), pp. 925–942. Reprinted with permission of The Society for Research in Child Development, Inc. Copyright © 1965 by the Society for Research in Child Development, Inc.

The present methods of reading training were formulated, and the present paper written, by the first author as part of a long-term project applying learning principles and procedures to the experimental study of language-learning and reading. The methods were applied by the second author in his position as an officer of the Maricopa County Juvenile Probation Department. The second author also collected and tabulated the data and aided in its graphic presentation. He wishes to express appreciation to Chief Probation Officer John H. Walker for lending cooperation in the conduct of the study; also to Mary J. Butterfield, who made important contributions in the preparation of the reading materials used in the study; to Brenda Shields, who typed the materials; and to Janet Munir, who typed the manuscript.

acquire the behavior involved, even though the conditions of learning have been entirely adequate.

It would be expected, however, that behavioral deficits would also arise in cases where the conditions of learning have been defective. Learning conditions can be defective in different ways. For example, the child may never have received training in the behavior he must later exhibit. Or the training may be poor, even though the "trainers," parents or teachers, and so on, have the best intentions.

In addition, however, a child may be exposed to learning conditions that are appropriate for most children but, due to the particular child's past history of learning, are not appropriate for him. It is especially in these cases that people are most likely to conclude erroneously that since other children learn in the same circumstances, the child's deficit must be because of some personal defect. For example, in cases where the training is long term, adequate reinforcement must be available to maintain the attentional and work behaviors necessary for learning. As Staats has indicated (1964c; Staats and Staats, 1963; Staats, Staats, Schutz, and Wolf, 1962), the reinforcers present in the traditional schoolroom are inadequate for many children. Their attentional behaviors are not maintained, and they do not learn. Thus, a deficit in an individual's behavioral repertoire may arise although he has been presented with the "same" training circumstances from which other children profit. Learning does not take place because the child's previous experience has not provided, in this example, the necessary reinforcer (motivational) system to maintain good "learning" behaviors. It would seem that in such a circumstance the assumption that the child has a personal defect would be unwarranted and ineffective.

However, after a few years of school attendance where the conditions of learning are not appropriate for the child, he will not have acquired the behavioral repertoires acquired by more fortunate members of the class—whose previous experiences have established an adequate motivational system. Then, lack of skilled behavior is likely to be treated aversively. That is, in the present case, the child with a reading deficit (or other evidence of underachievement) is likely to be gibed at and teased when he is still young and ignored, avoided, and looked down upon when he is older. Although the individuals doing this may not intend to be aversive, such actions constitute the presentation of aversive stimuli. Furthermore, this presentation of aversive stimuli by other "successful" children, and perhaps by a teacher, would be expected to result in further learning, but learning of an undesirable nature. These successful children, teachers, academic materials, and the total school situation can in this way become learned negative reinforcers, which may be translated (see Staats, 1964b) to say the child acquires negative attitudes toward school.

At this point, the child is likely to begin to "escape" the school situation in various ways (daydreaming, poor attendance, and so on) and to behave aversively in turn to the school and its inhabitants (vandalism, fighting, baiting teachers and students, and the like). Thus, a deficit in behavior, resulting from an inappropriate motivational system, can lead to the further development of inappropriate reinforcers and inappropriate behaviors.

The foregoing is by no means intended as a complete analysis of delinquency, dropouts, and the like. However, it does indicate some of the problems of learning that may occur in school. In addition, it does suggest that an analysis in terms of laboratory-established learning principles, when applied to problems such as in classroom learning of the above type, can yield new research and applied hypotheses. It was with this general strategy that the study of reading acquisition employing learning principles and reinforcement procedures were commenced (Staats, 1964a; Staats *et al.,* 1962; Staats, Finley, Minke, and Wolf, 1964a; Staats, Minke, Finley, Wolf, and Brooks, 1964b). The present study is a replication and an extension of these various findings to the development of a program for training nonreaders to read. The program, which adapts standard reading materials, is based upon the principle of the reinforcer system employed in the previous studies with the younger children, thus testing the principles of reinforcement in the context of remedial reading training, as well as the feasibility of using the type of reinforcement system with a new type of *S*. As such, the study has implications for the study of nonreading children of pre-adolescent, adolescent, and young adult ages. In the present case, *S* was also a culturally deprived delinquent child—and the study thus involves additional information and implications for the special problems associated with education in this population of children.

Methods

SUBJECT

The *S* was a 14-year-and-3-month-old boy of Mexican-American ancestry. He was the fifth child in a family of 11 children and the mother and father. The parental techniques for controlling their children's behavior consisted of physical and verbal abuse. Both parents described their own childhood conditions as primitive. The father was taken out of school after completing the fifth grade to help with his father's work. Each of *S*'s four older brothers had been referred to the juvenile court for misbehavior. The parents appeared to be at loss as to how to provide effective control for family members.

The *S* had a history of various miscreant behaviors, having been referred to the juvenile department nine times for such things as running away, burglary, incorrigibility, and truancy. During the course of the Study *S* was again referred on a complaint (with three other boys) of malicious mischief for shooting light bulbs and windows in a school building with a BB gun. He associated with a group of boys who had been in marked difficulty with the law. The *S* smoked, and on occasion he drank excessively.

The study commenced when *S* was residing with his family. However, after the complaint on malicious mischief *S* was sent to a juvenile detention home. During his stay there he was allowed to attend school in the daytime. The study was finally concluded when *S* was committed to an industrial school for juvenile-delinquent boys. This occurred because *S* baited the attendants at the detention home and caused disturbances which, although not serious, were very unpleasant and disruptive.

On the Wechsler Bellevue Form I, given when *S* was 13–10, he received Verbal and Performance IQ's of 77 and 106, respectively, for a Full Scale IQ of 90. The examiner concluded that *S* was probably within the normal range for this test. On the basis of this test and HTP Projective Drawings, *S* was characterized as having a poor attention span and poorly integrated thought processes and as lacking intellectual ambitiousness. He was also described as seeking satisfaction in fantasy and as having good conventional judgment.

The *S* had continually received failing grades in all subjects in school. He was described as having "been incorrigible since he came here in the second grade. He has no respect for teachers, steals and lies habitually and uses extremely foul language." The *S* had been promoted throughout his school career simply to move him on or to "get rid of him." He was disliked by the teachers and administrators in grade school because of his troublesome behavior and was described by the principal as mentally retarded even though one of the tests taken there indicated a score within the normal range. Another test taken there gave him an IQ of 75. During the study *S* was attending a local high school and taking classes for low-level students.

REINFORCER SYSTEM

In previous studies (Staats, 1966; Staats et al., 1964a; 1964b), a reinforcer system was demonstrated that was capable of maintaining attention and work behaviors for long-term experimental studies. This system worked well with preschool children of ages 2 to 6 and with educable and trainable retardates of ages 8 to 11. The principle of the system was based upon token reinforcers. The tokens were presented contingent upon correct responses and could be exchanged for items the child could keep. In the previous studies toys of various values could be obtained when a sufficient number of tokens had been accrued in visible containers.

This system was adapted for use with the adolescent *S* of the present study. In the adaptation there were three types of token, distinguished by color. The tokens were of different value in terms of the items for which the tokens could be exchanged. A blue token was valued at a tenth of a cent. A white token was valued at a fifth of a cent. A red token was worth half a cent.

The child's acquisition of tokens was plotted so that visual evidence of the reinforcers was available. The tokens could be used to purchase a variety of items. These items, chosen by the subject, could range in value from pennies to whatever the subject wished to work for. Records were kept of the tokens earned by *S* and of the manner in which the tokens were used.

READING MATERIALS

The reading material used was taken from the Science Research Associates (SRA) reading-kit materials. The SRA kits consist of stories developed for and grouped into grade levels. Each story includes a series of questions which can be used to assess the reader's comprehension of the story. The reading training program was adapted from the SRA materials as follows:

Vocabulary Words. A running list was made of the new words that appeared in the series of stories. The list finally included each different word that appeared in the stories that were presented. From this list, the new vocabulary for each story was selected, and each word was typed on a separate 3 × 5 card.

Oral Reading Materials. Each paragraph in the SRA stories was typed on a 5 × 8 card. Each story could thus be presented to *S* paragraph by paragraph.

Silent-Reading and Comprehensive-Question Materials. Each SRA story, with its comprehensive questions, was typed on an 8½ × 13 sheet of white paper.

PROCEDURE

Vocabulary Presentation. The procedure for each story in the series commenced with the presentation of the new words introduced in that story. The words were presented individually on the cards, and *S* was asked to pronounce them. A correct response to a word-stimulus card was reinforced with a mid-value token. After a correct response to a word, the card was dropped from the group of cards yet to be presented. The *S* was instructed to indicate words that he did not know the meaning of, and this information was provided in such cases.

When an incorrect response to a word stimulus occurred, or when *S* gave no response, *E* gave the correct response. The *S* then repeated the word while looking at the stimulus word. However, the word card involved was returned to the group of cards still to be presented. A card was not dropped from the group until it was read correctly without prompting. After an error on a word stimulus, only a low-value token was given on the next trial when the word was read correctly without prompting. The vocabulary-presentation phase of the training was continued until each word was read correctly without prompting.

Oral Reading.   Upon completion of the vocabulary materials, each paragraph was individually presented to *S* in the order in which the paragraph occurred in the story. When correct reading responses were made to each word in the paragraph, a high-value token was given upon completion of the paragraph. When a paragraph contained errors, *S* was corrected, and he repeated the word correctly while looking at the word. The paragraph was put aside, and when the other paragraphs had been completed, the paragraph containing errors was again presented. The paragraph was repeated until it was done correctly in its entirety—at which time a midvalue token was presented. When all paragraphs in a story had been completed correctly, the next phase of the training was begun.

Silent Reading and Comprehensive Questions.   Following the oral reading *S* was given the sheet containing the story and questions. He was instructed to read the story silently and to answer the questions beneath the story. He was also instructed that it was important to read to understand the story so that he could answer the questions.

Reinforcement was given on a variable interval schedule for attentive behavior during the silent-reading phase. That is, as long as *S* appropriately scanned the material he was given a low-value reinforcer an average of every 15 seconds. The exact time for reinforcement was determined by a table of random numbers varying from 1 to 30 seconds. Whenever he did anything else than peruse the material, no reinforcement was given. The next interval was then timed from the moment *S* returned to the silent reading, with the stipulation that no reinforcement be given sooner than 5 seconds after *S* returned to the reading. If the interval was less than 5 seconds, a token was not given until the next interval had also occurred. Timing was done by a continuously running stopwatch. The *S* was also given an extra midvalue token at the end of the silently read story on those occasions where he read without moving his lips.

Upon completion of the story, *S* wrote his answers to the questions typed below the story and gave his answers to *E*. For each correct answer, *S* received a high-value token. For an answer with a spelling error, *S* was reinforced with a midvalue token when he had corrected the answer. For incorrect answers *S* had to reread the appropriate paragraph, correct his answer, and he then received a midvalue token.

Vocabulary Review.   Some of the vocabulary words presented to *S* in the first phase of training were words he already could read. Many others, however, were words that the procedure was set up to teach. The oral-reading-phase performance indicated the level of *S's* retention of the words he had learned—and also provided further training trials on the words not already learned. A further assessment of *S's* retention of the words that he did not know in the vocabulary training was made after each 20 stories of the SRA materials had been read. This test of individually presented words, for each story, was started about 3 days after completion of the 20 stories and constituted fairly long-term retention.

This test was also used as a review for *S*, and further training on the words was given. This was first done by reinforcing *S* with a low-value token for every word he read correctly. However, *S's* attention was not well maintained by this reinforcement, and the procedure was changed to provide a midvalue token for correctly read words. When *S* could not read a word, or missed one, he was prompted and had to correctly repeat the name of the word while looking at the word. This word card was then put aside and presented later, at which time *S* was reinforced with a low-value token if he read it correctly. If not, the procedure was repeated until a correct unprompted trial occurred.

Achievement Tests. Prior to the commencement of the training, *S* was tested to assess his reading performance, and during the period of experimental training he was given two additional reading-achievement tests. The first one given was the Developmental Reading Test. (At this time the *S's* vision and hearing were also tested and found to be normal.) After 45 training sessions another reading test was given *S*, this time the California Reading Test, Form BB, for grades 1, 2, 3, and L–4. Twenty-five sessions later, just before the termination of the study, *S* was given the California Reading Test, Form BB, for grades 4, 5, and 6. The *S's* performance on the three reading tests constituted one of the measures of his progress. The tests were given at the Arizona State University Reading Center.

Training Sessions. The training sessions would ordinarily last for 1 hour or less, although a few sessions were as short as 30 minutes or as long as 2 hours. Not all of this time was spent in reading, however. A good deal of time was spent in arranging the materials, recording *S's* performance, keeping count of the reinforcers, plotting the reinforcers accrued, and so on. The time spent actually reading was tabulated. During the 4½-month experimental period, 70 training sessions were conducted, with an average of about 35 minutes spent per session for a total of 40 hours of reading training.

Results and Conclusions

During the period of training *S* made many reading responses. Figure 1 shows the number of single-word reading responses *S* made as a function of the hours of time spent in training. An estimate of the number of single-word reading responses was obtained from tabulating each presentation of a word card, the number of words in the stories, and the reading-comprehension questions at the end of each story, as well as the words presented to *S* in the later single-word retention test. Actually, the number of words in the stories was an estimate obtained from the mean number of words in two out of each five stories. Thus, rather than giving the true absolute number of reading responses made, the figure gives an estimate. However, the most important aspect of the figure is to indicate the rate of this single-word reading-response measure as a function of

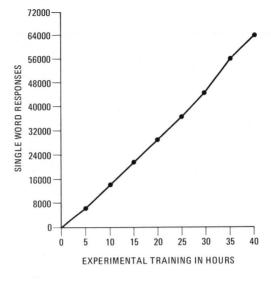

FIG. 1   *Number of single-word reading responses as a function of the time in experimental reading training*

time in experimental training. As can be seen, as the training progressed *S* covered the reading material at a slightly more rapid rate, as is shown by the slight positive acceleration in the curve. The importance of this result is to indicate that the child's behavior of attending to the task and making the appropriate reading responses did not diminish throughout the period of training. Thus, the reinforcement system employed was capable of maintaining the behavior for a long period of time. During this time the attentional and co-operative behaviors instigated resulted in many, many, learning trials—a *sine qua non* for the acquisition of achievement in any skill.

Before reading each story *S* was presented with individual cards for all the words included in that story which had not been presented in a previous story. When these words were presented, *S* would read a certain proportion correctly on first presentation, the other words being missed on the first presentation. The ones missed were considered to be new words for *S*, words that he had not previously learned. These words were separately tabulated. The cumulative number of these new words as a function of every 5 SRA stories read is shown by the top curve of Figure 2. (The data for the first 10 stories are not presented since they were not available for all three curves.) As this curve indicates, 761 new words were presented to *S* during the training.

Thus, *S* missed 761 words when they were first presented to him. However, he was given training trials on these words, and then he then read them again in the oral reading of the paragraph. The number of these words that he missed in this oral-reading phase is plotted in the bottom curve of Figure 2. This curve then indicates the number of errors made on the second reading test of the words that had been previously learned. Thus, only 176 words out of the 761 (about 23 per cent) were missed in the oral-reading phase—showing retention for 585 words. The results indicate that the criterion of one correct unprompted reading trial in the original vocabulary-learning phase produced considerable learning when the words were read in context.

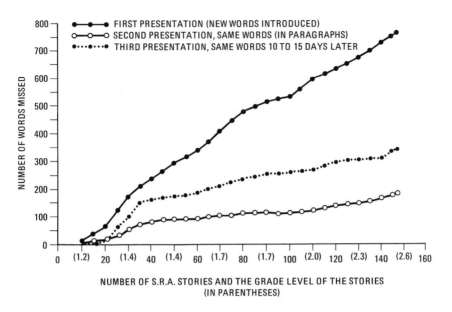

FIG. 2 *Number of words missed on first, second, and third presentations for the 150 SRA stories*

The middle curve in Figure 2 involves a measure of long-term retention of the words that had been learned. This measure was obtained by testing *S* on the words, presented singly, that had been learned in the preceding 20 stories. This test was given 10 to 15 days after the training occurred. The training thus included the previous single-word presentations of the words, as well as those same words read orally and silently. In addition, however, *S* had also learned a considerable number of other words by the time of this test. As the middle curve shows, when tested 10–15 days later, *S* read 430 of the 761 words correctly, or, conversely, 331 words (about 43 per cent) were missed. Thus, the procedures produced retention when the words were later presented out of context after a considerable intervening period.

The results appearing in Figure 2 indicate that the child covered a considerable amount of reading material, that he learned to read a number of new words when presented individually or in context, and that he retained a good proportion of what he had learned. The results also indicate that the child improved during the training in his retention. That is, his rate of getting new words in the first-presentation phase continues at a high rate throughout the study. (This supports the results shown in Figure 1 indicating that the child's behavior did not weaken during the training.) However, his "rate" of missing the new words on the second and third presentations decreased, that is, he retained more of the words he had learned. Thus, tabulation indicated that for the first 35 stories only about 33 per cent of the words learned were retained 10–15 days later, whereas *S's* subsequent retention increased to about 55 per cent. It should be noted that this improvement occurred even though the difficulty of the words (as shown in Figure 2 by the numbers in parentheses) became progressively greater during the training, moving from the 1.2-grade level of difficulty to the 2.6-grade level.

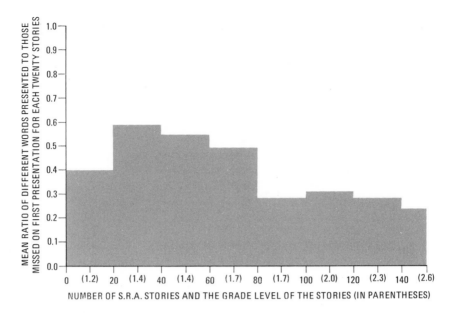

FIG. 3   *Ratio of words presented to those missed on first presentation for the 150 SRA stories*

These results receive support from the data presented in Figure 3. As already indicated, on the first presentation of the vocabulary of a story, some words were missed out of the total presented—and *S* was then presented with training on these words. Figure 3 shows the number of the words presented and missed in ratio to the total number presented, as this ratio is related to the number and difficulty of the stories presented. A smaller ratio indicates that *S* missed fewer of the total vocabulary words when they were presented for the first time. As can be seen in Figure 3, as the child read more stories in his training (even though they become more difficult), he missed fewer and fewer words that were presented to him. It should be stressed that he was thus improving in the extent to which he correctly responded to new words on *first* presentation. This improvement appeared to be correlated with other observations that indicated that *S* was also beginning to learn to sound out words as a function of the training. For example, he remarked when in the judge's office that he thought a sign said "information," because he could read the "in" and the "for" and the "mation." In addition, *S* reported a number of times that the training was helping him in school, that reading was getting easier for him in school, that he liked the reading training better as he went along, and so on. It would be expected (as will be supported by other data) that as the reading training improved his reading in school, the things he learned in school would also improve his performance in the reading training. It is this effect that may also be reflected in his increasing ability to read the new words presented to him.

In addition to this direct evidence of the child's progress in reading training, and the foregoing indirect evidence that the reading training was having general effects upon the child's behavior, the study was formulated to obtain other sources of information concerning the child's progress. One means of doing this was to give the child reading-achievement tests before beginning the reading

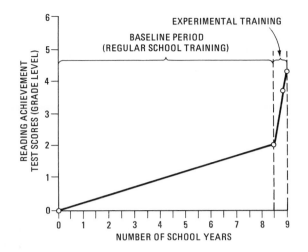

FIG. 4 *Reading-achievement test scores as a function of 8½ years of school training and 4½ months of experimental training*

training as well as during the training. The results of these tests are shown in Figure 4. The first point on the curve is a measurement obtained by use of the Developmental Reading Test giving a total score of reading achievement showing that *S* was performing at the grade-2 level. After 45 reading-training sessions, *S's* performance on the California Reading Test showed a gain to the 3.8-grade level. By the end of the training, after 25 more training sessions, *S* had advanced to the 4.3-grade level on the California Reading Test.

Another indication of the general effect of the reading training came from the child's performance in school, both in school achievement and deportment. The period of reading training concided with a school term. The boy received passing grades in all subjects: a *C* in physical education, a *D* in general shop, a *D* in English, and a *D* in mathematics. It should be emphasized that these grades represent the first courses that this child had ever passed, and thus his finest academic performance.

Furthermore, *S* began to behave better while in school. The boy had always been a behavior problem in school, and this continued into the period during which *S* received reading training. As Figure 5 shows, during the first month of the training *S* committed 10 misbehaviors that resulted in the receipt of demerits. The behaviors were as follows: disturbance in class (2 times), disobedience in class (five times), loitering (2 times), and tardiness. In the second month he was given demerits for scuffling on the school grounds and also for creating a disturbance. In the third month he was given demerits for cutting a math class and for profanity in class. As the figure shows, however, no misbehaviors occurred in the fourth month or in the half month after this until the conclusion of the school term.

The *S* requested that the tokens be exchanged for items that he wanted in sessions 12, 17, 25, 31, 35, 43, 49, 55, and in the last session he was given the value of the remaining tokens in cash. Items included were a pair of "beatle" shoes, hair pomade, a phonograph record, an ice cream sundae, a ticket to a school function, money for his brother who was going to reform school, and so on. Further information regarding the reinforcement system is given in

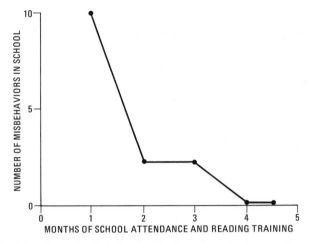

FIG. 5   *Number of official misbehaviors in school as a function of time in the experimental training*

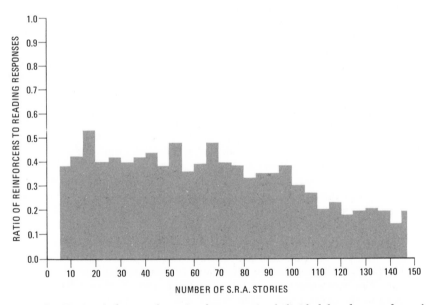

FIG. 6   *Ratio of the number of tokens received divided by the number of reading responses made as a function of the number of SRA stories read*

Figure 6. The vertical axis of the graph represents the ratio of the number of tokens obtained by *S* relative to the number of single-word reading responses which he emitted. Lesser ratios thus indicate more reading responses per reinforcer. This ratio was plotted as a function of the progress *S* made in the training program, as given by the number of SRA stories he had completed. As the training progressed *S* gradually made an increasingly greater number of reading responses per reinforcer. This effect was not accomplished by changing the rules by which the reinforcers were administered. The effect, which was planned in the training program, resulted from the fact that the SRA stories became longer as the grade level was raised. Since, for example, paragraph reading was reinforced by the paragraph, the longer the paragraph, the greater the number of reading responses that had to be emitted before reinforcement was obtained. At the end of training, thus, *S* was getting about half as much reinforcement per response as at the beginning of training. It should also be indicated that the stories were more difficult as the training progressed, so the effort involved in reading was increasing—although reinforcement for the reading was decreasing.

During the 4½ months of training, which involved 40 hours of reading training and the emission of an estimated 64,307 single-word reading responses, *S* received $20.31.

Discussion

In this section the various aspects of the reading-training procedures will first be discussed. Then the implications of the results and analysis will be outlined both for further studies of remedial reading training as well as for a learning conception of certain aspects of cultural deprivation and delinquency.

The method of reading training used in the present study was derived from previous study (Staats, 1964a; 1966; Staats et al., 1962) with pre-school children in which words were first presented singly, then in sentences, and finally in short stories. The present study indicated that SRA materials can be adapted for a similar type of presentation in conjunction with the type of reinforcer system previously developed (Staats et al., 1964a; 1964b). From the SRA materials it was possible to present single-word training trials and oral-reading training and to develop a silent-reading training procedure, all involving reinforcement.

When the training of reading, at least in part, is considered as operant discrimination learning, the learning task consists of having *S* emit the correct speech response while looking at the verbal stimulus—this process being followed by reinforcement. This basic procedure was elaborated in the present study to include two levels of reinforcement. An unprompted reading response on the first trial was reinforced more heavily than one that had been previously missed. This procedure appeared to produce learning that was retained very well when the child later read the words orally in a paragraph, with considerable retention also occurring when the child was tested on the individual words 10–15 days later.

It may seem incongruous at first to attempt to reinforce silent reading, since this behavior is not observable. However, it should be remembered that the subject actually has two types of behavior in the silent-reading act. He looks at the verbal stimuli—that is, attends—and he makes "reading" verbal responses to the verbal stimuli. While the reading responses cannot be monitored when they are covert, the attending behavior can be. Of course, there is a danger involved in reinforcing the behavior of just looking at something. Perhaps the child will do nothing else. If he is heavily reinforced for sitting and looking at a page, and the actual reading responses are effortful, he may not emit the reading responses. The present procedure was set up to eliminate this possibility by using a double contingency. The child was reinforced for simple attention, but the reinforcement was low in value. The opportunity for a greater amount of reinforcement came during the answering of the questions. Thus, although simple attention was reinforced lightly, attention and reading responses were reinforced much more heavily. In this way it was possible to use reinforcement in a procedure designed to maintain reading for "understanding," in addition to simple "word-naming." (These results could be generalized to other types of learning.) Furthermore, this procedure provided an opportunity to train the subject to read silently. Although he had a tendency to make vocal or lip responses while reading, it was possible to strengthen reading without these other responses through differentially reinforcing the correct silent reading.

Thus, it may be concluded that the reading program increased the child's reading vocabulary as shown by the various measures of retention used in the study, the tests of reading achievement, as well as the child's improved school performance and his verbal description of improved attitude toward and performance in reading in school. There were also suggestions that the child was acquiring a "unit-reading repertoire," that is, the general ability to sound out words through making the correct response to single letters and syllables. Thus, for example, the child made errors on fewer and fewer of the new words presented as the training progressed, even though the words were of greater difficulty. In addition, he retained a greater proportion of the words he learned as he went on. Further research of the present type must be conducted to test the possibilities for using a more phonic system of remedial reading training with the present type of subject.

A final point should be made concerning the training procedures used in the present study. The procedures are very specific and relatively simple. Thus, it was not necessary to have a person highly trained in education to administer the training. In the present case the trainer-experimenter was a probation officer. It might also be suggested that anyone with a high-school education and the ability to read could have administered the training. This has implications for the practical application of the present methods, since one of the questions that arises in this context concerns the economy of the procedures. Although the procedures as described involved a one-trainer-to-one-student ratio, as many remedial teaching procedures do, in the present case the simplicity of the procedures suggests the possibility that savings may be effected because the trainer need not be so highly trained. Thus, the procedures could be widely applied or adapted by various professionals, for example, social workers, prison officials, remedial teachers, tutors, and so on. In an even more economical application, helpers of professionals could be used to actually administer the procedures; for example, selected delinquents (or prisoners) could administer the procedures to other delinquents. Thus, the procedures could be utilized in various situations, such as settlement houses, homes for juvenile delinquents, prison training programs, parts of adult education, and so on. All that is needed is a suitable system of reinforcers to back up the tokens. These conclusions are supported by another study by A. W. Staats now being prepared for publication in which analogous methods developed for work with preschool children were applied by a graduate student who was untrained in teaching; the results suggest possibilities for economic innovations in education generally.

In the same context, it may be worth while pointing out that the results indicated that the child advanced as many years in reading achievement, as measured by the tests, during the experimental training as he had in his previous school history. A comparison of the relative costs—in the present case, about 70 hours of time of a person not necessarily trained in teaching and $20.31 for the reinforcers versus 8½ years of trained teachers' time, albeit in a group situation—suggests that the procedure introduced in the present study may not be uneconomical, even without improvements in the method. And, as will be further described, the child's failure in school may in many cases be considered as a contributor to the child's delinquency—which also carries a high cost to society. The present results, in suggesting that the training procedures may also effect general improvements in behavior, including misbehaviors in school, thus have further implications concerning the economy of the procedures.

The present study, among other things, tests the feasibility of using the type of reinforcing system, previously applied successfully to younger children, to the study of learning in older children—in this case a 14-year-old juvenile delinquent. The reinforcer system worked very well with the present *S*, maintaining his attention and working behaviors in good strength for a long period of time. And there was every reason to expect that the study could have been continued for a much longer period, probably as long as it would have taken to train the child to read normally.

It should be noted that although the amount of reinforcement given decreases during the training, as shown in Figure 6, the reading behavior is maintained in good strength throughout the study, as shown in Figures 1 and 2; thus, less and less reinforcement is needed to maintain the behavior even though the material increases in difficulty. As already described, this occurred because a progressively greater number of reading responses was necessary per reinforcer. This is analogous to gradually raising the ratio of responses to the reinforcers as considered in terms of ratio schedules of reinforcement. Staats has suggested that this type of gradual increase must occur to produce good work behaviors in humans (Staats and Staats, 1963).

This result in the present study is in part an answer to the question whether the use of extrinsic reinforcers in training will produce a child who is dependent upon these reinforcers. It is not possible to discuss this topic fully now. However, it may be said that the extrinsic reinforcement can be gradually decreased until, as was happening with the present child, reading becomes reinforcing itself, or other sources of reinforcement maintain the behavior.

A word should be said concerning the relevance of reinforcement variables in the treatment of nonlearning in culturally deprived children. Typically, as in the present case, such children do not, as a result of their home experiences, acquire "reinforcer systems" appropriate for maintaining learning in the traditional classroom. Rose (1956) has shown that, in the present terminology, lower-class children do not have experiences that make school achievement and learning itself positively reinforcing. This deficit, among others that affect the reinforcer system, can be expected to lead to poor school learning and other behavioral deficits. In such cases, there are increased opportunities for other poor social attitudes and undesirable behaviors to develop, as suggested in the introduction and exemplified in the present case.

The present study suggests that these conditions can be reversed through the application of learning principles and reinforcement variables to the task of repairing the child's behavioral-achievement deficit. There were indications that this treatment resulted in improvement in the reinforcement value of (attitudes toward) school for this child and consequently in the decrease in incidence of misbehaviors in school. The results thus suggest that under appropriate conditions the deficit in behavior stemming from the child's inadequate reinforcing system may be, at least in part, repaired by a properly administered, effective reinforcement system, resulting in a decrease in undesirable behaviors.

A comment should be made about the possibility of a Hawthorne effect, that is, that the social reinforcement by the E and possible extraexperimental reinforcement contributed to the results in the present study. It would be expected that such reinforcers could contribute to the overall effect—and in the present case the expenditure for the material reinforcers was small. In general, it can be expected that individuals will vary in the extent to which social reinforcers will be effective. For example, in preschool children social reinforcement is ineffective for long-term training (Staats, 1964c; Staats et al., 1962), and the same would be expected for many individuals with behavior problems. Ordinarily, it might be expected that the weaker other sources of reinforcement are for the individual; the stronger must be the reinforcer system of the treatment procedure.

In conclusion, the present study helps support and replicate the previous findings and extends the general procedures and principles to the study of an adolescent child who is culturally deprived and is also a juvenile delinquent. The various sources of data used suggest that the present procedures and principles are applicable to this population also. Based upon these suggestions, further studies will be conducted on culturally deprived children, delinquent and nondelinquent, as well as studies of other types of nonachieving or under-achieving readers.

It should also be indicated that the present study indicates the possibility for developing procedures for the objective application and test of laboratory-derived learning principles within the context of an actual problem of behavior. As previously indicated (Staats, 1964a), verification of learning principles in the context of a problem of human behavior constitutes one way to further the generality of the principles themselves. It may thus be suggested that such studies have two types of implication: they have implications for people interested in dealing with the problems of human behavior, as well as for those interested in the extension and verification of the basic science.

REFERENCES

Rosen, B. C. The achievement syndrome: A psychocultural dimension of social stratification. *Amer. sociol. Rev.,* 1956, 21, 203–211.

Staats, A. W. A case in and a strategy for the extension of learning principles to problems of human behavior. In Staats, A. W. (Ed.), *Human learning,* New York: Rinehart & Winston, 1964. (a)

Staats, A. W. Conditioned stimuli, conditioned reinforcers, and word meaning. In Staats, A. W. (Ed.), *Human learning.* New York: Holt, Rinehart & Winston, 1964. (b)

Staats, A. W. (Ed.) *Human learning.* New York: Holt, Rinehart & Winston, 1964. (c)

Staats, A. W. An integrated-functional learning approach to complex human behavior. In B. Kleinmuntz (Ed.), *Prob-* *lem solving: research, method and theory.* New York: Wiley, 1966.

Staats, A. W., Finley, J. R., Minke, K. A., and Wolf, M. Reinforcement variables in the control of unit reading responses. *J. exp. anal. Behav.,* 1964, 7, 139–149. (a)

Staats, A. W., Minke, K. A., Finley, J. R., Wolf, M., and Brooks, L. O. A reinforcer system and experimental procedure for the laboratory study of reading acquisition. *Child Develpm.,* 1964, 35, 209–231. (b)

Staats, A. W., and Staats, C. K. *Complex human behavior.* New York: Holt, Rinehart & Winston, 1963.

Staats, A. W., Staats, C. K., Schutz, R. E., and Wolf, M. The conditioning of textual responses utilizing "extrinsic" reinforcers. *J. exp. anal. Behav.* 1962, 5, 33–40.

18   Test of the Doman-Delacato Rationale with Retarded Readers

MELVYN P. ROBBINS

An empirical test of the central concept and treatment efficacy of the Doman-Delacato rationale was implemented by investigating the influence of a program based on the theory of neurological organization on the reading development of retarded readers. The study employed a traditional control group and a nonspecific program, thought to stimulate the placebo effect. The results failed to confirm the validity of the rationale —suggesting that verifiable, empirical evidence from carefully controlled studies is needed if the rationale is to be taken seriously by the scientific community.

The study was conducted to provide an empirical test of the central concept and treatment efficacy of the Doman-Delacato rationale. This was implemented by investigating the influence of a program based on the theory of neurological organization and a nonspecific program, thought to stimulate the placebo effect, on the reading development of retarded readers. The research being reported was a continuation of an earlier study of normal second graders which failed to confirm the usefulness of the rationale (1).

The Doman-Delacato rationale and treatment approach, developed at the Institutes for the Achievement of Human Potential (formerly the Rehabilitation Center) at Philadelphia, has seven basic tenets:

1. "The basic difference between the nervous system of man and that of slightly lower forms of mammals lies not in the number of cells, but in the differentiation and organization of those cells. Thus, we have for man the concept of neurological organization in addition to neurological development" (2—p. 5).

2. Man's ontogenic development proceeds via four distinct phases—medulla and spinal cord, pons, midbrain, and cortex—and it culminates in cerebral hemispheric dominance. According to the rationale, the phases of man's development recapitulated phylogenic development of the species via fish, amphibian, reptile, and primate (3).

3. Neurological organization ". . . provides the organism with all the capabilities necessary to relate it successfully to its environment" (4) and, as a measure of ontogenic progress, it is an indicator of man's development, both motor (ie, mobility, language, and manual competence) and sensory (ie, stereopsis, stereophonetics, and stereognosis) (3).

From *The Journal of the American Medical Association*, Vol. 202, No. 5 (October 30, 1967), pp. 389–393. Reprinted with permission.

   The Roman Catholic Archdiocese of Chicago gave permission to conduct the study. Financial support and a two-month residency with Glenn J. Doman and Carl C. Delacato at Philadelphia were supplied by the Institutes for the Achievement of Human Potential and the Given Foundation, New York. This study was supported in part by the Midwest Administration Center, University of Chicago, and by the Cooperative Research Program of the Office of Education. U.S. Department of Health, Education, and Welfare, project S-349, and the Public Health Service research grant MH 07346 from the National Institute of Mental Health.

   The University of Illinois' IBM 7094 was made available in part by a grant from the National Science Foundation. The program, Balanova V, was written by Paul Herzberg and was run under the statistical service unit research program SSUPAC. Programming and statistical advice were supplied by Marian Frobish, Gene Glass, and Henry I. Lippert.

4. Neurological organization is measured along a continuum beginning with neurologically disorganized individuals who suffer from frank brain abnormality, continuing through average or above-average children with reading problems associated with poor neurological organization, and culminating in physically and intellectually superior individuals with complete neurological organization (4).

5. Walking, writing, auditory understanding of language, tactile competence, (4) as well as "Speech and reading are the final *human* result of neurological organization and hence are clinical indices of the nature and the quality of neurological organization of an individual" (3—p. 7).

6. Neurological organization can be evaluated by existing procedures advocated by the Institutes for the Achievement of Human Potential (2–5).

7. Simple, nonsurgical exercises, actively or passively imposed on the nervous system, lead to improved sensory-motor functioning through the enhancement of neurological organization (3–4).

This report presents the results of a study testing the fifth, sixth, and seventh tenets of the Doman-Delacato rationale. The paper is divided into five sections: Background; Procedures; Hypotheses, Test, and Findings; Conclusions; and Implications.

Background

In two books (3, 5) purported to be ". . . a totally new approach to reading and language problems" (5), Delacato introduced the concept of neurological organization. He claimed success in treating diverse problems associated with deficiencies in neurological organization caused by either frank brain injury or improper environmental opportunities, including the following: inadequate mobility, poor handwriting, hyperactivity, delayed speech, articulation disorders, stuttering, aphasia, spelling difficulties, reading problems, and low college entrance examination scores. His primary evidence consisted of brief case presentations.

Publishing in *The Journal,* September 1960, the Philadelphia group reported "significant improvement" in mobility for 76 severely brain-injured children when they compared their current treatment approach to "classical procedures" (6). The study failed, however, (a) to define the "classical procedures," (b) to utilize a control group, (c) to present or cite references for evidence of the validity, reliability, and objectivity of the mobility scale utilized in the study, and (d) to analyze the data statistically.

While the mass media have bestowed much favorable publicity on the work of the Institutes (*Life* 55:31–36 [Aug. 23] 1963; *Good Housekeeping* 155:324 [Sept.] 1962; *Reader's Digest* 43:135–140 [Oct.] 1964 and 45:259–300 [Nov.] 1966), writers addressing the professions of medicine, reading, psychology, and education have not shared this enthusiasm (7–10).

Procedures

The theoretical and practical implications of the Doman-Delacato rationale with retarded readers were tested to answer the following questions: (a) Are purported indicators of neurological organization—creeping and laterality—

directly related to reading ability (tenets 5 and 6)? (b) Will active participation in a program based on the rationale improve the subjects' reading development (tenet 7)?

SUBJECTS

Approximately 250 students from grades three through nine of several nearby schools attended a summer reading program conducted by the Chicago Roman Catholic Archdiocese. Two sessions were taught each morning. The first session met from 9 to 10:15 A.M.; the second from 10:45 A.M. to 12 noon. Twelve regular archdiocesan teachers, who had received help in working with retarded readers, taught two sessions a day. Class size ranged from 6 to 13 pupils. The class assignments were made on the basis of reading level and age. The research study did not interfere with nor affect the assignment of students or teachers to various classes.

Eight of the 12 classes from each session were chosen at random. Within each class, children were randomly assigned to one of the three groups: control, experimental, or nonspecific (placebo). Assignment of students from each class to the three groups alleviated differential effect of a teacher on reading development of her own students, thus assuring equivalent development among all three groups, subject to sampling error. Allowance was also made for unusual occurrences in any class, as students in each group would be equally affected. One hundred and forty-nine children participated in the study. (Background information is reported in Table I.)

TABLE I *Background Information on Study Groups**

Item	Total Sample	Experimental Group	Non-specific Group	Control Group	F Ratio	Probability F Is Chance†
Mean age in months (July 1, 1965)	136.2	134.9	136.5	137.4	0.17	$P>0.75$
Mean school grade (1965–1966 school year)	6.1	5.9	6.2	6.1	0.37	$P>0.50$
Mean intelligence quotient (from school records)	97.6	97.6	98.5	96.5	0.54	$P>0.50$
Mean reading grade score (spring, 1965)	4.4	4.4	4.5	4.3	0.27	$P>0.75$
Number of subjects	149	51	51	47		
Sex						
Male	94	34	34	26		
Female	55	17	17	21		

* The mean reading deficit for the total sample ranged from 1.7 grade units, when mean schooling completed was compared with mean reading grade score, to 2 grade units, when mean age was compared with mean reading grade score. The probabilities for each F-ratio were determined from a standard statistical text (11).
† None of the F ratios were statistically significant at the 5% level. (A one-way analysis of variance with 2 and 146 degrees of freedom was performed.)

BASIC DESIGN

The first group, serving as a traditional control group, carried out its normal curriculum. The second group, designated as the experimental group, was subjected to a program described by Delacato in addition to its regular curriculum. As a control for the influence of the Hawthorne or placebo effect, a third group, identified as the nonspecific group, was subjected to a general program of activities, not known to be correlated with reading achievement, in addition to its normal curriculum.

The experimental and nonspecific programs were conducted during June and July, 1965. The children participated in the program on a daily basis.

EXPERIMENTAL GROUP: HOME PROGRAM

Before the experiment was begun, parents were requested by letters accompanied by appropriate instructions and illustrations to encourage their child's daily participation in the following activities: (a) two 15-minute periods of cross-pattern creeping; (b) two 15-minute periods of cross-pattern walking; (c) elimination of all musical activities; (d) utilization of the Delacato sleep position at night; and (e) lateralization activities wherever appropriate. The parents were also asked to complete a daily record chart indicating whether the program was being carried out at home (12).

EXPERIMENTAL GROUP: SCHOOL ACTIVITIES

During the half-hour period between teaching sessions (10:15 to 10:45 A.M.), the program for the experimental group consisted of five minutes devoted to the appropriate sleep position, 15 minutes of cross-pattern creeping, and ten minutes of cross-pattern walking. During the regular class period, the children used the Delacato color filtration procedures, purportedly useful in the lateralization of an individual, for remedial reading and writing activities (12).

NONSPECIFIC GROUP: HOME PROGRAM

Preexperiment letters were also sent to the parents of children in the nonspecific group. In the placebo-type program, to control for the experimental effect, parents were requested to encourage their child's daily participation in the following activities: (a) two 15-minute periods of active sports; (b) one 15-minute period of quiet games; (c) a general increase in all musical activities; and (d) the utilization of the nonspecific sleep position at night. A daily record chart was also included, on which the parents were to indicate which activities were carried out (12).

NONSPECIFIC GROUP: SCHOOL ACTIVITIES

During the half-hour period between classes, the nonspecific group met in a separate room for the experimental group and spent five minutes in the nonspecific sleep position and 25 minutes in miscellaneous musical activities, including singing, games, and dances. During their regular remedial reading class, the students engaged in the nonspecific color filtration program — a placebo-type activity— for all reading and writing exercises.

IMPLEMENTATION

The color filtration and nonspecific color filtration activities were carried out by teachers who had been instructed at a staff meeting. The principal investigator supplied equipment necessary for the visual activities (special folders, glasses, pencils, colored cellophane sheets). He also visited each class to insure that each teacher understood her own special program and the children understood their specific activities. With the exception of the visual tasks, the normal archdiocesan remedial reading program was conducted (12).

Each of the preceding terms has been defined elsewhere (12). The following definitions are examples of how the nonspecific program was patterned after the experimental program.

In color filtration activities, a red-colored, translucent, plastic lens was placed over the nondominant eye so that the visual image could be seen only by the dominant eye (3). During writing activities, a red pencil was used. The red lens over the nondominant eye filtered out the image so only the dominant eye could detect what was being written. During reading, green cellophane was placed over the book. This combination caused the image to be filtered out by the red lens, and hence only the dominant eye was able to detect the printed material.

In an activity designed to parallel the Delacato color filtration activity, the children in the non-specific group were required to wear glasses covered with green cellophane. The green lenses did not have a filtration effect for the non-dominant eye during reading or writing.

INSTRUMENTATION

Subjects in each of the three groups were administered tests measuring their initial level of creeping and laterality and their concluding reading ability.

Creeping was measured on a three-point scale (Table II). The examiner requested the child to creep across the room. If the child indicated a good coordinated cross-pattern style, he was rated good; if his creeping was slightly uncoordinated but still retained a cross-pattern style, it was rated fair; all other forms of creeping were rated poor. Creeping was measured by two professional

TABLE II   *Pretest Mean Reading Grade Scores Analyzed by Creeping and School Grade Level*

	Creeping							
Grade	**Good**		**Fair**		**Poor**		**Total**	
	Mean Reading Score	No of Students	Mean Reading Score	No of Students	Mean Reading Score	No of Students	Mean Reading Score	No of Students
4	2.7	9	2.7	12	2.4	2	2.6	23
5	3.9	10	3.6	17	3.3	5	3.6	32
6	4.4	16	4.3	17	4.4	4	4.4	37
7	4.9	9	4.9	11	4.6	1	4.9	21
8	5.4	5	5.7	8	5.9	5	5.6	18
9	7.4	6	6.8	6	8.1	2	7.3	14
Total	4.8	55	4.7	71	4.8	19		

Analysis of Variance*

Source	Degrees of Freedom	Mean Square	F Ratio	Probability F Is Chance
Grade	5	3877.7	50.7	$P<0.001$
Creeping	2	15.4	0.2	$P>0.75$†
Interaction	10	54.8	0.72	$P>0.50$†
Error Term	127	76.5		

* The design is not balanced, and the analysis of variance is only approximate. The approximate method of unweighted means has been used (13, 14).
† Not statistically significant at 5% level.

reading consultants of the archdiocese. The two consultants had previous experience in measuring creeping and had spent time at the Philadelphia Institutes for the Achievement of Human Potential where Delacato is a director.

The laterality score represented a summary of a series of tests measuring eyedness, handedness, and footedness (Table III). A child indicating a consistent preference to either the left or right side was considered lateralized. A child not indicating this type of consistent preference was considered nonlateralized.

TABLE III   *Pretest Mean Reading Grade Scores Analyzed by Laterality and School Grade Level*

Grade	Lateralized		Nonlateralized		Total	
	Mean Reading Score	No. of Students	Mean Reading Score	No. of Students	Mean Reading Score	No. of Students
3	2.1	2	1.8	2	1.9	4
4	2.3	4	2.7	19	2.6	23
5	3.3	8	3.7	24	3.6	32
6	4.6	7	4.3	30	4.4	37
7	4.9	5	4.9	16	4.9	21
8	5.2	2	5.7	16	5.6	18
9	7.3	5	7.2	9	7.3	14
Total	4.4	33	4.4	116		

Analysis of Variance*

Source	Degrees of Freedom	Mean Square	F Ratio	Probability F Is Chance
Grade	6	3333.3	45	$P<0.001$
Laterality	1	15.6	0.21	$P>0.50$†
Interaction	6	29.4	0.4	$P>0.50$†
Error Term	135	74		

* The design is not balanced, and the analysis of variance is only approximate. The approximate method of unweighted means has been used (13, 14).
† Not statistically significant at 5% level.

Eye preference was determined by five individual tests. Each of the tests was individually scored to indicate whether the child preferred his left eye, right eye, or seemed to oscillate between both eyes.

The first test involved the child looking through a telescope. The second involved an 8½- by 11-inch cardboard with a hole in the center. The child was instructed to hold the card at arms length and to sight a distant object. The third test involved looking through a 3-inch tube which simulated a microscope. The kaleidoscope was used for the fourth measure of eyedness. The telebinocular, administered by a trained reading consultant, provided the fifth test.

The hand tests involved pantomiming four activities: brushing one's teeth, using scissors, throwing a ball, and eating. In addition, a fifth test was utilized wherein the child was asked to write his name. These tests were scored for left-handedness, right-handedness, or mixed if the child chose to use both hands in solving the task.

Foot preference was determined by asking the child to kick a bean bag on two occasions. He was then asked to kick the bag with his nonpreferred foot. Both his choice and the quality of his kicking were taken into consideration in rating foot preference as either left, right, or mixed.

The appropriate level of the Stanford Achievement Test (15) was employed to measure reading (Table IV).

TABLE IV   *Post-test Mean Reading Grade Scores Analyzed by Treatment Group and School Grade Level*

Grade	Experimental Group		Nonspecific Group		Control Group		Total	
	Mean Reading Score	No. of Students	Mean Reading Score	No. of Students	Mean Reading Score	No. of Students	Mean Reading Score	No. of Students
4	2.8	7	2.5	8	2.6	8	2.7	23
5	3.5	14	3.7	12	3.5	6	3.6	32
6	4.3	12	4.2	11	4.2	14	4.3	37
7	5.4	7	5.1	7	5.3	7	5.3	21
8	6.2	4	6.1	8	5.6	6	6.0	18
9	7.0	5	6.3	5	6.2	4	6.5	14
Total	4.9	49	4.7	51	4.6	45		

Analysis of Variance*

Source	Degrees of Freedom	Mean Square	F Ratio	Probability F Is Chance
Grade	5	4610.8	36.3	$P<0.001$
Treatment Group	2	103.1	0.81	$P>0.25$†
Interaction	10	31.6	0.25	$P>0.99$†
Error Term	127	127		

* The design is not balanced, and the analysis of variance is only approximate. The approximate method of unweighted means has been used (13, 14).
† Not statistically significant at 5% level.

Hypotheses, Tests, and Findings

The first two null hypotheses based on preexperimental, normative data, compared reading achievement with two purported indicators of neurological organization—creeping and laterality.

HYPOTHESIS 1

Reading is not related to creeping: A one-way analysis of variance failed to disclose a statistically significant difference in mean reading scores among good, fair, and poor creepers. The respective mean reading scores were 4.3, 4.3, and 4.7 grade units. There were 2 and 146 degrees of freedom. The F ratio was 0.51. The probability of this F ratio being due to chance exceeds 0.50. A second two-way analysis of variance was performed to analyze the mean reading scores of the children by the interaction of the quality of creeping and grade level (Table II). Because grade 3 contained empty cells, it was eliminated from the analysis. The null hypothesis could not be rejected.

HYPOTHESIS 2

Reading is not related to laterality: A one-way analysis of variance comparing the mean reading scores of lateralized and nonlateralized children was performed. The rounded mean reading scores of both groups were 4.4 grade units. There were 1 and 148 degrees of freedom. The F ratio was 0.01. The probability of this F ratio occurring by chance is in excess of 0.99. A two-way analysis of variance comparing the mean reading scores through the interaction between laterality and grade level was also performed (Table III). The null hypothesis could not be rejected.

The final null hypothesis, relevant to data resulting from the experimental aspect of the study, compared the mean reading improvement of the experimental, control, and nonspecific groups associated with active participation in the Doman-Delacato program.

HYPOTHESIS 3

Reading improvement is not related to exposure to the experimental or nonspecific program: A one-way analysis of variance was performed to test statistical differences among post-test reading scores for the experimental, non-specific, and control groups. The respective mean scores were 4.4, 4.5, and 4.3 grade units. There were 2 and 146 degrees of freedom. The F ratio was 0.14. The probability of this F ratio occurring by chance exceeds 0.75. A two-way analysis of variance was also performed to test differences in the mean reading scores for the interaction between the treatment group and grade level (Table IV). The null hypothesis could not be rejected.

Conclusions

None of the three null hypotheses could be rejected on the basis of data gathered in the study. These findings led to the following conclusions applicable to the retarded readers who participated in this investigation:

1. The data did not support the postulated relationship between neurological organization (as measured by creeping and laterality) and reading achievement (hypotheses 1 and 2).
2. The data from the study did not support the contention that the addition of the Delacato program to the ongoing curriculum of the retarded readers in any way enhanced their reading development (hypothesis 3) when compared to similar children not exposed to the experimental program.

Implications

First, three null hypotheses were chosen to test the practical aspects and basic assumptions of the theory of neurological organization. The fact that the theory was not supported by any of the findings casts doubt upon its validity.

Second, Delacato has indicated that neurological organization can be measured by behavioral tasks (in this study creeping and laterality were used) and that reading can also be used as a clinical index of the quality of neurological organization (3). Since the central concept of the theory—the relationship between neurological organization and reading—has not been supported by the findings (hypotheses 1 and 2), the entire theory is suspect.

Third, the lack of independent research supporting the Doman-Delacato rationale and the failure of this study to support the theory suggests that verifiable, empirical evidence from controlled studies, with the use of generally accepted research methods, is needed if advocates of the theory wish to gain acceptance and recognition for the theory from the scientific community.

REFERENCES

1. Robbins, M. P.: A Study of the Validity of Delacato's Theory of Neurological Organization, *Exceptional Children* 32: 517–523 (April) 1966.

2. Delacato, C. H.: *Neurological Organization and Reading,* Springfield, Ill.: Charles C Thomas, Publisher, 1966.

3. Delacato, C. H.: *The Diagnosis and Treatment of Speech and Reading Problems,* Springfield, Ill.: Charles C Thomas, Publisher, 1963.

4. LeWinn, E. B., et al: "Neurological Organization: the Basis for Learning," in Hellmuth, J. (ed.) *Learning Disorders,* Seattle: Special Child Publications, 1966, Vol. 2, pp. 51–93.

5. Delacato, C. H.: *The Treatment and Prevention of Reading Problems,* Springfield, Ill.: Charles C Thomas, Publisher, 1959.

6. Doman, R. J., et al: "Children with Severe Brain Injuries: Neurological Organization in Terms of Mobility," *JAMA* 174: 257–262 (Sept. 17) 1960.

7. Brown, J. R.: "The Diagnosis and Treatment of Reading Problems" by C. H. Delacato, *Neurology* 14: 599–600 (June) 1964.

8. Hudspeth, J. W.: "The Neurobehavioral Implausibility of the Delacato Theory," in Douglass, M. P. (ed.): *Claremont Reading Conference Yearbook,* Claremont, Calif.: Claremont Reading Conference, 1964, Vol. 28, pp. 126–131.

9. Wepman, J. M.: "The Diagnosis and Treatment of Speech and Reading Problems" by C. H. Delacato, *Contemporary Psychology* 9: 351–352 (Sept.) 1964.

10. Cole, E. M.: "The Diagnosis and Treatment of Speech and Reading Problems" by C. H. Delacato, *Harvard Educational Rev.* 34: 351–354 (spring) 1964.

11. Dixon, W. J., and Massey, F. J., Jr.: *Introduction to Statistical Analysis.* New York: McGraw-Hill Book Co., Inc., 1957, p. 402.

12. Robbins, M. P.: *Influence of Special Programs on the Development of Mental Age and Reading: Cooperative Research Project No. S–349,* Washington, D. C.: Cooperative Research Program of the Office of Education, U.S. Department of Health, Education, and Welfare, 1965.

13. Winer, B. J.: *Statistical Principles in Experimental Design,* New York: McGraw-Hill Book Co., Inc., 1962, pp. 224–227.

14. Scheffe, H. A.: *The Analysis of Variance,* New York: John Wiley & Sons, Inc., 1959, pp. 362–363.

15. Kelly, T. L., et al: *Stanford Achievement Test* (Form X, Primary I, Primary II, Intermediate I, Intermediate II, and Advanced), New York: Harcourt, Brace & World, 1963.

19   A Hierarchy of Educational Tasks for Children with Learning Disorders

FRANK M. HEWETT

Abstract: *This article presents the concept of a hierarchy of educational task levels for children with learning disorders. An attempt is made to formulate a set of working hypotheses which would enable educators to outline realistic goals for this type of child. The theoretical framework is an outgrowth of experiences with hospitalized, emotionally handicapped children at the Neuropsychiatric Institute School, University of California, Los Angeles.*

The child who fails to learn in school is communicating vital information about himself. He may be revealing his general intellectual limitations or some specific sensory or perceptual-motor handicap. He may be apprising us of the inadequacy of his previous schooling due to poor teaching methods or sporadic attendance. He also may be communicating an inability to cope with social and emotional stress which is manifest through poor concentration, comprehension, and recall in the classroom.

Seldom is such a child's message clearly understood, and seldom is the explanation for his learning problem a simple and specific one. Constitutional, environmental, and psychological factors usually overlap, making it difficult for the educator to properly program the child according to his most basic needs.

In the search for remedial and educational guidelines, teachers have looked to the clinical psychologist, the educational psychologist, and the child psychiatrist for assistance. While these child specialists offer relevant generalizations regarding learning and behavior, their contributions are not always practical in the classroom setting. The battle strategies laid down by the military advisors in the tactical planning room may need alteration and clarification before they are useful to the field general on the front lines.

It is this gap between theory and practice that the concept of a hierarchy of educational tasks for children with learning disorders attempts to narrow. The basic assumption underlying the hierarchy holds that an effective educational program for children with learning disorders depends on the establishment of a point of meaningful contact between the teacher and the child. Such a point of contact is only possible when the child is experiencing gratification in the learning situation and the teacher is in control.

There is a wide range of types of gratification which the child may experience while learning (from a candy reward for each correct response to recognition for academic efforts by a place on the honor roll), and there are many levels of teacher control (from permissiveness in structuring to careful setting of behavioral limits and academic expectations). It is establishing this point of contact while providing appropriate student gratification and teacher control that is a crucial consideration for the teacher of children with learning problems. The normal achiever may be motivated by grades, competition with other students, and a variety of other social and intellectual rewards, but the nonachiever may be deterred from entering into the learning situation by these same factors. While

From *Exceptional Children*, Vol. 31 (December, 1964), pp. 207–214. Reprinted with permission.

The author acknowledges the assistance of James Q. Simmons, M.D., Chief, Children's Service, the Neuropsychiatric Institute, in formulating the educational tasks discussed in this paper.

normal classroom procedures may dictate that all students be held for definite academic and behavior standards, the child with a learning problem may have to be viewed within a broader educational frame of reference.

The theoretical framework to be presented in this paper has grown out of three years experience teaching hospitalized emotionally handicapped children and adolescents with learning problems at the Neuropsychiatric Institute School (NPI) at the University of California, Los Angeles. It is the result of a felt need on the part of the staff teachers for a set of working hypotheses with which to formulate realistic goals for their complex and highly variable students.

Meaningful contact and varying degrees of student gratification and teacher control are possible on seven educational task levels. These will be discussed following a brief historical review of the concept of a hierarchy of human development and behavior.

Review of Hierarchies

Hierarchies of developmental tasks and human motives are basic to the writings of Freud (Munroe, 1955), Erickson, Havighurst, and Maslow.

Freud's psychosexual stages of development form such a hierarchy and presuppose mastery and gratification at each earlier level before an individual is free to devote his energies to succeeding stages. Thus, an individual who experiences a faulty oral stage of development may have to divert a disproportionate amount of his energies toward oral gratification during later years. In Freud's own metaphor, an army general is less likely to win a war if he must leave a number of his troops to deal with unfinished battles along the way.

Erickson (1950) and Havighurst (1952) have described developmental tasks of early and middle childhood, adolescence, and adult life. Learning a sense of trust in others, learning social and physical realities, building a wholesome attitude toward one's self, and developing a clear sense of identity are a few of the tasks to be mastered for successful ascension up the ladder of life.

Maslow (1954) has suggested that human motives arrange themselves in a hierarchy from the most basic biological needs for self-actualization. Beginning with body needs such as hunger and thirst and moving step by step through safety needs for self-preservation, love needs for approval of others, esteem needs for self-enhancement, and finally, at the top of the scale, self-actualization needs for realization of one's utmost potential, Maslow has constructed a hierarchy within which he attempts to explain all human motivation. Maslow postulates that successful achievement and satisfaction of higher level needs is dependent upon reasonable fulfillment of needs at the lower levels.

The hierarchy of educational tasks which makes up the subject matter of this paper represents an attempt to organize and formulate psychological principles of development into practical terms for the educator. Each level is concerned with the reciprocal tasks of student and teacher in the formation of a working educational relationship. In an ascending order, the hierarchy of educational tasks consists of primary, acceptance, order, exploratory, relationship, mastery, and achievement task levels.

Primary Task Level

The most primitive level on which teacher and child may interact is the primary task level. Here, the teacher's task is to provide maximum gratification and to establish contact on the student's own terms, thus laying the groundwork for future interactions in which more control and direction may be exercised. This level is generally only applicable in cases of severe learning disability where the student is inaccessible to social controls or totally resistant to learning. The child's task is minimal at the primary level. The teacher may appeal to such basic needs as a desire for candy or money rather than to more complex social needs. It is at this level that operant conditioning work with severely regressed schizophrenics and autistic children is undertaken. Lindsley (1956), Ferster (1961), Isaacs (1960), and Weiland (1961) have demonstrated that such inaccessible individuals may take note of a teacher or therapist who has a piece of candy, gum or the like, pay attention and begin to learn or re-learn appropriate behaviors in order to obtain the desired reward.

Related work starting at the primary level has been done by Slack, (in a lecture to NPI Staff, 1963), who has shown how a desire for money may be an effective motivator for getting a school dropout with serious motivation and learning problems to learn to read. Slack approached such individuals and asked them to help him evaluate a teaching-machine reading program. For their efforts these boys were given a penny for each frame of the reading program. In the course of acquiring $30 and exposure to a basic reading vocabulary, many of these boys actually learned to read. More important, many manifested a new interest in school and learning and continued their formal education. Similar methods have proven successful with inmates in state prisons.

In the NPI school, a two year educational program was recently completed with a twelve year old autistic boy who had never developed speech (Hewett, 1964). The goal of the program was to teach this withdrawn and unsocialized boy to read and write and thus enable him to communicate more appropriately with the environment.

Candy gumdrops established the first point of contact between teacher and student. The boy paid attention and engaged in simple reading activities such as pictureword matching in order to obtain an immediate candy reward. Once this contact was established, the boy was given higher level tasks. This is an important characteristic of the hierarchy; while the teacher may initiate contact with the child on the lowest appropriate level, the eventual goal is to engage him in higher level tasks.

Acceptance Task Level

The second task level consists of acceptance tasks for both teacher and child. At this level, the teacher communicates complete acceptance of the child and attempts to establish the beginning of a relationship with him, still primarily on the child's terms. While the child may have perceived the teacher as an undifferentiated means to immediate gratification at the primary level, he now has the task of relating to the teacher as a social object. The child acknowledges the teacher's presence and responds more attentively to verbal interaction. This is only the very early stage of a genuine interpersonal relationship between teacher and child which will be the focus of a later level. At the acceptance level the teacher sets few behavioral limits and usually works on a one-to-one basis with the child. The student competes only with his own record and no grades are given. In addition, academic demands are minimal and the teacher's main goal is to make the child secure and successful in the learning situation. Toward this end a variety of activities such as playing games and taking walks may be utilized.

The child who refuses to get out of his parents' car and come into the classroom may be joined in the back seat by the teacher who initiates contact through reassurance and gradual building of an accepting relationship. At the NPI school, teachers often go on the wards and into the bedrooms of frightened withdrawn children who refuse to get out of bed and come to school. The teacher may sit on the bed next to the child and use a small projector to show him colored slides on the ceiling, or read him stories, or play simple games with him. The teacher who hopes to be successful with children who have serious learning problems and who are threatened by the prospect of further failure should be prepared to settle for the minimal but significant tasks on the acceptance level.

Order Task Level

Once the child feels accepted and is secure enough to form a limited relationship with the teacher, he is ready to be held for order tasks on the next level of the hierarchy. The teacher's task at this level is to increase her control and gradually impose structure, routine, and definite limits in the learning situation. Although academic deficiencies are still completely accepted, the student is now held for more appropriate behavior. He no longer works on his own terms and must accept certain conditions for learning. The work of Cruickshank (1961), Haring and Phillips (1962) suggests that well structured classroom environments facilitate learning among hyperactive and distractible students with learning problems. The concept of order and routine is basic to an effective learning situation for all children but particularly important for children with learning disorders whose erratic patterns of functioning in the classroom have contributed to their failure to learn. At the order level the teacher carefully judges the child's capacity for choice, presents him with small realistically attainable units of work and removes extraneous stimuli which are distracting in an effort to promote maximum gratification and success in the classroom.

At the NPI school, a resistant, nonconforming child who has failed to learn is often brought into the classroom for periods of ten to fifteen minutes a day. During this short period, the child's task is to function at the order level as a "student"—sit at a desk, follow simple directions and routines, and control his behavior. Longer periods are introduced as the student is able to tolerate them. During this time the child may be given certain order tasks to do such as sorting objects on the basis of size and color, puzzle making, or map coloring and labeling.

Recently a seventeen year old boy with a severe physical disability who had never learned to read was provided with an elaborate experiential reading program based solely on his great interest in rockets. The teacher spared no amount of effort in providing the boy with stimulating and interesting material. The boy, however, came to school when he pleased, would only work as long as he wished, and in essence set his own limits in the learning situation. Despite the ingenuity and total dedication of the teacher, the reading program was a complete failure. It was only after a staff conference during which the lack of limits and teacher control in the program were examined that a change was made. The boy was later told that an instructional program in reading was available for him but only at certain specific times. If he wanted to learn to read, he had to participate exactly as the teacher directed; otherwise, he did not have to come to school. The results were surprising. The boy showed up in class regularly and began to learn to read. He worked diligently and functioned on the teacher's terms. While for some students, an experiential or exploratory program, such as the one first tried with this boy, would be successful, it was necessary in this case to engage the student in tasks at the order level before learning could take place. Exploratory educational activities, to be discussed at the next level, are more likely to be successful once the student is functioning on the order-task level.

The task of maintaining order may be overlearned by the rigid and obsessive-compulsive child with a learning problem. It will be the teacher's task to direct such a child's energies from, rather than toward, more order and routine. This is another characteristic within all levels of the hierarchy. It is the teacher's task to help students who display extreme behavior to achieve a healthier balance.

Exploratory Task Level

Exploratory tasks are found on the next level of the hierarchy. Once the teacher and child have formed a beginning working relationship, they may explore the environment together. Now it is the teacher's task to introduce learning by offering the child a rich variety of multisensory experiences. The child's task is to reach out and explore the real world around him with his eyes, ears, hands, nose, and even his taste buds. It is the appeal that exploratory activities have for the child, not their appropriateness for his chronological age or grade level, that is important.

The teacher assesses the sense modalities by which the child learns best. Where sensory and perceptual motor problems exist, particular attention is paid to making the child's learning experience as reinforcing as possible. The work of Kephart (1961) and others has stressed the importance of readying a child for more complex educational tasks by special emphasis on the basic perceptual motor components of learning; these are undertaken at the exploratory level. Concrete experiences are utilized as a basis for instruction. The stimulus value and impact of all materials is enhanced and immediate feedback is provided the child following each exploratory experience. Exploratory activities such as music, simple games, imaginative play, story telling and arts and crafts, are often useful in reaching a child who is not ready for academic instruction.

The Fernald (1948) method of kinesthetic word tracing and experiential story writing as a means of teaching remedial reading and spelling is an example of an educational program organized at the exploratory level. The child is given a highly reinforcing means of word learning which provides him with visual, auditory, and kinesthetic cues. In addition he writes a daily story in class about anything of interest to him. This combination approach which reinforces reading and spelling offers an opportunity for expression of personal interest through written expression and is a highly successful approach with children with learning disorders.

An eleven year old catatonic schizophrenic boy in the NPI school was carried to school in a rigidly immobilized state. After several weeks he interacted and cooperated with his teacher for the first time by pushing a lever which turned on a slide projector and exposed a series of colored pictures of prehistoric animal life in front of him. The boy was motivated by a strong personal interest in prehistoric animals. A teacher of sixth grade normal children observed this boy's daily lever pushing interaction with the teacher and remarked that it was "interesting" but expressed concern because no regular sixth grade science curriculum in her school included the study of prehistoric life. Needless to say, the concept of a hierarchy of educational tasks and the necessity for establishing a point of contact with such a severely handicapped child was alien to her.

Relationship Task Level

Relationship tasks are found on the next level of the hierarchy. The teacher has the task of increasing her value as a social reinforcer and forming a genuine interpersonal relationship with the child. This implies more than mutual acceptance which was the focus of the acceptance task level, for the interpersonal relationship now becomes an important source of motivation. The child is concerned with gaining the teacher's approval and recognition. The teacher expresses more personal interest in the child and uses social approval and disapproval more freely as a means of motivation and control. It is at this level that the child's peer relationships also are of greater concern to the teacher. Students with similar interests and needs may be paired and more group instruction may be utilized.

Since the child who has failed to learn in school has often been subjected to considerable social devaluation, the tasks at this level are of particular importance. The teacher who sets realistic academic goals for the nonachiever and who helps him achieve success resulting in deserved praise and recognition will be shaping positive academic and social attitudes which may have far-reaching implications. A relationship with an adult who objectively deals with one's shortcomings while communicating respect and acceptance may be highly significant to the child with a learning disorder who has had previous faulty relationships with rejecting parents and unreasonable teachers.

A bright thirteen-year-old boy in the NPI school who was deficient in all achievement areas, particularly long division, had adopted the position that he was far too intelligent to concern himself with mundane educational matters. He was going to design a computer that would solve all mathematical problems in order to prove his genius. This boy's fear of facing the reality of his educational needs was prompted by achievement-conscious parents who would not settle for anything but an all "A" report card. The teacher devoted almost an entire semester forming a relationship with this boy. The relationship was developed while working on science experiments at the exploratory level. The turning point occurred when the boy completed a simple electrical device with the teacher's help. He found he could diagram and explain its function mathematically. The boy explained to the teacher, "This is the first thing I ever made that worked and that I really understand." From this point on, the boy talked less and less of his grandiose and unrealistic aspirations and began to work on his existing school problems.

The five previously discussed levels are essentially readiness levels for formal academic work. They have been stressed more than will be the remaining two levels because their importance may be overlooked by the teacher who views the child with a learning disorder as primarily in need of remedial academic help. Not until the child has shown the capacity to handle the lower level tasks is he seen as really ready to undertake remedial work solely on the mastery level. While remedial work may be given on any level, the emphasis will not be on academic accomplishment but on more basic educational needs as implied by the hierarchy.

Mastery Task Level

When the child is ready to deal with his academic deficiencies and concentrate on basic curriculum, mastery tasks on the next level of the hierarchy are undertaken.

The teacher's task at the mastery level is to help the student acquire essential information and understanding about the environment and to develop the intellectual and vocational skills necessary for social survival. The students learn reading, writing, and arithmetic since these skills are basic for all learning. The emphasis is on practical application of these skills to daily living. Intelligence and achievement testing are important at the mastery level. The teacher carefully assesses a given child's learning potential as well as his specific academic deficits before formulating a program on the mastery level. In addition, the use of progress tests and grading may be introduced.

Since the emotionally handicapped child with a learning disorder may have a marginal if not faulty reality orientation and limited resources for communication and social interaction, mastery skills are vitally important to him. One of the characteristics of emotionally handicapped children is that they often complete tasks on the hierarchy out of sequence. The schizophrenic child may learn to read, spell, and master number concepts while relating to the teacher on the primary level. Despite these academic gains, such a child may make no progress on the acceptance, order, exploratory, and relationship level. In the broadest sense, despite academic progress, the child is still suffering from a serious learning disorder and the teacher's goals should be set accordingly.

Achievement Task Level

Not a great deal needs to be said about achievement tasks which constitute the highest level on the hierarchy. The child who is consistently self-motivated, achieving up to his intellectual potential, eager for new learning experiences, and socially well-integrated in the classroom, is functioning on the achievement level. All teachers know the joy of working with such children. These are the children who have successfully completed all the tasks described on the lower levels and who are in a position to devote their energies to learning.

Discussion

The staff teachers of the NPI school have found it useful to describe and program all students within the framework of the educational task levels on the hierarchy. The student's observed functioning level is plotted for each task shortly after his enrollment and an educational program is formulated for him. In the charting of these plans, the following considerations are made:

1. The most significant goals will be set on the lowest task levels where the student is either deficient or given to extremes. The chances that a student will be successful at a given task level are greatly increased if he is adequately functioning at all lower levels.
2. The educational program may be best instituted on a task level where the student is functioning reasonably well. This initial level may be above or below the level viewed as most in need of emphasis. Therefore, the schizophrenic overachiever may be reached initially on a purely academic and intellectual level with the more important tasks of the relationship and exploratory levels emphasized as soon as possible.

3. Once contact has been established with a student on a particular level the teacher attempts to deal with unmet tasks on lower levels, and then to move up the hierarchy as quickly as possible.
4. Several task levels may be worked on concurrently and seldom will a teacher restrict an educational program to only one level. However, lower, unmet task levels will receive greater emphasis.
5. From time to time, students may regress in their functioning at a particular task level necessitating a reassessment of goals and a possible alteration of the educational program.

Hierarchy of Educational Tasks

Description	*Program*
Achievement	
Not functioning at this level.	
Mastery	
Underachieving in all subjects. Claims can't do basic addition and subtraction which he has previously demonstrated. Will do some silent reading at approximately third-grade level but has poor comprehension.	De-emphasize academic accomplishments, particularly in arithmetic, and give easy third-grade reading.
Relationship	
Becomes very anxious when singled out by the teacher for praise. Relates with other students only through provoking them to test classroom limits.	Maintain distance both physically and interpersonally. Respect his preference to be dealt with as member of group.
Exploratory	
Demonstrates few interests. Holds back in all activities and claims no interest in anything. Has shown some interest in movie projector and how it works.	Arrange to have science teacher let him experiment with an old projector. Start him on a simple electrical project when he seems ready.
Order	
Overcontrolled, rigid in his behavior. Refuses to have haircut or remove his red jacket in the classroom.	Arrange seating so he will not be next to volatile class members. Encourage some freedom of movement. Avoid discussion of jacket or haircut at present.
Acceptance	
Suspicious, guarded in relation to teacher. Withdraws when teacher approaches. Asks to work in study booth alone.	INITIATE CONTACT HERE Permit independent study in booth. Give small units of work and request he bring to teacher's desk. Approach initially in businesslike but friendly manner. Attempt to find some simple classroom chore he might do for teacher while other students working.
Primary	
Not functioning at this level.	

FIG. 1 *Hierarchy of Educational Tasks — Student Program of Steven*

Figure 1 provides an example of the description and program of Steven, an eleven-year-old boy who had refused to go to school for more than a year prior to hospitalization. The teacher's initial observations appear in the left column and her suggestions for the educational program in the right column. In the case of Steven, the basic task for teacher and student was set at the acceptance level. The teacher was most concerned with communicating an attitude of acceptance and helping this boy feel secure in the classroom at the expense of higher level tasks. While this was her major concern, the boy was held for some level of functioning with higher tasks.

Most children with learning problems are given tasks at all levels with the possible exception of the primary and achievement levels which are not applicable in the majority of cases. Once establishing contact at the acceptance level, the teacher carefully weighed the factors of student gratification and her own control and initiated the program as described. Her educational plan was not a static one; it changed from day to day. The teacher increased her control step by step until after a six month period, she had the student functioning effectively on the mastery level. He was able to tolerate interaction with teacher and peers, explore the classroom environment more freely, and display a consistent level of performance in his class work.

It is hoped that this concept of a hierarchy of educational tasks may make psychological principles of development more meaningful to teachers and provide them with a measure of educational economy in understanding and adequately programing for children with learning disorders.

REFERENCES

Cruickshank, W. *A teaching method for brain injured and hyperactive children.* New York: Syracuse University Press, 1961.

Erickson, E. *Childhood and Society.* New York: W. W. Norton Company, Inc., 1950.

Fernald, G. *Basic techniques in remedial school subjects.* New York: McGraw-Hill, Inc., 1948.

Ferster, C., and De Meyer, M. The development of performances in autistic children in automatically controlled environments. *Journal of Chronic Diseases,* 1961, 13, 312–345.

Haring, N., and Phillips, E. *Educating emotionally disturbed children.* New York: McGraw-Hill, Inc., 1962.

Havighurst, R. *Developmental tasks and education.* New York: Longmann-Green and Company, 1952.

Hewett, F. Teaching reading to an autistic boy through operant conditioning.

The Reading Teacher, 1964, 17, 613–618.

Isaacs, W., Thomas J., and Goldiamond, I. Application of operant conditioning to reinstating verbal behavior in psychotics. *Journal of Speech and Hearing Disorders,* 1960, 25, 8–12.

Kephart, N. *The slow learner in the classroom.* Columbus, Ohio: Charles E. Merrill Books, Inc., 1961.

Lindsley, O. Operant conditioning methods applied to research in chronic schizophrenia. *Psychiatric Research Reports,* 1956, 5, 118–139.

Maslow, A. *Motivation and personality.* New York: Harper and Brothers, 1954.

Munroe, R. *Schools of psychoanalytic thought.* New York: The Dryden Press, Inc., 1955.

Weiland, H., and Rudnick, R. Considerations of the development and treatment of autistic children. In Ruth S. Eissler et al. (Editors), *The psychoanalytic study of the child.* Vol. 16. New York: International Universities Press, 1961.

Part Six

The Case Report

One of the basic needs of a remedial teacher is a plan for gathering and systematizing pertinent information about individuals and passing that information on to others who may become involved at a later stage. Obviously there is no standard form or approach, for needs differ with the situation as well as with the individuals involved; but certain guidelines and conventions are useful. We chose the selections in this chapter—a general introduction to clinical reporting and two actual case studies—because we felt they would enable the reader to consider a potentially useful approach to the case report—the case report conceived both as a vehicle for communication and as a guide to diagnosis and teaching.

The English and Lillywhite article is addressed specifically to speech pathologists, but the basic message is relevant for any specialist or teacher confronted with the task of organizing and communicating information about children with learning problems. Writers of case studies who have clearly in mind the four levels of communication discussed in the article are likely not only to communicate better with others but also to be less prone to let their subjective feelings about a case becloud the facts. Clinical hunches can serve a real purpose, but they are only a short distance away from clinical biases.

Ray's case report includes a description of the kind of learning problem that is encountered frequently. The report is well organized to show the sequence that leads from diagnosis to specific recommendations for teaching. The subject of Jansky's case report appears to have a more complex problem, but again the sequence of the diagnostic and remedial process is apparent. Although the formats of the two reports are quite different, both writers have managed to remain essentially objective in viewing their cases.

20   A Semantic Approach to Clinical Reporting
in Speech Pathology

ROBERT H. ENGLISH

HEROLD S. LILLYWHITE

Disordered oral communication may be considered, for all practical purposes, the speech and hearing clinician's business. It rightly becomes his "stock in trade." Not only must the clinician possess the knowledge and skill for "evaluating," "correcting," or "improving" the oral communication of others, but he must have the ability to communicate with his patient, with other individuals interested in the patient, and with colleagues in regard to his patient.

The ability of the clinician to communicate via several media and on several levels, then, is one area of importance to the attainment of professional competency. The purpose of the present discussion is to consider a method of reporting or communicating diagnostic and therapeutic information relative to persons with disorders of communication. More specifically, the discussion will be concerned with four levels of communication and with the language of clinical reporting, all of which may be applied either to oral or written forms. The four levels of communication to be described, not only provide an organized method of reporting, but they also provide a technique for structuring the examination procedures.

The Four Levels of Communication

OBSERVATION LEVEL

Examination procedures should begin with informal and formal techniques of observation. At this level the clinician puts his five senses to work and perhaps a "sixth sense" if one considers the so-called "clinical sense." Lillywhite (4, p. 105) states that ". . . it is a time at which we observe, we hear, or we feel some 'thing' or somebody." Sondel (6, p. 57), in analyzing the work of Ogden and Richards, contends that observation is made through "cold and impersonal eyes" . . . "there should be no good or bad, beautiful or ugly, useful or not useful, important or not important, etc." In short, at this level the clinician "senses," merely this, nothing more.

A special comment probably should be made concerning the sense of hearing. If hearing is compared with the other senses it is, perhaps, the least efficient of the five senses. Nichols contends that listening is the most used of the communication skills. Reasoning from extensive testing of the listening ability of subjects under controlled conditions, Nichols (5, p. 5) concludes: ". . . After the average person has listened to someone talk, he remembers only about half of what he heard—no matter how carefully he thought he had listened." The speech clinician should be an astute listener; however, during the examination session many speech clinicians become so concerned with procedures that they frequently forget to listen. In diagnostic and therapeutic sessions there is a strong temptation for the clinician to over-verbalize while the patient tends to

From *Journal of the American Speech and Hearing Association,* Vol. 4 (June, 1963), pp. 647–650. Reprinted with permission.

under-verbalize. Under such conditions much observational data, which might be useful in reaching evaluations and rendering judgments, is missed or over-looked. If we are to become more competent clinical observers, we must, among other things, learn to listen more efficiently to our clients. Lillywhite (4, p. 103) supported this view when he wrote:

> There is no other occupation that depends so much on the ability to listen accurately and understandingly as that of working with the handicapped. People with problems, that is, the handicapped and their parents, generally are more concerned about being heard than they are about being told. Although they come asking questions, they do not seek answers so much as they seek a sympathetic, understanding listener who will help them verbalize ways to their own solutions . . . . To listen with understanding requires courage; to listen with accuracy requires skill. Many people seem to assume that because they hear, their listening habits are adequate. This is far from the truth. We might transpose Emerson's statement slightly to read "What you are speaks so loudly you cannot hear what I say." It works the same whether you are speaking or listening. Your own motivations, your problems, your needs and your maturity, or lack of it, get in the way of accurate evaluations of what you hear. We need to attack the problem of listening directly and consciously.

During this step the clinician uses many observational devices. Such devices, to name only a few, may include: (a) the oral examination, (b) the language examination, (c) the speech sound inventory, (d) the sound discrimination test, (e) the tests of auditory acuity (informal and/or formal), (f) the several tests of personality and/or tests of mental ability, (g) the interview (parent, patient, spouse, etc.), (h) the existing case-history data.

The astute clinician does not always rely upon controlled methods of observation, but quickly learns to make incidental or informal observations of behavior from the moment he meets the patient until the patient departs. He makes a mental note of these observations and later attempts to verify them and weave them into the overall observational pattern.

DESCRIPTIVE LEVEL

Once satisfied that he has a satisfactory sample of the patient's speech and language ability the clinician moves to a second level of communication, the verbal level of description or reporting. The clinician begins to describe, in oral or written forms, what he has observed. Very often this level may begin on an informal basis during the observational level in the form of informal notes or symbols to be organized later into a composite report. Care should be exercised to record or report only "pure observation." No attempt should be made, at this point, to evaluate the data observed. The experienced clinician will have some evaluational ideas, but he will refrain from "snap judgments" (4, p. 102) and will withhold reporting these until "all" of the observational data has been gathered and reported. At this point the language of the clinician is most important. He consciously avoids being influenced or influencing others with his language structure. Sondel (6, pp. 57–60) points out that the scientist is constantly striving to avoid bias; thus, he attempts to give uncolored descriptions of what exists, insofar as he is able. He is constantly aware that there are times when "emotive language" is out of order and he must depend upon unbiased description. The following excerpt from a clinical report illustrates a semantically oriented behavioral description:

The patient's language behavior is characterized by "jargon-like" utterances, and concretisms accompanied by a well-developed gesture language. He also tends to use a great deal of onomatopeia with associated gesture. The correct number of syllables is frequently used in polysyllabic words although the consonants are incorrect. His parents report that he uses the same sound combinations for words, even though they are unintelligible, to refer to the same things, for example: [ɔwaɪ]/all right; [waɪ]/write; and [mɛidouwoun]/merry-go-round.

Descriptive reporting, as simple as it might appear, is a difficult task. The difficulty arises not from the mechanics of grammar, but from our own mental mechanisms. Sondel (6, p. 59) reminds us that ". . . we express ourselves every time we describe something. Our purposes color our words. Our slant creeps in —almost in spite of everything we can do. . . . It requires a very special and clear headed effort to stay with symbols that do, indeed, refer to things." This may be by choice or omission. For invaluable assistance with descriptive reporting, the clinician might refer to Sondel's (6, pp. 56–62) discussion of "symbolic language" in reporting.

EVALUATIONAL LEVEL

When the clinician is certain that he has sufficient facts he may feel confident enough to move on to the level of evaluation. Evaluation, as description, is another verbal level of communication. The clinican begins to interpret what he has observed. He attempts to make judgments, to formulate tentative hypotheses, develop certain inferences, and to reach a number of "guarded" conclusions as to causes, effects, etc. He takes particular care not to allow his evaluation to exceed his observations. He shows caution in his use of language style by using such phrases as: "These observations tend to show. . . ." "Based upon these tests and observations it would appear that . . ." etc. Language style is illustrated further in the following paragraph from a clinic report. From description, in the first part of the paragraph, the clinician proceeds to evaluation in the italicized portions.

The patient had very little difficulty with items at the 7 year level; however, performance on items above and below the 7 year level was "spotty" and, in some cases, answers seemed bizarre. By way of example, at the 6 year level she had no trouble with number concepts but when asked to deal with "similarities and differences" she was unable to do so. *This performance places the Verbal Comprehension at or slightly below the 7 year level. This represents a delay of about 1 year, 10 months. Verbal Expression is at or slightly above the 5 year, 6 month level* in that the subject uses 5 and 6 word sentences: however, most of her sentences are simple sentences with some compound sentences and no complex sentences.

FEELING LEVEL

The fourth and final level involved in clinical reporting is the level at which we tend to verbalize how we feel about what we have seen, felt, heard, etc. This level provides for at least two attitudinal degrees of feeling, one of which is an asset to good clinical reporting, the other a liability.

Feeling Level as an Asset to Clinical Reporting. This attitudinal degree or stage of feeling frequently is employed by the experienced clinician. It provides for a listing of impressions about certain observations made of the patient and the situation which cannot be developed into conclusions, inferences, and/or hypotheses. Representative feelings here are sometimes referred to as "hunches," "guesses," or "the clinical sense." At best, it represents those feelings possessed by a clinician for which, at the moment, he has no objective, supportive evidence. They are factors that require further observational check-out before hypotheses can be formulated and, once again, tested by additional observation-description-evaluation. The recheck may be a simple matter of a second look which utilizes observational techniques, or it may require observation which uses different or specially designed techniques. A caution to be observed here is that one might be prone to develop a "blind-spot" and allow it to color his reporting adversely.

One may "feel" that the data are not exactly accurate; that, although organic, emotional, and/or mental retardation components are not tapped by present methods, such may exist. Such items are identified in the language structure such as in the following excerpt from a report:

> Although the subject's speech was within normal limits and language was only moderately delayed, *this examiner feels* that an emotional component with a mild mental retardation over-lay *might be operative* in this case. The *examiner* also *is of the impression that* a broader language deficit *might be present* as suggested by the bizarre nature of the subject's language structure.

FEELING LEVEL AS A LIABILITY TO CLINICAL REPORTING

This attitudinal stage might be termed as the "trigger-stage" of feeling. Too frequently this degree of feeling is allowed to "color" the entire report. At this stage the clinician often is tempted to make "snap judgments," to render "all-ness" evaluations, and to be guilty of the "tragedy of is" (4). There is a tendency to use such statements as: "Johnny *is* incorrigible"; "The parents *were* unreasonable and annoying"; "He *was* impossible in the testing situation"; "The mother *is* dirty and uncooperative; no wonder Mike *doesn't get* very far in therapy"; "David *is* just like all C. P. kids . . ."; "He behaved *like* a brat."

Statements like these reveal more about the clinician's feelings than about the individuals he thinks he is evaluating.

The Language of Clinical Reporting

Clinical activities or procedures, according to a number of writers (1, 2, 3, 4), should be patterned after the scientific method. The notion of the four levels presented in the preceding discussion is based essentially upon a consideration of the scientific method. Briefly stated the scientific method is a method whereby we begin (after preliminary wonder, etc.) by asking pertinent questions and formulating hypotheses; we then set out to make unprejudiced observations in an effort to answer our questions and either validate or invalidate our hypotheses; the next task is to report our observations accurately without bias; and finally, we make an honest effort to revise our original assumptions or hypotheses based upon our newly acquired data (2, p. 49).

The use of the scientific method is predicated upon a scientific orientation. Such an orientation is largely an attitude or "mental set" that leads to a way of behaving in a logical manner. Semantically speaking, it is a way of "thinking," and a way of "talking." The basic features of a scientific orientation have been outlined by Johnson (2, pp. 83–86) in the following manner:

1. The fundamental notion of the process character of reality.
2. Adaptability, a readiness to change as changing conditions require—fostered by the basic notion of process differences.

3. The basic method of problem solving (scientific method).

4. The language of a scientific orientation is designed to be factually meaningful, directly or indirectly, and clear and valid.

5. Scientific language is oriented around factually clear, answerable questions.

6. In a scientific orientation, the natural process of projection is carried out with a high degree of awareness ("to-me-ness").

7. In a scientific orientation, there is little or no tendency to speak as though with a voice of another (ventriloquizing).

8. Accurate prediction, or foresight, is a clearly recognized objective in a scientific orientation.

In applying the method of science to clinical procedures in speech correction we should be concerned with the language of our clinical reporting for "the language of science is the better part of the method of science" (2). Our language should reflect our awareness of the several violations of the principles of general semantics, which include: identifications, allness evaluations, hasty signal reactions or "snap judgments," self-defensive tensions or ego involvement, unconditionality of response, etc.

To avoid semantic violations our "mental set" should reflect certain important semantic concepts. We should be aware that our words about a given person, object, or the behavior of the person or thing are not that person, object, or behavior of that person or thing. We also must keep in mind that our verbal descriptions of a given person, object, or action do not represent all of that person, object, or action. Lastly, we must realize that the language we employ is a way of talking about language itself, that is, we make statements about statements, evaluations about evaluations, abstracts about abstracts, etc. In short, our verbal abstracts are self-reflexive in nature.

The clinician's language also must reflect his awareness of three important semantic principles as he works with patients and colleagues alike. First, he must be concerned with the principle of probability which states that in a world of process-change predictions and reports can be given only with some degree of probability, there is no absolute certainty. What was "true" yesterday may not be "true" today, and what is so today may not be so tomorrow. A second principle is that of symbol reaction. Briefly stated, symbol reaction refers to an awareness that words, statements, objects, events, stimuli, etc., are merely abstracts of something else, and in reacting one does not react to the symbol solely but to "all" that the symbol supposedly might represent. A third principle, extensionalization, in a general sense refers to an awareness of what has already been described as the scientific method and as the process of abstracting, carried on consciously and adequately. More specifically, it refers to an orientation on the nonverbal levels of communication. In other words, our language is an extension of our nonverbal levels of communication.

The profound effect of language upon the behavior of "self" and that of "others" led Korzybski (3) to advocate the use of specific terms, devices, and techniques on a verbal level, as a reminder to self and to others of the very real dangers inherent in our language. We, as clinicians, might do well to employ some of the linguistic aids suggested by Korzybski as we conduct therapy and report our observations in order that we might reflect the scientific and semantic orientation of this discussion.

The terms, devices and techniques described below should serve to make the language of clinical reporting more representative of a reality process. First, there are certain actional or operational terms which refer to descriptions of what happens or what is done. Such terms tend to counteract the subject predicate nature of our language. Rather than saying, "Jean *was* nervous," we might say, Jean appeared nervous, in that she shifted about in her chair almost continuously; bit her fingernails frequently; and demonstrated tremors in her lips and hands throughout the therapy sessions.

Second, there are certain conditional terms that we might use which serve to qualify our statements, to show exceptions, and to indicate conditions. Such terms might include: "except," "but," "under conditions of—," etc. By way of example: "Under verbal expression he appeared to be at the five-year level in the average number of words used per running sentence, *but* syntax was not much above the three-and-one-half year level. Thus, at this time it would appear that the child's verbal expressive ability might be placed somewhere between the four and four-and-one-half year levels."

Third, the tendency to date individuals, objects, and/or things will serve to index times. There is no time, as such, in nature, but there are times. No two dates are alike nor are there two times which are identical. Thus, we may say that David, *1960,* is not David, *1961,* or, as a matter of fact, David *yesterday* may not be exactly the same as David *today.*

Fourth, the employment of indexes will help us to identify individuals, objects, and/or things. Through indexing we demonstrate to ourselves and others the ability to recognize and communicate differences in our language structure. In short, we accept the premise of nonidentity. For example, "A is not A," that is, "stutterer$_1$ is not stutterer$_2$," nor are stutterer$_1$ and stutterer$_2$ typically like "all" stutterers.

Fifth, we may use certain projective terms which will serve to indicate to "self" and to "others" that we are conscious of our own feelings or projections. Such terms might include: "to me," "in my opinion," "as I see it," "from my view point," "I feel that—," etc. Such terms act as reminders to be cautious of evaluations and judgments based upon the data reported. They usually identify data that go beyond the observable facts. They also may indicate the clinician is capable of "feeling" or "emotion," in the clinical setting.

Space and purpose do not permit a discussion of the many aids available to the clinician in semantically structuring his "thinking," his "language," and his "behavior" toward a more scientifically oriented method. Some of these additional semantic devices and techniques available to the clinician are: "etcetera," "plurals," "quantity," "underlining," "quotations," etc. However, in using the "tools" of general semantics, the clinician should remember that he must be understood, not solely on verbal levels as something to be talked about, but on nonverbal levels, extensionally, as something to be used.

Conclusion

The present discussion has been concerned with a general semantic approach to clinical reporting in clinical speech correction. More specifically, an organized method of communicating diagnostic and therapeutic information has been described under two general headings: the four levels of communication and the language of clinical reporting.

The four levels of communication, based upon a scientific orientation, included: observation, description, evaluation and feeling (or hunch). It should be recognized that the first three are inter-related, mutually dependent levels involved in reporting or communicating pertinent data concerning a given subject. The experienced clinician often is able to move quickly from one to the other as he works with a subject. This is true particularly if he is highly familiar with his methods and techniques of examination and treatment. If, in addition to his knowledge of the "tools," he also has in mind a plan or particular organization for diagnosis and therapy he will be more prone to move back and forth among the first three levels. The important point to be made here is that he should be conscious at all times of the level where he is working. As he works he may jot down brief working notes, or he may be capable of making accurate mental notes to be recorded later. Such notes are used in his organized report concerning a given subject. When the clinician reaches level four, he shows his awareness of the level by reporting only the "asset stage." He presents this latter, identifying it and qualifying it so that it may not be interpreted as "fact." If he reaches the "liability stage," however, he should indicate this on a "conscious level" and should probably call for an impartial judgment and reevaluation or a readjustment in a therapy situation.

The language of cliniclal reporting, from a general semantics point of view, is a way of "thinking" and "talking" about people and things in the clinic environment. It is a language that reflects the scientific orientation through the use of certain concepts, general principles, devices, and terms. Thus, the scientifically oriented speech clinician might do well to bear in mind, to paraphrase Johnson (2), "The language of the speech clinician (speech correction) is the better part of the method of the speech clinician." In a sense, the language would appear to act as a guide to the method.

REFERENCES

1. Hayakawa, S. I., *Language in Thought and Action.* New New York: Harcourt, Brace & Co., 1949.

2. Johnson, Wendell, *People in Quandaries.* New York: Harper, 1946.

3. Korzybski, Alfred, *Science and Sanity.* Lakeville, Conn.: International Non-Aristotelian Library Publishing Co., 1948.

4. Lillywhite, Herold, A point of view for those working with the handicapped. *Exceptional Children,* 25, 1958, 101–105.

5. Nichols, Ralph G. and Stevens, Leonard A., *Are You Listening?* New York: McGraw-Hill, 1957.

6. Sondel, Bess, *The Humanity of Words: A Primer of Semantics.* Cleveland: World Publishing Co., 1958.

21   GARY ... A Case Report

DARREL D. RAY

This case report introduces the reader to Gary (age 9 years, 8 months). Gary is a third grader, his school history reveals only failure and frustration; his parents reflect hopelessness, anxiety, and puzzlement. His teachers refer to Gary in terms of laziness, indifference, immaturity, and emotional maladjustment.

A Reading Center examined Gary. This diagnostic procedure was followed: (1) determining potential, (2) evaluating reading performance (including sub-skill growth), (3) examining physical and environmental limitations, and (4) preparing recommendations based on the diagnosis.

The report, sent to the remedial reading teacher, the school psychologist, the classroom teacher, and in a modified form, to the parents, clearly reveals the nature of Gary's reading problem.

I. Tests Administered

A. *Peabody Picture Vocabulary Test—Form B,* American Guidance Service, Inc., Philadelphia.

B. *Wechsler Intelligence Scale for Children,* Psychological Corporation.

C. *Wide Range Achievement Test* (Reading Section), Psychological Corporation.

D. *Gates-McKillop Reading Diagnostic Test—Form 11,* Bureau of Publications, Teachers College, Columbia University.

E. *Durrell Analysis of Reading Difficulty* (New Edition), World Book Company, New York, New York.

F. *Gates Primary Reading Test—Form 1* (PPR, PWR, PSR), Bureau of Publications, Teachers College, Columbia University.

G. *Gray Oral Reading Test—Form D,* Bobbs-Merrill Company, Inc.

H. *The Informal Reading Inventory,* Lyons-Carnahan Publishing Company, Inc.

I. *Keystone Visual Survey Tests,* Keystone View Company, Meadville, Pennsylvania.

II. Observed Behavior

Gary was found to be cooperative, responsive, and remained in a happy frame of mind in spite of the numerous errors made. Gary did not complain of fatigue, and no fatigue was apparent at any time. School records revealed a failure in reading beginning "from the very start of school." Gary's potential as reported by the school is in accord with his performance at the Reading Center.

The observations made at the Reading Center concerning behavioral characteristics concur with the school and home reports, both of which indicate many recessive characteristics.

III. Test Results

A. *Peabody Picture Vocabulary Test—Form B*
  C.A. 9–8   M.A. 10–4   I.Q. 103

From *The Oklahoma Reader,* Vol. 1 (1966), pp. 11–15. Reprinted with permission.

B. *Wechsler Intelligence Scale for Children:* Results of this test place Gary in the average classification of general intelligence. This test is divided into two parts, each designed to test specific areas of general intelligence. Part I (verbal) includes test of general information, comprehension, arithmetic, vocabulary, similarities, and digit span. Gary had average success with all portions of this sub-test. Part II (performance) includes tests of picture completion, picture arrangement, block design, and object assembly. Gary had average scores on all portions of the sub-test.

The general intelligence classifications as determined by this test indicate that intellectual capacity should not account for Gary's reading difficulty. Considering intelligence alone, Gary should have average progress in the classroom.

C. *Wide Range Achievement Test* (Reading Section)—Grade Equi 1.8

D. *Gates McKillop Reading Diagnostic Test—Form 11*

	Grade Score	Rating
1. Oral Reading	1.7	VL*
2. Words: Flash	1.7	N*
3. Words: Untimed	2.1	High
4. Phrases: Flash	1.3	L*
5. Knowledge of Word Parts		
Giving Letter Sounds	3.0	High
Naming Capital Letters	2.0	High
Naming Lower-case Letters	2.0	N*
6. Recognizing the Visual Form of Sounds		
Initial Letters	3.0	High
Final Letters	3.7	High
Vowels	3.3	High
7. Auditory Blending	4.0	High

E. *Durrell Analysis of Reading Difficulty* (New Edition)

Oral Reading Time—Below the scoring on the test below 1st Grade.
                Comprehension—Fair.
Silent Reading Time—Below the scores given for test below 1st Grade.
                Comprehension—Poor.

F. *Gates Primary Reading Test—Form 1*

	Reading Grade	Reading Age
Word Recognition	2.33	7.6
Sentence Reading	2.45	7.7
Paragraph Reading	2.1	7.3

G. *Gray Oral Reading Test—Form D:* Grade Equivalent 1.0 (Total Passage Scores 0)

H. *The Informal Reading Inventory*—Lyons and Carnahan
Pre-Primer 1 83% Word Recognition, about 35 w.p.m.
Pre-Primer 2 89% Word Recognition, about 32 w.p.m.
Primer 60% Word Recognition, 23 w.p.m.

IV. Test Interpretation

Both the *Informal Reading Inventory* with a score below the Pre-Primer level for instructional purposes and the *Durrell Analysis of Reading Difficulty* indicate

---

* VL—Very low in relation to oral reading performance indicates area of weakness.
  N—Normal progress in relation to oral reading performance.
  L—Low in relation to oral reading performance indicates area of weakness.

that Gary's reading at the present time is at the first stage of beginning reading. This is further substantiated by the *Gray Oral Reading Test* (Grade Equivalent 1.0) and by the *Gates McKillop Reading Diagnostic Test* as well as the *Wide Range Achievement Test* record scores, which place Gary at a grade equivalent of 1.7 and 1.8 respectively. In checking Gary's errors made during the testing, it was found that at least 16 of his errors were in words at the Pre-Primer II level. From this information it is felt that Gary is retarded by at least 2.4 years, as his reading expectance is 4.1 years when computed from the intelligence test and using the Bond Formula. Instructional reading should begin at the Pre-Primer II level, with special emphasis on:

A. Developing a sight vocabulary.

B. Developing word recognition skills in a meaningful setting.
   Visual Perception—Word Parts

   1. Initial: (Although Gary scored high on "Giving letter sounds" from *Gates McKillop Reading Diagnostic Tests,* he failed to use this knowledge in several instances while reading. Examples: hide-ride, cock-rock, limb-climb, was-saw, we-he, make-like, I-and, said-was.
   2. Medial: (In short sound of vowels, especially, Gary was unable to give any sound of a vowel other than its long sound). Developing an awareness of observing the middle of words, and using his knowledge of letter sounds here also.
   3. Final: Expand Gary's observation of the ending of words.

V. General Recommendations

It is recommended that an adjusted developmental reading program beginning at the Pre-Primer II level should be inaugurated by the classroom teacher and particular attention given to:

A. Developing a sight vocabulary. It is recommended that a sight vocabulary be developed before an intensive phonic program is initiated. These sight words should include phonetically consistent words of one syllable developed through the use of verbal context clues, picture clues. etc. For example: bat, cat, rat, hat, all have concrete referrents and also could be used effectively to teach phonic generalizations.

The word recognition program should begin with visual and auditory discrimination of initial consonant and substitution of consonants in the initial position to form new words. The program should proceed from that point in a developmental approach (outlined in the teacher's manual for any good basal series).

At the level of initial instruction a vocabulary that is instantly recognizable consists of two major types of words.

   1. *Type One*
      a. Noun markers (a, the, some, etc.)
      b. Verb markers (am, are, is was, have, etc.)
      c. Phrase markers (up, down, in, out, etc.)
      d. Clause markers (if, because, that, why, etc.)
      e. Question markers (who, why, how, etc.)
      f. Certain common nouns, useful and necessary to understand simple material (man, boy, dog, girl, mother, father, kitten, etc.)

2. *Type Two:* Phonetically consistent words to be used in phonics instruction

These sight words serve two important functions in a child's reading program: (1) provide consistent recognition practice for many of the words most frequently used, and (2) provide the basis for a structured phonics program. Words from *Type One* (above) should be presented in context, *Type Two* can be presented using picture clues, verbal clues and context clues.

A check of the words from the Pre-Primer I level is suggested. These words may be taken from the manual of the basic series which is followed. The check may be followed by presenting words from the Pre-Primer II level in a flash and also untimed presentation.

A variety of materials is now available which is high in interest and low in vocabulary. Several series, e.g., *Sailor Jack, The Buttons, Jim Forest,* and *Cowboy Sam,* to mention a few, are most helpful in developing word recognition in a meaningful setting. Sight vocabulary is further developed and strengthened by exercises in which the words being emphasized at the time are utilized.

B. Developing word recognition skills in a meaningful setting, beginning with the following:

1. Visual Perception—Word Parts
   a. *Initial* (Emphasis on Gary's using his knowledge of letter sounds in recognizing words. Errors noted during the testing were the substitutions of y-u, w-y, z-x, a-i, p-q. Make certain Gary is scanning the words from left to right as the reversal of was-saw was noted several times.)
   b. *Medial* (Learning the sort sound of vowels; emphasizing an awareness of both the consonant and vowel sounds in words.)
   c. *Final* (To develop observation of the ending of words, and make use of his knowledge of these sounds in recognizing the word.)

Gary's rate of reading as indicated from the *Gates McKillop Diagnosis Tests* and the *Durrell Analysis of Reading Difficulty,* as well as the *Informal Reading Inventory,* needs to be increased. It is felt that when a sight vocabulary is built up, the rate of reading will increase. No attempt should be made at this time to increase the rate of reading other than through increased speed of perception of known words and phrases.

VI. Specific Recommendations

A. To develop a sight vocabulary and word recognition skills the following are suggested materials which might be used.

1. Because of the number of confusions, reversals, etc., it is recommended that a Kinaesthetic approach (the Fernald-Keller Technique) be used with Gary for at least a portion of his reading program. An outline of the use of the approach is available at the Developmental Reading Center.
2. Basal Manual and accompanying workbooks (Pre-Primer II level). It is recommended that a basal reader other than the one adopted by the school be used with Gary.

3. Exercises using basic vocabulary being developed:
   a. Exercises in which a word is so much expected that the recognition will be rapid. Example: We can ride a————(tree, horse, farm).
   b. Exercise in which a child finds the correct word in a list on the blackboard as the teacher gives the clue. Example: Find the word in the list which tells us where we (clue) eat dinner, play. ("Words": out-doors, table.)
   c. Exercises which require meaningful scanning of a list. Example: See how fast you can draw a line around all the things which run.

horse	run	house	cat	girl	store
tree	dog	boy	road	pig	three

4. Remedial procedures used for correcting:
   a. Initial errors (designed to focus attention on beginning of words).
      1. Building of a picture dictionary by the child.
      2. Exercises in alphabetizing words.
      3. Sorting labeled pictures for filing.
5. Multiple-choice questions in which attention is given to initial element.
   a. Example: The man put on his——(boat, goat, coat).
6. Classification exercises that emphasize initial sounds and word meanings.
   a. Find every word that starts like "crack" and is something we can eat.

crab	candy	cradle
apple	dried	crumbs
creep	crown	cream

   b. Middle errors (result of limited knowledge of vowel sounds).
      1. Exercises which teach the phonetic sounds of vowels.
      2. Methods that encourage the child to inspect words in an orderly fashion.
      3. Copying some of the words which cause difficulty may help.
      4. The use of context as a check on accuracy.
      5. Multiple-choice exercises which help by forcing the child to attend to the middle parts of words.
         a. Example: The pig was in the——(pen, pan, pin).
   c. Ending Errors (Not to be overemphasized to the neglect of initial elements)
      1. Exercises designed to increase knowledge of variant endings, families of words, and suffixes. Exercise should be in contextual settings.
         a. Example: Finish the word; it should rhyme with *call*.
            The boy was playing with a b—— (tall, back, ball).
7. Fish pond game, in which words are attached to paper clips and a child uses a pole with a magnet on the end of the line. If the child can read the word that he fished out of the pond at a glance, it is caught. If he has to study the word, the fish got away.
8. Kottmeyer and Ware, *Conquests in Reading,* Webster Publishing Company, St. Louis, Missouri (Consonant Sounds and Vowel Sounds, pp. 1–4, 8, 14, 15, 20, 21, 25, 26); later pages 42–43, 64, 66). (Sight Words, pp. 11, 17, 23, 28, 45, 52, 59); (Word Recognition Skill, Development of, pp. 42, 49, 50, 53, 56, 61).
9. Word flash cards and phrase cards.

10. Cynthia Buchanan, *Programmed Primer,* McGraw-Hill Book Company, Inc.

B. To promote reading in interest areas:
   1. Edith McCall, *Buttons at the Zoo,* Benefic Press, Chicago.
   2. Edna Walker Chandler, *Cowboy Sam and Freckles,* Benefic Press.
   3. Robinson, Monroe, Artley, *Fun with Our Family,* Scott Foresman, Chicago, Ill.
   4. Selma and Jack Wasserman, *Sailor Jack and Eddy,* Benefic Press.

C. It is recommended that the parents be asked to provide tutorial assistance for Gary. The present level of development indicates that the reading problem will become more severe. The parents should be made aware of the fact that Gary's problem is severe enough that tutoring, special grouping, and special help will continue for a lengthy period of time.

D. It is recommended that Gary be encouraged to participate in a summer remedial program.

---

22   A Case of Severe Dyslexia with Aphasic-like Symptoms

JEANNETTE JANSKY

The following is a case report of Dick, who is now twelve and one-half years old. Therapy for his severe dyslexia will be terminated in a few weeks. Dick was originally referred for speech evaluation when he was six years old. The following facts were elicited at that time:

Family history showed difficulty in the language area on both sides. The maternal grandfather's speech was hesitating and somewhat disorganized. The mother's speech was severely blocked during adolescence. A paternal uncle and nephew were very poor spellers, as was Dick's older brother, who stuttered for a while and had trouble telling a story. Dick's older sister also had occasional speech blocks.

Motor development was not deviating, but Dick's motor speech patterns had always been poor. They improved somewhat by the time he was four or five, but there had been comparatively little progress since.

During the examination, the boy's coordination of large muscle groups was found to be excellent, and, indeed, he had gained considerable prestige among peers because of his facility in sports. However, fine coordination, as manifested in graphic activities, was poor. Laterality was not firmly established, though the boy preferred his right hand. His Goodenough Draw-A-Man and Bender Gestalt productions showed striking immaturity in terms of spatial organization, and visuomotor control was very poor. Both drawings were primitive. Auditory memory span was four nonsense syllables and hence adequate for his age.

From *The Reading Teacher,* Vol. 15 (November, 1961), pp. 110–113. Reprinted with permission of Jeannette Jansky and the International Reading Association.

Dick had a marked interdental lisp, and he also occasionally missed other sounds. The intelligibility of his speech fluctuated as a function of complexity of sentence structure. When he was involved in a complicated story, rate increased, output was poorly structuralized, and speech became indistinct. His story telling suffered, thus, both in terms of organization and delivery. It was noted that he had a marked difficulty in word-finding and lacked simple concepts like "stove." Verbal definitions were concrete, being more descriptive than functional. As a result of an intelligence evaluation, the psychologist felt that Dick's intelligence was probably superior, though there was marked scatter in subtest scores.

In view of the appearance of so many positive signs, there was little question that Dick suffered from a specific language disability. The parents were warned that on the basis of language evaluation it was highly likely the boy would find reading difficult, and it was suggested that they watch his progress in that area closely. However, since Dick did not suffer socially on account of his mild speech problem, it was suggested he not come for speech therapy.

Exactly a year later Dick came back to the office in trouble over his reading. First grade reading instruction had not made the slightest impression on Dick, and at the end of a full year he could not read a single word and could name only the letter *A*. Dick started work on his reading in November of 1955. He came only three times a week, although it would have been desirable for him to come more often. The number of periods was increased to four as soon as possible.

Dick proved to be ambitious and showed a capacity for hard work, but even so, it took him three painful months to learn the names of the letters of the alphabet. It was here that his anomia—trouble with naming—was first clearly demonstrated. While he remembered letter shapes and could write "Dick," he simply could not remember the names of the letters. Like an aphasic, he learned letter names mainly by oft-repeated descriptive phases, such as "*h* is the chair shape." He made up the clues himself and many of them were highly personalized.

The sound equivalents for vowels were hard for him to learn, since he forgot the names of key pictures illustrating the sound. For example, he drew a picture of an orange and colored it to remind him of the short *o* sound, but Dick had difficulty remembering even so concrete a stimulus. He finally managed by remembering the shape the lips made when producing the sound.

At the age of seven he still could not always recall color names; he did not know the names of the days of the week. He knew neither the names of the months, nor the date of his own birthday, despite repeated coaching. He did not know that he lived in New York State. He confused the meal names and was not sure if breakfast came in the morning or evening. He had no word concepts for "tomorrow" or "yesterday." His anomia was the source of considerable embarrassment in his contacts with other people.

Time as a framework meant little to Dick. This is understandable when one realizes he had no word concepts for demarking its passage. He was entirely dependent on his nurse to get him on time to his various appointments. He did not respond appropriately to being told something would happen in several days or in several hours. Both were extremely vague references to the future.

Temporal sequences were difficult for the boy. Since Dick confused the beginning and the end of the word when he heard it, he reversed the order of letters. One might ask him what letter *bat* begins with and get the answer "*t*." As to spatial disturbance: one could not help feeling that physiologically Dick lacked a clear feeling of separation from the surrounding space. He melted, so to speak, into the couch in the waiting room. While most children like a large playroom, he preferred to work in a small room because, as he explained it, "I feel lost in the playroom—this one is not so loose." Dick lost his way easily.

Especially impressive was the way spatial difficulties interfered with the boy's learning in terms of visual verbal symbols. One got the feeling that for him the letters *b-p, d-q, m-w,* and *n-u* pivoted perversely. He looked at *big* and *pig* and insisted they were just the same. When he was told to start sounding at the beginning, not the end of the word, he repeatedly observed, as he had done during oral spelling, that the beginning could just as easily be the end. It is apparent that for the boy, left to right progression was still an arbitrary matter, despite months of coaching. Dick found it hard to hold to the line when reading. One was impressed by the excessive mobility and plasticity individual letters and words as a whole had for him. In helping Dick it felt exactly as if one were up against trying to embed something permanently in very wet sand.

Even when words finally became familiar, this was true only for the situation in which the words were originally learned. For example, Dick was able to recognize a word printed on a yellow sight card, but not the same word when printed on a white one, or when the print varied. This inability to transfer a Gestalt from one situation to another—to generalize—is a mark of concreteness, and in this sense Dick was concrete. He also had trouble recognizing the word when it was embedded in a page. This was a figure-background problem more than anything else. Electroencephalographic and neurologic findings were negative, but we regard Dick's pervasive difficulties as being in the nature of an aphasic disturbance.

The aim in therapy for this plastic youngster was to establish numerous signposts, to fix a more stable frame of reference. In the areas of both reading and spelling he was given techniques for analyzing large configurations into smaller ones and synthesizing small configurations into larger ones. It was a matter of constant re-enforcement, and required endless patience on Dick's part. In general, the phonic method was used, though at first he had great difficulty since his analytic and synthetic abilities were so poor. It was when these "clicked" that Dick began to make more rapid strides.

When we first knew him, Dick was repeating the first grade. He has been able, because of the school's patience and flexibility, to remain with his group each year and is now finishing sixth grade. He has until this year lagged considerably behind the group in most academic areas. However, driven by his need to keep up with the class, Dick's study skills have improved—each year he has done more of his own home work, and this past spring he had no help at all.

On recent Independent School Tests (for youngsters in private schools) Dick rated Grade 8 in Reading Comprehension and middle of Grade 5 in Spelling and Speed of Reading. Dick now enjoys reading, and although his spelling still is primitive, though he reads rather slowly, and though there are residuals of his language deficit in a number of areas, we feel that in the coming year Dick will be ready for a regular tutor who can help him close the gaps in a number of academic areas.

Despite the fact that through success Dick has gained in self-confidence, one can see in his defensiveness that he still has many fundamental doubts as to his competence. We are referring him to a psychological counsellor in the hope that he will get some insight into, among other things, his own strength and intelligence.

In observing and working with Dick during the past six years, it has been fascinating to watch the interdependence in terms of progress of development and remediation. This case provides some information about the kind of gains which can be expected under optimum circumstances from an intelligent youngster with a severe and pervasive language deficit.

‪▬▬▬▬▬▬▬▬▬▬▬▬▬▬▬▬▬▬▬▬▬▬▬▬▬▬▬▬▬▬▬▬▬▬▬▬‬

Part Seven

Reading

The papers included in this part present some characteristics of two different populations of disabled readers as well as comments on (1) general principles of teaching word recognition, (2) teaching a "low reading" group, and (3) the applicability of phonic generalizations. Finally there is a follow-up study of the long-term effects of remedial reading instruction.

Rabinovitch and Ingram present a psychiatrist's clinical classification of the characteristics of emotionally disturbed children who are also disabled readers. Their differentiation between "primary" and "secondary" reading disability seems to be approaching classic status. After noting Rabinovitch's major diagnostic groupings, the reader perhaps may find that the use of Capobianco's views on diagnosis and remedial teaching (Part Four) as some sort of scale will serve to put the groupings into perspective for him.

Sawyer deals with a second population of poor readers: those who do not have emotional problems. She finds some differences in mental functioning between severely and mildly disabled readers in this category and concludes that this warrants differential instruction. The next step seems to be development of the necessary instruction techniques. One other comment about Sawyer's article is appropriate: The instruments used to measure word recognition and comprehension are not given. This information is necessary since operational definitions of comprehension differ.[1] Furthermore, the term "instructional reading level" as used by Sawyer does not have a commonly accepted comprehension criterion.[2]

The articles by Bryant on remedial principles, by Reid and Beltramo on instruction of low reading groups, and by Clymer on applicability of phonic generalizations have implications both general and specific in the teaching of disabled readers.

Bryant's principles for teaching dyslexics are based on general learning theory and are specifically relevant to the teaching of a sight vocabulary. The term "dyslexia" as defined by Bryant in the first sentence of his article is widely held, though his definition is not the only one. Reid's and Beltramo's report of an action study involving variations in method of instructing low reading groups is a summary of a longer project report. A problem in many action studies such as this one is how to cope with the differences in teaching methods used. One way is to assign teachers randomly to a specific method of teaching. Other suggestions have been to rotate teachers from method to method or to have each teacher teach several methods at various times of the same day. The logical and

---

[1] J. Atwater, "Toward Meaningful Measurements," *Journal of Reading,* Vol. 11 (1968), pp. 429–434.
[2] J. P. Kender, "How Useful Are Informal Reading Tests?" *Journal of Reading,* Vol. 11 (1968), pp. 337–342.

expedient practice of holding in-service meetings for teachers of each method—a practice used by Reid and Beltramo—also aids in reducing the Hawthorne effect by raising general teacher competency and enthusiasm. Of course, if one group of teachers is initially superior, there can be no guarantee that in-service will equalize this difference.

Clymer's comments on the "per cent of applicability" of forty-five phonics generalizations that he selected from the 121 used in four basal series are presented for two reasons: (1) When the student's needs are numerous and time is limited, a priority must be placed upon what is to be taught. In these cases Clymer's conclusions about the usefulness of certain popular phonic generalizations may serve the teacher as a limited guide in the selection of course content. (2) Though it cannot be said that Clymer is the first person to look at phonic generalizations, his study can be considered as the foretoken of present research in the usefulness of specific phonic generalizations.[3]

The final study is Balow's comparison of the long-term effects of ten weeks of intensive remedial reading instruction with and without follow-up sessions. It seems to have implications for summer school programs for the disabled reader. Buerger[4] in a similar study followed the progress of students who received year-long remedial instruction. His conclusion is identical to that of Balow, although it would seem his subjects were not as severely retarded as those of Balow.

An explicit, though arbitrary, scope and sequence of reading skills developed by Otto *et al.*[5] is included here for three reasons: (1) A remedial teacher should have access to a sequential list of reading skills that can function as the basis for the differential diagnosis and instruction of a disabled reader. (2) It also seems logical to assume that the scope of the reading skills that can be evaluated by standardized paper-and-pencil tests is restricted to those skills that lend themselves to this format. (3) Finally, the sequential development of reading skills in a basal series may be implicit.

Otto *et al.* have developed a sequence within each of six broad reading skill areas: word recognition, comprehension, study skills, self-directed reading, interpretive skills, and creative skills. This list follows.

I. WORD RECOGNITION

Kindergarten

1. Listens for rhyming words and sounds, phrases, and verses.
2. Listens for initial consonant sounds.
3. Notes likenesses and differences in letters, words, and phrases.
4. Distinguishes sizes.
5. Distinguishes colors.
6. Distinguishes shapes of objects.

Grade 1

1. Has sight word vocabulary of 50 to 100 words.
2. Follows left-to-right sequence.
3. Has phonic analysis skills.
   a. Consonant sounds
      (1) Beginning
      (2) Ending
   b. Consonant blends

3 L. E. Burmeister, "Usefulness of Phonic Generalizations," *Reading Teacher,* Vol. 21 (1968), pp. 349–356. L. E. Burmeister, "Vowel-Pairs," *Reading Teacher,* Vol. 21 (1968), pp. 445–452. R. Emans, "When Two Vowels Go Walking and Other Such Things," *Reading Teacher,* Vol. 21 (1967), pp. 262–269. P. Fuld, "Vowel Sounds in VCC Words," *Reading Teacher,* Vol. 21 (1968), pp. 442–444.
4 T. A. Buerger, "A Follow-up of Remedial Reading Instruction," *Reading Teacher,* Vol. 21 (1968), pp. 329–334.
5 W. Otto, Ruth Saeman, Camille Houston, Betty McMahan, and Patricia Wojtal, *Prototypic Guide to Reading Skill Development in the Elementary School,* Working Paper No. 7 (Madison: Wisconsin Research and Development Center for Cognitive Learning, 1967).

I. WORD RECOGNITION (cont.)

c. Rhyming elements
d. Short vowels
4. Has structural analysis skills.
   a. Compound words
   b. Contractions
   c. Base words and known endings
   d. Plural and possessive forms

Grade 2

1. Has sight word vocabulary of 100 to 170 words.
2. Has phonics skills.
   a. Consonants and their variant sounds
   b. Vowel sounds
      (1) Long
      (2) Vowel plus *r*
      (3) *a* plus *l*
      (4) *a* plus *w*
      (5) Dipthongs *oi, oy, ou, ow*
      (6) Long and short *oo*
   c. Vowel rules
      (1) Short vowel generalization
      (2) Silent *e* rule
      (3) Two vowels together
      (4) Final vowel

   (5) Final vowel in two-syllable word
3. Has structural skills: base words, prefixes, and suffixes.
4. Distinguishes among homonyms, synonyms, and antonyms.
5. Has independent and varied word attack skills.
6. Chooses appropriate meaning of multiple-meaning words.

Grade 3

1. Has sight word vocabulary of 170 to 240 words.
2. Has phonic analysis skills.
   a. Three-letter consonant blends.
   b. Common consonant digraphs
   c. Simple principles of silent consonants
3. Has structural analysis skills.
   a. Simple syllabication principles
      (1) Polysyllabic words
      (2) Syllabication patterns
      (3) Single vowel sound per syllable
   b. Accent
   c. The Schwa

II. COMPREHENSION

Kindergarten

1. Develops listening skills.
   a. Has attention and concentration span suitable for his age.
   b. Is able to remember details.
   c. Can relate details to each other in reconstructing story read to him.
   d. Can follow two oral directions.
2. Increases vocabulary through listening.
3. Is able to recall stories in sequential order.
4. Anticipates outcome of stories.
5. Interprets pictures critically.
6. Can identify main characters in a story.

Grade 1

1. Uses picture and context clues.
2. Is able to gain meaning from:
   a. Words
   b. Sentences
   c. Selections
3. Uses punctuation as a guide to meaning.

Grade 2

1. Is able to gain meaning from:
   a. Words
   b. Phrases
   c. Paragraphs
2. Reads in meaningful phrases.

Grade 3

1. Selects main idea of paragraphs.
2. Reads for facts.
3. Reads for sequence of events.

Grades 4–6

1. Adjusts reading rate to:
   a. Type of material
      (1) Factual
      (2) Fiction
   b. Level of difficulty
   c. Purpose
      (1) Identification
      (2) Reading for general information.
      (3) Skimming for specific information
   d. Familiarity with the subject

II. COMPREHENSION (cont.)

2. Gains additional skill in use of punctuation as guide to meaning (semicolon, colon, dash, and added uses of the comma).

3. Is able to gain meaning from:
   a. Words
   b. Sentences
   c. Paragraphs

III. STUDY SKILLS

Kindergarten

1. Follows simple directions.
2. Demonstrates elementary work habits.
   a. Shows independence in work.
   b. Accepts responsibility for completion and quality of work.
3. Shows development of motor coordination (eye and hand).

Grade 1

1. Follows directions.
   a. Follows directions when working in a group.
   b. Follows directions when working independently.
2. Has adequate work habits.
3. Uses table of contents.
4. Uses picture clues to find answers to questions.
5. Recognizes organization of ideas in sequential order.
6. Summarizes material.
7. Begins to make judgments and draw conclusions.

Grade 2

1. Uses picture dictionaries to find new words.
2. Groups words by initial letters.
3. Explores library as a research center.
4. Shows increasing independence in work, reads own directions, table of contents, dictionary, etc.

Grade 3

1. Begins to use index of books.
2. Begins to read maps.
3. Finds main idea in paragraph.
4. Has basic outlining skills.

Grades 4–6

1. Gains skill in locating information.
   a. Acquires and broadens dictionary skills.
      (1) Uses alphabetical sequence in looking up words.
      (2) Uses guide words as aid in finding words.
      (3) Uses simple diacritical markings (to check pronounciation).
      (4) Uses primary accent marks as a guide to pronounciation.
      (5) Uses secondary accent marks as a guide to pronunciation.
      (6) Understands the function of pronunciation key and symbols.
      (7) Uses dictionary to find exact spelling of a word.
      (8) Understands the special sections of a dictionary.
      (9) Selects appropriate meaning of a word to fit context.
      (10) Recognizes need for additional meanings of known words.
   b. Utilizes encyclopedia.
      (1) Uses guide letters to find information on a given subject.
      (2) Uses alphabetical arrangement to locate information.
      (3) Understands the purpose of topical headings.
      (4) Understands the index.
      (5) Uses encyclopedia with greater facility to find information.
      (6) Understands and uses:
         (a) Topical headings
         (b) Cross references
         (c) Bibliographies
      (7) Uses the index volume efficiently.
   c. Uses maps, charts, and graphs.
      (1) Gains skill in reading and interpreting political maps.
      (2) Begins to read and interpret simple graphs.
      (3) Reads and interprets several kinds of maps.
      (4) Reads and uses captions, keys, and legends of maps.
      (5) Selects appropriate maps to determine:
         (a) Direction
         (b) Distance
         (c) Land formation
         (d) Climates
         (e) Time zones
         (f) Populations

III. STUDY SKILLS (cont.)

(6) Reads and interprets additional kinds of graphs.

(7) Answers questions requiring the interpretation of maps, graphs, tables.

(8) Gains skill in using many potential types of sources to solve a problem.

d. Uses IMC or library effectively.

  (1) Understands fiction books are alphabetized according to author.

  (2) Uses card catalog to find information.

  (3) Understands and uses author, title, and subject cards.

  (4) Locates books on shelves.

  (5) Uses cross reference cards.

  (6) Uses other reference materials.

    (a) Atlases

    (b) *World Almanac*

    (c) Pamphlet file

    (d) Magazines and subject index to children's magazines.

  (7) Locates and uses audio-visual materials.

    (a) Card catalog

    (b) Equipment

e. Recognizes and uses with facility the various parts of texts and supplementary books and materials.

2. Organizes information.

a. Gains skill in note-taking.

  (1) Begins to take notes in own words.

  (2) Learns to take notes selectively.

(3) Arranges ideas in sequence.

(4) Selects main ideas.

(5) Selects supporting details.

(6) Keeps notes brief.

(7) Shows ability to work from notes.

(8) Identifies sources of materials by use of:

  (a) Bibliography

  (b) Footnotes

b. Understands and uses outlining in work.

  (1) Uses correct form of outline.

  (2) Can find main idea.

  (3) Makes simple outline.

  (4) Outlines topics in more detail.

  (5) Uses own outline for oral and written reports.

  (6) Uses outline to organize thinking in appropriate areas.

c. Summarizes material.

  (1) Writes summary of a story in three or four sentences.

  (2) States important points expressed in a discussion.

3. Evaluates information.

a. Realizes printed statements may be either fact or opinion.

b. Checks statements with those in other sources to evaluate validity.

c. Evaluates relevancy of material to topic.

d. Compares various viewpoints on the same topic.

e. Evaluates information in terms of his own experience.

f. Identifies propaganda.

IV. SELF-DIRECTED READING

Kindergarten

1. Cares for books properly.
2. Is aware of sequential order of books.
3. Begins to show initiative in selecting picture books.

Grade 1

1. Begins to apply independent word study skills.
2. Is able to find answers to questions independently.
3. Begins to do recreational reading.
4. Begins to select suitable reading materials independently.

Grade 2

1. Broadens skills listed at above two levels.
2. Develops increasing fluency.

Grade 3

1. Develops varied purposes for selecting material.
2. Begins to do independent research assignments.
3. Is able to locate sources of information
4. Applies reading skills to subject matter areas.

IV. SELF-DIRECTED READING (cont.)

Grades 4–6

1. Conducts research independently.
   a. Applies work study skills to independent work.
   b. Uses bibliography as guide to materials.
   c. Makes own bibliography in research work.
   d. Uses multiple sources to find information.
   e. Broadens application of reading skills to all areas.
   f. Understands the function of footnotes.
2. Reads independently.
   a. Enjoys reading and reads widely.
   b. Selects reading materials:
      (1) Appropriate for his reading level.
      (2) Of a variety of kinds (magazines, newspapers, etc.).
      (3) That holds his interest.
   c. Keeps a brief record of his library book reading.
   d. Enjoys sharing his reading experiences with others.
   e. Seems to use his independent reading to initiate activities (e.g. independent projects, intellectual or manipulative; creative activities; hobbies).
3. Appreciates literature.
   a. Enriches vocabulary through wide reading.
   b. Cherishes and rereads favorite books and stories.
   c. Begins to evaluate a selection of literature and analyze why it did or did not appeal to him.
   d. Shows interest in building a personal library.
   e. Becomes more discriminating in his reading.
   f. Uses reading increasingly as a leisure-time activity.

V. INTERPRETIVE SKILLS

Kindergarten

1. Reacts to pictures and relates to own experiences.
2. Shows interest in stories read.
3. Begins to react to mood of poems and stories.

Grade 1

1. Sees humor in situations.
2. Reads with expression.
3. Has empathy with characters.

Grade 2

1. Recognizes implied ideas.
2. Identifies character traits.
3. Begins to make judgments.
4. Begins to draw conclusions.

Grade 3

1. Recognizes reactions and motives of characters.
2. Has ability to relate to stories set in backgrounds different from his own.
3. Makes simple inferences about characters and story outcomes.

Grades 4–6

1. Reaches conclusions on the basis of stated facts.
2. Relates isolated incidents to the central idea of a story.
3. Understands character roles.
4. Recognizes and analyzes subtle emotional reactions and motives of characters.
5. Handles implied ideas.
6. Recognizes story or plot structure.
7. Gains skill in interpreting and appreciating types of language (figurative, idiomatic, picturesque, dialectal).
8. Senses subtle humor and pathos.
9. Reacts to writer as well as writing.
   a. Begins to identify elements of style.
   b. Begins to identify his purpose in writing.
   c. Begins to evaluate and react to ideas in light of the author's purpose.
10. Forms and reacts to sensory images.
11. Perceives influence of different elements within selection.
    a. Notes impact of time and place.
    b. Follows sequence of events.

V. INTERPRETIVE SKILLS (cont.)

c. Understands cause-effect relationship.

12. Identifies and reacts to tone and mood.

13. Selectively assimilates ideas.
    a. Uses ideas gained from reading to solve a problem in other areas.
    b. Integrates ideas read with previous experience.
    c. Modifies behavior and thinking as a result of reading.

14. Gains increased skill in critical reading.
    a. Weighs evidence.
    b. Combines materials from various sources in making decisions and solving problems.
    c. Understands the importance of checking facts and conclusions frequently.
    d. Develops understanding that critical thinking is necessary in a democracy.

VI. CREATIVE SKILLS

Kindergarten

1. Engages in creative dramatic play based on stories read by teacher.
2. Reflects mood in use of voice.

Grade 1

1. Has ability to enjoy rhythm in words.
2. Has ability to see and hear rhyming words.
3. Can interpret ideas and stories through discussions, dramatizations, drawing, etc.
4. Has ability to do cooperative planning.
5. Is able to share ideas.
   a. Shares with individuals.
   b. Shares with groups.
6. Participates in development of experience charts.
7. Tells original stories.

Grade 2

1. Shows initiative in large group activities.

2. Uses voice intonation creatively.
3. Writes original stories.

Grade 3

1. Shares in creative dramatics.
   a. Acts out stories read.
   b. Creates own plays.
2. Identifies with people and situations encountered in stories.

Grades 4–6

1. Participates in choral speaking.
2. Memorizes poems.
3. Tells stories to the group.
4. Plans dramatizations of stories and poems.
5. Reads selections of his choice and to the group.
6. Shares books with others.
7. Composes original stories and poems.
8. Reads orally to entertain.
9. Pantomimes.
10. In artistic media expresses ideas gained from reading.

23 Neuropsychiatric Considerations in Reading Retardation

RALPH D. RABINOVITCH

WINIFRED INGRAM

A close, interdependent relationship between our schools and our psychiatric clinics and hospitals is generally recognized as essential for effective work with school age children. Two relatively new developments have further highlighted the need for this integration of effort. On the one hand there is the rapid growth of special education classes for the emotionally disturbed in the public schools, and on the other hand expansion of specialized classroom programs in psychiatric day-care and in-patient centers (6).

In our work in both public school and psychiatric settings we have been impressed with the high incidence of reading and language problems among the total referrals. We have been particularly interested to note that in those schools that have developed special psychiatric or social adjustment rooms, the regular classroom teachers have tended to recommend children with both personality and gross reading problems. Even severe disturbance tends to be found tolerable in the classroom if the child is making adequate academic progress. This was not anticipated when some of these programs were established, and we now find teachers trained to work with the emotionally disturbed faced with virtually illiterate children whose special remedial needs they do not feel competent to meet. Similarly, through bitter experience, we have learned that for a significant percentage of the *boys* admitted to Hawthorn Center's day-care or in-patient units, psychotherapy and milieu therapy alone are insufficient for rehabilitation; intensive specific remedial reading therapy must be added. Of necessity, then, our multidiscipline group has been forced to give major research and clinical attention to reading problems.

A severe burden imposed on child, family and clinic worker alike, is the tendency of many school people and pediatricians to refer the child with the assumption that the psychiatric clinic will find the learning problem to be due to an "emotional block" and that through the magic of psychotherapy, perhaps limited to a few interviews, the child will be "released" to learn adequately. Unfortunately some of us in child psychiatry and clinical psychology have fostered this attitude in the past, overgeneralizing dynamic formulations. The problem in much more complex and there is a need for careful differential diagnosis in each case studied.

Two broad factors in the child's reading functioning must be assessed:

1. The mastery of specific techniques and skills necessary for reading.
2. The application of skills in the learning situation.

In recent years there has been a valid emphasis by educators on content in learning, on the social meaningfulness of what is taught, and this has led to many positive changes in curriculum. Repetitive drill work has been reduced in both language and arithmetic, much to the benefit of the victims of schooling. In the large majority of children, reading skills tend to evolve spontaneously,

From *The Reading Teacher,* Vol. 15 (May, 1962), pp. 433–438. Reprinted with permission of Ralph D. Rabinovitch, Winifred Ingram, and the International Reading Association.

stimulated and directed by good teachers. With these children content becomes the major concern. But, unfortunately, there are some for whom written material remains meaningless and for whom there can be no content because the *technique* of reading itself is lacking. Despite the highest level of motivation and effort, they have difficulty learning to translate letter symbols into concepts. The *process of symbolization* is impaired and learning through "normal" teaching methods cannot be expected.

In some of these cases history indicates brain injury (encephalopathy) as the probable cause of the disability. In other cases no such history is found and the disability is felt to be due to a developmental neurological deficit.

Using the broad term "reading retardation" to describe all cases in which there is a significant discrepancy between mental age on performance tests and level of reading achievement, we can, then, define three major diagnostic groupings (7, 8).

1. Capacity to learn to read is impaired without definite brain damage suggested in history or on neurologic examination. The defect is in the ability to deal with letters and words as symbols, with resultant diminished ability to integrate the meaningfulness of written material. The problem appears to reflect a basic disturbed pattern of neurologic organization. Because the cause is biologic or endogenous, these cases are diagnosed as *primary reading retardation*.

2. Capacity to learn to read is impaired by frank brain damage manifested by clear-cut neurologic deficits. The picture is similar to the early-described adult dyslexic syndromes. Other definite aphasic difficulties are generally present. History usually reveals the cause of the brain injury, common agents being prenatal toxicity, birth trauma or anoxia, encephalitis, and head injury. These cases are diagnosed as *brain injury with resultant reading retardation*.

3. Capacity to learn to read is intact but is utilized insufficiently for the child to achieve a reading level appropriate to his mental age. The causative factor is exogenous, the child having a normal reading potential that has been impaired by negativism, anxiety, depression, emotional blocking, psychosis, limited schooling opportunity or other external influence. We diagnose these as *secondary reading retardation*.

Unfortunately the criteria for definite differential diagnosis are still uncertain and the problem is complicated by much overlap in etiology in individual cases. It is difficult to be certain in the cases of suspected secondary reading retardation, the problem being to rule out a basic developmental deficiency mild in degree. Through the years our research group has come to view the incidence of secondary retardation as lower than we had at first anticipated. While the meaningfulness to the child of what he reads will be strongly conditioned by his life experience and personality, and while the rapidity of his progress in learning will be much influenced by his social opportunities, his basic mastery of symbolization is probably much more neurologically determined than we had once thought. Detailed studies of the reading skills of severely disturbed inpatients, presenting a wide range of psychopathology and attending school in residence, should prove helpful in assessing effects of specific relationship and life experience distortions on the reading process and its application. Such studies are now in progress at Hawthorn Center.

Of all the children with reading problems those with primary retardation present the greatest challenge. In our research we have devoted major attention to this group. Beginning with the surface symptom we can define the syndrome in terms of the following levels of process disturbance:

1. Reading Retardation

The level of disability is usually severe, and apart from a small sight vocabulary, learned by rote, and sporadic simple phonic skills there may be almost no functional reading ability. Arithmetic competence is usually also low although it may be somewhat higher than the reading level. Greatest impairment may be in spelling, reflected in the child's attempts at writing to dictation.

2. Reading Process Disturbance

Analysis of the child's reading performance indicates difficulties in both visual and auditory areas, and directionality also tends to be impaired. Visual recognition and discrimination on a perceptual level are intact but letter forms and combinations cannot be translated into meaningful concepts. In a similar way, in the auditory sphere, differences in vowel sounds are appreciated when presented orally, but the sounds cannot be translated into their letter symbols. For example, when a series of short vowel sounds "i, i, e, i" are presented orally, the "e" is readily recognized as different from the "i's" but the crucial step required for reading and spelling, the translation of the sound into its appropriate letter symbol, is impaired. The difficulty then is in symbolization in both visual and auditory fields. Complicating the problem may be left-right directional confusion with or without mixed laterality. Some typical illustrative examples of writing to dictation by children with a severe primary syndrome follow (5):

Paul is aged twelve, referred for psychiatric study because of severe depression. He is in the fifth grade, having repeated both the third and fourth grades. On the Wechsler Test, performance I.Q. is 114, verbal I.Q. 82. Tested reading level is pre-primer despite a performance mental age of fourteen years. Diagnosis is severe primary retardation. Paul produces the following when asked to write to dictation "The boy came home":

(Ciⁱⁱ ßiL L let GYLe

Paul's production reveals total confabulation with no capacity to deal with letters as symbols. Both visual and auditory skills are grossly deficient.

Bill, aged nine, was referred because of school truancy and acting-out behavior in the classroom. Originally considered mentally retarded because of inability to learn at school, psychometric testing indicates that Bill is of normal intellectual potential, performance I.Q. being 94; verbal I.Q. is 72. Reading level is low first grade. Bill writes "The boy came home" as follows:

The doy nor house

This child depends totally on his visual memory and has virtually no phonic skills. He recalls "nor" as a word and just hopes that by chance it will turn out to be "came." He struggles with "boy," but cannot differentiate from "dog" and the contamination "doy" emerges.

Tom is diagnosed as having primary reading retardation at age seven, midway through the first grade, which he had repeated. At that time he wrote "The boy came home" as follows:

⊤Ⅼⅉ ⊤ ⅬoⅼⅩ

An intensive remedial program was instituted, and at age nine he was progressed to this point:

†hℯ doy caⁿℯ hoⁿℯ

Tom still reverses "b's" and "d's," but he is well on the road to reading competence.

3. Broader Language Deficits

While in everyday conversation the child may appear to manage relatively well, careful attention to the language pattern reveals frequent difficulties in specific name finding, imprecise articulation and primitive syntax. Typical examples drawn from the responses by severe primary cases to test questioning follow:

> Why is it better to build a house of brick than of wood? "Well just in case a hurricane the house can break down, but you put the brick on, it can just hit it but not break nothing down" (age nine years).

> What must you do to make water boil? "You should put it under a fire" (age ten years).

> How did he get hurt? "He sprang a thing, a arm when he felled out of that tree" (age eleven years).

> Is it night-time or day-time now? "Day-time. It's, well, clouds are out and stuff. It's white the clouds, it's lightsen up, the clouds and stuff" (age nine years).

> Is it morning or afternoon? "It's in the noon-time. Noon. In the noon" (age nine years).

These tend to represent extreme examples, but we look for similar disturbances in expressive language in all cases of the primary syndrome.

4. Specific Concept-Symbolization Deficiency in Orientation

The symbolization defect is not limited to the reading processes alone, but is found to be more basic. There is difficulty in translating orientational concepts into symbols. Thus while the child has no trouble appreciating which of two people is taller, he cannot define their height in feet. Similarly, while he knows clearly that he wakes up in the morning, he may be unable to express this knowledge in terms of a specific hour. To explore further this orientational factor we have devised the Hawthorn Center Concept-Symbolization Test with questions relating to personal information, time, quantity and dimension, number, directionality, and laterality. Drs. Ingram, Katz, Kauffman, Langman, and Lynn of our group are now completing standardization of the test, which we hope may prove helpful as a diagnostic and prognostic instrument, especially with young children, and as a partial key to therapy need (4).

5. Body Image Problems

Even more basic, there may be disturbances in personal-orientation or body image, but these have been much less clearly demonstrated. Now we are using Benton's Laterality and Finger Localization Test and other approaches to study further this aspect of the pathology (1).

All of us working with children with severe reading problems recognize the need for more precise differential diagnostic criteria. We are approaching this problem in two ways. First, a longitudinal study of reading progress of classes of children in public schools is under way. A large battery of tests has been given, starting with first grade, and two groups have been isolated for detailed comparative investigation, those at the highest and at the lowest end of the scale of reading competence; from this study, now in its fourth year, we hope to isolate prognostic indices. Second, our psychologists are attempting to refine differential diagnostic criteria through detailed analysis of psychologic test data, obtained from children presenting a wide range of psychopathology, including language and reading disabilities. Tests used are the Wechsler, the Stanford-Binet LM, Bender-Gestalt, Draw-A-Family, Hawthorn Center Concept-Symbolization Scale, and Benton Laterality and Finger Localization Battery. Thus far all data point at least in one direction: the problem is not one in perception per se, but rather in the translation of perceptions and concepts into meaningful symbols that can be used in reading and related language functions.

The total symptom complex of the primary reading retardation syndrome gives, we feel, a clue to the etiology: a neurological deficit, often familial in origin, and expressing parietal cerebral dysfunction (2, 3).

No discussion of neuropsychiatric considerations in reading problems can avoid mention of the inordinate suffering experienced by otherwise normal children, cut off from communication channels, increasingly vital for survival today. With limited resources to meet their specific needs, we are obliged all too often to limit our involvement with them to documenting their successive psychological reactions from initial anger to guilt feelings, depression and ultimate resignation and compromise with their aspirations. Work in clinics throughout the country has encouraged us to hope that early intervention by well trained language therapists may permit many children with primary reading retardation to develop at least functional reading competence. Major needs are for early diagnosis and the provision of intensive remedial programs in the public schools. In addition, an adjusted curriculum throughout the school years, relying minimally on literacy, must be devised for some students. It is interesting, if disconcerting, to note how much further advanced our speech correction programs are, in comparison with those for reading therapy. It may be that the speech correction workers have been more aggressive in presenting their reasonable demands and have in the past had more clear-cut programs to offer. But now, as reading diagnostic issues are becoming clarified and as specific remedial techniques are evolving, the time is ripe for implementation of large-scale special education reading services in our public schools. Such programs, financed by special reimbursements available in many states, must take their place alongside those already established for children with speech, visual, hearing, orthopedic and other handicaps. In view of the fact that no responsibility of the public school is greater than to teach all children to read, the inclusion of remedial reading as a recognized branch of special education would seem as logical as it is essential.

REFERENCES

1. Benton, A. L.: Right-Left Discrimination and Finger Localization: Development and Pathology. New York, Hoeber, 1959.

2. Critchley, M.: The Parietal Lobes. Baltimore, Williams and Wilkins, 1953.

3. Drew, A. L.: A neurological appraisal of familial congenital word-blindness. Brain. 79:440, 1956.

4. Langman, M. P.: The reading process: a descriptive, interdisciplinary approach. Genetic Psychol. Monographs. 63:3, 1960.

5. Missildine, H., and Eisenberg, L.: Physician's Role in Management of Retarded Reader. Feelings. Vol. 3, No. 9, October, 1961.

6. Morse, W. C.: Education of the socially maladjusted and emotionally disturbed children (Cruickshank, W. M., and Johnson, G. O., Eds.), Education and Exceptional Children and Youth, New York, Prentice Hall, 1958.

7. Rabinovitch, R. D.: Learning and reading disabilities (Arieti, S., Ed.), Handbook of Psychiatry, New York, Basic Books, 1959.

8. Rabinovitch, R. D., Drew, A. L., DeJong, R. N., Ingram, W., and Withey, L.: A research approach to reading retardation (McIntosh, R., Ed.), Neurology and Psychiatry in Childhood. Baltimore, Williams and Wilkins, 1956.

---

24   Does the Wechsler Intelligence Scale for Children Discriminate Between Mildly Disabled and Severely Disabled Readers?

RITA I. SAWYER

Educators dream of opportunity for all, but they know that for those who do not develop adequate reading skills opportunities are limited. The reasons why some children do not make progress can be listed: they are absent from school at crucial times; they have limited capacity; their environment does not help build positive attitudes; or they are hostile toward learning.

These are understandable, if regrettable, reasons for reading difficulties. Yet these reasons do not apply to all children who have problems in reading. Research continues to probe for other explanations.

A recent investigation conducted at the Syracuse University Reading Center was based on the assumption that there would be a difference between the intellectual functioning of mildly disabled readers and the intellectual functioning of severely disabled readers. It was assumed that the difference would exist even though the group was limited to those whose full-scale intelligence quotient was between 90 and 119, as measured by the Wechsler Intelligence Scale for Children.

Reprinted from *The Elementary School Journal,* Vol. 66 (November, 1965), pp. 97–103, by permission of The University of Chicago Press. Copyright 1965 by The University of Chicago.

Since mental test performance remains the best predictor of reading achievement, good readers as well as poor readers have been investigated and compared on the basis of their results on intelligence tests (1). The retarded reader emerges as having poor auditory memory (2), as being less able to maintain sustained abstract attention as indicated by the various parts of the intelligence tests, and as being more anxious than the normal reader (3). The retarded reader does not necessarily have a poorer vocabulary, and he does not always have a poorer visual memory (2), but he is frequently found to be limited in visual memory (4). In memory growth (5) and auditory discrimination development (6), he seems to mature more slowly than the good reader does.

Since intelligence is a construct, it is usually evaluated on the basis of whatever makers of intelligence tests say it is. Some intelligence tests, because of their structure, lend themselves to analysis more readily than others. The Wechsler Intelligence Scale for Children is such a test, and it has been used to investigate whether good and poor readers differ significantly on its various subtests (7, 8). There is some agreement that the poorer reader does less well on the subtests of Arithmetic, Information, and Coding (7, 9, 10).

The results have been neither conclusive nor definitive, perhaps because of a lack of precise delineation of the structure of the groups being compared (11). In some studies, conclusions have been drawn on the basis of a sample of twenty-five pupils whose grade placement extended from Grades 3 through 8 (9). In one study comparisons were made between thirty-one poor readers and only eleven good readers (7).

Some confusion may be due to the different interpretations of *reading* used in classifying the sample. Most frequently, word recognition alone has been used to determine reading level.

The Syracuse University study interpreted *reading* as including both word recognition and comprehension. Both of these factors were used in determining the level of accomplishment of those included in the sample. A disabled reader was defined as one whose instructional-reading level was at least a year below what might be expected considering the pupil's years in school and intelligence quotient as indicating a probable rate of progress (12). Those who had not made at least half the progress in reading that might be expected of them were considered severely disabled. Those who were disabled but had made more than half the progress that might be expected were considered mildly disabled. With the help of corrective techniques used in the classroom, the mildly disabled might be able to function in the regular situation; the severely disabled would have grave difficulty and would present a problem beyond the scope of the average teacher.

The sample consisted of ninety mildly disabled readers and ninety severely disabled readers who ranged in age from eight years to fifteen years and five months. The pupils were randomly selected. The sample was stratified so that thirty mildly disabled and thirty severely disabled readers fell into one of three arbitrarily chosen age levels: 8.0 through 10.4 years, 10.5 through 12.9 years, and 13.0 through 15.4 years. One hundred and forty of the total number were boys. Proportionately more boys fell in the severely disabled group.

Table I presents data on the sample. For the two groups it shows the range and the mean for chronological age, for intelligence quotient, for grade placement at the time of diagnosis, and for instructional-reading level determined at the time of diagnosis.

TABLE I   *Ranges and Means for Chronological Age, Intelligence Quotient, Grade Placement, and Instructional Reading Level for Ninety Mildly Disabled Readers and Ninety Severely Disabled Readers*

Category	Mildly Disabled		Severely Disabled	
	Range	**Mean**	**Range**	**Mean**
Chronological age	8.4–15.5	11.8	8.1–15.5	11.7
Intelligence quotient	91–119	107	91–118	103
Grade placement	3–10	6.0	2–9	5.4
Instructional-reading level	2–9	4.7	Reading Readiness—3	1.0

The pupils in the sample were drawn from children who had come to the Syracuse University Reading Center between September, 1958, and June, 1963, for diagnosis of reading difficulty. Children whose primary difficulty had been designated as emotional were not included in the sample.

A statistical comparison, based on the raw scores of the subtests of the Wechsler Intelligence Scale for Children, was made using Fisher's Discriminant Function. This is a special application of multiple regression that takes into consideration not only the mean difference between scores on subtests but also the interrelationship between scores on subtests.

Comparisons were made to answer the following questions:

Do the subtests for the Wechsler Intelligence Scale for Children discriminate between a group designated as mildly disabled in reading and a group designated as severely disabled?

Is the discrimination arrived at when the total group is considered the same as when only the boys are considered?

Is there a difference in the ability of the subtests of the Wechsler Intelligence Scale for Children to discriminate when various age levels are considered?

Is it possible to discriminate between the two groups of reading disability by using fewer than the eleven subtests that are usually used to determine a full-scale intelligence quotient?

By using the discriminant equations developed in this study, is it possible to assign a disabled reader chosen from outside the sample to either the mildly disabled category or the severely disabled category?

Table II summarizes the weights associated with the various subtests and the level of significance for each of the statistical considerations. When the eleven subtests were considered in relation to either the total group or just the boys in the sample, discrimination between the groups was statistically significant.

When the boys in the sample were considered alone, some of the weights shifted proportionately from what they were when the total group was considered. These weights are numbers, either positive or negative, which when multiplied by the individual's raw subtest scores determine to which reading disability group he will be assigned.

When the weights for the total group were inspected, the first six variables in descending order of influence were Arithmetic, Digit Span, Comprehension, Object Assembly, Picture Completion, and Vocabulary. When only the boys were considered, the order of influence as determined by the size of the weight

TABLE II   *Summary of Discriminant Functions Developed on the Basis of Eleven and Seven Variables Used to Distinguish Between Mildly Disabled Readers and Severely Disabled Readers*

Variables	Weights for Eleven Variables				
	Total	Boys	Age Groups (years)		
			8–10.4	10.5–12.9	13.0–15.4
Information	− 2.4	−1	54.6	− 7	19.6
Comprehension	−20.7	−5.1	−25.1	− 4	−14.3
Arithmetic	36	7.5	63.6	8.3	17.9
Similarities	12.8	2.8	21.3	− 1	28.3
Vocabulary	17.3	6.9	− 5.3	11.3	− 1
Digit Span	23	8.4	9	30	−19.5
Picture Completion	−19	−5.9	− 1	−12.9	−20.8
Picture Arrangement	−11.2	−4.2	− 9.9	− 2.2	3.9
Block Design	− 1	1.1	− 6.5	2.6	1
Object Assembly	−20	−5.4	21.2	− 7.8	−34
Coding	8	1	−16.6	3.1	13.1
Level of Probability	.0005	.0005	.07	.10	.25

Variables	Weights for Seven Variables			
Information	−1	−1	10.5	− 7.5
Comprehension	—	—	—	—
Arithmetic	6.5	8.2	7.8	36.1
Similarities	1.6	3.4	2.8	− 1
Vocabulary	3.3	7.2	−1	28
Digit Span	—	—	—	—
Picture Completion	—	—	—	—
Picture Arrangement	−3.2	−6	−1.9	−13.5
Block Design	—	—	—	—
Object Assembly	−6	−6.4	1.6	−28.2
Coding	2.7	1.9	−2.6	21
Level of Probability	.0005	.0005	.025	.025

was Digit Span, Arithmetic, Vocabulary, Picture Completion, Object Assembly, and Comprehension. Thus, it would seem that different subtests play different parts in the discrimination when only boys are considered.

When the group was classified by age, the ability of the subtests to discriminate declined in effectiveness as chronological age increased. It is also apparent from an inspection of the weights that the contributions of the subtests to the discrimination varies with age. Picture Completion is increasingly associated with the severely disabled at the older age levels. With the increase in chronological age, Picture Arrangement shifts from contributing to membership in the mildly disabled group to membership in the severely disabled group. High scores in Coding, which seem to be characteristic of the severely disabled at the youngest age level, are more closely associated with the mildly disabled at the oldest age level. The reverse may be said about Digit Span.

When the two groups were compared using fewer subtests than in the original analysis, the discrimination was highly effective. In the second analysis, three of the subtests dropped had the lowest reliability coefficients at age seven years and six months (13). These subtests were Comprehension, Digit Span, and Picture Completion. The fourth subtest eliminated was Block Design; it seemed to be contributing very little to the discrimination. The decision about which subtest to drop was conditioned by the ultimate goal of the study, which is a first step toward the refinement of a procedure for use in the early identification of children who might have difficulty in learning to read.

It would seem that it is possible to discriminate between a group of severely disabled readers and a group of mildly disabled as described in this study by using either eleven subtests or seven subtests. There is also indication that the discrimination is more effective at the younger age levels.

How efficient would the equations developed be in assigning disabled readers from outside the sample to either the mildly disabled or the severely disabled groups? The question is a practical one. Two small-sample cross-validations were carried out. Mean values of the subtests for the mildly disabled and the severely disabled were computed, and a midpoint was calculated for each of the discriminant functions developed in this study. These midpoints are presented in Table III. Those having a total score less than the midpoint resemble the severely disabled. A score higher than the midpoint resembles the mildly disabled readers.

TABLE III   *Midpoints Associated with the Five Discriminant Functions Using Eleven Subtests and Four Discriminant Functions Using Seven Subtests to Distinguish Between Mildly Disabled Readers and Severely Disabled Readers*

Category	Midpoint
Eleven Subtests	
Total group	264.58
Boys only	98.84
Level 1 (ages 8.0 through 10.4)	1,145.70
Level 2 (ages 10.5 through 12.9)	399.22
Level 3 (ages 13.0 through 15.4)	200.96
Seven Subtests	
Total group	65.4
Boys only	126.4
Level 1 (ages 8.0 through 10.4)	82.9
Level 2 (ages 10.5 through 12.9)	1,103.3

The cross-validation for the eleven variable functions, based on a sample of twenty, presented evidence that it is possible on the basis of the equations developed from this study to classify with considerable accuracy individuals into appropriate categories, of either mildly disabled or severely disabled readers. The equation for the total group was clearly incorrect only once out of the twenty times tried, a rating of .95. When the record of the age equations was inspected, the age equation associated with Level 2 (10.5 through 12.9 years) was incorrect once out of nine times applied. The equation for boys would have misclassified one out of thirteen pupils. When two equations were used on the same individual, he would never have been unanimously assigned to a group incorrectly.

The cross-validation for the seven variable functions was equally effective in assigning pupils. The equations for a given individual were in agreement and correct 80 per cent of the time. Disagreement as to group assignment sometimes could be accounted for by the fact that the individual's score fell on the boundary between the two disability classifications. Subsequent follow-up study on the current status of such individuals indicates that they seem more closely related to the severely disabled reader. The functions were incorrect one out of twenty-seven times applied, an accuracy rating of 96 per cent.

This study seems to have two main implications for education. The severely disabled reader described in this study can be identified as being different from the mildly disabled reader. An investigation of the reading progress made by the severely disabled as they grow chronologically indicates that as a group they do not improve appreciably in skill in spite of their potential capacity to learn as indicated by full-scale intelligence-quotient scores. Since the severely disabled reader can be identified, and since he seems to make little progress in overcoming his handicap as he is being currently taught, the first implication is that schools need to present such pupils with a different kind of learning situation.

The second implication for education is the need for early identification of children who may be severely disabled readers potentially. The ability of the Wechsler Intelligence Scale for Children to discriminate seems more effective at the younger ages. Early identification is part of the school's responsibility. Providing special learning situations that will permit such children to make gains commensurate with their abilities is a necessary corollary.

More research is needed on the questions explored in this study. To put the study in proper perspective, it ought to be replicated using a school population that would include a third group, the achieving reader. It would also be of value to extend this investigation so that data on younger children would be available. The use of several equations for the same child seems to prevent misclassification. A longitudinal study with periodic testing beginning in the first grade would provide information leading to early identification of the severely disabled. Such a study would also be valuable in establishing specific instructional methods designed to promote successful learning for this special group.

REFERENCES

1. Irving Anderson and Walter Dearborn. *The Psychology of Teaching Reading,* p. 10. New York: Ronald Press, 1952.

2. Mildred Post. "Differences in Performance on Stanford-Binet Items of Children Who Function Above or Below Grade Level in Word Recognition." Unpublished doctoral dissertation. Syracuse: Syracuse University, 1958.

3. Jules C. Abrams. "A Study of Certain Personality Characteristics of Non-Readers and Achieving Readers," *Dissertation Abstracts,* XVI (1956).

4. Nicholas Rizzo. "Studies of Visual and Auditory Memory Span with Special Reference to Reading Ability," *Journal of Experimental Education,* VIII (December, 1939), 208–39.

5. L. F. Alwitt. "Decay of Immediate Memory for Visually Presented Digits Among Non-Readers and Readers," *Journal of Educational Psychology,* LIV (1963), 144–48.

6. Bertha Boya Thompson. "A Longitudinal Study of Auditory Discrimination," *Journal of Educational Research,* LVI (March, 1963), 376–78.

7. Harold Burks and Paul Bruce. "Characteristics of Poor and Good Readers as Disclosed by the Wechsler Intelligence Scale for Children," *Journal of Educational Psychology,* XLVI (1955), 488–93.

8. Donald Neville. "A Comparison of the WISC Patterns of Male Retarded and Non-Retarded Readers," *Journal of Educational Research,* LIV (November, 1957), 195–97.

9. Grace T. Altus. "A WISC Profile for Retarded Readers," *Journal of Consulting Psychology,* XX (1956), 155–56.

10. Lynne Schellberg Hirst. "The Usefulness of a Two-Way Aanalysis of WISC Subtests on the Diagnosis of Remedial Reading Problems," *Journal of Experimental Education,* XXIX (December, 1960), 153–60.

11. Alfred A. Baumeister and Claude J. Bartlett. "Comparison of the Factor Structure of Normals and Retardates on the WISC," *American Journal of Mental Deficiency,* LVI (1962), 641–46.

12. Guy Bond and Miles Tinker. *Reading Difficulties: Their Diagnosis and Correction.* New York: Appleton-Century-Croft, 1957.

13. Wechsler Intelligence Scale for Children (Manual). New York: Psychological Corporation, 1949.

25   Some Principles of Remedial Instruction for Dyslexia

N. DALE BRYANT

Specific, severe disability in word recognition (dyslexia) is usually resistant to standard remedial procedures. Many children with dyslexia remain virtual non-readers in spite of years of remedial work. Dyslexia cases can learn to read, but only if the teacher recognizes the nature and extent of the child's difficulties and uses procedures appropriate for dealing with those difficulties. Teachers need a frame of reference for planning remediation of these cases—some principles as well as techniques. The points outlined below represent an application of learning principles to the specific disabilities found in working with several hundred reading disability cases. The principles are not inappropriate for teaching retarded readers other than those with dyslexia. Characteristics of dyslexic children have been discussed by many authors, notably Money (3) and Bryant (1). The relationship of dyslexia to other reading problems has been discussed by Rabinovitch (4) and Bryant (2). Bibliographies in these references provide a more comprehensive introduction to this extensive literature.

The following principles are not a method of remediation but are, instead, a partial framework on which effective remediation can be built. Several principles are common to all efficient learning. They are emphasized here because the learning difficulties of dyslexic children necessitate close adherence to general learning principles.

Principle 1

Remediation should initially focus on the simplest, most basic perceptual-associational elements in reading: perception of details within the Gestalt of words and association of sounds with the perceived word elements.

From *The Reading Teacher,* Vol. 18 (April, 1965), pp. 567–572. Reprinted with permission of N. Dale Bryant and the International Reading Association.

This paper results from an investigation supported in part by a project grant OM 225 from the National Institutes of Mental Health, Public Health Service, and a research grant from the Association for the Aid of Crippled Children.

A child with dyslexia does not readily abstract and make generalizations like those that allow the normal child to improve basic skills of reading on his own. If a child is reading second grade material, merely practicing at this level can benefit some retarded readers, but a child with dyslexia is likely to continue to be confused. The teacher should focus remediation upon the child's difficulties and simplify the work so that confusion is avoided and the basic perceptions and associations are learned so well that they will not be forgotten.

One of the major problems exhibited by dyslexia cases is the difficulty in perceiving and retaining a detailed image of a word. This is seen clinically when a child recognizes a word on one line and is unable to recognize it, or incorrectly identifies it, on the very next line. The child is operating on rather minimal cues (often the initial letter, the length and general shape of the word) and the context of the selection being read. *Calling attention to the details within a word is an important aspect of remedial teaching.* Writing or even tracing the word is useful not only because of possible kinesthetic-tactile facilitation of memory but, perhaps more important, because the child's attention is called to each letter within the word. Another effective technique consists of presenting the word with one or more letters left out. As the child fills in blanks and finds that he is right, he is forced to become aware of the missing details. Flash cards or tachistoscopic practice can insure the rapid recognition of the details within words that is necessary in actual reading. Practice in rapid discrimination of words from other words that differ only slightly insures that the perception of details is well established.

A second major problem for dyslexia cases is the difficulty in associating sounds with letters and perceived word parts. This is a basic element of all reading by children who have usable hearing, and it functions in recognizing "sight words" as well as in its more obvious role in sounding out new words. Until basic symbol-sound associations are established, learning new words and increasing reading level are likely to provide only inconsistent gains. To get around the inability of the dyslexia case to abstract these associations from words he learns, the remedial teacher should focus on a single association or, at most, a few associations until practice has firmly established the relationship.

To be effective in reading, when the letter is presented as a part of a word, the associated sound must be quickly blended with other sounds to produce the word. The child should, therefore, practice with words rather than individual letters. The words should be chosen so that the particular sound association is the only process requiring effort for the child. Every word that is written, every letter filled in, or word briefly seen should be pronounced aloud so that practice of symbol perception and sound association takes place. *Always the pronunciation should be correct, aloud (so you know it is correct), and immediate.* If the child ever falters, the word should be pronounced for him.

Principle 2

Perceptual and associational responses should be overlearned until they are automatic.

An automatic response occurs when a response to a letter or word part becomes so well established that a person does not have to consciously try to select an appropriate response. For example, an immediate association of sound with a letter (or common combination of letters) is usually made by normal readers. All common associations should become automatic for good reading, including the modification of a sound because of another part of the word (as in the rule of silent *e*). In quickly recognizing a word, many component discriminations and associations are automatically made that otherwise would confuse or distract from other discriminations or associations.

To develop automatic responses for the basic discrimination of letters, and for the association of sounds, the child needs to overlearn these basic skills and to practice them in complex words. Flash cards, tachistoscopic practice to discriminate from similar words, or the rapid reading of sentences are useful in establishing automatic responses. *The teacher should not encourage laborious sounding out.* Simple enough tasks should be used in learning so that recognition is always quick. As learning progresses, the difficulty of the task can be increased until, even in difficult words, the association of sound responses to the word parts is relatively quick and automatic.

Typically, dyslexia cases cannot deal at any one time with many discriminations or associations that are not automatic, and this is probably a major reason for failure of remediation with these cases. Even three-letter words often cause confusion. Dyslexic children cannot single out the perceptual and associational elements basic to word recognition on their own, so the remedial teacher must present tasks which will cause the child to develop automatic responses in the basic elements of reading one at a time.

Principle 3

The remedial teacher should plan the learning experience and modify the presentation of the task and material on the basis of the child's performance so that the child is correct in nearly all of his responses, regardless of whether they are made aloud or to himself.

Incorrect responses can produce negative learning and confusion, as well as damage the confidence and motivation of the student. Every teacher has seen a child make an error and then have other errors snowball, even for tasks the child was previously able to do. This is particularly characteristic of dyslexia cases. They seem unusually vulnerable to confusion, perhaps because they have less depth and stability in their previous learning. Learning is based primarily on increments of correct response with immediate knowledge that the response is correct. *Any remedial session in which the child is allowed to make predominantly incorrect responses, particularly when he thinks even for a minute that they may be correct, is damaging to the child.* He may lose what he has gained, and may handicap future learning. Any time a child, who is trying, makes several errors in a row, it is likely that the teacher has made an incorrect judgment is selecting materials or tasks. Long delay in a response that should be automatic is in itself an error. Many concepts and techniques for keeping tasks within the capability of the child are the same as those described in articles on programmed learning.

Principle 4

When two discriminations or associations are mutually interfering, the following steps should be taken consecutively: (a) one of the discriminations or associations should be learned to an automatic level; (b) the second should then be learned to an automatic level; (c) the first should be briefly reviewed; (d) the two should be integrated, starting with tasks where only the difference between the two need to be perceived; and, finally, (e) in graduated steps both should be made automatic when the task requires discriminations and associations in addition to the mutually interfering ones.

Mutually interfering discriminations or associations occur frequently and remain a source of confusion to the dyslexic learner. Probably the best example is the association of several sounds for a particular letter. Vowels look somewhat alike and are often used interchangeably by dyslexia cases. Complicating the situation is the fact that every vowel has more than one sound and that the sounds are very similar to those of other vowels. This is a major stumbling block for dyslexia cases because it is a basic perceptual-associational element of even simple reading (Principle 1). It is important to overlearn each symbol-sound association until it is automatic (Principle 2). Not only will this over-learning contribute to phonic skills in sounding out new words, but the associa-tion of the sound seems to give more definite structure to the visual image of a letter and facilitates its rapid recognition within a word. The problem facing the dyslexic child is that he has difficulty in abstracting the different letters and sounds in a normally complex situation, so *the remedial teacher must limit the discriminations and associations required* to the point that the child can success-fully handle them (Principle 3). When presented visually with a particular vowel, the dyslexic child is likely to respond with any one of five short vowel sounds or with any other sound with which vowels are associated. These are mutually interfering discriminations and associations (Principle 4). Even his visual discrimination of vowels is often poor, perhaps because the vowels are not clearly differentiated in terms of sounds.

If the reading teacher can stabilize the discrimination of each letter and the correct association of a *short* vowel sound with the appropriate sound, most of the confusion can be eliminated. The child will then possess the stable skills which will allow him to go on and learn conditions under which specific vowels have long or other sounds. Following this principle, a teacher might work with simple words using a single vowel, such as short *a*, until the child correctly and automatically responds with a short *a* sound any time this vowel occurs in a word. Then a second vowel (e.g., *o*) would similarly be associated with its short sound until the perception and association became automatic. A review of the short *a* association would be made to insure that the later learning had not caused the forgetting of the earlier learning (retroactive inhibition). Then, since both of these associations would have been established, whenever the child knows that a word is going to contain a short *a* or that it is going to contain a short *o* sound, the remedial teacher would start with words which differ only in the medial vowel. All should be words that the child has previously perceived and sounded automatically.

The flash card presentation of pairs of words such as *cat* and *cot, hat* and *hot* would give the child practice in rapidly discriminating which vowel is present and also practice is giving the correct short sound associated with it. If the child has some trouble, the teacher should limit practice to a single pair of words (e.g., let the child know the word is going to be either *cat* or *cot*) so that little discrimination is required of him. If his recognition skills are somewhat more advanced, or after practice with simpler discrimination tasks, the child might know only that a card will be drawn from four specific pairs of words with which he has previously practiced.

Eventually, the task should be such that in flash card presentation or in the reading of sentences the child can rapidly and correctly discriminate the vowel and give the correct short sound association at the same time that he is discriminating any other combination of consonants. At that point he would be able to recognize and immediately pronounce any three-letter word having as its medial vowel either short *a* or short *o*. In fact, he should be able to perform correctly with nonsense syllables in which the medial vowel is either short *a* or short *o*.

Once he is stable in his discrimination of short *a* and short *o*, the entire cycle can be repeated with his learning a third vowel. After the sound association of a short sound with this third vowel is well established, the short *a* and short *o* words should be briefly reviewed. Discrimination of words containing this third vowel (e.g., *cut*) from similar words containing either the short *a* or the short *o* (e.g., *cat* and *cot*) could be practiced in increasingly more demanding tasks until any three- or four-letter word containing one of the three vowels can be identified in less than a second. The same procedure would be repeated with the fourth short vowel and the fifth short vowel with integration and practice each time.

Rates of progress will depend upon the child's impairment. Some children can establish automatic association of short vowel sounds with their respective letters in a few sessions. Other children may require months to become stabilized in even a few short vowel associations.

Of course, the foregoing example is only one illustration of the application of the principles. Such procedures would have to be incorporated in a comprehensive program. A full discussion of the application of the principles would be too long for this paper. Nevertheless, some examples of other areas might include the following: As nonphonic words are needed, they can be taught as sight words, reminding the child not to sound them out. Sight words should be overlearned with attention given to discrimination of details within the word. Once a child can recognize any brief short vowel word, his perceptual and associational skills are likely to be well established. Polysyllabic words can be introduced by combining known words. (The child is likely to introduce them himself and with reasonable skill.) Long vowel sounds can be taught by starting with words the child knows and showing him how they change when, for example, silent *e* is added, or when the vowel ends the word. Once basic skills are stabilized at an automatic level, routine remedial procedures using small steps and lots of reading will take a dyslexic child the rest of the way to adequate reading achievement.

Principle 5

There should be frequent reviews of basic perceptual, associational, and blending skills, and as rapidly as possible these reviews should involve actual reading.

Dyslexia cases are often thought to have poor memory, and, indeed, they do for reading material. This may be because their learning is not well established. It is essential that every skill that a child learns be frequently reviewed. This occurs normally in reading, but because of the low level of skill of most dyslexia cases and their avoidance of the reading situation, review must be planned within the remedial session itself. Review should always be slanted towards rapid perception, rapid discrimination, and rapid association—all need to be automatic skills. It is possible to obtain or to construct reading exercises which utilize only the skills the child has already learned, thus giving him practice in what he has learned and avoiding skills not yet established, thus avoiding confusion.

Remedial activities based upon the principles discussed above are not intended to be mechanically applied. Successful remedial instruction of dyslexia will be influenced by the extent to which the teacher can couple the richness of previous teaching experience with (a) skill in identifying the cause of the child's difficulty at any point in the lesson, and (b) ability to modify instruction so that only the most basic difficulty is worked on until it is solved and integrated. Within the scope of the principles outlined for work with dyslexic cases, many procedures can be used effectively—and finding new techniques should be a creative challenge to the teacher.

REFERENCES

1. Bryant, N. D. "Reading Disability: Part of a Syndrome of Neurological Dysfunctioning." In J. A. Figurel (Ed.), *Challenge and Experiment in Reading.* New York: Scholastic Magazine Press, 1962.

2. Bryant, N. D. "Learning Disabilities in Reading." In J. A. Figurel (Ed.), *Reading as an Intellectual Activity.* New York: Scholastic Magazine Press, 1963.

3. Money, J., Ed. *Reading Disability: Progress and Research Needs in Dyslexia.* Baltimore: Johns Hopkins Press, 1962.

4. Rabinovitch, R. D., Drew, A. L., DeJohn, R. N., Ingram, W., and Withey, I. "A Research Approach to Reading Retardation." In R. McIntosh and C. C. Hare (Eds.), *Neurology and Psychiatry in Childhood.* Baltimore: Williams & Watkins, 1954.

---

26   Teaching Reading to the Low Group in the First Grade

HALE C. REID

LOUISE BELTRAMO

To many a first grade teacher, getting a low reading group off to a good start presents a challenge. Often it is the lack of success experienced by these low group children which brings criticism upon a specific reading program. Concern for these children led to a study designed to develop and to investigate various methods of beginning reading instruction for the low reading group in first grade.

Methods and Subjects

Seven methods of beginning reading instruction were identified and developed from four of the possible approaches to teaching reading:

1. The first, included because of widespread interest in the effect of a broad language experience upon a child's success in reading, became known as the Language method. The 1–1 Ginn Elementary English materials (Reid and Crane) were selected for their emphasis on the combined skills of listening, writing, speaking, and reading as the basis for this method.

From *The Reading Teacher,* Vol. 19 (May, 1966), pp. 601–605. Reprinted with permission of Hale C. Reid and the International Reading Association.

2. The second approach became known as the Letter-Sounds method. Importance is currently attached to the recognition of the letters of the alphabet and their sounds and to the use of context clues as aids in learning to read. The McKee-Harrison materials published by Houghton Mifflin were selected as the most suitable source materials.

3. The third approach, functional reading, became known as the Literature method. Built around easy-to-read books, this method capitalized upon a basic principle of learning, i.e., we learn by being involved. Twenty-five titles of the Little Owl Series, published by Holt, Rinehart and Winston, served as the main source of instructional material.

4. The fourth approach, evolving from interest in perceptual development in recent years, became known as the Skills Development method. Materials from Continental Press supporting development of visual motor and visual discrimination skills, as well as rhyming, thinking skills, and beginning sounds, were chosen as core material.

Writing activities have been a part of the first grade curriculum in Cedar Rapids for fifteen years. In an effort to assess the effect of writing activities on reading achievement, three additional methods were developed: Method V, a combination of Method I (Language) and Method II (Letter Sounds); Method VI, a combination of Method I (Language) and Method III (Literature); and Method VII, a combination of Method I (Language) and Method IV (Skills Development). In each of these combinations writing was included through the Language program.

Selection of the 424 subjects in the study was determined by use of the Metropolitan Readiness Test, Form A, at the beginning of the 1964–65 school year. All first grade children in the Cedar Rapids (Iowa) public schools who scored at or below the 60th percentile were eligible as subjects. Fifty-one classrooms having at least six and not more than twelve pupils scoring at or below the 60th percentile for the low group were automatically included in the study.

Procedure

During the first semester each of the 51 groups received 35 minutes daily of teacher-directed reading instruction in their respective methods.

At midyear all children were to start in a basal reading program. However, since some of the first semester methods did not include guided experience with books, it seemed advisable to provide a transitional period of two weeks, in which all pupils could be introduced to hardback books. Transitional instruction was designed to teach how to handle a book, how to note page sequence, how to follow word and sentence order, and how to interpret punctuation marks.

At the completion of the two-week transition period, 40-minute daily instruction in a basal reading program was begun. The Ginn preprimers and primers were selected for exclusive use with the research pupils. Other titles were also selected for extension, maintenance, and use of reading skills taught. Lesson plans incorporating first semester findings about how these pupils learned and what types of experiences generated their interest were written to accompany all second semester material.

These special lessons included a literary approach to the use of the basal readers, in which stories in the preprimer were often considered as a whole, or two or more preprimer stories were treated together as a unit when the content lent itself to such treatment. Sometimes these were then read at one sitting. To maintain the enjoyment of stories, the pupils were allowed to skim or give a cursory perusal to the whole story before actual reading. After the pupils had had time to examine a story the teacher was directed to ask a question, such as, "Now, shall we read the story in a different way?" Lesson plans provided suggestions for weaving together the story background in such a way that the text logically grew from the teacher's narration.

Word study lessons, which began at the preprimer level, were spaced intermittently throughout the semester, with use of word knowledge in independent word recognition as the ultimate goal.

During the second semester, beginning at the preprimer level, training in independent reading was given. Lessons were included which would lead to creative thinking and creative activities.

Eight half-day, regularly spaced in-service meetings, including lesson demonstrations, were held during the year for all teachers.

At the beginning of the year, in addition to the Metropolitan Readiness Tests, the following tests were administered: Murphy-Durrel Diagnostic Reading Readiness Test (Rev.); the Pintner-Cunningham Primary Test, Form A; the Thurstone Primary Perception Tests; and the Wechsler Intelligence Scale for Children. (The range on the WISC Verbal was 70–126 with a median of 97 and a mean IQ of 95.7.)

At midyear, a specially constructed battery of tests was given to all pupils to measure gain. Eleven selected subtests of the beginning of the year tests were arranged under the three general categories of visual discrimination, auditory discrimination, and comprehension.

End-of-the-year testing, at the beginning of May, for the 309 remaining pupils was centered on the Stanford Achievement Test, Primary I Battery (excluding Arithmetic). A sample of twenty randomly selected pupils from each of the seven first semester methods were individually tested on: the Gates Word Recognition, Fry Oral Reading Test of Phonetically Regular Words, and Gilmore Oral Reading Test.

Attention should probably be called to the fact that tests were administered after only two and one-half months of formal book instruction.

Results

The results were analyzed by methods of analysis of covariance in three different phases: (1) a comparison analysis of midyear performance of group means by method for 11 criterion variables, (2) an analysis of end-of-year group means for the final criterion test, (3) a comparison analysis of an intensive sample of 20 pupils from each of the seven methods. Teacher competence, in WISC Verbal, and the Metropolitan Readiness Tests total raw score served as control variables on all three phases of the testing.

Of the seven methods studied, Method VII, the combination of Language and Skills Development, produced the best results on the mid-year tests. Method III, Literature, ranked low on these tests. All of the midyear test results showed a definite tendency for children to score higher in those tests which measured the skills in which they had received direct training. The closer the test resembled the learning situation, the more likely a significant difference was found between two methods, favoring the method with closer learning-testing resemblance.

Since there was only one significant difference on the Stanford Achievement Test at the end of the year (Word Study Skills: Method I over Method VI), the table presents the number of times on each of the five subtests the adjusted mean for a given method was superior to another method. These results support the original hypothesis that no one method would prove markedly superior in all aspects of reading achievement measured by the SAT.

TABLE I   *Number of Times the Adjusted Mean for a Given Method Was Superior to Another Method on Stanford Achievement Subtests*

Subtest	Methods						
	I	**II**	**III**	**IV**	**V**	**VI**	**VII**
Word Read.	5+	2+	1+	3+	6+	0	4+
Par. Mean.	5+	1+	6+	2+	4+	0	3+
Vocab.	2+	6+	5+	1+	4+	0	3+
Spelling	6+	1+	3+	4+	2+	0	5+
Word Study	6+	2+	1+	3+	5+	0	4+
Total	24	12	16	13	21	0	19

One of the primary objectives of this study was to identify outstanding features of methods which could conceivably be combined to produce an effective method for teaching beginning reading to the low group pupil. The following elements have been, within the framework of the methods studied, tentatively selected as worthy of consideration in such a method:

1. From the Language method, which had a greater number of positive differences than all other methods on all end-of-year tests, the following elements might be included: (1) a structured approach which interrelates listening, speaking, reading, and writing; and (2) an emphasis on the early teaching of the lower- and upper-case letters of the manuscript alphabet and on opportunities for independent composition work.

2. From the combination of Letter-Sounds and Language (Method V), which generally showed strength in Word Recognition, Vocabulary, and Word Study Skills subtests on the SAT, those aspects of intensive training for associating written symbols with their spoken referrants. Interrelating these skills with all areas of communication seemed to prove stronger than teaching the Letter-Sounds method alone.

3. From the Literature method, which ranked higher than all other methods on the Paragraph Meaning subtest of the SAT, one might suggest the early use of hard-back easy-to-read books for their motivational value and for their content in a functional reading situation.

4. From the combination of Skills Development and Language (Method VII), which had superior ranking on the midyear testing and almost consistently better-than-average ranking on the end-of-year tests, might be suggested the intensive use of certain skills including motor and visual discrimination exercises specifically chosen to aid the child with perceptual difficulties.

It is obvious that the careful selection and combination of the outstanding strengths of the seven methods investigated in this study would be the critical factor in creating such a program. Method VI (the combination of Language and Literature), for example, which might be considered a logical combination, fared poorly in the end-of-the-year group tests, although on the individual tests its rank moved to near or above the middle.

Test results of the intensive sample showed further that (1) Method I (Language) maintained a consistently high rank, (2) Method II (Letter-Sounds) showed superiority on both tests involving reading words in isolation, (3) Method III (Literature) again demonstrated superiority in a typical reading situation (Gilmore Oral Reading Test, Accuracy).

Observations

Experienced teachers and observers generally agreed that the sustained interest among the research pupils seemed higher than they had previously witnessed in a low reading group.

Observation and teacher recommendation in this study point to the positive value of having, within a heterogeneous classroom, different methods and materials for the low reading group pupil.

For a typical low group population, training in isolated skills of reading to the exclusion of a more general program seems questionable, unless the pupils have been definitely identified as needing reinforcement in a particular area.

Regularly-spaced in-service meetings for all teachers seemed to contribute markedly to the successful instigation of programs that departed radically from the ordinary.

Perhaps one of the unmeasurables in this study is the effect of the early use of hard-back books on the attitude of pupils toward reading. In addition, serious thought should be given to the poor showing of the Literature method at mid-year against its very high performance in reading comprehension at the end of two and a half months of formal book instruction. The question might be raised: Do readiness tests measure what really contributes to an enthusiastic, successful reader?

It seems significant that this group appeared, through deliberately planned and carefully developed lessons, to assume responsibility, to show independence of thought, and to perform many activities in a creative manner.

Perhaps the teachers in this study felt more than usually free to allow the children to develop to their capacities because they were not aware of the IQ's, were not held to predetermined achievement levels, and expected that the children could learn to read.

27   The Utility of Phonic Generalizations in the Primary Grades

THEODORE CLYMER

The origins of this study go back to Kenneth, an extraordinary elementary pupil. Prior to my encounter with Kenneth I had completed a reading methods course in a small teachers college which provided a background in the principles of teaching reading as well as a good introduction to techniques. Among these techniques were procedures to develop phonic generalizations and also *the* list (not *a* list) of the most valuable generalizations to develop. (To those of you who might like copies of the list, I am sad to report that somehow through the years it has been lost.)

Difficulties with Kenneth began as the class reviewed phonic generalizations at the start of the school year. Our procedures were like those used in many classrooms: Groups of words were presented, and the class analyzed their likenesses and differences with a view toward deriving a generalization about relationships between certain letters and sounds or the position and pronunciation of vowels.

Throughout these exercises, following the dictum of my reading methods teacher, we were careful not to call the generalizations "rules," for all our statements had a number of exceptions. As the class finally formulated a generalization regarding the relationships of letters, letter position, and sounds, such defensive phrasing as "most of the time," "usually," and "often" appeared as protective measures. We also spent time listing some of the exceptions to our generalizations.

At this point Kenneth entered the discussion. While the class was busily engaged in developing the generalization, Kenneth had skimmed his dictionary, locating long lists of exceptions to the generalization. In fact, he often located more exceptions than I could list applications. When I protested—somewhat weakly—that the dictionary contained many unusual words, Kenneth continued his role as an educational scientist. He turned to the basic reader word list in the back of his text and produced nearly similar results. Today, of course, Kenneth's behavior would be rated as "gifted," "talented," or "creative"—although I remember discussing him in other terms as I sat in the teachers' lounge.

As Kenneth had provided a memorable and even a "rich" learning experience for me, he furnished the impetus for a series of studies which will attempt to answer three questions: (1) What phonic generalizations are being taught in basic reading programs for the primary grades? (2) To what extent are these generalizations useful in having a "reasonable" degree of application to words commonly met in primary grade material? (3) Which of the generalizations that stand the test of question 2 can be learned and successfully applied to unknown words by primary children?

From *The Reading Teacher*, Vol. 16 (January, 1963), pp. 252–258. Reprinted with permission of Theodore Clymer and the International Reading Association.

This paper is an extension of a report given at a joint meeting of the International Reading Association and the National Conference of Research in English, May, 1961. Thomas Barrett, Harriette Anderson, Joan Hanson, and David Palmer provided invaluable assistance in various phases of the study.

What Generalizations Are Taught?

Four widely used sets of readers were selected to determine the phonic generalizations being taught in the primary grades. After a preliminary study of the manuals, workbooks, and readers, the manuals were selected as the source of the generalizations. The manuals presented the generalizations in three ways: (1) statements to be taught to the pupils, (2) statements to be derived by the pupils after inductive teaching, and (3) statements with no clear indication as to what was to be done. Generalizations presented by all three means were included in the analysis.

Five general types of generalizations emerged from the study of the teachers manuals. These types dealt with (1) vowels, (2) consonants, (3) endings, (4) syllabication, and (5) miscellaneous relationships. Arbitrary decisions were made in assigning some generalizations to one or another of the five types since certain statements might easily be classified under two or more headings.

If we eliminate from our consideration the miscellaneous type of generalization, a total of 121 different statements were located. There were 50 vowel generalizations, 15 consonant generalizations, and 28 generalizations in each of the ending and syllabication groups. In evaluating these figures it should be kept in mind that any statement was considered a separate generalization when its phrasing excluded or included different sets of words than another statement. For example, the generalization, "When there are two vowels side by side, the long sound of the first is heard and the second one is usually silent" and "When *ea* come together in a word, the first letter is long and the second is silent" were counted as two separate generalizations, although the second statement is a special application of the first.

While not directly related to our discussion here, note should be made of the wide variation of grade level of introduction, emphasis, and phrasing of the generalizations. Of the 50 different vowel generalizations, only 11 were common to all four series. None of these 11 was presented initially at the same half-year grade level in all four series. Some series gave a much greater emphasis to the generalizations than did other series. One publisher introduced only 33 of the 121 generalizations, while another presented 68. These comments are not meant to detract from the usefulness of basic materials, but simply to point out some of their differences. These differences do call for careful adjustments in the classroom when pupils are moved from one set of materials to another. The teacher who changes from series X to series Y may need to make some important revisions in his word recognition program. These findings may indicate also the need for further experimentation on emphasis and the developmental aspects of our word recognition program.

Which Generalizations Are Useful?

Forty-five of the generalizations given in the manuals were selected for further study. The selection of these was somewhat arbitrary. The main criterion was to ask, "Is the generalization stated specifically enough so that it can be said to aid or hinder in the pronunciation of a particular word?" An example or two will make our criterion clear. The generalization, "Long *o* makes a sound like its name," is undoubtedly a valuable generalization, but it was not specific enough to meet our criterion. On the other hand, the statement, "When a vowel is in the middle of a one syllable word, the vowel is short," was included because we could judge by reference to a word list how often one syllable words with a vowel in the middle do in fact have a short vowel sound.

Our next problem was to develop a word list on which we could test the generalizations. A reasonable approach seemed to be that of making up a composite list of all the words introduced in the four basic series from which the generalizations were drawn, plus the words from the Gates Reading Vocabulary for the Primary Grades. Once this list of some twenty-six hundred words was prepared, the following steps were taken:

1. The phonetic respelling and the syllabic division of all words were recorded. Webster's *New Collegiate Dictionary* was used as the authority for this information.

2. Each phonic generalization was checked against the words in the composite list to determine (*a*) the words which were pronounced as the generalization claimed and (*b*) the words which were exceptions to the generalization.

3. A "per cent of utility" was computed for each generalization by dividing the number of words pronounced as the generalization claimed by the total number of words to which the generalization could be expected to apply. For example, if the generalization claimed that "When the letters *oa* are together in a word, *o* always gives its long sound and the a is silent," all words containing *oa* were located in the list. The number of these words was the total number of words to which the generalization should apply. Then the phonetic spellings of these words were examined to see how many words containing *oa* actually did have the long *o* followed by the silent *a*. In this case thirty words were located which contained *oa*. Twenty-nine of these were pronounced as the generalization claimed; one was not. The per cent of utility became 29/30 or 97. This procedure was followed for all generalizations.

When the per cent of utility was computed for each generalization, we set two criteria as to what constituted a "reasonable" degree of application. We have no scientific evidence to demonstrate that these criteria are valid; it can only be said that they seem reasonable to us.

The first criterion was that the composite word list must contain a minimum of twenty words to which the generalization might apply. Generalizations with lower frequencies of application do not seem to merit instructional time.

The second criterion was a per cent of utility of at least 75. To state the matter another way, if the pupil applied the generalization to twenty words, it should aid him in getting the correct pronunciation in fifteen of the twenty words.

The table gives the results of our analysis of the forty-five phonic generalizations. An inspection of the data leaves me somewhat confused as to the value of generalizations. Some time-honored customs in the teaching of reading may be in need of revision.

Certain generalizations apply to large numbers of words and are rather constant in providing the correct pronunciation of words. (See, for example, generalizations 19, 35, and 36.)

A group of generalizations seem to be useful only after the pupil can pronounce the word. Generalizations which specify vowel pronunciation in stressed syllables require that the pupil know the pronunciation of the word before he can apply the generalization. (See, for example, generalization 33.) This criticism assumes, of course, that the purpose of a generalization is to help the child unlock the pronunciation of *unknown* words.

The usefulness of certain generalizations depends upon regional pronunciations. While following Webster's markings, generalization 34 is rejected. Midwestern pronunciation makes this generalization rather useful, although we reject it because we used Webster as the authority. Such problems are natural, and we should not hold it against Mr. Webster that he came from New England.

If we adhere to the criteria set up at the beginning of the study, of the forty-five generalizations only eighteen, numbers 5, 8, 10, 16, 20, 21, 22, 23, 25, 28, 29, 30, 31, 32, 40, 41, 44, and 45 are useful. Some of the generalizations which failed to meet our criteria might be useful if stated in different terms or if restricted to certain types of words. We are studying these problems at the present time. We are also examining other generalizations which we did not test in this study.

TABLE I *The Utility of Forty-five Phonic Generalizations*

*Generalization	No. of Words Conforming	No. of Exceptions	Per Cent of Utility
1. When there are two vowels side by side, the long sound of the first one is heard and the second is usually silent.	309 (bead)†	377 (chief)†	45
2. When a vowel is in the middle of a one-syllable word, the vowel is short.	408	249	62
Middle letter	191 (dress)	84 (scold)	69
One of the middle two letters in a word of four letters	191 (rest)	135 (told)	59
One vowel *within* a word of more than four letters	26 (splash)	30 (fight)	46
3. If the only vowel letter is at the end of a word, the letter usually stands for a long sound.	23 (he)	8 (to)	74
4. When there are two vowels, one of which is final *e,* the first vowel is long and the *e* is silent.	180 (bone)	108 (done)	63
*5. The *r* gives the preceding vowel a sound that is neither long nor short.	484 (horn)	134 (wire)	78
6. The first vowel is usually long and the second silent in the digraphs *ai, ea, oa,* and *ui.*	179	92	66
ai	43 (nail)	24 (said)	64
ea	101 (bead)	51 (head)	66
oa	34 (boat)	1 (cupboard)	97
ui	1 (suit)	16 (build)	6
7. In the phonogram *ie,* the *i* is silent and the *e* has a long sound.	8 (field)	39 (friend)	17
*8. Words having double *e* usually have the long *e* sound.	85 (seem)	2 (been)	98
9. When words end with silent *e,* the preceding *a* or *i* is long.	164 (cake)	108 (have)	60

* Generalizations marked with an asterisk were found "useful" according to the criteria.
† Words in parentheses are examples—either of words which conform or of exceptions, depending on the column.

TABLE I (cont.)   *The Utility of Forty-five Phonic Generalizations*

*Generalization	No. of Words Conforming	No. of Exceptions	Per Cent of Utility
*10. In *ay* the *y* is silent and gives *a* its long sound.	36 (play)	10 (always)	78
11. When the letter *i* is followed by the letters *gh*, the *i* usually stands for its long sound and the *gh* is silent.	22 (high)	9 (neighbor)	71
12. When *a* follows *w* in a word, it usually has the sound *a* as in *was*.	15 (watch)	32 (swam)	32
13. When *e* is followed by *w*, the vowel sound is the same as represented by *oo*.	9 (blew)	17 (sew)	35
14. The two letters *ow* make the long *o* sound.	50 (own)	35 (down)	59
15. *W* is sometimes a vowel and follows the vowel digraph rule.	50 (crow)	75 (threw)	40
*16. When *y* is the final letter in a word, it usually has a vowel sound.	169 (dry)	32 (tray)	84
17. When *y* is used as a vowel in words, it sometimes has the sound of long *i*.	29 (fly)	170 (funny)	15
18. The letter *a* has the same sound (ô) when followed by *l*, *w*, and *u*.	61 (all)	65 (canal)	48
19. When *a* is followed by *r* and final *e*, we expect to hear the sound heard in *care*.	9 (dare)	1 (are)	90
*20. When *c* and *h* are next to each other, they make only one sound.	103 (peach)	0	100
*21. *Ch* is usually pronounced as it is in *kitchen, catch*, and *chair*, not like *sh*.	99 (catch)	5 (machine)	95
*22. When *c* is followed by *e* or *i*, the sound of *s* is likely to be heard.	66 (cent)	3 (ocean)	96
*23. When the letter *c* is followed by *o* or *a* the sound of *k* is likely to be heard.	143 (camp)	0	100
24. The letter *g* often has a sound similar to that of *j* in *jump* when it precedes the letter *i* or *e*.	49 (engine)	28 (give)	64
*25. When *ght* is seen in a word, *gh* is silent.	30 (fight)	0	100
26. When a word begins *kn*, the *k* is silent.	10 (knife)	0	100
27. When a word begins with *wr*, the *w* is silent.	8 (write)	0	100
*28. When two of the same consonants are side by side, only one is heard.	334 (carry)	3 (suggest)	99
*29. When a word ends in *ck*, it has the same last sound as in *look*.	46 (brick)	0	100
*30. In most two-syllable words, the first syllable is accented.	828 (famous)	143 (polite)	85

* Generalizations marked with an asterisk were found "useful" according to the criteria.
† Words in parentheses are examples—either of words which conform or of exceptions, depending on the column.

TABLE I (cont.) *The Utility of Forty-five Phonic Generalizations*

*Generalization	No. of Words Conforming	No. of Exceptions	Per Cent of Utility
*31. If *a, in, re, ex, de,* or *be* is the first syllable in a word, it is usually unaccented.	86 (belong)	13 (insect)	87
*32. In most two-syllable words that end in a consonant followed by *y*, the first syllable is accented and the last is unaccented.	101 (baby)	4 (supply)	96
33. One vowel letter in an accented syllable has its short sound.	547 (city)	356 (lady)	61
34. When *y* or *ey* is seen in the last syllable that is not accented, the long sound of *e* is heard.	0	157 (baby)	0
35. When *ture* is the final syllable in a word, it is unaccented.	4 (picture)	0	100
36. When *tion* is the final syllable in a word, it is unaccented.	5 (station)	0	100
37. In many two- and three-syllable words, the final *e* lengthens the vowel in the last syllable.	52 (invite)	62 (gasoline)	46
38. If the first vowel sound in a word is followed by two consonants, the first syllable usually ends with the first of the two consonants.	404 (bullet)	159 (singer)	72
39. If the first vowel sound in a word is followed by a single consonant, that consonant usually begins the second syllable.	190 (over)	237 (oven)	44
*40. If the last syllable of a word ends in *le*, the consonant preceding the *le* usually begins the last syllable.	62 (tumble)	2 (buckle)	97
*41. When the first vowel element in a word is followed by *th, ch,* or *sh*, these symbols are not broken when the word is divided into syllables and may go with either the first or second syllable.	30 (dishes)	0	100
42. In a word of more than one syllable, the letter *v* usually goes with the preceding vowel to form a syllable.	53 (cover)	20 (clover)	73
43. When a word has only one vowel letter, the vowel sound is likely to be short.	433 (hid)	322 (kind)	57
*44. When there is one *e* in a word that ends in a consonant, the *e* usually has a short sound.	85 (leg)	27 (blew)	76
*45. When the last syllable is the sound *r*, it is unaccented.	188 (butter)	9 (appear)	95

* Generalizations marked with an asterisk were found "useful" according to the criteria.
† Words in parentheses are examples—either of words which conform or of exceptions, depending on the column.

Conclusion

In evaluating this initial venture in testing the utility of phonetic generalizations, it seems quite clear that many generalizations which are commonly taught are of limited value. Certainly the study indicates that we should give careful attention to pointing out the many exceptions to most of the generalizations that we teach. Current "extrinsic" phonics programs which present large numbers of generalizations are open to question on the basis of this study.

This study does not, of course, answer the question of which generalizations primary children can apply in working out the pronunciation of unknown words. The answer to the question of the primary child's ability to apply these and other generalizations will come only through classroom experimentation. Also, this study does not establish the per cent of utility required for a generalization to be useful. The percentage suggested here (75) may be too high. Classroom research might reveal that generalizations with lower percentages of utility should be taught because they encourage children to examine words for sound and letter relationships.

The most disturbing fact to come from the study may be the rather dismal failure of generalization 1 to provide the correct pronunciation even 50 per cent of the time. As one teacher remarked when this study was presented to a reading methods class, "Mr. Clymer, for years I've been teaching 'When two vowels go walking, the first one does the talking.' You're ruining the romance in the teaching of reading!"

---

28   The Long-Term Effect of Remedial Reading Instruction

BRUCE BALOW

Somewhat after the situation in psychotherapy, much of the belief in the effectiveness of remedial reading programs is a matter of faith. The practitioners know they are successful and can point to individual cases to prove it, but there are few research reports available to provide the evidence needed. One type of evidence is the change in performance in reading following a period of intensive remedial instruction. A few studies of this nature have been published, but usually they report only the immediate post-instruction results with no evaluation of the maintenance over time of gains established during intensive tutoring.

Previous Studies

Bond and Fay reported on a summer reading clinic in which twenty-three pupils in grades one through six were given two hours of daily reading instruction for a five-week period (2). The average gain over the five weeks was five school months, which compared very favorably with the expected gain of one month based on the average growth in reading achieved by these pupils during

From *The Reading Teacher,* Vol. 18 (April, 1965), pp. 581–586. Reprinted with permission of Bruce Balow and the International Reading Association.

regular school years. These authors also tabulated an expected rate of gain by adding I.Q. into the formula. With I.Q. included, the expected rate of gain was 1.3 months, which when compared with the obtained gain of five months again supported the value of the remedial program.

In a public school program which offered remedial reading instruction to nearly one thousand pupils in grades four through eight in a two year period, Mouly and Grant (5) reported an average gain of over two months in reading age for each month in the remedial program. Their sample was quite different from the usual clinical sample, however, in that the subjects were twelve months or more below mental age in reading, but few were below chronological age in reading. Inasmuch as fourth grade was the lower grade limit, it is logical to assume that these pupils generally had established independent word recognition skills prior to remediation. Most reading teachers would probably agree that the initial three or four years of reading skill development are much the hardest and that marked gains are more readily obtained after independent word recognition skill has been established. It should also be noted that in the Mouly and Grant study remedial instruction was given thirty minutes daily in addition to the regular classroom instruction and that gains were statistically adjusted for I.Q. That is, any pupil of I.Q. below 100 had his reading gain score adjusted upward and vice versa for pupils above 100 in I.Q.

Bliesmer, in an article discussing methods of evaluating progress in remedial programs (1), includes a report of gains in another public school reading clinic program. His sample of eighty-one pupils from grades four through eight made gains during remedial instruction substantially greater than their average yearly gains in previous years. In one clinic the remedial rate was approximately one and one-half times the pre-tutoring average yearly gain and in the second clinic more than three times the pretutoring rate.

A British study of remedial gains with a subsequent follow-up to provide an estimate of the staying power of those gains was reported by Lovell, Byrne, and Richardson (4). The average gain in reading score among 240 full-time remedial class pupils had been two years during an average instructional time of one year. Sixteen months or more following return to regular class the authors reassessed the reading scores of the group and found that the pupils had continued to improve in reading but at a slower rate than the increase in age. Thus, although continuing to progress in reading, these pupils were once again dropping farther behind the average of their age group.

Another study, also from England, was reported by Johnson and Platts (3), who surveyed 284 pupils who had received individual or small-group remedial instruction. This group showed an average age of ten, average I.Q. of 90, and primary level reading skills prior to remedial assistance. While in remedial teaching they gained at a rate of two to three times the normal rate of nondisabled pupils; on follow-up after two years the rate of improvement had fallen off markedly. As in the Lovell, Byrne, and Richardson study, the youngsters continued to make progress in reading, but at a slower rate than their growth in age, and consequently were falling farther behind their classmates with each passing day.

These studies support the belief that remedial reading instruction produces substantial gains while the pupil is actively receiving assistance. Further, this evidence suggests that remedial instruction enables the disabled reader to continue to progress in reading skills after his return to regular classes. The follow-up data indicate, however, that despite his continued progress the disabled pupil increasingly falls behind his classmates, because after his remedial assistance is terminated he does not progress as rapidly as does the normal reader.

The Present Studies

It is the purpose of this paper to summarize the results of three separate investigations which provide evidence on the effect of intensive remedial instruction for severely disabled readers. Each investigation was conducted in the Psycho-Educational Clinic at the University of Minnesota. Two elements of remedial work will be considered: first, immediate growth in reading skill and second, the continued growth of the pupils after termination of intensive tutoring.

The Psycho-Educational Clinic at the University of Minnesota is a training center for graduate students preparing to do remedial education and psychological service work in the schools. In conjunction with this training the clinic offers diagnostic and remedial education services to children and their parents. The clients who find their way to the clinic are quite often those who persist in difficulty despite a variety of remedial efforts in home and school for a number of months or years prior to referral. Services are offered year round, but the bulk of remedial reading instruction is carried out during the ten-week summer program of two hours daily individual and small-group instruction.

The methods and techniques of the Psycho-Educational Clinic are governed by the needs of the pupil—both psychological and educational needs are responded to. An a priori orthodoxy does not exist, and youngsters are not forced into any mold based on staff commitment to a given "system" of remediation. All of the clients come with severe disability. Rarely does one of our youngsters read above fifth grade level upon entrance; most are at second or third grade level of skill, and all have gross deficiencies in word recognition. Of necessity independent skill in word recognition receives the major emphasis in our remedial program. Comprehension is the object of substantial but lesser concern, while the development of favorable attitudes toward reading and toward himself as a person of worth is pervasive. Speed is seldom if ever taught directly because the pupils are not ready for it.

Nearly the full range of current and past materials and techniques is brought into play. A thoroughly eclectic outlook is vigorously pursued, with various students receiving synthetic phonics, analytic phonics, combined phonics, basal readers and workbooks, independent workbooks, tracing and writing approaches, machines, remedial kits, linguistic approaches, nonoral work, cloze technique, library reading, programmed materials, and most frequently a combination of several such approaches.

All of the subjects in these studies were selected from among a larger population of clinic clients, primarily on the basis of diagnostic classification and place of residence. Those studied were clients whose primary problems were diagnosed as disability in reading and whose homes were within fifty miles of the greater metropolitan area surrounding the university. None was included who was judged to have serious emotional disturbance or sensory handicap, but many showed moderate adjustment problems in home and school, low self concept, and distractibility. The full range of socio-economic levels is represented; the majority of clients, however, tend toward lower middle-class and working-class background. Both boys and girls are included, although the proportion of girls is only 20 per cent of the total.

Summary data on the mean intelligence quotient, age, and reading grade equivalent score of each of the samples are found in Table I. The clients represented in these groups are average in measured I.Q., though tending toward the upper part of the average range. Since all intelligence scores were obtained from the full Binet or Wechsler intelligence scales administered by qualified psychologists in the Psycho-Educational Clinic, the results represent relatively accurate estimates of the general mental ability of the subjects. Each group distributes in an approximate bell-shaped curve around the mean I.Q. recorded in Table I. Similar distributions were also found for age and reading scores. The average age at initial contact, as indicated in Table I, is the age at the beginning of clinical tutoring for Sample I and Sample II. Sample III was selected as a diagnosed group only, not necessarily tutored in the clinic, thus the figure utilized for that sample is age at time of initial diagnostic study. The average age of each sample is approximately that of fifth and sixth grade pupils.

It will also be noted in Table I that these bright youngsters of average fifth and sixth grade age produced mean reading test scores at third grade level. Thus they were two to three years below age level on standardized tests of reading, which will be recognized by experienced reading teachers as indicating a level of functional reading skill three to four years below age level, or approximately at second grade.

TABLE I   *Summary Data for the Samples at Initial Contact with the University of Minnesota Psycho-Educational Clinic*

Sample*	N	Mean I.Q.	Mean Initial C.A.	Mean Initial Reading Grade	Mean Months Regular Class Instruction	Mean Months Reading Growth in Reg. Class
I	36	109	11–0	3.5	45	25
II	43	100	12–1	3.9	55	29
III	52	107	10–6	3.3	42	23

* The raw data for each of these samples came from unrelated clinic studies over a ten-year period, 1950 to 1960. The author expresses his appreciation for the use of the raw data in Sample I to Arline E. Reetz, Sample II to Ann P. Cerney, and Sample III to Maynard C. Reynolds and John L. Schummers, all previously associated with the Psycho-Educational Clinic.

To briefly summarize the three samples, each consisted of boys and girls bright enough to achieve at or above their fifth and sixth grade average age level but who were in fact achieving in reading three years or more below expectancy. Most of the subjects were of middle-class background, with far greater representation from the lower middle and working class than from the upper middle class. All lived within fifty miles of the metropolitan area surrounding the Twin Cities of Minneapolis and St. Paul, Minnesota.

Findings

The findings are summarized in Table II.

Among these three samples the consistency of regular class growth prior to special remedial assistance is noteworthy. In each instance the subjects were making progress in regular class instruction at approximately half the rate of the normal pupil. A remarkable change occurred during remedial instruction,

TABLE II   *Growth in Reading* During Periods of Instruction*

Sample	Ratio Pre-remedial Period	Ratio Remedial Period	Months Post-remedial Interval	Ratio Post-remedial Period†
I	.56	6.61	9	−.01
II	.53	4.79	13	.75
III	.55	unknown	36	.75

* Based on growth per 20 days of instruction of 2 to 3 hours daily reading activity. Each regular class year is assumed to consist of 9 months of 20 instructional days.

† Over a 13-month post-remedial period, 50 per cent of Sample II had had additional remedial assistance through school reading center, remedial clinic, or private tutoring. Over the 4-year period following the initial clinic contact, Sample III received a mean of 174 hours of special remedial instruction, less than an hour per week.

however. These severely disabled readers, most of whom had not established independence in word recognition prior to the the remedial program described above, progressed at a rate twelve times their regular class rate in Sample I and nine times their regular class rate in Sample II. (The data were not available for calculation of this figure for Sample III.) Beyond this substantial change by comparison with their own previous record of growth, these disabled readers also clearly surpassed the normal growth rate of normal pupils. Assuming the normal pupil makes one month growth in reading skill for one month in school, these severely disabled readers bettered normal growth by more than six times in Sample I and nearly five times in Sample II.

The rate of continued growth in reading following a period of intensive assistance is reflected by the post-remedial period column in Table II. Several judgments can be made from those figures. Continuing growth seems to depend upon continued attention to the problem. While the second and third groups received additional remedial assistance throughout the follow-up period, few of the pupils in Sample I had any further special help. Sample I pupils did not lose the reading skill they had acquired during the time in the clinic, but neither did they continue to develop on their own. Quite in contrast is the continuing progress of the second and third groups. Given far less intensive, but nonetheless supportive, help over the follow-up period, these pupils continued to develop in reading at a pace more rapid than that preceding intensive tutoring. Rate of growth over the follow-up period was approximately 75 per cent of normal growth.

These findings are consistent with previously reported research in supporting the effectiveness of remedial instruction for disabled readers. They extend the evidence in support of remedial effectiveness to include the very severely disabled pupil who is referred to a university clinic after years of failure, at about sixth grade age and functioning in reading at second grade level.

The unfortunate but highly instructive element of these findings is that severe reading disability is not corrected by short-term intensive courses of treatment, even though it is ameliorated by such help. Neither, it would appear, is the cure to be found in intensive treatment followed by maintenance sessions of an hour or so per week, although again such a program is far superior to no special help at all. The implication which follows naturally from these conclusions is that severe reading disability is probably best considered a relatively chronic illness needing long-term treatment rather than the short course typically organized in current programs.

As far as it reaches, remedial assistance appears to be effective. A reasonable question for research is whether intensive instruction over an extended period of months or years would eventually enable severely disabled readers to take their place among normal youngsters making normal progress in school.

REFERENCES

1. Bliesmer, Emory T. "Evaluating Progress in Remedial Reading Programs," *Reading Teacher,* 15 (Mar. 1962), 344–350.

2. Bond, Guy L., and Fay, Leo C. "A Report of the University of Minnesota Reading Clinic," *Journal of Educational Research,* 43 (Jan. 1950), 385–390.

3. Johnson, L. R., and Platts, D. "A Summary of a Study of the Reading Ages of Children Who Had Been Given Remedial Teaching," *British Journal of Educational Psychology,* 32 (Feb. 1962), 66–71.

4. Lovell, K., Byrne, C., and Richardson, B. "A Further Study of the Educational Progress of Children Who Had Received Remedial Instruction," *British Journal of Education Psychology,* 33 (Feb. 1963), 3–9.

5. Mouly, G. J., and Grant, Virginia. "A Study of Growth to Be Expected of Retarded Readers," *Journal of Educational Research,* 49 (Feb. 1956), 461–465.

‸‸

Part Eight

Handwriting

Difficulties in handwriting, reading, and spelling are likely to be highly inter-related. Most basically, a child who is failing in reading and spelling usually has negative feelings toward verbal activities in general, and these may be mani-fested in careless, illegible handwriting. Illegibilities may result, too, from a kind of negative motivation: the desire to hide misspellings. In certain instances poor handwriting may be caused by deeply rooted emotional problems, and a child may be, in effect, agraphic. Or difficulty in writing may be a direct result of a physical disability, but such cases are rare.

Whatever the cause, the most efficient way—and probably the single most effective way—of tackling the problem of illegibilities is to focus upon specific illegibilities. In a context in which realistic models for handwriting performance are provided and a reasonably high level of motivation is sustained, such a focus can be the nucleus for a program of remedial instruction in handwriting. The worth of nonspecific exercises and of other traditional activities supposedly aimed at improving handwriting has not been demonstrated.

The first article in this chapter is a report of an investigation of the effect of three methods of instruction upon the handwriting performance of third- and fourth-graders. While Tagatz *et al.* were not concerned with remedial instruction as such, the results of the study have implications that are as clear for remedial teachers as for regular classroom teachers. The subsection of the paper in which the collection of data is discussed may be of particular interest, for the same procedure can be followed by a remedial teacher interested in sampling hand-writing produced under a variety of conditions. If a child's best handwriting is legible but his normal handwriting is not, the teacher can assume that the basic problem is one of habit, not inability to produce acceptable letter forms.

The studies by Newland and by Quant are classics. Both are the result of careful analyses of the factors that cause handwriting to be illegible, and as such they provide the framework for a diagnostic inventory. Newland's findings in particular should be useful in helping a remedial teacher to focus upon the relatively few but frequent faulty habits in producing letter forms that cause handwriting to be illegible. Quant's results have to do with the importance of spacing, alignment, slant, and quality of line as well as letter formation; but he argues that the most important factor in determining the legibility of handwrit-ing is good letter formation.

While the studies by Newland and by Quant are still useful in providing focus for diagnosis of handwriting problems, the fact is that the Newland study was done more than thirty years ago and the Quant study more than twenty years ago. In the interim not only have changes taken place in handwriting instruction, but the shift toward conceptualizing handwriting more as a tool than an art has quickened. As a result, the nature of the handwriting product has probably changed, and the types of malformations and other factors that influence legibility may have changed. Both studies, therefore, need to be replicated with contemporary handwriting samples.

While there is still much value in focusing upon the specifics of illegibility during the remedial teaching sequence, a need to look occasionally at the handwriting product in an overall way exists. The total impression of quality made by a particular handwriting sample results from the sum of letter formations, spacing, alignment, and quality of line; and the total product is the ultimate concern of both student and teacher. Demonstrations of progress through sequentially closer approximations of a model can serve as a motivational device, and relative ratings based upon general quality can aid the teacher in assessing progress. Scales consisting of handwriting samples from discrete quality levels can be useful, for they serve to define operationally the sometimes elusive notion of quality of handwriting.

This is not the place to become involved in a discussion of what actually does constitute quality in handwriting, but the fact is that obvious differences may exist even among handwriting samples that are all easily readable. Handwriting quality is distributed along a continuum that ranges from unreadable to highly readable as well as from aesthetically unappealing to very appealing. Handwriting scales provide criteria that enable both pupils and teachers to judge the quality of handwriting samples in some systematic way. The point of the article by Otto, Askov, and Cooper is that once the criteria have become established, samples can be reliably rated even without reference to the scale that served initially to establish bases for judgments.

Whereas the Newland and Quant articles are reports of analyses of errors in cursive writing, the Lewis and Lewis article is a report of an analysis of errors in the manuscript (printing) writing of first-grade pupils. Virtually all first-grade pupils are introduced first to manuscript writing, and only later, usually sometime during the second or third grade, is the transition made to cursive writing. In addition to the immediate value of the error analysis as a guide to diagnostic work with primary children, the study appears to have heuristic value, for the authors have pointed out some interesting possibilities for further research. The classification scheme given in the method section for letter-construction errors is worth particular study. Finally, the suggestion that the feasibility of modifying the structure of the most troublesome letter forms be studied merits consideration. Present letter forms[1] seem to be derived more from whimsy and convention than from empirical analysis of writers' perceptual-motor abilities and limitations.

Groff has suggested new norms for handwriting speed to supplant those constructed by Ayres. Groff's questions about the Ayres procedure are legitimate, and the new norms are more realistic in terms of everyday handwriting tasks. Remedial teachers need to be concerned about their pupils' handwriting speed, because unless their writing is reasonably fluent, it cannot serve as the tool they need for normal schoolwork. If handwriting must be painstakingly drawn to be legible, the demands of the task are likely to inhibit expression through writing.

---

1 See V. E. Herrick and W. Otto, *Letter Form Models Advocated by Commercial Handwriting Systems* (Madison, Wis.: School of Education, University of Wisconsin, 1961) for a presentation of the most widely used manuscript and cursive letter form models.

29   Effect of Three Methods of Instruction upon the Handwriting Performance of Third- and Fourth-Graders

GLENN E. TAGATZ

WAYNE OTTO

HERBERT J. KLAUSMEIER

WILLIAM L. GOODWIN

DORIS M. COOK

One of the interesting generalizations arising from a national survey of practices in the teaching of handwriting (Herrick and Okada, 1963) was that although most respondents claimed to favor the teaching of handwriting in all subject areas, few reported attempts to help pupils develop a personal style or recognize their own errors. This is true even though (a) relatively few types of errors account for a great proportion of the illegibilities in handwriting (Newland, 1932; Quant, 1946), and (b) commercial materials reflect consensus that in the upper elementary grades instructional time in handwriting may best be devoted to remedial work, i.e. identifying general and specific inaccuracies in letter forms, slant, size, spacing, and alignment (Committee for Research in Basic Skills, 1960). The gap between an apparent need and actual practice appears to be responsible for considerable dissatisfaction with the provisions for and the results of handwriting instruction.

The present study was designed to secure more precise information about instructional methods and handwriting performances of children enrolled in the third and fourth grades of an urban elementary school. The specific purpose of the study was to determine the effects of three different instructional approaches upon handwriting performance. For convenience the approaches were designated (a) formal group, (b) formal-individualized and (c) individualized-diagnostic. The basic question in regard to the individualized approaches was whether pupils would do better with a set of commercially prepared materials or with teacher devised and directed procedures.

Method

SUBJECTS

Eighty-eight third-grade and 75 fourth-grade pupils served as subjects. They were randomly assigned to one of the three instructional groups following stratification by sex and previous achievement/ability level. The latter stratum was determined by equally weighting previously obtained general mental ability

From *American Educational Research Journal,* Vol. 5, No. 1 (January, 1968), pp. 81–90. Reprinted with permission.

The research reported herein was performed pursuant to a contract with the United States Office of Education, Department of Health, Education, and Welfare, under the provisions of the Cooperative Research Program. Center No. C-03/Contract No. OES 10-154. Personnel in the R & I Units at Giese School in Racine, Wisconsin, included a learning specialist, Marillyn Kletecka, and three certified teachers, Anne Buchanan, Charles Leonard, and Mary Rounds, at the fourth level; and at the third level, learning specialist Maxine Vohs and teachers Janet Hansen, Beverly Schinderle, and Sammye Woods. The building principal is Earl Nelson.

scores and scores on standardized achievement tests and categorizing the subjects within each grade into high, average, and low groups.

PROCEDURE

Each group was given 15 minutes of handwriting instruction each day for the nine-week duration of the study. Teachers systematically rotated across groups to control for teacher variance. That is, the three third-grade teachers and the three fourth-grade teachers who participated in the study taught each of their respective grade level groups for one-third of the total nine weeks, changing groups each week. The assignment of the children randomly to the three instructional treatments and the changing of teachers among the three groups were possible because all the teachers and children for each grade have been organized into one research and instructional unit, rather than remaining in three self-contained classrooms. The R and I Units, designed to facilitate controlled experimentation in the classroom, is explained fully elsewhere (Klausmeier, *et al.*, 1966).

The approaches taken with the three instructional groups were dissimilar by design; each had a salient feature that might be expected to have measurable impact in a comparative study. The approaches are briefly described.

Formal Group Approach. This is the approach that had been used in the preceding years. The standard procedure was to follow the instructional plan outlined in the adopted commercial system for teaching handwriting for the entire group. In Grade Three the Peterson Directed Handwriting system, published by the Macmillan Company in their *Adventures in Handwriting* series, was used; and the *Correlated Handwriting Series,* published by Zaner-Bloser, was used in Grade Four.

Formal-Individualized Program. The procedure here was to follow the programed sequence of instruction presented in the *Penskills Individualized Handwriting Skills Program,* published by Science Research Associates. The program is individualized in that it permits pupils to proceed at their own pace and, within the limits of the materials provided, to focus upon their own problems. It is formal in that the instructional materials are prescribed and restricted to the contents of the *Penskills* kit.

Individualized-Diagnostic Approach. With this approach there was no systematic use of commercially prepared materials. The procedure was similar to that outlined by Otto and McMenemy (1966, Chapter 10); individuals were assisted and encouraged to recognize errors and malformations in their own writing and to work specifically on the elimination of personal difficulties. In general, an attempt was made to help each pupil focus on a limited number of his own problems at the beginning of an instructional sequence, and then he was permitted to practice while doing writing of his own choosing. All pupils were systematically encouraged to develop the habit of continuously evaluating their own handwriting, e.g. once each week they wrote a standard sentence which they evaluated in terms of a normative scale.

COLLECTION AND ANALYSIS OF DATA

Handwriting samples were obtained at the beginning and at the end of the nine-week period. To expedite later scaling, a standard sentence, which includes all letters of the alphabet, was used: *Big oxen, quick zebras, fighting monkeys, and wild pigs have jungle homes.* Two facts were considered in gathering the samples: legible handwriting is sometimes produced at the cost of an extremely slow rate; and some habitually careless writers may be able to produce legible handwriting if they so choose. Thus, the decision was to compare handwriting performance in terms of speed of writing and legibility of the handwriting product and also to gather samples under three conditions. The three conditions in which data were gathered were:

Normal Condition.   Teachers had their pupils continuously write the standard sentence after instructing them to write *as they usually* wrote. A five-minute work sample was secured. A total word count was obtained for each subject, and the third sentence (or the last completed sentence for slower pupils) was rated for legibility by three independent judges.

Best Condition.   Pupils were instructed to write the same sentence four times *as well as* they could. The third sentence was judged for legibility as above.

Fastest Condition.   Teachers instructed their pupils to write the same sentence continuously *as fast as* they could. Word counts of a five-minute work sample were obtained for each pupil, and the third sentence produced was judged for legibility.

The 978 sentences collected under the three conditions in two testing sessions were coded and scrambled before scoring. Three independent judges who were naive as to the instructional treatment, session of testing, and grade level of the subjects assigned a rating of one to five (low to high legibility) to each sample of writing. The SRA *Penskills* scale, which comprises 20 criterion samples from five quality levels, was used as a guide in assigning ratings. The three ratings were averaged to determine a single final score for each of the two samples of writing for each subject.

Three-way analyses of covariance were performed separately for Grade Three and Grade Four for the following measures: number of words produced under the normal and fastest conditions, and ratings of legibility under normal, best, and fastest conditions. The covariate in each analysis was the score on the same pre-instruction measures. Newman-Keuls procedures were used to test the significance of differences between adjusted means following the analyses of covariance. These means were adjusted to account for initial differences on the pre-instruction measures.

Results

Inter-judge reliability indexes were .72, .81 and .78. The high coefficients support the legibility rating scheme that was employed.

The *F*-ratios generated by the analysis of covariance for Grade Three are presented in Table I. Instruction was significant for the normal and fastest legibility ratings. Previous achievement/ability level was significant only for the number of words written in five minutes under normal instructions, while sex was significant on every measure except number of words written under the fast condition. The number of words written under fast instructions did not reach significance for any of the main effects. The covariate was highly significant for each performance measure.

TABLE I *Summary of F-Ratios by Dependent Variable for Grades 3 and 4*

Source	Grade	df	No. of Words Normal	No. of Words Fast	Normal Rating	Best Rating	Fastest Rating
Instruction (I)	3	2/69	2.54	1.40	5.31**	1.25	4.38*
	4	2/56	3.04	—	1.61	3.29*	—
Previous Achievement/ Ability Level (P)	3	2/69	3.91*	1.56	—	—	1.64
	4	2/56	2.61	1.99	3.34*	6.73*	—
Sex (S)	3	1/69	4.24*	—	5.76*	7.74**	9.11**
	4	1/56	—	—	12.15***	13.99***	8.99**
I X P	3	4/69	2.05	—	—	—	1.11
	4	4/56	—	—	—	—	3.38
I X S	3	2/69	—	1.38	2.14	1.43	5.09**
	4	4/56	—	—	—	—	—
P X S	3	2/69	3.00	—	1.02	1.05	—
	4	4/56	—	—	—	—	—
I X P X S	3	4/69	1.48	—	1.51	—	—
	4	4/56	1.09	—	1.51	—	—
Covariate	3	1/69	69.85***	65.90***	23.84***	27.98***	20.24***
	4	1/56	19.93***	30.68***	43.87***	21.79***	35.57***

* $p < .05$
** $p < .01$
*** $p < .001$

TABLE II *Adjusted Means for Number of Words Written and Legibility Scores for Significant Main Effects by Dependent Variable, Grades 3 and 4*

Main Effect	Level	Grade	Normal No. of Words	Normal Rating	Best Rating	Fastest Rating
	Formal Group	3	NS	1.47	NS	1.35
		4	NS	NS	2.83	NS
Instruction	Individualized	3	NS	1.94	NS	1.71
	Diagnostic	4	NS	NS	2.75	NS
	Formal Individual	3	NS	1.69	NS	1.47
		4	NS	NS	3.15	NS
Previous	High	3	28.98	NS	NS	NS
		4	NS	2.68	3.22	NS
Achievement/Ability	Average	3	25.11	NS	NS	NS
		4	NS	2.91	3.08	NS
Level	Low	3	24.47	NS	NS	NS
		4	NS	2.44	2.44	NS
	Male	3	24.80	1.54	1.65	1.34
		4	NS	2.41	2.62	1.95
Sex						
	Female	3	27.58	1.86	2.05	1.68
		4	NS	2.95	3.20	2.44

Relevant adjusted means for the significant main effects are presented in Table II. From the table, the superiority of the individualized-diagnostic approach (1.94, 1.71) over the formal group method (1.47, 1.35) is clear, but the difference between the individualized-diagnostic and the formal-individualized approach (1.69, 1.47) did not reach statistical significance. The high previous achievement/ability group made significantly greater gains than the average and low groups on speed of writing under normal instructions. Third-grade girls not only wrote faster than boys under normal instructions, but they also wrote more legibly under all three sampling conditions, i.e. normal, best, and fastest. The significant instruction by sex interaction for the fastest rating (Table I) occurred because of the exceptional performance of the girls in the individualized diagnostic group.

Somewhat different results were obtained from the Grade Four data. These results are summarized in Table I. Generally speaking, fewer treatment significances were found at level four. Only the best rating was significantly different in the instructional treatments part of the analysis. Previous achievement/ability level was significant for the normal and best ratings, while sex reached significance on all three ratings. It can be noted that no significant effects occurred relating to either of the analyses of number of words written. Covariates were highly significant in all five analyses as they had been for Grade Three.

Relevant adjusted means are presented in Table II for the significant *F*-values. The formal individualized instruction group scored significantly higher than the individualized diagnostic group on the best rating, but not significantly different from the formal group. Differences among the three groups were not significant, as noted, for the normal rating and the fastest rating. Under the normal writing condition, pupils at the average previous achievement/ability level made significantly greater gains in legibility than the pupils in the low stratum. Under the best writing condition, fourth-graders in both the high and average strata outgained pupils in the low level. Performance among groups in the fastest condition was not significant. Female fourth-graders performed better than their male counterparts on all three ratings. The significant instruction by previous achievement/ability level interaction for the fastest rating was primarily due to relatively high adjusted means for the low stratum pupils under all three treatments and the marked low rating for the average stratum pupils with formal group instruction.

Discussion

There seems to be considerable evidence that the traditional handwriting approach examined in this study is not as effective as the individualized approaches, particularly at the third-grade level. With one exception—where the difference was not statistically significant—the individualized approaches to teaching handwriting produced greater increases in legibility than the formal group approach. In Grade Three, the best performance resulted from the individualized diagnostic instruction in which no commercial materials were used. There seems to be sufficient support for an individualized approach to merit a longer term replication study with a view toward ultimate replacement of the traditional approach if such is merited. It is recognized that the traditional approach probably suffered from a lack, or at least a tarnishing, of the halo effect. To counterbalance this, however, the teachers had least prior experience with the individualized diagnostic approach, and it is the most difficult to execute.

Results at the fourth-grade level were not so definitive. In only one case was the instructional treatment effect significant, i.e., best rating: in this case the formal group approach was most effective; and the individual-diagnostic approach was least effective. It should be kept in mind, however, that third- and fourth-graders may be quite dissimilar where handwriting is concerned. A marked development in handwriting skill probably occurs in the intervening year between late third and late fourth grade; and, in addition, the fourth-graders had received an additional year of traditional handwriting instruction before the experiment began. Perhaps the critical factor in the early development of legible handwriting is individualized attention, yet this same individualization may not be nearly so effective after pupils' handwriting habits have been fairly well established. Perhaps, too, some combination of the individualized diagnostic and formal individualized methods would produce the most efficient performance in Grade Three. Though no treatment was clearly most effective in Grade Four on all of the performance measures, it is interesting to note that the absolute gains in legibility from pre- to post-instruction measures were much greater under all three treatments than in the third grade.

Girls were consistently and significantly better than males on most of the measures. Female superiority in tasks of manual dexterity is, of course, commonplace; but it must be remembered that in the present analyses adjustments were made for differences in initial skill through covariance. Thus, the girls' consistent advantages were generated in just nine weeks. It is possible, however, that a bias favoring some feminine handwriting characteristic, e.g. aesthetic appeal as opposed to readability *per se,* exists among the judges or in the scale employed.

Differential gains in handwriting skill by pupils in the three previous achievement/ability levels were not entirely consistent. More often than not, however, students from the lowest stratum progressed the least.

In conclusion, it seems likely that the gap between the apparent need to individualize handwriting and actual practices employed in the schools should be bridged through curricular modification in the early grades—probably before Grade Four—and not in the middle elementary grades as suggested in many commercial materials.

REFERENCES

Committee for Research in Basic Skills. *Comparison of Practices in Handwriting Advocated by Nineteen Commercial Systems of Handwriting Instruction.* School of Education. University of Wisconsin, 1960. 111 pp.

Herrick, Virgil E., and Okada, Nora. "The Present Scene: Practices in the Teaching of Handwriting in the U.S.—1960." In Herrick, Virgil E., (Ed.) *New Horizons for Research in Handwriting.* University of Wisconsin Press, 1963. pp. 17–38.

Klausmeier, Herbert J., Goodwin, William L., Prasch, J., and Goodson, M. R., *Project Models: Maximizing Opportunities for Development and Experimenta-tion in Learning in the Schools.* Madison, Wisconsin: Research and Development Center for Learning and Re-education, Occasional Paper No. 3, 1966. 29 pp.

Newland, T. E. "An Analytical Study of the Development of Illegibilities in Handwriting from the Lower Grades to Adulthood." *Journal of Educational Research* 26: 249–258, December 1932.

Otto, Wayne, and McMenemy, R. *Corrective and Remedial Teaching.* Boston: Houghton Mifflin, 1966. 377 pp.

Quant, Leslie. "Factors Affecting the Legibility of Handwriting." *Journal of Experimental Education* 14: 297–316; June 1946.

30   An Analytical Study of the Development of
Illegibilities in Handwriting from the
Lower Grades to Adulthood

T. ERNEST NEWLAND

Summary.—*Analyses by twenty-four different persons of 1,344,905 letters writ-ten by 2381 different individuals, ranging in age from first grade children to adults in different occupations, resulted in the tabulation of 42,284 specific il-legibilities. A study of these indicated that:*

   1. There were more forms of illegibilities peculiar to the different age groups than there were common to two or more age levels.
   2. The illegibilities of only four letters (a, e, r, t) contributed 45, 46, and 47 per cent to the elementary, high-school and adult groups respectively.
   3. Only fourteen forms of illegibilities in the elementary and high school levels and nine in the adult group contributed 50 percent of all the illegibilities recorded.
   4. Only four types of difficulties in the formation of letters caused over one-half of all illegibilities.
   5. The gross frequency with which illegibilities appeared tended to increase with age.

These results indicate that while remedial or preventive work should be adapted to the different age levels, either the prevention of illegibilities in the writing of the letters "a," "e," "r," and "t," the correction of from nine to fourteen forms of illeg-ibilities, or the correction or prevention of four types of bad letter-formation habits would decrease the number of illegibilities by one-half. Corrective or preventive work directed along all three of these lines would probably eliminate at least three-fourths of all illegibilities.

Introduction

The problem of illegibilities is essentially a social one; correspondence of all sorts is illustrative of this, whether it be in terms of confusions on personal checks or in terms of undecipherable parts of social correspondence. In spite of the fact that this problem is of such importance, illegibilities have not at-tracted sufficient scientific attention. That they are deserving of such considera-tion should seem apparent to anyone who will recall instances in which errors have occurred on account of confusions. While recorded instances such as the one which appeared in the *Church World:* "And they were married and lived happily even after," and a London dispatch to the *New York Sun* in which this statement was made: "We have not done any business with firms or persons in America since Prohibition came into farce in that country" may be amusing now, there may have been times when humor was not the predominating note.[1]

   This study is an attempt to answer the following questions: (1) What letters are most frequently illegible? (2) In what way or ways do these illegibilities occur? That is, are certain letters illegible in one or more ways? Do the different forms appear with approximately the same frequencies? Are any differences

1 "Humor in Error," *The Reader's Digest,* November, 1931, p. 67.

From *Journal of Educational Research,* Vol. 26, No. 4 (December, 1932), pp. 249–258. Reprinted with permission.

apparent in the comparison of results at different age levels? And (3) do the answers to these questions suggest any remedial or preventive measures?

While a sizable number of studies has been made on the general aspect of quality of cursive handwriting, very few have been recorded where the specificity of the illegibility problem has been even mentioned. Ayres,[2] in 1913, and Freeman,[3] in 1915, referred to a few specific letter illegibilities which they considered deserving of attention, but they pushed the matter no further. Nothing other than implied expert opinion was cited in light of which they seem to have made their statements. In 1927, S. L. and L. C. Pressey[4] published the results of the pioneer investigation in the field of specific analysis of illegibility.[5] The study summarized here is similar to that of the Presseys' with the exception that this one had a wider and more adequate sampling of ages, the resulting mass of material analyzed was greater and the data of this study were submitted to a more elaborate analysis.

Materials and Methods

The material used for this analysis consisted of regular periodic papers collected from a total of 1500 pupils in the eight grades of the elementary school, from 452 students in the four grades of the high-school level, from 297 college students represented mainly by sophomores but including also juniors and seniors, and letters written by 132 different adults to editors of two different city newspapers. The schools from which the specimens were collected were in widely separated states and can reasonably be considered to be typical of the general school situation. Both city and country schools supplied material. No one system of handwriting instruction contributed an overwhelming portion. No papers were prepared expressly for this study. A part of them were done with pencil and a part with pen. In all, 341,315 words, or 1,344,905 letters, written by 2381 different persons provided the basis for this analysis. Table I shows the distribution of the material among the different groups.

Some 24 different persons contributed their analyses to one or more parts of this study. They were instructed to record each time they encountered something in their reading of the specimens which made them stop and look a second time at what they were reading in order to determine what the writer meant.[6] Specific directions were given to the effect that they were not to let such things as misspellings, re-writings, crowdings or erasures enter their results as illegibilities. Such things as these were recorded, but separate from the specific illegibilities. If the readers were unable to record the illegibilities in some such category as "a like o," "g like cj" or "e closed," they copied as best they could

2 Ayres, L. P., "A Scale for Measuring the Quality of Handwriting of School Children," Bulletin No. 113, Russell Sage Foundation, Division of Education, 1913.

3 Freeman, F. N. *The Teaching of Handwriting*. Boston: Houghton Mifflin Company, 1915.

4 Pressey, S. L., and Pressey, L. C. "Analyses of Three Thousand Illegibilities in the Handwriting of Children and Adults," *Educational Research Bulletin*, VI, September 28, 1927.

5 Related to this general problem is the study on illegibilities in numerals. See: Newland, T. E. "A Study of the Specific Illegibilities Found in the Writing of Arabic Numerals," *Journal of Educational Research*, XXI, March, 1930.

6 This procedure may seem to have been unreliable, but quite the contrary was found to be the case. Not only the gross correlational method of comparison but also a minute analysis of the particular forms of illegibilities showed a high agreement, for this type of study. In the case of the former method, a rank correlation between the frequencies of letter illegibility, as recorded by one person, and the frequencies of letter illegibility, as recorded by two other persons working together on the same set of over 400 high school papers, was found to be +.80 ±.05. Similar computation on the results of one person's analyzing twice the same set of 45 high school English papers, without his knowing the purpose of the duplication of the work, gave +.96 ±.01.

TABLE I   *Scope of the Material Analyzed*

Groups	Number of Persons Writing	Number of Words Analyzed	Number of Letters	Number of Specific Illegibilities	Number of Readers
Elementary Grades					
1	60	434	1,573	29	1
2	133	3,449	12,503	242	1
3	174	6,813	24,697	560	1
4	178	17,744	64,322	1,917	6
5	316	27,029	97,980	2,581	7
6	202	17,999	65,246	1,015	5
7	263	35,795	129,757	845	2
8	174	40,653	147,367	581	2
Total	1,500	149,916	543,445	7,770	14
High School Grades					
1	159	29,304	116,776	4,383	3
2	140	26,880	107,117	2,580	3
3	108	17,820	71,013	2,177	3
4	45	8,284	33,012	1,963	3
Total	452	82,288	327,918	11,103	3
Adult Group					
College	297	67,474	292,837	10,915	8
Letters	132	41,637	180,705	12,496	1
Total	429	109,111	473,542	23,411	9
Grand Total	2,381	341,315	1,344,905	42,284	24*

* Does not equal the sum of the readers on the different parts because some readers worked on more than one part.

the specific form of the illegibility and entered a tally mark opposite the reproduction. In case of doubt as to what the letter might be, the intent of the writer was checked by means of the context. Tabulations were kept separate for each grade or group, and were later combined into totals which were used to characterize some major grouping such as the elementary grades, high school, or adult. The actual illegibility frequencies were transmuted into terms of frequency-per-one-hundred-thousand running letters. Throughout the study, an attempt was made to have all tabulations as specific and extensive as possible, the assumption being that it was at all times more desirable to have a mass of specific data that could later be synthesized than it was to have gross records which could only with great difficulty and much inaccuracy be further analyzed.

Results

A total of 499 different forms of illegibilities were recorded. According to Table II, only 16 per cent of this total were common to all three of the major age groups used—the elementary, the high school, and the adult. An additional 20 per cent were common to only two of these three groups. The fact that 64 per cent of the forms were peculiar to one group or another is suggestive remedially.

TABLE II *Number and Percentages of Forms of Illegibilities Common to All Three Levels, Common to Any Two of Them, and Peculiar to Any One of Them*

Letter	Forms Common to						Forms Peculiar to				Total Number of Forms
	All Levels	%	El.& H.S.	H.S.& Ad.	El.& Ad.	%	El.	H.S.	Ad.	%	
a	5	25	1	—	2	15	4	6	2	60	20
b	4	14	3	1	3	24	4	9	5	62	29
c	3	38	1	—	—	12	2	—	2	50	8
d	4	17	1	2	2	21	6	7	2	62	24
e	3	33	—	—	—	—	4	—	2	67	9
f	3*	8	4	3	4	28	5	12	8	64	39
g	2	8	2	3	2	27	6	9	2	65	26
h	3	13	2	2	2	26	6	4	4	61	23
i	6	32	2	—	3	16	2	2	4	52	19
j	—	—	—	—	—	—	4	1	1	100	6
k	2	12	4	2	2	47	3	4	—	41	17
l	2	15	—	—	1	8	3	3	4	77	13
m	3	25	1	—	1	8	2	1	4	67	12
n	3	15	2	1	4	30	4	3	4	55	20
o	7	29	2	2	2	25	7	2	2	46	24
p	1	3	5	2	2	25	8	9	9	72	36
q	—	—	—	—	—	—	1	4	1	100	6
r	6	22	3	—	2	19	9	4	2	59	26
s	5	19	1	3	1	19	6	9	1	62	26
t	6	19	1	1	1	10	8	10	4	71	31
u	4	19	—	—	2	10	9	3	3	71	21
v	3	21	1	—	2	21	1	4	3	58	14
w	4	18	1	—	2	14	7	4	4	68	22
x	—	—	—	—	—	—	1	1	—	100	2
y	2	9	3	—	—	14	5	8	3	77	21
z	1	25	—	—	—	—	—	2	1	75	4
Totals	82	16	40	22	40	20	117	121	77	64	499

* This means that three forms, or practically eight per cent of the forms in which "f" appeared illegible, were common to all three age levels, four were common to only the elementary and high-school levels, three were common to only the high-school and adult levels, etc.

Only six letters—"c," "e," "j," "q," "x," and "z"—had less than ten forms in which they appeared illegible. Five letters had from 10 to 19 illegibility forms, while three had over 30 forms of illegibilities. Nearly half (12) of the letters of the alphabet, then, appeared illegible in from 20 to 29 different forms. The implications concerning the specificity of remedial procedure, with respect to the different age-level groupings, seem quite obvious.

Table III shows the frequencies per 100,000 running letters with which the letters of the alphabet appeared illegible and the extent to which each letter contributed to the total number of illegibilities at each level, as expressed in percentages. It can be seen that the illegibilities of the four letters "a," "e," "r," and "t" were among the first five in importance in each major age group and that they together contributed 45, 46, and 47 per cent to the elementary, high-school, and adult groups respectively. Taking all the letters together, the high-school students wrote 136 per cent more illegibly than did the elementary school children, but were surpassed 52 per cent by the adults. It is interesting to note that the adults wrote more than three times more illegibly than did the elementary school children.

TABLE III *Frequencies per 100,000 Running Letters with Which Each Letter Appeared Illegible and the Percentages of the Totals the Illegibilities of Each Letter Represented*

Letter	Elementary		High School		Adult		Total	
	Fr.	**%**	**Fr.**	**%**	**Fr.**	**%**	**Fr.**	**%**
a	153	11	277	9	377	8	269	8
b	89	6	278	9	180	4	172	5
c	16	1	47	1	70	1	44	1
d	126	9	260	8	266	5	214	7
e	167	12*	392	12	904	18	495	16
f	39	3	120	4	155	3	102	3
g	31	2	53	2	66	1	50	2
h	80	6	154	5	235	5	157	4
i	57	4	158	5	362	7	195	6
j	1	—**	2	—	1	—	1	—
k	19	1	49	2	30	1	31	1
l	34	2	49	2	100	2	62	2
m	16	1	10	—	27	1	19	1
n	55	4	63	2	457	9	205	6
o	73	5	181	6	185	4	143	5
p	15	1	113	3	84	2	65	2
q	1	—	3	—	1	—	1	—
r	167	12	290	9	440	9	302	9
s	47	3	132	4	273	6	152	5
t	134	10	515	16	600	12	402	13
u	23	2	8	—	15	—	17	1
v	11	1	22	1	35	1	23	1
w	22	2	47	1	35	1	34	1
x	—	—	—	—	—	—	—	—
y	10	1	25	1	31	1	22	1
z	1	—	4	—	2	—	2	—
Total	1,387		3,252		4,931		3,179	

* This shows that the letter "e" was found illegible 167 times in every 100,000 running letters written by the elementary group, and contributed 12 per cent of the total number of illegibilities of that group.

** These dashes indicate percentages of less than .5.

When one considers the most frequent forms of illegibilities which accounted for approximately one-half of all the illegibilities among lower case letters, as shown in Table IV, one is impressed by two things, namely, the small number of forms, as compared with the total number recorded at each level, and the degree of consistency with which certain forms appeared at the different levels. Of particular interest is the fact that, of the nine forms of illegibilities which accounted for 50 per cent of all the illegibilities recorded for the adult level, six were common to all three levels. The illegibility "e closed" accounted for nearly twice as many illegibilities in the elementary and adult groups and practically 50 per cent more than its nearest competitor in the high-school group. With one exception, the other five, "d" like "cl," "r" like "i," "i" not dotted, "h" like "li," and "n" like "u" showed no marked tendency either to increase or to decrease in relative importance going from the elementary grades to the adult group. This exception, "n" like "u," had a percentage from four to five times greater among the adult illegibilities than among those in the lower age groups.

As for the analysis of capital letter illegibility, out of a total of 753 illegibilities tabulated for these letters, 439 of them were recorded for the letter "I."

TABLE IV   *The Most Frequent Forms of Illegibilities Accounting for Approxi-mately Fifty Per Cent of all Illegibilities Among Lower Case Letters, Their Frequencies, and the Percentages They Contributed to All Illegibilities*

Elementary			High School			Adult			Total		
Fr.	%	Form	Fr.	%	Form	Fr.	%	Form	Fr.	%	Form
145	11	e closed*	373	11	e closed	882	18	e closed	473	15	e closed
81	6	d like cl	265	8	t like l	363	7	n like u	155	5	n like u
56	4	a like o	152	5	a like u	216	4	d like cl	148	5	d like cl
47	3	a like u	146	4	d like cl	200	4	i, no dot	131	4	t like l
45	3	a like ci	120	4	r like i	188	4	a like o	114	4	r like j
42	3	t, cross above	94	3	i, no dot	185	4	r like i	111	4	i, no dot
			91	3	o like a	182	4	t, cross above	103	3	a like o
41	3	r like i	84	3	h like li				102	3	a like u
36	3	b like li	63	2	r like s	151	3	a like li	93	3	t, cross above
35	3	t like l	55	2	t, cross right	148	3	t, cross right			
35	3	i, no dot							88	3	h like li
34	2	r like half n	53	2	r like half n	51			68	2	b like li
33	2	o like a	52	2	t, too short	(9 of 220 forms)			51		
30	2	h like li	50	2	n like u				(11 of 498 forms)		
27	2	n like u	50	2	d like cl						
50			53								
(14 of 279 forms)			(14 of 264 forms)								

* This means that "e closed" occurred 145 times in every 100,000 running letters written at the elementary level and accounted for 11 per cent of all the illegibities at that level.

The malformation of "I" accounted for at least 55 per cent of the capital letter illegibilities in the elementary group, and for no less than 43 per cent of all the illegibilities at the high-school level, but what were overshadowed by the importance of the failure of adults to close their "D's," which latter condition accounted for at least 30 per cent of the illegible capitals of adults.

A grouping of the different illegibilities with respect to common types of errors in the writing process provided very interesting possibilities remedially and preventively. For instance, the failure to close letters, Type 1, Table V, was found to be the most consistently serious illegibility habit, as indicated by the percentages of 24, 20 and 16 for the elementary, high-school and adult groups respectively. The tendency to close loops unnecessarily, especially above the lines, rose from 13 per cent in the elementary level to 20 per cent in the adult level. The tendency to loop strokes unnecessarily fluctuates from a 12 per cent importance in the elementary group to one of 27 per cent in the high-school, and goes back to 12 per cent for the adults. While Types 20 to 24 contribute less than one-half of one per cent to the total of the illegibilities recorded, they are included here as interesting negative findings.

The upshot of this phase of the work seems to be that the concentration on three or four types of difficulties would focus attention on those groups of faulty habits which account for about one-half of the total illegibility problem. Each of the eight illegibility habit groupings shown in Table V contributed five per cent or more of the 42,284 illegibilities. The possibilities of recombining the 24 groupings in this table are numerous and the remedial and preventive implications of these new types of difficulty should be of great importance to those interested in the teaching of handwriting.

TABLE V   *Analysis of Letter Malformations*

Type		Percentages Contributed			
		El.	**H.S.**	**Ad.**	**Total**
1	Failure to close letters (a, b, f, g, j, k, o, p, q, s, y, z)	24	20	16	18
2	Top loops closed ("l like t," "e like i")	13	14	20	18
3	Looping non-looped strokes ("i like e")	12	27	12	16
4	Using straight up-strokes rather than rounded strokes ("n like u," "c like i," "h like li")	11	10	15	13
5	End stroke difficulty (not brought up, not brought down, not left horizontal)	11	6	9	9
6	Difficulty crossing "t"	5	5	9	7
7	Difficulty dotting "i"	3	5	5	5
8	Top short (b, d, f, h, k, l, t)	6	7	3	5
9	Letters too small	4	5	4	4
10	Closing c, h, r, u, v, w, y	4	3	3	3
11	Part of letter omitted	4	4	3	3
12	Up-stroke too long	2	3	1	2
13	Letters too large	2	1	—*	1
14	Beginning stroke off line	—	3	1	1
15	Bottom short (f, g, j, q, y, z)	2	1	—	1
16	Using rounded up-strokes instead of straight ones ("i like e," "u like ee")	—	1	2	1
17	Down-loop turned incorrectly	1	1	1	1
18	Excessive flourishes	—	1	1	1
19	Part added to letter	—	—	1	1
20	Down-stroke too long	1	1	—	—
21	Up-loop turned incorrectly	—	—	—	—
22	Down-loop closed	—	—	—	—
23	Printing	—	—	—	—
24	Palmer "r"	2	1	—	—
25	Unrecognizably recorded	2	1	3	3
26	Unclassified	10	9	9	9

* These dashes represent frequencies which accounted for less than one-half of one per cent of the total.

Conclusions

In light of the above data, certain general statements can be made for the whole study:

1. There were more forms of illegibilities peculiar to the different age groups than there were common to two or more age levels. Only 16 per cent of the 499 different forms of illegibilities were found common to the elementary, high-school, and adult groups, while 64 per cent of them were peculiar to some one level.

2. The illegibilities of only four letters (a, e, r, and t) contributed 45, 46, and 47 per cents to the elementary, high-school, and adult groups respectively.

3. Only fourteen different forms of illegibilities in the elementary and high-school groups and nine in the adult group contributed one half of all the 42,284 specific illegibilities recorded; six of these were common to all three levels. Writing "e" like "i" resulted in 15 per cent of all illegibilities.

4. Only four types of difficulties in the formation of letters caused over one-half of all the illegibilities. These were: (a) the failure to close letters, (b) closing looped strokes, (c) looping non-looped strokes, and (d) using straight up-strokes rather than rounded strokes.

5. The gross frequency with which illegibilities appeared tended to increase with age. The high-school students wrote 136 per cent more illegibily than did the elementary school children, per constant amount of material, while the adults wrote 52 per cent more illegibily than did the high-school students, or over 350 per cent worse than the elementary pupils.

Implications

The major implications of these conclusions seem to be at least two. In the first place, preventive and corrective work in handwriting can be not only quite definite but also highly concentrated on a very few aspects of the total problem.[7] Any one of at least three lines of evidence would seem to substantiate this. It will be recalled that the illegibilities of only the four letters "a," "e," "r," and "t" contributed no less than 45 per cent of all the illegibilities recorded at any age level. The fact that only a very small number of forms of illegibilities occurred so frequently that they represented one-half of all illegibilities found is at once suggestive of the specificity of the preventive or remedial measures. And then it will be remembered that the prevention or correction of only four types of bad writing habits would improve legibility at least 50 per cent. It does not seem unreasonable to hazard the guess that preventive and remedial efforts directed along a combination of all three of these lines might eliminate three-fourths of all illegibilities encountered.

The second suggestion is this. It would be possible, and probably highly desirable, to evaluate existing systems of teaching cursive handwriting in light of the analyses made in this study. For instance, knowing the types of incorrect movements made in the formation of letters and knowing the relative importance of these movements, as determined either by the frequencies with which they appeared or by the percentages which they contributed to the whole illegibility situation, it would be possible to analyze in a similar way the amount of practice on different types of strokes or movements recommended in the manuals of the various handwriting systems in order to determine whether or not greater emphasis might be placed on certain aspects heretofore neglected. If such a study were made and instructional procedure modified accordingly, it would be a relatively simple matter to analyze the product of the new system and compare the results it produces with the data presented here, the efficacy of the new method being determined by the extent to which illegibilities had been reduced.

---

7 Illustrative of devices that can be of use in such an approach are two charts which greatly facilitate the analysis of handwriting from the standpoint of specific illegibility. The Presseys have prepared a "Chart for Diagnosis of Illegibilities in Handwriting" and the writer has constructed a "Chart for Diagnosis of Illegibilities in Written Arabic Numerals," both of which are published by the Public School Publishing Company, Bloomington, Illinois. The successful use of the former in an experiment to determine the extent to which specific illegibility habits could be corrected as well as the extent to which general quality and legibility could be improved was reported by Hilda Lehman and Luella C. Pressey in an article "The Effectiveness of Drill in Handwriting to Remove Specific Illegibilities" which appeared in *School and Society*, XXVII, May 5, 1928.

31   Factors Affecting the Legibility
of Handwriting

LESLIE QUANT

Introduction: the Problem

The investigation here reported is an attempt to show how various factors modify the legibility of handwriting. The data are derived from an objective study of the eye-movements of subjects as they read paragraphs of handwriting. In this study legibility is considered as synonymous with readability. Legibility is not considered as a unitary characteristic, but is regarded as a composite made up of simpler elements. Dr. Frank N. Freeman in his Chart for Diagnosing Faults in Handwriting[1] has selected five characteristics for measuring the quality of handwriting: (1) letter formation, (2) spacing, (3) alinement, (4) slant, and (5) quality of line. The present study will be organized around these characteristics.

As far as the writer has been able to discover, no previous attempt has been made to show how these characteristics enter into the legibility of handwriting. Investigators in the field have assumed that handwriting that presented a good appearance was legible, but no attempt has been made objectively to analyze handwriting to see how any of the factors which Freeman studied determines the legibility of a selection of handwriting. Breed and Culp[2] conducted an investigation to determine the relationship between legibility (quality of handwriting) and speed, based on the Ayres Handwriting Scale. They later suggested a weighting[3] for factors in the form of handwriting which make for legibility. The Presseys made an investigation of the illegibilities in handwriting, in which persons who read the material were asked to note any letter formations that gave any trouble in reading. Illegibilities were checked by the criterion[4] that "if they [the subjects] had to look twice at a word, they were to check that part of the word which gave them trouble."

In the present study each factor is considered separately from the other factors, in an attempt to determine the relative importance of each in the total composite which is called good writing or poor writing on the basis of legibility. The ease with which the handwriting can be read is to be considered through an attempt to answer the following questions:

1. What effect, if any, do variations in letter formation have on legibility of handwriting?

[1] Frank N. Freeman, "An Analytical Scale for Judging Handwriting," *Elementary School Journal,* XV (1915), pp. 432–441.
[2] Frederick S. Breed and Vernon Culp, "An Application and Critique of the Ayres Handwriting Scale," *School and Society,* II (1915), pp. 639–647.
[3] Frederick S. Breed and Vernon Culp, "Note on the Relation of Legibility and Form in Handwriting," *School and Society,* IV (1916), p. 872.
[4] Luella C. Pressey and Sydney L. Pressey, "Analyses of Three Thousand Illegibilities in the Handwriting of Children and Adults," *Educational Research Bulletin,* VI (September 27, 1927), p. 270.

From *Journal of Experimental Education,* Vol. 14, No. 4 (June, 1946), pp. 297–316. Reprinted with permission.

The paragraphs of handwriting which constitute the reading selections used in this study were omitted in the Journal's printing but may be found in the complete dissertation in the library of the University of Chicago. In this reprinting references to these plates have been deleted and ellipses used to indicate same; also, inconsistencies in the original text have been corrected.

2. What effect, if any, does variation in spacing have on legibility of handwriting?

3. What effect, if any, does irregularity of alinement have on legibility of handwriting?

4. What effect, if any, does irregularity of slant have on legibility of handwriting?

5. What effect, if any, does the quality of line have on legibility of handwriting? (Quality is used here in a restricted sense, and refers to the weight of the line of writing.)

Procedure

As a preliminary step the author observed the handwriting of numerous persons, in order to discover very good and very poor quality of handwriting. These individuals were then asked to vary their habitual manner of writing in certain respects. For example, a person who wrote with good alinement of letters was asked to write exactly as he would write normally, except that he would use poor alinement. If the individual wrote with poor letter formation, he was asked to improve this characteristic so that his writing would be changed only by having good letter formation. Otherwise his writing was not to be changed in any respect. Repeated trials with a large number of persons, both good and poor writers, showed that modification of one characteristic of handwriting results in some degree of accompanying changes in other characteristics also. If a person writes habitually with even slant, and then attempts to write with uneven slant, he alters the letter formation, writes with uneven alinement, or even changes the quality of line, and modifies the spacing between letters. This method of deriving samples of handwriting which would be comparable in all respects except one selected characteristic was finally abandoned as impracticable.

The next step was an investigation of a large number of samples of handwriting in an effort to locate, if possible, certain "types" of handwriting. Prospective Freshman students at the University of Chicago formerly were asked to submit, as a part of their personnel record, an autobiography in their own handwriting. A careful search through approximately 750 of these records revealed the fact that there are no "types" of handwriting. On the contrary, handwriting shows a great variety of individual differences from person to person. The poor handwriting in these records was usually poor in several respects, and the good writing was good in most respects. All possible variants of good and poor seemed to be present in numerous combinations. The attempt, therefore, to select samples of "typical" handwriting was likewise considered futile.

The author next selected a paragraph, designated in this study as Selection 2, produced in his habitual style of writing with a medium-point fountain pen. After a period of intensive practice the writer found it possible to modify his own handwriting so that other selections could be written similar to Selection 2 in all respects but one. For example, one paragraph was written in which the letter formation was poor, but in all other respects (spacing, slant, etc.) the writing was of the same quality as the original paragraph (Selection 2).

In order that the difficulty of the content of the selections would remain constant throughout the study, the standardized paragraphs—"Peter's Dream"— were used.[5]

5 These paragraphs were devised by Dr. W. S. Gray for testing oral reading ability.

The following selections were read by the subjects participating in this investigation:

Selection 1—a printed paragraph.

Selection 2—a paragraph of normal handwriting in the author's habitual style of writing.

Selection 3—handwriting with poor letter formation.

Selection 4—normal handwriting with reduced spacing between letters, but with normal spacing between words.

Selection 5—normal handwriting, but with reduced spacing between letters and between words.

Selection 6—normal handwriting, but with the spacing reduced to ¼ inch between the lines of writing.

Selection 7—normal handwriting, but with increased spacing between letters and between words.

Selection 8—a paragraph written with uneven alinement of letters.

Selection 9—a paragraph written with irregular slant.

Selection 10—a paragraph written with a heavy line.

Selection 11—a paragraph written with a light line.

. . .

Further description of these experimental paragraphs of handwriting will show the extent to which they vary from the original paragraph of normal handwriting (designated as Selection 2).

Table I shows that Selection 2, with a total of 155 letters, has 148 letters that may be classified as having good letter formation—95 per cent of the total number. There is no objective standard by which letter formation can be judged to be poor or good, since the different handwriting systems in general use are not in perfect agreement, but in this study, any departures from accepted good form have been the criterion by which a letter is said to have poor form. As examples, failure to close the loop of the "a", "d", or "o", "m" and "n" which are not rounded at the top of the strokes, failure to complete the loop of "b", "g", "h", "j", "l", and "y", incorrect formation of "r", "w", "v", confusion of "i" and "e", or of "a" and "o", or any malformation of a letter—all these

TABLE I   *Letter Formation in Selections 2 to 11**

Selection	Number of Letters with Good Formation	Number of Letters with Poor Formation	Total Number of Letters	Per Cent of Good Letters	Per Cent of Poor Letters
2	148	7	155	95	5
3	25	127	152	16	84
4	160	4	164	98	2
5	126	5	131	96	4
6	125	7	132	95	5
7	138	7	145	95	5
8	138	9	147	94	6
9	140	5	145	97	3
10	128	6	134	96	4
11	134	4	138	97	3

* Data are not included for Selection 1, since it is printed material.

indicate the basis on which letters have been judged as having poor formation. Comparison of the data in Table I shows a high degree of uniformity of all paragraphs with respect to letter formation—varying from 94 per cent to 98 per cent except for Selection 3—the paragraph which was written expressly to provide a selection characterized by poor letter formation. Selection 3, with a total of 152 letters, contains 127 letters—84 per cent—that are classified as having poor formation.

Selections 4 to 7 differ from Selection 2 (Normal Writing) with respect to the spacing. Dividers were used to measure the space between each letter and between each word in every selection of handwriting. Table II shows the average spacing between each letter and between each word in Selections 2 to 11.

TABLE II   *Average Spacing Between Words and Between Letters in Selections 2 to 11 (in Units of Sixteenths of an Inch)*

Selection	Average Spacing (in $\frac{1}{16}$ inch)	
	Between Words	Between Letters
2	3.4	1.4
3	3.8	1.6
4	3.1	0.7
5	1.2	0.8
6	4.0	1.9
7	5.2	2.9
8	3.1	1.8
9	3.1	1.8
10	3.0	1.5
11	3.5	1.5

Selection 4 was written in the author's normal handwriting, but the spacing was greatly reduced between the letters in each word. However, the spacing was normal between each word. In Selection 5 the spacing was greatly reduced between letters and also between the words of the paragraph. Table II shows that the average spacing between words is 3.1 sixteenths of an inch, and 0.7 sixteenths of an inch between letters for Selection 4, and 1.2 sixteenths between words and 0.8 sixteenths of an inch between letters for Selection 5, compared to 3.4 and 1.4 between words and letters, respectively, for Selection 2 (Normal Handwriting).

Selection 6 was written in normal handwriting, but the space between lines was reduced to ¼ inch, to discover whether this reduction would affect the legibility of the selection. The spacing between letters and between words for Selection 6 is 4.0 sixteenths and 1.9 sixteenths, respectively.

In Selection 7 the spacing was increased between words and between letters, and the average space between words and between letters is 5.2 sixteenths and 2.9 sixteenths, respectively—the greatest average spacing for the entire group of selections.

Selection 8 was written in such a manner that a large number of the letters would have uneven alinement. A letter is considered to be imperfectly alined if it does not extend to the horizontal line of writing (except letters like "g", "j", and "y", parts of which normally extend below the line). Guide lines, drawn on thin paper, were placed over the selections of writing in order to discover which letters were imperfectly alined. Table III shows data for alinement for Selections 2 to 11. This table shows that the amount of properly alined letters varies from 87 per cent for Selection 9, to 96 per cent for Selections 4 and 5, except for Selection 8 (poor alinement) in which only 45 per cent of the letters show proper alinement, with 16 per cent of the letters written above the line, and 39 per cent below the line.

TABLE III   *Alinement of Letters in Selections 2 to 11*

Selection	Number of Letters				Percentage		
	Above Line	Below Line	On Line	Total	Above Line	Below Line	On Line
2	10	0	167	177	6	0.	94
3	13	1	138	152	8	.6	91
4	5	1	158	164	3	.6	96
5	5	0	126	131	4	0.	96
6	10	0	123	133	8	0.	92
7	9	3	133	145	6	2.	92
8	24	57	66	147	16	39.	45
9	17	2	126	145	12	1.	87
10	9	0	125	134	7	0.	93
11	7	0	131	138	5	0.	95

Selection 9 was written in the author's usual style except that the slant was varied. A protractor was used to measure the angle of slant (with the base line of writing) of all the letters in Selections 2 to 11. There is no standard slant that is considered "correct" for handwriting, but experts are in agreement that the slant should not exceed 30 degrees from vertical with the base line.[6] Regularity of slant is considered more important in writing than is the degree of slant. Table IV presents data for each selection of handwriting in this study, and shows the amount of variation of slant for the letters in Selection 9, compared with all other selections.

Selection 10 was written with the heaviest writing pen available—Esterbrook #788. Writing was done with heavier lettering pens, but the ink did not spread uniformly on the paper, and unsatisfactory records resulted, except when the size of the writing was appreciably increased.

Selection 11 was written with the finest writing pen available—Spencerian #1. Fine lettering pens were tried, but the records produced by their use showed great variation in the width of the line, and the use of pens finer than Spencerian #1 changed markedly the quality of the handwriting.

In Freeman's studies of handwriting he uses "quality of line" to refer to "evenness in the thickness of the line and to smoothness as distinguished from waviness."[7] In the present study "quality of line" will be used in a more restricted sense, and Selections 10 and 11 are studied to determine how the use of a light or heavy line in writing affects the legibility of the writing, compared to the use of a line of medium weight.

[6] Frank N. Freeman, *The Teaching of Handwriting* (Boston: Houghton Mifflin Company, 1915), p. 99.
[7] Frank N. Freeman and Mary L. Dougherty, *How to Teach Handwriting* (Boston: Houghton Mifflin Company, 1923), p. 170.

TABLE IV *Angle of Slant of Letters (with Base Line of Writings) for Selections 2 to 11*

Angle (in degrees)	Frequency for Each Selection									
	2	**3**	**4**	**5**	**6**	**7**	**8**	**9**	**10**	**11**
114								1		
107								1		
105								2		
103								3		
102								1		
101								1		
100								3		
97								1		
96								1		
95							1	3		
94								1		
93		1						2		
92		2						6		
91		1						7		
90	1	3	1	1	1	2		15		2
89	2					1		5		
88	1	1	1		2		3	6		
87	3	8	5	1	8	7	7	13	2	1
86	1	6	4	2	4	5	7	3		1
85	27	2	8	3	14	9	20	8		12
84	2		3	2	5	8	4	3	2	16
83	12	14	11	13	23	14	37	1	18	6
82	7	16	16	13	22	14	16	2	14	5
81	9	5	10	13	10	4	1		8	32
80	21	25	30	30	17	19	22	3	27	12
79	17	17	12	6	7	10	1	2	2	30
78	21	15	19	14	9	16	20	10	28	6
77	1	13	12	18	8	8	1	5	2	
76	8	2	10	5	2	13		6	5	8
75	17	7	10	5	1	7	3	3	11	5
74			4	2		4		5	6	2
73	2	12	5	2		2	1	6	1	
72		2	1	1		2	3	2	3	
71	1							4	1	
70			1					1	4	
69								1		
68			1							
67								1		
66								3		
65										
64										
63								2		
55								1		
54								1		
Total	12292	12198	13059	10442	10897	11652	12060	12200	10577	11024
No. of Letters	153	152	164	131	133	145	147	145	134	138
Mean	80.3	80.2	79.6	79.7	81.9	80.3	82.0	84.1	78.9	79.9

Apparatus and Technique

Legibility might be measured by the distance at which it is necessary to place the material so that it may be read at a stated rate with given accuracy. Degree of legibility may be measured also by the rate and accuracy with which the material can be read at a given distance. The latter method was chosen for this study. The subjects were asked to read paragraphs of handwriting, and a photographic record of eye-movements was made by means of a camera equipped with 35 mm. motion picture film.

The technique of recording eye-movements by means of photographs is sufficiently familiar not to require extended description here. The reader is referred to a detailed account of the technique presented by C. T. Gray in his monograph.[8] The subjects read under favorable conditions, unaffected by distracting influences. Before reading, the camera and the equipment were explained to those subjects for whom the laboratory was unfamiliar. A large number of the subjects were students in the Department of Education to whom the eye-movement apparatus was already familiar. The subject and the experimenter were alone in the room during the reading, and there were no disturbing factors to modify the performance of any subject.

The subjects were asked to read through the paragraph once, silently, in their accustomed manner of reading any material that they wished to remember. They were told that at the end of the reading of each paragraph simple questions would be asked to test how well the reading had been done. The questions were not standardized, but were designed only as an incentive for the subjects to read the selections with care. No comment was made, either favorable or unfavorable, on the answers that the subjects gave to questions, since the experimenter did not wish to influence the performance of the subjects by introducing any factors extraneous to the reading of the material.

Before beginning the reading of each paragraph the subject was asked to "close your eyes as soon as you have finished the last line." The precaution precluded the possibility of additional eye-movements back over the material which had already been read.

The developed films were placed in a projector, and the enlarged image of the eye-movements was adjusted exactly to fit the length of the line of handwriting of each selection. The eye-movements for each subject for each selection were plotted. In this manner an exact record was obtained for each subject of the number, location, and duration of every eye pause during the reading of each paragraph.

Subjects

Adults were selected as subjects for this study, on the assumption that the reading of handwriting is more largely an activity of adults than of children. The subjects were selected at random, on the basis of availability. Many were University students, both undergraduates and graduates. Some records were discarded owing to the fact that the subjects wore glasses habitually, and the necessity of reading without glasses before the camera modified the reading to so large an extent that the eye-movement record obtained did not show typical reactions for the subject. The records of 35 subjects were used—11 women and 24 men. Twenty subjects read the entire series of eleven selections. Selection 3 (poor letter formation) and Selection 7 (wide spacing between letters and between words) consistently produced a marked change in the character of reading for all subjects. Hence, these selections were omitted from the reading performance of the remaining fifteen subjects for this study.

The Reading of Printed Material

The paragraph of printed material (Selection 1) was used in order to get a measure of the reading ability of the subjects. The lines of print in this para-

8 C. T. Gray, *Types of Reading Ability as Exhibited Through Tests and Laboratory Experiments,* Supplementary Educational Monographs, Vol. I, No. 5 (Chicago: University of Chicago Press, 1917), pp. 83–90.

graph are shorter than the lines of handwriting used in the other paragraphs used in this study. In the progress of reading printed material the eye covers less distance in the line, but encounters more words per line than in the handwriting selections. The printed characters have more uniformity than those in handwriting. The reaction which readers make to printed material is known; hence, we may discover, through examination of the records of the subjects for the printed material whether the subjects are effective or ineffective readers.

We can then compare the performance of these subjects as they read paragraphs of handwriting. Apparent differences between a subject's reading records for the printed material and the handwriting selections may be accounted for by the variation between the printed and the written paragraphs. It can be determined at what point the reader may be experiencing difficulty if a study of eye-movements is made as he proceeds from paragraph to paragraph. Since the difficulty of the content of the paragraphs of handwriting is constant, any variation in the reading records for any subject from paragraph to paragraph can be assigned to factors in the handwriting itself, rather than to the difficulty of the content of the paragraphs.

.　　.　　.

The difference between effective and ineffective reading can be determined by a study of the eye-movement records. Effective reading has relatively few fixations per line. Five to six should be sufficient for a line of print such as is found in Selection 1. If the subject has mature reading habits, these fixations should be more or less regularly spaced within the lines, because mature reading is characterized by rhythmical movements of the eyes along the line of print. The immature reader, on the other hand, fixates frequently, and the distance between the fixations within the line is likely to show irregularity. Frequent fixations in the line indicate that it is necessary for the reader to break up the line of print into small units in order to comprehend the material. The necessity for small units may be accounted for by the form of the material, or may be occasioned by the difficulty of the content. The presence of a large number of fixations is evidence, therefore, that the reader is encountering difficulty, either on account of the form, or because the content is difficult to comprehend. The subject who has developed mature reading habits shows little variation in the duration of the pauses. The fixations are not altogether uniform, but the variation in the duration of the fixations is not marked. If a reader encounters anything unusual in the reading process he may involuntarily increase the duration of the fixations in order more deliberately to perceive the material. In effective reading of ordinary easy material such as Selection I pauses of unusual length should be infrequent.

Another characteristic of effective reading is the regularity of eye-movement from left to right. If the subject has developed good reading habits the eye moves along the line from the beginning to the end in a series of short movements, followed by a long return sweep of the eye to the left to the beginning of the next line. An occasional regressive movement back toward the left is not unusual even in effective reading, especially near the beginning of lines. These regressive movements at the beginning of lines are caused by a failure to make a long enough return sweep to carry the eye the entire distance back from the end of one line to the beginning of the following line. As the subject reads, if he encounters difficulty so that his rhythm is disturbed, he is also likely to make regressive movements in order more effectively to recognize what is printed in the line. The control of the eye, in an attempt to hold it in one position for any great length of time, is difficult, and for this reason, when a subject pauses for a considerable period of time at any point in the reading, the record is likely to show not one long fixation, but rather a series of separate movements, shifting irregularly backward and forward along the line. The subject who has failed to develop good reading habits will manifest this shifting tendency of the eye to a much more marked degree than will the subject who has developed good habits. A large number of regressive movements means that the reader is encountering difficulty in his reading.

These characteristics of eye-movements in reading will be more apparent if a comparison is made between the records of the most effective and of the least effective readers among the subjects used in this study. The record of an effective reader shows a relatively large average number of words per fixation, the duration of the fixations is short, and the average number of words per regressive movement is large. Ineffective readers have a relatively small number of words per fixation, the duration of the fixations is likely to show considerable variation, and the reading records are likely to show a smaller number of words per regression than in the records of effective readers.

Table V presents data for Selection 1 (printed paragraph) for all subjects with reference to the average number of words read per fixation, the average duration of fixations, and the average number of words read per regression.

The average number of words read per fixation for all subjects is 1.4, ranging from 0.9 for Subject 19 to 2.0 for Subject 6. The average duration of fixations in units of 1/25 second is 6.5, with a range from 4.5 for Subject 32 to 8.6 for Subjects 1 and 5. The average number of words read per regression is 19.4, with a range from 5.7 for Subject 19 to 40+ for the six subjects whose records contain no regressive movements. It is apparent that the variation from subject to subject is not consistent for the number of words read per fixation, the average duration of fixations, and the average number of words per regression. Some subjects who are effective readers may have a high average number of words per fixation, but use relatively long fixation time. Most of the subjects had few regressive movements. Subject 19, with seven regressive movements, had the largest number of the entire group.

The variation in the reading records for the entire group will be more apparent if the records of the eight most effective readers are compared with the records of the eight least effective readers.

In selecting the eight most effective readers and the eight least effective readers of the subjects used in this study the following method was used. The reading record for Selection 1—the printed paragraph—for each subject was assigned a rank order, according to each of these criteria: (1) average number of words read per fixation, with highest rank to subjects having the largest number, (2) the duration of fixations, with the highest rank to subjects having the shortest duration, (3) average number of words per regressive movement, with highest rank indicating the largest number of words read per regression. The average of these three rankings was used as an index of the relative rank of each subject in the effectiveness of his reading.

On this basis Subjects 4, 6, 10, 21, 25, 26, 32 and 34 may be regarded as the eight most effective readers of the entire group, and the eight least effective readers are Subjects 3, 13, 16, 18, 19, 20, and 23.

TABLE V *Number of Fixations, Average Number of Words Read per Fixation, Average Duration of Fixations, and the Average Number of Words Read per Regression for Selection 1*

Subject Number	Number of Fixations	Average Number of Words Read per Fixation	Average Duration of Fixations	Average Number of Words per Regression*
1	21	1.9	8.6	10.0
2	33	1.2	5.5	40.00
3	29	1.4	7.7	8.0
4	27	1.5	6.0	40.0+
5	26	1.5	8.6	40.0
6	20	2.0	5.5	40.0
7	22	1.8	7.8	40.0
8	26	1.5	6.1	40.0
9	31	1.3	5.0	20.0
10	23	1.7	6.9	40.0+
11	24	1.7	6.5	40.0
12	31	1.3	5.9	40.0
13	36	1.1	6.1	8.0
14	21	1.9	8.5	20.0
15	26	1.5	6.5	40.0
16	32	1.2	7.0	13.3
17	32	1.2	7.3	40.0
18	32	1.2	7.0	10.0
19	44	0.9	6.8	5.7
20	37	1.0	7.0	10.0
21	24	1.7	4.9	20.0
22	28	1.4	7.1	20.0
23	36	1.1	8.2	13.3
24	30	1.3	5.8	40.0+
25	24	1.7	6.0	40.0+
26	14	2.8	7.2	40.0+
27	28	1.4	6.8	40.0
28	27	1.5	5.5	40.0
29	33	1.2	5.5	40.0
30	34	1.2	6.0	40.0
31	34	1.2	7.4	10.0
32	29	1.4	4.5	40.0
33	34	1.2	5.1	20.0
34	26	1.5	5.4	40.0+
35	31	1.3	6.5	8.0
Total	1005			
Mean	28.7	1.4	6.5	19.4

* The records followed by plus signs in the last column are records of subjects who made no regressions in the entire selection. The plus sign indicates that the records might have been higher with a longer selection.

Table VI presents data for the eight most effective readers and for the eight least effective readers in the group of subjects.

It is evident that the most effective readers are superior to the group of least effective readers in every characteristic. The most effective group shows a mean of 23.8 fixations for the paragraph, compared with 35.0 for the least effective group. In comparing the average number of words per fixation the most effective readers show a mean of 1.8 compared with 1.1 for the least effective readers. In average duration of fixations the most effective readers have a mean of 5.8

TABLE VI   *Average Number of Words Read per Fixation, Average Duration of Fixations, Average Number of Words Read per Regression for the Most Effective and for the Least Effective Readers, for Selection 1*

Subject Number		Number of Fixations	Average Number of Words Read per Fixation	Average Duration of Fixations	Average Number of Words Read per Regression
		Most Effective Readers			
4		27	1.5	6.0	40.0+
6		20	2.0	5.5	40.0
10		23	1.7	6.9	40.0+
21		28	1.7	4.9	20.0
25		24	1.7	6.0	40.0+
26		14	2.8	7.2	40.0+
32		29	1.4	4.5	40.0
34		26	1.5	5.4	40.0+
	Total	191	14.3	46.4	300.0
	Mean	23.8	1.8	5.8	37.5
		Least Effective Readers			
3		29	1.4	7.7	8.0
13		36	1.1	6.1	8.0
16		32	1.2	7.0	13.3
18		32	1.2	7.0	10.0
19		44	0.9	6.8	5.7
20		37	1.0	7.0	10.0
23		36	1.1	8.2	13.3
31		34	1.2	7.4	10.0
	Total	280	9.1	57.2	78.3
	Mean	35.0	1.1	7.1	9.8

twenty-fifths of a second, compared with 7.1 for the least effective readers. A large difference exists between the two groups with respect to the average number of words per regression, with 37.5 as the mean for the most effective readers and 9.8 for the least effective readers.

The most effective readers use fewer fixations in reading the paragraph, with a larger average number of words per fixation. They employ shorter fixation time than is found in the records of the least effective readers. They also use few regressive movements. The least effective readers invariably make regressive movements in reading Selection 1.

The Reading of Normal Handwriting

Selection 2 may be regarded as the normal selection of handwriting for this study, since it has good letter formation, regular spacing, even alinement, uniform slant, and a medium weight of line. It will be considered as the standard for comparison with other paragraphs of written material used in the study. It has been pointed out that printed material exhibits regularity of spacing within the line. Handwriting, on the other hand, shows variation within the selection. Because it is handwriting there will necessarily be some modification in spacing (between letters and between words), letter formation will show some imperfections, the slant will lack perfect uniformity, and the variations in pressure during the writing process will result in modification in the weight of line. The eye of the reader must, of necessity, be accommodated simultaneously to these variations during the process of reading the handwriting. For this reason it is to be expected that the reading records for normal handwriting will be to some extent dissimilar to the records for the printed material.

In effective reading of printed material the eyes move from left to right along the lines, in a series of regular, rhythmic pauses. For simple material the pauses are infrequent, the duration of the fixations is short, there is considerable uniformity of distance between the fixations, and few regressive movements are present. These general characteristics of the reading of printed material show some degree of modification when the subjects read a selection of handwriting. A comparison of the reading records for Selection 1 and Selection 2 will show the extent of this modification.

Table VII shows data for all the subjects who read the paragraph of normal handwriting (Selection 2).

The first difference to be noted in the reading of the two selections is that handwriting requires more eye-movements than printed material. The eye-span is narrowed in reading the paragraph of handwriting, necessitating more pauses as the subject progresses along the lines. For the entire group of subjects in reading printed material the average number of words per fixation is 1.4. In reading handwriting the average number of words per fixation for the group drops to 1.0. The difference is large enough to indicate that the handwriting presents greater difficulty to the reader than does the printed selection. This difference is consistent when the individual subjects are considered. Every subject, with the exception of Subjects 16 and 32, shows a smaller number of words read per fixation in Selection 2 than in Selection 1. Subject 16 shows an average of 1.2 words per fixation for both selections, and Subject 32 shows an average of 1.4 words for print and 1.8 for handwriting. Subject 32 is the one subject in the group whose record for reading handwriting shows a larger average number of words per fixation for handwriting.

A second criterion by which to judge the difficulty of material is the duration of the fixations of the eye. Long durations indicate a deliberate reaction to the characters in the material being read. Table VII shows an average duration of 6.0 twenty-fifths second for the fixations for all subjects in reading handwriting, compared with the average duration of fixations of 6.5 twenty-fifths second for all subjects in reading Selection 1 (printed paragraph). In reading handwriting the subjects employ shorter pauses than in reading printed material. Instead of increasing the duration of fixations in reading handwriting the subjects use fixations of shorter duration, but they increase the number of fixations.

A third difference between the reading of handwriting and printed material is to be noted in the number of regressive movements in the records. As material increases in difficulty the subject tends to retrace the material already read in order to increase his perception. Hence, the presence of regressive movements in a reading record is indicative of difficulty, or at least of uncertainty on the part of the reader. Absence of regressive movements in a reading record is an indication that the reader finds the material easy to comprehend, without the necessity for additional backward movements in the line. Table VII shows an average of 10.1 words per regressive movement for the entire group of subjects, compared with an average of 19.4 words per regressive movement for the printed paragraph. It is evident that the reading of handwriting is more difficult than printed material, since the average number of words per regression shows such a marked decrease below the average for the printed material—47.9 per cent.

TABLE VII *Number of Fixations, Average Number of Words Read per Fixation, Average Duration of Fixations, and Average Number of Words Read per Regression for Selection 2*

Subject Number	Number of Fixations	Average Number of Words Read per Fixation	Average Duration of Fixations	Average Number of Words per Regression
1	41	0.9	6.3	4.7
2	—	—	—	—
3	36	1.0	7.7	7.6
4	37	1.0	5.7	38.0
5	40	0.9	6.6	12.7
6	29	1.3	6.0	38.0
7	28	1.3	6.6	38.0
8	31	1.2	5.0	38.0
9	39	0.9	5.5	19.0
10	32	1.2	7.6	38.0
11	40	0.9	5.7	9.5
12	33	1.1	6.7	19.0
13	51	0.7	6.4	3.8
14	32	1.2	7.0	19.0
15	36	1.0	6.0	7.6
16	32	1.2	5.4	19.0
17	49	0.8	6.0	7.6
18	45	0.8	6.5	5.4
19	46	0.8	6.3	3.1
20	46	0.8	6.9	9.5
21	35	1.1	4.9	38.0
22	—	—	—	—
23	44	0.8	7.5	5.4
24	35	1.1	6.3	19.0
25	23*	1.2	5.1	28.0
26	34	1.1	5.3	19.0
27	38	1.0	6.4	12.7
28	38	1.0	5.3	6.3
29	41	0.9	5.4	12.7
30	40	0.9	5.5	12.7
31	36	1.0	6.0	12.7
32	35	1.8	4.1	38.0+
33	38	1.0	5.6	7.6
34	40	0.9	4.7	5.4
35	41	0.9	5.8	7.6
Total	1241	—	—	—
Mean	37.6	1.0	6.0	10.1

* Record is for five lines.

Not only is the average number of words read per regression less for handwriting than for printed material, but the differences are consistent when the records for the two selections are compared. The records for all subjects show a smaller number of words read per regression except Subjects 21 and 31. These two subjects show a larger average number of words read per regression for the handwriting than for the printed material. It is evident that the reading of handwriting causes more regressive movements than does printed material.

These differences in the averages for the entire group between the records for the paragraph of print and the paragraph of handwriting are borne out in an examination of the records of the most effective readers, and their comparison with the records of the least effective readers. The records of both groups show a superior performance for the reading of the selection of printed material.

TABLE VIII   *Average Number of Words Read per Fixation, Average Duration of Fixations, Average Number of Words Read per Regression for the Most Effective and for the Least Effective Readers, for Selection 2*

Subject Number		Number of Fixations	Average Number of Words Read per Fixation	Average Duration of Fixations	Average Number of Words Read per Regression
			Most Effective Readers		
4		37	1.0	5.7	38.0
6		29	1.3	6.0	38.0
10		32	1.2	7.6	38.0
21		35	1.1	4.9	38.0
25		23	1.2	5.1	28.0
26		34	1.1	5.3	19.0
32		35	1.8	4.1	38.0+
34		40	0.9	4.7	5.4
	Total	265	9.6	43.4	242.4
	Mean	33.1	1.2	5.4	30.3
			Least Effective Readers		
3		36	1.0	7.7	7.6
13		51	0.7	6.4	3.8
16		32	1.2	5.4	19.0
18		45	0.8	6.5	5.4
19		46	0.8	6.3	3.9
20		46	0.8	6.9	9.5
23		44	0.8	7.5	5.4
30		40	0.9	5.5	12.7
	Total	340	7.0	52.2	67.3
	Mean	42.5	0.8	6.5	8.4

Table VIII shows data for the eight most effective readers and the eight least effective readers in the entire group of subjects.

Table VIII shows a mean of 1.2 words per fixation for the most effective readers for Selection 2, compared with 1.8 words for Selection 1. The number of words read per fixation is less for the most effective readers for handwriting than for the printed paragraph. Table VIII shows that for the less effective readers there is an average of 0.8 words per fixation, compared with 1.1 words per fixation for the printed selection. For both groups of subjects the selection of handwriting was more difficult, judged by the number of words read per fixation.

An examination of the data for the average duration shows a consistent use of shorter fixations in reading handwriting than in reading the printed selection. The eight most effective readers show an average duration of 5.4 twenty-fifths second per fixation in reading handwriting, compared with 5.8 for the printed selection. The eight least effective subjects have an average duration of 6.5 twenty-fifths second per fixation for handwriting, compared with 7.1 for the printed paragraph. Both groups are consistent in the use of shorter fixations in reading handwriting.

Both the most effective and the least effective readers show a smaller average number of words read per regression for handwriting than for printed material. Table VIII shows an average of 30.3 words per regression for the most effective readers, compared with 37.5 for the same group for printed material. The least effective readers have an average of 8.4 words per regression for handwriting, compared with 9.8 words per regression for the printed paragraph. It is evident that for both the most effective and the least effective readers there is a decided increase in the number of regressive movements employed in reading handwriting, compared with the reading of printed material.

Poor Letter Formation and Legibility

Previously the reading of normal handwriting was compared with the reading of printed material. The reading records show that there is a significant difference between the difficulty of the reading of printed material and of handwriting, judged by the criteria of the average number of words read per fixation, average duration of fixations, and average number of words read per regression. The general character of the reading process is the same for printed material and for handwriting, but there is a consistent decrease in the average number of words read per fixation, and in the average number of words read per regression for handwriting, compared with printed material. Subjects use a shorter average duration of fixations in reading handwriting than in reading printed material.

In order to determine the effect of poor letter formation on legibility it is necessary to employ a selection of handwriting that is comparable to normal handwriting in every respect, except that the letter formation shall be poor. Selection 3 is the paragraph with all the characteristics of good handwriting except good letter formation. Eighty-four per cent of the letters in Selection 3 are poorly formed. Any differences observed in the reading records for this paragraph, compared with the paragraph of normal handwriting (Selection 2), are to be accounted for on the basis of the quality of letter formation employed in the two selections.

In the conduct of the investigation the subjects showed such a high degree of consistency of performance in reading this paragraph (with poor letter formation) that no subjects beyond Subject 20 read this selection. Table IX shows data for the twenty subjects who read this selection.

For Selection 3 the average number of words read per fixation is 0.8, the average duration of the fixations is 6.4 twenty-fifths second, and the average number of words read per regression is 4.3.

Since only twenty subjects read Selection 3 it will be necessary, in comparing the records of readers for Selection 2 and Selection 3, to include the records of only the first twenty subjects in Table VII. For Subjects 1 to 20 for Selection 2 (Table VII) the average number of words read per fixation is 1.0, the average duration of fixations is 6.3 twenty-fifths second, and the average number of words read per regression is 17.7.

Poor letter formation reduces the average number of words read per fixation from 1.0 for normal handwriting to 0.8, for all subjects. The subjects use a narrower eye-span in reading the material with poor letter formation. Three subjects show no change in eye-span for the selection with poor letter formation, since the average number of words read per fixation is the same for both Selection 2 and Selection 3. All other subjects show a consistently smaller number of words per fixation for handwriting with poor letter formation. The decrease varies from 0.1 to 0.3 words per fixation for each subject. No subject shows a larger average number of words per fixation for the selection with poor letter formation.

The average duration of fixations for the selection with poor letter formation varies only slightly from the average duration of fixations for the selection of

TABLE IX *Number of Fixations, Average Number of Words Read per Fixation, Average Duration of Fixations, and Average Number of Words Read per Regression for Selection 3*

Subject Number	Number of Fixations	Average Number of Words Read per Fixation	Average Duration of Fixations	Average Number of Words Read per Regression
1	53	0.8	7.0	2.7
2*	40	0.9	5.5	18.5
3	54	0.8	7.0	2.8
4	45	0.9	5.9	6.1
5	52	0.8	6.2	2.8
6	41	1.0	7.6	5.4
7	38	1.1	7.2	10.8
8	38	1.1	5.0	21.5
9	44	0.9	6.5	5.4
10	45	0.9	6.8	6.1
11	66	0.6	6.0	4.3
12	44	0.9	5.8	14.3
13	67	0.6	5.8	2.1
14	44	0.9	7.0	6.1
15	53	0.8	5.7	2.8
16	41	1.0	5.9	8.6
17	51	0.8	6.0	4.3
18	56	0.8	6.5	3.0
19	75	0.6	6.4	1.9
20	62	0.7	7.1	4.3
Total	1009			
Mean	50.4	0.8	6.4	4.3

* Record is for six lines.

normal handwriting, with 6.3 twenty-fifths and 6.4 twenty-fifths, respectively, for the two selections. Four subjects use fixations of the same durations for both selections, nine subjects use longer fixations, and the other subjects use fixations of shorter average duration in reading the selection with poor letter formation. The subjects do not show any consistent trend in the duration of their fixations. The reading of handwriting with poor letter formation does not equally affect the fixation time for all subjects, when compared with the fixation time for normal handwriting.

In comparing Selection 2 with Selection 3 with respect to regressive movements it is clear that poor letter formation increases the number of regressions. The average number of words read per regressive movement for twenty subjects for Selection 3 is 4.3, compared with 17.7 for the same subjects for Selection 2. Not only is the average number of words decreased for the selection with poor letter formation, but there is also a consistent decrease when the records of individual subjects are considered. Every subject shows a smaller average number of words per regression for the selection with poor letter formation, when compared with normal handwriting. Poor letter formation increases the number of regressive movements for every subject.

Spacing and Legibility

In order to study the effect of spacing on the legibility of handwriting, four selections were read by the subjects: (1) Selection 5, in which the spacing was reduced between the letters, and also between the words; (2) Selection 4, in which the spacing was reduced between the letters, but normal spacing was kept between the words; (3) Selection 6, in which normal spacing was kept between letters and words, but narrower spacing (one-fourth inch) was used between the lines of handwriting; (4) Selection 7, in which the spacing was increased between letters and between words. Each selection will be considered, in turn, in order to discover the effect of each spacing on the ease with which subjects can read the handwriting.

How is the legibility of handwriting affected, if the spacing is altered? Comparison of the selection of normal handwriting with other selections in which only the spacing has been modified, shows these results:

1. When spacing is reduced between letters and between words: The reduction of spacing shortens the line of handwriting and permits the subject to read a significantly larger average number of words per fixation than in normal handwriting. The average duration of fixations does not show any significant change when the spacing is reduced. The average number of words read per regression shows some reduction in reading the shortened line, but the difference is not significant. The reduction of spacing does make handwriting more legible, by increasing the number of words per fixation.

2. When spacing is reduced between letters, but normal spacing is maintained between words: The reduction in spacing increases significantly the average number of words read per fixation. The duration of fixations does not show any significant change. The average number of words per regression does not show any significant change. Decreasing the spacing results in improvement in legibility over normal handwriting, by increasing the average number of words per fixation.

3. When spacing is reduced to ¼″ between the lines of handwriting: There is no significant change in legibility. The ease with which the handwriting can be read is not conditioned by the spacing between lines. Handwriting with ¼″ spacing between the lines is as easily read as the handwriting with ⅝″ spacing. The average number of words read per fixation, the duration of fixations, and the average number of words read per regression show that subjects read one selection as well as the other, when normal handwriting with the two spacings is compared.

4. When spacing is increased between the letters and between the words: There is a significant decrease in the average number of words read per fixation, and in the average number of words read per regression. It is clear that the legibility of handwriting decreases when the spacing between letters and between words is increased.

Compactness in the lines of handwriting increases legibility of handwriting, but lack of compactness in handwriting decreases legibility.

Slant and Legibility

Selection 9, written with irregular slant of letters, is comparable to Selection 2 in all respects except the slant. Table IV shows variation in the amount of slant for Selection 9 compared with all other selections used in this study. The slant of the letters in Selection 2 varies from 71 to 90 degrees with the base line of writing. The slant of the letters in Selection 9 varies from 54 to 114 degrees with the base line of writing.

The data for the subjects will be analyzed to discover what effect the irregularity of slant has on the legibility of the handwriting.

Table X presents the data for the reading records of the thirty-five subjects who read Selection 9.

TABLE X *Number of Fixations, Average Number of Words Read per Fixation, Average Duration of Fixations, and Average Number of Words Read per Regression for Selection 9*

Subject Number	Number of Fixations	Average Number of Words Read per Fixation	Average Duration of Fixations	Average Number of Words Read per Regression
1	48	0.9	5.8	3.2
2	39	1.1	4.9	14.0
3	39	1.1	6.9	8.4
4	35	1.2	5.1	14.0
5	39	1.1	6.1	7.0
6	34	1.2	7.9	21.0
7	29	1.4	6.6	21.0
8	33	1.3	5.0	42.0
9	37	1.1	6.5	14.0
10	36	1.1	6.4	14.0
11	42	1.0	5.1	8.4
12	45	0.9	5.1	7.0
13	68	0.6	5.7	2.2
14	36	1.1	7.4	8.4
15	31	1.3	5.7	8.4
16	36	1.1	5.7	10.5
17	45	0.9	6.2	8.4
18	47	0.9	7.2	3.5
19	46	0.9	6.2	3.8
20	46	0.9	6.3	7.0
21	33	1.3	4.9	14.0
22	38	1.1	6.4	42.0
23	41	1.0	8.3	8.4
24	39	1.1	5.6	8.4
25	36	1.1	5.4	10.5
26*	22	1.4	6.0	31.0
27	37	1.1	7.6	21.0
28	48	0.9	5.1	2.8
29	49	0.8	5.2	7.0
30	46	0.9	5.3	10.5
31	41	1.0	5.6	14.0
32	39	1.0	4.4	21.0
33	45	0.9	5.2	8.4
34	39	1.0	4.8	8.4
35	40	1.0	5.8	7.0
Total	1404			
Mean	40.1	1.0	5.9	7.8

* Record is for five lines.

Table X shows for all subjects an average of 1.0 word read per fixation, with a range from 0.8 to 1.4. The average number of words read per fixation is the same as for normal handwriting, but only four subjects have the same average for Selection 9 and for Selection 2. Eighteen subjects have a larger average number of words read per fixation for Selection 9, and eleven have a smaller average for Selection 9. The average number of words read per fixation is not consistently larger for all subjects in reading Selection 9.

The average duration of fixations for all subjects is 5.9 twenty-fifths second for Selection 9, compared with 6.0 for Selection 2, normal handwriting. Not all subjects show consistently a longer average duration of fixations for one selection. Four subjects have the same average duration of fixations for both selections, eleven have a larger average duration of fixations for Selection 9, and the remaining subjects have a longer average duration of fixations for normal handwriting. The slight difference in average duration—0.1 twenty-fifths second—does not indicate any great difference in reading difficulty in the two selections.

The average number of words read per regressive movement for all subjects is 7.8, compared with 10.1 for the selection of normal handwriting. No subjects show the same average number of words per regressive movement for both Selection 9 and Selection 2. Eleven subjects show a larger average number of words read per regression for Selection 9, but all other subjects show a larger average for Selection 2. It is clear that the number of regressive movements increases when subjects read handwriting that has irregular slant.

Table XI shows data for the most effective and the least effective readers for Selection 9.

For the most effective readers the average number of words read per fixation is 1.1 compared with the average of 1.0 for the entire group of subjects. The average number of words per fixation for this same group is 1.2 for normal handwriting, indicating that the most effective readers find normal handwriting

TABLE XI *Average Number of Words Read per Fixation, Average Duration of Fixations, Average Number of Words Read per Regression, for the Most Effective and for the Least Effective Readers for Selection 9*

Subject Number		Number of Fixations	Average Number of Words Read per Fixation	Average Duration of Fixations	Average Number of Words Read per Regression
		Most Effective Readers			
4		35	1.2	5.1	14.0
6		34	1.2	7.9	21.0
10		36	1.1	6.4	14.0
21		33	1.3	4.9	14.0
25		36	1.1	5.4	10.5
26		22	1.4	6.0	31.0
32		39	1.0	4.4	14.0
34		39	1.0	4.8	8.4
	Total	274	9.3	44.9	126.9
	Mean	34.2	1.1	4.6	15.8
		Least Effective Readers			
3		39	1.1	6.9	8.4
13		68	0.6	5.7	2.2
16		36	1.1	5.7	10.5
18		47	0.9	7.2	3.5
19		46	0.9	6.2	3.8
20		46	0.9	6.3	7.0
23		41	1.0	8.3	8.4
30		46	0.9	5.3	10.5
	Total	359	7.8	51.6	53.9
	Mean	44.9	0.9	6.4	6.9

slightly easier to read than handwriting with uneven slant. The most effective readers show an average duration of 4.6 twenty-fifths second for Selection 9, and 5.4 for Selection 2. The fixation time is shorter for the selection with irregular slant than for normal handwriting. The most effective readers have an average of 30.3 words read per regression for normal handwriting, compared with 15.8 for handwriting with irregular slant. Writing that has irregular slant is more difficult for the effective readers as judged by the average number of words read per regressive movement.

The least effective readers have an average of 0.9 word read per fixation for Selection 9, compared with 0.8 for Selection 2. The average duration of fixations is 6.4 for Selection 9, compared with 6.5 for Selection 2. The average number of words read per regressive movement is 6.9 for Selection 9, compared with 8.4 for Selection 2. The least effective readers show little difference in the records for normal handwriting and the selection with irregular slant. Irregular slant apparently does not alter the reading procedures of ineffective readers to any noticeable degree.

Summary

The foregoing study of reading records for the different selections of handwriting may be briefly summarized.

1. Handwriting is less legible than printed material. In printed material the spacing between words is regular, and the length of lines can be regulated to make one line as long as every other line. The height and form of a letter in a certain style of print is always uniform, no matter how often the letter occurs on the page, or in what combination with other letters. In handwriting the spacing between letters varies to some degree, and the length of all lines is not exactly the same. The height of letters varies even in one word where the same letter may be repeated. The form of letters varies to some extent also. These factors do not vary separately in normal handwriting, but when one factor varies it is quite likely that other factors will also show some degree of variation. For that reason the legibility of letters is not always uniform throughout any selection of handwriting. Therefore the average performance must be used in a consideration of handwriting. Analysis of the data for the selection of print and the selection of normal handwriting show that handwriting is less legible than print. The relationship is consistent, measured by the average number of words per fixation, the average duration of fixations, and the average number of words read per regressive movement.

Table XII shows for all subjects the average number of words read per fixation, the average duration of fixations, and the average number of words read per regression for each selection used in this study.

2. Good letter formation is the most important factor in determining the legibility of handwriting. Conversely, poor letter formation reduces legibility more than any other single factor considered in this investigation.

When handwriting has poor letter formation the reader must pause frequently in the line, because the words are not recognized in large wholes. Words are perceived when the eye is at rest, and the eye pauses in the line in order that perception may take place. At each pause the reader perceives groups of letters. If the letters are poorly formed he recognizes them less easily, consequently the units of recognition become smaller, and the number of fixations per line increases. Table XII shows clearly the effect of poor letter formation, with 0.8 word read per fixation for Selection 3, characterized by poor letter formation.

TABLE XII   *Average Number of Words Read per Fixation, Average Duration of Fixations, and Average Number of Words Read per Regression for Selections 1 to 11*

Selection	Average Number of Words Read per Fixation	Average Duration of Fixations	Average Number of Words Read per Regression
1	1.4	6.5	19.4
2	1.0	6.0	10.1
3	0.8	6.4	4.3
4	1.1	6.0	9.2
5	1.0	6.1	9.7
6	1.0	5.8	8.0
7	0.8	6.2	4.4
8	1.1	5.9	11.4
9	1.0	5.9	7.8
10	1.0	5.8	8.6
11	1.1	6.0	8.8

Other evidence of the reduction of legibility when poor letter formation is found in handwriting is furnished by the duration of the fixations. The duration of the fixations is an index to the speed with which the reader recognizes words. If the reader has rapid recognition the pauses are short in duration. In reading the selection with poor letter formation the duration of fixations is longest for all handwriting selections used in this study. The subjects recognize the words least rapidly in this selection.

If material is legible the reader can recognize the written words in the lines with few fixations, and the movement of the eye is from left to right, without the necessity of backward movement. When the handwriting has poorly formed letters the number of words recognized per regression decreases. Table XII shows that Selection 3 has the smallest average number of words read per regression. The data in Table XII show clearly that poor letter formation reduces legibility of handwriting.

Selection 2, normal handwriting, was compared with all other selections used, by means of Fisher's t-test. A summary of all comparisons is given in Table XIII, with reference to the average number of words per fixation, average duration of fixations, and average number of words per regression.

TABLE XIII   *Comparison of Selection 2, Normal Handwriting, with All Other Selections, for t-Test*

Selections Compared	Average Number of Words per Fixation		Average Duration of Fixations		Average Number of Words per Regression	
	t	P	t	P	t	P
2 minus 1	−8.40	<.01	−3.196	<.01	−4.48	<.01
2 minus 3	5.745	<.01	− .5304	.6<P<.7	6.032	<.01
2 minus 4	−3.5926	<.01	.7923	.5<P<.6	− .3659	.8<P<.9
2 minus 5	−2.430	.01<P<.02	− .546	.6<P<.7	− .3691	.8<P<.9
2 minus 6	.1206	>.9	1.571	.2<P<.3	1.5369	.2<P<.3
2 minus 7	3.8745	<.01	0.00		3.18	<.01
2 minus 8	−2.253	.02<P<.05	1.54	.2<P<.3	−1.5970	.2<P<.3
2 minus 9	− .522	.7<P<.8	.616	.6<P<.7	3.58	<.01
2 minus 10	−1.7024	.05<P<.1	2.548	.01<P<.02	1.9700	.02<P<.05
2 minus 11	−2.7666	<.01	0.00		.0855	>.9

There is greater difference between the selections in the number of words per fixation than in the other criteria used. Of the ten comparisons with Selection 2 seven significant ratios occur, one is of questionable significance, and only two are too small to have significance. The variations in handwriting produce significant changes in the number of words read per fixation, compared with normal handwriting. The variations in handwriting do not produce a corresponding change in the average duration of the fixations. Of the ten ratios shown in Table XIII only two are significant. The variations in handwriting result in significant change in the average number of words read per regression. Of the ten ratios five are significant. Variation from normal handwriting did not produce any significant difference, judged by the average number of words read per regression.

3. The compactness of handwriting affects its legibility. Reduction of spacing between letters and between words appears to improve legibility, but the evidence is not conclusive. The reduction of space shortens the line of writing, and results in a decrease in the number of fixations necessary in reading the shortened line. The average number of words read per fixation is increased significantly. The average duration of fixations is decreased, but the decrease is not significant in amount. The average number of words read per regression shows also a slight increase, but not enough to be significant.

Reduction of spacing between letters only, with no reduction between words, shows the same tendency as the reduction of spacing between words and between letters. The average number of words per fixation is increased over the number in normal handwriting, but there is no significant change in the average duration of fixations or in the average number of words read per regression. The reduction of spacing between letters only probably does increase legibility, but the data are not conclusive.

Reduction of spacing from ⅝″ to ¼″ between lines does not noticeably affect the legibility of handwriting. Reference to Table XIII shows that the difference between normal handwriting and handwriting with the narrower spacing (Selection 2 and Selection 6) is too slight to have any significance.

Increasing the spacing between words and between letters reduces legibility. The increase in spacing results in a longer line, which in turn increases the number of fixations. The number of words per fixation is perceptibly and significantly decreased. The average duration of fixations remains exactly the same as for normal handwriting. The average number of words read per regression is significantly decreased. The selection with wide spacing between letters and between words ranks next to the selection with poor letter formation in illegibility.

Compactness in handwriting favors legibility, and lack of compactness decreases legibility. The compactness results from decreasing the spacing between the letters and between words: it does not result from a crowding of the letters, or from changing the style of letters in the handwriting. A change in the size or style of letters might show a different result, but this aspect of writing was not investigated in the present study.

4. Evenness of alinement apparently is not an important factor in the legibility of handwriting. Comparison of the results of reading a paragraph with poor alinement and one with good alinement shows that poorly alined handwriting is not less legible than handwriting with good alinement. The poorly alined paragraph shows a significantly larger average number of words read per fixation than does the selection of normal handwriting. When the two paragraphs are compared there is no significant difference in the average duration of fixations,

and in the average number of words read per regression. Word recognition is more rapid in the selection of uneven alinement.

5. The regularity of the slant of letters is an important factor in the legibility of handwriting. When the slant of the letters becomes irregular the legibility of handwriting is decreased. Irregular slant does not result in any marked change in the number of words read per fixation. The average duration of fixations is not altered to any significant extent by irregularity of slant, and the records show an average duration of fixations that differs in no significant way from the average duration of fixations from normal handwriting. Handwriting that has irregular slant does show a decrease in the average number of words read per regression. Since regressions occur only as an index of difficulty for the reader, it is evident that irregular slant does decrease the legibility of handwriting. No attempt was made in this study to determine what slant is best, with respect to legibility, but the data do show that the irregularity of slant does decrease the legibility of handwriting.

6. The results of this investigation are inconclusive, with respect to the influence of weight of line on legibility of handwriting.

A heavy line produces handwriting that is probably more legible than handwriting produced with a medium line. The difference between handwriting produced with a heavy line and handwriting produced with a medium weight of line is doubtful, when judged by the average number of words read per fixation. The number of words is somewhat larger for the selection with the heavier line, but since P lies between .05 and .1, according to Fisher's t-test, the difference cannot be said to be significant. There is a difference in the average duration of fixations for the selection with a heavy line and the selection with medium weight of line, with the longer duration for the heavy line. The average number of words read per regression is larger for normal handwriting than for the handwriting produced with the heavy line. It cannot be definitely stated that a heavy line produces more legible handwriting.

Handwriting that is characterized by a light line is more legible than handwriting that has a medium weight, when judged by the average number of words read per fixation, and the difference is significant. The average duration of fixations for the two selections is exactly the same, showing no difference between the two selections. The average number of words per regression is slightly more for the selection with medium weight, but the difference is very small—not large enough to have any significance. It cannot be stated that the use of a light line in handwriting is an important factor in the legibility of handwriting.

Determination of the effect of weight of line on legibility is not clearly shown in the results of this investigation. Further study is needed to clarify the issue of weight of line and its effect on legibility of handwriting.

Implications

Several implications for the teaching of handwriting grow out of the results of this investigation.

1. No one characteristic of handwriting exists separately from other characteristics, but they are interrelated in the handwriting process. In any attempt to improve the quality of handwriting it is necessary to keep clearly in mind the fact that one characteristic is dependent on others. Letter formation is closely related to spacing, slant, alinement, and weight of line. Any change in one characteristic is accompanied by a corresponding change in the others.

2. Since letter formation is the most important factor in determining the legibility of handwriting, this aspect of writing should receive the greatest emphasis in teaching children to write.

In recent years handwriting instruction has emphasized the use of simplified letter forms, free from flourishes and extra strokes, containing only the essentials of the letters. The results of this study indicate that, from the point of view of legibility, this emphasis is correct.

In teaching children to write, the development of good letter formation should be the chief outcome, and the development of other characteristics should be related to the improvement of letter formation. The chief concern of teachers should be the improvement of other aspects of the handwriting process only as they contribute to good letter formation—not as ends in themselves. Slant, alinement, spacing, and quality of line should receive attention only as they improve letter formation. Principles that result in improvement of letter formation are probably reliable guides to teachers in improving handwriting.

3. Pupils should be taught to use a compact type of handwriting. This should not be developed at the sacrifice of good letter formation, but should emphasize compactness of spacing between letters. A medium or narrow spacing between letters is to be preferred to wide spacing between letters. Since the use of wide spacing in handwriting can develop into a type of writing which results in malformation of letters or in the development of flourishes, pupils should be taught in such a manner that correct letter formation is used even with relatively narrow spacing between letters.

It need not be a matter of concern whether or not children use a particular width of ruling on paper. There is no difference in the legibility of handwriting with ⅝″ and ¼″ between the lines of writing. The selection of either ruling should be made on the basis of other factors than the legibility of handwriting, since legibility is not modified by the use of either spacing.

4. Evenness of alinement need not receive special emphasis in the teaching of handwriting. Uneven alinement adds slightly to the legibility of handwriting, but is not of sufficient importance to be considered as an end in itself. If correct letter formation is emphasized sufficiently in the teaching of handwriting, the letters will be well alined. Uneven alinement is likely to be caused by poor letter formation. For that reason it is not desirable to teach children to write with uneven alinement. It is quite probable that, aside from a possible esthetic effect, no end is served by insisting that handwriting be perfectly alined. If good letter formation is set up as the chief outcome of handwriting instruction even alinement will probably be an accompanying result. Handwriting of good quality is produced by rhythmic movements of the hand and forearm, and even alinement is a natural outcome of rhythmic movements in the writing process.

5. The regularity of slant is important as a component of legibility of handwriting. It is important, therefore, if the writing is to be legible, that the slant of writing be more or less uniform. Uniformity of slant is closely related to good letter formation in the writing process. No attempt was made in this study to determine what slant is best for the sake of legibility, but the investigation does show that the regularity of slant is important. The teaching of handwriting, therefore, should emphasize regularity of slant as an important item. The slant of handwriting is conditioned by the muscular control and skill of the writer. Teachers should emphasize regular slant as an important aspect of correct letter formation in order to increase the legibility of handwriting.

6. The weight of line employed in handwriting is not an important matter, judged from the point of view of legibility. It is probably best that children

should use a medium weight of line. Neither a heavy line nor a light line is clearly superior to a medium weight with respect to legibility. The manipulation of a medium weight of pen is probably more satisfactory, from the point of view of the pupil who is learning to write, than is the use of a fine pen or a coarse pen. Since there is no clear-cut case for either the light or the heavy pen, it is probably best to use a pen of medium weight.

7. Handwriting has social value only as it provides a more or less permanent record which can be read by someone. Children should be made aware of the necessity for producing a legibly written record, and should be made to understand the extent to which the different characteristics of handwriting enter into the composite characteristic designated as legibility. Slant, alinement, and the other characteristics should receive attention, not as important outcomes in themselves, but because they contribute to improved legibility of the handwriting.

---

32   Legibility Ratings for Handwriting Samples: A Pragmatic Approach

WAYNE OTTO

EUNICE ASKOV

CARIN COOPER

Rating pupils' handwriting samples for legibility at fairly frequent intervals can yield information useful in motivating pupils and in establishing a basis for corrective teaching. Yet, in practice the awkwardness of using the typical legibility rating scales probably prevents most teachers from making such assessments very often. The notion underlying this study was that once teachers have established a set of criteria for making legibility judgments by using scales, they should be able to make reasonably reliable judgments even when the formal use of scales is discontinued.

Handwriting samples were obtained by having 240 fourth and sixth grade pupils write a paragraph containing two sentences which include all the letters in the alphabet and which are the standard sentences for the California and Wisconsin scales, respectively: "The quick brown fox just came over to greet the lazy poodle" and "The quick brown fox jumps over the lazy dog." Thus, there were two standard sentence samples from each pupil. Three judges independently rated the samples for legibility. First, the California scale, a 7-point scale that is provided as a part of the California Achievement Test battery (Tiegs and Clark, 1957), and the Wisconsin scale, a 7-point scale devised for the present study by procedures outlined by Herrick and Erlebacher (cf. Herrick, 1961, pp. 207–231), were used to assign a legibility rating to the appropriate sample from each pupil. Then the judges assigned a legibility rating of 1 to 7 to each sample without using a scale.

Inter-judge reliability coefficients (Pearsonian) were .77, .72, and .69 with the California scale and .85, .80, and .74 with the Wisconsin scale; the between-

---

From *Perceptual and Motor Skills*, Vol. 25 (1967), p. 638. Reprinted with permission of authors and publisher.

scales correlation was .79. When ratings were made without scales, the inter-judge coefficients were .79, .91, and .85 with the California sentence samples and .72, .74, and .86 for the Wisconsin sentence samples; the between-samples *r* was .82. The judges did about as well, then, without the scales as with them, and there was no loss in the reliability of the ratings for individuals when the scales were not used. When each judge's ratings of the California sample sentences with and without the scale were correlated, the *r*s were .77, .83, and .76; with the Wisconsin sentences *r*s were .76, .85, and .73.

These results indicate there was no significant loss in the magnitude of judges' reliability ratings when the use of scales was discontinued. The implication appears to be that, given a background of experience in making such judgments, teachers do not need to use scales to make reliable judgments regarding the legibility of pupils' handwriting. Further research is needed to determine optimum procedures for establishing criteria for judging. Meanwhile, a preliminary period of scale-based judging appears to be useful.

REFERENCES

Herrick, V. E. (Ed.) *New horizons for research in handwriting.* Madison: Univer. of Wisconsin Press, 1961. Pp. 207–231.

Tiegs, E. W., and Clark, W. W. *California Achievement Tests, Elementary.* Monterey, Calif.: California Test Bureau, 1957.

---

33 An Analysis of Errors in the Formation of Manuscript Letters by First-Grade Children

EDWARD R. LEWIS

HILDA P. LEWIS

Problem

Although the manuscript style of handwriting is taught to first graders in most American schools, few detailed analyses of the specific difficulties inherent in manuscript letter formation exist. As a result, instructional programs are planned without the benefit of knowledge from relevant research. To meet this need, the present investigation determined the relative difficulty of the 52 letter forms of the manuscript-style alphabet, the incidence of various types of error by letter form, and the relationship of errors to certain personal variables of first-grade children.

Answers were sought to the following questions:

1. What is the order of difficulty of the 52 letter forms of the manuscript-style alphabet?
2. What is the incidence of various types of error in each of these 52 letter forms?

From *American Educational Research Journal*, Vol. 2 (1965), pp. 25–35. Reprinted with permission.

3. When the letter forms are grouped into classes according to structural characteristics, do the classes differ in frequency of error?

4. Is there a differential effect of instruction in eliminating errors?

5. Are frequency and type of error related to (a) sex? (b) chronological age? (c) mental maturity? (d) visual perception? (e) quality of handwriting? (f) handedness?

6. Is there a difference between the incidence of error in functional writing and that in copying letters?

Subjects

The subjects consisted of all the nonrepeating pupils in the 15 first-grade classrooms of one school district in a middle-class California suburb and totaled 354. The numbers of boys and girls were approximately equal.

Procedure

1. In September 1960, samples of manuscript handwriting before instruction were obtained from the subjects. They copied the 52 letter forms of the manuscript alphabet from a set of 26 one-foot-square cards, each bearing the capital and lower-case forms of one letter drawn in black in the style found in the California State Series (California State Department of Education, 1959), as shown in Figure 1, and oriented to three horizontal blue lines corresponding to the lines on the pupils' one-inch-lined newsprint. To randomize the effect of fatigue, the order of presentation of the letters was determined in each class by randomly selecting the first letter to be shown, proceeding in alphabetical order from the selected letter to *Z,* then to *A,* and continuing alphabetically until all letters were presented.

2. In April 1961, after the children had had 6 months of formal instruction in manuscript handwriting, the procedure described above was repeated.

3. At the same time (after 6 months of instruction), samples of the children's functional writing were collected.

4. The chronological age and sex of each subject were obtained from his cumulative record. The "Draw-a-Man" and "Matching" subtests of the *Metropolitan Reading Readiness Test,* Form R, provided mental-maturity and visual-perception scores, respectively. Teachers identified left-handed pupils.

5. Two judges, using the Freeman manuscript-handwriting scale for grade 1 (Freeman, 1958) rated the quality of the post-instruction samples of copied letters. The two ratings were averaged and a quality score assigned to each sample on a five-point scale.

6. Errors in letter construction were classified into the following 11 types:

(1) *Reversal:* the mirror image of a letter form.

(2) *Partial omission:* any part of a letter form missing.

(3) *Addition:* inclusion of a part not shown on the model.

(4) *Incorrect relationship of parts:* any letter form in which a part is not correctly oriented.

(5) *Incorrect size of letter form or parts of it:* a letter form (or part) that is too large or too small in relation to the guide lines.

(6) *Incorrect placement relative to line:* incorrect orientation to the writing line.

FIG. 1 *Manuscript letter forms used in study*

(7) *Misshapenness:* distortion of all or part of a letter form.

(8) *Rotation:* a letter form rotated more than 15 degrees from an imaginary line drawn vertically through its axis.

(9) *Retracing:* any letter form (or part) that has been reconstructed after an initial effort.

(10) *Inversion:* any letter form upside down.

(11) *Total omission:* any letter form not attempted.

7. In instances of multiple errors in a single letter form, each error was recorded. To determine reliability of scoring, two judges independently scored a randomly selected group of 50 copying samples. The per cent of agreement was 90.

Findings

For the two samples of copied letters combined, Table I gives the number of errors of each type for each letter form, the total number of errors of each type, and the total number of errors for each letter form. Errors were most frequent for *q*, with *g*, *p*, *y*, and *j* following. Errors were least frequent for *l*, with *o*, *L*, *O*, and *H* next in order of increasing frequency of error. The most frequent type of error was *incorrect size;* the least frequent was *inversion.*

The letter form most frequently *reversed* was *N*, with *d*, *q*, and *y* following; *k*, *K*, *C*, *F*, and *E* were least frequently *reversed.* The greatest number of *partial omissions* was for *m*, with *U* and *I* next, but with the error occurring much less frequently. *Additions* were most frequent for *q*, with *C*, *k*, *m*, and *Y* following. *Incorrect relationship of parts* was a rather common error, occurring most frequently in *k*, with *R*, *a*, *M*, and *m* next in decreasing order of frequency.

Although *incorrect size* was more evenly distributed among the letter forms than were other errors, it was found more frequently in the descenders, *p*, *g*, *y*, *q*, and *j*, than in other forms. *Incorrect placement relative to line* was also a common error in the descenders and a less frequent and rather evenly distributed error in the remaining letter forms. The forms most frequently *misshaped* were *j*, *G*, and *J*.

The stability of the data in Table I was determined as follows: The 354 subjects were divided randomly into two equal groups and a table similar to Table I made for each group. The frequencies in each column of the group-one table was correlated with the frequencies in the corresponding column in the group-two table. The resulting coefficients are reported in Table II and indicate that, in groups of children like the subjects of this study, error frequencies of all types except 3, 10, and 11 are likely to be similar to those in Table I.

To determine whether differences in error frequency exist among classes of letter forms grouped according to structural characteristics, the letter forms were assigned to classes on the following bases:

I. Those constructed of only vertical or horizontal and vertical lines

II. Those containing only slanted lines or slanted lines combined with horizontal or vertical lines

III. Those containing circles or parts of circles that do not merge with vertical lines

IV. Those in which curves and vertical lines merge

To see whether differences in error frequency among the four classes were statistically significant, the errors occurring in nine randomly selected letter

TABLE I *Frequency of Errors by Type and by Letter Form in Two Samples (Combined) of Copied Manuscript Letter Forms from Each of 354 First-Grade Pupils*

Letter Form	Type of Error ‡											Total
	1	2	3	4	5	6	7	8	9	10	11	
q	42	2	34	115	251	226	3	5	74	2	21	775
g	8	1	10	123	266	246	2	11	80	5	19	771
p	13	1	11	74	291	229	2	2	65	1	12	701
y	40	1	11	59	263	229	*	23	37	0	18	681
j	17	11	12	4	230	281	30	6	41	1	12	645
m	5	90	21	156	198	31	1	5	54	0	18	579
k	1	1	24	229	177	22	*	4	32	0	13	503
U	18	33	16	141	135	24	3	8	107	4	13	502
a	15	3	7	175	129	49	4	10	55	*	23	470
G	2	2	26	85	146	35	25	17	70	10	15	433
R	3	3	10	206	109	20	3	10	38	0	11	413
d	44	4	10	90	167	28	3	0	49	4	7	406
Y	*	2	20	104	177	36	*	20	31	0	12	402
u	21	9	8	105	122	31	3	7	67	5	18	396
M	*	7	11	160	135	17	*	13	27	8	13	391
S	24	0	8	30	115	21	16	83	65	*	16	378
b	24	0	15	73	152	35	2	5	43	4	14	367
e	7	3	11	32	171	53	6	24	39	4	17	367
r	4	3	6	66	156	34	1	6	64	0	23	363
Z	23	0	18	43	160	28	*	24	38	*	19	353
n	7	11	5	64	171	23	3	4	42	0	22	352
s	25	0	14	15	122	32	8	73	42	*	17	348
Q	7	8	14	94	136	23	14	3	33	2	7	341
B	6	1	12	141	118	23	7	4	20	*	6	338
t	*	1	8	37	191	27	*	5	53	0	11	333
z	31	0	9	38	124	47	*	19	42	*	23	333
K	2	1	19	101	131	23	*	7	23	*	8	315
W	*	3	13	72	143	10	*	21	26	13	11	312
A	*	1	7	63	110	27	*	53	36	1	9	307
N	47	1	11	69	109	18	*	8	26	*	12	301
C	5	0	17	*	128	25	15	31	57	*	11	289
f	4	2	16	29	125	16	3	5	67	1	16	284
J	25	0	14	*	110	29	20	8	43	0	11	260
w	*	3	11	57	99	26	*	14	17	13	20	260
h	6	0	2	52	140	13	2	4	27	0	12	258
T	*	0	7	30	113	16	*	3	60	0	9	238
x	*	1	5	24	95	32	*	43	18	*	18	236
c	4	0	13	*	106	25	12	24	36	*	15	235
V	*	0	5	22	91	13	*	51	25	5	14	226
F	2	1	14	24	114	27	*	5	27	0	12	226
P	5	0	14	11	127	26	6	3	20	0	11	223
E	2	3	10	22	110	31	*	4	30	*	10	222
X	*	0	5	29	103	10	*	41	21	*	13	222
I	*	16	8	6	96	17	*	3	50	*	14	210
v	*	0	4	15	79	24	*	47	17	2	17	205
i	*	2	3	13	122	19	3	1	23	1	13	200
D	6	1	4	6	111	17	14	3	25	*	7	194
H	*	2	3	14	108	14	*	5	24	*	9	179
O	*	0	6	*	114	12	15	*	22	*	8	177
L	3	2	3	10	91	19	*	6	26	1	12	173
o	*	0	5	*	97	25	6	*	26	*	9	168
l	*	*	4	*	101	9	*	5	17	*	13	149
Total	498	236	574	3,128	7,285	2,373	232	786	2,097	87	714	18,010

‡ See text for description of each numbered type.
* Not scored in this category because the letter form does not lend itself to the error.

TABLE II *Product-Moment Correlation Coefficients Showing Stability of Data in Table I*

Type of Error	r
1. Reversal	.86
2. Partial Omission	.96
3. Addition	.57
4. Incorrect Relationship of Parts	.97
5. Incorrect Size of Letter Form or Parts of It	.96
6. Incorrect Placement Relative to Line	.99
7. Misshapenness	.86
8. Rotation	.94
9. Retracing	.86
10. Inversion	.68
11. Total Omission	.40
All types combined	.99

forms from each class were compared. Table III gives the letter forms for each class and the total number of errors for each group of letter forms. (The number of errors for each letter form was obtained from the right-most column of Table I.)

TABLE III *Groups of Nine Letter Forms Randomly Selected from Each Structural Class and Total Number of Errors for Each Group*

Class	Letter Forms	Total Number of Errors
I	E,F,H,I,L,T,i,l,t,	1,930
II	N,V,W,X,k,v,w,x,y	2,946
III	R,S,B,C,D,a,b,o,s	2,965
IV	J,U,f,h,j,m,n,r,u	3,639

Errors were most frequent in letter forms in which curves and vertical lines merge; they were least frequent in letter forms constructed of vertical lines or horizontal and vertical lines. The Friedman Two-Way-Analysis-of-Variance Test (Siegel, 1956) was applied to the data in Table III and indicated that the differences among the classes are significant beyond the .001 level.

For both the pre- and the post-instruction samples of copied letter forms, Table IV gives the mean number of errors of each type for boys and girls separately and the significance level of the difference between each pair of means (when .20 or better). The significance levels were determined by the Mann-Whitney *U* Test (Siegel, 1956). Before instruction, boys made significantly more *partial omissions, inversions,* and *total omissions* than did girls; girls *retraced* letters more often. After instruction, boys made significantly more *size* errors, more *rotation* errors, more *misshapen* letters, and more errors of all types put together (total row in Table IV) than did girls. For each error type, the frequency with which each child made that kind of error was correlated with his chronological age. The resulting coefficients were all very low, both before and after instruction.

The subjects were assigned to five groups according to their mental-maturity scores on the "Draw-a-Man" subtest, on which a score of 5 indicates a high degree of mental maturity and a score of 1, a low degree. Table V presents the

TABLE IV *Mean Numbers of Errors for Boys and Girls Separately and Significance Levels of the Differences Between These Means, by Type of Error and for Pre-Instruction and Post-Instruction Copying Samples*

Type of Error	Mean Number of Errors				Significance Level of Difference Between Boys' and Girls' Means	
	Pre-Instruction		Post-Instruction			
	Boys (N = 180)	Girls (N = 174)	Boys (N = 180)	Girls (N = 174)	Pre-Inst.	Post-Inst.
Reversal	1.11	1.15	.29	.59		.20
Partial Omission	.61	.36	.17	.17	.05	
Addition	1.39	1.02	.44	.40	.10	
Incorrect Relationship of Parts	5.60	5.49	3.49	3.13		
Incorrect Size of Letter Form or Parts of It	18.09	15.76	4.08	3.29	.20	.05
Incorrect Placement Relative to Line	5.88	5.48	1.23	.90		.20
Misshapenness	.52	.54	.21	.07		.01
Rotation	1.80	1.66	.53	.44		.05
Retracing	3.43	4.92	1.88	1.66	.05	
Inversion	.26	.18	.02	.01	.05	
Total Omission	1.66	1.10	.59	.67	.05	
All types combined	40.41	37.70	12.93	11.33		.05

TABLE V *Mean Numbers of Errors, Before Instruction, of Subjects Grouped by Mental-Maturity Scores and Significance Levels of the Differences Among the Means of the Five Groups, by Type of Error*

Type of Error	N	Mental Maturity Scores					Significance Level
		1 32	2 71	3 105	4 85	5 21	
		Mean Number of Errors					
Reversal		1.93	1.53	.96	1.08	.85	.05
Partial Omission		1.06	.76	.45	.31	.19	.01
Addition		1.68	1.42	1.45	.89	.57	.20
Incorrect Relationship of Parts		8.46	6.19	5.82	5.40	3.76	.01
Incorrect Size of Letter Form or Parts of It		28.59	22.32	18.52	12.01	11.48	.01
Incorrect Placement Relative to Line		8.65	6.77	5.68	5.15	3.47	.01
Misshapenness		.71	.60	.76	.38	.19	.20
Rotation		3.18	2.04	2.14	1.17	.80	.01
Retracing		3.09	4.19	4.65	5.18	3.90	
Inversion		.68	.18	.30	.08	.09	.01
Total Omission		3.53	1.54	1.60	.82	.28	.01
All types combined		61.62	47.59	42.38	32.52	25.62	.01

mean frequency, before instruction, of each error type in each group and the significance levels of the differences among the means. Table VI presents analogous data for the samples collected after instruction. The significance levels were determined by the Kruskal-Wallis *H* Test (Siegel, 1956). Before instruction, errors of all types except *retracing* tended to decrease with higher mental maturity. Differences were significant at or beyond the .05 level for all error types except *addition, misshapenness,* and *retracing.* After instruction, the only differences significant at or beyond the .05 level were in *rotation* and in *incorrect placement relative to line.*

TABLE VI *Mean Numbers of Errors, After Instruction, of Subjects Grouped by Mental-Maturity Scores and Significance Levels of the Differences Among the Means of the Five Groups, by Type of Error*

Type of Error	N	Mental-Maturity Score					Signifi-cance Level
		1 32	2 71	3 105	4 85	5 21	
		Mean Number of Errors					
Reversal		.40	.38	.25	.28	.09	.20
Partial Omission		.15	.18	.16	.20	.14	
Addition		.53	.41	.55	.36	.28	
Incorrect Relationship of Parts		3.53	3.37	3.71	2.94	2.71	
Incorrect Size of Letter Form or Parts of It							
Incorrect Placement Relative to Line		2.03	1.17	1.49	.60	.47	.01
Misshapenness		.21	.14	.27	.04	.04	
Rotation		1.18	.68	.56	.20	.04	.01
Retracing		1.78	1.54	2.00	1.97	1.28	
Inversion		.00	.02	.02	.00	.04	
Total Omission		.65	.24	1.26	.50	.09	
All types combined		15.19	11.73	15.43	9.83	7.47	.10

For each error type, the frequency with which each child made that kind of error was correlated with his visual-perception score (derived from the "Matching" subtest). The correlations were low and negative before instruction and, in general, lower (closer to zero) and negative after instruction, indicating that pupils with better visual perception have a small initial advantage, which is reduced by instruction.

The subjects were assigned to five groups according to the manuscript-handwriting quality scores obtained on their post-instruction copying samples, and the mean frequency of each error type computed for each group. As would be expected, the frequency of errors tended to increase markedly as the quality of the writing decreased. For all types of errors combined, the mean frequencies for the five groups arranged in descending order of quality were 2.6, 5.4, 9.6, 13.0, and 26.2. As determined by the Kruskal-Wallis *H* Test, the differences among the groups were significant at the .01 level or beyond for every type of error except *partial omission* and *inversion.*

The subjects were divided into two groups according to handedness (about 14 per cent were left-handed). Table VII presents the mean number of errors of each type, before and after instruction, for each group and the levels of significance (when .20 or better) for the differences between the groups. The

TABLE VII   *Mean Numbers of Errors for Right-Handed and Left-Handed Subjects Separately and Significance Levels of the Differences Between These Means, by Type of Error and for Pre-Instruction and Post-Instruction Copying Samples*

Type of Error	Mean Number of Errors				Significance Level of Difference Between Means of Right- and Left-Handed Groups	
	Pre-Instruction		Post-Instruction			
	Right-Handed (N = 304)	Left-Handed (N = 50)	Right-Handed (N = 304)	Left-Handed (N = 50)	Pre-Inst.	Post-Inst.
Reversal	1.07	1.48	.42	.55	.05	.05
Partial Omission	.43	.84	.17	.20	.01	
Addition	1.17	1.46	.40	.53		
Incorrect Relationship of Parts	5.34	6.78	3.23	3.79	.05	
Incorrect Size of Letter Form or Parts of It	16.64	18.80	3.65	3.89		
Incorrect Placement Relative to Line	5.56	6.42	1.02	1.34	.20	.10
Misshapenness	.51	.62	.15	.12		
Rotation	1.61	2.44	.42	.85	.05	.10
Retracing	4.27	3.52	1.79	1.71		
Inversion	.19	.46	.00	.06	.01	.01
Total Omission	1.22	2.40	.69	.26	.10	
All types combined	38.07	45.22	12.01	13.35	.05	

levels of significance were determined by the Mann-Whitney *U* Test. For all types of errors combined, the mean frequency of errors, before instruction, in the left-handed group exceeded that in the right-handed group at or beyond the .05 level. The left-handed children, as a group, made significantly more errors of *reversal, partial omission, part relationships, rotation,* and *inversion.* After instruction, the mean frequency of all types of error combined was again lower for the right-handed group but the difference between the means of the two groups was no longer statistically significant. However, the left-handed children, as a group, still made significantly more *reversals* and *inversions.*

To find out whether the incidence of errors in functional writing differs from that in copying letters, the number of errors in the initial appearance of all letter forms in each pupil's functional writing was compared with the number of errors in the corresponding letter forms in his post-instruction sample. The Wilcoxon Matched-Pairs Test (Siegel, 1956) was used to determine the significance of the mean difference in number of errors. The frequency of errors in free writing exceeded that in the sample of copied letters beyond the .01 level of significance.

Suggestions for Future Research

1. Since the letter forms of the manuscript alphabet vary considerably in incidence of error, teachers and research workers might find it profitable to assess the efficiency of instructional practices in which relative difficulty

(as determined by frequency of error) is a factor in the order of introduction of the forms.

2. Since it is likely that immaturity of visual perception and lack of motor control were factors in the three most common types of error—*incorrect size, incorrect relationship of parts,* and *incorrect placement relative to line,* research might contribute to an understanding of the function of each of these factors and their interrelationships.

3. Since errors were most frequent in those letter forms in which curves and vertical lines merge (*J, U, f, h, j, m, n, r, u*), the merits and feasibility of modifying the structure of these forms might be studied. Teachers might test the value of providing special exercises for these particularly difficult letter forms and more opportunities for practicing them.

4. Both before and after instruction, boys made more errors than did girls. The differential reduction in type of error for each sex warrants further investigation.

5. Although chronological age within the limited range of 69 to 81 months bore little relationship to errors, the variation in their incidence over a wider age range might be determined.

6. Mental maturity as indicated by scores on the "Draw-a-Man" subtest was related to incidence of errors before, but not after, instruction. It would be interesting to see whether this finding would be confirmed if other mental-maturity tests were used.

7. Although the relationship of visual perception, as indicated by scores on the "Matching" subtest, to incidence of errors was slight, it might be worth while to try more refined measures of perception.

8. As a group, left-handed subjects before instruction made more errors of all types (except *retracing*). After instruction, they still made significantly more *reversals* and *inversions*. Directional confusion in left-handed children merits further study.

9. The incidence of errors in free writing was greater than in copying letters. The effect of mental set on handwriting errors needs more investigation.

10. In the present study, relative difficulty of the letter forms was determined from *combined* pre-instruction and post-instruction samples. The tasks of putting them in order according to the incidence of errors before instruction and again after instruction, comparing the error frequencies, and interpreting any differences remain.

REFERENCES

California State Department of Education. *Handwriting Made Easy.* California State Series. Sacramento: the Department, 1959. 95 pp.

Freeman, Frank N. *Evaluation Scales for Guiding Growth in Handwriting.* Columbus, Ohio: Zaner-Bloser Co., 1958.

Siegel, Sidney. *Nonparametric Statistics for the Behavioral Sciences.* New York: McGraw-Hill Book Co., 1956. 312 pp.

34   New Speeds of Handwriting

PATRICK J. GROFF

Ayres in 1917[1] measured the speed of handwriting by large numbers of pupils, and set norms that are used to this day. It has been noticed by some, however, that these speeds of handwriting seem excessively high when compared with the actual time it takes a pupil to finish a written composition. Frustrations are surely to follow if a teacher or child expects that under normal conditions the rate of written composition will approximate the Ayres norms.

These differences between the norms set by Ayres and the rate at which pupils usually are able to compose written language are due probably to the procedures that Ayres used in his study. First, he had his subjects in grades five through eight read the first three sentences of Lincoln's *Gettysburg Address* until they were familiar with it. These sentences were written by the administrator of the test of handwriting on the chalkboard, presumably in cursive handwriting. Then, the subjects copied these sentences until they were "familiar" with them. After this, the sentences were copied for two minutes from the model written on the chalkboard.

Reasonable objections can be made to this procedure for measuring the speed of handwriting. Why should norms of speed of handwriting be established on material that has been copied repeatedly until the writer is "familiar" with it? In addition, what constitutes "familiarity" in this case, that is, how many times should the sentences be copied by individual children before each is "familiar" with it? Looking to other tests, one would not likely learn that a pupil reads or practices in some way a reading, spelling or language usage test before taking the same test. Why then should a pupil practice handwriting a specific material before taking a speed of handwriting test on the same material? The lack of control here over the influence of practice on the test achievement seems abundantly clear. Each administrator of the test in the Ayres' study apparently was left to his own decision as to how much practice to give before the test began. Would not the actual or expected speed of handwriting of pupils as they write stories, reports, letters, etc., differ greatly in speed from the relatively artificial speed they could achieve after repeatedly copying a passage? If so, the norms set by Ayres seem to be less useful than is normally thought for establishing grade-level expectancies in the speed of handwriting.

To overcome these objections in measuring the speed of handwriting, the writer investigated the handwriting speed of 4834 middle-grade pupils by having them write the three beginning sentences from the *Gettysburg Address* under different conditions. In this writing the pupils first read the sentences written on the chalkboard by their teacher, not in cursive but in manuscript, until they were familiar with them. That is, they read the words until all the pupils could recognize them. This familiarity was more readily ascertained, of course, than familiarity gained through copying. The teacher discovered which children could not read each word during a rereading of the passage after it had been read aloud by the teacher. All unfamiliar words then were reread aloud until

1 Ayres, Leonard P. *Measuring Scale for Handwriting.* New York: Russell Sage Foundation, 1917.

From *Elementary English,* Vol. 38 (1961), pp. 564–565. Reprinted with permission of the National Council of Teachers of English and Patrick J. Groff.

the teacher was satisfied that each pupil could recognize all the words. It can be seen that while a constant of word recognition of the passage by all the pupils was maintained, a constant of unfamiliarity with writing the passage as a whole was maintained also. Writing the passage on the chalkboard in manuscript rather than cursive ruled out the possibility of gaining familiarity with the passage in cursive which added another constant to this procedure.

It is suggested that the speeds of handwriting resulting from the above investigation and presented in Table I more nearly approach the actual speeds of handwriting that a pupil can maintain under natural writing conditions than do the Ayres norms. If this is so, these speeds are more useful and valid for determining grade-level expectancies in the speed of handwriting than are the speed norms set by the older study. In addition, in the writer's opinion, these procedures described above seem to have greater administrative reliability by removing as nearly as possible variance in the preparation of the pupil for the test. Because of these advantages, it is suggested that this procedure be used to measure the speed of handwriting rather than the procedure described by Ayres.

TABLE I   *Speeds of Handwriting in Letters per Minute of Pupils Studied by Ayres and by Groff*

Letters per Minute	Per Cent of Pupils					
	Grade		Grade		Grade	
	4 Ayres	4 Groff (N = 1563)	5 Ayres	5 Groff (N = 1522)	6 Ayres	6 Groff (N = 1749)
10–19	Not reported	6.8	1	3.8		1.5
20–29		25.4	2	13.5	2	5.5
30–39		31.5	5	31.5	3	18.4
40–49		21.3	12	26.0	8	27.1
50–59		9.9	20	12.6	14	21.2
60–69		3.6	22	7.6	19	12.9
70–79		.8	19	3.2	21	7.9
80–89		.3	12	.8	16	3.6
90–99		.1	5	.4	10	.9
100–109			2	.4	5	.8
110–119					2	.4
	M=55	M=35.06	M=64	M=40.65	M=71	M=49.65

Part Nine

Arithmetic

It seems appropriate to mention prior to commenting on the papers in this section that Suydam[1] has developed an instrument for the evaluation of educational research and has established its reliability on research found in *The Arithmetic Teacher*. The appropriateness and possibly the value of Suydam's instrument seem to be enhanced by the fact that three of the following five articles concerning arithmetic were originally published in *The Arithmetic Teacher*.

In the first of the five papers, Capps' comparison of IQ and personality test scores of superior students and underachievers in arithmetic serves as an introduction to that population designated as underachieving in arithmetic. It is interesting to note that the emotional, mental, and sex characteristics of Capps' sample tend to be similar to the characteristics of samples of disabled readers.

Both Balow and Chase report studies of children's ability to solve arithmetic problems. On the basis of the data Balow concluded that even when IQ is controlled, the abilities of reading and arithmetic computation are related to problem solving. Also, Balow's first conclusion is of special significance because it alerts the teacher to the fact that classroom exercises may differ from tests in the relative amounts of abilities (i.e., reading and arithmetic computation) which influence problem-solving success.

For those interested in research methodology, Balow used a factorial design and analyses of variance and co-variance in a type of situation in which some researchers tend to use correlation. This is not to say Balow's design or analyses are suspect; indeed, the methodology is straightforward.

As previously stated, Chase also studied mathematical problem solving; but in contrast to Balow, Chase's concern was with the diagnostic value of a set of formalized steps used to solve a problem. In essence, Chase evaluated a four-step, formal-analysis technique as a method of diagnosing problem-solving difficulties among the students. It seems likely that Chase's discussion would be of value to all who desire to teach a formal method of problem solving to the slower or disabled learner.

Caldwell's plan for using standardized tests to identify specific arithmetic skills in which all or part of a class needs additional instruction is applicable to any academic subject. In essence, Caldwell has presented a step-by-step procedure that leads to corrective or remedial teaching, i.e., the students in a classroom who have not mastered a skill are identified, and further instruction is initiated at the student's level of understanding.

1 Suydam, M. N. An instrument for evaluating experimental educational research reports. *Journal of Educational Research,* 1968, 61, 200–203.

Moench, unlike Caldwell, who was concerned with remedial/corrective teaching, writes about a small study of the effects of individualized arithmetic skill practice in a developmental setting. The value of the article for the remedial teacher seems to be (1) that the place of the remedial program in a developmental program is shown and (2) that limited experimental evidence reveals the value of matching child and practice material. The latter finding is shown to be especially true for the slower children in the study.

An additional note about the Moench study: Moench has provided sufficient detail for the teacher interested enough to want to check Moench's procedures in his class.

---

35   A Comparison of Superior Achievers
          and Underachievers in Arithmetic

LELON R. CAPPS

Until the teaching profession squarely faces the problem of the underachiever in our schools, the goals of education in America will not be fully realized. Although underachievement exists in all areas of the curriculum, this article focuses on arithmetic. All too often, we assess the slow learner's problem as one of inadequate mental capacity or unsatisfactory emotional adjustment.

Many people cite emotional adjustment as one of the most influential determinants of success in school and in life. However, to ascribe lack of success to poor emotional adjustment or to lack of ability appears at times to be a questionable practice. Some information is available to support the view that emotional adjustment contributes in an important way to achievement in arithmetic. The problem is somewhat analogous to the question: "Which came first—the chicken or the egg?"

One remedial clinic that studied twenty-two children who were underachieving in arithmetic concluded that fifteen of them were probably retarded because of emotional difficulty (1). Immediately the question arises, "What about the other seven?" Another investigator, reporting observations of thirteen children who were underachieving in arithmetic, pointed to the fact that emotional problems rather than low intelligence were the principal cause of retardation (2). Conversely, one study reported that mathematics is a refuge for introverts and people who do not adjust satisfactorily to their environment (3). It is obviously difficult to establish a cause-and-effect relationship between achievement in arithmetic and emotional adjustment or vice versa.

The investigation reported here was designed to examine characteristics of children who were accelerated or retarded in arithmetic achievement. A total of 188 fourth- and sixth-graders who were accelerated or retarded in arithmetic achievement were selected from sixteen schools. The accelerated children were those who scored one standard deviation above their national grade norm. The

Reprinted from *The Elementary School Journal,* Vol. 63 (December, 1962), pp. 141–145, by permission of The University of Chicago Press. Copyright 1962 by The University of Chicago.

retarded children were those who scored one standard deviation below their national grade norm.

In terms of years of achievement on the standardized test, the accelerated group scored one year or more above the average score for the particular grade. The retarded pupils scored one year or more below the average score for the particular grade. To measure arithmetic achievement the SRA Achievement Series, Grades 4 through 6, was used. To obtain an index of individual adjustment, the California Test of Personality, Grades 4 through 8, was administered. Intelligence scores were obtained from the California Test of Mental Maturity, Grades 4 through 8.

After the initial selection, the sample was divided into four groups. Forty-three fourth-grade pupils were classified as retarded in arithmetic, and forty-five fourth-grade pupils were classified as accelerated in arithmetic achievement. Forty-six sixth-grade pupils were retarded in arithmetic, and fifty-four sixth-grade pupils were accelerated in arithmetic. The results for boys and girls were analyzed separately.

After the data were organized into the appropriate groups, scores for each of the four arithmetic areas were correlated with scores on the fifteen areas in the California Test of Personality. Coefficients of correlation between the total scores on the two tests were also computed. Differences were tested by means of the appropriate F or t test.

As Table I indicates, the average accelerated sixth-grader had an intelligence quotient of 117, while the average retarded sixth-grader had an intelligence quotient of 97. Within the two groups, the boys and the girls did not differ significantly in intelligence quotient. However, the accelerated group had more girls than boys. The retarded group had more boys than girls. A reading factor may explain in part the difference in numbers of boys and girls in the accelerated and the retarded groups. It should also be pointed out that the number of boys and girls in the two fourth-grade groups were more nearly equal.

TABLE I   *Mean Intelligence Quotients and Mean Chronological Age for the Sixth-Grade Group*

Group	Number of Pupils	Mean Intelligence Quotient	Standard Deviation	Mean Chronological Age	Standard Deviation
Accelerated					
Boys	23	116.2	9.4	142.7	3.7
Girls	31	118.2	14.6	138.8	3.2
Total	54	117.4	12.8	140.4	3.4
Retarded					
Boys	29	96.3	14.3	143.4	3.1
Girls	17	99.1	12.3	143.3	2.4
Total	46	97.2	12.9	143.4	2.8

As may be seen from Tables I and II, the number of boys and girls was about equal in both the accelerated groups. However, in the accelerated groups in both the fourth grade and the sixth grade, the girls were more variable than the boys. This was not so in the underachieving groups. Intelligence differences between boys and girls were not significant in either the retarded or the accelerated groups. However, special consideration should be given to the mean intelligence

TABLE II   *Mean Intelligence Quotients and Mean Chronological Age for the Fourth-Grade Group*

Group	Number of Pupils	Mean Intelligence Quotient	Standard Deviation	Mean Chronological Age	Standard Deviation
Accelerated					
Boys	21	122.8	5.2	117.4	4.1
Girls	24	123.1	13.3	118.2	2.8
Total	45	122.8	12.3	117.8	3.3
Retarded					
Boys	22	104.3	18.7	118.0	3.2
Girls	21	101.5	17.4	111.6	3.0
Total	43	102.9	17.5	114.9	3.1

quotient for the retarded groups. In the fourth-grade retarded group as in the sixth-grade retarded group, the average intelligence quotient was about 100. The implication of this finding will be discussed later.

Table III shows the mean scores and the standard deviations for four arithmetic areas. The four areas measured by the SRA arithmetic achievement test are reasoning ability, concepts, computational ability, and total arithmetic achievement. The mean scores for boys and girls were not significantly different. However, in the group of accelerated fourth-graders, the boys varied significantly more than the girls. In the three remaining groups, differences were not significant.

Examination of Table IV reveals that the girls in all groups scored higher on the personality test than the boys. In general, there was more variance in the accelerated groups than in the retarded groups. This may be partially explained

TABLE III   *Mean Scores and Standard Deviations for Arithmetic Achievement for the Fourth- and the Sixth-Grade Groups*

Group	Reasoning	Standard Deviation	Concepts	Standard Deviation	Computation	Standard Deviation	Total Arithmetic	Standard Deviation
Sixth Grade								
Accelerated								
Boys	7.8	.7	8.0	.5	7.0	.5	7.6	1.3
Girls	7.9	1.4	8.5	.9	7.2	1.3	7.8	.8
Total	7.8	1.2	8.2	.7	7.1	1.0	7.7	1.0
Retarded								
Boys	4.2	.9	4.4	1.1	4.7	1.2	4.4	.5
Girls	4.3	.8	4.3	.9	4.7	.6	4.5	.5
Total	4.2	.9	4.4	1.1	4.7	1.1	4.6	.5
Fourth Grade								
Accelerated								
Boys	5.9	.9	5.9	1.0	4.9	1.7	5.5	1.7
Girls	5.8	.7	5.9	.7	4.8	.5	5.5	.3
Total	5.8	.8	5.9	.9	4.8	1.1	5.5	1.4
Retarded								
Boys	2.5	.2	3.0	.8	3.1	.9	2.8	.4
Girls	2.6	.9	3.0	.1	3.1	.9	2.9	.3
Total	2.6	.9	3.0	.6	3.1	.9	2.9	.4

TABLE IV   *Mean Scores and Standard Deviations for the Test of Personality for the Fourth- and the Sixth-Grade Groups*

Group	No. of Pupils	Personal Adjustment		Social Adjustment		Total Adjustment	
		Mean	Standard Deviation	Mean	Standard Deviation	Mean	Standard Deviation
Sixth Grade							
Accelerated							
Boys	23	63.7	21.5	56.4	23.6	61.1	25.1
Girls	31	64.9	20.6	65.8	24.2	67.1	21.4
Total	54	64.6	21.0	61.8	23.9	65.5	23.2
Retarded							
Boys	29	39.5	18.0	39.5	20.6	39.5	19.0
Girls	17	47.4	22.2	45.9	20.4	46.3	21.1
Total	46	42.6	20.9	42.1	20.6	42.0	19.7
Fourth Grade							
Accelerated							
Boys	21	58.4	24.8	51.9	24.0	55.2	23.3
Girls	24	71.7	19.2	69.8	18.7	71.6	20.2
Total	45	64.1	22.9	61.6	22.8	63.8	22.3
Retarded							
Boys	22	34.5	10.8	34.3	16.5	34.4	10.9
Girls	21	40.7	22.7	47.1	24.5	43.3	17.6
Total	43	38.0	14.8	43.4	22.6	40.9	14.7

by the possibility that the accelerated groups, being more intelligent, were test-wise. Consequently, in their attempt to answer the questions "correctly" regardless of their true feelings, a greater range of variability resulted. The children in the retarded groups were perhaps more honest in their appraisal and choice of answers. Since the test depends on honesty in choosing the answer, it is possible that the results for the accelerated groups are less valid than the scores for the retarded groups. It should also be pointed out that the accelerated groups had significantly higher mean scores than the retarded groups.

Table V indicates the mean scores for the total groups in total arithmetic achievement and total personality adjustment. By using the Behrens-Fisher method for testing the equality of means on the personality measure, it was found that in both the fourth- and the sixth-grade groups the differences were significant at the 5 per cent level. Since only the 1 per cent level was being considered, it can be concluded that children who are accelerated in arithmetic achievement do not score significantly different (1 per cent level) on the personality inventory than children who are retarded in arithmetic achievement.

TABLE V   *Summary of Total Test Scores on the Arithmetic Test and the Test of Personality for the Fourth- and the Sixth-Grade Groups*

Group	Number of Pupils	Total Arithmetic Score	Total Adjustment Score
Sixth Grade			
Accelerated	54	7.7	65.5
Retarded	46	4.6	42.0
Fourth Grade			
Accelerated	45	5.5	63.8
Retarded	43	2.9	40.9

Coefficients of correlation among the subscores on the arithmetic achievement test and the personality test were also computed. The coefficients were negligible in every instance.

Tables I and II indicate that boys and girls are not significantly different in intelligence in accelerated or retarded groups chosen on the basis of arithmetic achievement. It can be concluded that the relationship of intelligence to arithmetic achievement is the same for either sex. The lack of significant difference in intelligence quotient between the accelerated and the retarded groups suggests that good work habits coupled with low or average intelligence will not result in superior arithmetic achievement for most children.

Table III supports the conclusion that boys who are accelerated in arithmetic tend to achieve the same scores on achievement tests as girls do. That is, boys and girls who are accelerated in arithmetic achievement do not differ significantly in the areas of reasoning, conclusions, computation, and total scores on the SRA arithmetic achievement test. The same statement may be made of children who are retarded in arithmetic achievement.

In general, the data from Table IV would lead to the conclusion that girls tend to score higher on personality tests than boys in samples chosen on the basis of acceleration or retardation in arithmetic. Though these differences were not significant, they do indicate trends. One possible interpretation of this phenomenon is that girls tend to receive better adjustment scores because they mature earlier.

Differences in total adjustment reported in Table V are significant at the 5 per cent level. A tentative conclusion that retardation in arithmetic tends to be related to personal adjustment seems to be warranted. The exact nature of this relationship is difficult to ascertain. It is most logical to assume that it is reciprocal in nature. That is, emotional difficulties tend to foster difficulties in arithmetic achievement and vice versa.

A final and most important conclusion is related to the data in Tables I and II. Examination of the mean intelligence quotient for the retarded groups in both the fourth and the sixth grades indicates that these children have average mental ability. Consequently, it is quite possible that a considerable portion of the cause for retardation may center in the area of arithmetic instruction. This finding certainly points to the necessity for teachers and principals to make a critical examination of their instructional practices and the total curriculum in arithmetic.

REFERENCES

1. Lesta Hoel, "An Experiment in Clinical Procedures for Arithmetic." 222–32. *The 22nd Yearbook of National Council of Teachers of Mathematics.* Washington: National Council of Mathematics, 1954.

2. Emma N. Plank, "Observations on Attitudes of Young Children Toward Mathematics," *Mathematics Teacher,* XLIII (October, 1950), 252–63.

3. Ira Rochlin, "Nonintellectual Factors in the Learning of General Mathematics." Unpublished Ph.D. thesis. University of Chicago, 1952.

36   Reading and Computation Ability
as Determinants of Problem Solving

IRVING H. BALOW

Since 1918, when Monroe (1) showed that a given problem could be verbally stated in twenty-eight different ways, research workers have been interested in the relationship between reading ability and arithmetic achievement. The resulting research has not been clear on what relationship exists, often because of the confounding effects of intelligence.

Intelligence is a recognized factor in arithmetic achievement and in reading achievement. The correlation between reading achievement and intelligence tends to be high, but fluctuates with specific tests used. Monroe (2), using mental age derived from the Revised Stanford Binet Intelligence Test, found correlations from .56 to .65 with reading ability. Strang (3), using the language score on the California Tests of Mental Maturity, found correlations between .80 and .84 with reading achievement.

Brueckner and Grossnickle (4) have specified the inter-correlations between intelligence and various arithmetic skills, with a low of .35 between IQ and computation and a high of .766 between IQ and vocabulary.

Recognizing that any apparent relationship between reading achievement and arithmetic achievement might be spurious and really attributable to intelligence, Fay (5) controlled chronological and mental age in comparing his groups. Working with good and poor readers, he found no differences in arithmetic achievement between the groups with intelligence held constant.

That reading achievement would not be related to computation skill with the effects of intelligence controlled is reasonable. Little reading skill is involved in finding solutions for examples. The subject need only read numbers and operations signs. This minimum reading knowledge required in computation would result in a very low correlation between reading and computation (if the effects of intelligence were controlled).

It is in the area of problem solving or arithmetic reasoning that reading would seem to be important. Problems are specified by words. In problem solving, the subject must determine the question being asked, the information given, the arithmetical operations required, and must find this information through reading. Obviously, reading ability is involved. However, general reading ability has not been found to correlate highly with problem-solving ability as measured by standardized tests (6). Hanson (7), studying problem solving in arithmetic, found no significant differences between good and poor students in comprehension abilities, but he did find that the poor achievers in arithmetic were, on the average, faster readers.

Comparison of the reading skills of "good" and "poor" achievers in arithmetic leaves much to be desired. If reading skill is important in problem-solving ability, a continuum may well exist, with each increase in reading ability being accompanied by an increase in problem-solving achievement. It is also possible that a minimum level of reading ability is required to do well in problem solving at any given grade level.

From *The Arithmetic Teacher,* Vol. 11 (January, 1964), pp. 18–22. Reprinted with permission.

The relationship of computation skill to problem solving or arithmetic reasoning would appear to be more direct. Problem solving requires computation skill—the child who is unable to compute is unable to solve problems requiring computation. However, tests of problem-solving ability rely upon computation skills taught at the grade level for which the test is designed. That is, a sixth-grade test of problem solving will have very few, or no, requirements for computation skills not taught prior to grade seven. This being the case, what accounts for the above grade level scores in problem solving? Is it the result of above grade level computation skill (measured only by grade level and below computation requirements), above grade level reading skill, or a combination of these factors?

The Problem

This study was designed to determine if level of general reading ability is significantly associated with problem-solving ability, if level of computation skill is significantly associated with problem-solving ability, and if a high level of ability in one of these areas will compensate for a low level of ability in the other.

Previous studies have generally compared good and poor problem-solvers or arithmetic achievers on reading ability, or have compared good and poor readers on arithmetic achievement or problem solving. Either of these comparisons eliminates a large middle group of students and may distort whatever relationship does exist. In this study, all levels of reading ability were secured, as well as all levels of computation skill, in determining the effect of these factors on problem solving.

Design and Analysis

This study involved all sixth-grade students in a southern California community. A total of 1400 children completed the testing. The Stanford Achievement Tests, Intermediate, Form KM: Reading and Arithmetic, were administered in February. The grade placement in reading (average of the scores on the Word Meaning and Paragraph Meaning subtests) was used as the criterion measure of reading ability, grade placement on the Computation subtest as the criterion measure of computation skill, and grade placement on the Reasoning subtest as the measure of problem-solving ability. The California Short-Form Test of Mental Maturity, Elementary, 1957 S Form, was administered and the total IQ used as the measure of intelligence.

The children were then classified according to level of computation ability and level of reading ability. Four levels of ability were used and were determined by the grade placement score: 1.0 to 5.0, 5.1 to 5.9, 6.0 to 6.9, and 7.0 to 11.5. This double classification resulted in sixteen cells. The grade placement score on the Reasoning subtest and the IQ were recorded in the proper cells for each child. Twenty-three scores were then randomly selected from each cell and were used in the analysis.

The null hypothesis to be tested was: There are no significant differences in problem-solving ability associated with general reading ability, computation ability, or an interaction of these factors, when intelligence is controlled.

The analysis of variance and covariance was used to test the hypothesis.

TABLE I   *Mean IQ and Reasoning Scores for Children Classified by Level of Reading and Computation Ability*

Average Reading		Arithmetic Reasoning			
		1.0 to 5.0	5.1 to 5.9	6.0 to 6.9	7.0 to 11.5
7.0 to 11.5	IQ	108.74	112.30	115.57	124.17
	Reasoning	6.200	6.408	7.373	8.365
6.0 to 6.9	IQ	100.57	107.74	110.04	116.83
	Reasoning	5.560	6.221	6.878	7.295
5.1 to 5.9	IQ	96.17	101.73	106.57	105.83
	Reasoning	5.165	5.552	6.213	7.030
1.0 to 5.0	IQ	88.87	90.70	96.48	100.26
	Reasoning	4.582	5.204	5.908	6.134

Table I shows the mean IQ and the mean reasoning scores for the 368 children in the analysis. An inspection of Table I shows that in this sample, as in previous studies, a direct relationship exists between IQ and reading ability and between IQ and computation skill. In each column, the lowest average IQ is in the bottom cell with an increase in IQ in each cell to the highest IQ in the top cell. Similarly, in each row, the lowest IQ appears in the left-hand cell and IQ increases to the right as computation level increases. It is this difference in average IQ between the cells that is controlled in covariance. Similar differences exist in the mean reasoning scores. With each increase in average reading or arithmetic computation there is an increase in reasoning score.

The differences in mean reasoning scores shown in Table I were tested for significance through analysis of variance (ignoring differences in IQ). The results of this analysis are shown in Table II.

TABLE II   *Results of the Analysis of Variance of the Reasoning Scores of Table I*

Source of Variation	Degrees of Freedom	Mean Square	F-Ratio	Hypothesis
Computation	3	58.701	72.291	Reject $P < .01$
Average Reading	3	44.555	54.870	Reject $P < .01$
Interaction	9	1.373	1.690	Accept $P > .05$
Within Groups	352	.812		
Total	367			

Table II shows very large *F*-ratios for computation and reading, differences which would arise by chance less than one time in one hundred if the null hypothesis were true. The interaction of these factors is not significant.

To determine if the same results would obtain with intelligence controlled, the common within-classes regression coefficient was used to adjust the reasoning scores (8). For the 368 children, the average IQ was 105.16 and the regression coefficient was .06074. Thus, all cells with average IQ below 105 will show increased reasoning scores and all cells with average IQ above 105 will show decreased reasoning scores. Table III shows the results of this adjustment.

From Table III it can be seen that increases in computation skill seem to be associated with higher achievement in reasoning. It is, however, more difficult to see that increases in reading ability are associated with higher reasoning scores. Table IV shows the results of the analysis of covariance, controlling intelligence.

TABLE III   *Adjusted Mean Reasoning Scores for Children Classified by Arithmetic Computation and Reading Ability*

Average Reading	Arithmetic Computation				
	1.0 to 5.0	**5.1 to 5.9**	**6.0 to 6.9**	**7.0 to 11.5**	**Total**
7.0 to 11.5	5.983	5.974	6.741	7.210	25.908
6.0 to 6.9	5.839	6.064	6.581	6.586	25.070
5.1 to 5.9	5.711	5.760	6.128	6.990	24.589
1.0 to 5.0	5.572	6.083	6.435	6.432	24.522
Total	23.105	23.881	25.885	27.218	

TABLE IV   *Results of Analysis of Covariance of Reasoning Scores Controlling IQ*

Source of Variation	Degrees of Freedom	Adjusted Mean Square	F-Ratio	Hypothesis
Computation	3	20.208	27.456	Reject P < .01
Average Reading	3	2.347	3.188	Reject P < .05
Interaction	9	1.125	1.528	Accept P > .05
Within Groups	351	.736		
Total	366			

The analysis of covariance results in the rejection of the null hypothesis as it refers to reading and computation, and acceptance where it refers to interaction. When intelligence is controlled, there are significant differences associated with computation ability, higher levels of computation resulting in higher scores in problem solving. When intelligence is controlled, there are significant differences associated with reading ability, higher levels of reading resulting in higher scores in problem solving. A comparison of the totals in Table III and the *F*-ratios in Table IV indicates that computation is a much more important factor in problem solving than is reading ability. This may be the result of constructing tests with the fewest possible reading problems in order to get as pure a measure as possible of problem-solving ability.

A comparison of the *F*-ratios in Table II with those in Table IV gives an idea of the importance of controlling intelligence in a study of this nature.

Summary and Conclusions

Fourteen hundred sixth-grade children were given reading, arithmetic, and IQ tests, and were then classified according to reading level and computation level. From the resulting classification, children (twenty-three from each cell) were randomly selected and their arithmetic reasoning scores compared, using the analysis of covariance and controlling IQ, to determine the importance of reading ability, computation ability, and interaction on problem solving.

The following conclusions seem warranted:

1. General reading ability does have an effect on problem-solving ability. The findings of this study may differ from previous studies because the total range of reading ability was used rather than two groups defined as good and poor readers. Also, the effect of intelligence was controlled.

It is suggested that the vocabulary and reading difficulty control of standardized tests (which differs from grade level texts) may actually minimize the effect of reading, and that if a more normal reading situation were employed reading skill might prove to be more important.

2. When IQ is not controlled, much of the apparent relationship between reading and problem-solving ability is the result of the high correlation of each of these factors with IQ. Controlling IQ drastically reduces the degree of relationship.

3. Computation ability does have a significant effect on problem-solving ability. With the effects of IQ controlled, above grade level scores on the reasoning test appear to bear a closer relationship to computation ability than to reading ability.

4. The lack of a significant interaction suggests that for a given level of computation ability, problem solving increases as reading ability increases, and that for any given level of reading ability, problem solving increases as computation ability increases.

5. The findings of this study point out the importance of considering children's reading ability as well as computation ability when teaching problem-solving skills. Both of these factors are important to the child if he is to deal adequately with verbal problems in his school work.

REFERENCES

1. Walter S. Monroe, "The Derivation of Reasoning Tests in Arithmetic," *School and Society,* VIII (Sept., 1918), 295–99, 324–29.

2. Marion Monroe, *Children Who Cannot Read* (Chicago: University of Chicago Press, 1932).

3. Ruth Strang, "Relationships Between Certain Aspects of Intelligence and Certain Aspects of Reading," *Educational and Psychological Measurement,* III (1943), 355–59.

4. Leo J. Brueckner and Foster E. Grossnickle, *Making Arithmetic Meaningful* (Philadelphia: The John C. Winston Company, 1953), pp. 434–35.

5. Leo C. Fay, "The Relationship Between Specific Reading Skills and Selected Areas of Sixth-Grade Achievement," *Journal of Educational Research,* XLIII (March, 1950), 544–47.

6. David H. Russell, "Arithmetic Power Through Reading," *Instruction in Arithmetic,* Twenty-fifth Yearbook, Chap. 9 (Washington: National Council of Teachers of Mathematics, 1960), pp. 211–12.

7. C. W. Hansen, "Factors Associated with Superior and Inferior Achievement in Problem Solving in Sixth-Grade Achievement" (unpublished Ph.D. dissertation, University of Minnesota, 1943).

8. Palmer O. Johnson and Robert W. B. Jackson, *Modern Statistical Methods* (Chicago: Rand McNally & Company, 1959), pp. 410–24.

37 Formal Analysis as a Diagnostic
Technique in Arithmetic

CLINTON I. CHASE

For years various writers have proposed that pupils be expected to follow a series of steps as an aid to solving written or story problems in arithmetic. This approach is known as formal analysis.

Although variations have appeared in the procedure proposed, the following sequence is an example of the steps pupils are expected to follow: What does the problem ask me to find? What information is given? What number process should I use? What would a reasonable answer be?

In an early study the formal-analysis approach was tested by Newcomb, who found evidence in favor of this step-by-step method of arriving at solutions to problems (1).

Sister Mary Jacqueline has also found conventional analysis effective in bringing about improvements in problem-solving ability (2); and Herriott, through practical experience, corroborated these results (3). In another study Adams showed that the step-by-step approach was a problem-solving aid for children of low intelligence (4).

However, Hanna produced competent data suggesting that the conventional formula for analyzing problems was less effective than no prescribed method at all (5). Rather, it was more effective to have pupils determine what the conditions of the problem depended upon than to follow a scheme of analysis like that used by Newcomb. Clark and Vincent supported this conclusion (6). Washburne and Osborne found that just practice in dealing with problems produced more proficiency in reaching solutions than experience with a conventional formula did (7).

In an effort to identify skills in which good problem-solvers were superior to poor problem-solvers, Hansen found that the steps in formal analysis distinguished between pupils who were capable in solving problems and pupils who were not (8).

Following these findings, Spache proposed the scheme as a means of diagnostic measurement: by using it the teacher could identify the point at which children were having difficulty in arriving at solutions to problems (9). The validity of this procedure, however, depends on the pupil's thinking in a sequence of steps like those provided in the conventional formula.

In this regard, Burch found that success in only one step of the formal-analysis procedure was followed by the correct solution of the problem. He found that, on the whole, children did better in solving the problems than in carrying out the steps of analysis (10).

The research reviewed here may cast doubt on the efficacy of the formal-analysis scheme as an aid to problem-solving and may also suggest that more evidence is appropriate on the value of this device as a diagnostic tool.

The purpose of the present study was to investigate the use of the problem-analysis approach in the diagnosis of problem-solving difficulties. In accordance with Spache's findings, the hypothesis to be tested is that good problem-solvers

Reprinted from *The Elementary School Journal*, Vol. 61 (February, 1961), pp. 282–286, by permission of The University of Chicago Press. Copyright 1961 by The University of Chicago.

do not achieve higher scores than poor problem-solvers in each step of the formal-analysis process.

To establish the criterion of problem-solving ability, Test D: Basic Arithmetic Skills, Iowa Every-Pupil Tests of Basic Skills, Form N, was administered to a group of 151 sixth-grade pupils in an urban area of northern California. The problem section of the test was taken as the criterion, and the distribution of scores on this test was divided into thirds. The pupils whose scores fell in the high third were labeled good problem-solvers, while the pupils whose scores fell in the lowest third were called poor problem-solvers.

Since intelligence may play a part in determining a pupil's rank on the problem test, the final groups used for the study were equated on intellectual factors. Three scales—Verbal, Reasoning, and Number—from the SRA Primary Mental Abilities were used for the matching. Scores on these scales were used instead of a total score because the test manual describes them as being most closely related to arithmetic ability. From these three scales a mean mental age was determined for each child, and this average was used for matching good and poor problem-solvers.

Between any two pupils in a matched pair the maximum difference allowed in mental age was three months; however, for most of the pairs the difference was less than three months. The average mental age of the good problem-solvers was 138.7 months, and the average mental age for the poor problem-solvers was 137.8 months.

Through this procedure forty-two pupils from the groups whose scores were in the upper and the lower thirds on the problem-test distribution were matched on intellectual ability. Since differences in arithmetical skills do exist between the sexes, some effort was made to match pupils by sex as well as by mental age. Of the twenty-one pairs used in the study, nineteen were of the same sex.

One other test was administered to the groups: the Problem Analysis Test, the instrument on which the present study centers. To construct this test, problems were taken from several textbooks used in the upper elementary grades. Two problems were taken from a fourth-grade textbook, four problems from a fifth-grade textbook, and nine items from a sixth-grade textbook. The selection provided a range of difficulty though most of the problems were at the grade level to be tested in the study.

In presenting the items on the examination the problems were placed on the left-hand side of the page and the steps in analysis in sequence to the right of each problem. The analysis consisted of three steps:

A. What should I find?

B. What should I do to get the answer?

C. The answer would be about ___?___.

For each step in the analysis the pupil could choose one of three answers. A sample item is shown on this page.

Pupils were given a copy of the test and instructed on how to complete it. Special emphasis was placed on finishing all the steps in one problem before going on to the next problem.

After the pupils had completed the test, the papers were scored, one point being allowed for every correct choice in each of the three scales of the examination. Then for every child a total score was obtained for each of the three steps of the analysis.

.   .   .

Problem	What Should I Find?	What Should I Do to Get the Answer?	The Answer Would Be About ___?___ .
If you bought a 4¢ stamp how much change should you get back from a quarter?	*a*) The number of 4¢ stamps that can be bought for 25¢. *b*) How much of 25¢ is left after spending 4¢. *c*) How much a 4¢ stamp costs.	*a*) Divide 25¢ by 4¢. *b*) Subtract 4¢ from 25¢. *c*) Add 25¢ and 4¢.	*a*) 8¢ *b*) 30¢ *c*) 20¢

To estimate the reliability of the examination, the tests of each of the three steps were analyzed separately by the odd-even, split-half method. The resulting coefficients, with the Spearman-Brown extension for the whole test, were Step A, .86; Step B, .87; and Step C, .85.

After the tests were marked, a separate distribution of scores was made for good problem-solvers and for poor problem-solvers on each of the three scales in the formal analysis. The significance of the difference between the means of the good problem-solvers and the means of the poor problem-solvers was tested for each of the three scales in the analytic process.

Besides the test of problem analysis, two sections of the Iowa Every-Pupil tests were given—the section on computations and the section on fundamental knowledge—to see whether these tests might also reveal skills in which pupils who are good at solving problems are different from pupils who are not so successful in dealing with problems. The significance of the difference between the means of the good problem-solvers and the means of the poor problem-solvers was likewise tested for these two scales.

The results of the statistical procedures described are reported in Table I. None of the steps in the problem-analysis test distinguished between good and poor problem-solvers. But the means on the tests of skills in handling computations and in dealing with the fundamental arithmetical concepts showed significant differences between the pupils who solved the problems successfully and the pupils who had less success. Also, the pupils in both groups averaged higher scores in determining what the problem asked them to find (Problem Analysis A)

TABLE I   *Mean Scores on Arithmetic Tests of 21 Good Problem-Solvers and 21 Poor Problem-Solvers*

Variable	Mean Scores		
	Good Problem-Solvers	Poor Problem-Solvers	
Problem Analysis A	9.57	7.95	1.91
Problem Analysis B	7.38	6.43	.73
Problem Analysis C	7.09	6.76	.46
Computation	12.14	7.00	3.36*
Fundamental Knowledge	13.43	9.45	2.38†

* Significant at the 1 per cent level.
† Significant at the 5 per cent level.

than they did in the steps involving the number processes in arriving at a solution (Problem Analyses B and C).

If a test is to be truly diagnostic, the skill under observation should be allowed to operate as it does in real-life situations. Therefore, a test designed to identify difficulties in problem-solving should allow the reasoning process to function without hindrance or distraction.

Burch's evidence suggests that a formal-analysis procedure does not meet this criterion (10). Further, Buswell has demonstrated that children may use several approaches to solving problems and that valid answers may be achieved in more than one way (11).

This evidence appears to indicate that coercing children into a prescribed scheme of attack may be incompatible with the process actually used in problem-solving. If this contention is true, it would seem to cast doubt on the efficacy of a formal-analysis test as a means of diagnosis, since such a test might force the child to depart from his preferred approach in order to use the prescribed steps. Thus the test may not allow the problem-solving process to operate in its customary manner but attempts to assess a progression of acts that is not necessarily characteristic of the child's approach to problems. Thus, as Burch has suggested, the child may have greater difficulty with the analytic steps themselves than in solving the problem.

Still, to think about arithmetical situations, the child must be acquainted with certain basic ideas that govern the manipulations of quantitative relationships in any problem, regardless of how it is approached. After observing the relationships in the situation at hand by whatever approach the child prefers, he must do the required computations to arrive at the solution. It is possible, therefore, that success in problem-solving is related more closely to certain academic skills that provide for versatility of attack on problems than to the ability to follow a series of prescribed steps toward a solution.

This rationale may explain the fact that the tests of computation and of fundamental knowledge produced significant differences between good problemsolvers and poor problem-solvers. Computation and fundamental knowledge are tools that may be applied in a variety of approaches to the arithmetical situation, while formal analysis does not provide for such versatility of attack.

If this reasoning is correct, measures using the formal-analysis approach cannot be expected—because of the rigidity of this procedure—to discriminate consistently between good problem-solvers and poor problem-solvers. In contrast, measures of arithmetical skills, like computation, may discriminate.

The present study, which was designed to evaluate the formal-analysis technique as a means of diagnosing difficulties in solving arithmetic problems, provided evidence to support the conclusion that the formal-analysis approach is not a successful means of identifying differences between good and poor problem-solvers. The technique cannot be relied upon, at least in sixth grade, to point up the causes of unsuccessful performance in solving arithmetic problems.

REFERENCES

1. Newcomb, R. S. "Teaching Pupils How to Solve Problems in Arithmetic," *Elementary School Journal,* XXIII (November, 1922), 183–89.

2. Sister Mary Jacqueline, "An Experiment in Remedial Teaching in Arithmetic," *Elementary School Journal,* XLI (June, 1941), 748–55.

3. Herriott, Robert E. "An Aid in the Analysis of Verbal Problems," *Arithmetic Teacher,* V (April, 1958), 143–45.

4. Adams, Ray E. *A Study of Comparative Value of Two Methods of Improving Problem Solving Ability in Arithmetic.* Philadelphia: University of Pennsylvania, 1930.

5. Hanna, Paul R. "Methods of Arithmetic Problem Solving," *Mathematics Teacher,* XXIII (November, 1930), 442–50.

6. Clark, John R., and Vincent, E. Leona. "A Comparsion of Two Methods of Arithmetic Problem Analysis," *Mathematics Teacher,* XVIII (April, 1925), 226–33.

7. Washburne, Carleton, and Osborne, Raymond. "Solving Arithmetic Problems," *Elementary School Journal,* XXVII (November, 1926), 219–26; *ibid.,* XXVII (December, 1926), 296–304.

8. Hansen, Carl W. "Factors Associated with Successful Achievement in Problem Solving in Sixth Grade Arithmetic," *Journal of Educational Research,* XXXVIII (October, 1944), 111–18.

9. Spache, George. "A Test of Abilities in Arithmetic Reasoning," *Elementary School Journal,* XVLII (April, 1947), 442–45.

10. Burch, Robert L. "Formal Analysis as a Problem-Solving Procedure," *Journal of Education,* CXXXVI (November, 1953), 44–47.

11. Buswell, Guy T., with the co-operation of Bert Y. Kersh, *Patterns of Thinking in Solving Problems.* University of California Publications in Education, Vol. XII, No. 2. Berkeley: University of California Press, 1956.

---

38 Group Diagnosis and Standardized Achievement Tests

EDWARD CALDWELL

Many of the performance reports for standardized tests are now machine-processed and are in a language that is difficult for teachers to utilize in the classroom. This is especially true if the teacher is interested in comparing student performance on specific parts or questions in the test with student knowledge of the subjects being taught. Even when tests are hand-scored, the converted or normative scores are of limited value to the teacher who wants to determine what the students know about a specific skill, such as addition or subtraction of fractions.

This paper describes a method that can be used to identify class difficulties with specific content in the basic skills. Group diagnosis is chosen because teachers are finding it increasingly difficult to find sufficient time to work with individual students in the classroom. The procedure requires essentially no statistical background, and the only materials needed are completed answer sheets and a copy of the test or an item guide. It is concrete to the extent that results are based on simple counts of right or wrong answers. To insure clarity the procedures are presented here in demonstration form with actual data from a fifth

From *The Arithmetic Teacher,* Vol. 12 (February, 1965), pp. 123–125. Reprinted with permission.

grade class chosen at random. Since achievement tests are most frequently administered in the fall, the results used herein and the procedures listed are recommended for application during the first half of the school year. For the sake of brevity the data will be limited to the arithmetic fundamentals subtest of the California Achievement Tests.

Step 1: Identify the essential skills taught during the previous year. This can be done fairly quickly by an examination of the textbook or curriculum guide used in the school system. The identified skills should be placed in logical order and listed on a sheet of paper.

Step 2: Examine the questions in the standardized test to determine which questions measure the skills listed in Step 1 and to what extent. Both the item and the item number, or one representative item, should be placed alongside the skill on the list. No test items may be found for some skills and several may be found for other skills. Items measuring the same skill may vary in complexity, length, and presentation.

Step 3: Now you are starting what is essentially an item analysis. Count the numbers of students in the class having right and wrong answers to the listed items. In some instances it may be desirable to count omitted responses. For example, the teacher may wish to know the degree of guessing that occurs. Handcounting from separate answer sheets is most easily accomplished by fixing the eyes on the right response and flipping through the stack with the thumb. Counting can also be done by scoring machines, but this is usually not feasible for small groups. The proportions of right and wrong answers will give you an index of "success" on each item from which you can make a judgment about the competency of the class on the skill represented. If the papers are separated into low-scoring and high-scoring halves, an index of discrimination can be secured with the same tabulation of responses. It is this latter index which will yield insight into which group needs work on which skills. Remember that these three steps deal with skills previously taught and may not always be necessary. If dependable information is already available from extended work with the class, the steps may be eliminated.

Step 4: Attention is now directed to skills which are being taught during the current year. The skills to be taught are listed, representative test items are written alongside the skills, and right-wrong counts are made just as they were for skills taught in the previous year. Some of the same skills may appear in more difficult form, and some new ones will appear. By comparing and studying the performances on items from both periods, the teacher can determine which skills need instructional emphasis.

Demonstration

The procedures outlined above are demonstrated with actual data in Tables I and II. Some of the skills listed for fourth- and fifth-grade pupils were secured from the state guide for arithmetic in Florida schools. Test answer sheets for a beginning fifth-grade class were secured to complete the analysis and to show how the test items can be related to the course content.

The sample of items in Table I shows a number of deficiencies for this beginning fifth-grade class in the skills that were taught during the previous year. If the list were assumed to be complete, the teacher would have concrete

TABLE I *Class Count on Fourth-Grade Skills*

Skill	Item No.	Rights	Wrongs	Total
1. Three-Digit Addition with Carrying	51	25	2	27
2. Adding Like Fractions	55	8	19	27
3. Subtracting Like Fractions	76	10	17	27
4. Recognizing Money in Decimal Form	6	17	10	27
5. Multiply with Two-Place Multiplicand and Carry	89	10	17	27
6. Divide with One-Place Divisor	108	23	4	27
7. Divide with Carrying	110	12	15	27
8. Divide with Zero in Quotient	111	11	16	27

evidence for the direction to take in review before he moved on to material scheduled for the fifth grade.

The results in Table II clearly indicate that this class has not experienced the skills normally scheduled for Grade 5. This, of course, could have been predicted from the deficiencies which were apparent with fourth-grade material. The small number of right answers was probably the result of guessing, which is a factor that must be considered when multiple-choice items are taken separately. The first example is a reminder that the test does not necessarily contain items dealing with all skills taught.

TABLE II *Class Count on Fifth-Grade Skills*

Skill	Item No.	Rights	Wrongs	Total
1. Changing Large Units of Mea- to Small ones	None			
2. Averaging	40	8	19	27
3. Dividing with Two-Place Divisor	113	5	22	27
4. Adding Like Fractions with Unlike Denominators	58	5	22	27
5. Subtracting Like Fractions with Unlike Denominators	78	5	22	27

Discussion

It is obvious that modifications of this procedure may be appropriate when circumstances differ from those described here. More than one item of the same type may be used to increase the reliability. Items not related to the course content may be included if the teacher has interest in them. If the test is given at midyear, performance could be analyzed in terms of skills taught and to be taught at the same grade level.

One may be confronted with a problem in the interpretation of proportions on the right-wrong counts. For example, from Table I it is fairly clear that the class as a whole is competent with three-digit addition. But, if two-thirds of the class misses an item, as in subtracting like fractions, the teacher must decide whether to teach the skill to the whole class, leave it alone, or try to find out which individuals are deficient and teach them separately. If the latter course is chosen, caution must be applied in the use of single items to diagnose individuals. How the information is applied in teaching is an arbitrary decision which must be left to the teacher. In some instances the teacher may wish to construct additional tests to measure skills in some areas.

The procedures described here are not a substitute for individual diagnosis nor a foolproof method for determining all pupil assets and deficiencies. Standardized tests only sample student skills in each of the grades, and must not be considered a complete measure of all learning that occurs or needs to occur in the classroom.

The method described here is also not a substitute for the statistical operations that may be recommended for sound purposes. It is essentially a method of group analysis which avoids the statistical complexity of normative scores, insofar as the teacher is concerned, and provides data which is more concretely related to course content.

39 Individualized Practice in Arithmetic —A Pilot Study

LAUREL MOENCH

In an article entitled "Meeting Individual Differences in Arithmetic," Frances Flournoy stated that, "At this time we have no significant published research in the field of Arithmetic which aids a school faculty or a teacher in the decision as to what variations to make, how, and how much (in providing for individual differences in the regular classroom with heterogeneously composed groups of children)" (1).

Most of the research plans which have been proposed recently can only be carried out effectively under preferential conditions with ability-grouped or ungraded classes, departmentalization, supervisors or specialists as teachers, laboratory school facilities, and so forth. Only modified plans similar to those proposed can be carried out in the regular self-contained classroom, and even then the results have not always been gratifying.

The following description of a pilot study which utilized one very definite idea as to "what variations to make, when, how, and how much" is written in the hope that it might help to serve as a link to the type of research Flournoy seeks.

Flournoy lists two basic ways of varying the program: (a) variation of instruction, which includes variation of learning time, content variations, and varying teaching methods and materials; and (b) altering class organization. Variations here include class-as-a-whole, combination of whole class and small group, grouping according to achievement, and completely individualized instruction. Flournoy found that "the majority of the teachers appear to teach

From *The Arithmetic Teacher*, Vol. 9 (October, 1962), pp. 321–329. Reprinted with permission.

This study was conducted during 1959–1960 while the author was employed by the University of Illinois Arithmetic Project, Dr. David A. Page, Director. The project was supported by funds from the Carnegie Foundation. The author wishes to thank the faculty, parents, and pupils of the Leal School in Urbana, Illinois, without whose cooperation and assistance this experiment could not have been conducted and to acknowledge with gratitude the technical advice and assistance afforded the author by various members of the University of Illinois Staff.

arithmetic in a class-as-a-whole organization"[1] (2). Research workers might well keep in mind that the more marked our departure from class-as-a-whole becomes, the greater the burden on the teacher.

The combination of whole class and small group arrangement was followed in the present study with a variation in materials and such variation in method as to be consistent with the material change.

More specifically, the pilot study was primarily concerned with providing practice for pupils on different levels of difficulty through a more independent use of textbooks. Or, hypothetically, the child who is permitted to begin his practice *at his own individual level of performance for a given topic* (whether it be subtraction, multiplication, or division) *and to proceed in his practice at his own rate will tend to achieve at a higher level than will the child who practices at an average level which has been arbitrarily set.*

By putting the child's practice work into his own hands and thus permitting him to set his own goals to a certain extent, we are meeting Wright's requirements for "cognitively well-structured school situations." We are (a and b) helping children to refine goals and the paths leading to the goals; (c) setting definite barriers (by setting beginning and ending points and class time limits); (d) letting the child in on what lies ahead; and (e) adjusting "things to be done" to abilities (3).

Our first question then, *"What* shall be individualized?" has been answered in the selection of our problem. Before deciding *how* this should be accomplished, let us look briefly at practice as it fits into the total program.

We know that practice plays a subordinate and supportive role in the meaningful arithmetic program, and, when used judiciously and selectively after meaning has been fully developed, it seals in meaning and improves speed, ease, and control of operation (4).

Too much practice may lower achievement scores, as Donald E. Shipp has found[2] (5); too little practice may make reteaching necessary; and the wrong kind of practice, as J. R. Hilgard demonstrated (6), is simply a waste of time because material which has been committed to memory will be forgotten if it does not possess structure, does not have organization, nor "belong" to some meaning core.

For the purposes of the present study, however, we shall assume several things. We shall assume that the children in the middle elementary-grade class have had good, meaningful instruction; that the class will have arrived at the proper point in sequence for the practice to take place or that practice "readiness" exists before practice is begun; that the teacher has at her fingertips the kind of practice program that is right in time allotment as well as in type of material selected for practice; and that correctness of form is inherent in the program itself. We are solving for only one unknown and that is: Is individualized practice important enough to warrant making a place for it in our program?

---

1 Flournoy's findings in this regard are further substantiated in a broad study made by Effie G. Bathurst in which it is reported that forty-seven cities out of fifty-two queried stated that in policy they were committed to the self-contained class unit as the basis of organization within the elementary school. Effie G. Bathurst and others, *Fourteen Questions on Elementary School Organization,* Pamphlet 105 (Washington, D.C.: U.S. Office of Education, Superintendent of Documents, 1948).
2 In a study of four types of classes in which time allotted to development work as compared with time allotted to practice varied from 25, 40, 60, or 75 per cent of the total time spent in arithmetic, Donald E. Shipp found that the classes which spent 25 or 40 per cent of their time in practice showed higher achievement scores than the classes which spent 60 or 75 per cent of their arithmetic time in practice.

Procedure

Given a fourth-grade Urbana, Illinois, class heterogeneously grouped as regards performance in arithmetic and a working expense budget of $100, the teacher-investigator set up the experimental operations. The first step was to spend the expense money. So, after the class range in arithmetic ability was found from the California test scores (7) and the subtraction scores on the Tailor Tests[3] (8), a spread of additional textbooks from Grades 2 through 7 in the series currently in use in the system was purchased (9).

The experimental design followed in this study was originally built around a textbook series other than the one in use in the Urbana class. It is believed that the plan here employed could be adapted to any method, any set of textbooks, and any middle elementary-school class.

In providing for individual differences in reading, M. Duren and W. A. Lewis conceived the idea of removing the covers from a number of readers and setting the individual stories into separate booklets. Each story had its own vocabulary study at the beginning of the booklet and adapted comprehension exercises at the end (10).

The same basic idea was followed with the newly purchased arithmetic texts. The covers were removed and all of the practice pages from all of the books from Grades 2 through 7 were removed. These practice pages were regrouped into three sets of practice booklets, each of which covered a three-level grade range. *No level identification of any kind* appeared on the covers of these booklets. This was considered to be very important because of the experiences of some of the teachers in the ungraded classroom field. Months of careful ungrading efforts were defeated when parents or children counted stars or boats and defined the child's grade level.

Authoritative support for the "erasing" of level identification marks can be found in an article by W. W. Cook, wherein he states that "the practice of labeling school books by grade should be discontinued. A code number indicating to the teacher the difficulty of the material is sufficient. . . . The grade levels at which certain knowledge, skills, and abilities should be learned cannot be determined with any degree of specificity (11). More support is found in L. J. Brueckner's *Making Arithmetic Meaningful:* "The wide range in ability of pupils in any grade group shows that the traditional concept of 'grade' must be discarded. It violates all that we have learned about individual differences in any group of pupils" (12).

The second step was concerned with class organization, and, as previously stated, a combination whole-class and small-group organization was to be followed.

The overall plan was that the teacher would follow class-as-a-whole organization *except during work-study time practice periods,* at which time terminal subgrouping at three levels would be operative.

Two tests, a subtraction facts test and a diagnostic test, the Tailor Test, were administered as an aid to setting up the sub-groups and in introducing the topic, which in this case was subtraction. Some may question the advisability of using

---

3 The Tailor Tests are simple diagnostic tests designed for use in the middle elementary grades in subtraction and multiplication. The pre-test form is designed to establish level of individual and class performance in the topic *before* the topic teaching is begun. It points a way for the teacher to place the emphasis of her instruction, whether the test is to be used for grouping purposes or not. The post-test form, given at the end of the unit, serves a comparative and checkup function.

tests to "introduce" a topic. However, we were thinking in terms of the middle elementary grades, where pupils are already acquainted with addition, subtraction, multiplication, and division. It is not new teaching but rather "telescoped reteaching" as Morton terms it (13).

With the Urbana class attention also needed to be given to the fact that experimental conditions were to be observed. For experimental purposes, therefore, one-half of the class was to serve as the experimental group while the other half acted as their evenly matched paired controls. This gave four "real" subgroups: (A_3) experimental low performers, (A_2) experimental medium performers, (A_1) experimental superior performers, and ($B_{3,2,1}$) controls (treated in the classroom as one group but for experimental record comprising low, medium, and superior performers).

A more complete description of the manner by which groups were set up so as to yield the desired experimental data is given below.

Using the subtraction facts test and the Tailor Test as a base, a profile was set up by which the desired groups could be derived. Frequency distribution tables of the scores were made from which the mean score for the entire class was calculated. Frequency histograms and polygons were plotted from the distribution tables and the class mean score was graphed with the histograms determining the sub-classes. However, in most cases it was possible to select the sub-classes on the basis of natural distribution alone.

The cut-off points for superior performers (as yet unclassified as to experimental or control) was 16.7 or better above the class mean on subtraction facts; Tailor Test, Part I, 7.5 or better above the mean; and Tailor Test, Part II, 14.9 or better above the mean. The cut-off points for the low performers (experimental and control) was as follows: Facts, 23.3 or more below the class mean; Tailor Test, Part I, 22.5 or more below the class mean; and Tailor Test, Part II, 13.1 or more below the class mean. Scores falling between the cut-off points for the superior and the low performers established the medium performers' (experimental and control) groups.

Matching equal pairs was then effected. Portions of the Iowa Every Pupil Test (Form O), the California Achievement Test, and intelligence quotient scores were used in conjunction with the achievement divisions (superior, medium, and low) which had been established.

Starting with the superior performers, as many high I.Q. pupils were assigned to the experimental group as to the controls. Moving on down the I.Q. scale, this equality was respected. In some cases, but not in every case, the divisioning was made in conjunction with the California and/or the Iowa scores. When the A_1 (experimental) and B_1 (control) groups had been set, the same process was repeated for the medium and low performers, thus creating Groups A_2 and A_3 (experimental), B_2 and B_3 (controls).

With materials and the terminal sub-groups set, our "how" answer is all but complete. Turning now to the class, using class-as-a whole organization, it remains only for us to follow the text and teach and/or add enrichment or remedial instruction as needed; and to change over to the terminal sub-group operation in work study periods when and where practice is indicated, permitting the child to begin his practice *at his own individual level of performance and to proceed in his practice at his own rate.*

In the Urbana experimental class, when the point of readiness for practice was reached, the controls were asked to work the practice pages from the fourth-grade book, whereas sub-groups A_{1-3} were given the practice booklets which most nearly suited them and were assigned only the starting page. The children took it from there. Some worked hard, others easy, but everyone worked. No change in seating arrangement was made; no reference was made to ability groups, except that the children knew that each of them had a partner of equal ability and that a comparison would be made at the end of our experiment. The children were asked not to work from their books outside of class but were given material of an enrichment nature for homework or extra-credit purposes. Every possible precaution was taken to keep individualized practice as the only variable in the experimental setup.

The total time spent in the "individualized" or group work-study periods for the subtraction topic was approximately one week (but not, however, one week of consecutive days). When mastery seemed evident, a post-test on subtraction facts and a post-test form of the Tailor Tests were administered. Per cent gains scores over pre-test scores is shown in Figure 1. Experimental groups are indicated by means of the solid bar, the controls, open bar.

The same basic procedure as above described was observed in multiplication. The topic time was five and one-half weeks; the grouping time, two weeks. Per cent gains over pre-test scores is shown in Figure 2. Other short topics were interspersed throughout this period. These included such topics as Roman numerals, measures, weights, area, perimeter, magic squares, enrichment material from the University of Illinois Arithmetic Project, and so forth.

At the conclusion of the work in multiplication, the experiment proper was brought to a close, thus completing the answer to the question of "how" and "how much" to vary the program for the Urbana class. Since the class had not as yet been introduced to long division, the teacher-investigator felt that there

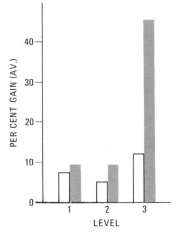

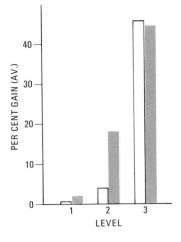

FIG. 1 *Short-term (three weeks) advance in fundamental subtraction operations as measured by the Tailor Tests. (Solid bar = experimental group; open bar = control group.)*

FIG. 2 *Short-term (five and one-half weeks) advance in fundamental multiplication operations as measured by the Tailor Test. (Solid bar = experimental group; open bar = control group.)*

would not be enough formal practice to warrant individual practice in this topic. All that remained to be done was to administer the tests on long-term retention.

It might be noted at this point that complete flexibility is one of the advantages of this type of grouping. The sub-groups can be set aside and taken up again at any time without interruption of the ongoing program. Also complete mobility is possible from topic to topic. As G. C. Pinney found, social status problems often attend ability grouping (14). Yet when rigid grouping is observed in the *total* arithmetic program, the ability gaps widen rapidly and the more difficult a return to heterogeneity becomes. Intra class grouping in practice makes greater control possible through flexibility.

The post-test form of the Iowa test was administered during the second week of May (seven months after the experimental program began). Gains over pre-test scores, expressed in months, are indicated in Figure 3. Figures 3a–d give a break-down of these scores. Included are scores in addition (a pre-experimental topic) and division (a post-experimental topic).

The following October (one year after the experimental program began), the post-form of the California test was administered. Gains over pre-test scores are shown in months in Figure 4 (computation) and Figure 5 (reasoning).

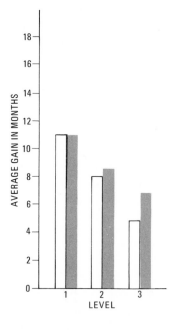

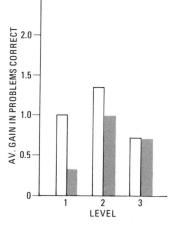

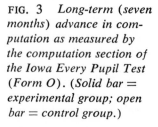

FIG. 3 *Long-term (seven months) advance in computation as measured by the computation section of the Iowa Every Pupil Test (Form O). (Solid bar = experimental group; open bar = control group.)*

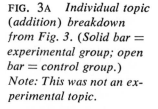

FIG. 3A *Individual topic (addition) breakdown from Fig. 3. (Solid bar = experimental group; open bar = control group.) Note: This was not an experimental topic.*

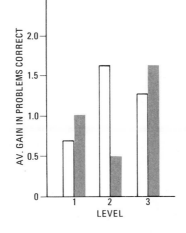

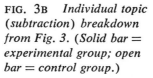

FIG. 3B *Individual topic (subtraction) breakdown from Fig. 3. (Solid bar = experimental group; open bar = control group.)*

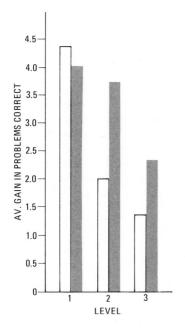

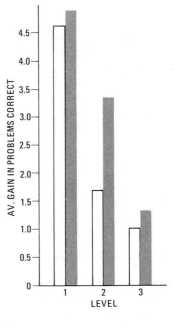

FIG. 3C *Individual topic (multiplication) breakdown from Fig. 3. (Solid bar = experimental group; open bar = control group.)*

FIG. 3D *Individual topic (division) breakdown from Fig. 3. (Solid bar = experimental group; open bar = control group.) Note: This was not an experimental topic.*

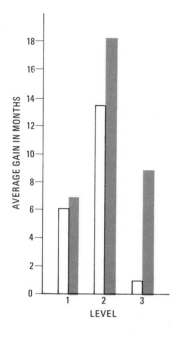

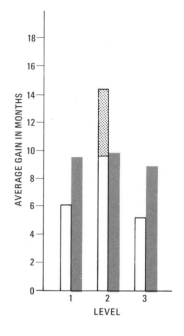

FIG. 4   *Long-term (twelve months) advance in fundamental operations as measured by the California Achievement Test. (Solid bar = experimental group; open bar = control group.)*

FIG. 5   *Long-term (twelve months) advance in reasoning as measured by the California Achievement Test. (Solid bar = experimental group; open bar = control group; dotted extension describes the Level 2 average when it includes one child's unusually high [thirty-four months] gain.)*

Results and Interpretation

In interpreting the results as indicated by the graphs, the reader's attention is called to the following points:

1. The hypothesis that *the child who is permitted to begin his practice at his own individual level of performance for a given topic and to proceed in his practice at his own rate will tend to achieve at a higher level than will the child who practices at an average level that has been arbitrarily set* was not tested until the long-term findings (Figures 4 and 5) were completed one year after the study was begun. At this time experimental groups *did* excel more than the controls both in reasoning and in computation. This held for the low and superior performers with something of a "tie" effect appearing in the medium-performance groups.

The investigator had expected some differences to appear at the close of each topic when the post-form of the Tailor Test was given (Figures 1 and 2) and/or with the administration of the second Iowa test at seven months (Figures 3, 3a–d). But as the graphs indicate, these differences were negligible, so that at the close of school in the spring, the investigator had conceded that individualized practice insofar as the study was concerned held no appreciable achievement advantage over practice procedures followed in the traditional manner.

However, like the penicillin that grew on the discarded material in the scientist's window sill, something in the nature of the children "grew" over the summer vacation, and for the purposes of this study this "something" showed that individualized practice even when observed for as little as a period of three weeks (total but not consecutive days) *did* have a measurable concomitant advantage over the traditional procedure.

2. While addition and division did not serve as experimental topics, graphs in these areas show two things. Addition was a *pre*-experiment topic. The fact that at the end of seven months the controls excelled the experimental groups in this area lends support to the validity of the initial pairing. At the outset of the experiment, the control groups were equal to the experimental groups from the standpoint of achievement.

In the case of division, a post-experimental topic, the experimental groups showed themselves to be stronger than the controls. Somehow, the pupils in the experimental groups had developed either a better approach to work study or better work study habits than did the controls.

3. The reader is cautioned to remember that the sample, one single class, with correspondingly small sub-groups necessarily deriving, cannot be considered large enough to stand as a final positive proof of the hypothesis. Until it has been repeated with a larger sample, this pilot study can only be said to have indicated a trend.

4. In Figures 1 and 2, it is shown that superior and medium performers in both the experimental and control groups did not demonstrate as great an advance in computational skills in multiplication as did the low performers. Yet seven months later (Figure 3c) the opposite effect was recorded. This may indicate that the low performers had been practicing before they were ready and that there may not have been sufficient understanding and core in this area. This would have an important implication as regards the meaning portion of the program. Thus, the *patterns* practice follows are an aid to the improvement of the program. A sharp advance in computational skill in a learner who ordinarily advances at a slow rate *may* be a symptom of internal or external pressuring rather than the sudden attainment of complete understanding.

5. Results at the end of the twelve-month period may be summarized as follows: Of the high performers (Level 1, Figures 4, 5), the experimental group averaged a three and three-quarter-month advantage over the control group in reasoning and a one and one-quarter-month advantage over the control group in fundamental operations. Of the low performers (Level 3), the experimental group averaged a four-month advantage over the control group in reasoning and an eight-month advantage over the controls in fundamental operations.

Since one child's score may have prejudiced the average of the medium performers in the control group in reasoning, this average is indicated with and without his gain (shown by the dotted portion of the bar). By including his score, the controls excelled the experimental group by four and three-fifths months; excluding it gave the experimental group a one-quarter month advantage. The advance of medium performers (Level 2), experimental group, exceeded that of the control group in fundamental operations by four and one-half months. Each experimental group appeared to have benefited from the individualized practice.

In summary, the present pilot study has demonstrated that pupils in one self-contained, heterogeneously grouped classroom who were permitted to begin their practice at their own level and to proceed in their practice at their own rate gained in achievement more markedly than did the pupils who practiced at the level arbitrarily set for the grade.

Since the teacher-investigator followed class-as-a-whole organization except for short, strategic periods, a minimum of extra teacher planning and instructional time was required. It is believed that the plan here employed could be adapted to any method, any set of textbooks, and any middle elementary class. The sub-groups can be observed or disbanded at any time without interruption to the on-going program.

The study stands as one teacher-investigator's answer to Frances Flournoy's question as to, "what variations to make, how, and how much?" in providing for individual differences in a typical self-contained classroom.

REFERENCES

1. Frances Flournoy, "Meeting Individual Differences in Arithmetic," *The Arithmetic Teacher,* VII (February, 1960), 85.

2. *Ibid.,* p. 86

3. H. F. Wright, in A. P. Coladarci (ed.), *Educational Psychology, a Book of Readings* (Dryden Press, 1955), pp. 352–4.

4. L. J. Brueckner and F. E. Grossnickle, *Making Arithmetic Meaningful* (Philadelphia: The John Winston Company, 1953), p. 122.

5. Donald E. Shipp, "An Experimental Study of Achievement in Arithmetic and the Time Allotted to Development of Meanings and Individual Pupil Practices," *Dissertation Abstracts* (Baton Rouge: Louisiana State University, 1958), p. 492.

6. J. R. Hilgard, in A. P. Coladarci, *op. cit.,* p. 48.

7. W. Tiegs, and W. W. Clark, *California Achievement Tests.* Grades 4-5-6, Form W, 1957 edition.

8. L. Moench, "The Arithmetic Curriculum in the Elementary School,"

Unpublished Master's thesis, University of Illinois, 1959.

9. J. Osborn, A. Riefling, and H. F. Spitzer, *Exploring Arithmetic* (St. Louis: Webster Publishing Company, 1958).

10. M. Duren and W. A. Lewis, "One Way to Meet Individual Differences," *National Elementary School Principal,* XXXV (September, 1955), 74–75.

11. W. W. Cook, "Individual Differences and Curriculum Practice," *Journal of Educational Psychology,* XXXIX (March, 1948), 146–7.

12. L. J. Brueckner, *op. cit.,* p. 95.

13. R. L. Morton, "The Review Versus the Telescoped Reteaching of the Work of Preceding Grades," *The Mathematics Teacher,* XXXVIII (May, 1946), 228.

14. G. C. Pinney, "Grouping by Arithmetic Ability—An Experiment in the Teaching of Arithmetic," *The Arithmetic Teacher,* VII (March, 1961), 120–3.

Part Ten

Spelling

Some writers have concluded that reading and spelling ability are relatively discrete, while others have reported fairly high correlations between the two skills. The disagreement may be due, at least in part, to two things: (1) the fact that researchers obviously do not agree as to what magnitude of correlation constitutes a *psychologically*—as opposed to *statistically*—significant relationship and (2) the fact that the magnitude of the relationship is not the same for samples of pupils from different intelligence and general achievement levels. The fact is, though, that poor readers are almost always poor spellers. The interrelationships among reading, handwriting, and spelling were discussed briefly in the chapter devoted to handwriting and need not be repeated here. But it is also true that good readers are not necessarily good spellers. Although poor performance in both areas can be attributed to a common array of limitations and skill lacks, certain abilities that make for good performance in reading—e.g., ability to respond to minimal cues, ability to fill in from context—may tend to limit performance in spelling, which requires one to attend explicitly to the letter arrangements in irregularly spelled words.

The point here is simply that pupils who read well and who write legibly may, nevertheless, need special help in spelling. The tendency may be to provide help only for pupils with all the problems and to ignore those who have a single, specific disability.

The content of a spelling improvement program is likely to be influenced greatly by the point of view of the person by whom it is devised. More specifically, two distinct schools of thought regarding the content of the spelling program exist; and perhaps the advocates of an eclectic approach that makes extensive use of the essential points from both sides constitute a third school. Practitioners probably will generally find themselves in the third school, for pure applications of theory are rare in the real world of the classroom. In fact, the majority of practitioners are probably not fully aware of the debate that has been going on for a number of years. The first two articles in this chapter, by Hodges and by Yee respectively, help to clarify the issues in the debate.

Hodges' article includes (1) discussions of the Hanna-Moore and the Horn studies and the divergent conclusions drawn by those researchers and (2) a presentation of the rationale for and the implications from a subsequent study by Hanna and his associates. While it should be noted that Hodges was one of the Hanna associates involved in running the expanded study, the presentation is reasonably free from bias. Three specific points from the article merit particular attention:

1. As Hodges points out, the extended study by Hanna *et al* was an analysis of American-English orthography, *not* a study in elementary school curriculum and instruction. The direct results of the study are only the bases for curriculum development and research that must follow. Yee also has made this point in his article.

2. Rudorf's finding that half of Hanna's 17,310 words could be spelled correctly on the basis of sound-to-letter patterns is interesting, particularly because it could be used either to support or to condemn the placement of emphasis upon the regularity of sound-to-letter patterns in spelling instruction.

3. An ideal solution to the problem, as noted in the final paragraph of the article, would be a revised orthography, in which grapheme-phoneme relationships are more regular.

Yee also presents an overview of the two sides of the spelling debate, but the essential theme of his article is that seemingly conflicting points of view can be complementary if they are intelligently placed in juxtaposition. The point that there is danger in adopting an either-or stance is well taken. Yee has done well in identifying the basic issues in the debate, and his discussion of needed research efforts deserves a careful reading.

Hunt *et al* have identified four factors that affect performance in spelling: phonetic ability, ability in structural analysis, visual memory, and ability to spell the "demons." Their finding that the four factors are relatively independent —at least among college freshmen—points up the need for differential diagnosis before a program of remedial teaching is begun with an individual. The way in which the study was designed to provide a test of the stated hypotheses and the construction of the four spelling tests merit attention as possible paradigms for further research in spelling and in related areas. The article points out the need for research (1) to ascertain whether other independent determiners of spelling performance exist and (2) to assess the worth of methods devised to develop these underlying abilities that determine spelling performance.

The article by Personke and Yee includes a model of spelling behavior and an interpretation of the model. Analysis of spelling behavior in terms of the five suggested channels helps not only to clarify the nature of the process but also to focus attention upon the specific difficulties—or breakdowns in the operation of all channels—being experienced by pupils who are poor spellers. Such a comprehensive view of spelling behavior ensures that neither strengths nor weaknesses will be overlooked when spelling problems are diagnosed and when remedial teaching is planned. The writers' point that efforts to demonstrate the superiority of particular approaches may serve only to establish dichotomies which do not really exist is well taken.

The last article in this chapter, by Jensen, is the report of an examination of spelling behavior in terms of "principles derived from the experimental psychology of learning." As such, it is an example of an all too rare phenomenon: an attempt to bridge the gap between the laboratory study of learning and the classroom study of learning. Unfortunately, the most obvious implication for practice of the demonstrated classic serial-position effect—i.e., that the apparently troublesome middle portions of words be made the focus of special attention—is negated by Jensen's reference to studies that have shown the futility of emphasizing difficult parts of words in directed study. The latter results are not so definitive, however, as to preclude further study. Perhaps more effective means for focusing upon the difficult portions of words can be devised.

40   The Case for Teaching Sound-to-Letter
Correspondences in Spelling

RICHARD E. HODGES

In 1953, Paul R. Hanna of Stanford University and one of his doctoral students, James T. Moore, published in the *Elementary School Journal* a report of their study of American-English orthography (1). The results of this study indicated that there is a much closer relationship between the sounds of spoken American English and their representation in writing than is usually supposed (2). Later, other researchers in spelling curriculum and instruction, and textbook publishers, critically examined the rationale and the findings of Hanna and Moore. Some accepted the findings. Others saw basic weaknesses in the rationale and the design of the research and in the conclusions drawn from it.

In 1957, the *Elementary School Journal* published a critique of the Hanna-Moore study, a critique that stemmed from another analysis of American-English orthography conducted by Ernest Horn, of the State University of Iowa (3). Horn's study cast serious doubt on the findings of Hanna and Moore, or at least on their interpretations of the findings. Horn found less consistent relationships between spoken and written American English than those indicated by Hanna and Moore. A later article by Horn (4) elaborated further the weaknesses of the case for regularity in the orthography. In brief, the positions taken by Hanna and Moore and by Horn represent a major division between those who believe that American-English spelling has considerable regularity and those who contend that such regularities are contrived.

Recently this controversy has been kindled anew. Hanna recognized that his study was not a conclusive examination of sound-to-spelling relationships in American-English orthography and that his research did indeed have serious weaknesses. Accordingly, Hanna, in collaboration with E. Hugh Rudorf and the present writer, undertook a much more extensive examination of our writing system and the degree to which it reflects oral language. A report of this research (5), like the research it superseded, has generated further criticism of the case for teaching spelling on the basis of patterns of sound-to-letter correspondences.

What, then, are the issues on each side of the controversy, and how has this recent research attempted to provide definitive insights into the nature of American-English orthography?

The Hanna-Moore Study

The rationale of the Hanna-Moore research rested on certain assumptions. First, these researchers assumed that the child entering school is the master of a rather large vocabulary of spoken words and that he soon acquires an increasing repertoire of words used in reading. Therefore, spelling programs should seek to enable the child to associate his speaking vocabulary with his reading vocabulary and to reproduce these associations in their accepted written forms.

Second, Hanna and Moore assumed that the orthography of the American-English language is alphabetically based; that is, American-English spelling is a

Reprinted from *The Elementary School Journal*, Vol. 66 (March, 1966), pp. 327–336, by permission of The University of Chicago Press. Copyright 1966 by The University of Chicago.

system in which graphemes (the letters of the alphabet and their combinations) are used in writing to represent phonemes (the constituent sounds of English speech). An alphabetic writing system is in contrast to other types of orthographies in which written symbols may represent syllables or words. Accordingly, the ability to spell depends to a large extent on the ability to associate the appropriate graphemes with the phonemes that comprise the words of American-English speech.

With these two basic assumptions in mind, Hanna and Moore intended to analyze an American-English spelling vocabulary of three thousand words that were believed to represent the spelling words most common in children's usage and those most often taught in the first eight grades. From this list Hanna and Moore wanted to determine the extent to which each phoneme in the words comprising the spelling vocabulary of the elementary-school child is represented consistently in writing by a specific letter or combination of letters. In sum, the investigators intended to assess whether there are consistent relationships between phonemes and graphemes so that a speller could, with some assurance, select the correct written symbol for a given speech sound he heard and said in a word.

Hanna and Moore derived a standard pronunciation system of forty phonemes (including eight diphthongs; for example, *uy* as in *buy*) of spoken American English that included vowels, single consonants, consonant blends, suffixes, and final blends. This system used the *Thorndike Century Senior Dictionary* (6) as an authority and included only the preferred pronunciations given in that reference. The effects of syllable stress or lack of syllable stress on the pronunciation of phonemes were not considered unless these stress factors actually produced a different phoneme.

Each of the three thousand words (most of which were monosyllabic because of the sources from which they were taken) was then broken down into its component phonemes. The number of occurrences of each phoneme was then tabulated according to its position in a word or syllable. The tabulation was to show:

1. The number of different spellings of each phoneme.
2. The frequency of these spellings in the list of three thousand words.
3. The per cent of phonemes in the three thousand words that were regularly spelled.

A *regular spelling* was defined as that letter or combination of letters that is most frequently used to represent a given phoneme. The less frequently used letter representations of a phoneme were classified as *irregular spellings*.

What were the more important findings of this research? Generally, the investigators found that:

1. About four-fifths of the phonemes in the list of three thousand words have regular spellings.
2. Approximately three-fourths of the vowel phonemes in the words that had been analyzed are spelled by regular letter representations about 57 per cent to 99 per cent of the time.
3. Seven of the vowel phonemes have quite inconsistent letter representations (the vowel sounds in such words as *about, he, book, food, verb, all,* and the *y* sound in *onion*).
4. Single consonant phonemes are represented by their regular spellings about 90 per cent of the time they occur (as are the beginning consonant phonemes of *bed, dog,* and *gas*).

5. Doubled consonant letters (as in *address*) occur less than 1 per cent of the time in the word list.

6. Two consonant phonemes (the initial sound in *jam* and *gem* and the final sound in *jazz* and *has*) are quite irregularly represented in writing.

7. The so-called suffixes *le* and *on* (as in *table* and *lemon*) are also spelled quite irregularly.

8. About 82 per cent of the consonant blends are spelled in only one way (as is the initial consonant blend in *black*).

From these findings Hanna and Moore concluded that elementary-school spelling programs could profitably be organized to help pupils take advantage of the alphabetic nature of the American-English orthography (1). These programs, the researchers suggested, should capitalize on the regularity of the sound-to-letter patterns in learning to spell. The recognition of their work is testified to, at least in part, by researchers who subsequently have sought to verify or to reject their findings and by the references made to their study in many of the current spelling textbooks.

The Horn Study

The conclusions that Hanna and Moore drew from their study, however, were subject to careful analysis, particularly by spelling authorities who maintained that the orthography is not a consistent reflection of American-English speech. The most forthright and the most substantial critique of the Hanna-Moore research was made by Ernest Horn, an eminent spelling scholar. Horn pointed out critical elements in the rationale and the design of the Hanna-Moore research which suggested that their findings were suspect (3). The most telling criticisms follow:

1. A list of the three thousand most commonly used words in writing is an inconclusive sample. Research based on many more words is necessary to demonstrate the consistency, or lack of consistency, of American-English orthography.

2. There is more than one accepted pronunciation of words. For example, American-English pronunciation differs in formal and informal speech and by regional dialects.

3. The definition of *regularity* is obscured because the investigators did not account for the frequency of the sounds or for the number of exceptions to the "regular" spellings they identified. In short, regularity is not insured merely because a given spelling of a phoneme is the most frequent representation of that sound. The spelling of a phoneme should be highly predictable (have few exceptions) and should be generalizable to large numbers of words before the label of *regularity* can be applied.

To lend strength to these criticisms, Horn replicated the research of Hanna and Moore but made several adaptations. Horn analyzed a sample of ten thousand words. He also attempted to account for multiple pronunciations of these words by checking several dictionaries. As a final authority, he used Kenyon and Knott's *A Pronouncing Dictionary of American English* (7). Further, he assigned any so-called silent letters in a word (for example, the letter *b* in *debt*) to some sound in the word, a procedure that Hanna and Moore did not use.

What were some of the principal findings of Horn's study? Generally, Horn concluded that Hanna and Moore were correct in their estimation that English speech sounds do have common spellings; however, their interpretations of the findings were misguided, if not somewhat naïve. The limitation of their sample, Horn noted, caused them to make generalizations that did not hold up when a larger sample of the language was examined. Horn reported that:

1. Over a third of the words in *A Pronouncing Dictionary of American English* have more than one accepted pronunciation.
2. Over half of the ten thousand words contain silent letters in which an arbitrary judgment must be made when assigning them to a particular sound in a word. Further, about a sixth of the words contain doubled letters, and typically only one of the letters is pronounced.
3. Not only do several letters often represent a given sound, but a given letter often represents several sounds.
4. Many words commonly used in writing are polysyllabic and therefore contain unstressed syllables. The concept of regularity breaks down in unstressed syllables particularly (3).

Consequently, Horn drew sharply different conclusions regarding the feasibility of constructing spelling programs that emphasized sound-to-letter patterns in American English. In a later statement (4), Horn proposed that spelling generalizations be taught only when they are extremely powerful (that is, when they apply to large numbers of words and have few exceptions), because generalizations can easily be misapplied as well as correctly applied. He further indicated that large numbers of common words do not conform to any orthographic rule and therefore cannot be learned by children through a process of associating speech sounds and written symbols. Finally, children should be helped to learn the ways in which sounds are represented in writing rather than their most common spellings.

Horn's basic views have been reiterated elsewhere by various critics of the Hanna-Moore study, but often with embellishments that directly concern spelling curriculum and instruction. A recent critique (8) of the Hanna-Moore research indicates that:

1. Subjectivity is involved in assigning silent letters to some phonemic value.
2. Dialect differences and variability of word pronunciation in different sentence contexts complicate associating written symbols with given speech sounds.
3. There is a danger in generalizing about sound-to-letter correspondences from a narrow sample of American English to a more comprehensive sample.
4. Many "function" words (for example, *says, the*) do not fit any orthographic rules yet need to be learned by children early in their school career; these words weaken the case for teaching spelling on the basis of regular sound-to-letter correspondences.
5. It is necessary to consider the frequency of particular sounds in words.
6. A strong case could also be made for teaching spelling on the basis of inconsistencies in the language rather than supposed consistencies.

The Stanford Spelling Project

Regardless of the position one takes on the research by Hanna and Moore, it is clear that their study is quite important for at least one basic reason: it raises significant questions and foments critical analyses. The fact that the Hanna-

Moore study still continues to generate interest is testimony that the area these researchers explored is an important one and that their general premises have substance.

Yet, even their proponents were not able justifiably to claim that Hanna and Moore had made a truly comprehensive analysis of American-English orthography. What was obviously needed was a definitive analysis of American-English orthography, one that would be comprehensive and would be designed to obviate the weaknesses that were evident in the earlier study by Hanna and Moore.

Therefore, in 1961 Hanna proposed to the Cooperative Research Branch of the United States Office of Education that such a study be undertaken. The purpose of the research would be to determine how consistently the phonemes of American English are represented by particular written symbols in the orthography in a sample that included far more than three thousand words or ten thousand words. Further, using linguistic concepts and computer technology, this research would attempt to explore the nature of the orthography in much greater detail than had previously been done. Thus, the research would be, in part, an attempt to go beyond this earlier work by considering additional elements of American-English orthography. This research proposal received the sponsorship of the United States Office of Education, and the research was carried out from January, 1963, to December, 1964.

More detailed results of this research are available elsewhere (5, 9, 10). In general, however, the data from this study indicate that the orthography does indeed reflect spoken language with considerable consistency, particularly when the several components of the phonology (the sound system) underlying the orthography are taken into account.

It is certainly true that most phonemes are represented graphically in more than one way. And it is also true that the fact that phonemes are represented in many ways in large numbers of different words makes it difficult to sort out measures of consistency. For these reasons it was decided to examine the relationships between phonemes and their written representations in their positions in syllables and also to take into account the stress given to these syllables.

Let us examine the rationale and the design of this research to illustrate how it proposed to overcome the basic weaknesses of the Hanna-Moore research and to indicate the depth to which this study plumbed the nature of American-English orthography.

The research team wished to examine as large a sample of American-English words as would be definitive and practical to analyze. Accordingly, the first twenty thousand words from *The Thorndike-Lorge Teachers Word Book of 30,000 Words* (11) were used. Certain words were eliminated including proper names, contracted word forms, hyphenated words, abbreviations, archaic and poetic words, foreign words, trade names, slang and dialectal words, and words listed as "rare" in standard dictionaries. The elimination of these words resulted in a basic list of 15,284 words. This list was then supplemented by an additional 2,026 words taken from *Webster's New Collegiate Dictionary* (12), which included words that had entered the lexicon in recent years, and additional words of standard usage that were not included in the basic list. In no case, however, were derived forms of base words added to the list lest the "deck be stacked" by increasing the frequencies of certain phoneme-grapheme correspondences that are consistently spelled in prefixes and suffixes. Accordingly, derivations were included only when affixes were uncommon or when they changed the pronunciation of the base form of the word.

The list of 17,310 words was felt to be extensive enough to insure that many polysyllabic words were included. Further, the extensiveness of the word list enabled the research team to analyze phoneme-grapheme correspondences at several levels of the phonology underlying the orthography. These levels were sound-to-letter correspondences wherever they occur in *words,* sound-to-letter correspondences as they occur in positions in syllables, and sound-to-letter correspondences as they occur in positions in stressed and unstressed syllables.

Careful attention was paid to the selection of graphemic symbols that represent speech sounds in American-English writing. It must be agreed that compiling such lists of letter representations is a subjective task; but not entirely so. The so-called silent letters often have historical antecedents (for example, the vestigial letter *k* in *knock* at one time represented a phoneme, the initial sound one hears in *kit*). Furthermore, letters do not have sounds; they represent them. Letters do have names, but we do not spell words in writing by saying the names of the letters; we say the names of the letters only when we wish to spell words orally. In addition, it might be argued that, pedagogically, it is more meaningful and simpler to indicate that the initial *n* sound is written *kn* in *knock* than to point out repeatedly the silent letters that permeate our writing system. In any case, all letters in a given word were assigned to some sound (for example, the ending *o* sound in *though* is spelled *ough*) after carefully examining several references that discussed American-English orthography (13–16) and by consulting with linguists and language arts specialists who advised the project team.

Similarly, the doubled letters that often represent consonant phonemes were assigned to single speech sounds whenever the dictionary pronunciation indicated that this was appropriate. Indeed, a case might be made for the reformulation of the teaching of syllabication in elementary school, since the standard practice of separating words such as *follow* and *fellow* between doubled letters is a typographer's rule, not a reflection of the way such words are pronounced.

An important, if not crucial, consideration is the pronunciation system used in research of this nature. Obviously, language is dynamic; sounds in words used in running speech vary among dialect groups as well as among individuals. But the spelling of such words is another matter. Each word to be spelled is isolated from its context for the purposes of spelling and writing, and words that are unfamiliar to the speller are often pronounced in isolation from the context in which they occur.

As an aid to spelling, the pronunciation system used to analyze the consistency of the orthography is better based on lexical (or dictionary) pronunciations than on pronunciation systems that describe words occurring in running speech. Furthermore, the minor variations in speech sounds that occur in spoken discourse are not phonemic, that is, the substitution of one minor sound change for another does not alter the meaning of a word. Fortunately, for those who speak American English, such minor changes in sound, or allophonic variations, are assimilated without awareness; otherwise, the cognitive load of remembering all such allophones from several dialects and in different sentence patterns would be prodigious.

Thus, on logical grounds (and practically, too, in order to maintain a consistent sound system throughout the analysis), a pronunciation system was employed that included thirty consonant phonemes and twenty-two vowel phonemes. Actually, this coding system reflects the conventional phonemic codes used by linguists. The additional sounds included in this pronunciation system included vowel sounds before *r* sounds and certain diphthongs.

The decision to use a standard pronunciation system is not meant to argue that dialect differences in American English are negligible in the task of learning to spell. However, admonitions concerning the role of dialect in spelling are based primarily on logical rather than empirical grounds. That is, no concerted study has been made of how dialect differences affect spelling standard English. It is hoped that the results of this research will provide bases for undertaking studies that will compare spellings of words in the standard orthography with spellings of those words by individuals in various dialect communities. The author is at present formulating such studies.

To recapitulate, a sizable list of words was analyzed. The research used a consistent pronunciation system and a carefully prepared list of letter representations to determine the degree to which these two systems (speech and writing) are related at several levels of the phonology underlying the orthography. The results of these analyses clearly indicate that the orthography is alphabetically based: large numbers of consistent phoneme-grapheme correspondences occur at least 80 per cent of the time in some position in stressed and unstressed syllables (9).

What do these findings indicate for the spelling curriculum of the elementary school? They suggest that a mastery of American-English spelling might be made easier by a conscientious programming of spelling materials that capitalizes on consistent sound-to-spelling correspondences and on the "rules" for making correct associations between phonemes and graphemes.

But such spelling programs require careful preparation and testing. For this reason, the research was intended as an analysis of American-English orthography and was not a study in elementary-school spelling curriculum and instruction. In short, the research has laid the conditions for curriculum construction and experimentation.

Clearly, the frequency with which consistent sound-to-letter correspondences occur in spelling large numbers of words is an important factor to be considered. To assess this factor, the present author tabulated the frequencies and percentages of all phoneme-grapheme correspondences occurring in the list of 17,310 words as well as the frequencies and percentages of the distribution of phonemes as they occur throughout the word list (9).

The research team also wished to test the value of the observable consistent phoneme-grapheme relationships found in the word sample for spelling words in the conventional American-English orthography. Accordingly, a second major phase of the total research project was undertaken by E. Hugh Rudorf. This phase involved the development of a computer program by which the 17,310 words can be spelled on the basis of these phoneme-grapheme relationships (10). For each phoneme a set of rules for predicting its spelling was derived from an analysis of the data obtained in the first phase of the research. The rules indicated how a particular phoneme would be spelled under the various conditions of position and stress, and how a preceding or following phoneme in the same syllable or word as the phoneme in question might affect its spelling.

To accomplish this analysis, the computer was provided with an "oral vocabulary" of 17,310 words, the sets of rules, and a list of the graphemes that stand for phonemes in the orthography. The computer was programmed to spell these words on the basis of the rules given. The findings of this analysis indicate that about half of the 17,310 words can be spelled on the basis of sound-to-letter patterns and that additional thousands of words can be spelled correctly if such morphological factors as affixation and compounding are taken into account.

The findings support the contention that there are productive relationships between the American-English writing system and the sounds in words that this writing system represents. The fact that many words, including some frequently used words, do not conform to these alphabetic principles does not require that we ignore the basic alphabetic structure of our orthography in our efforts to help children efficiently and effectively master the complexities of American-English spelling. Obviously, the spelling of some words can most easily be mastered by visual memorization. Other words contain certain uncommon spellings that require the pupil's special attention; yet parts of these words usually contain highly regular sound-to-letter correspondences when their positions in syllables and syllable stress are considered. Plainly, learning to spell is a more complex process than simply learning to make correct associations among phonemes and graphemes (17, 18).

An ideal solution to many of the vagaries of American-English orthography is some system of spelling reform. It is quite unlikely, however, that the problems that impede the development and acceptance of a revised form of American-English orthography can be overcome at this time (19). Meanwhile, it would be unfortunate, and a disservice to elementary-school children who are learning to spell, to underscore the negative aspects of an orthography which, in the main, is based on a consistent, and a historically interesting, sound-to-letter system.

REFERENCES

1. Paul R. Hanna and James T. Moore, Jr. "Spelling—from Spoken Word to Written Symbol," *Elementary School Journal,* LIII (February, 1953), 329–37.

2. James T. Moore, Jr. "Phonetic Elements Appearing in a Three Thousand Word Spelling Vocabulary." Unpublished doctoral dissertation. Stanford, California: Stanford University, 1951.

3. Ernest Horn. "Phonetics and Spelling," *Elementary School Journal,* LVII (May, 1957), 424–32.

4. Ernest Horn. "Spelling," *Encyclopedia of Educational Research,* pp. 1337–54. Chester W. Harris (editor). New York: Macmillan, 1960.

5. Richard E. Hodges and E. Hugh Rudorf. "Searching Linguistics for Cues to the Teaching of Spelling," *Elementary English,* XLII (May, 1965), 527–33.

6. E. L. Thorndike. *Thorndike Century Senior Dictionary.* Chicago: Scott, Foresman and Company, 1941.

7. John S. Kenyon and Thomas A. Knott. *A Pronouncing Dictionary of American English.* Springfield, Massachusetts: G. and C. Merriam Company, 1953.

8. Walter T. Petty. "Research Critiques." Edited by Patrick Groff. *Elementary English,* XLII (May, 1965), 584–87.

9. Richard E. Hodges. "An Analysis of the Phonological Structure of American-English Orthography." Unpublished doctoral dissertation. Stanford, California: Stanford University, 1964.

10. E. Hugh Rudorf. "The Development of an Algorithm for American-English Spelling." Unpublished doctoral dissertation. Stanford, California: Stanford University, 1964.

11. E. L. Thorndike and Irving Lorge. *The Teacher's Word Book of 30,000 Words.* New York: Bureau of Publications, Teachers College, Columbia University, 1944.

12. *Webster's New Collegiate Dictionary.* Edited by John P. Bethel. Springfield, Massachusetts: G. and C. Merriam Company, 1961 (sixth edition).

13. Godfrey Dewey. *Relative Frequency of English Speech Sounds.* Cambridge, Massachusetts: Harvard University Press, 1923.

14. W. Nelson Francis. *The Structure of American English.* New York: Ronald Press Company, 1958.

15. Robert A. Hall, Jr. *Sound and Spelling in English.* Philadelphia: Chilton Company, 1961.

16. Axel Wijk. *Regularized English.* Stockholm: University of Stockholm, 1959.

17. Paul R. Hanna and Richard E. Hodges. "Spelling and Communications Theory: A Model and an Annotated Bibliography," *Elementary English,* XL (May, 1963), 483–505, 528.

18. Richard E. Hodges. "The Psychological Bases of Spelling," *Elementary English,* XLII (October, 1965), 629–35.

19. Richard E. Hodges. "A Short History of Spelling Reform in the United States," *Phi Delta Kappan,* XLV (April, 1964), 330–32.

41 The Generalization Controversy on Spelling Instruction

ALBERT H. YEE

An enduring and sometimes confusing controversy involving leading authorities in spelling continues today. Most school leaders and teachers have been unaware of this prolonged debate and do not realize that the issues of concern involve them most significantly. Elementary school teachers and their classes have been involved in the debate insofar as their choice and use of spellers and particular methods of instruction may be concerned. The purpose of this article is to clarify conflicting points of view and offer a critique of the problem.

Very simply, the debate centers on the question of whether competency in spelling can be obtained through a general use of spelling generalizations (rules) or not. Some authorities say that English-American language spelling forms are highly irregular and offer learners and their teachers only a confusing and contradictory mass resistant to any broad systematized set of spelling rules. For example, Horn (22) wrote: "The sound of long *a* (a) . . . was found 1,237 times, with 601 exceptions to the commonest spelling; the sound of *k* was found 2,613 times, with 932 exceptions; and the sound of *s* in *sick,* 3,846 times, with 1,278 exceptions. One is hardly justified in calling spellings 'regular' or in teaching the commonest spellings as principles or generalizations when the exceptions are numbered not merely by the score but by hundreds." Therefore, spelling instruction by this point of view becomes a gradual accumulation of necessary and practiced words, including the introduction of generalizations whenever warranted by applied research evidence.

The contrasting point of view by other authorities argues that there is greater phonetic regularity or sound-to-letter relationship in spelling than opponents claim and that spelling would become more efficient and easier by learning spelling rules to generate effective spelling ability. For example, according to

From *Elementary English,* Vol. 43 (February, 1966), pp. 154–161, 166. Reprinted with permission of the National Council of Teachers of English and Albert H. Yee.

Rudolf Flesch (7) in his well-known publication of 1955, *Why Johnny Can't Read,* "About 13 per cent of all English words are partly irregular in their spelling. The other 87 per cent follow fixed rules." Hanna and Moore (17) wrote, "Words learned in splendid isolation are likely to remain in isolation with no relation to words of similar sound and construction . . . children should learn early the techniques which will enable them to proceed successfully in making letter-sound relationships." In describing how various approaches to spelling should be balanced in a modern spelling program, Hanna and Hanna (15) wrote:

> A phonetic analysis of words and an inductive study of the letter symbols used to spell the sounds in words *provide a firm base for the spelling program* [italics the writer's]. This new approach, coupled with a word-study plan which uses the visual and the hand-learning for reinforcement, gives us hope of a day when all our pupils can spell correctly the words they need to write.

We will now review research findings and conclusions for both sides of the debate.

None or Limited Teaching of Spelling Rules

One question in the debate has dealt with the ability of learners to apply spelling rules to their general spelling requirements. In 1912, Cook (6) found that out of seven spelling rules learned earlier by college and high school students, only one rule was of real value. That rule states that words ending in *ie,* such as *lie,* change the *ie* to *y* before adding the suffix *ing.* Also in 1912, Turner (37) reported that results with a group of 16 pupils taught by the method of direct drill without reference to spelling rules were superior to results obtained from another group of 16 pupils taught with reference to spelling rules. The two groups were matched prior to the study of spelling rules.

In 1930, Archer (3) reported negative transfer operating in pupils' (5th and 7th grades) spelling of certain words; his findings showed that children generalized from experience with one type of words and misapplied the generalization to other words. Archer, therefore, concluded a rule must be justified on its lack of ambiguity in application.

In 1931, Sartorius (35) concluded from her study of generalization in spelling that "rules should be treated with caution until experimental evidence concerning their functional value is secured." In 1932, King (29) reported that the teaching of spelling rules appeared to be impractical, considering unsatisfactory results in a study where a limited set of spelling rules were taught. King concluded that it would be very hard for children to learn to apply the many complicated rules that would be necessary for comprehensive spelling ability. Jackson (28) reported in 1953 that no statistically significant increase in spelling achievement was found in comparison between classes receiving extra phonetic instruction in spelling and classes acting as controls. Jackson concluded that extra phonetic instruction for the experimental classes was not worth the time spent in overlearning phonetic relationships. It may well be, however, that inefficient teaching methods made significant contributions to the failure and hindered benefits from teaching generalizations.

A more specific concern has dealt with the ability to spell efficiently, *i.e.,* without hindrance and a minimum of spelling errors. Hahn (11) found in 1960 that additional teaching of phonics in reading to pupils in grades three through six produced no significant difference in spelling errors compared to results obtained from pupils in similar grades receiving "no phonics" instruction. In 1964, Hahn (10) tested pupils in three schools in three separate school districts in Pennsylvania matched on socio-economic background, teacher training, and children's group IQ tests. Spelling instruction was varied in the three schools to test different methods of teaching. According to Hahn, ". . . pupils in School A had received much formal training in phonics for two years, while pupils in Schools B and C had received a *normal* [italics the writer's] amount of such training as a part of their regular reading program. No special phonics work was done in spelling classes in any school." According to the investigator, the results of the spelling tests for the three school districts showed that there was no statistical difference between the mean scores of phonics and "normal" groups. The phonics group scored lowest of all three districts on a spelling test made up of words that none of the pupils had studied and upon whose phonics training should have helped most if phonics training has transfer validity. Since no special phonics training was provided in School A's spelling program and the phonics training was provided through the *reading* program, phonics training in *spelling* may have provided more significant differences.

Another area of concern in the debate has been the nature of the language and logical assessments of available research findings and the problems involved in spelling effectiveness. Ernest Horn, who for many years contributed much writing and research in this area, has consistently expressed doubts that spelling rules based on sound-to-letter relationships can replace direct instruction of words. In 1919, he wrote:

> Most of the articles dealing with the subject contain a peculiar fallacy, namely, that by discovering that words are covered by a given rule, one may discover the efficiency of teaching that rule . . . one must show . . . that a rule can be easily taught, that it will be remembered, and that it will function in the stress of actual spelling. Evidence seems to cast a doubt on all three of these assumptions. . . . (25)

In 1954, Horn (23) found it possible to conclude that "the limited success in attempts to teach pupils to learn and apply even a few spelling rules suggests that we should not be too optimistic about the practicability of teaching the more numerous and complicated rules or principles in phonetics." With greater finality, Horn (22) wrote in 1957 that, "There seems no escape from the direct teaching of the large number of common words which do not conform in their spelling to any phonetic or orthographic rule." Later in 1957, writing for the *Encyclopedia of Educational Research,* Horn (21) listed the type of evidence which he considered must be recognized as possible limitations to the benefits of teaching phonetic generalizations:

> 1. Over one-third of the words in *A Pronouncing Dictionary of American English* have more than one acceptable pronunciation due to regional and cultivated differences.
> 2. Many different spellings can be given most sounds and even the most common spellings have numerous exceptions.
> 3. A majority of words contain silent letters, and about a sixth are spelled with double letters even though only one of the letters may be pronounced.
> 4. Responses become uncertain when more than one reasonable choice is available, such as *"bizzy* for *busy, honer* for *honor."*
> 5. Unstressed syllables characterized by the schwa or short *i* sound are very hard to spell by sound.

6. Any spelling rule, phonetic or orthographical, can be used incorrectly as well as correctly.

7. Some spelling elements are fairly consistent, such as word positions and the adding of prefixes and suffixes. More adequate evidence is needed to realize the value of relating sounds to symbols, but it appears that such value "should be utilized as an aid to spelling rather than as a substitute for the direct study of these words."

Horn's view is not one-sided, however, as he demonstrates in his research pamphlet, *Teaching Spelling:*

When dependable evidence is available . . . it is entirely possible that teaching sound-letter relationships will be regarded as an essential part of the spelling program. . . . Even though the evidence is meager on some important matters, it seems to justify considerable emphasis upon phonics. . . . Instruction in phonics should be regarded, however, as an aid to spelling rather than as a substitute for the systematic study of the words in the spelling list (20).

Greater Phonetic Emphases in Spelling

We turn now to the research findings and conclusions of those supporting a greater emphasis on teaching spelling rules utilizing phonetic or sound-letter relationships.

In 1917, Lester (30) countered critics of the use of spelling rules with a well-argued article stressing the helpful and short-cut nature of common spelling rules. Lester, however, emphasized the point that spelling rules should be taught as "necessary tools with which to perform a piece of work," and wrote in a manner which did not place him entirely in an "either-or" position.

In 1926, Watson (38) reported two studies dealing with competency in spelling. In one study, individual high school students were taught either spelling rules or spelling words by drill; in the second study, two different high school classes were compared—one received instruction in spelling rules and the other received class drill. In both studies, the results favored instruction in spelling rules.

In 1930, Carroll (4) presented findings of a comparative study of the ability of bright and dull children to make use of spelling generalizations. Carroll found positive results in the use of spelling rules by bright children and negative results for dull children, and concluded that the group differences in spelling errors were due to "the marked superiority of the bright over the dull in phonetic generalization ability."

In 1930, Archer (2) pursued a suggestion he gained from his earlier study (3) that a spelling rule would be useful if the rule could be applied to enough words to justify its use and taught to be applied in proper situations through inductive and deductive methods. In the follow-up study, Archer (2) reported statistically significant results supporting the instruction of one spelling generalization. He wrote: "We must . . . recognize that the question as to *how* a rule is taught is just as important as *what* is taught. We must develop the rule in a psychological manner and teach it in a way that will function in the words to be spelled."

The most elaborate efforts to emphasize the value of spelling generalization and the relationship of sound and letter have been made by Paul R. Hanna and his colleagues at Stanford University. Their main contention is that the "American-English language is not based upon a one-to-one relationship between phoneme and grapheme, but that there are patterns of consistency in the orthography which, based upon linguistic factors, may be said to produce correspondences that are surprisingly consistent" (14).

In 1953, Hanna and Moore (17) presented an article that has received much attention. It has become well-known, because it has been cited as evidence for the support of instruction in spelling rules dealing with letter representations of sounds; and it has drawn considerable criticism from opponents, such as Horn (22) and Petty (33), for the interpretations Hanna and Moore made from the results of their study. The study dealt with an investigation of a 3,000 word spelling list "to determine the extent to which each speech sound in the words comprising the spelling vocabulary of the elementary school child is represented consistently in writing by a *specific* letter or combination of letters." According to the researchers, the results indicate that sounds to a high degree were consistently represented by particular letters. One finding showed that "approximately four-fifths of the phonemes contained in the words comprising the spelling vocabulary of the elementary school child are represented by a regular spelling."

More recently, Hodges and Rudorf (19), working under the direction of Hanna, presented the first of a series of five articles dealing with the relationships of linguistics to spelling instruction. Capitalizing on the advances in computer technology, the researchers conducted an impressive investigation of the relationships between phonemes and graphemes in over 17,000 different words, thus exceeding by far Moore's earlier study of 3,000 words. The two-phase study[1] also was designed to provide an analysis of the structure of American-English orthography in general. In Phase I, the orthography was found to be "a far more consistent reflection of spoken language than had been assumed, particularly when the several components of the phonology (sound system) underlying the orthography are examined." Granting that phonemes have more than one way of being spelled, Hodges and Rudorf, however, point out that "a remarkable amount of consistency is found" when positions of phonemes in syllables and in monosyllabic words and the amount of stress given to syllables are considered.

In Phase II, a second computer program called for "predicting" the spelling of the sample of 17,000 different words. The process in Phase II was as follows:

> For each phoneme a set of rules (an algorithm) was constructed which indicated which spelling of that phoneme should be used under various conditions of position, stress, and environment. The algorithm was then utilized to process the 17,000 words from their phonemicization to their graphemic representation (19).

This computer process showed that of the 17,000 words 49 per cent were spelled correctly, 37.2 per cent were spelled with only one error, 11.4 per cent with two errors, and 2.3 per cent with three or more errors. As interpreted by the researchers, the results strengthened "the phonological approach to spelling," since "many of . . . (the) errors may not constitute a serious spelling problem. Many of them could be obviated with the mastery of simple morphological rules." Suggestions, therefore, by Hodges and Rudorf are that "regularities exist in the relationship between phonological elements in the oral language and their graphemic representations . . . and that a pedagogical method based upon oral-aural cues to spelling may well prove to be more efficient and powerful than present methods which rely primarily upon visual and hand learning approaches." Thus, results of the two linguistic analyses by Hanna and his students

---

1 A 1,500-page report of the study, USOE sponsored Project No. 1991, has been published by the United States Government Printing Office.

showed certain consistencies in sound-to-letter relationships. From such results, the researchers felt that more emphasis on instruction of phonetic relationships may be more valuable than the usual "drill" method. In stressing greater applica- cation of sound-to-letter patterns in spelling, the Stanford group has attempted to further this particular point of view through much writing and research. Nevertheless, they have insisted that a balanced perspective toward the total spelling program must be maintained. With their efforts directed primarily to one approach, mistaken impressions that they believe spelling depends *wholly* on oral-aural means must be guarded against. In 1959, Hanna and Hanna (12) wrote:

> While we know that the brain acts as a unit, we can still educate the brain for spelling through first emphasizing one type of input and imagery, and then stressing another type. Each of the types—visual, oral-aural, and haptical— must be systematically planned and learned in the spelling program. And as each type of imagery is learned, it must be systematically joined and coordi- nated with the other types of imagery so that the net result is a reinforcement by each of the other.

Spelling instruction stressing a greater combination of approaches may prove that what have been held to be conflicting points of view can become comple- mentary in a concerted program. Schonell (36) believes that spelling instruction should be based on grouping words with auditory and visual similarities and emphasizing the necessary articulatory and graphic responses with the utilitarian worth of the words being learned. Investigating the spelling achievement of Scottish children, most of whom were being taught to spell with the Schonell speller, Personke (32) found that the Scottish sample (ages 7, 11, and 14) ranged from 18 months to 28 months above the American norms on the Metro- politan Spelling Test (1947 edition; Primary II Battery, Forms; Intermediate Battery, Form V; and the Advanced Battery, Form V).

Discussion

There is always the danger of assuming an "all-or-none" or "either-or" stance, as the reader may well realize, on any complex issue involving many variables and alternatives. In the past, many writers have tended to write in dichotomous terms on the question of instruction in spelling generalizations. Definitive writ- ings by spelling authorities have argued for balanced spelling programs which incorporate a variety of approaches, including phonological methods. However, one main source of confusion in the spelling controversy has been basic disagree- ment over which instructional approach predominates over others in interpreta- tions of what constitutes "balanced" spelling programs. In reading discussions of spelling programs, one must try to perceive how writers rank alternative ap- proaches in their instructional strategies. For example, is the use of sound-to- letter generalizations to be considered the predominant approach in spelling programs or should generalizations be merely aids supplementary to "drill" ap- proaches? Although all authorities call for "balanced" spelling programs, writers have emphasized favored approaches and sought deemphasis of other ap- proaches. Readers, therefore, must guard against drawing "either-or" conclu- sions themselves by reading more than what writers intend. Researchers pursuing certain aspects of their total spelling programs in depth, such as the Stanford group at this time, must continue to make clear to readers how their present emphases relate to their conceptual views of total spelling programs. Accordingly, the Stanford group has recently presented a number of definitive statements, *e.g.,* (13) (14) (18).

At this time, the most relevant issues to be clarified appear to be as follows: (a) The question as to why the Stanford group inferred so much greater regularity of sound-letter relationship than did Horn (22) from a linguistic study of his own raises at least two issues. First, are the bases used to establish the degree of regularity debatable? Second, should spelling instruction be based upon some assumed or controversial degree of regularity? (b) In a phonologically oriented spelling program, how can we effectively teach pupils the many phoneme-grapheme relationships they would require for a comprehensive command of English-American spelling? (c) How should we relate such instruction to other proven methods? (d) Would such instruction significantly improve the learner's spelling ability? Hodges and Rudorf rightly called for research to answer such methodological and evaluative questions. The burden of proof for pedagogical applications, therefore, rests on the shoulders of advocates. Yet the classroom results may still be similar to earlier studies on the question of instruction in spelling rules, for the preponderance of studies appear to question the effectiveness of strict phonetic approaches. The degree of benefits and the extent of limitations obtained through predominant reliance on spelling generalization in spelling programs have yet to be established by empirical research on such application. Significant results supporting the use of a few rules provides little proof that a major emphasis on rules in spelling would be successful. However, attention should be given the fact that broad formulations of consistently valid generalizations were not feasible by conventional means prior to the computerized investigation of a 17,000 word corpus at Stanford. Previous research findings on the value of generalizations in spelling instruction may be of less value if the studies utilized generalizations now found to be invalid.

Certainly new research efforts on the issue of spelling generalizations need to be better designed and conducted. Hypotheses need to be stated in the clearest possible terms and tested by rigorous statistical analyses. The need for an improvement in research design and analysis can be seen in many studies that merely report the numbers of spelling errors and per cent of words spelled correctly without any statistical test of significance applied to differences found in results. Proof or disproof of a hypothesis does not depend merely on higher or lower spelling scores secured for an experimental group of subjects as compared to a control group. The differences in scores may not be statistically significant, *i.e.,* the difference may have a high probability of occurring by chance alone. Also, design defects involving pupil or teacher variables may invalidate test results.

Interestingly, there are still those in education who seek simple answers to complex questions. Sometimes the questions are stated so only simple answers seem adequate or no reasonable answer can be given. A teacher may be classed with the "drill" group of research subjects on the basis of her speller which deemphasizes phonetic relationships (actually, all spelling textbooks provide for some instruction in sound-to-letter relationships), but the teacher may be supplying her own supplementary phonics instruction when she teaches spelling. Any further research on teaching methods in spelling should carefully consider the variables dealing with the teacher, her actual methods of instruction, and the pupil's background and spelling needs. As an example, the pupil's vernacular speech would seem that in writing with phonetic rules the pupil will spell as *he* pronounces.

Another matter that has tended to contribute to educators' finding simple answers to complex concerns has been the manner in which researchers have generalized conclusions from their research results. Quite often, researchers have overstated their cases; almost all have generalized their conclusions beyond their unrandomized samples of classrooms. For example, would results for two classes of tenth graders in Kalamazoo be the same in the majority of tenth-grade classes in the U.S.A.? Would such results be the same in other grades, such as grades 2 and 3? Further research should have provisions for the careful consideration of the proper randomization of samples. Unless such provisions are made, any claim by researchers in generalizing conclusions beyond the specific sample tested are highly questionable and scientifically unsound.

Interpretation and discussion of results should be stated in unequivocal and objective terms. Inferences made beyond the limitations of results, such as lack of randomization and direct investigation of certain concerns, have been misread unless writers add more definite precautionary notes or do not venture too boldly into inferences beyond the scope of their study. The conclusions of Gates and Chase's (9) study generalizing from a sample of deaf children did not lend support to phonetic approaches, but did support others. Nevertheless, the study has been cited quite often as support for phonetic emphases in the teaching of spelling due to the report's last seven lines which commented on Watson's (38) study. School personnel responsible for the choice and purchase of spellers may want to give more deliberate attention to the theoretical nature of available spellers under consideration and the references cited to support the authors' points of view.

The controversy of phonics versus "looksay" in reading methods has been largely demolished by the vast majority of educators and parents who realize that the controversy is a false dichotomy, *i.e.*, both methods and others together help provide the most effective reading program for children. Likewise, in the controversy between spelling rules or no spelling rules, the false dichotomy should be apparent. A review of the more carefully written works on the issue show that the question of spelling generalization may be maturing into one of degree and points to the need to fully investigate classroom applications before curriculum materials and methods are recommended for widespread use.

REFERENCES

1. Aaron, Ira E., "The Relationship of Audio and Visual Discrimination to Spelling Ability," unpublished doctoral dissertation, University of Minnesota, 1954.

2. Archer, C. P., "Shall We Teach Spelling by Rule?" *Elementary English,* 7 (March, 1930), 61–63.

3. Archer, C. P., *Transfer of Training in Spelling.* University of Iowa, Studies in Education, Volume 5, No. 5, 1930.

4. Carroll, H. A., *Generalization of Bright and Dull Children.* Contributions to Education, No. 439. New York: Bureau of Publications, Teachers College, Columbia University, 1930.

5. Clymer, Theodore, "The Utility of Phonic Generalization in the Primary Grades," *The Reading Teacher,* 16 (January, 1963), 252–258.

6. Cook, W. A., "Shall We Teach Spelling by Rules?" *Journal of Educa-*

tional Psychology, 3 (June, 1912), 316–325.

7. Flesch, Rudolf, *Why Johnny Can't Read.* New York: Harper, 1955.

8. Gates, Arthur, *Generalization and Transfer in Spelling.* New York: Bureau of Publications, Teachers College, Columbia University, 1935.

9. Gates, A. I. and E. H. Chase, "Methods and Theories of Learning to Spell Tested by Studies of Deaf Children," *Journal of Educational Psychology,* 17 (May, 1926), 289–300.

10. Hahn, William P., "Phonics: A Boon to Spelling?" *Elementary School Journal,* 64 (April, 1964), 383–386.

11. Hahn, William P., "Comparative Efficiency of the Teaching of Spelling by the Column and Contextual Methods," unpublished doctoral dissertation, University of Pittsburgh, 1960.

12. Hanna, Jean S. and Paul R. Hanna, "Spelling as a School Subject: A Brief History," *National Elementary Principal,* 38 (May, 1959), 8–23.

13. Hanna, Paul R. and Jean S. Hanna, "Applications of Linguistics and Psychological Cues to the Spelling Course of Study," *Elementary English,* 42 (November, 1965), 753–759.

14. Hanna, Paul R. and Jean S. Hanna, "The Teaching of Spelling." *National Elementary Principal,* 45 (November, 1965), 19–28.

15. Hanna, Paul R. and Jean S. Hanna, "Spelling Today," *The Instructor,* 70 (November, 1960), 6, 106.

16. Hanna, Paul R. and Richard E. Hodges, "Spelling and Communications Theory: A Model and an Annotated Bibliography," *Elementary English,* 40 (May, 1963), 484–506.

17. Hanna, Paul R., and J. T. Moore, "Spelling—from Spoken Word to Written Symbol," *Elementary School Journal,* 53 (February, 1953), 329–337.

18. Hodges, Richard E., "The Psychological Bases of Spelling," *Elementary English,* 42 (October, 1965), 629–635.

19. Hodges, R. E., and E. H. Rudorf, "Searching Linguistics for Cues for the Teaching of Spelling," *Elementary English,* 42 (May, 1965), 527–533.

20. Horn, Ernest, *Teaching Spelling.* American Educational Research Association, Department of Classroom Teachers Research Pamphlet. Washington, D.C.: National Education Association, 1963.

21. Horn, Ernest, "Spelling," *Encyclopedia of Educational Research,* 3rd edition. C. W. Harris (Ed.). New York: Macmillan Company, 1960, 1337–1354.

22. Horn, Ernest, "Phonetics and Spelling," *Elementary School Journal,* 57 (May, 1957), 424–432.

23. Horn, Ernest, "Phonics and Spelling," *Journal of Education,* 136 (May, 1954), 233–235, 246.

24. Horn, Ernest, "A Source of Confusion in Spelling," *Journal of Educational Research,* 19 (January, 1929), 47–55.

25. Horn, Ernest, "Principles of Methods in Teaching Spelling as Derived from Scientific Investigation." 18th Yearbook, NSSE, Part II, Bloomington, Illinois: Public School Publishing Company, February, 1919, pp. 52–77.

26. Horn, Ernest and E. J. Ashbaugh, "The Necessity of Teaching Derived Forms in Spelling." *Journal of Educational Psychology,* 10 (March, 1919), 143–151.

27. Horn, T. D., "Research in Spelling," *Elementary English,* 37 (March, 1960), 174–177.

28. Jackson, J., "The Influence of Word Analysis upon Spelling Attainment," *Journal of Educational Research,* 47 (October, 1953), 106–115.

29. King, Luella M., *Learning and Applying Spelling Rules in Grades Three to Eight*. Contributions to Education, No. 517. New York: Bureau of Publications, Teachers College, Columbia University, 1932.

30. Lester, John A., "Delimitation of the Spelling Problem," *English Journal*, 6 (June, 1917), 402–411.

31. O'Reilly, Robert, "Phonics and Spelling," *Elementary English*, 42 (February, 1965), 126–127, 210.

32. Personke, Carl, "A Comparison of the Spelling Achievement of Groups of Scottish and American Children," unpublished doctoral dissertation, The University of Michigan, 1963.

33. Petty, Walter, "Research Critiques— II" *Elementary English*, 42 (May, 1965), 584–587.

34. Russell, David H., *Characteristics of Good and Poor Spellers*. New York: Bureau of Publications, Teachers College, Columbia University, 1937.

35. Sartorius, Ira C., *Generalization in Spelling*. Contributions to Education, No. 472. New York: Bureau of Publications, Teachers College, Columbia University, 1931.

36. Schonell, Fred, *Backwardness in the Basic Subjects*. London: Oliver and Boyd, 1942.

37. Turner, E. A., "Rules Versus Drill in Teaching Spelling," *Journal of Educational Psychology*, 3 (October, 1912), 460–461.

38. Watson, Alice E., "Experimental Studies in the Psychology and Pedagogy of Spelling," unpublished doctoral dissertation, Teachers College, Columbia University, 1926.

---

42   The Elements of Spelling Ability

BARBARA   HUNT

ALICE   HADSELL

JON   HANNUM

HARRY   W.   JOHNSON

Unfortunately, we who write English in the twentieth century are caught in a squeeze between tremendous pressure for conformity in spelling, if we wish to be considered educated, and the non-phonetic nature of many of our words. It devolves upon our educational psychologists to show us how to walk the narrow line.

In a completely phonetic language, to be a perfect speller one need only learn the sounds for a small number of letters and letter combinations and a few rules for combining them. But in English, spelling ability depends on the ability to do that and on several other abilities as well. The present study was carried out to determine whether the abilities that make up spelling ability vary independently. If they do, spelling instruction should be differentiated, even among pupils at the same over-all level.

Previous workers in the field of spelling instruction seem to have identified four factors, besides general intelligence, that affect the ability to spell English words. These factors are:

Reprinted from *The Elementary School Journal*, Vol. 63 (March, 1963), pp. 342–350, by permission of The University of Chicago Press. Copyright 1963 by The University of Chicago.

The ability to spell words that are phonetic

The ability to spell words that involve roots, prefixes, suffixes, and the rules for combining them

The ability to look at a word and to reproduce it later and

The ability to spell the demons

Findings of researchers will be briefly reviewed in that order.

A doctoral dissertation by Aaron investigated "the relative contributions of nine auditory-visual discrimination measures" to the spelling ability of fourth-graders. It was found that "spelling of phonetic syllables was the largest contributor to the estimate of the spelling of non-phonetic words as well as those which were phonetic" (1: 1164–65). Aaron has interpreted this finding to mean that "phonetic skills may be important in the spelling of all types of words" (1: 1165).

In another study, conducted with high school and university students, it was found that "spelling ability at the high school and university level depends to a large extent upon the ability to handle phonetic associations" (2). Together, these studies certainly suggest that phonetic ability operates in spelling at all levels.

Aaron found that a second factor in predicting success in spelling was "visual analysis of words," otherwise referred to as "structural analysis." The three factors "important in predicting each of the five spelling measures were visual analysis of words, recognition of beginning and ending sounds in words, and spelling of phonetic syllables . . ." (1: 1164).

The "recognition of beginning and ending sounds in words" and the "spelling of phonetic syllables" are both part of the ability to spell phonetic words. But the first factor, "visual analysis," is a separate and distinct ability: the ability to spell roots, prefixes, and suffixes—whether or not they are phonetic—and combine them properly into English words.

"Visual perception, visual discrimination and visual memory" constitute a third factor or group of factors that have been identified, for they "have been found to be highly related to spelling ability" (3). In an article on the relative influence of visual and auditory factors on spelling ability Hartmann concluded that spelling ability "does not seem to be closely related to the *special* [ability] involved in reproducing tachistoscopically-exposed stimuli of a meaningful nature. . ." (4).

Spelling demons are also frequently mentioned in discussions of spelling problems. The English language, with its complex history of change and development, has many words that are not spelled phonetically. One advocate of a simplified method of spelling has pointed out that English spelling is inefficient because it tries to show the history of the word and the present pronunciation of the word at the same time (5). The result is that our language is replete with words affectionately called "spelling demons."

Certainly, the four factors discussed here can be shown to be interrelated in their influence on the ability to spell. In fact, cogent arguments can be presented to prove that each one is influenced by all the others.

The purpose of the present study, however, is to show that the interrelations are not very great and that two people with the same total spelling score may have problems of an entirely different sort. The problem of the present study was to determine whether, among poor spellers in English, the four factors listed earlier vary independently.

The hypothesis actually tested was whether the scores of the poor spellers would vary independently on items devised to tap the four types of abilities. Consequently, the proof of the hypothesis rested to some extent on the validity and the reliability of the instrument developed to test it. But the face validities of the four sections of the test seemed so palpably high that validity has not been a matter of serious concern, and the reliability of the test is checked by the very design of the experiment.

To render the hypothesis amenable to statistical testing, it was recast as two hypotheses:

Hypothesis A—Intercorrelations among the four sections of the test would be of no statistical significance.

Hypothesis B—Simple, two-factor analysis of variance would yield a significantly high test-section by individual interaction variance.

The testing of these hypotheses was undertaken as a research project for a master's thesis in psychology (6).

The test items and the accompanying instructions developed to test the hypothesis of this study were designed with a view to producing the most sensitive possible experimental plan. The experimental instrument was a collection of one hundred items, which were divided into four sections of twenty-five items each. Each of the four sections was to measure one of the four types of abilities. So far as possible, we chose items that about 50 per cent of the subjects could pass. To arrive at this kind of test and to refine and polish the instructions to be used with each of the four sections, a pre-pilot form of each section was given to subjects randomly selected from a college course in remedial English, and a pilot form of each section was given to other randomly selected subjects from the same group. The test in final form was given to the remaining available subjects as the experiment proper.

A detailed description of the preparation of the test follows.

Phonetic Ability

To check knowledge of phonetic principles, nonsense words of one and two syllables were used. The words were dictated carefully, and to respond correctly, the subject had to employ the following rules:

In a word or accented syllable made up of a consonant, a vowel, and a consonant, the vowel usually takes the short sound, as, for example, in *baf, sug.*

In a word or accented syllable made up of a consonant, two vowels, and a consonant, the vowels usually take the long sound of the first one, as, for example, in *loat, maib.*

In a word or accented syllable made up of a consonant, a vowel, a consonant, and a final *e,* the first vowel takes its long sound, and the *e* is silent, as, for example, in *lote, mabe.*

A consonant in the middle of a two-syllable word must be doubled, ordinarily, if the first vowel is to be short, as, for example, in *diffet, dattal.*

A consonant(s) may be substituted for the initial consonant(s) in a familiar word, very often, to form a new word; for example, given the spelling of *game,* to spell *trame, stame.*

As we explained earlier, it was desirable to have items that about 50 per cent of the subjects could answer correctly. With this in mind, a pre-pilot test was given to four students. Items that were answered correctly by two or three subjects were given as a pilot test to fifteen students. Of these items, the twenty-five that were nearest to being answered correctly by 50 per cent of the subjects on the second trial comprised the final form of the section on phonetic ability.

Structural Analysis

The purpose of the second part of the test was to sample ability to spell words that involved common roots, prefixes, suffixes, and knowledge of the rules for combining them. To avoid the influence of familiarity with real words, actual prefixes and suffixes were to be added to nonsense root words.

For example, the students were told, *"G-a-m* spells *gam."* They were then asked to write words such as *pregam* and *nongam.* Nonsense words were also devised to check knowledge of whether a consonant is doubled when a suffix is added. The students were to write such words as *gams, gammed, bames,* and *bamed,* as they were pronounced.

A pre-pilot test was given to four students. The words that were spelled correctly by two or three subjects were selected for the pilot test, which was given to fifteen students. The twenty-five words nearest to being spelled correctly by exactly 50 per cent of the subjects on the pilot run were selected to compose the final section on structural analysis.

Visual Memory

The section to evaluate visual memory was intended to measure ability to look at a word and then spell it correctly from memory.

Nonsense words were used in this section of the test so that actual knowledge of words might not influence the scores. The words were nonsense words selected from Stevens' list of nonsense words of low meaning value and words constructed from such nonsense words (7).

In preparing the cards for administration of this section of the test, nonsense words of three, four, five, and six letters were printed in lower-case manuscript letters that varied from 1½ to 2 inches in height, on white cardboard cards 7¾ inches by 11½ inches; nonsense words of seven or more letters were printed in lower-case manuscript letters that varied from 1½ inches to 2 inches in height, on white cardboard cards, 7 inches by 22 inches.

The words used were so selected that no vowel appeared more than once in a given item, and the items were constructed according to the patterns in Table I. The ultimate aim in constructing this section was to draw up a list of twenty-five nonsense words that varied in length in some such manner as that described in Table II. To make the experimental design as sensitive as possible, it was desirable that the average score on this section be about 50 per cent correct and, thus, that the average item be correctly answered by 50 per cent of the subjects.

Each word, regardless of the number of letters in the nonsense word, was to be shown to the students for three seconds. After each card was exposed, the students were to be asked to reproduce what they had just seen.

A pre-pilot test, made up of fifteen words that varied from three to fifteen letters in length, was given to ten students. Results showed that words of fifteen letters were too difficult. So these words were discarded; a few other changes

TABLE I   *Patterns of Nonsense Words to Test Visual Memory*

Length of Word in Number of Letters	Pattern of Word*
3	C-V-C
4	C-V-C-C
	or C-C-V-C
	or V-C-C-V
5	C-V-C-C-V
6	C-V-C-C-V-C
7	C-V-C-C-V-C-C
	or C-C-V-C-C-V-C
8	V-C-C-V-C-C-V-C
	or C-V-C-C-V-C-C-V
	or C-V-C-C-V-C-V-C
9	C-V-C-C-V-C-C-V-C
12	C-V-C-C-V-C-C-V-C-C-V-C
15	C-V-C-C-V-C-C-V-C-C-V-C-C-V-C

* In the above patterns, *C* stands for *Consonant* and *V* stands for *Vowel*. Thus, *C-V-C* would indicate a word composed of a consonant, a vowel, and a consonant, such as *feg*.

TABLE II   *Hypothetical Distribution of Word Lengths for Visual Memory Test*

Length of Words in Number of Letters	Number of Words of That Length
15	1
12	2
9	3
8	3
7	4
6	5
5	4
4	2
3	1
Total	25

were also made to refine the location of the 50 per cent level of difficulty. A pilot test, using fifteen students, was then conducted with the revised instrument, and the twenty-five words closest to the 50 per cent level of difficulty on this second trial were retained for the final form of the test.

Spelling Demons

The spelling demons used in this test were selected from three lists, which were themselves compilations from other studies. Only those words that appeared in all three of the following lists by Edna L. Furness and Gertrude A. Boyd were included: "231 Real Spelling Demons for High School Students," "335 Real Spelling Demons for College Students," and "Ninety-eight Spelling Demons for High School and College Students" (8, 9, 10). This method of selection yielded a list of eighty-seven demons.

A pre-pilot test consisting of those eighty-seven words was given to ten students. The words were dictated, given in a sentence, and dictated again. The students were asked to write the words in the ordinary fashion of spelling tests.

Only sixty-eight of the eighty-seven words given in the pre-pilot test were found to be usable for the pilot test. The pilot test was given to ten other students, and from this test the twenty-five words that fell closest to the 50 per cent level were selected to compose the final section on spelling demons.

Since the experimental design was one that would be most sensitive if about half of the subjects could answer each item correctly, subjects were sought at the level of ability likely to provide such ideal conditions. The subjects used were University of Omaha Freshmen who were taking English 109 in the spring semester of 1961.

At the University of Omaha, students who fail to pass the entrance examination in English (11) at a sufficiently high level are required to take English 109. They are, on the average, very poor spellers. As noted earlier, some of these students were used as subjects for the pre-pilot run and the pilot run of the test. The remaining twenty students, all men, were used for the experiment proper.

The experimental design of the present study was essentially very simple. The four sections of the test in its final form were given to the twenty subjects, and the results were analyzed.

The twenty-five items in each section of the test were divided into subtests of five items each. Thus, a subject could get a score of from zero to five correct on each subtest, and his score for the section would be the sum of five such subtest scores. The highest possible score on all four sections of the test was 100.

Before the statistical analysis was begun, Bartlett's check was run to determine whether the data would lend themselves to analysis of variance without a correction (12). A B' of 95.78 indicated that variance among the cells was not great enough to be significant at the .05 level, since the critical value was 101.88. A correction was not deemed necessary.

To determine whether the individual's test scores on the four sections varied independently, intercorrelations of the four sections were run. To determine whether the scores varied to a significant extent, an individual by test-section interaction variance was computed.

The results were very clear-cut. Regarding the independence of the scores on the four sections, the intercorrelations among the sections varied from .29 to −.14, as shown in Table III. Since a correlation coefficient of .444 would have been necessary for significance at even the .05 level, these results certainly indicated that the four sections were measures of four relatively independent types of ability.

TABLE III   *Intercorrelations Among Sections of the Spelling Test*

Test	Memory Visual	Structural Analysis	Phonetic Ability
Demons	.29	−.14	−.10
Visual Memory		.11	.28
Structural Analysis			.23

Thus, Hypothesis A, a null hypothesis, may be accepted without serious risk. It may be said that the abilities measured by the four sections are unrelated. To this extent, the theory represented by Hypotheses A and B is substantiated.

But this result could be achieved if the scores on the various sections of the test were unrelated simply because they were random and meaningless. We can check this possibility of complete randomness, because among completely random scores all variations would be random variations from section to section, random variations from person to person, or random interaction variations, that is, variations from person to person in the patterns of the scores on the sections of the test. Analysis of variance makes it possible to separate these three kinds of variations and to see whether there are significant variations of the third kind. Hence we turn to Hypothesis B.

The analysis of variance performed to test Hypothesis B is reported in Table IV. The crucial result, as suggested earlier, is the F value of 1.58 for the interaction variance. This F value is significant at the .01 level. The other F values are all comfortably below the .05 level of significance. This result suggests that our subjects and our test items were reasonably well chosen.

TABLE IV   *Analysis of Variance of Spelling-Test Scores*

Source	df	msq	F
Among Subtests	3	14.67	8.48
Among Subjects	19	3.95	2.28
Interaction	57	2.73	1.58
Within Blocks	320	1.73	

Hypothesis B, then, another null hypothesis, may be rejected, and our theory is borne out again. The results have indicated, at a high level of significance, that if all our subjects were exactly equal in total spelling ability, and all the sections of the test were exactly equal in difficulty, there would still be significant variations among the section scores simply because the person with a high score on one section of the test would have a low score on another, and these differences would represent real differences in ability.

The results clearly indicate that the four sections of the test have diagnostic value and should be put to practical use. The person with a spelling deficiency should be given a differential spelling test, and then appropriate corrective training should be applied.

Apparently it can safely be said that four of the elements involved in spelling ability vary to a large extent independently of one another. Much now remains to be done.

This study should be replicated at various academic levels. Presumably, the four factors considered here operate among poor spellers at every academic level. But this conclusion cannot be taken for granted.

The existence of other significant factors should be checked. A multiple correlation or similar technique should be employed to determine how much of spelling ability is accounted for by the elements already identified. The experimental work for such a study has been completed by one of the writers and will be reported as a master's thesis.

Presumably specific spelling training, such as training in phonics, is appropriate for only one of the four types of deficiency. But the same specific spelling training should be applied to subjects with different profiles to see whether those with low scores on a single section of the test used here respond especially to training designed to foster the ability tapped by that section and whether differential instruction so selected will improve spelling ability as a whole.

Methods for developing each of the four types of ability need to be worked out and evaluated. Renshaw's technique (13) should be compared with Fernald's technique (14) for the development of visual memory. Study of Pollock and Baker's *The University Spelling Book* (15) and use of the Spelling Laboratory (16) should be evaluated in terms of their effect on the ability to spell phonetically and the ability to spell with roots, prefixes, and suffixes.

For the evaluation of methods of teaching spelling demons, Johnson (17) suggested a series of studies using Horn's method (18) as a universally recognized yardstick by which to evaluate any method suggested. He urged a simple, parallel-group design. His application of that approach, which yielded inconclusive results with a very promising new technique, should be replicated until some conclusion can be reached.

Clearly, before theory can move forward much further, new research will need to be done. But the problem now seems to be laid open, and fruitful directions for experimentation lie all about us.

Practice, on the other hand, can now range ahead of theory. The possible hypotheses implied here are so patently tenable that the teacher, it seems certain, can quite safely assume that they are sound. Furthermore, instruction of the kinds suggested is worth a try: it could hardly do much harm. Nothing should be left undone that might improve instruction in spelling in the English language.

REFERENCES

1. Ira A. Aaron. "The Relationship of Auditory-visual Discrimination to Spelling Ability." Doctoral dissertation, University of Minnesota; summarized in *Dissertation Abstracts*. Ann Arbor, Michigan: University Microfilms, 1954.

2. Jack Holmes. "A Substrata Analysis of Spelling Ability for Elements of Auditory Images," *Journal of Experimental Education*, XXII (June, 1954), 347.

3. Chester W. Harris (editor). *Encyclopedia of Educational Research*, third edition, p. 1348. New York: Macmillan Company, 1960.

4. George W. Hartmann. "The Relative Influence of Visual and Auditory Factors in Spelling Ability," *Journal of Educational Psychology*, XXII (December, 1931), 691.

5. Ralph D. Owen. "Those Spelling Demons—They Make the Children Shrique," *Illinois Education*, XL (January, 1952), 165.

6. Jon Hannum. "An Analysis of the Differential Test of Spelling Ability." Unpublished master's thesis, Omaha University, 1961.

7. Stanley Smith Stevens. *Handbook of Experimental Psychology*. New York: John Wiley and Sons, 1951.

8. Edna L. Furness and Gertrude A. Boyd. "231 Real Spelling Demons for High School Students," *English Journal*, LXVII (May, 1958), 267–70.

9. Edna L. Furness and Gertrude A. Boyd. "335 Real Spelling Demons for College Students," *College English*, XX (March, 1959), 292–95.

10. Edna L. Furness and Gertrude A. Boyd. "Ninety-eight Spelling Demons for High School and College Students," *Educational Administration and Supervision*, XLIV (November, 1958), 353–56.

11. G. S. Wykoff, J. H. McKee, and H. H. Remmers. *The New Purdue Placement Test in English*. Boston: Houghton Mifflin Company, 1955.

12. M. S. Bartlett. "Some Examples of Statistical Methods of Research in Agricultural and Applied Biology," *Journal of the Royal Statistical Society: Supplement*, IV (1937), 137–70.

13. Samuel Renshaw. "The Visual Perception and Reproduction of Forms by Tachistoscopic Methods," *Journal of Psychology,* XX (October, 1945), 217–32.

14. Grace M. Fernald. *Remedial Techniques in Basic School Subjects,* pp. 181–210. New York: McGraw-Hill Book Company, 1943.

15. Thomas Pollock and William Baker. *The University Spelling Book.* Englewood Cliffs, New Jersey: Prentice-Hall, Inc., 1955.

16. Don H. Parker and Frederic R. Walker. *Spelling Laboratory IIa.* Chicago: Science Research Associates, 1960.

17. Harry W. Johnson. "A Method for Teaching the Spelling of Words Evaluated, I: By Truncation." Unpublished study, University of Minnesota, 1951.

18. Ernest Horn. *Principles of Method in Teaching Spelling as Derived from Scientific Investigation,* pp. 52–77. Eighteenth Yearbook of the National Society for the Study of Education. Edited by Guy M. Whipple. Bloomington, Illinois: Public School Publishing Company, 1919.

---

43   The Situational Choice and the Spelling Program

CARL PERSONKE

ALBERT H. YEE

In a 1957 paper critical of one-sided phonetic spelling methods, Ernest Horn stated an implied need for a theoretical model of spelling to organize present evidence and to provide some frame of reference for further research. As Horn wrote:

> Attempts to account for a pupil's choice of the spelling of an unlearned word at a given time are largely conjecture. Why did one pupil in attempting to spell *awful* write *offul,* while others wrote *awfull, offel,* or *offle?* There must have been some influence or influences that, if known, would explain why these particular spellings of the sounds were written. Presumably, any of the laws of association may operate in a given attempt to spell and sometimes in combination. Both common sense and the evidence from research suggest that when a number of reasonable choices are available, responses are uncertain (1).

In each of the situations described by Horn, the speller had a choice of several alternate options. Selection of the most effective option determined whether the word was spelled correctly or incorrectly.

In the March 1966 issue of *Elementary English,* the writers presented a theoretical model of spelling behavior which offered in fact five options or channels of spelling behavior. It was proposed that these channels: (a) represented the totality of possible spelling behavior; (b) were complementary in nature; and (c) suggested the need for a new aspect of spelling behavior, the situational

---

From *Elementary English,* Vol. 45 (1968), pp. 32–37, 40. Reprinted with permission of the National Council of Teachers of English and Carl Personke and Albert H. Yee.

THEORETICAL MODEL OF SPELLING BEHAVIOR

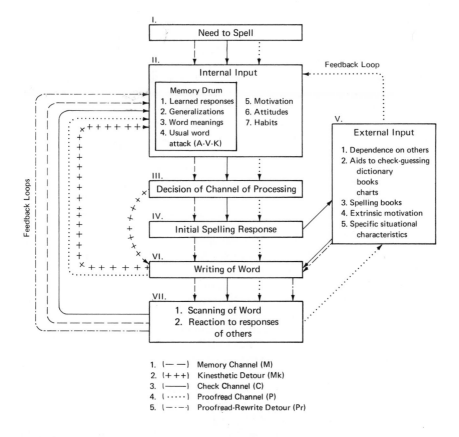

1. (— —) Memory Channel (M)
2. (+ + +) Kinesthetic Detour (Mk)
3. (———) Check Channel (C)
4. (·····) Proofread Channel (P)
5. (— · —) Proofread-Rewrite Detour (Pr)

choice. It was further suggested that the model demonstrated that any one-sided spelling program would leave the speller unprepared for the total of possible spelling situations he might face.

The reader is referred to the original article (4) for a description of the model and the rationale for the proposed multi-channel approach. In this paper, attention is turned toward interpretation of the model with emphasis on the complementarity of the channels and the situational choice.

Operation of the Model

In the model, the writers propose five distinct yet complementary channels of spelling behavior. In each case the behavior began with a felt need, that is, a desire to spell a word. Based on a systems processing approach, the model then took the speller through all or part of seven phases or operations. The number and order of these operations is a function of the channel chosen. Ultimately all channels provide for feedback into the memory drum, an essential component of the system.

The memory channel (M) is the process of extracting learned words or generalizations from the memory drum and using these to produce a written response. The kinesthetic bypass (Mk) of this channel occurs when the spelling of a word is so well known that it can be written without an overt response. The remaining three channels require the use of an external input—a dictionary, spelling book, or perhaps another person. The checking channel (C) occurs when the speller refers to the external input prior to a written response. When the speller checks on a written response through use of an external input, he is using the proofread (P) channel. If the check proves that his initial response was incorrect, he must then rewrite the word correctly. This is the proofread-rewrite detour (Pr).

The operation of the theoretical system will perhaps be better understood by describing how spellers might perform in several spelling situations. In contrast to the previous article describing the system of various processes as if they were discrete and separate entities, the illustrations here will be more realistic by focusing upon the speller and the means by which he processes his spelling needs.

Suppose a pre-schooler faces his first need to spell. The child draws a picture of a cat and wants to label it *cat*. A quick search of his internal input yields nothing but the meaning of the word. He may decide to try spelling the word with letters he has seen in his story books, and he makes an initial response of something like *a-b-c*. Satisfied with what he has written, he reinforces himself in this response. This is an example of selection of a channel of behavior, in this case (M), which proved to be ineffective.

Suppose the same child runs to show his mother what he has written. He seeks her approval and observes her behavior intently as she scans the word. When she tells him that he has misspelled the word, he may react to her behavior by asking for the correct spelling. Seeing the child's interest and need, the mother will more than likely provide the correct spelling and thereby act as an external input. Thus, the child uses the proofread-rewrite channel (Pr) and is reinforced both by actually spelling *cat* correctly and by the satisfactory use of his mother as an external input. The child begins to "learn" how to spell. The content of his memory drum may be said to increase by one and he begins to learn to select appropriate channels of processing his spelling needs. It should be observed that although the first instance was described as use of the (M) channel and the second described his use of the (Pr) channel, the two were identical until the child reacted to his mother's scanning behavior (Phase VII).

Suppose a child has already faced situations when he was unable to produce the satisfactory response by himself but had discovered that Mother could help him. His course of action in subsequent spelling situations may be to turn to his mother or some other person with spelling information for all of his spelling needs. Those previous experiences may cause the child to rely less on his internal input than external input when faced with spelling needs. His initial response becomes turning to another person for the satisfactory spelling response. It can be said that the child's spelling behavior has become programmed for the checking channel of processing spelling needs (C). The child's tendency to utilize the (C) channel exclusively in this illustration demonstrates the importance of helping the pupils realize the complementary nature of all channels and their own role in selecting appropriate channels.

As the child progresses through school, his store of internal inputs increases with learned words, generalizations for spelling unfamiliar words, attitudes toward spelling and toward the use of external input, and preferred methods of word attack. In school, the pupil's store of internal inputs becomes vastly more developed than had been the case at home. Since the pupil's internal input becomes structured along the lines of his teacher's teaching strategies, especially his elementary school teachers', the role of the teacher in helping develop the pupil's mature, independent spelling behavior must be considered second to none.

Suppose a teacher gives the child the word *fight* on a spelling test. Before the test, the word was presented by the teacher, who instructed the child to practice writing the word and to check his writing. The student would use the (C) channel or the (P) channel, or both, as he practices the word. The teacher's aim is that reinforcement through the feedback loop as the pupil practices will help him internalize the spelling of the word and, hopefully, its development as a meaningful unit of expression in the larger cognitive sense. During the spelling test, the child retrieves the internalized response from his memory drum and spells the word. After scanning the pupil's responses, the teacher reinforces the correct responses by approving his work in some form. This represents use of the (P) channel and is best represented by Thomas D. Horn's *corrected test* technique (2).

Suppose, however, that the child did not practice and check sufficiently prior to the test. During the test the word *fight* cannot be retrieved, because it has not been fixed in his memory drum. In this case he may revert to a learned generalization and spell the word as *fite*. After scanning the pupil's response, the teacher indicates to the pupil that the spelling is incorrect. The speller may then be instructed to refer to his original spelling list and rewrite the word, *i.e.,* to make use of the proofread-rewrite channel (Pr). It can be seen that the use of the corrected test results always involves the pupil in one of the proofreading channels. It can also be seen that since some feedback will take place on the first instance of the child writing the word, that if the teacher does not make use of the test for anything other than an evaluative technique, feedback other than for the incorrect response may never reach the memory drum; thus, the child will be reinforced in the use of an incorrect spelling of a word.

Since such proofreading behavior under testing conditions occurs more or less involuntarily, the following illustrates a spelling instance that is less structured and artificially imposed upon the pupil. Suppose the pupil desires to spell *fight* in a creative writing situation. If he has already stored the word in his memory drum, the process is simply to retrieve the needed information and respond accordingly. On the other hand, he may not be familiar with the spelling of the word and seek a solution through a learned spelling generalization. In that case, he may write *fite*. If the pupil receives no indication that his spelling is incorrect and is satisfied that he has made the correct spelling response, he will be reinforced in his response. However, he may choose to check his response before writing it, that is, to use the (C) channel, because he feels *fite* may not be correct. Or he may write *fite* with the intent to check his response when he has finished his writing. Such behavior would be voluntary proofreading. In any case, it is apparent that the processing channel chosen will depend upon the speller's past spelling experience, his store in his internal input, and the situational conditions and choices. An individual's motivation to spell properly and continually improve his spelling efficiency can be seen to be most influential in these processes.

All spelling behavior does not, of course, involve the correction of a misspelled word. An example might be a sixth grader who needs to spell the word *receive*. Suppose he does not have the word encoded in his memory drum but he does know the generalization "i before e except after c." Using the rule, the pupil spells *receive*. Satisfied with his spelling he is reinforced in this response. In this case, the (M) channel was selected to process the spelling need and proved to be effective.

It has already been noted that there is a very efficient channel of processing available to the mature speller, the kinesthetic bypass of the memory channel (Mk). This is the channel that the writer is using at this very moment. The words written here are so familiar to the writer that they can be spelled without conscious effort. It is not even necessary for some to see what they write as they spell; ask any teacher who can write on the chalkboard while facing her class!

The preceding discussion offers many examples of the complementarity of the spelling channels. Behavior in one situation and along one channel will ultimately affect behavior in another situation and perhaps along another channel. This complementary behavior is especially noted in three places: (a) in the early processes, until the Initial Response, all channels of behavior are identical; (b) the speller may switch from one channel to another during the scanning behavior (Phase VII); and (c) the feedback loop will affect and perhaps alter behavior in future situations.

Critique of the Channels

It has also been noted that the choice of channels for processing a spelling response will depend upon the specific situation in each case. That is, certain channels are more suitable for one situation than for another and the suitability will be determined by an evaluation of the strengths and weaknesses of each of the approaches. It should be noted that although some comparison on an absolute basis may be necessary to facilitate this critique, the complementarity of channels cannot be overemphasized.

It almost goes without saying that the quickest and most efficient type of spelling behavior lies in the (Mk) or kinesthetic bypass channel. The goal of each speller and each teacher of spelling should be to enlarge the individual's store of words that can be handled in this way. Fluency in writing is almost dependent on a large store of words which can be "written without thinking."

However, there are weaknesses in this approach which make it necessary for the speller to use alternate channels in specific situations. For one thing, the channel can be used only with previously stored words. If used with an unknown word, the speller must retrieve a response from his store which is an approximation of the correct response. Use of the response will tend to reinforce the possibility that it will be used again, whether it is correct or incorrect.

The (Mk) channel offers the same relative strengths and weaknesses, except that (M) will be somewhat less efficient in that this channel requires a conscious thought process. Thus, the added process of conscious thought consumes time and the speller's attention. Involving the speller's conscious attention to the spelling of a word produces a *conceptual break;* the writer momentarily thinks of the spelling of a word, rather than the message he is attempting to communicate.

The conceptual break becomes an even greater problem if the student processes his response through the checking (C) channel. When using this channel, the speller stops the writing process in order to get the correct response from among the external inputs. The break in attending to the message thus becomes more complete and extended than when the (M) channel is used. However, channel (C) can provide effective spelling behavior when the speller is confronted with an unfamiliar word. By using this channel the speller can be assured of a correct response when writing the word. This response alone will be entered into the internal input and reinforced by way of the feedback loop. It becomes apparent that the surest methods for learning a new word must be through use of the (C) channel. This is in effect what the speller does when he copies a word from his spelling book. However, it is doubtful that this is a good method when one is writing a thesis, a story, or even a personal letter.

The (P) channel, like the (C) channel, checks unfamiliar words. However, (P) has the disadvantage that while it offers a guaranteed reinforcement of a correct response, it also makes possible the reinforcement of an incorrect response. If the speller writes the word with the intent that it is correct, the feedback loop will immediately reinforce that response, even though it may be incorrect. Subsequent feedback of the correct response after turning to the external inputs will not necessarily eliminate the tendency to make an incorrect response in a similar situation. However, if the speller initially writes the word with the intent that it may not be correct, there will be little danger of undesirable feedback occurring. The subsequent feedback of a correct response after use of any of the available external inputs will help insure the possibility that the correct response will be used in a similar situation. At the same time, the (P) channel has the important advantage of avoiding at least the more complete and extended conceptual break of the (C) channel. Consideration of the strengths and weaknesses of each of these channels offers the possibility that the (C) channel might better be used for learning words in a spelling list whereas the (P) channel or (Pr) channel might better be used in a writing situation.

In any case, it is readily seen that while the (M) and (Mk) channels are desirable as goals of any spelling program, they are not suitable as means of learning to spell new words. For this purpose the (C), (P), or (Pr) channels are absolutely necessary. These are the learning channels of spelling behavior. Since it is almost inconceivable that anyone will ever learn by memory the spellings of all words he may need to write, these channels should always remain as a part of his total spelling behavior. As a matter of fact, simple observation leads one to believe that they may fall into disuse. The eventual atrophy in the use of these learning channels may be the result of failure to teach the situational choice in the spelling program.

Conclusions

Acceptance of the proposed spelling model offers many suggestions for teachers and researchers. Perhaps the most important suggestion and one which could ultimately affect all future research and development in methods for spelling is that any program which does not include learning in the use of all five channels of spelling behavior is going to leave the child ill equipped for all of his spelling needs.

The teacher must prepare the child in all facets of the internal and external inputs. Her spelling program must present the child with a large store of memorized words and generalizations; skills in auditory visual and kinesthetic attacks; good attitudes and habits in spelling; skills in using dictionaries, spellers, and other books in spelling; and study skills to facilitate the internalization of more words for future use. At the same time she must teach her pupils how to make the best situational choice in terms of available resources. There is ample evidence that present methods generally fall in one or more of these factors. As an example, a recent study indicated that only one spelling series in current use contained exercises in the skills of proofreading (3).

For the researcher, the model suggests that efforts to demonstrate that one approach is superior to another serve to establish dichotomies which do not really exist. Total spelling behavior demands that children be instructed in all approaches. Research might better be directed towards seeking the best means to teach each aspect of the total skills needed, the effects of changes of one channel of behavior on another channel, specifically in those Phases noted as crucial—the scanning and the feedback phases, and the best means to approach the only entirely new factor presented by this model, the situational choice.

REFERENCES

1. Horn, Ernest. "Phonetics and Spelling," *Elementary School Journal,* 57 (May, 1957) 424–432.

2. Horn, Thomas D. "The Effect of the Corrected Test on Learning to Spell," *Elementary School Journal,* 47 (1947) 277–85.

3. Oswalt, William W. "The Effects of Proofreading for Spelling Errors on Spelling Achievement of Fifth Grade Pupil," unpublished doctoral dissertation, Temple University, 1962.

4. Personke, Carl and Albert H. Yee. "A Model for the Analysis of Spelling Behavior," *Elementary English,* 43 (March, 1966) 278–284.

44   Spelling Errors and the Serial-Position Effect

ARTHUR R. JENSEN

The relative frequencies of spelling errors as a function of letter position have been examined for 7-, 9-, and 11-letter words selected at random from the Thorndike-Lorge word list. These were administered to 150 eighth-graders, 158 tenth-graders, and 89 junior college freshmen, respectively. The distribution of errors according to letter position was found to closely approximate the classical, skewed, bow-shaped, serial-position curve for errors generally found in serial rote learning. Other features in common between spelling and serial learning were discussed. It is suggested that a theory of serial learning and of the serial-position effect may be germane to the psychology of spelling.

Perusal of the research on spelling reveals that this subject has been traditionally dominated more by a linguistic than by a psychological orientation (Horn, 1960). Spelling difficulties have been analyzed largely in terms of phonetics, syllabication, parts of speech, and frequency of word usage. Spelling research is also predominantly characterized by a rather simple, unanalytical, correlational approach. Relationships have been found between measures of spelling ability and measures of reading, MA, IQ, achievement in various school subjects, and numerous other variables (Horn, 1960). Seldom, however, is spelling studied as a learning phenomenon or examined in terms of principles derived from the experimental psychology of learning. The investigator has conceived of what might be called a psychological theory of spelling based primarily on

From *Journal of Educational Psychology,* Vol. 53 (June, 1962), pp. 105–109. Copyright 1962 by the American Psychological Association. Reprinted with permission.
    This study was supported in part by a Faculty Research Grant from the University of California and in part by the National Science Foundation.

concepts in learning theory. The purpose of the present investigation is to examine only one aspect of the formulation, viz., the serial-position effect. The similarity of the distribution of spelling errors, when errors are plotted according to their position in the word, to the distribution of errors in serial rote learning—the so-called serial-position effect—has never before been noted. The correspondence between spelling and serial learning would seem to offer some clues concerning the nature of spelling errors.

When a series of words, nonsense syllables, symbols, or figures is learned, the errors made before mastery are distributed according to the position of each item in the series, producing the familiar, skewed, bow-shaped serial-position curve. Various theories have been proposed to account for this phenomenon (Jensen, 1962a; McGeoch and Irion, 1952, pp. 125–134). Since a word consists of a series of letters, and since spelling a word consists of putting each letter in its proper order, we might ask whether the serial position effect, which is generally manifested in every form of serial learning investigated in the laboratory, is also manifested in spelling. If so, the distribution of spelling errors should be similar to the serial-position curves produced by the serial learning of other materials. That is to say, errors should generally be most frequent in the middle of a word, with fewest errors at the beginning and end of the word. That spelling errors occur more frequently in the middle of words has probably been noted before, but apparently not with sufficient precision to reveal the more subtle features of the serial-position effect.

Variations in the shape of the serial-position curve are mainly a function of the number of items in the series. The curve for a short series is markedly skewed, with the largest proportion of errors occurring well past the middle of the series. As the series becomes longer, the serial-position curve becomes more symmetrical (McGeoch and Irion, 1952, p. 123). It would be interesting indeed if this were found to be the case also for the distribution of spelling errors in words of different lengths. The present investigation was addressed to this question.

Method

SPELLING

So that word selection would be unbiased with respect to the purpose of the present study, every 7-letter, 9-letter, and 11-letter word of the Thorndike-Lorge word list (1944, pp. 1–208) was typed on a slip of paper. The slips were thoroughly shuffled to eliminate alphabetical order, and then 75 eight-item word lists were made up separately for 7-, 9-, and 11-letter words by drawing the words at random from the total word pool. Foreign words and proper nouns were eliminated.

In order to maximize spelling errors while at the same time presenting words that were reasonably familiar to the subjects, it was decided to give the 7-letter words only to the eighth-graders ($N = 150$), the 9-letter words only to tenth-graders ($N = 148$), and the 11-letter words only to junior college freshmen ($N = 89$).

The spelling tests were selected at random from all the eight-item spelling lists. Every eighth-grader was given 24 7-letter words; every tenth-grader was given 24 9-letter words, but different lists were used in different classes, so the total number of different 9-letter words was 96. Each of the junior college students was given 48 11-letter words.

The subjects had mimeographed forms on which to print the words. For a 7-letter word, for example, a row of seven adjacent squares was provided, with the instructions to put one letter in each square. Similar forms were used for 9- and 11-letter words. This procedure permitted the position of each spelling error to be easily tabulated.

For all groups of subjects, the words were read aloud by the regular class-room teacher in the fashion of the usual spelling test. Students were not given the words for study before the test. Neither the teachers nor the students knew the purpose of the test.

SERIAL LEARNING

To permit a detailed comparison between the position of errors in spelling and in serial rote learning, serial learning data were obtained. Sixty subjects (college students) learned by the anticipation method a nine-item serial list composed of nine colored geometric forms: triangles, squares, and circles, colored red, blue, and yellow. The stimuli were projected automatically one at a time at a 3-second rate with a 6-second intertrial interval. (A detailed description of the apparatus is given elsewhere—Jensen, Collins, and Vreeland, 1962.) Never were figures of the same shape or color adjacent in the series. A green light of 3-seconds duration served as the signal for the subject to anticipate the first item in the series. Subjects responded by saying "red triangle, blue square," etc. All subjects learned to a criterion of one perfect trial. Two different orders of stimuli were used, with 30 subjects assigned to each order.

Results

All the serial-position curves are presented as the percentage of total errors that occur at each serial position, so that the area under all the curves is the same. This method of presentation was adopted since the interest here does not concern the absolute number of errors but only the relative shapes of the curves for serial learning errors and for spelling errors. For the color-form serial-learning data, the percentage of errors at each position was determined for each subject individually and then averaged over all subjects, in order to weight each subject equally in the group curve. A similar method was applied to the spelling data. Since some words were misspelled much more frequently than others, the percentage of the errors at each position was determined for each word and these were averaged over all words so that every word is weighted equally in the final curve.

Figure 1 shows the distribution of errors as a function of letter position for 96 9-letter words and for the serial position of errors made by 60 subjects in learning the color-form series. Both curves evince the essential features of the serial-position effect, that is, a bowed curve with the greater proportion of errors occurring after the middle position. The intraclass correlation between the pairs of data points for the two curves may be regarded as an index of the degree of similarity in the shapes of the curves (Haggard, 1958). The intraclass r was .81 between the spelling and the color-form curves. When the curves produced by the two serial orders of the color-form test were intercorrelated, the r was .96, which may be regarded as an equivalent-forms reliability of the shape of the serial-position curve.

The error curves for 7- and 11-letter words are shown in Figure 2. These curves closely resemble serial-position curves found in the literature on serial

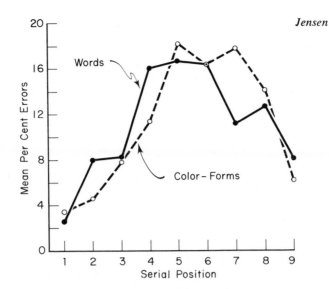

FIG. 1 *Serial-position curves for errors in 9-item color-form serial learning (60 subjects) and for spelling errors in 9-letter words. (The latter is based on a total of 3,864 spelling errors, i.e., incorrect letters, made on 96 words by 148 tenth-graders.)*

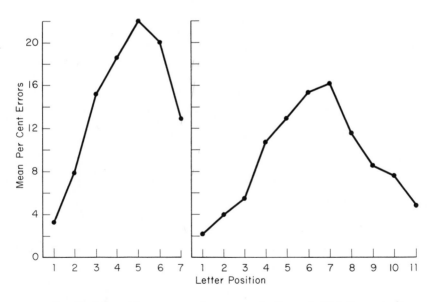

FIG. 2 *Serial-position curves for errors in 7- and 11-letter words. (The curve for 7-letter words is based on a total of 1,546 spelling errors made on 24 words by 150 eighth-graders. The 11-letter curve is based on a total of 2,262 spelling errors made on 48 words by 89 junior college freshmen.)*

learning (Jensen, 1962a; McGeoch and Irion, 1952, p. 123) with the degree of skewness varying as a function of the number of items in the series. The peak of errors for a 7-item list is generally at Position 5, and for an 11-item list it is at Position 7. The spelling errors conform perfectly to these expectations.

Since the usual method of learning to spell words is not the anticipation method generally used in serial learning experiments, but involves simultaneous viewing of all the letters in the word, one might ask if learning the color-forms by this method also evinces the serial-position effect. If it did not, it would be doubtful that the resemblance of the error curves for spelling to those of serial learning was indicative of a common psychological process underlying both forms of learning. To investigate this question, an additional 30 subjects (college students) were given a color-form test that involved simultaneous presentation of all the items in the series. Nine colored plastic forms (red triangle, green square, blue triangle, yellow diamond, red circle, yellow triangle, blue circle, pink square, and green diamond) were placed in a row before the subject. After the subject had studied the order of the objects for 10 seconds, the objects were disarranged haphazardly and the subject was asked to rearrange them in the proper order. This procedure was repeated, always with the same serial arrangement of the objects, until the subject learned to reconstruct their order perfectly. There was a different order for each subject.

Figure 3 shows the serial-position curve obtained by this method of simultaneous presentation. It may be regarded as a spatial, rather than the usual temporal, form of serial learning. The serial-position effect clearly is not limited to learning by the anticipation method (Jensen, 1962b). It should be noted that the curve in Figure 3 more closely resembles the curve for misspellings in words in Figure 1 than does the serial anticipation curve in Figure 1. In brief, the distribution of spelling errors more closely corresponds to the spatial serial-position effect than to the temporal. This is what we would expect, since the

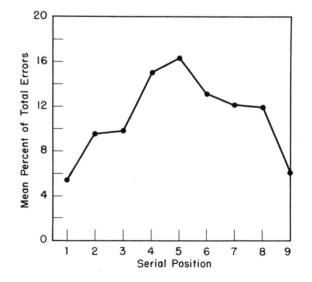

FIG. 3 *The serial-position curve for errors on a spatial serial learning task in which all nine items were presented simultaneously on each trial (30 subjects).*

letters of words are viewed simultaneously as in the spatial serial learning procedure. The intraclass correlation between the words curve in Figure 1 and the curve in Figure 3 is .90, which indicates a degree of correspondence between these curves that is almost as high as the "reliability" of the curves would permit.

Discussion

A strictly linguistic, rather than psychological, interpretation of these findings is not readily apparent. The obvious linguistic explanation of these results is in terms of the relative easiness of spelling the common prefixes and suffixes in words, which would tend to make for fewer spelling errors at the beginnings and ends of words having these elements. This explanation is unconvincing for several reasons. If prefixes and suffixes, most of which are composed of two or three letters, are learned as units, and if these prefixes and suffixes account for the shape of the error curve, then we should expect quite a differently shaped curve than was actually found in the present study. Each of the first three and last three letter positions should have an almost uniformly small proposition of errors. Furthermore, the differences in the skewness of curves for words of different lengths would be difficult to explain by the prefix-suffix hypothesis. It is apparent that even if the first and last three positions of the error curves are ignored, the middle portion of the word still manifests the bowed serial-position effect. Note the curve for 11-letter words in Figure 2; even without the first and last three positions the errors are distributed in a fashion typical of serial-position curves. Furthermore, only a small proportion of the words used in this study had either suffixes or prefixes. Using as a criterion a list of 46 common Greek and Latin prefixes (McCrimmon, 1950, p. 186), it was found that only 16% of the 9-letter words had prefixes. The mean number of errors on the first three positions for these words was 5.60; for nonprefix words the mean number of errors was 6.80. This small difference, in addition to the fact that only 16% of the words had prefixes, could not account for the markedly bow-shaped error curves found in the present study.

It is not claimed that spelling errors are solely a function of serial position. Certainly some words are phonetically more difficult than others, and this factor is undoubtedly a large source of spelling errors. Each word has its own peculiar difficulties, and it appears that these difficulties can occur at any letter position in the word. It is only when the errors that are peculiar to individual words are "averaged out" by combining the position errors of a large number of words, as was done in the present experiment, that the distribution of errors associated with the serial-position effect becomes evident. Thus, a phonetically difficult element is probably more or less difficult according to its position in the word.

There is still another interesting point of correspondence between spelling and serial learning. A number of studies (reviewed by Horn, 1960, pp. 1346–1347) have found that emphasizing difficult parts of words, in presenting the words in a lesson, by underlining, writing the letters in capitals, using bold-faced type, etc., is of little or no value in increasing the probability that the word will be spelled correctly. Emphasis of particular letters in a word corresponds to the so-called von Restorff procedure in serial learning, in which an item in the series is perceptually emphasized in some manner. The emphasized item is usually learned more readily than would be a nonemphasized item in the same position, but the difficulty of learning the list as a whole remains the same as if no item had been emphasized (Jensen, 1962c; Newman and Saltz, 1958). When errors are reduced at one position, they are correspondingly increased at other positions, so that there is no overall advantage from emphasizing a particular element in the series. This seems to be true in spelling as well as in serial learning.

REFERENCES

Haggard, E. A. *Intraclass correlation and the analysis of variance.* New York: Dryden, 1958.

Horn, E. S. In C. W. Harris (Ed.), *Encyclopedia of educational research.* New York: Macmillan, 1960. Pp. 1337–1354.

Jensen, A. R. An empirical theory of the serial-position effect. *J. Psychol.,* 1962, 53, 127–142. (a)

Jensen, A. R. Temporal and spatial serial-position effects. *Amer. J. Psychol.,* 1962, in press. (b)

Jensen, A. R. The von Restorff isolation effect with minimal response learning. *J. exp. Psychol.,* 1962, in press. (c)

Jensen, A. R., Collins, C. C., and Vreeland, R. W. A multiple S-R human learning apparatus. *Amer. J. Psychol.,* 1962, in press.

McCrimmon, J. M. *Writing with a purpose.* Boston: Houghton Mifflin, 1950.

McGeoch, J. A., and Irion, A. L. *The psychology of human learning.* New York: Longmans, Green, 1952.

Newman, S. E., and Saltz, E. Isolation effects: Stimulus and response generalization as explanatory concepts. *J. exp. Psychol.,* 1958, 55, 467–472.

Thorndike, E. L., and Lorge, I. *The teacher's word book of 30,000 words.* New York: Teachers College, Columbia University, Bureau of Publications, 1944.

Part Eleven

Written Expression

The five studies of written expression included in this part may be categorized as either establishing relationships among the language arts or testing methods of or assumptions about instruction. Although not all consider the varying degrees of ability among students including the underachiever, the findings and conclusions seem to be bases for judgments about remedial or corrective instruction in written expression.

In the first study Fea correlated various measures of reading, written expression, and oral expression in an attempt (1) to find the best common measure and (2) to establish a developmental hierarchy in the language arts. In addition, Fea has presented a noteworthy review of the literature concerning the relationship among the several language arts and observed a few phenomena that may serve as partial support for some practices described in later studies: (1) The material read previous to writing seemed to be more closely related to the written product than the child's reading ability. (2) Fairly high correlations between various measures of the quality of oral and written expression existed. (3) Writing *after* reading was followed by an oral performance better than one that followed the reading immediately.

The last four articles fall in the second category described in the first paragraph above. These studies, treating various methods of instruction and assumptions underlying instruction, are by Humphrey, Kraus, Heys, and Wheeler.

Humphrey compared language learning of two groups, one of which used a workbook while the other group participated in a game designed to teach the same principle. The description of the games and the results of the study may serve as an example of the method and the rationale for use of games in language instruction.

Kraus also reported a comparison of methods of instruction but differed from Humphrey in that she focused on improvement of the sentence structuring of her subjects. The findings, which tend to support individual diagnosis and instruction, hence remedial/corrective procedures, have led Kraus (1) to make four recommendations about the process of improving children's sentence structuring and (2) to pose four questions that provide food for thought for remedial teachers.

Both Heys and Wheeler report comparisons of the effects of frequent writing and "reading" on subsequent compositions and measures of writing ability. In essence the practice of writing a theme a week was tested, and the effects on various populations and measures were noted. The two reports are presented because (1) the "reading" programs and populations differ and (2) the relationship between an original study and a follow-up can be seen. Furthermore, the remedial teacher will find that the conclusions can serve as a basis for the establishment of a program of instruction that features the enhancement of specific skills or selected aspects of written instruction.

---

45   Interrelationships Among Materials Read, Written, and Spoken by Pupils of the Fifth and Sixth Grades

HENRY R. FEA

The close relationships among the four language arts—speaking, listening, reading, and writing—have been explored by research workers and advocated by curriculum-makers. A more intensive study of interrelationships among speaking, reading, and writing was attempted in the present study by applying nine measures to materials read, written, and spoken on the same topic by a group of fifth- and sixth-grade pupils. The study employed measures which had previously been used for reading, oral language or written language and applied them simultaneously to samples of all three forms of communication. This made possible comparisons of the different language arts abilities at these grade levels and an analysis of the measures themselves.

More specifically, the study attempted to answer the following questions:

1. What is the level of development in each of the three language arts for the same children in grades five and six?
2. Does varying the oral-written order of reproduction affect the quality of oral or written samples of pupils' work?
3. Does the developmental level of oral and written samples vary more with level of material read than with reading ability of the pupil?
4. Is level of development revealed by one measure comparable with that revealed by others?
5. Are any measures suitable as multiple-measures of the different language arts?
6. If measures prove suitable as multiple-measures, what is the order of development in each factor considered?

Previous Studies

There have been few studies which attempted to measure development in more than one of the language arts simultaneously. Lorge and Kruglov (18) investigated the relationship between intelligence and readability level of written compositions, for eighth- and ninth-grade pupils. They noted that readability level of compositions was approximately two grades below expected reading status.

Bushnell (2) attempted an analytical contrast of some factors of the oral and written English of tenth-grade pupils. Each pupil gave a short narrative

From *The Journal of Educational Psychology,* Vol. 44 (1953), pp. 159–175. Reprinted with permission.

oral composition. Later, the pupils wrote themes on the same subject matter. Bushnell found only nine cases in which oral compositions were superior as measured by the opinion of judges using the Van Wagenen Composition Scale. Errors in sentence structure were more numerous in oral compositions. There were on the average three overloaded or disjointed sentences in every oral theme. but only one such sentence in every eight written themes. Bushnell gives his opinion that oral language is less subject to training in the schools and remains on an immature level as judged by number of words, number of sentences, and number of words per sentence as well as in general quality. He admits that sentence length may not be a valid measure because of its dependence on punctuation.

Schonell (25) found more cases of backwardness in written language than in spelling or reading. He suggested environment as a reason, stating that reading and spelling are more dependent on direct teaching. He believes that reading affects vocabulary in oral and written language by unconscious assimilation. This does not operate with the same potency on the subtler characteristics of sentence structure. Thus, style and structure do not transfer to the same extent as vocabulary.

Dow and Papp (5) investigated relationships among test scores of reading ability, language ability, and grades in fundamentals of speech, public speaking, and literary interpretation. Their subjects were students in sophomore English courses. Reading scores and scholastic aptitude scores were determined from tests given in freshmen year. Scores on fundamentals of speech, public speaking, and literary interpretation were taken from grade books of instructors. They admit that, in light of measures used, validity of their findings may be open to question, but conclude that no significant relationships appeared among reading ability, language ability, and speech ability.

Lemon and Buswell (16) investigated errors in oral and written expression of twenty ninth-grade children. Oral samples were recordings of informal conversation by a concealed microphone. Written samples were themes obtained as class assignments. For comparison they equalized the two samples from each pupil to the sample containing the smaller number of words. Since the coefficient of correlation between oral and written errors was −.289 they questioned methods of teaching which they felt yielded no transfer in a situation conducive to transfer.

Watts (29) studied oral and written language development in children. He contends that success in written language is dependent upon success already having been achieved in oral language. He believes that children will not use the prearranged form characteristic of good prose but use the style of everyday speech which has no prearranged form. Thus he infers that speech is a groping process of clarification of thought and that this is not true of written language. This point may be open to question. Careful writers "get something down," then rewrite for good form.

Mathews, Larsen and Gibbon (19) investigated the importance of reading ability for freshmen taking rhetoric classes. They performed three experiments involving teaching composition purely by reading materials. Scholastic aptitude, reading, and rhetoric levels showed all of the high grade group to be in the upper quarter in reading skill. The low grade group was only slightly above average in reading skill. All experimental groups showed appreciable improvement in reading and no appreciable lag in grammar as compared to the control group who were given direct instruction in rhetoric.

Rossignol (21) explored relationships among hearing acuity, speech production, and reading performance of primary-grade children. Hearing acuity was tested by a pure-tone audiometer, speech production by two examiners using an articulation test and a sound-repetitions test. Reading performance was checked by the Gates Primary Reading Test. She found a small but significant relationship between reading performance and speech production.

The Measures

The experimental material consisted of three samples of language from each pupil.

1. A transcription of the oral reading by each pupil of the story *Golden Harvest* by Elizabeth Yates (23). This story had been adapted previously by use of the Lorge Formula (17) to an exact 4.5 reading level.
2. A transcription of the oral reproduction of the same story by each pupil.
3. A transcription of the written reproduction of the same story by each pupil.

The samples were then analyzed by the following measures:

1. Vocabulary—number of words.
2. Vocabulary—number of different words.
3. Vocabulary—number of words not found on the Dale list (3).
4. The Type-token Ratio—This measure was used by Johnson (14). It is an expression of the ratio of the number of different words (types) to the total number of words (tokens).
5. The Lorge formula for readability (17). This is a measure of the reading difficulty of materials written for children, using the number of words, number of difficult words, number of sentences and number of prepositional phrases.
6. The mean and standard deviation of sentence length. This measure was used by Schonell (24).
7. Degree of subordination. This measure was used by La Brant (15). It is expressed as a ratio of the number of dependent clauses to the number of independent clauses.
8. Number of prepositional phrases. This measure has been used widely; one example is that of Watts (29).
9. Some measure of ideas expressed.

The Subjects

The one hundred forty cases were selected from children of the fifth and sixth grades of four elementary schools in two California cities. Basis for selection of subjects was:

1. Reading ability of grade three or better as revealed by results of the Van Wagenen Unit Scales of Attainment.
2. All children were of the white race and came from homes where English was the only language spoken.
3. Normality of sight, speech, and hearing as revealed by school records.

Since it was possible to vary the order of reproduction of oral and written samples, and because variation of such order might affect the quality of the samples, two groups were used. Group A followed the order; reading, telling, writing: Group B followed the order; reading, writing, telling. The groups were equated on a basis of sex, grade, age, reading grade scores, and socio-economic background.

Conduct of the Experiment

Each subject was taken to a small room in his school containing an Audograph recorder. The pupil was informed of the three tasks expected of him, shown the operation of the machine, and told that his reading and telling of the story would be recorded. For recording, the child remained seated, and a lapel microphone was used. Each child was given two minutes to organize his thoughts before telling the story he had just read. To write the story, the pupil was taken to a second small room containing several desks.

When all samples had been procured they were subject to the following transcription and analysis:

1. Oral reading recordings—analyzed according to the Gray Oral Reading Analysis (8) for fluency (time required to read the story), mispronunciations, omissions, substitutions, insertions, repetitions, reversals, and faulty phrasing (excessive pausing where no pause is indicated in the text, as used by Hahn (9)).
2. Oral reproduction recordings—analyzed for repetitions, unintelligible remarks, punctuation, number of words, number of different words, number of words not appearing on the Dale list (3), number of prepositional phrases, number of sentences, number of run-on sentences, number of incomplete sentences (as defined by Hoppes (12)), degree of subordination, and number of correct verbal memories (this is a measure of the number of reproduced facts).
3. Written reproductions—analyzed for the same factors as oral reproductions with exception of repetitions and unintelligible remarks.

Analysis of the Results

An analysis of the original story as read by the children was made for comparison with their later oral and written samples. Results of this analysis are given in Table I.

TABLE I *Results of Measures Applied to the Story,* Golden Harvest

Measures	Results
Total Number of Words	750.
Total Number of Different Words	327.
Total Number of Hard Words	70.
Total Number of Phrases	65.
Total Number of Sentences	63.
Degree of Subordination	.39
Total Number of Facts	109.
Average Sentence Length	11.90
SD of Sentence Length	5.97
Type-token Ratio	.44
Lorge Grade Rating	4.50

The second step was statistical analysis of the children's language samples. Are the measures appropriate as measures of material read, spoken, and written? Does application of these measures show relationship among the language samples? Two statistical measures are used in an attempt to answer the second question: correlation, to reveal the degree of relationship; level of significance of difference between means when a measure is applied to two of the media. Obtained correlation coefficients are listed in Table II. Means, standard deviations, and critical ratios between means are illustrated in Table III.

TABLE II   *Correlation Coefficients of Relationships of Language Arts Factors*

Factors	r
Total Number of Verbal Memories: Oral with Written	.82
Total Number of Different Words: Oral with Written	.67
Total Number of Hard Words: Oral with Written	.64
Total Number of Phrases: Oral with Written	.63
Total Number of Words: Oral with Written	.62
Total Number of Minutes for Reproduction: Oral with Written	.50
Total Number of Sentences: Oral with Written	.43
Type-token Ratio: Oral with Written	.42
Reading Grade with Number of Written Verbal Memories	.40
Reading Grade with Number of Oral Verbal Memories	.37
Number of Repetitions in Reading with Number of Repetitions in Oral Reproduction	.33
Excessive Phrasing in Reading with Excessive Phrasing in Oral Reproduction	.32
Average Sentence Length: Oral with Written	.17
Lorge Rating: Oral with Written	.16
Reading Grade with Lorge Rating of Oral Reproductions	.11
Number of Minutes for Reading with Number of Minutes for Oral Reproduction	.07
Number of Minutes for Reading with Number of Minutes for Written Reproduction	.06
Number of Mispronunciations in Reading with Lorge Rating of Written Reproductions	−.002
Reading Grade with Lorge Rating of Written Reproductions	−.004
Number of Mispronunciations in Reading with Number of Oral Verbal Memories	−.03
Number of Mispronunciations in Reading with Number of Written Oral Memories	−.11
Number of Mispronunciations in Reading with Lorge Rating of Oral Reproductions	−.11

From these results some twenty conclusions may be advanced about the interrelationships of the three language arts and their measures.

1. Relationship among the number of minutes to read, tell, and write the story. This measure is misleading because a pupil who speaks or writes quickly with occasional long pauses receives the same score as one who speaks or writes slowly with no long pauses. Table II shows negligible correlation except for oral and written reproduction correlation coefficient of .5. Investigations have shown positive correlation of reading comprehension and speed. Therefore, pupils who read quickly should have greater degree of comprehension and remember more. Because they remember more they should have more to tell and write. Thus, reading time should correlate negatively with oral and written reproduction time. This reasoning disregards the possibility of a general verbal

TABLE III *Means, Standard Deviations, and Critical Ratios Between the Means of Factors in Oral Reproductions and Written Reproductions of One Hundred Forty Pupils*

	Oral Samples		Written Samples		Critical Ratio
	Mean	**SD**	**Mean**	**SD**	
Total Number of Words	291.21	124.15	196.48	81.36	7.55
Number of Hard Words	18.26	7.96	13.38	6.31	5.67
Number of Different Words	115.39	39.16	94.16	31.02	5.03
Number of Sentences	15.21	6.91	11.35	6.02	4.99
Number of Phrases	19.77	10.09	15.47	7.82	3.98
Number of Run-on Sentences	1.96	1.82	1.33	1.38	3.26
Number of Verbal Memories	35.01	15.45	30.38	13.60	2.66
Degree of Subordination	.32	.09	.32	.10	.01
Average Sentence Length in Words	19.99	5.86	22.85	23.01	−1.43
Number of Incomplete Sentences	.29	.62	.43	.82	−1.57
Lorge Rating	4.50	.37	4.81	1.41	−2.53
Type-token Ratio	.43	.08	.50	.08	−8.17

fluence factor which would tend to produce positive time relationships. Perhaps both factors operate to cancel the effect of either. Mean reading speed is approximately one hundred seventeen words-per-minute; oral reproduction speed, one hundred eight words-per-minute; written reproduction, eight words-per-minute. The last figure is low in relation to speed of handwriting usually quoted for these grade levels.

2. Relationship of reading grade to number of oral and written verbal memories. The positive relationship shown in Table II would appear normal. Most reading tests make considerable demand upon immediate memory. It would seem natural that a pupil receiving a high oral score would receive a high written score. The critical ratio of 2.66 is of such magnitude that separate norms would be necessary if the measure were used for both oral and written language.

3. Relationship of the number of reading mispronunciations to the number of oral and written memories. Table II shows negligible relationship. Probably two opposing factors produce the result. If a pupil cannot pronounce a word and does not know its meaning he will not use it orally or in writing; if he knows the meaning but has difficulty with the pronunciation, extra time spent trying to pronounce it should fix it in his memory.

4. Relationship of the number of reading mispronunciations to Lorge rating of oral and written samples. The Lorge formula seems excellent as used with oral samples. Its use in written language samples of children who show no evidence of sentencing is questionable.

5. Relationship of reading grade to Lorge rating of oral and written reproductions. Results, shown in Table II, indicate little relationship between pupil reading-level and level of difficulty of style of his oral and written samples. However, they may indicate that level of material read has more influence on level of maturity of reproductions than reading level of the pupil.

6. Relationship of excessive phrasing in reading to excessive phrasing in oral reproduction. Results support the findings of Hahn (9) that it is a habit.

7. Relationship of the number of repetitions in reading to the number of repetitions in oral language. Table II shows a definite tendency for those who repeat in reading to do the same in oral language reproduction.

8. Relationship of the total number of words used in oral and written language situations. Results of Table II indicate a definite tendency for those who use more words orally to do the same in writing. In only seven cases did a pupil write more words than he spoke. The critical ratio is of such magnitude as to require different norms for the two media but the measure appears to be valid.

9. Relationship of the number of different words used in oral and in written language samples. The relationship here is greater than for total number of words. But, again, separate norms would be necessary. Pupils in this situation used in speaking approximately thirty-five per cent, and in writing approximately twenty-nine per cent of the number of different words encountered in reading.

10. Relationship of the number of hard words in oral and written language. Results are similar to those of the two previous measures so this measure is probably superfluous in measuring similarities when the other two are used.

11. Relationship of the number of phrases in oral and written language. Studies in oral language have been limited to consideration of the age at which phrases appear in the language of the child. Stormzand and O'Shea (27) used the measure in written language. On the basis of their findings the present study should have shown the mean number of phrases in oral and written language as approximately thirty-five and twenty-four. Actual results as shown in Table III are 19.77 and 15.47 phrases per sample. Perhaps difference in material would account for this discrepancy as Stormzand and O'Shea used original material. Table II shows a definite relationship for this measure; therefore, it is valid but separate norms would be necessary.

12. Relationship of the number of sentences in oral and written language. Placing responsibility with the pupil for indication of sentencing has been used here. Previous investigators have considered the thought-unit as synonymous with a sentence. This makes the sentence count subjective, and it has been condemned by Watts (29), Johnson (14), Seegers (26) and La Brant (15) for this reason. In this study the sentence-unit appears sufficiently valid in oral language to justify its use. But due to inability of a few pupils to use punctuation, results obtained from written samples are questionable. Results are at variance with those of Bushnell (2) and Bear (1) in that the present study shows more sentencing.

13. Relationship of the number of run-on sentences in oral and written language. Results shown in Table III substantiate the findings of Wiswall (30). The measure is vulnerable to the extent that the definition of a sentence is subjective.

14. Relationship of the number of incomplete sentences in oral and written language. This measure tends to be more objective than a sentence count. Table III shows this to be the first measure considered where the mean for written samples exceeds that for oral samples. Also, this measure could be applied in both media using the same norms. However, it is an unsuitable measure at these grade levels as only thirty-one oral and thirty-nine written samples contained incomplete sentences.

15. Relationship of the degree of subordination in oral and written language. This measure has been used by many previous investigators such as Heider and Heider (10) and La Brant (15). From evidence of Tables II and III this would appear to be a suitable measure of oral and written language samples. The same norms would be suitable for both media.

16. Relationship of the number of correct verbal memories in oral and written language. There is high degree of relationship here.

17. Relationship of the average sentence length in oral and written language. There is, according to Table II, low degree of relationship. The questionable validity of the sentence as a measure has been previously discussed.

18. Relationship of the standard deviation of sentence length in oral and written language. Result for oral language is similar to the original story: result for written language is very largely due to lack of pupil punctuation.

19. Relationship of the type-token ratio in oral and written language. There is close similarity among the original story, oral samples, and written samples. However, this measure is invalid because of the high rate of repetition of some words in the English language. A pupil who writes one sentence will obtain a higher type-token ratio than an author who writes a book. It could be a valid measure if an identical number of words were allowed for each sample.

20. Relationship of the Lorge grade rating in oral and written language. The low degree of relationship as indicated in Table II is to be expected because of the dependence of the Lorge rating on sentencing.

Summary of Analysis of Language Samples

It would seem, from material presented in the preceding section, that there is substantial degree of relationship among reading material, oral language samples, and written language samples of fifth- and sixth-graders in the following: verbal memories evoked, number of words used, number of different words employed, number of hard words, number of phrases and degree of subordination. Further, in situations similar to this study, such factors may be reliably measured. If such measures are used, different expectations or norms must be established for all factors except degree of subordination.

Factors considered in the preceding section which indicate some degree of relationship among the three media are: number of minutes for reading and reproduction, number of sentences, and type-token ratio. These have not proved suitable as measures of all three types of language behavior. While the number of minutes for oral and written reproduction are positively related, there is little relationship of reading time with oral and written reproduction time. Differences of opinion as to what constitutes a sentence invalidates this as a measure. The type-token ratio is not a valid measure unless all samples are equated for number of words.

Factors which indicate little relationship among the media or are not applicable to more than two of the media are: average sentence length, the Lorge rating, mispronunciations, repetitions, and excessive phrasing. Average sentence length and Lorge rating are suitable measures, but both are dependent on the definition of a sentence.

Comparison of the Two Equated Groups

Statistical evidence of the result of comparison of oral and written language performance on the basis of order or presentation is given in Table IV. Group A first reproduced the story orally, then in writing. This order was reversed with Group B.

The only significant difference is in the number of sentences in oral samples. The writer is of the opinion that pupils who have just read the story rush through oral reproduction in the hope that facts will not be forgotten. Those who write the story prior to oral reproduction have undergone a sufficient time lapse to assure that facts still remembered will remain so for a period of time.

Although no significant differences exist, with the exception of oral sentencing, the general trend as shown in Table IV is interesting. On those measures

TABLE IV   *Means, Standard Deviations, and Critical Ratios of Differences Between the Means of Oral Language Samples and Written Language Samples for Seventy Pupils in Each of Groups A and B*

	Group A		Group B		Critical Ratio
	Mean	SD	Mean	SD	
Oral Reproductions					
Total Number of Words	272.84	120.91	309.58	124.64	1.77
Number of Different Words	111.38	38.17	119.40	39.73	1.22
Number of Hard Words	17.41	8.28	19.10	7.57	1.26
Number of Phrases	18.78	10.02	20.76	10.01	1.16
Number of Sentences	13.64	6.38	16.78	7.06	2.76
Number of Run-on Sentences	2.00	1.80	1.91	1.83	.28
Number of Incomplete Sentences	.33	.67	.26	.55	.26
Degree of Subordination	.31	.10	.32	.09	.91
Number of Verbal Memories	34.18	15.59	35.84	15.26	.64
Average Sentence Length in Words	20.79	5.85	19.20	5.74	.63
Type-token Ratio	.44	.09	.42	.06	1.95
Lorge Rating	4.58	.35	4.42	.38	.14
Written Reproductions					
Total Number of Words	188.63	72.72	204.33	88.49	1.15
Number of Different Words	91.30	27.48	97.01	33.98	1.09
Number of Hard Words	12.97	5.46	13.80	7.01	.78
Number of Phrases	15.17	7.32	15.77	8.29	.45
Number of Sentences	10.73	6.36	11.97	5.58	1.22
Number of Run-on Sentences	1.14	1.21	1.51	1.50	1.61
Number of Incomplete Sentences	.30	.66	.58	.94	1.88
Degree of Subordination	.33	.11	.31	.09	1.23
Number of Verbal Memories	30.01	12.66	30.76	14.45	.32
Average Sentence Length in Words	26.00	30.31	19.71	10.82	1.64
Type-token Ratio	.51	.07	.50	.08	.34
Lorge Rating	5.04	1.84	4.58	.69	1.98

which were accepted as valid in the preceding section, Group B is superior in all but degree of subordination. Thus, according to evidence from the present study, pupils who write the story before telling it use, in both oral and written samples, a greater number of words, a greater number of different words, a greater number of hard words, a greater number of phrases, and a greater number of verbal memories.

Conclusions

1. The level of development in the three language arts appears to be in the order: material read, oral language, and written language. However, this result in a reproductive situation does not apply with equal validity to any other

combination of language activities because the assumption is that the material read is the standard.

2. Varying the order of oral and written reproductions does not affect the quality of the samples, except for the number of oral sentences, to a significant degree. However, there is a general trend toward superior language usage in both oral and written samples when written reproduction is performed first.

3. The level of development of oral and written language is more dependent upon the level of the material read than upon the reading level of the pupils according to evidence of this study. The average level of maturity for oral language samples is identical with the difficulty of the passage read, both with Lorge rating of 4.5. Further experiments using reading material on various levels of difficulty would be necessary before this statement can be made with any degree of certainty.

4. Level of development revealed by one measure is not comparable with that revealed by another. Studies comparable to the present one have not been sufficient to establish levels of comparison among the measures. For example, it is not possible to state that one sample containing fifty more words but five fewer phrases than another sample is of less, equal, or greater degree of language maturity.

5. Measures which appear suitable as multiple-measures. . . . which could be applied to material read, spoken and written in situations and with material comparable to the present study are: verbal memories, number of words, number of different words, number of hard words, number of phrases, and degree of subordination. The Lorge formula may prove to be an acceptable multiple-measure although such was not clearly the case in the present study. All of these measures except degree of subordination would require separate norms for the three media.

6. Assuming that the measures are suitable multiple-measures, the level of maturity of development in each factor could be determined only by further investigations. Comparable studies are not sufficient to establish levels of development. However, the present study indicates that, in similar situations, the mean number of written-language words may be approximately two-thirds that of oral reproduction; number of different words in oral samples may be about one-third the number of words in reading material; and the number of hard words one-tenth the total number of words, with written samples comparable on a reduced scale. There is further indication that in similar situations pupils may be expected to produce approximately one-third of the facts which they have read orally and that the ratio of subordinate clauses to total number of clauses used may be approximately one to three.

7. The hypothesis of Hahn (9), that excessive phrasing in oral reproduction is a habit caused by nervousness or excitement and tending to persist, appears to be substantiated here to the extent that this factor is related to reading and oral reproduction. The same relationship seems to be true for repetitions in oral reading and oral reproduction.

8. From evidence of the present study, the best single index of measurement in reading material, oral and written language samples would appear to be the degree of subordination.

REFERENCES

1. M. V. Bear. "Children's growth in the use of written language," *Elementary English Review*, 16: 312–319, December, 1939.

2. P. P. Bushnell. *An Analytical Contrast of Oral with Written English.* (Teachers College Contribution to Education, No. 415.) New York: Bureau of Publications, Teachers College, 1930, pp. 87.

3. E. Dale. "A comparison of two word lists," *Educational Research Bulletin*, 10: 484–489, December, 1931.

4. E. A. Davis. "The subordinate clause in oral and written language," *Child Development*, 12: 333–338, 1941.

5. C. W. Dow and S. R. Papp. "The Relation of Reading Ability and Language Ability to Speech Ability," *Speech Monographs*, published by the National Association of Teachers of Speech, 10: 107–108, 1943.

6. A. M. Edwards. *Alphabetical Index of Occupations and Industries.* Washington: United States Government Printing Office, 1940, pp. 607.

7. A. I. Gates. "Character and Purposes of the Yearbook," *Forty-eighth Yearbook of the National Society for Study of Education*, Part II, 1949, pp. 1–9.

8. W. S. Gray. *Studies of Elementary-School Reading Through Standardized Tests.* Supplementary Educational Monographs, No. 1, University of Chicago Press, Chicago, 1917, pp. 157.

9. E. Hahn. "The speech of first-grade children in audience situations," *Elementary English*, 25: 39–46, January, 1948.

10. F. Heider and G. M. Heider. "Comparison of sentence structure of deaf and hearing children," *Volta Review*, 43: 364–367 and 406, June, 1941, 536–540 and 564, September, 1941, 599–604 and 628–630, October, 1941.

11. G. Hildreth. "Reading Progress in Grades II and III," *Forty-eighth Yearbook of the National Society for the Study of Education*, Part II, 1949, pp. 54–126.

12. W. C. Hoppes. "Some aspects of growth in English expression," *Elementary English*, 10: 67–70 and 121–133, March and May, 1933.

13. E. Horn and J. F. Curtis. "Improvement of Oral Reading," *Forty-eighth Yearbook of the National Society for the Study of Education*, Part II, 1949, pp. 254–265.

14. W. Johnson and Others. *Studies in Language Behavior*, Psychological Monographs, 56: No. 2, 1944, pp. 111.

15. L. L. La Brant. *Studies of Certain Language Developments of Children in Grades Four to Twelve*, Genetic Psychology Monographs, 14: 387–494, November, 1933.

16. B. K. Lemon and G. T. Buswell. "Oral and written expression in grade IX," *School Review*, 51: 544–549, November, 1943.

17. I. Lorge. "Predicting reading difficulty of selections for children," *Elementary English Review*, 16: 229–233, October, 1939.

18. I. Lorge and L. Kruglov. "The relationship between the readability of pupils' compositions and their measured intelligence," *Journal of Educational Research*, 43: 467–474, February, 1950.

19. E. G. Mathews, R. P. Larsen, and B. Gibbon. "Experimental investigation of the relation between reading training and achievement in college composition classes," *Journal of Educational Research*, 38: 499–505, March, 1945.

20. P. McKee. *Language in the Elementary School.* Boston: Houghton Mifflin Co., 1939, pp. 591.

21. L. J. Rossignol. *The Relationships Among Hearing Acuity, Speech Production, and Reading Performance in Grades 1A, 1B, and 2A.* Teachers College Contribution to Education, No. 936. New York: Bureau of Publications, Teachers College, 1948, pp. 50.

22. D. H. Russell. "Evaluation of Pupil Growth In and Through Reading," *Forty-eighth Yearbook of the National Society for the Study of Education,* Part II, 1949, pp. 284–301.

23. D. H. Russell, C. M. McCullough, and D. Gates. *Trails to Treasure.* Boston: Ginn and Co., 1949, pp. 45–56.

24. F. J. Schonell. "Diagnostic Tests in English," *The Yearbook of Education.* London: Evans Brothers, 1935, pp. 963.

25. _____. *Backwardness in the Basic Subjects.* London: Oliver and Boyd, 1942, pp. 560.

26. J. C. Seegers. "Form of discourse and sentence structure," *Elementary English,* 10: 51–54, March, 1933.

27. M. J. Stormzand and M. V. O'Shea. *How Much English Grammar?* Baltimore: Warwick and York, 1924, pp. 224.

28. E. L. Thorndike. "Reading as reasoning," *The Journal of Educational Psychology,* 8: 323–332, June, 1917.

29. A. F. Watts. *The Language and Mental Development of Children.* London: George G. Harrap and Co., Ltd., 1944, pp. 354.

30. Z. E. Wiswall. "A study of sentence structure in eighth-grade composition," *Elementary School Journal,* 26: 441–448, February, 1926.

46   Comparison of the Use of Active Games and Language Workbook Exercises as Learning Media in the Development of Language Understandings with Third-Grade Children

JAMES H. HUMPHREY

Summary.—Two equated groups of children were taught language understandings, one group through active games and the other through language workbook exercises. Using the differences between pre- and post-test scores as criteria, the results suggested that children learned through both media. It also appeared that learning through active games was greater than with the language workbook exercises.

The use of an active game in a more or less scientific way as a learning medium in other curriculum areas might well be considered a relatively recent innovation. In view of this it seems appropriate that certain basic considerations concerned with this approach to learning be taken into account.

From *Perceptual and Motor Skills,* Vol. 21 (1965), pp. 23–26. Reprinted with permission of author and publisher.

The author expresses grateful appreciation to Dr. Matthew Yarczower, Associate Professor of Psychology, University of Maryland, for his critical reading of this report and helpful suggestions regarding certain aspects of the study.

More pronounced emphasis is being placed on the important role in the learning process that is played by kinesthetic "feedback" produced by body movement. Although there appears to be an abundance of empirical evidence which suggests that this notion is very useful from a child development point of view, as far as the active game medium is concerned there have been relatively few attempts to test the hypothesis objectively. The present study represents an effort to provide more objective and scientific evidence relative to this view.

In essence, this procedure involves the selection of an active game which is taught to the children and is used as a learning activity for the development of the skill or concept in a specific subject area. It is hypothesized that young children tend to learn better when the learning takes place through pleasurable physical activity, i.e., when the *motor* component operates at a maximal level in concept development in school subject areas predominantly oriented to *verbal* learning. This is *not* to say that "verbal" and "motor" learning are two mutually exclusive kinds of learning, although it has been suggested that at the two extremes the dichotomy appears justifiable. It is recognized that in verbal learning which involves almost complete abstract symbolic manipulations there may be, among others, such motor components as tension, subvocal speech, and physiological changes in metabolism which operate at a minimal level (2). It is also recognized that in active games where the learning is predominantly motor in nature, verbal learning is evident, although perhaps at a minimal level. For example, in teaching an active game there is a certain amount of verbalization involved in developing a kinesthetic concept of the particular game that is being taught.

Method

A previous study (1), undertaken to determine whether children could actually learn through this medium, employed the Single Group Experimental Procedure. In the present study the Parallel Group Experimental Procedure was used to determine how well a group of third-grade children might develop language understandings through the active game medium as compared with how well another group might develop the same understandings through the language workbook medium.

Twenty third-grade children were pretested on 10 language understandings. There were 10 test items for each concept, making a total of 100 test items. A reliability coefficient of .87 for the test was derived by using a test-retest procedure with a similar group of third-grade children. The children were divided into two groups on the basis of the test scores. One group was designated as the *active game* group and taught through that medium. The other group used the language workbook. Both groups were taught by the same teacher.

In order to facilitate an understanding of the types of learning activities used for each group, an example for each group is presented. The examples are concerned with *distinguishing between words that use "c" or "s" in making the "s" sound*. For the active game group the learning activity used to develop this understanding was a game called "Cs and Ss," which is an adaptation of the game "Crows and Cranes" (see Fig. 1).

As shown in Fig. 1, the children were divided equally into two groups, the "Cs" and the "Ss," who lined up facing each other, with their lines about 5 feet apart. A goal line was drawn a given distance behind each group. The teacher called out a word that is spelled with either a "c" or an "s." If the word

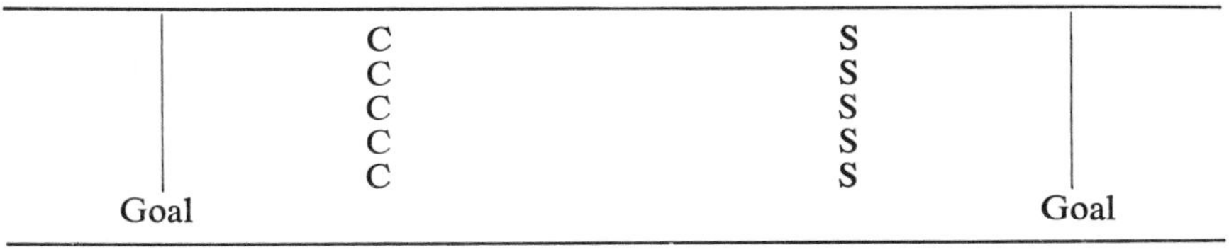

C	S
C	S
C	S
C	S
C	S
Goal	Goal

FIG. I   *Example of active, game-learning activity*

required a "c," all of the "Cs" ran to reach their goal line before being tagged by a member of the "S" group. All of those tagged became members of the opposite group. The groups then returned to their respective lines, and the same procedure was followed with another word. The group having the greater number of players on its side at the end of a specified playing time won.

For the language workbook group the learning activity was a standard language workbook exercise. This consisted of a list of 12 words containing both "c" and "s" sounds. In the exercise there were questions concerning which letters spelled the "c" or "s" sounds. In addition, this exercise required that the children write the words that used the "c" or "s" sounds. The test contained a list of 10 words with both the "c" and "s" in each of the words, and the children were asked to cross out the letter so that the word would be spelled correctly.

Comparisons of the pre- and post-test scores of the language workbook group and the pre- and post-test scores of the active game group were handled by using the standard error of the mean difference and the t ratio. The comparison of the post-test scores of both groups was computed by using the Wilcoxon signed-rank test of differences.

Results and Discussion

The obtained t value of 2.857 for the language workbook group was significant at the .05 level, showing gain from pre- to post-test. The obtained t of 3.333 for the active game group was significant at the .01 level. The signed-rank test of differences applied to the post-test scores of both groups indicated significance at .05 in favor of the active game group.

For a clearer picture of the trend of differences between both groups the per cents of differences in gain on a paired per-pupil basis are shown in Table I. Eight of the children in the active game group had a greater per cent difference

TABLE I   *Difference in Per Cent Gain on Test 2 for Each of 10 Ss*

Subject Pair	Diff. in % Gain	Medium
1	6	Workbook
2	18	Active Game
3	3	Active Game
4	26	Active Game
5	12	Active Game
6	7	Workbook
7	30	Active Game
8	73	Active Game
9	1	Active Game
10	16	Active Game

in gain than their counterparts in the language workbook group, while two of the children in the language workbook group had a greater per cent difference in gain.

CONCLUSIONS

In recognition of the limitations imposed by a study of this nature one should be cautious in drawing conclusions. If one accepts the significant differences in the test scores as evidence of learning, these third-grade children could develop language comprehension through either medium, although the active game medium produced greater changes.

REFERENCES

1. Humphrey, J. H. A pilot study of the use of physical education as a learning medium in the development of language arts concepts with third-grade children. *Res. Quart.*, 1962, 33, 136–137.

2. Johnson, G. B. Motor learning. In W. R. Johnson (Ed.), *Science and medicine of exercise and sports*. New York: Harper, 1960. Ch. 30.

---

47   A Comparison of Three Methods of Teaching Sentence Structure

SILVY A. KRAUS

From the research of the past several decades we have learned that skill in the recognition of grammatical concepts has little influence on the ability to express one's thought accurately (ability of children to explain verb usages doubles between grades seven and nine, but their ability to use verbs remains relatively stable),[1] that errors in sentence structure are more serious and persistent than are the more mechanical errors of grammar and punctuation,[2] that language development follows a genetic pattern of growth similar to the human infant's predictable pattern of physical development, and that the individual's achievement in language is due largely to his general mental development.[3]

These discoveries concerning the general nature of language and the seriousness of errors in sentence structure prompted research into specific methods for the improved teaching of the sentence. These studies indicate that (1) clarity in sentence structure is more readily gained by an emphasis upon the thought to be expressed than upon grammatical explanations, (2) the motivation of

[1] Catherine Catherwood, *A Study of Relationships Between a Knowledge of Rules and Ability to Correct Grammatical Errors and Between Identification of Sentences and the Knowledge of Subject and Predicate*, unpublished M. A. thesis, University of Minnesota, August 1932.

[2] Roy I. Johnson, *A Study of Errors in English Composition*, unpublished M. A. thesis, Department of Education, University of California, 1917.

[3] A. T. Watts, *The Language and Mental Development of Children*.

From *English Journal*, Vol. 46 (1957), pp. 275–281. Reprinted with permission of the National Council of Teachers of English and Silvy A. Kraus.

The research summarized in this article was carried out for a doctoral study at the University of Minnesota.

writing through means of challenging situations seems to solve many perplexing problems, and (3) more attention to individual needs results in greater achievements.[4]

The basic problem in the teaching of sentence structure is clear: what motivations, what methods of teaching sentence structure in relation to the thoughts to be expressed will prove most effective in teaching students of divergent abilities, working in the same classroom, to express their thoughts clearly? Is the presentation by the "thought method" the determining factor? Can the effectiveness of the thought approach be increased? Is it possible to use this thought approach effectively in various ways? To improve sentence structure, is it necessary to present the major elements of sentence structure in a predetermined order? How can differing levels of ability be utilized to hasten writing improvement? Under what conditons will original writing prove most beneficial? How effective is instruction in sentence structure when it is given as the need arises?

Purpose and Procedure of the Study

To explore some of these problems, the writer set up experimental classes in the eleventh grade in Eugene High School, Eugene, Oregon, to study three methods of teaching sentence structure. The general purpose of the study was to determine whether any one of the following methods was superior in helping students to express their thoughts clearly:

1. A procedure in which five units of sentence structure were logically presented and taught according to the thought approach but in which the students did no original writing. All activities (with the exception of occasional reading) were concerned with the study of sentence structure.
2. A procedure in which these same sentence structure items were taught exactly in the same way but in which the students wrote weekly themes which were not discussed after their return. Again, in these sections, all activities (with the exception of the weekly theme writing and occasional reading) were concerned with the study of sentence structure.
3. A procedure in which all sentence structure items were taught only as the result of errors made in weekly themes which students wrote in connection with a literature unit. Sentence structure was studied in these sections only as errors in themes written in connection with the literature unit indicated a need.

ITEMS CHOSEN FOR STUDY

An analysis of research concerning errors in the writing of high school students and of sentence structure items presented in high school texts dictated the choice of the following sentence structure items for study:

1. Completeness
2. Coordination
3. Subordination
4. Clarity
5. Effectiveness: Unity, Variety, Conciseness

4 Irvin O. Ash, "An Experimental Evaluation of the Stylistic Approach in Teaching Written Composition," *Journal of Experimental Education,* IV (September 1935), p. 551.

Completeness. The logical expression of a complete idea was considered a complete sentence. Imperative sentences and bits of dialogue which, though grammatically incomplete, are a special form and logically complete were classified as complete sentences. The following are examples of incomplete constructions:

1. As they went to a senior conference at Wind Mountain. (Subordinate idea used as complete sentence)
2. I've had fun what I have done though. (Omission of words)
3. Fortunately not too serious but she still walks with a limp. (Subject of first thought omitted)
4. He saw an airplane. Looking up between the buildings (Incomplete sentence)
5. The guilty boy ran when he saw them coming. The neighbors, his father, and his sisters. (Appositive used as a sentence)
6. Helen returned home recently, she has been touring in Europe. (Two ideas run together)

Coordination. Ideas of equal value within a sentence must be so expressed that their coordinate relationship is evident. These sentences illustrate improper coordination.

1. I was invited to the party while he was not. (Coordinate and contrasting value of ideas dictates use of *but*.)
2. It rained and they postponed the picnic. (First idea the cause of the second. They postponed the picnic *because* it rained.)

Clarity. Sentence clarity is dependent upon many factors such as unity, proper subordination and coordination, the effective ordering of parts, the avoidance of unnecessary detail, agreement of subject with verb and pronoun with antecedent, properly placed modifiers, logical expression of ideas, and correct choice of connectives. The following sentences illustrate errors which prevent sentence clarity.

1. At the age of five my parents decided to move to California. (Illogical expression of idea.)
2. I have not traveled much which I wish I could have. (Misuse of connective.)
3. They say we can go with you. (To whom does *they* refer?)
4. I am told I was afraid of the black smoke that comes from trains and just many other exciting things happened to me when I was younger. (Lack of unity.)
5. Then I went to Colin Kelly for the seventh grade which is a wonderful school. (Misplaced modifier.)
6. Turning the corner on two wheels, the old lady was hit by the truck. (Misplaced modifier.)

Emphasis. A sentence is emphatic when its important ideas are so arranged that their message is unmistakable and forceful.

Weak—Nothing tastes better than hot, spicy cinnamon buns, fresh from the oven, in my opinion.
Forceful—Nothing, in my opinion, tastes better than hot, spicy cinnamon buns, fresh from the oven.
Awkward—He likes to play tennis and swimming.
Improved—He likes to play tennis and to swim.
or
He likes swimming and playing tennis.

Variety. The usual pattern in an English sentence is subject—verb—object. Monotony can be avoided through modification of this pattern.

Swiftly the canoe glided over the black waters of the bayou.
There is no sauce in the world like hunger. (Cervantes)
At any one place a tornado lasts about half a minute.
Swooping low, the planes come in at the boats, spitting death.

Conciseness. The most effective sentences communicate their thoughts simply and directly.

Padded—One should not spend a great deal of his time explaining why he has made mistakes; he should instead work hard to attain some measure of achievement.
Concise—Don't make excuses; make good. (Elbert Hubbard)
Padded—Every once in a while he will remember.
Improved—Once in a while he will remember.
Padded—I want to tell you that Joan will be here next week.
Improved—Joan will be here next week.

MATERIALS USED IN THE STUDY

Six original units of work were constructed for use in the study. Five of these were sentence structure units which contained explanatory and drill material for the sentence structure problems chosen for study—completeness, subordination, coordination, clarity, and effectiveness. The organization of each unit is indicated below.

Unit I. Completeness

I. The complete sentence, the basis of communication
II. Problems of completeness
    A. Recognition of the complete sentence
        1. Recognition of the key words
        2. Hearing the complete sentence
    B. Most common violations
        1. Subordinate thoughts punctuated as complete sentences
            a. Segments that explain preceding sentences
            b. Segments that describe neighboring thoughts
        2. Word placement and punctuation which interfere with easy understanding of completeness

Unit II. Subordination

I. Nature of subordination
II. Clear relationship between principal and subordinate ideas
    A. Relationships that tell cause, time, purpose, etc.
    B. Relationships that describe
    C. Other methods of subordinating ideas
    D. Pitfalls in the subordination of one idea to another

Unit III. Coordination

I. Nature of coordination
II. Ideas that are coordinate
III. Punctuating coordinate ideas

IV. Words that often introduce coordinate ideas
V. Coordinate elements within a single idea

Unit IV. Clarity

   I. Agreement
  II. Logical completion of each thought
 III. Avoidance of excessive detail
 IV. Logical comparison
  V. Inclusion of all necessary words
 VI. Proper connectives between thoughts
VII. Careful placement of words

Unit V. Effectiveness

  I. Coherence
 II. Emphasis
    A. Placing important parts of thought in strategic positions
    B. Arranging ideas in order of climax
III. Conciseness
    A. Avoiding unnecessary words
    B. Avoiding words that prevent direct statements
    C. Condensing subordinating ideas
    D. Avoiding long connectives
    E. Avoiding choppy sentences
 IV. Point of view
  V. Variety

A literature unit was carried on in the experimental groups which studied sentence structure only as errors in themes written in connection with the unit indicated a need.

METHODOLOGY

Six classes, each a random sample of the entire junior class, became our experimental group for a period of eleven weeks. Two instructors were involved, each teaching a Method I, a Method II, and a Method III class.

Method I. Students in the two Method I sections were taught the elements of sentence structure previously noted. They engaged in no other activity except the occasional reading of selections listed in the unit on mythology.

The following instructions were given for the teaching of these sections:

1. You are teaching sentence structure according to the logic of the ideas to be expressed. Follow the letter and the spirit of the handbook.
2. Make discussions interesting and lively.
3. Attempt to draw all students into the discussion.
4. Do not set students to long periods of exercise marking. Use exercises as resource material to reinforce principles discussed. Check and discuss the marking of a small portion of an exercise before proceeding.
5. On the basis of class discussion, exercise marking, and tests determine the individual needs of students. Do not allow students to waste time on principles which they have mastered. Assign group work carefully. (Once a week students marked a review sheet, the results of which determined their assignments to groups working on sentence completeness, proper subordination, agreement, etc.)

6. Any time not spent in work on sentence structure should be spent in the reading of material in Christ, *Myths and Folklore*.

The following is the typical routine of the Method I sections:

First five minutes: Individual seat work on principle of previous day's work. (Teacher indicated page of sentence structure booklet to be considered. Exercises in these booklets directed students to choose between complete and incomplete sentences, to underline a faulty connective, to choose a correct verb or pronoun, to choose the best of four sentences, etc. Such exercises were used because of the necessity of controlling the amount of original writing in an experiment attempting to determine the effect of original writing upon improvement in sentence structure.)

Ten minutes: Checking of work, answering of questions.

Fifteen minutes: Discussion of work at hand. (Presentation of a new principle or further discussion of a troublesome point.)

Fifteen minutes: Group work.

Method II. Identical instructions were given for the teaching of Method II with the added stipulation that on one day each week students were to write a short theme in class on subjects of their own choosing. (A list of topics common to the home, school, and community life of high school students aided those who had difficulty in choosing a subject.) These themes were marked, graded, and returned; but no work was done on the basis of the errors. All instruction in sentence structure was presented in the same predetermined order as in Method I classes, where no writing was done.

With the exception of this one day reserved for writing, the routine of Method II classes was identical with that of the Method I groups.

Method III. The following instructions were given for the teaching of students in Method III groups:

1. You are teaching a unit of literature in connection with which attention will be given to all the language art skills, especially the skill of writing.
2. Please follow the unit instructions carefully so that:
   a. The selections read by all are interestingly discussed.
   b. As many students as possible are drawn into the discussions.
   c. Enriching experiences presented to the class interest the largest possible number.
   d. Activities chosen for individual or group projects are within each student's range of ability.
   e. Students write a short theme in class each week on topics which have been discussed in class or in which the student is interested because of his project. (List possible topics each week.)

While marking the compositions, each teacher tabulated the sentence structure errors. Often sentences containing the errors were duplicated. The typical routine for the day when papers were returned was as follows:

1. Reading of a particularly effective paper. (Discussion of ideas presented and the effectiveness of the composition.)
2. Discussion of basic errors as found in sentences on duplicated sheets.
3. Division of class into groups to work on sentence structure items of which their compositions demonstrated a need. (Students were placed in groups of not more than five and directed to specific pages of *Warriner's Handbook*.)

They were told to discuss these pages, to correct on a separate sheet of paper the sentences in which they had made their errors, and to attach these sheets to their themes. Each student was to approve the corrections made by his classmates before the corrections and themes were returned to the teacher and to initial the correction sheets as a sign of his approval.

Method III groups wrote themes during one period a week, worked on sentence structure approximately one and one-half periods a week, and engaged in the activities as outlined in the literature unit during the remaining two and one-half periods.

The total amount of time spent in the study of sentence structure by the students in the three experimental groups during the eight weeks of instruction was approximately as follows:

Method I: Forty-five minutes a day, five days a week for eight weeks—thirty hours.
Method II: Forty-five minutes a day, four days a week for eight weeks—twenty-four hours.
Method III: Seventy-five minutes a week for eight weeks—ten hours.

Results and Conclusions

To obtain an accurate estimate of the efficacy of the three experimental methods in the teaching of sentence structure it was necessary to choose a statistical method which would hold all factors constant except the one being studied. To study the effect of teacher difference, method difference, and the interaction of teacher and method on improvement in sentence structure, analyses of variance and covariance were used to compare pre-tests and pre-themes with post-tests and post-themes. These analyses revealed the following:

1. A method of teaching sentence structure by a thought approach which also took into consideration the varying needs of students resulted in significant gains in the ability to choose the punctuation and usage items which correctly completed sentences.
2. These gains were significant for all methods alike. However, the gains were effected in classes taught by Method III in one-third of the time required for all other methods.
3. Significant gains were also shown in the ability of all students to detect weaknesses in sentence structure. The difference in gains effected by the three methods was also significant, Method III appearing to be the most effective.
4. No one method was more effective than another in causing students to use more mature sentences in original compositions.
5. The method of attacking points of difficulties in students' writing appears to be as effective in promoting sentence structure growth as is a more complete presentation of sentence structure principles offered in a pre-determined order. This method effected its results in approximately one-third of the time required for the other methods.
6. It appears that the method of teaching sentence structure in connection with actual writing done in the classroom is as effective in promoting growth as are long periods of drill in sentence structure principles.

The results of this study indicate that the following classroom procedures are effective in promoting growth in sentence structure:

1. The explanation of sentence structure according to the relationship of the idea to be expressed rather than according to grammatical rule.

2. The provision of opportunity for students to work on the items most difficult for them after they have worked on errors common to all.

3. The discussion of experiences about which students are to write.

4. The teaching of the sentence structure items for which students' writing indicates a need. This does not mean that the instruction in sentence structure should be incidental or haphazard. Basic errors should be attacked first, other items being added in an ascending order of difficulty. All items presented should thereafter be checked in all writing; they should be emphasized and retaught as need indicates.

Much remains to be done. The following questions remain unanswered:

1. Is the presentation of sentence structure by the thought method or the attention paid individual differences in the classroom the more important factor in effecting improvement in sentence structure?

2. How can differing levels of ability be utilized to hasten improvement in writing?

3. Will the presentation of sentence structure according to the structural patterns suggested by C. C. Fries and others hasten improvement in writing?

4. How can students' experiential backgrounds best be utilized to effect the maximum contribution to writing growth?

---

48   The Theme-a-Week Assumption:

A Report of an Experiment

FRANK HEYS, JR.

How do students learn to write? Obviously, the answer goes, they learn to write by writing. How much writing should high school students do? Obviously, we are told, a theme a week is the prescribed minimum. Ah, then if we have our students write at least a theme a week, we can be sure they will learn to write well? At this point an embarrassed silence ensues, since practically every teacher who has "taught" his students to write by having them write a theme a week has had his failures as well as his successes—failures in numbers large enough that they cannot be dismissed as insignificant.

At a time when the magic number of "a theme a week" has attained the sanctity of Holy Writ, it is difficult to call for evidence to support such a prescription. It is equally difficult, in the face of authoritative advice, to ask if frequent practice in writing is necessarily the best way to teach students to write. Nevertheless, it is the purpose of this article to ask such questions and to indicate some possibly controversial answers.

In 1958 the teachers of English at the Lincoln-Sudbury Regional High School in Sudbury, Mass., discussed the need to improve instruction in composition. Aware of our own dissatisfactions with students' ability to write well, we were

From *English Journal,* Vol. 51 (1962), pp. 320–322. Reprinted with permission of the National Council of Teachers of English and Frank Heys, Jr.

also aware of increasing pressure to boost the amount of written work as a means of curing the ills of composition. While we were willing to stand on our heads, if need be, to teach students to write better, we wanted to be sure that standing on our heads *would* do the job. Thus we sought evidence to support the recommendations of a theme a week. When we found none, we decided to conduct our own study, a very limited one.

Two eleventh-grade classes were involved. One of them wrote the equivalent of a theme a week, and the other was excused from practically all composition work for the entire year and used the time thus freed for an increased amount of in- and out-of-class reading. The results at the end of the year indicated that both groups had improved in their ability to write; that both groups had improved about the same; but that if either class could be said to have made the greater improvement, it was the class that had done little or no writing.

Design of the Study

With those inconclusive but disquieting results before us, we decided to seek additional information. Accordingly, in the fall of 1960, with the support of a small grant from the Fund for the Advancement of Education, we began a more precise experiment. This time eight classes were involved, two in each grade. The two classes in each grade, as closely matched as was possible under the normal sectioning practices of the school, were both taught by the same teacher. The teacher designated one class as a "writing" class, and students in the writing class wrote the equivalent of a theme a week, which was rigorously corrected by the teacher and revised or rewritten by the student. The other class was designated as a "reading" class, and the students in these classes wrote, on the average, a theme every third week. These students, however, spent one period each week reading in class books which they had selected and brought to class. In all other respects students in these classes followed the curriculum appropriate for their grade.

The experiment thus consisted of giving students in two classes in each of four grades a year's experience that differed in but one respect: the amount of reading and writing done.

The job of evaluation was a knotty one. We were aware of all the difficulties involved in any attempt to assess improvement through reading student compositions. Accordingly we decided to use the STEP Writing Test, and all students took Form 2A in the fall of the year and Form 2B the following spring. At the same time, however, we were also aware of objections to purely objective evaluations of writing, so we decided to have all students write two test compositions, one in the fall and one in the spring. To read and evaluate these compositions, which could be identified only by a code number, we employed three experienced readers of the College Board's English Achievement Test, paying them from grant funds. The decision to use these readers was an arbitrary one, but it was made in the hope that the disciplinary training they had undergone while reading the interlinear passage would increase the validity of their grading since each reader was asked to evaluate the papers for a specific quality. In evaluating the papers, the readers assigned each paper to one of nine groups and entered as a score for that paper the number of the group, with 1 as the lowest grade and 9 as the highest. The evaluation in the experiment was completed by comparing initial and final scores on the STEP Tests, class by class and group by group within each class, and by comparing initial and final scores assigned to each paper in each of the three categories, class by class and group by group.

Results

What were the results? Lumping all students together for the moment, we found the following:

	Average Increase— "Reading" Classes	Average Increase— "Writing" Classes
STEP Writing Tests	+6.5	+3.5
Compositions read for:		
Content and Organization	+ .70	+ .45
Mechanics	+ .38	+ .11
Diction and Rhetoric	+ .70	+ .07

Of course, we did not lump all students together. We broke down the results for each class and compared those students in the matching classes who had low, middle, and high initial scores. Without inserting here the complicated tables of data that resulted, I list instead the generalizations that we reached as a result of our analysis:

1. Frequent writing practice probably yields greater dividends in grade 12 than in grades 9, 10, and 11.
2. Frequent writing practice probably yields greater dividends with low groups than with middle or high groups.
3. Frequent writing practice with low groups probably yields greater dividends within the area of content and organization than within the area of mechanics or of diction and rhetoric.

Or, to put it the other way around, except for some seniors (but not all) and except for some low groups (but not all) and except for the area of content and organization (but not always), we got consistently better results from those students in reading classes.

It is difficult to do other than generalize since the two methods of evaluation do not always confirm each other. Specifically, the STEP Tests indicate that the middle groups, taken as a whole, learn to write about equally well with either method; the composition evaluations on the other hand, contradict this finding and indicate a superior gain for those students in reading classes. To set down more specific conclusions, then, would first mean deciding in favor of one method of evaluation. This we do not feel competent to do.

Conclusions

Readers of this article should not be left with the feeling that this experiment is definitive and that it sounds the death knell of the theme a week. In all fairness I must report that Paul Diederich of the Educational Testing Service, while calling these "by far the most carefully determined figures on this sort of experiment I have ever seen," nonetheless is of the opinion that they are "chancy." Chancy or not, however, it seems strange that we were not able to demonstrate a superiority for the much-touted "theme a week" method, that instead we demonstrated the converse. As a result, the teachers involved in the experiment agreed that the following conclusions were, for the time being, definitely indicated by the evidence:

1. The claim that "the way to learn to write is to write" is not substantiated by this experiment.
2. The claim that ability to write well is related to the amount of writing done is not substantiated by this experiment.
3. For many students reading is a positive influence on writing ability.
4. The influence of reading on the ability to write appears to be a separate factor, not directly related to the teacher's personality and enthusiasm.

It is our strong feeling that much more experimentation remains to be done before these findings are translated into curriculum design. We need to find out, for example, if these findings will be repeated in similar experiments in other schools. We need to find out how much reading, and what kind, will produce the optimum effect on ability to write. Above all we need to reduce or remove the "chancy" nature of the data obtained. We would welcome the assistance of other schools in an enlarged experiment to achieve these ends.

The question of teaching composition appears to be a complex and highly sophisticated one; perhaps it should be rephrased to read: "How best teach which students in which grades to write well?" But until we have the answer to that question, the case for a theme a week must receive the old Scottish verdict of "Not proven."

---

49   An Experimental Study of Means to Improve Writing

FRED WHEELER

The assumption that frequent writing is necessary to improvement of writing ability, together with the related assumption that compositions must be heavily corrected, was studied by Burton and Arnold (1). The weekly theme failed to justify itself. The null hypothesis that there are no significant differences in the writing performance of high school students that can be associated with frequency of writing, or with intensity of teacher evaluation, or with ability levels of pupils, or with any combination of these factors, has been sustained by their study.

Another study by Heys (2) tested the hypothesis that increased reading (taking the time formerly devoted to in-class writing) would improve the ability of students to write. Heys' study showed no statistically significant differences between the gains of the "Reading" group and the "Writing" group.

The present study was designed to test the hypothesis that less frequent writing—together with certain systematic and analytical readings—would result in

From *Journal of Secondary Education*, Vol. 40 (Nov., 1965), pp. 331–335. Reprinted with permission.

improved use of vocabulary, mechanics, rhetoric, critical thinking, and organization in written composition. Carefully selected and pointedly discussed reading of essays, it was postulated, would be of greater value than student-selected free reading, varying from student to student (as in the Heys study).

Six junior classes were selected, four English 5y[1] classes and two English 5x classes. Three teachers were asked to participate, each having two like classes in order to eliminate, as far as possible, the influence of teacher variation. One group was called the Experimental Group and the other the Control Group.

Students in each teacher's experimental and control classes were matched as closely as possible on two criteria: the DAT verbal ranking and the student's grade in the previous English class.

The three teachers taught the control classes according to the approved courses of study, requiring one composition each week. The three teachers taught the experimental classes by following the approved courses of study, except that there were less frequent writing assignments (one every three weeks). There was, in addition, very close reading and evaluation of this less frequent composition, with emphasis upon revision and improvement.

In the time released by less frequent writing in the experimental classes, the teachers would do the following:

Assign reading in the book of essays (*World-Wide Essays* by Greene and Bromberg, Globe, 1963).

Hold individual conferences with students about their writing.

Read student compositions to the class for discussion.

Conduct discussions about the content, organization, use of diction, use of connectives, use of argumentation and critical thinking in essays assigned in text.

Duplicate a student's composition and have students analyze it.

Encourage students to speak articulately about how they organize their ideas and why they selected words, examples, arguments, transitions, etc.

In order to measure the improvement of the matched experimental and control groups, the STEP Writing Test 2A was administered near the beginning of the semester and readministered at the end of the semester. One teacher-made essay test was administered at the beginning of the semester and another at the end of the semester. The STEP Writing Test was especially appropriate for use in this study because the test has been item-analyzed in the following categories:

1. *Organization:* reasonable ordering of ideas, events, facts, etc.
2. *Use of Conventions:* attention to syntax or sentence structure, diction in the sense of gross errors of word choice, punctuation, spelling.
3. *Critical Thinking:* detection of unstated assumptions, perception of cause-and-effect relationships, and anticipation of the needs of the reader.
4. *Effectiveness of Expression:* adequacy of emphasis, adequacy of development, exactness of expression, economy, simplicity, and variety.
5. *Appropriateness of Expression:* choice of a level of usage suitable to the purpose and to the reader.

1 English 5y students were low junior students of average ability. English 5x students were low junior students of high ability.

The STEP Writing Test was scored by machine so that there was a sub-score for each of the five categories (above) and a total score for each answer sheet. The teacher-made essay tests were evaluated by groups of five or six teachers, according to the same categories given for the STEP test. Teachers were asked to mark each paper in each of the five categories, on a scale from 1 to 4 (best). These marks were then averaged to give five sub-scores for each essay, the five sub-scores then being averaged to give a total score for the paper.

When all the data had been gathered, it was possible to derive statistics that demonstrate whether the hypothesis of the study may be accepted.

Analysis of Test Results

Significance at the $P = .05$ level
(Based on the work of Educational Research Services and its director, G. Arthur Jensen.)
A. Comparisons between initial and final test scores for each group on each of the sub-tests and the total test.
 1. The STEP Writing Test
  a. The x-ability groups
   (1) The experimental group made significant gains, on the average, on the total test and on each of the sub-tests except "appropriateness."
   (2) The control group made significant gains, on the average, on the total test and on each of the sub-tests except "critical thinking" and "appropriateness."
  b. The y-ability groups
   (1) The experimental group made significant gains, on the average, on the total test and on each of the sub-tests.
   (2) The control group made significant gains on the average, on the total test and on each of the sub-tests except "critical thinking."
 2. The teacher-made essay test
  a. The x-ability groups
   (1) The experimental group obtained decreases in the mean score on all of the sub-tests. However, none of the differences in mean test scores are significant except for the "conventions" sub-test. In this case the experimental group scored significantly lower, on the average, on the final test than on the initial test.[2]
   (2) The control group obtained mean scores on the initial and final essay sub-tests that are not significantly different.
  b. The y-ability groups
  Neither the experimental nor control group made scores that were significantly different, on the average, between the initial essay sub-tests and the final essay sub-tests.
B. Comparisons of the differences in improvement in test scores between the experimental and control groups
 1. STEP Writing Test
  a. The x-ability groups
  The differences between the average improvement of the experimental and control groups are not significant for any of the tests.

---

2 On the day of the composition the class teacher predicted such a drop because the class was rebellious about writing the essay at the end of the semester.

b. The y-ability groups

(1) The experimental group made significantly greater improvement, on the average, on the "critical thinking" sub-test and significantly smaller improvement on the "appropriateness" sub-test than did the control group.

(2) The differences in average improvement were not significant for the other sub-tests.

2. The teacher-made essay test

The differences between the average gains for the experimental group and the average gains of the control group are not significant for any of the sub-tests for the y-ability pupils. This same situation was true for the x-ability pupils.

C. Correlations between total STEP test scores and total essay test scores.

TABLE I

Group		Initial Test	Final Test
X-ability	Exp.	.30	.76
	Cont.	.29	.25
Y-ability	Exp.	.53	.01
	Cont.	.50	.48

1. Two correlations stand out as unique. Both of these pertain to the relationship between the final STEP and final essay test scores obtained by pupils in the experimental groups. In the first instance, the relationship of the scores of the x-ability pupils was found to be fairly high (.76). In the second instance, the relationship of the scores of the y-ability pupils were found to be close to zero (.01).

2. All other correlation coefficients indicate only a small relationship exists between the scores pupils made on the STEP test and the scores the same pupils made on the essay test.

The Objective STEP Writing Test 2A: There seems to be no reason to consider x-ability and y-ability students separately. On the objective test, all groups made significant gains in organization, use of conventions, and effectiveness of expression. The y-ability students all gained in appropriateness of expression, while the scores of the x-ability students were already so high on this subtest as to make a significant gain unlikely.

However, both x and y experimental groups made significant gains on the "critical thinking" sub-test, while both x and y control groups did not. Because the groups were carefully matched, it seems fair to conclude that the differences in classroom teaching and the systematic analysis of the essays contributed to this result.

1. On the teacher-made essay tests, none of the groups gained significantly, on the average, on the sub-tests or on the total tests. In the case of the significantly lower scores on the final essay for the x group, the explanation of poor motivation has been offered.

The well-known difficulty of evaluating essay tests objectively may well account for the lack of significance in this area of measurement. The question is analyzed in parts A and B of the Appendix.

2. The correlations between total scores of the objective STEP Writing Test and those on the teacher-made writing test are probably meaningless. Certainly six of the eight correlations are too small to bear the weight of any definite conclusion. The two unusual correlations, (.76) and (.01), if they have any explanation, may perhaps be accounted for by the variation in teacher judgment of essays.

The results of the present study differ from the results of other studies in this area in one respect only—the area of "critical thinking." All of the studies seem to demonstrate that frequent writing (the theme-a-week assumption) is not justified insofar as it does not result in improved ability to write. Neither does less frequent writing result in a lessened ability to write, as judged in the present study by a standardized objective test and a teacher-made essay test.

The fact that both experimental groups made significant gains in "critical thinking" on the objective test suggests that the time given to in-class writing might well be devoted to careful reading of essays and analytical discussions of ideas.

It would seem from the results of this study that ability to write can be bolstered as much, or more, by purposeful reading as by a routine weekly writing assignment.

The time that the teacher spends in correcting five sets of weekly compositions is about twenty-five hours each week. This study suggests that—with appropriate changes in classroom activities—the work load of the teacher might well be reduced, while at the same time improving the critical thinking of the students.

At present there is no rigorous knowledge of effective ways to teach writing to all students. Many of the cherished prejudices of the English teacher have been shown to be unfounded. Systematic research is needed to discover what kinds of reading experiences, writing exercises, and classroom techniques will improve the students' learning to write.

REFERENCES

1. Burton and Arnold, "Effects of Frequency Writing and Intensity of Teacher Evaluation Upon High School Students' Performance in Written Composition," Cooperative Research Project, No. 1523, United States Office of Education, 1963, 99 pp.

2. Frank Heys, Jr., "The Theme-a-Week Assumption: A report of an Experiment," *The English Journal,* May, 1962, pp. 320–322.